GROWING FRUITS & VEGETABLES ORGANICALLY

GROWING FRUITS & VEGETABLES ORGANICALLY

The Complete Guide to a Great-Tasting, More Bountiful, Problem-Free Harvest

Edited by Jean M. A. Nick and Fern Marshall Bradley

Contributors: Helen Atthowe, Melody Aumiller, Elizabeth Clark, George DeVault, Barbara W. Ellis, Elizabeth Henderson, Lewis Hill, Louise Hyde, Robert Kourik, Debbie Leung, Sharon L. Lovejoy, Sally McCabe, Susan McClure, Lynn McGowan, Deborah L. Martin, Scott Meyer, Patricia S. Michalak, Sheelagh Oliveria, Nancy J. Ondra, Pamela K. Peirce, Cass Peterson, Barbara Pleasant, Joanne Poncavage, Miranda Smith, and Marian Van Atta

RODALE PRESS, EMMAUS, PENNSYLVANIA

Our Mission

We publish books that empower people's lives.

RODALE BOOKS

Executive Editor: **Margaret Lydic Balitas**
Managing Editor: **Barbara W. Ellis**
Editors: **Jean M. A. Nick** and **Fern Marshall Bradley**
Contributing Editors: **Deborah L. Martin** and **Nancy J. Ondra**
Senior Research Associate: **Heidi A. Stonehill**
Copy Manager: **Dolores Plikaitis**
Copy Editor: **Laura Stevens**
Office Manager: **Karen Earl-Braymer**
Administrative Assistant: **Susan L. Nickol**
Editorial assistance: **Deborah Weisel**
Senior Designer: **Linda Jacopetti**
Cover and Book Designer: **Frank Milloni**
Cover and Book Layout: **Linda Brightbill-Bossard**
Cover Photographer: **Mitch Mandel**
Illustrators: **Kathy Bray, Pamela Carroll, Rae D. Chambers, Julia S. Child, Ed Courrier, Jean Emmons, Frank Fretz, Kathryn D. Kester,** and **Elayne Sears**
Indexer: **Ed Yeager**

If you have any questions or comments concerning this book, please write to:
Rodale Press
Book Readers' Service
33 East Minor Street
Emmaus, PA 18098

Library of Congress Cataloging-in-Publication Data

Growing fruits & vegetables organically : the complete guide to a great-tasting, more bountiful, problem-free harvest / edited by Jean M. A. Nick and Fern Marshall Bradley ; contributors, Helen Atthowe . . . [et al.].
    p.   cm.
   Includes bibliographical references (p.   ) and index.
   ISBN 0–87596–586–5   hardcover
   1. Vegetable gardening.   2. Fruit-culture.
3. Organic gardening.   I. Nick, Jean M. A.
II. Bradley, Fern Marshall.   III. Atthowe, Helen.
IV. Title: Growing fruits and vegetables organically.
SB324.3.G75   1994
635'.0484–dc20   93–37830
                       CIP

Distributed in the book trade by St. Martin's Press

2 4 6 8 10 9 7 5 3 1   hardcover

....

....

CONTENTS

PART 2

THE HOME FOOD GARDEN

A Practical Encyclopedia of Vegetables,
Fruits, Herbs, and More • 270

CREDITS

The Writers

Helen Atthowe is plant production manager for Bitterroot Native Growers, a wholesale nursery specializing in native plants, located in Corvallis, Montana. She has a master's degree in horticulture from Rutgers University. She also manages her own organic farm.

Elizabeth Clark is a free-lance writer from Texas. Her articles have appeared in the *Dallas Times Herald* and in *Texas Gardener* magazine.

George DeVault is the U.S. editor of *Novii Fermer,* a Russian-language farming magazine published by Rodale Press, and the former editor of *The New Farm.*

Elizabeth Henderson and her partner David Stern manage Rose Valley Farm in Rose, New York. They grow vegetables, garlic, and small fruits.

Lewis Hill owns and operates Vermont Day Lilies in Greensboro, Vermont, with his wife, Nancy. He is the author of *Cold-Climate Gardening* and *Fruits and Berries for the Home Garden.*

Robert Kourik is a free-lance writer, publisher, consultant, and landscape designer in Occidental, California. He is the author of *Drip Irrigation for Every Landscape and All Climates.*

Debbie Leung is a market gardener from Olympia, Washington, who grows Asian vegetables and other specialty produce.

Susan McClure is a free-lance garden writer from Ohio. She is the author of *The Harvest Gardener.*

Lynn McGowan is a free-lance writer from Pennsylvania. She is a former associate editor for *American Horticulturist* magazine.

Scott Meyer is a senior editor at *Organic Gardening* magazine.

Patricia S. Michalak has a master's degree in entomology from Michigan State University. She is a free-lance writer and organic market gardener in Kempton, Pennsylvania.

Pamela K. Peirce is a garden writer, horticultural photographer, and photo editor from San Francisco, California. She is the author of *Golden Gate Gardening.*

Cass Peterson and her partner Ward Sinclair own Flickerville Mountain Farm and Groundhog Ranch in Dott, Pennsylvania. They raise more than 70 kinds of vegetables, flowers, and herbs.

Barbara Pleasant is a contributing editor to *Organic Gardening* magazine and the author of *Warm-Climate Gardening.*

Joanne Poncavage is a senior editor at *Organic Gardening* magazine.

Miranda Smith is an agriculture writer and organic market gardener from Belchertown, Massachusetts. She is a co-author of *Rodale's Chemical-Free Yard and Garden.*

Marian Van Atta is the author of *Growing and Using Exotic Foods.* She has grown tropical and subtropical foods for over 20 years.

The Editors

Fern Marshall Bradley has a master's degree in horticulture from Rutgers University. She has managed an organic market garden, is an avid vegetable gardener, and is an editor of garden books at Rodale Press.

Barbara W. Ellis is managing editor of garden books at Rodale Press. She has a bachelor's degree from Kenyon College and a bachelor's degree in horticulture from the Ohio State University. She is a former publications director/editor for *American Horticulturist* magazine.

Deborah L. Martin has a bachelor's degree in horticultural writing from Purdue University and has worked as a Cooperative Extension agent for urban gardeners in Indianapolis. She is an associate garden book editor at Rodale Press.

Jean M. A. Nick has a master's degree in horticulture from Rutgers University and has worked in the greenhouse industry and a commercial vineyard. She is an associate garden book editor at Rodale Press and grows vegetables and small fruits on her farm in eastern Pennsylvania.

Nancy J. Ondra has a bachelor's degree in agronomy from Delaware Valley College and is an associate garden book editor at Rodale Press. She collects and propagates perennials and trees and keeps a large composting area on her farm near Pennsburg, Pennsylvania.

The Experts

We gratefully acknowledge the garden professionals from North America who took time to talk with us, answer our questions and share their secrets. In particular we thank Linda C. Askey, garden editor of *Southern Accents;* Molly and Ted Barlett, owners of Silver Creek Farm in Hiram, Ohio; Allen Boettcher, home horticulture agent for the University of Arizona Cooperative Extension, Maricopa County; David Cavagnaro, preservation garden manager at Heritage Farm for Seed Savers Exchange in Decorah, Iowa; Lynn Coody, a farming consultant for Organic Agsystems Consulting in Cottage Grove, Oregon; Richard de Wilde, owner of Harmony Valley Farm in Chaseburg, Wisconsin; Veet Deha, agricultural consultant with Crest Lane Designs in Ithaca, New York; Judith Dilkie, an organic gardener in Stittsville, Ontario; Daniel J. Donnelly, extension agent, agricultural science, for the University of Maryland Cooperative Extension Service; Sue and Craig Dremann, owners of Redwood City Seed Company in Redwood City, California; Sylvia and Walter Ehrhardt, owners of Ehrhardt Organic Farm in Knoxville, Maryland; Yvonne Freeman, agriculture adult education coordinator for the University of California Cooperative Extension; Grace Gershuny and Stewart Hoyt, market gardeners in Barnet, Vermont; Fred and Barbara Hoover, owners of Fre-Bar, Inc., in Phoenix; Rob Johnston, president of Johnny's Selected Seeds in Albion, Maine; Holly Kennell, county agent, Washington State University, King County; Wendy Krupnick, trial gardens manager for Shepherd's Garden Seeds in Felton, California; Rose Marie Nichols McGee, president of Nichols Garden Nursery in Albany, Oregon; Pat Murray, associate vice-president of Raindrip, Inc., in Chatsworth, California; Ellen Ogden, co-owner of The Cook's Garden in Londonderry, Vermont; Sheelagh Oliveria, the assistant manager of the organic garden at Fetzer Valley Oaks Food and Wine Center in Hopland, California; Jan Riggenbach, free-lance garden columnist from Glenwood, Iowa; James M. Stephens, professor, state extension vegetable specialist at the University of Florida, Gainesville; Paul Talalay, M.D., of Johns Hopkins Hospital in Baltimore; Kent Taylor, president of Taylor's Herb Gardens in Vista, California; Judy Tiger, executive director of Garden Resources of Washington in Washington, D.C.; Lynn Tilton, a writer and gardener from Sierra Vista, Arizona; Allen Wilson, a professor of landscape horticulture at Ricks College in Rexburg, Idaho. We also acknowledge *Herb Gundell's Complete Guide to Rocky Mountain Gardening* by Herb Gundell as a source of planting recommendations for the Rocky Mountain region.

INTRODUCTION

Your mom told you fruits and vegetables were good for you, and she was *right*. These days, eating lots of fresh fruits and vegetables is more important than ever. Nutritionists suggest we need five to eight servings of fruits and vegetables every day. Feature articles in health magazines and even the daily newspaper talk about the disease-preventing benefits of foods such as cabbage, broccoli, garlic, strawberries, and many others.

The best way to know that you're eating truly fresh, vitamin-rich fruits and vegetables is to grow them yourself. And when you grow them organically, you *know* they're 100 percent good for you—without the possibility of synthetic chemical residues—and that your garden is a safe, natural environment for you, your family, and your neighborhood.

Growing food organically is not hard to do, but it helps to get some expert advice now and then. Most of us don't have access to a real live expert, so we look to gardening books and magazines to answer our questions.

Growing Fruits and Vegetables Organically has the expert answers you need to grow a great garden. It gives you everything you need to know about backyard food gardening in an easy-to-access format. To create this book, we had a technical researcher, Helen Atthowe, who is an organic grower, consultant, and scientist in her own right, read hundreds of research papers on organic growing. She interviewed many of the researchers who wrote those papers. She also tapped into her extensive network of colleagues to get their ideas and the very latest growing and pest control information.

We gave this information to our writers, all of whom are also experienced organic gardeners or growers. They talked to dozens more researchers and organic growers all over North America to get real answers to common questions and up-to-the-minute information on new techniques. And you're holding all of that expert knowledge in your hands right now.

Getting the Most from This Book

Growing Fruits and Vegetables Organically is organized so you only need to read what you want to know today. Keep it near your back door for handy reference before or during a gardening session. It will get you back out to your garden fast, and that's really where you want to be, isn't it?

Here's a brief overview of the book to help guide you in finding the answers to your questions of the day. (Don't forget—the book also has a complete index, which is a great way to find *specific* information fast.)

Part 1: From Planting to Harvest

Part 1 covers the nuts and bolts of specific gardening techniques. From deciding what to grow in your garden, selecting a site, and improving the soil to putting your garden to bed for the winter, our experts tell you exactly how to do it right and without wasting your precious time. Here are a few highlights.

Chapter 1: Your First Food Garden. Novice gardeners will want to start with this chapter, written especially as a guide for starting a small, successful, first garden. Experienced gardeners can browse through it for a quick review of site selection and garden care basics.

Chapter 2: Starting Out Right. Every gardener will benefit from this chapter's quick course in evaluating a garden's soil fertility. Then use the "Rating Soil Fertility" table to decide if your soil has low, medium, or high fertility. Armed with that knowledge, you'll be able to choose the soil improvement recipes that are just right for your soil from the "custom care" regimes that round off the chapter. These regimes offer specialized fertilizing instructions for three different classes of vegetable crops, for small fruits, and for fruit trees.

Chapter 3: Planning and Record Keeping; and Chapter 4: Planting. These chapters cover everything you need to know about laying out your garden, planning crop rotations, setting up succession plantings, growing your own transplants, and getting the plants into the ground.

Chapter 5: Caring for Your Crops. This chapter covers feeding, watering, and training your plants. "Watering 101" is a unique approach to watering that offers three specific approaches for figuring out when to water and how much water to apply. You can choose between a simple weekly guideline, a method based on monitoring your soil, or a precise mathematical calculation.

Chapter 6: Preventing and Controlling Problems. This preventive-based chapter gives you the knowledge you need to beat 90 percent of your problems *before* they even occur. Just in case the other 10 percent stop by uninvited, we've included an illustrated quick-reference table of the most common insects and diseases you may encounter on your vegetables or pestering your fruit. Once you've located the culprit, the table tells you how to defeat it with safe, organic control methods.

Chapter 7: Gathering the Harvest; and Chapter 8: Ending and Extending the Season. These chapters provide detailed information on harvesting and storage, after-harvest care of your plants, and techniques for extending your harvesting season.

Chapter 9: Gardening in Containers. This chapter tells you how to grow everything from tomatoes to herbs to dwarf apple trees in containers. From making your own potting mix to choosing the best type of container, this chapter has it all.

Chapter 10: Specialty Gardens. We asked some talented garden designers to give you some small food garden designs and ideas to show you that growing fruits, vegetables, and herbs can be exciting, creative, and fun—as well as practical. For example, Louise Hyde of Well-Sweep Herb Farm designed a little garden of tea herbs and flowers, complete with a sheltered bench to sit on to drink them in. Sharon Lovejoy, author of *Sunflower Houses,* has shared some of her child-pleasing magic for enticing children into the garden.

Chapter 11: Seed Saving and Propagation. This chapter shows you how to save seeds, divide plants, and graft to make new plants from existing ones.

Part 2: The Home Food Garden

Part 2 is a complete, alphabetical guide to growing hundreds of different vegetables, fruits, herbs, grains, and nuts.

Eighty-eight entries give complete and specific cultural information on major food plants such as apple, corn, and tomato. Hundreds more food plants are grouped into entries such as Herbs and Spices, Greens, Mexican Specialties, and Exotic Crops. If you're looking for information on a specific plant, your best bet is to flip straight to the index. Every plant included in the book is listed in the index by common name.

We've organized each entry the same way to make it easy for you to find what you need to know fast. Each starts with planning and plant selection. It then moves on to planting, care through the season, problem prevention, harvesting, and after-harvest care.

In entries on many popular crops, you'll find critical facts, such as best site and proper spacing, summarized in the "At a Glance" feature. Seedling illustrations for many of the more common vegetables show you which of those little green sprouts to keep.

Look for the "Problem Prevention" section in each entry to find practical, specific steps you can take to prevent insects, diseases, and animal pests from damaging your crops. It's set up like a calendar, but instead of months we've used seasons (such as "in late winter") or plant development stages (such as "when buds start to show green") to tell you when to perform a particular task. That way you'll be right on time whether you live in Maine or New Mexico. For example, in the Apple entry, we recommend "In late winter, hang codling

moth traps." Then we go on to explain how to monitor the traps and what to do when you catch moths (see page 276). Successful gardening couldn't be any easier.

So you can see that you'll want to keep your *Growing Fruits and Vegetables Organically* handy for quick reference before and during your sessions in the garden. It will become a valued friend you turn to again and again for advice.

May your garden be healthy and bountiful. Happy growing!

Jean MA Nick

Fern Marshall Bradley

Jean M. A. Nick
Fern Marshall Bradley
Editors

PART 1

FROM PLANTING TO HARVEST

❂

A How-To Guide for Planning,
Planting, and Maintaining
Your Home Food Garden

1 YOUR FIRST FOOD GARDEN

An Introduction to Planting and Harvesting a Home Vegetable Garden

First-time gardeners are often amazed by what they call their "beginner's luck." To their delight, seeds come up, plants grow, and food practically leaps onto the table. It's not surprising this is such a common experience, because many vegetables and herbs—and even some fruits—are among the easiest plants to grow.

If you haven't yet grown your first garden (or if you just want a quick review of the basics), this chapter is for you. It will help get you off to a running start with your first garden. You'll learn what it takes to select plants and get them in the ground and how to keep them thriving through the year.

Sure, there is plenty more to learn and plenty of fine-tuning you can do later. Gardeners are always looking for ways to get a bigger harvest, extend the growing season, or grow a new and different crop. That's half the fun of gardening. But after you've used this quick guide to a first-year garden, you can read about the fine-tuning at leisure while you munch some of your delicious, homegrown food.

LOOK FOR LOCAL INFORMATION

A good use for some of your early gardening enthusiasm is to find out what other local gardeners are doing. See if you can find a planting chart for your area that lists crops to plant and the approximate dates when they can be planted in the garden. Check your Cooperative Extension Service. You may also be able to get them from local gardening organizations, your local newspaper, or books on local gardening. You should also ask the average dates of the last spring frost and first fall frost for your area.

One good way to find local gardeners to talk with is to take a stroll in your neighborhood and look for food gardens. If you can't see into backyards from the street, ask around to find where the gardens might be hidden. Then try to find the gardener working in the garden, or arrange an introduction through another neighbor. Gardeners often love to chat about what they are doing. Here are some good questions to ask:

1. Do you grow cabbage (or whatever crop you're interested in planting)? If so, when do you plant it? Old-time gardeners sometimes use signs of the season to time vegetable plantings. For some typical signs, see "Planting by Nature's Signs" on page 97.

2. If the gardener doesn't grow cabbage (or whatever crop you're interested in planting), ask why not. The answer may be that he or she doesn't like that crop. Or it may be that something about local soil or climate or pest problems make the crop difficult to grow. Listen and learn, but if you really want to grow that crop, don't give up on it solely on the basis of what one gardener says.

3. What are your favorite cultivars of cabbage (or whatever crop you're interested in planting)? Why do you like them? Do you order them from particular catalogs?

4. What pests bother your garden? What plants do they damage and when do they strike? Which pests need to be controlled quickly and which do little actual damage?

5. Is there a typical kind of soil or soil problem in the neighborhood (for example, sandy, clayey, rocky, poorly drained, or acidic)?

6. Do you know of a free or cheap source of organic soil amendments (materials that enrich the soil) or mulch?

7. Can you show me what rich, well-amended garden soil looks like?

8. Which local nurseries have the best selection of high-quality plants?

Nearby gardeners may become gardening friends. It's fun to share information about successes and failures and also to trade extra seeds and homegrown seedlings.

GUIDELINES FOR FIRST-TIMERS

While it's tempting to rush out and start digging and planting, it's a good idea to take time first to plan your attack. Here are some guidelines to keep in mind that will ensure your debut garden is a big success.

Start small. Enthusiasm is important, but don't let first-year ambition inspire you to take on too large an area for your first garden. It isn't hard to *plant* a large garden and get it growing. But it may be very hard to *keep up* with that garden through the season and to cope with storing and processing a large harvest in your first gardening season.

How big is big enough? It depends in part on how much time you'll have for gardening. If you have little time, be assured an area as small as 16 square feet (4×4 feet) will provide you with a surprising amount of food. And an area of about 200 square feet (10×20 feet) is plenty of room for most first-year gardeners.

Grow easy crops. For your first food garden, it's best to start with mostly annual vegetables and herbs. Annuals are plants that grow and are harvested in under a year. They will give you encouraging results fairly quickly. Concentrating on annual crops for the first year also allows you to defer decisions about permanent plantings until you have more experience. Although you may want to plan out your entire yard right away, deciding where to plant the fruit trees and berry bushes or where to build the grape arbor, it's wise to save these more permanent plantings and structures until after you have gardened for a season or more.

Choose a sunny site. The best location for a vegetable-and-herb garden is a spot that gets direct sun all day. An ideal garden site is level or slopes slightly to the south or southwest to catch the most sun. Leafy crops, such as lettuce and greens, require at least four hours of direct sunlight; six or more is better. Fruiting crops, such as tomatoes and beans, need at least six sunny hours and will produce better with eight or more.

Trees, buildings, or fences on the south side of a garden cause the most problems because they cast the most shade; ones on the west side are nearly as bad because they block the warm afternoon sun. For more ideas on what to look for, see "Selecting the Best Site" on pages 6 and 7.

Plan for easy care. Perhaps the next-most-important guideline is to locate your first garden near your house or in a place that you will pass daily. It should be convenient to stop by every day to do a bit of this and that. If your garden is near your kitchen, you'll be able to run out easily and harvest your vegetables and herbs whenever a recipe comes to mind. Consider your water source, too. In most regions, you'll need to water at least occasionally, and in some regions, you'll need to water most of growing season. It is best if a garden hose will reach your site—carrying water in buckets is always discouraging.

Consider All of Your Options

If you don't have a large, sunny, ideally situated site, don't despair. Get creative! You don't have to grow all of your vegetables and herbs in one plot. Consider using a small section of your sunny front yard for tomatoes and peppers, a strip of side yard for some leafy greens and herbs that can take partial shade, and a sunny corner of the backyard for beans and squash. In urban settings, a container garden on the roof or on a deck may be the best option. Just be sure to have a structural engineer approve your roof for the extra weight, and be sure you set up your container garden so excess water will drain off the roof or deck easily and not collect under the containers.

If you truly have no place to garden where you live, consider obtaining a plot in a community garden. Community gardens are generally on land leased from a public or private agency such as a school, church, utility company, or community center. Community gardens are less convenient than a home garden, but they offer valuable benefits for beginners. The best part is that other community gardeners are usually generous with encouragement and advice. In addition, the soil is likely to be partially or fully prepared. If there is a waiting list for a community garden near you, the sooner your name is on it, the sooner you will be gardening!

SITE AND SOIL PREPARATION

Once you've decided where to put your garden, you're ready to begin clearing and preparing the site. Clearing will be easiest if you're lucky enough to have inherited a recently abandoned garden plot. In this case, you will need only to pull out any dead crop plants and a season or two of weeds. In such a plot, most of the weeds are likely to be annuals, ones that spread only by seeds. (You may also have some perennial crops worth saving, so try to get an experienced gardener to take a look before you start.) If the area has been untended for years, the weeds will be more numerous. More of them are also likely to be perennials that spread by underground bulbs or runners. You may even have small shrubs and trees growing there.

Start by cutting or pulling all of the weeds and unwanted plants from your site. If the weeds have gone to seed, it's best to dispose of them with your household trash. If they haven't, you can use them to start a compost pile. Compost is decomposed organic matter (plant and animal material), and it is one of the best

SELECTING THE BEST SITE

This simple map of a typical yard illustrates some of the factors you should consider when selecting a site for your garden. Although trees, buildings, and fences cast shade at various times of day, there are still plenty of options for planting vegetables and fruits.

Look at your yard to see which areas are sunny and which are shady. You can create a map of your property like the one on the opposite page. When selecting a site, you'll also want to consider some of the following factors:

1. If there is a vegetable garden site in your yard prepared by a former resident, take advantage of it to minimize the work required.

2. Sites used as flower beds may also be easy to use and may have amended soil.

3. Lawn areas are not hard to clear, but the soil may be compacted and not amended.

4. Windy sites are not suitable. Trees or shrubs make good windbreaks; walls and fences take up less room. Windbreaks that allow some air through are most effective. You can plant a vine on an open fence to slow the wind.

5. Avoid low areas were water stands after rains. If the only site available is wet, plan on using raised beds.

6. Avoid steep slopes. If you can't avoid them, plan on building terraces.

7. Avoid planting your garden across pathways through the yard—the path to the garage, for example—and play areas.

8. Avoid sites shaded by trees and areas where tree roots will compete with food plants. If you're planning in early spring, don't forget to take into account shade cast by overhead tree branches that will leaf out by late spring.

9. Compost piles can be in partial or full shade. Keep them out of the main part of the yard but handy to the garden and the kitchen.

10. Avoid sites abutting heavily traveled roads. Exhaust fumes and runoff of oil-tainted water can contaminate crops.

11. A deck, such as the one shown, can be an ideal site for a barrel of herbs or some vegetables in containers.

things you can add to your garden soil to improve its quality. For more information on how to make and use compost, see "Making and Using Compost" on page 36.

If your site is now a lawn, use a spade to cut the turf into manageable pieces (maybe 12 to 15 inches square). Slice under the turf with the spade and lift it in thin slabs. You can pile the cut turf, grass-side-down, in a broad pile a foot or two high. Keep the pile moist so the grass will decay. The following year, it will be a great soil amendment to add to your garden. You can also use the displaced turf to patch dead spots in the rest of your lawn. Just dig out

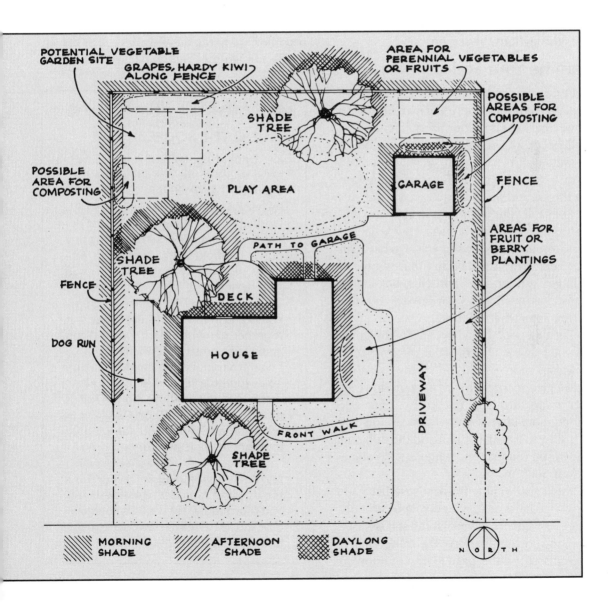

POTENTIAL VEGETABLE GARDEN SITE

GRAPES, HARDY KIWI ALONG FENCE

AREA FOR PERENNIAL VEGETABLES OR FRUITS

SHADE TREE

POSSIBLE AREAS FOR COMPOSTING

POSSIBLE AREA FOR COMPOSTING

PLAY AREA

GARAGE

FENCE

PATH TO GARAGE

AREAS FOR FRUIT OR BERRY PLANTINGS

SHADE TREE

FENCE

DECK

DOG RUN

HOUSE

SHADE TREE

DRIVEWAY

FRONT WALK

MORNING SHADE   AFTERNOON SHADE   DAYLONG SHADE

NORTH

enough of the dead spot so that the patch will lie flush, and water it well until the roots take hold. Create paths by leaving strips of lawn between garden beds. Paths at least the width of a lawn mower will be easy to keep trimmed.

Weeds will sprout anew as the season progresses. Remove all of the weed roots you see as you dig your garden, but no matter how carefully you do that, you'll also have to fight weeds throughout the season.

Examine Your Soil

Once you've uncovered your soil, take time to examine it more closely. Dig up a little with a trowel and hold it in your hand. If it is sandy, it will feel gritty between your fingers. When you wet it and squeeze it, it will not hold together well. Clay soil feels slippery between your fingers and sticks together well when it's wet. In fact, if your soil's high in clay, you will be able to roll it into a snake between the palms of your hands. Loamy soil is in between sandy and clayey. You'll be able to feel some of the larger, grittier sand particles, but loamy soil also has smaller clay particles, so it holds together somewhat when wet.

The type of soil you have affects the problems you may encounter in your garden. Sandy soil warms more quickly in spring, which is good for getting crops off to a fast start. However, water drains through it quickly, so it must be watered more often. Clay soil holds moisture but is slow to warm. For more on the different types of soil you may encounter, see "Evaluating Your Soil" on page 25.

You'll also want to find out whether your soil will be hard or easy to dig. You can only judge this well on a day when the soil is moist but not soggy. See "Tricks of the Trade: Do the Squeeze Test" on this page to find out how to tell if soil is the right consistency to dig.

When your soil is ready to dig—moist but not soggy—push a shovel deep into it, lift out some soil, and turn it over in a pile next to the hole. If your soil is high in clay or if it's very compacted, this will be hard to do. Clay soil is especially difficult to dig if it has been worked while too wet or has had lots of foot traffic or vehicles passing over it. Sandy soil can also become hard to dig if it is walked on or driven on for a long time. Tightly packed soil is best

---

✍ TRICKS OF THE TRADE ✍

DO THE SQUEEZE TEST

One of the easiest ways to ruin good soil or make bad soil worse is to dig or till it when it's either too wet or too dry. Soil that's too wet when it's worked will form large clumps that dry hard and solid, without the many tiny pores that hold soil water and air. Soil that's worked when it's too dry can turn to fine dust.

To tell if soil is right for digging, hold some in your hand and squeeze it together gently to form a clod. Then apply light pressure to the clod with a finger from your other hand. If the clod holds together but breaks apart easily under pressure, you can dig the soil. If the clod doesn't break apart easily, your soil is too wet. If the clod doesn't hold together at all, it's too dry.

If your soil is too wet to dig, wait a few days and test it again. If your soil is too dry, set a sprinkler to soak it deeply and thoroughly. Then wait a couple of days and test to see if it has dried enough to be safe to work.

opened up with a rotary tiller before you try to plant it.

Also look for rocks in your soil. A few aren't a problem, except if you want to grow root crops such as carrots. But rocks make digging more difficult. Soil that is mostly rocks is not suitable for growing vegetables. If your shovel hits an impenetrable layer of rock or very hard soil within a foot of the surface, the soil is too shallow for a vegetable garden. In this case, look for deeper soil elsewhere on your property, or build raised beds for your garden. Fill these raised beds with soil you purchase or carry from elsewhere. For more on building and using raised beds, see "Making Raised Beds" on page 54.

Plan for Soil Amendments

Soil that's ready for planting is easy to dig. It is usually dark or nearly black because it contains lots of decayed organic matter. The organic matter holds the particles in soil together to give the soil a good crumb structure, which creates soil that gardeners often describe as fluffy. If your soil doesn't look or feel like this, don't despair. You can add enough organic matter and fertilizer this year to get started. In years to come, you'll continue adding organic matter to improve your soil.

Soil that already contains some organic matter puts you ahead of the game. Your soil is most likely to be rich in organic matter if it is in the east, north central, or northwest part of the country, if it has been under a forest or meadow, or if someone has been gardening it well for several years. It is likely to be low in organic matter if it is in the mountains or the southeast or southwest part of the country, if it has recently been in scrubby wild land or desert, if it is on a graded construction site, or

if it has been gardened poorly for several years.

Soils are practically never *too* high in organic matter, so plan on adding an organic soil amendment such as compost when you dig your garden. To find more information on soil amendments, see "Using Fertilizers" on page 45.

Consider Soil Testing

Testing your soil doesn't tell you how smart it is, but it is a smart thing to do before planting. A soil test will tell you if your soil provides the nutrients plants need. Although you can use a home test kit, you'll learn the most if you send a soil sample to a lab because their written report will recommend what to do to correct any problems they find. For more on soil tests, see "Chemical Tests" on page 28.

If you add plenty of organic soil amendments and some organic fertilizer, you'll probably do fine your first year without testing for soil nutrients. However, it's still a good idea to find out the soil pH, which is a measure of the acidity or alkalinity of your soil. You can do it yourself with an inexpensive pH test kit available at garden centers or with litmus paper, which is available at pharmacies.

Most vegetable and herb crops grow best when the pH is near neutral (7.0). Large regions of North America typically have acidic or alkaline soil, and these soils need special pH-changing amendments before crops will thrive. You can't assume that your soil is the same pH as a typical soil in your region. For example, Lewis Hill, author of *Cold-Climate Gardening,* says that while much of the soil of New England is acidic, the soil in his garden in northern Vermont turned out to be alkaline. For more information on pH and its effects in your garden, see "Soil pH" on page 24.

Working Your Soil

You may dig or till your garden a couple of days before you intend to plant, or you may prepare the soil up to several months in advance. Where winters are cold, gardeners often turn the soil in the fall to get it ready for spring planting.

If your initial assessment indicates that your soil will be relatively easy to work, just spread the organic soil amendments you've decided to add, along with any organic fertilizers, over the surface. Then dig it in by hand or use a rotary tiller. In a new garden site, hand-digging offers a big advantage. If your soil contains the roots, runners, or other parts of perennial weeds that can grow into new weed plants, hand-digging allows you to remove these as you work. Using a tiller, on the other hand, can make the problem worse by breaking the weed roots up into smaller parts. All too often, a new weed plant can grow from every fragment!

Digging by hand is often no more difficult than renting and wrestling with an unfamiliar tiller. The illustration below shows you how to dig to get the most work done with the least effort. Remember to let your weight and your leg muscles, not your back muscles, do the work.

If your soil is compacted, you may want to loosen it with a rotary tiller. You can rent a tiller from a tool-rental business or you may

Wrong

Right

Keep your knees slightly bent when you dig and move soil, and hold the shovel close to your body when it's full. It's more efficient and easier on your back. Turn each shovelful of soil halfway over before dropping it in place. To rest your back, stop work every few minutes, put your hands on your hips, and lean back slightly.

be able to hire someone to till your garden. Hard soil generally requires more than one pass, each time digging a bit deeper. When the soil is loosened to a depth of 6 to 8 inches, spread amendments and fertilizers evenly over the top and make one last pass with the tiller to work them in.

You can use a shovel or a digging fork to dig by hand. A digging fork is best if you are removing the roots and runners of perennial weeds because it's less likely to break them up. A fork is also the best tool for digging rocky soil. As you dig, work from one end of the bed to the other, turning over the soil to the depth of your shovel or fork. Break up any large clods, and remove rocks and weed roots as you go. It's best to work in rows so it's easy to see where you've already worked the soil.

The main goal of digging or tilling a new garden site is to loosen the soil so air and water can penetrate it—along with the roots of your new seedlings. Don't stand on the freshly turned area as you work or walk on it after you've finished. Walking on the soil will destroy the loose, fluffy texture you've worked so hard to create. (One reason paths between small garden beds are popular and practical is that the beds can be tended from the sides and never need to be walked on.)

PLANNING YOUR GARDEN

Long before your soil is ready, you'll begin planning what to plant. Go ahead and think big. Imagine a home orchard, berries by the garage, and bountiful vegetable beds. Then choose a few annual vegetables and herbs from your big list to try in your first season.

Think about what you like to eat. The crops you use in your kitchen are the ones you'll remember to harvest. If no one in your family likes lettuce salad, it won't matter how easy it is to grow lettuce. For some good first-garden choices, look at "Easy Crops by Region and Season" on page 503. There you'll find a list of easy-to-grow crops for your region, based on soil conditions, climate, and pests. You will have the most rewarding first experience if you limit yourself to ten or fewer vegetables and herbs from one of these lists. You can also look through the plant entries in Part 2 of this book to find possible crops. Skim the text to get a general idea of the care they will need and whether they will grow well in your climate and fit into your available space.

While planning, look for seed and nursery catalog ads in gardening magazines, and send for at least two or three of them. Look particularly for ones specializing in crops suited to your region. Even if you buy seeds from local seed racks your first year, you'll enjoy planning catalog orders for your next gardening season.

Choose a Planting Time

With final list in hand, you need to find out when each crop should be planted. Gardeners often divide crops into two general groups: cool-season crops and warm-season crops. Cool-season crops, such as cabbage, lettuce, and broccoli, can withstand some cold weather or even frost, but their growth suffers in hot weather. Warm-season crops, like tomatoes and peppers, won't tolerate frost and grow well in hot weather. If you live in an area with a short summer (100 to 150 days) wedged between spring and fall frosts, it's fairly simple to decide when to plant. Plant cool-season crops a couple of weeks before the last expected spring frost date for your area. Plant warm-season crops a few weeks later, when the soil is warm and danger of frost is well past. (If you have missed these starting times this year, try a planting of the fastest-growing cool-season crops such as lettuce, mustard greens, and radishes, planting them at least a month before the first expected fall frost.)

In areas with longer frost-free seasons, you can also make a second planting of many cool-season plants in mid- to late summer. You can even try second plantings of some warm-season crops in midsummer.

In the Deep South and the desert Southwest, summers are too hot for even some warm-season crops. The warm-season crops planted earliest beat the worst heat. In milder parts of the Southwest, gardeners often replant tomatoes and other warm-season crops in early fall for a second harvest. See page 93 for an illustration of where the planting seasons fall in different climates.

For help in tying your crop list to a planting time, see "Easy Crops by Region and Season" on page 503. (For crops not on this list, check the crop's plant entry in Part 2 to determine the best time to plant.) Jot down a planting schedule on your calendar so you'll know when each crop should go into the garden.

Don't make the common beginner's mistake of planting everything at once. For example, in many areas, if you hold off planting everything until it's safe to put your tomatoes out, it will be too late for cool-season crops such as lettuce and peas, which will not grow well when weather turns hot. Where seasons are longer and winters milder, such as in the South, there are more opportunities to start new crops. Very early spring and late summer to fall are excellent planting times in that part of the country.

Decide How Much to Plant

Once you're a gardening pro, you may grow most of the fresh food your family eats. But for your first garden, a good goal is to just produce a little of some of the foods you enjoy. Gaining experience with judging planting amounts and timing will help you plan your next garden.

Even in the best-planned gardens, production is not completely predictable. Sometimes pest damage, weather, or one of your mistakes limits production. Other times, a crop will out-produce your wildest dreams. Still, it is possible to make good estimates of production. Chapter 3 describes in detail how to make estimates. Also, in Part 2, each plant entry contains information on how much to plant.

Although a very small garden is not likely to produce too much of any one crop, a few crops are so productive that relatively few plants can overload your kitchen. Fast-maturing, fast-declining crops, such as radishes, lettuce, green onions, spinach, mustard greens, and cilantro, can present this problem. When you grow these, plant no more at one time than your family can eat in two to three weeks. For example, if your family can eat about 10 radishes a week, plan to grow no more than 30 at one time. If you want more and the season permits, you can replant the same amount when the first planting is half-grown.

The other kind of crop that can overwhelm with its bounty is one that can, under good conditions, produce a huge crop on each plant. Prime examples are summer squash, such as zucchini, and tomatoes. In this case, plant only one or two plants per person the first year.

Plan to Prevent Problems

Gardening will inevitably introduce you to certain insects, plant diseases, and pesky animals that want a share of your harvest. As you decide what crops to grow and draw up a garden plan, start thinking about the problems you'll encounter through the season. Actually, basic good organic gardening practices are the first line of defense against pests. If you take good care of your soil and plants, your garden will be healthier and have fewer problems with insects, diseases, and weeds. Healthy plants attract fewer insect pests, are less susceptible to disease, and beat out weeds.

Start by making a list of the potential problems mentioned by local gardeners. If you don't know what causes them, try to find out. The more you know, the better able you'll be to pick effective control methods. Problem prevention is often more simple than you might think. Before you go to buy plants for your garden, take a look at the illustration below to help you determine which plants are healthy and which aren't. The tips that follow will help

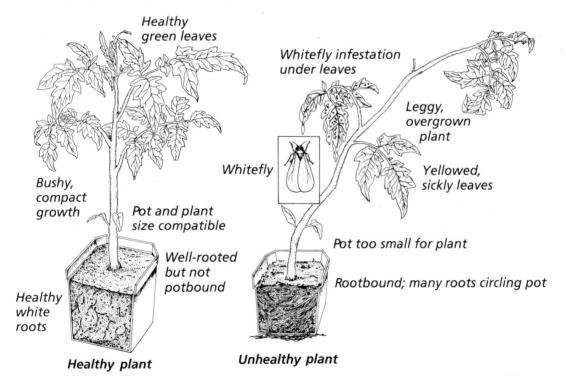

When you're buying transplants, look for plants that are a good green color and at least as wide as they are tall. Don't buy plants with scars on the stem—an indication that leaves have fallen from the plant.

you maintain a healthy garden and minimize problems in it.

Look for problems regularly. Walk through your garden daily—or at least once a week—looking carefully at your plants. Turn over leaves, note overall appearance, and look for signs of pests, diseases, or damage.

Plant resistant plants. Buy vegetables and fruits that are insect- or disease-resistant. Resistance is often mentioned in catalog copy or on the seed packet. Tomatoes marked VFNT, for example, are resistant to Verticillium and Fusarium wilts, nematodes, and tobacco mosaic. Check the individual plant entries in Part 2 for more information on resistant cultivars.

Don't bring in problems. Check all new plants for signs of insects, diseases, or weeds before you buy. Don't buy from nurseries that offer unhealthy-looking stock.

Handle plants carefully. Bruised leaves and stems are more susceptible to attack by diseases and insects. Also, stay out of the garden when it's wet. Disease organisms spread easily on the film of water on wet leaves.

Use barriers to keep pests at bay. Deny larger animal pests like rabbits and deer access to your garden riches with fences, barriers, repellents, and scare tactics. Floating row cover is an easy, effective way to control insect pests such as cabbage maggots, flea beetles, and Mexican bean beetles.

Protect transplants with cutworm collars. Cutworms cut down transplants under cover of darkness. To make protective collars for your plants, cut strips of lightweight cardboard about 8 inches × 2½ inches, overlap the ends to make a circle, and fasten with tape or a staple. When transplanting, slip a collar over each plant and press it into the soil around the stem so about half of the collar is below the soil line.

There are many other preventive methods for dealing with specific pests. For complete information on preventing and controlling pest problems, see Chapter 6.

Laying Out the Garden

After deciding what and how much to plant, it's time to figure what goes where in the garden. Whether or not you draw up a plan on paper before you plant, it is important to remember which plant is which. To learn the ins and outs of drawing up a plan on paper, refer to "Putting a Plan on Paper" on page 81. If you don't draw a plan before you plant, make a rough sketch of your garden afterward. Or, at a minimum, put a label next to each kind of plant.

Usually, you'll want to plan so that each plant gets as much sun as possible. The midday sun shines from slightly to the south. Therefore, plants will get the most sunlight if you plant east-west rows of crops. Plant the tallest crops on the north side of the garden, planting progressively shorter crops until you get to the south side. Read seed packets or see the plant entries in Part 2 to find out how tall each crop will grow and how far apart the rows should be spaced. To determine the correct distance between rows of two different kinds of crops, add together the correct distance between rows for each crop and divide the sum by two.

You don't have to plant in rows, but they have one big advantage for a beginning gardener: It's obvious where you put the seeds. Later, when you are trying to tell weed seedlings from crop seedlings, you will probably be glad you followed a pattern that is easy to recognize.

You may want to arrange your garden to provide shade for certain crops. If you are growing a crop that needs cooler conditions, such as lettuce, into a warm time of year, plan to shade it. If you plant the lettuce on the east side of a north-south row of a taller crop such as corn, it will get afternoon shade. You can even plant the lettuce on the north side of an east-west row so it receives shade most of the day.

Plant perennial crops in their own area—a block or a row at the edge of the garden is fine. That way, when you want to dig the soil for the next season's annual plants, the perennials won't be in the way.

For your first garden, don't worry too much about which crops to plant together or apart. You can find lots of advice in gardening books and magazines concerning what to plant next to what, but quite simply, commonly grown vegetables seem to share the same garden space pretty well. In years to come, you'll want to refine your garden management style as you learn more about techniques such as companion planting, interplanting, and crop rotation. (See Chapter 3 for more information on these techniques.)

Buying Seeds and Plants

Once you have a plan in hand, you're ready go shopping. See "Easy Crops by Region and Season" on page 503 to see which crops are best started as seeds and which should be grown from sets or transplants.

Buy fresh seeds. Discounted seed packets are all too often last year's stock. While they may germinate just fine, don't add any uncertainty your first gardening year. Buy sets, such as potatoes or garlic, from a source intended for gardeners, rather than from a grocery, to be sure they are disease-free.

Buy seedlings or transplants from a repu-table nursery on the day you plan to plant or only a few days earlier. See the illustration on page 13 for tips on buying healthy plants.

PLANTING YOUR GARDEN

It's miraculous to watch tiny seedlings pushing up through the soil. While they're powerful for their size, seedlings have a hard time growing if there are clods of soil, bits of wood, or rocks around them. Taking care to prepare seedbeds before planting will mean that more of your seeds make it through to become productive members of your garden.

Finish preparing your garden for planting on a day when the soil is moist but not soggy. (See "Tricks of the Trade: Do the Squeeze Test" on page 8.) Use your shovel or digging fork to break up the largest clods. Rake the soil to break up smaller clods and to smooth and level the soil surface. Use a light touch, or you'll end up with a planting bed less level than when you began. As you work, remove large rocks or chunks of undecayed organic matter.

Planting Seeds

Your final preparation will be just in the places where you plant. In areas where you are going to plant seeds—that is, in the row or an inch or two on each side—use your fingers to feel 2 or 3 inches under the surface and break up any remaining clods. Where you'll be planting small seeds such as lettuce, beet, or radish seeds, prepare a fine seedbed by removing rocks or other material bigger than $\frac{1}{4}$ inch in diameter. For larger seeds such as bean, squash, and corn seeds, you can leave slightly larger rocks and organic material.

Read the seed packet for advice on the depth and distance apart to plant the seeds. If your soil is heavy clay or if you are planting early while weather is still cold, use the shallower depth suggested. If your soil is sandy or if the weather is quite warm, use the deeper one.

To plant small seeds, use your finger or the corner of a rake to prepare a shallow trench of the proper depth. Next, open the seed packet and shake a few seeds into the palm of your hand. Put the seed packet down, upright, out of the way of your work. Pick up a few seeds between your fingers and scatter them down the planting trench. Getting them the right distance apart takes a little practice, but it doesn't have to be perfect. The seed packet generally recommends sowing seed closer than the final spacing because having too many seedlings is better than having too few. You can always thin some seedlings—pull them out or cut them off at soil level—once they come up.

To plant larger seeds, use your finger to poke holes in the soil the correct depth and distance apart. Pick out individual seeds and drop one in each hole. This allows you to decide the spacing exactly, but you'll still usually plant a few extra and thin later on. Sometimes larger seeds, such as squash or pole beans, are planted in hills. Hills are small groups of seeds planted with wide distances between the groups. In a hill, you generally plant about twice as many seeds as you want to mature and then thin to the biggest seedlings.

Cover large or small seeds once you have planted a hill or a few feet of row. Sprinkle soil carefully over the row or into individual planting holes. As you cover the seeds, roll the soil between your fingers or palms to break up even tiny clods. It may help to mark off short sections of a row with sticks or rocks and cover the sections one at a time. When a section has been covered to the correct depth, use your hand to pat down the soil. This pushes soil against the seeds so that when you water the seedbed, the water makes good contact with the seeds. Once you've finished planting for the day, be sure to give all of your newly seeded rows a gentle but thorough watering.

Planting Transplants

With a little basic care, healthy, well-grown transplants will all generally survive being moved to the garden. You can buy just the number you plan to have in your mature garden. For best results, move transplants to the garden on a cool, still, overcast day, or in the late afternoon. Otherwise, sun and wind can dry out the seedlings, checking their growth or even killing them.

When you're ready to plant transplants, check the individual plant entries in Part 2 for spacing recommendations and measure to figure out where planting holes should be. Mark the spots with small stakes. Use a trowel to dig a hole as deep as the container that holds the transplant and about 1½ times as wide. Remove any large objects from the soil you dig out of the planting hole. Then feel into the 2 to 3 inches of soil at the bottom of the hole for any more obstructions. If you want to add an extra amendment or fertilizer at planting time, dig the hole a few inches deeper. Place the amendment or fertilizer in the hole, and mix it into the soil. Put about 1 inch of plain soil on top of this mixture.

Next, remove a transplant from its container. If the container is flexible plastic, you should be able to gently squeeze the sides of the container to loosen the plant and push it up so you can remove it. If the plant is not in a flexible container, cover the soil surface with your hand, overturn the plant, and tap firmly on the container. If the plant is stuck, turn the container right-side-up, run a knife around the inside of the pot, and then overturn it again.

Put the container aside and examine the root ball. If the roots are circling around at the bottom, loosen them gently. Then, using your other hand to steady the root ball, turn the plant over and into the prepared hole. To minimize root damage, try to keep the soil on the root ball as much as possible. If the hole proves too deep, lift the transplant very gently by reaching under the root ball, and move some more soil under it. If it is set too shallowly, lift the plant and remove a bit of soil.

Fill the hole around the root ball with the soil you removed when you dug the hole. Steady and center the plant stem with one hand while you sweep soil in with the other. When the hole is filled, pat the soil down firmly. If this creates a depression, add a bit more soil and pat again. Do not build a mound of soil around the stem; the soil should be level.

You can create a little basin to hold water around the plant by making a low circular ridge of soil around the transplant. Make the circle 6 to 12 inches in diameter, depending on the size of the transplant. New transplants need water fairly soon, so if you are planting many at a time, empty a quart of water gently at the base of each one as soon as you plant it.

When you are done planting for the day, water thoroughly. You can use a sprinkler for this, even for plants that you shouldn't water from above later on. Sprinkling helps reduce evaporation from the new transplants, and gentle droplets of water falling to the ground will not wash away the seeds that you have planted. Use an oscillating sprinkler, or water

by hand. If you hand sprinkle, move the hose around frequently so that water won't run off the soil surface.

If you had to plant on a sunny day or if the weather is likely to be sunny and hot for the next few days, give the transplants a little shade. To shade transplants from the afternoon sun, stick something into the soil on the southwest side of the rows. Propped up shingles, pieces of cardboard, or small screens made of newspaper stapled or taped to two sticks will do the trick.

If the weather is still a little too cool, protect transplants by putting paper bags over them at night. Cut partway up the sides of the bags and weight down the flaps with soil or small rocks. Warm just-planted seedbeds by covering them with black plastic. Look under the plastic daily and remove it as soon as you see the seedlings breaking through the ground. For more tips on protecting your seedbeds and transplants from cold and from pests, see "Season Extension Techniques" on page 209.

CARING FOR YOUR CROPS

Transplants and newly sown seeds need to be kept constantly moist for the first few weeks. Water your new garden lightly every time the surface is dry or up to twice a day in hot, dry weather. Seedlings should begin to emerge from the ground in a week or two. If the weather is cool, emergence will take a bit longer.

Transplants need to repair root damage during the first few days in the garden. The lower leaves may yellow and the plants may wilt slightly. Then they'll appear to sit unchanged for a week or longer. You'll know you succeeded when the plants begin to grow again.

Controlling Weeds

Unfortunately, the first green leaves you see in your seedbeds are likely to be weeds. Competition with weeds can seriously slow the growth of your crops. Weed early and often to show who's in charge. Some seed packets have pictures of the crop seedling, so you'll know what to pull and what to preserve. Or to grow your own weeding guides, see "Make Your Own: Seedling ID Guides" on the opposite page.

Between transplants and rows of seedlings, use a hoe or a hand cultivator to control weeds all through the season. Scrape just below the surface, cutting off weed roots. Hand-pull weeds that come up close to your plants. For the weeds that sprout up nearest your plants, it's safest to use scissors to cut off the weeds at the ground. That way, you won't damage crop roots.

Weed regularly throughout the season. Your goal is to keep weeds from going to seed in your garden. This tactic reduces the number of weed seeds around to sprout next year.

Thinning Seedlings

Thinning is a heartbreaker for beginning gardeners. It can be painfully sad to pull out the little plants you worked so hard to grow, but that's exactly what you must do. Seed-sowing recommendations are designed to ensure that plants fill the row, but that means sowing extra seeds as insurance. Crowded plants grow more slowly and will be stunted, so don't neglect this all-important step. Once your seedlings are well up and growing, check the final recommended spacing and pull or use scissors to clip off extra seedlings at ground level. You'll find recommendations for final spacing on seed packets and in the plant entries in Part 2.

The good news is that sometimes you can eat your thinnings. Add those tiny lettuce plants or baby radishes to a salad! You may even be able to thin in two stages. For example: Thin your lettuce plants to half the final spacing—say, 2 to 4 inches apart—the first time and eat the small thinnings. Later, thin to the final spacing—say, 6 to 8 inches—again eating the thinnings.

Watering

Like weeding, watering is most important early in the season. Newly planted seeds and transplants can require daily watering. As your plants grow deeper roots, they need deeper, less frequent watering. Varied weather conditions and different soil types make it impossible to give an exact schedule. One rule of thumb frequently cited is that vegetable crops require about a 1-inch layer of water per week. This rule is too simplistic to apply to all of the varying climatic conditions found in North America. It may work well if you garden in humid regions—as long as you're not having an unusually dry summer!

If it hasn't rained and you suspect your plants need watering, check the top inch or two of soil. If the soil is dry, water deeply and thoroughly. Allen Wilson, a professor of landscape horticulture at Ricks College in Idaho, reports that beginners who have moved to the arid West from eastern areas with plentiful rainfall frequently don't water often enough. On the other hand, Jan Riggenbach, a free-lance garden columnist from Iowa, cautions to check soil moisture before watering plants that droop a bit at the end of a hot day. If the soil is already moist, the plants will revive once the sun goes down. To add more water could drown the roots. For more thorough

✦ MAKE YOUR OWN ✦

SEEDLING ID GUIDES

You can grow some extra insurance that will come in handy once seeds begin germinating in your garden. Seedling jars are a great way to be sure you'll be able to tell the seedlings you planted from the weed seedlings. Plant one for each kind of seed you plant on the same day you plant seeds outside. If you are growing more than one ID guide at a time, you'll want to label each one by writing the name of the seeds on a bit of masking tape and sticking it to the outside of the jar. Then use the jar seedlings as a living field guide when you're weeding so you'll know which seedlings to leave and which to pull. Here's how to make your own seedling ID guide:

1. Select a small juice glass or a pint jar with relatively straight sides. Fold a single paper towel into thirds. Roll it into a tube a bit narrower than the glass or jar.

2. Insert the paper towel tube into the jar, then open it slightly so it's pressed up against the sides of the jar. Pour about 1 inch of water into the jar and wait for it to soak up and moisten the entire paper towel. If this uses up all of the water you added, add more so that there is about ½ inch of water in the bottom of the jar.

3. Pull the paper towel away from the glass in one place and drop in a seed. Try to position the seed partway down. If it falls all the way to the water at the bottom, it will probably rot. Repeat this step two or three times, placing a seed in two or three more places around the jar.

4. Check your jar daily for growth. Keep a ½-inch reservoir of water in the jar at all times. Keep the jar in a warm, dark cupboard until the seeds germinate, then move it to a sunny location. After you've used the seed-jar seedlings to guide you when weeding your garden, discard them, since plants started in this manner rarely thrive.

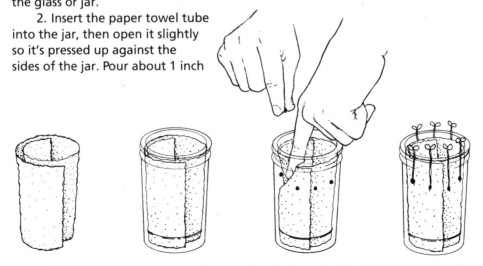

guidelines on the best ways to water your garden, see "Watering 101" on page 117.

Mulching Your Garden

For weed control and keeping the soil moist and cool, nothing is better than a good layer of mulch. Vegetable gardeners often use organic mulches, such as straw, compost, or grass clippings, because they add all-important organic matter to the soil as they decay.

To apply a mulch, weed the garden completely, water it well, then spread a 1- to 4-inch layer evenly on the surface. Mulch pathways as soon as you plant. But in spring, delay mulching around your plants until the soil has a chance to warm. Keep mulch away from transplants until they start to grow and away from seedlings until they have a few leaves and are growing vigorously. Then push mulch up closer to the plants but still not so near that it touches plant stems. For more on using mulches, see "Mulching" on page 35.

BASIC HARVEST KNOW-HOW

As your crops thrive and grow, you will be approaching the main event: the harvest. But don't assume that it is something that happens months from planting time. If you planted quick-growing crops such as radishes or lettuce, you can be pulling crisp roots and picking tender greens in as few as 20 days!

Don't expect your harvest to happen all at once, either. Many crops bear over a long period of time. In fact, vegetable cultivars for the home garden are often bred to produce a longer harvest because picking a little at a time for a long time is best for daily kitchen use. Keep an eye on your garden throughout the season so you won't miss either early or ongoing harvests.

Harvesting your crops is pleasant work, but it does take time and must be done when the crops are ready. Everyone knows what a ripe tomato looks like, but the harvesting clues aren't quite as clear for every crop. For example, snap beans should be picked when the enlarging seeds are just visible and okra when the pods are 3 to 5 inches long. Read the plant entries in Part 2 for tips on when to harvest each of your crops.

Some crops need to be picked regularly to prolong the harvest. Among these are beans, peas, cucumbers, and zucchini. If even one fruit on any of these plants is allowed to become overripe, the plant will make fewer new fruits or even stop production. See the table "Making Fresh Flavor Last" on page 202 for more on harvesting your garden bounty.

You'll undoubtedly find that food gardening is most satisfying if you make good use of everything you grow. And that's a learned skill. As you continue to garden, you will get better at coordinating your garden with your kitchen. You will plant more of what you used well and less of what went to waste. You'll remember to harvest frequently and to coordinate your garden and vacation schedule. And you'll learn recipes that use the early and late bits of crops, as well as deal with the glut of the main harvest. The lessons you have learned in your first year will make the next year more rewarding. Soon, you'll become one of those experienced gardeners that novices in the neighborhood rely on to learn the lay of the gardening land.

2 MANAGING YOUR SOIL
Rating Your Soil's Fertility and Creating a Soil Management Program

Fertile, deep soil on a level, sunny site is a blessing for any gardener. Most of us have to work to create that blessing for ourselves because most soils aren't naturally perfect for growing fruits, vegetables, and herbs. But how do you decide what your soil really needs? What would benefit your plants most? And how can you put all of the details of fertilizers, compost applications, crop needs, and existing soil problems together into a basic plan for improving your soil? In this chapter, you'll learn the answers to all of these questions. You'll learn how to analyze what type of soil you have and how fertile it is. Then you'll use that knowledge to create a management program based on good gardening practices that increase the quality and productivity of your soil year by year, such as adding organic matter and fertilizing. You'll also learn how to work your soil, prepare planting rows or beds, and manage soil the right way.

If you're a new gardener, your first step will be to choose a site that meets your plants' basic needs for light and space. For information on site selection, see "Guidelines for First-Timers" on page 4, "Selecting the Best Site" on pages 6 and 7, and "Other Climatic Concerns" on page 93.

Once you gain experience with soil management or if you're already an advanced gardener, you may want to experiment with customized soil management programs for different types of vegetable and fruit crops. You'll find "custom care" regimes for fruiting vegetable crops, root crops, leafy crops, tree fruits, and small fruits beginning on page 56.

SOIL BASICS

You can't tune up a car engine if you don't know what all of the parts are. That's true about soil, too. A working knowledge of your soil—what it's made of, how it works, and what lives in it—will help you analyze its fertility and develop an effective management program for it.

Why is your soil so important? Soil supports your plants, not only physically, but also as the medium through which they receive water and nutrients. A healthy soil does a better job of these two critical functions than unhealthy soil does. When soil is healthy, it has lots of biological activity, a good balance of nutrients, and a loose, open structure. The way you manage and work the soil affects all of these aspects of soil health.

Roots are the channel from your soil to your plant's stems, leaves, and fruits. The most important function of roots is collecting water and nutrients. While plants manufacture their own food from carbon dioxide absorbed through their leaves, they can't do it without nutrients dissolved in water in the soil. As roots grow, young root tips are continually exploring new soil and mining it for nutrients. Managing your soil properly makes their search mission easier.

What Soil Is Made Of

Soil is wonderfully alive. If you're new to organic gardening, that statement may surprise you. But beneath the surface, the soil is full of living organisms that interact in a finely tuned living system. On a percentage basis, soil is mostly minerals (45 percent), followed by air (25 percent) and water (25 percent). The biological component is only 5 percent, but it is a very significant 5 percent. So watch your step in the garden! Your soil deserves as much respect and special care as your plants do.

In "Evaluating Your Soil" on page 25, you'll find a variety of tests you can use to look closely at your own soil.

Minerals

Tiny particles of rock called sand, silt, and clay make up the mineral portion of the soil. The exact percentages of each of these materials varies depending on where you garden and can have a significant effect on soil drainage and fertility. Gardeners generally refer to soils as sandy, loamy, or clayey. This relates to the proportions of the different sizes of mineral particles in the soil, also called its texture.

While all of these particles are tiny, on a comparative basis, sand particles are the biggest. Sand particles don't adhere, or stick together, when wet. Sandy soils often drain too fast and don't hold enough water for good crop production. These soils also tend to be lower in natural fertility.

Silt particles are smaller than sand particles. They will adhere when wet. Soils that have moderate amounts of sand, silt, and clay are called loam soils. They are generally considered the best soils for gardening.

Clay particles are extremely tiny. These particles adhere very tightly when wet. A clay soil can be slow to dry after rains. It tends to form heavy clods and surface crusts. It may hold nutrients so tightly to the surfaces of its particles that it doesn't easily supply enough nutrients for best plant growth.

Air and Water

Soil has spaces, or pores, between its particles, which are filled with air or water. Soil structure, meaning the arrangement of the soil particles, determines the size and the quantity of pore spaces in the soil. Many factors contribute to the creation of soil structure. Soil water freezes and thaws, plant roots grow and die, and earthworms move through the soil. All of these processes contribute to formation of soil pores and formation of soil clumps, or aggregates. Soil structure is also affected by soil pH, the amount of humus in the soil, and the combination of minerals in the soil. The ideal soil is friable—the soil particles clump together in clusters with air spaces between them.

Soil pore spaces are critical because they ensure that plant roots and soil organisms get the air and water they need. Ideally, pore spaces should vary in size and be evenly distributed. Large pore spaces allow water to drain through the soil to make room for soil air. Smaller pore spaces hold water in the soil for plant roots.

Both soil organisms and plant roots need soil air. Plant roots "breathe" and need air exchange between soil air and the atmosphere for good development. Many beneficial soil organisms cannot live without the oxygen in soil air, and nitrogen-fixing bacteria use the nitrogen in soil air as a raw material. These bacteria "fix" nitrogen into protein materials that are later broken down into nitrogen compounds called nitrates, which plants can absorb.

Plant roots take up soil water and pass it on to leaves and stems, where it serves as a nutrient, a coolant, and an essential part of all plant cells. Many mineral nutrients are also transported into roots and through plants in water.

If soil doesn't drain well, water fills up all of the pore spaces. This prevents roots from getting the air they need, thus suffocating the plants. Walking on the soil, driving power equipment over it, or digging in it when it's wet all destroy soil structure, causing these important pore spaces to collapse.

Organic Matter

Organic matter is material in your soil that was once alive. It includes plant residues (raw organic matter) and humus, the dark-colored, stable form of organic matter that remains after most of the plant and animal residues in it have decomposed.

Organic matter has different sizes of particles and pore spaces, which help retain air and water in the soil. It also provides a good environment for root growth and many of the nutrients plants need to grow. When clay, raw organic matter, and humus bind together in the soil, they form tiny, sticky particles called colloids. Colloids act like minute, negatively charged magnets. They attract nutrient particles that have a positive charge, such as potassium, magnesium, and calcium. These positively charged particles are called cations.

A soil's capacity to hold cations is called the cation exchange capacity (CEC). In general, it's good to have a high CEC, because it means your soil can hold on to lots of the nutrients your plants need to grow. However, a high CEC doesn't necessarily mean that the soil is fertile. That's because there are also cations, such as hydrogen and aluminum, that are not beneficial to plants. If your soil holds lots of aluminum cations, it may have a high CEC, but that won't help your plants because plants don't need this mineral!

Another benefit of organic matter is that as it decomposes, it is transformed into vitamins, hormones, and substances that stimulate plant growth. Decomposing organic matter also produces certain toxins that suppress weeds and plant disease organisms (called pathogens). Organic matter also provides a favorable environment for beneficial organisms that prey on pathogens.

Living Organisms

Earthworms, insects, mites, soil-dwelling mammals and reptiles, nematodes, bacteria, fungi, and other soil microorganisms live in the soil. As they move through it, they act as players and messengers in decay and nutrient cycles. Most of these animals and microbes are beneficial to your soil and your plants. They cause organic matter to decompose into humus and they transform some plant nutrients into forms your plants can absorb. Some even prey on pests and disease organisms that harm your plants. Mycoorhizae help plant roots take up nutrients and water.

If you keep the beneficial organisms happy and productive, 75 percent of your job as a gardener will be done for you. Think of the beneficial organisms in soil as your "microherd," and learn to tend it conscientiously. If you don't, you will inherit its job and find yourself becoming a soil chemist and mineral balancer. The illustration on pages 26 and 27 shows enlarged views of some of these organisms and explains their functions in the soil.

Soil pH

Soil pH is a characteristic that all gardeners read about but few understand. Soil pH is a measure of the acidity or alkalinity of the soil. In more technical terms, it is a measure of the concentration of hydrogen ions (charged molecules of hydrogen) in soil water. Soil pH is expressed as a number between 1.0 and 14.0. Neutral soil has a pH of 7.0. Acid soil has a pH less than 7.0; alkaline, or basic, soil has a pH greater than 7.0.

Soil pH is important because it influences the chemical forms of phosphorus and some micronutrients (nutrients needed in minute amounts for plant growth). When a plant nutrient is in the form that can be absorbed by plant roots, it is said to be available. Phosphorus is most available when soil pH is between 6.5 and 6.8. Micronutrients are most available at levels between 6.0 and 7.0.

As a gardener, your goal is to keep your

IS YOUR SOIL SAFE?

Toxic waste and heavy metals may not jump to mind as factors to worry about when choosing a site for your food garden. Unfortunately, contamination of soil is becoming a problem even in our backyards, especially in the city. Soil can be contaminated by materials dumped in the past, by substances leaching from waste dumps, and by pesticide residues, peeling paint, and air pollution.

Lead is the toxin of most concern to home gardeners. In the past, automobile exhaust showered lead on urban gardens. Flakes of lead-based paint can accumulate in soils around any old wooden structure, rural or urban.

If you suspect that your soil is contaminated, seek advice about whether to have soil tests done and which tests to try. To find out how to take a soil sample, see "Collecting a Soil Sample" on page 29. Contact your Cooperative Extension Service or state environmental regulatory agency to find out where to send it and how much it will cost.

---

soil pH in the ideal range from about 6.2 to 6.8. If your soil is too acidic (having a pH less than 6.0), it has too many hydrogen ions. You can add lime, which neutralizes some of these ions, and raise the pH so it is more balanced. If your soil is too alkaline (having a pH greater than 7.5), it doesn't have enough hydrogen ions. You can add sulfur or other substances to increase the number of hydrogen ions and balance the pH. Organic matter also tends to have a balancing effect on soil pH.

EVALUATING YOUR SOIL

To develop an effective soil management program, you need a clear picture of your soil's health, and that means giving your soil a thorough checkup. A few simple do-it-yourself tests combined with the results from a conventional soil test will give you a good picture of your soil's overall health. You'll use the results of these tests plus the information in the table "Rating Soil Fertility" on page 31 to help you decide whether your soil is low-, medium-, or high-fertility. Your soil checkup will also help you identify specific problems. With this information in hand, you'll be ready to make a plan to improve it.

Clues from Plants

The first step in investigating your soil's health is to investigate your plants. Soil problems usually cause plant growth problems. For example, yellow, patchy-looking leaves can indicate either too little or too much soil moisture. Plants will appear wilted. Dig them up, and you'll find stunted roots. Strangely shaped root crops also can indicate poor soil drainage. Poor root growth and pale, stunted leaves can also indicate nutrient deficiencies. For some specific examples, see "Signs of Soil Stress" on this page. You can also refer to the table "Troubleshooting Plant Nutrient Deficiencies" on page 175. Don't make a hasty diagnosis based on such signs alone. Also, remember that deficiency symptoms will look even worse if the soil is poorly drained and low in oxygen.

Weeds will also give you clues about your soil. Although you'll find weeds in every garden, look closely if you notice one species of weed dominating an area. Robust dandelions may indicate compacted soil. Chamomile and goosefoot usually mark soils that are alkaline, while sheep sorrel and horsetails prefer acid soils. Thistles grow well in heavy clay soils. Barnyard grass indicates a high water table.

Hands-On Tests

Getting more personal with your soil can also help you evaluate it. Taking a good look at its color, texture, smell, and structure will help you know how to improve it. Scoop up a handful of your soil. Are the particles held loosely together with what feels like moist flour paste? If so, your soil is well-aggregated, which means

(continued on page 28)

SIGNS OF SOIL STRESS

Sickly looking plants may not have a "bug." The culprit may be an unhealthy soil that's not providing well for your plants. Here are some telltale clues to soil woes:

• Poor growth of grains, grasses, or beets may indicate a nitrogen deficiency.
• Weakling legumes or potatoes may signal low potassium levels.
• Struggling root crops often indicate a deficiency of both potassium and phosphorus.
• Young potato vines may turn yellowish green if available nitrogen is insufficient or if soil microbes are sluggish and not busily cycling nutrients.
• Stunted, misshapen celery may be due to insufficient nitrogen and phosphorus.
• Lateral-growing, long, stringy roots with few visible root hairs indicate that nutrients aren't easily available.

LIFE IN THE SOIL

Beneath the surface of the soil is a dynamic world of biological and biochemical activity. Roots probe for water and dissolved nutrients, while insects, earthworms, bacteria, fungi, and other microorganisms take part in cycles of growth and decay. The following are some of the most important organisms found in healthy soil.

Actinomycetes. Actinomycetes are a specialized type of bacteria. They play an important role in organic matter decay and humus formation.

Bacteria. Bacteria are single-celled animals. Rhizobacteria stimulate plant growth. Nitrogen-fixing bacteria form protein materials from atmospheric nitrogen. Nitrifying bacteria convert nitrogen from organic matter into nitrate. Other bacteria convert sulfur compounds and phosphorus into forms that plants can absorb.

Earthworms. Earthworms tunnel through the soil. As they feed, organic matter passes through their bodies and is excreted as granular, dark castings. This enhances soil structure, and mixes and adds air to the soil. Earthworms

Beneficial nematodes

Actinomycetes

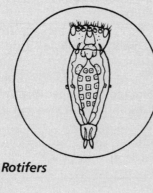

Rotifers

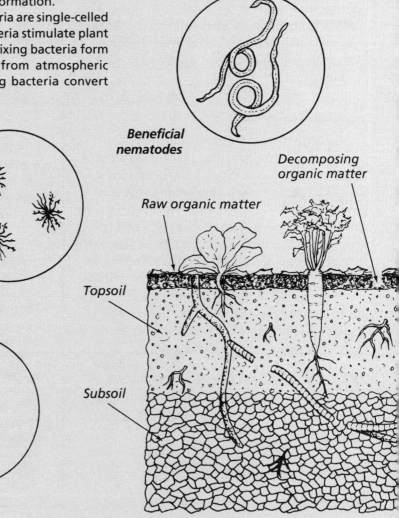

Decomposing organic matter

Raw organic matter

Topsoil

Subsoil

also eat microorganisms that cause plant diseases.

Fungi. Fungi are plants that don't produce chlorophyll. Some kinds play a role in decomposition; others are beneficial organisms that prey on organisms that cause plant diseases. Mycorrhizae are specialized fungi that help plant roots take up nutrients and water.

Protozoa. Protozoa are one-celled animals. They eat organisms that cause plant diseases and thus offer disease control.

Rotifers. Rotifers are microscopic animals. They live in moist soils and play a role in breaking down organic matter.

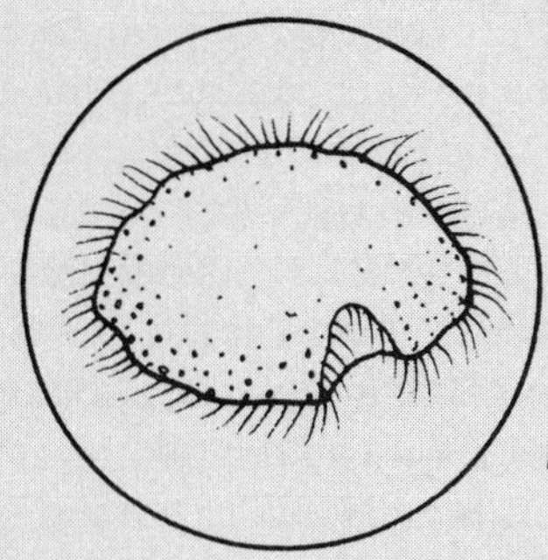

Protozoa

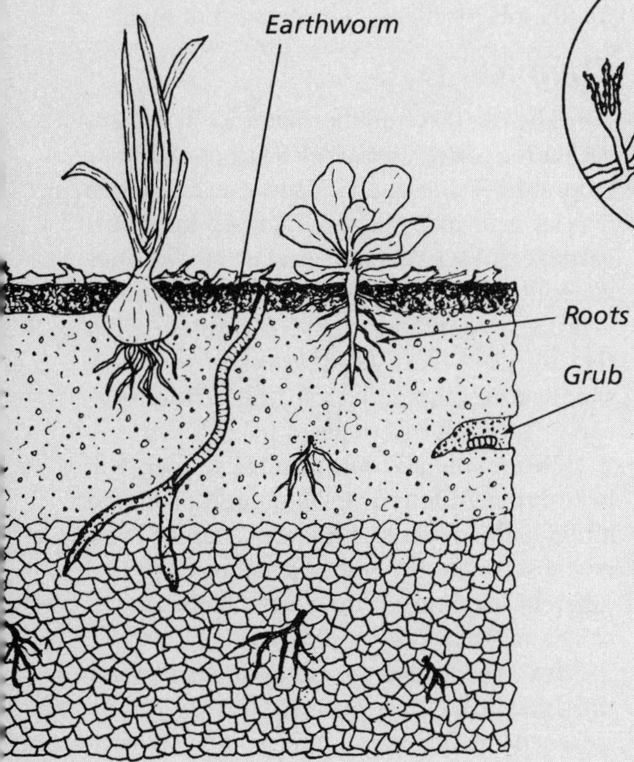

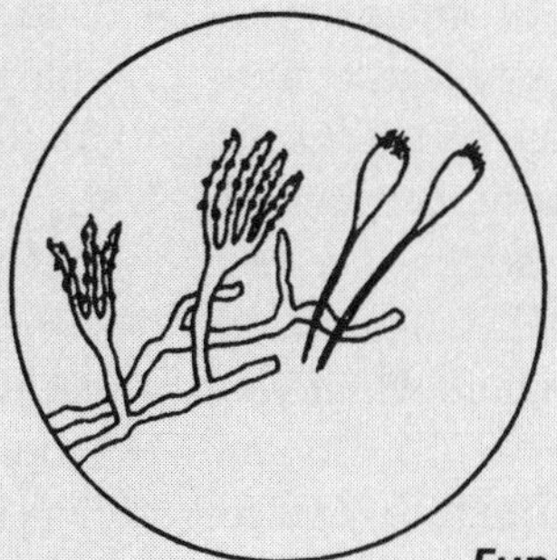

Earthworm

Fungi

Roots

Grub

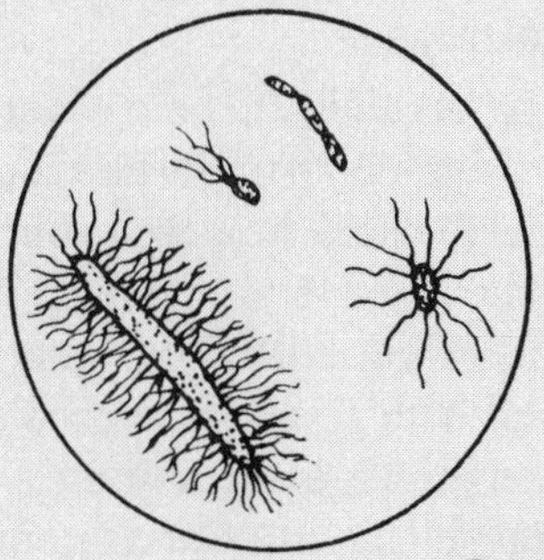

Bacteria

it has a structure that promotes strong root growth. Good soil tends to be dark brown or red in color. Poor soil tends toward the paler shades of brown and red. If your soil has gray or whitish streaks, suspect poor aeration and drainage. Humus—always present in productive soils—turns a dark black when wet.

Productive soil smells earthy. The scent arises from the presence of microorganisms called actinomycetes and also from fungi. A healthy soil quite literally smells alive.

Feeling for Texture

You can identify your soil's texture by feel. To do this, dig a hole 4 to 6 inches deep, and scoop out 1 tablespoon of soil from the bottom. Wet the soil with 1 teaspoon of water. Try to roll the soil into a ball. Sandy soil feels coarse and doesn't stick together when wet. Silt feels less coarse than sand. It feels fluffy, like powder, and will roll into a ball that sticks together loosely. Clay makes a firm ball when rolled together and clings to your fingers when you put the ball down.

Another simple test for soil texture is called fractional analysis. This test determines the relative percentages of sand, silt, and clay particles in your soil. Refer to "Testing for Texture" on the opposite page for instructions.

Checking Drainage

Soil drainage—its ability to hold water and to let it drain through—is an important indicator of soil health. To check how well your soil takes up water, dig a hole 6 to 12 inches deep and 6 to 12 inches wide. Fill it with water and let it drain. A soil with good drainage should absorb the water in 15 to 30 minutes. If it drains faster, your soil has low water retention. Slower draining indicates a soil with low permeability, poor structure, and/or lack of pore spaces between soil particles.

To test soil drainage, refill the hole after the water drains away. Record the time it takes for the water to disappear. If it takes longer than 2½ hours, your soil drainage is poor.

Counting Earthworms

Healthy soil is full of earthworms. Surface signs of earthworms include castings (small mounds of crumbly soil) and entrance holes. To get an estimate of the earthworm population in your soil, dig a hole 8 to 10 inches deep and 1 foot wide. (The best time to do this is when the soil is about 60°F and moist.) Count the earthworms in the soil you remove. More than ten earthworms is great. Six to ten indicate a relatively healthy soil. Five or fewer indicate possible problems: a soil with low organic matter, pH problems, and/or poor drainage.

Chemical Tests

The last piece of information you need to gather is a conventional soil test. Some private laboratories and the Cooperative Extension Service will analyze soil samples for home gardeners. Fees vary, but private laboratories generally charge more than the extension service does. Home soil test kits are available, but they're not usually as accurate as sending a sample to a commercial testing lab. Home kits can be useful for testing soil pH.

To provide accurate results, the lab will need either a composite soil sample, or several individual samples for separate testing. A composite soil sample combines soil from several different locations. It does not always give as clear a result as several separate samples will.

It's best to take a sample at least every third year from each section of the garden you treat separately. For example, you could sample your fruit tree soil this year; next year,

TESTING FOR TEXTURE

Fractional analysis is an easy way to determine soil texture. For this simple test, you'll need a clear glass jar with a lid, 1 cup of dry, finely pulverized soil, 1 teaspoon of nonsudsing dishwasher detergent, and a crayon or grease pencil. To get a soil sample that's representative of your entire garden, take tablespoon-size samples from several locations and depths, mix them, dry them thoroughly, and then pulverize them with a rolling pin or mallet.

Fill the jar two-thirds full of water, add the soil and detergent, and fasten the lid securely. Shake the jar vigorously for 1 minute, and then put it down.

Sand particles will settle to the bottom first. Let the jar sit for one minute, and then mark the side with a crayon or grease pencil to indicate the level of sand. After two hours, most of the silt will have settled. Mark its level on the side of the jar also. Then let the jar sit undisturbed for a few days. By this time the clay particles should have settled out, and the water will be clear. Mark the clay level.

By eye, estimate the relative amounts of each particle in your soil. If one type of particle is more than half of the total amount of soil in the jar, that is your dominant soil texture. If the three types are relatively equal, your soil is probably some type of a loam soil, such as a sandy loam or silty loam.

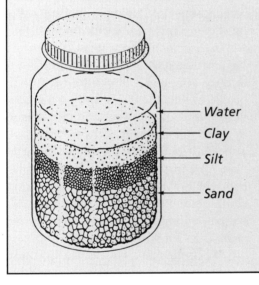

Water
Clay
Silt
Sand

sample your vegetable garden soil; the year after, sample your small fruit area; then, three years from now, sample the fruit tree soil again. Keep your results in a folder and look back at them. Over the years, they will help clear up the mysteries each soil holds far better than will the advice of any expert.

Collecting a Soil Sample

Before you can collect your soil sample, you'll need to pick up or send for a mailing kit from the agency that will be doing the test. Then follow these steps to take a sample:

1. Clear the soil surface in the sampling area.

2. Using a stainless steel tool, dig a narrow hole, 4 to 6 inches deep. Avoid touching the soil with anything other than the tool (even your hands), because it may throw off your test results if any impurities are introduced into the sample.

3. Take a slice of soil from the side of the hole as your sample.

4. If you're preparing a composite soil sample, repeat Steps 1 through 3 in eight to ten different places around your garden. Mix the samples in a plastic or stainless steel container using a stainless steel tool and not touching it with your hands.

5. Seal the resulting mix in a plastic bag and ship it in the mailing kit. If you're sending in several individual samples, simply place the soil collected at each sampling site in a separate bag and seal the bags. If you want the lab to recommend only organically acceptable materials, be sure to specify that when you send in your samples. When you are done, ship all of them to the testing agency.

Interpreting Your Soil Tests

Armed with your soil test results and your observations from your at-home tests, you're ready to evaluate your soil's overall health. Your soil test report can be read just like a school report card, as shown in the illustration on pages 32 and 33. One of the most important values on the report is your soil's organic matter content. In general, 4 percent is a good level for garden soils. However, organic matter content should be higher in clay soil than in loamy or sandy soil.

Your soil test report will include recommendations for amendments. If you have requested that they recommend only organically acceptable materials, that is what their recommendations should be for. If you are unsure whether something they have recommended is organic, call them and ask. You can simply follow the recommendations from the testing lab, but a more interesting and accurate way to use all of your results is as data for rating your overall soil quality. You'll find instructions for determining whether you have high-, medium-, or low-fertility soil in "Rating Soil Fertility" on the opposite page. Once you've decided on your soil's rating, you'll be ready to develop a soil improvement program.

CREATING A MANAGEMENT PROGRAM

The information you collected and analyzed using the "Rating Soil Fertility" table on the opposite page forms the basis of your soil management program. Besides determining whether you have low-, medium-, or high-fertility soil, you'll also have identified soil problems you'd like to solve, such as pH that needs adjusting, low organic matter content, or poor soil drainage. This information will also contribute to a good soil management plan. One important part of the plan will be managing soil organic matter by using mulches, compost, and cover crops. Your plan will also include adding fertilizers and using proper techniques for working the soil.

If planning and working for soil improvement is a new part of your gardening style, start small. Your overall plan may include building a compost bin, planting cover crops, adding amendments, and building raised beds. But if you try to put a grand plan like that in effect in a single season, you may never get around to planting your seeds and transplants!

A good first step is to keep your soil covered throughout the year. Bare soil loses humus faster than covered soil because nutrients are leached away more readily. Raindrops beating on bare soil also destroy the loose, open soil structure you are working to maintain. And, of course, bare soil is much more subject to wind and water erosion.

Keeping the soil covered can be as simple as planting more intensively and mulching unplanted areas. Over time, you can learn how to use cover crops to both cover and enrich the soil.

Rating Soil Fertility

Use this table to decide whether your soil's overall fertility is low, medium, or high. Decide which ranking your soil is for each characteristic in the table by comparing your soil observations and soil test results to the values listed. The majority of the values should fall under one category. That is your soil's overall fertility level. Keep in mind that no two soils ranked as low-, medium-, or high-fertility will respond in exactly the same way to a particular soil management program.

Drainage rate refers to results from the test described in "Checking Drainage" on page 28. Earthworm count refers to the test that is described in "Counting Earthworms" on page 28.

CHARACTERISTIC	LOW-FERTILITY SOIL	MEDIUM-FERTILITY SOIL	HIGH-FERTILITY SOIL
Drainage rate	Less than 15 minutes or more than 2.5 hours	30 minutes to 2.5 hours	15–30 minutes
Earthworm count	Less than 5	5–10	More than 10
pH	5.7 or below; 6.8 or above	5.8–6.2	6.2–6.8
Organic matter content	1–2%	2–4%	5% or greater
Cation exchange capacity	Less than 5	5–15	Higher than 15
Estimated nitrogen release	Less than 80 pounds per acre	80–140 pounds per acre	More than 140 pounds per acre
Available phosphorus	Less than 20 ppm	20–50 ppm	Greater than 50 ppm
Reserve phosphorus	Less than 55 ppm	55–90 ppm	Greater than 90 ppm
Potassium	Less than 120 ppm	120–199 ppm	200–300 ppm

HOW TO READ A SOIL TEST REPORT

Your soil test report will have columns headed by a word or abbreviation representing a component of the soil. For each component, there is a corresponding number indicating its amount. For some components, such as phosphorus, the report lists two values. One is the amount of a nutrient that is readily available—in a chemical form that plant roots can take up. The other is the amount in reserve, which can be thought of as all of the chemical forms of that nutrient that exist in the soil. Not every lab report will look exactly like this illustration. Some labs may report the values in meq/100g or some other units. If your lab report uses different units, just use their low/medium/high ratings to choose the appropriate column in the table "Rating Soil Fertility" on page 31.

Organic matter is reported in two ways. It is reported as a percentage of total soil components (% rate) and as estimated nitrogen release (ENR). ENR is a prediction of the amount of nitrogen that will be released by the soil in the course of one growing season.

Phosphorus (P) is reported as P_1 and P_2, or weak bray and strong bray ($NaHCO_3$-P). The weak bray test measures phosphorus that is readily available to plants. The strong bray test measures phosphorus in reserve.

Cations are potassium (K), magnesium (Mg), sodium (Na), and calcium (Ca). They are reported in parts per million (ppm).

SAMPLE NUMBER	ORGANIC MATTER % * RATE ** ENR	PHOSPHORUS P_1 (Weak Bray) ppm-P RATE	P_2 $NaHCO_3$-P ppm-P RATE	POTASSIUM K ppm-K RATE	MAGNESIUM Mg ppm-Mg RATE
1	2.9 84	14	16	104	162

pH is reported as soil pH and buffer pH. Soil pH measures active acidity—the amount of hydrogen and aluminum in the water in soil pore spaces. Buffer ph measures total acidity—the total amount of hydrogen and aluminum held in reserve in the soil. Buffer pH is the value used to determine lime requirements.

Cation exchange capacity (CEC) is reported in milliequivalents per 100 grams (meq/100g).

Nitrogen (N) is often reported as nitrate, a form of nitrogen that is available to plants.

Sulfur (S) is reported in parts per million (ppm).

Micronutrients are substances such as manganese (Mn), iron (Fe), copper (Cu), boron (B), and molybdenum (Mo), needed only in minute quantities for plant growth. They are reported in parts per million (ppm).

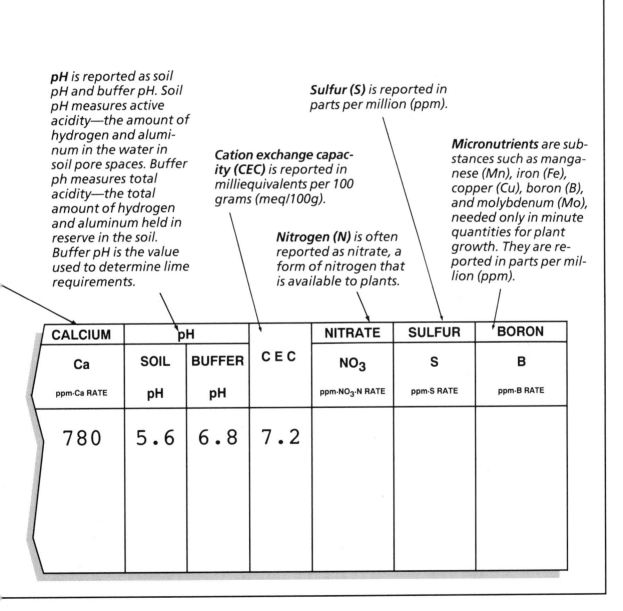

CALCIUM	pH		CEC	NITRATE	SULFUR	BORON
Ca	SOIL	BUFFER		NO$_3$	S	B
ppm·Ca RATE	pH	pH		ppm·NO$_3$·N RATE	ppm·S RATE	ppm·B RATE
780	5.6	6.8	7.2			

Start with pH

Deciding whether or not your pH needs adjusting is another good first step. If the your soil test indicates the pH is either above or below the ideal range for most crops (generally 6.2 to 6.8), you'll need to decide whether or not you need to raise or lower it. Here are some guidelines to help you.

Raising pH

Applying lime to the soil raises pH, but it's important to remember that too much lime can create nutrient imbalances in the soil, which lead to nutrient deficiencies in your plants. Don't add lime if the pH of your soil is higher than 6.1, because it may push the pH up out of the ideal range of 6.2 to 6.8.

Keep in mind that different soil types respond differently to lime applications. As a general rule, if your pH is between 5.0 and 6.0, add 5 pounds of lime per 100 square feet. Soils high in organic matter respond less to lime application. If your soil's organic matter is more than 4 percent, you can add 5 to 8 pounds per 100 square feet.

If the pH is lower than 5.0, add 10 pounds of lime per 100 square feet. Check the pH again the following year, and add more lime if the pH is still below 6.1. Don't add more than 10 pounds of lime per 100 square feet in any single year.

The best types of lime to use on most soils are high-calcium lime or oystershell lime (which is 96 percent calcium carbonate). Many garden centers sell only dolomitic limestone, which contains a healthy dose of magnesium. All three types work equally well to adjust the soil pH, but if you have a choice, choose high-calcium lime or oystershell lime unless your soil is low in magnesium.

You can apply lime with a small garden spreader. If you're only liming a small area, you can broadcast it by hand. Till or dig the lime into the top 3 to 4 inches of the soil.

Lowering pH

If your soil pH is above 7.0, you'll want to bring it down to the ideal range. To lower pH by about 1 unit (from 7.5 to 6.5, for example), spread 1 pound of sulfur per 100 square feet. To apply it, broadcast the sulfur by hand or spread it with a garden spreader, then till or dig it into the top 3 to 4 inches of soil.

Fertilizer and pH

Keep in mind that some fertilizers have an effect on pH. For example, 1 pound of rock phosphate or bonemeal has a liming value of about $\frac{1}{3}$ pound of lime. Either can slightly increase pH. Also, if you're adding sulfur as a fertilizer, it will, of course, decrease pH.

MANAGING ORGANIC MATTER

Feeding your soil a diverse diet of organic matter is an essential part of any management program. In fact, the secret to maintaining a balance between building organic matter and growing crops intensively is to add residues continually.

Mulching with organic matter, adding compost, and using cover crops (also called green manures) are the most common ways to add soil organic matter. All three add organic matter in various stages of decomposition, which helps your soil provide plants with more balanced nutrition. That's because decaying plant residue provides nutrients more rapidly than humus, which is stable organic matter. Humus is rich in nitrogen, phosphorus, and sulfur but low in calcium, magnesium, and potassium.

The best combination of mulch, compost, and green manure for your soil depends on the type of soil you have. Sandy soils do best when fed stable forms of organic matter like finished compost or well-rotted manure because they help the soil to retain more water and nutrients. If your soil is heavy clay, focus more on incorporating green manures and fresh mulches like hay. These coarser, less stable forms of organic matter will open up the soil and improve aeration.

You may wonder if you can add too much organic matter to your soil. The answer is yes. An excess of organic matter (especially fresh plant residues) added to any soil can create productivity problems. It can upset nutrient balances, and some of the initial by-products from fresh residues can be toxic to seedlings. Excessive fresh residues in soil can favor some insect pests and diseases, such as root-eating grubs and root rot.

How much is too much? It depends on the microbial health of your soil. If your soil has a thriving microbial population, it can handle more residue. One way to tell is too watch your plants for nitrogen or phosphorus deficiency symptoms such as stunted growth, yellowing or lower leaves, or purpling foliage. If the soil has been recently enriched and the symptoms persist for more than three or four weeks, you may be adding more residues than your microbes can handle.

When you make your plan, keep in mind that some gardening activities actually deplete soil organic matter. Tilling, for example, adds oxygen to the soil, which causes your micro-herd to take a deep "breath" and speeds up its activity. This quite literally burns up the organic matter in your soil. That's why you should always add organic matter to your soil whenever you till.

Mulching

If you love your soil, keep it covered. In most cases, your garden will be happiest if the soil is covered with an organic mulch. Mulches help retain water, are a source of nutrients (including micronutrients), and provide a good habitat for beneficial organisms like spiders and ground beetles.

Spread mulch in the fall on empty beds after garden cleanup. If you till it in before spring planting, remulch after planting. Renew the mulch as needed during the growing season. For perennial fruit trees and shrubs, put down a 3- to 4-inch layer of mulch in a circle out to the drip line of the plant annually. You'll also find specific suggestions for mulching individual crops in the plant entries in Part 2.

There are a few cases when it's better not to mulch. Use caution when applying mulch around seeds and seedlings because some mulches release substances that are toxic to seedlings. Wait until the plants are well-established.

Northern gardeners may find that organic mulches keep the soil too cool for warm-weather crops. And in cool, humid conditions, organic mulches can stay wet for extended periods, which increases some insect and disease problems. "The Plastic Mulch Option" on page 36 explains an alternative way to mulch in these situations.

Choosing a Mulch

Mention mulch, and most gardeners think of grass clippings or shredded leaves. But your choice of mulch could also be grass hay, legume hay, wheat or oat straw, corncobs, weeds (before they flower and form seed heads), wood chips, sawdust, peat moss, residues from food or grain processing, and garden plant residues. See "Fertilizer Options" on page 50 for information about nutrient content of these mulches.

There are some simple rules that will help you narrow down your choice of mulch. A first obvious rule is to use a mulch that's fairly easily and cheaply available. Other guidelines concern the effects of various mulches on your soil and plants.

THE PLASTIC MULCH OPTION

Black plastic mulch is a popular choice for weed control in home gardens. Garden beds covered with black plastic will show some soil temperature increase (about 10°F over bare soil temperature). Black plastic mulch also protects the fruits of vining crops such as strawberries, melons, and cucumbers from rotting and keeps them clean. Clear plastic increases soil temperature (about 18°F over bare soil temperature) even more than black plastic does and may thus increase yields in warm-season crops. However, clear plastic actually encourages weed growth. Photodegradable plastic mulches are designed to break down in the field by controlled photo- and bio-degradation. Unfortunately, the decomposition products may be toxic to soil microbes.

You may find clear or black plastic mulch helpful at times in your garden. Just don't confuse its benefits with those you get from organic mulch. Applying clear or black plastic mulch does not benefit your soil's health. It adds no organic matter and can block air movement into the soil.

The more coarse a mulch is, the less it will improve soil moisture retention. This means coarse mulches (like straw or corncobs) may be a good choice for cool, wet, or heavy soils, especially if you are mulching crops sensitive to wet feet. Sandy, light, or well-drained soils do well with fine-textured mulches, such as partially decomposed sawdust, that pack down tightly and hold in moisture.

Dry, woody materials should decompost partially before you apply them as mulch. When using materials such as wood chips and sawdust, be sure they have decomposed a bit before you use them. This will help prevent problems with toxins and nutrient tie-ups.

Crop choice sometimes influences mulch choice. A mulch may be fine to use on one crop but may adversely affect another. For example, residues from cabbage-family crops should not be used on other crops from the same family, but they are fine as mulch for mature fruit trees. Sawdust may have an acidifying effect and thus may be great for acid-loving crops like blueberries but terrible for celery.

Try to match your mulch choice with your soil conditions and crop requirements. Don't be afraid of trying a new and different material. If it can be broken down by soil microbes, it probably can be used as a mulch. First, test new mulches on a small portion of your garden to be sure they won't have any adverse effects on your plants.

Making and Using Compost

Making and using compost is one of the best things you can do for your garden. When you make compost and add it to the soil, you're not only making a tasty snack for your microherd, you're also adding a nutrient- and humus-rich soil amendment.

Finished compost has a uniform consistency and an earthy smell; you can no longer identify the original materials it was made from. Finished compost is also a near-perfect fertilizer, since it has a predictable carbon-to-nitrogen ratio and a high concentration of nutrients. You rarely need to worry about mistakes with compost. There is little chance of overfertilizing with one nutrient and ending up with imbalances. Nor is there fear that a mulch or crop residue will tie up phosphorus or nitrogen or produce plant toxins.

Making compost involves mixing different organic materials in a pile or bin and providing conditions that encourage decomposition. If you have time and interest in compost making, you can manage it intensively and produce a lot of it. Or you can let compost happen naturally by making a passive pile.

How Composting Works

Your compost pile is home for a hard-working microherd of composting organisms. Keep their comfort in mind as you build and manage your pile. The microbes that power the composting process transform raw organic materials into decomposed organic materials. This transformation involves breaking the materials into physically smaller pieces and into simpler and different biological compounds.

Composting occurs both by aerobic and anaerobic means. Aerobic bacteria require oxygen to do their work. They decompose material rapidly and are responsible for the buildup of heat in the compost pile. Anaerobic bacteria do not require air. Anaerobic decomposition is easy because all you do is let the pile sit. However, it is slow and can produce strong, unpleasant odors.

When microbes break down organic matter, they use the carbon in the organic matter to build their own populations because carbon is a primary ingredient of the microbial cells. However, like other plants and animals, microbes also need nitrogen, phosphorus, and other nutrients in order to reproduce. When the carbon and nitrogen content of the materials in a compost pile are in the right balance, microorganisms reproduce rapidly and the composting process moves along. When it is out of balance, the process will not be as successful.

It's possible to measure the average

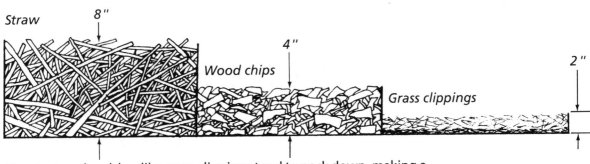

Fine-textured mulches like grass clippings tend to pack down, making a dense layer that seals moisture in, but they also can seal rainfall and air out. Apply thin layers of fine mulches, and renew them frequently. You can spread a very coarse mulch like straw several inches thick.

amounts of carbon and nitrogen in an organic material like straw and compare them as a ratio—the carbon-to-nitrogen (C/N) ratio. An initial C/N ratio between 20:1 and 30:1 in your pile will result in good compost. When a compost pile is made primarily from materials that have ratios below 20:1, there is too much nitrogen available in comparison to carbon. Microbes can't make use of all of the nitrogen, so it may convert into ammonia gas and be lost from the pile. When this happens, your compost pile will have an unmistakable ammonia odor.

If the C/N ratio is more than 30:1, nitrogen is low and microbial activity is sluggish. If the C/N ratio is higher than 50:1, decomposition is very slow. If you add this high-C/N compost to the soil, microbes may use nitrogen in the soil to help finish the decomposition of the compost. While this occurs, the nitrogen will be unavailable to your plants. Good-quality finished compost has a C/N ratio between 10:1 and 15:1 when it is ready to spread. See "Creating Compost Combos" on this page for a list of commonly used composting materials and their C/N ratios.

Making a Compost Pile

There's no single set of directions for making a compost pile. However, there are some general guidelines you should follow for better results.

Make your pile at least 3 feet × 3 feet × 3 feet. Smaller piles may not heat properly. Piles taller than 6 feet are not recommended because they may pack down and not be properly aerated. The pile also should feel moist, but you should not be able to squeeze water out of a handful of it.

The microherd that's making your compost for you needs oxygen to do its work. To

CREATING COMPOST COMBOS

When making compost, choose materials that are both coarse- and fine-textured. Check the nutrient levels and carbon-to-nitrogen (C/N) ratios of the materials you choose. It's difficult to tell the exact C/N ratios of the materials you have, or to tell the C/N ratio of a compost pile. Aim for a mix of coarse- and fine-textured materials and high C/N and low C/N materials. Here are the C/N ratios of some common compost ingredients.

INGREDIENT	C/N RATIO
Brush and tree trimmings	80:1–100:1
Crop refuse	20:1–100:1
Kelp (seaweed)	19:1
Kitchen wastes	5:1–35:1
Lawn clippings	20:1–30:1
Leaves	40:1–80:1
Legume hay	16:1
Manure, cow	18:1
Manure, horse	22:1
Manure, pig	14:1
Manure, poultry	7:1
Manure, sheep	16:1
Nonlegume hay	32:1
Straw	47:1–72:1
Weeds	20:1

get oxygen into your compost pile, design a bin with holes in the sides. Push metal or wooden spacers vertically or horizontally into the bin. Stirring the residues with the spacers as the bin fills helps to aerate the pile. The pitchfork method of moving a pile from one place to another is a tried-and-true method but is also a lot of work. For easier turning, make compost in a barrel with a removable lid. (Drill holes in the sides for better aeration as well.) When you want to "turn your pile," fasten the lid and roll the barrel around the yard! Or make a portable bin like the one shown in the illustration on this page; when the bin is full, just take it off of the pile and move it to another spot to begin a new pile.

For more ideas on composting systems, see "Tricks of the Trade: Compost Hints for Busy Gardeners" on page 40. You can also find many different commercial compost makers through garden supply catalogs.

Compost Ingredients

While you can make compost from just about any mixture of yard and kitchen wastes you have available, you may want to look beyond your own yard to get a better mix of high-carbon and high-nitrogen ingredients. Here are a few of the common compost ingredients.

Grass clippings. Grass clippings compost fast and hot but can mat down and lower aeration. Be sure to mix them with a bulky material. Adding hay to your pile will increase biological activity but may also add weed seeds.

Kitchen scraps. Vegetable and fruit peelings and any produce that has gone "over the hill" are great additions to the compost pile. Don't put animal products like meat scraps, fat, or eggs (eggshells are fine) in your compost pile because they may attract rodents. It's also best to reject kitchen scraps that are heavy with oil, because oils take longer to break down.

Leaves. Leaves are especially good for providing potassium and micronutrients to compost. They tend to be dry, however, and have a high carbon-to-nitrogen ratio. If you use leaves as an additive, you'll need to add supplemen-

tary water and nitrogen. Shred leaves before adding them. Unshredded leaves are very slow to decompose because they mat together, keeping oxygen and moisture out. If possible, mix them with lawn clippings.

Manure. If you can get it, manure is a great addition to the compost pile. If you can't get it, don't despair—you can make great compost without any manure. Poultry manure is very concentrated. Its nitrogen is rapidly available, and thus the chance of leaching loss is high. It decomposes rapidly and will speed up

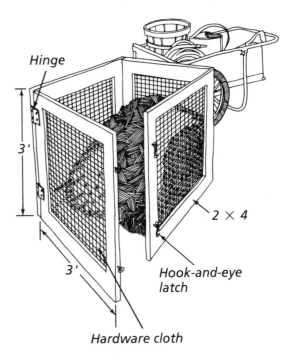

Hardware cloth is strong enough to support the weight of compost, yet lets air into the pile. This portable bin has four sides made of 3-foot-square pieces of ½-inch hardware cloth fastened to 2 × 4 s. To create a door, hinge one side and place hooks and eyes on the edge opposite the hinges to fasten it shut.

decomposition of high-carbon residues. Horse manure heats up rapidly and is a good, balanced additive. Cow manure and pig manure are balanced additives that rot easily with fairly low nitrogen losses.

Weeds and crop residues. Crop remains and weeds can go in the compost pile, with some precautions. Don't add weeds that are setting seed, and don't add crop residues that are diseased or infested with pests. You'll just create problems for future gardens, unless you're willing to manage your pile intensively to keep

---

∾ TRICKS OF THE TRADE ∾

COMPOST HINTS
FOR BUSY GARDENERS

Try these nifty methods for getting more and better compost.

Grow nitrogen-rich comfrey for your compost. Plant some comfrey near the compost pile. The plants are very vigorous. Whenever they get large, cut them down to 2 to 3 inches tall. Add the clippings to your pile for a quick nitrogen boost.

Plant a cover crop on your compost for winter protection. If it's nearing fall and you have a pile of unused, near-finished compost, plant a cover crop on it to stabilize the nutrients throughout the winter. Sprinkle legume seeds on the top and sides of the pile and water it in. The crop will thrive on a rich compost diet. In the spring (three to four weeks before you want to use the compost), use a fork or a tiller to uproot and mix the legume into your pile.

Compost with benign neglect. Try setting up a passive pile in a wooded part of your property. Position a portable, lightweight bin and an old truck or tractor tire side by side. Push two sturdy stakes or fence posts into the ground inside the bin. They should be long enough to extend 1 to 2 feet above the top of the bin. Fill the bottom of the bin with coarse material such as hay, straw, cornstalks, or seed-free weeds. Then, whenever it's convenient, empty kitchen trimmings into the bin. On these quick stops, aerate the compost by moving the stakes back and forth a couple of times.

Put matured crop plants, weeds, or leaves inside the tractor tire, since they decompose more slowly. When the bin is one-third to one-half full, add a few inches of the residue from the tire each time you add kitchen scraps. In the fall, the grove of trees will conveniently add leaf residue all on its own. The leaves on top will help insulate the pile through the winter. In two to six months, you'll have finished compost. When you need compost, tip the bin and scoop out the bottom layers.

Buy compost in a bag. Bagged compost is available at garden supply stores, or you can buy it by the cubic yard from commercial compost makers. Always check to make sure compost is well-decomposed. (You should not be able to distinguish the materials that went into making the compost.) Ask whether a nutrient content analysis of the compost is available. Check the pH with a home test kit; for best results, it should be between 5.5 and 7.5.

temperatures high enough to kill pathogens and weed seeds.

Fast Compost or Slow?

If you want compost fast, design a hot compost pile, also called a high-input or aerobic pile. Build a pile 5 feet wide × 5 feet high. Enclose the pile with bales of straw or wooden pallets to help maintain heat. Choose materials with a low carbon-to-nitrogen (C/N) ratio (between 20:1 and 25:1). Ideally, mix coarse material and manure or, if you can't get manure, use yard wastes and kitchen trimmings. Refer to "Creating Compost Combos" on page 38 for materials with low C/N ratios. Turn the pile every three to seven days, and keep it moist. Add a commercial microbial activator (a powder containing composting microorganisms) or a "tea" prepared by soaking finished compost in water. Aerobic composting can produce compost in five to eight weeks. The warmer the weather and the more you turn your pile, the sooner you will get a finished product.

If you are a patient compost maker, try a low-input, low-maintenance composting method. Enclose your pile and put stakes or holes in the sides of the compost pile for aeration. Turn the composting material one or two times a month. Use materials that have a higher C/N ratio (between 20:1 and 30:1). Choose a mixture of coarse- and fine-particle materials to provide aeration. Add soil layers as you build the pile. Be prepared to wait several months for finished compost.

When you push your hand into your compost pile, it should be warm to the touch. A hot compost pile can reach temperatures up to 160°F. These temperatures will kill many plant disease organisms and weed seeds, but they will also kill some beneficial organisms.

If you want to compost woody materials, fungi are the primary decomposers you want to encourage. Fungi do not survive at temperatures above 140°F, so do not encourage high temperatures in your compost pile if you are adding woody materials to it.

Compost Problem Troubleshooting

Making compost isn't quite the same as making a cake. There are no recipes with precise quantities, and the ingredients will never be quite the same from pile to pile. Here are some suggestions that may help if your compost just won't cook:

Make a bigger pile. It should be at least 3 feet by 3 feet square and 3 to 4 feet high.

Soften things up. If the residues in your pile are too tough, they won't break down. Mix in succulent plant material or manure.

Water it down. When your pile is too dry, it will have a whitish, powdery deposit inside. Add moisture until a sample handful feels moist, but not wet enough to squeeze excess water from.

Add a dry touch. If your pile is too wet, add dry soil and/or turn the pile to dry off excess water. A pile may also stay wet if it gets compacted. Add a layer of coarse material to the center of a continually wet pile.

Cover it up. If all else fails, or if the weather turns cold, insulate your pile by covering the top of it with hay or clear plastic.

Managing Cover Crops

Cover crops are the cheapest form of organic supplement that organic gardeners can use. Cover crops—also called green manure crops—cover bare soil and thus decrease soil loss through erosion. Planting a crop such as alfalfa or clover in your garden will add organic matter and nutrients, make nutrients more available, suppress weeds, and decrease leaching. Cover crops build up soil structure and increase biological activity.

Using cover crops does require some extra time and planning. They may not be the best choice for very busy gardeners. However, the rewards of using cover crops are more than worth the time it takes to learn how to use them. Below are the four basic ways to work cover cropping into your garden management program. (Refer to the illustration on the opposite page for examples of these four methods.)

1. Plant during the growing season to cover the ground temporarily, then till it under and plant a food crop.

2. Plant in fall, allow the crop to grow all winter, and till it under in spring.

3. Plant in fall, and allow the crop to grow and be killed by winter cold. Plant your spring food crop directly into the killed cover crop.

4. Plant during the growing season to grow among your food crop plants.

On a garden scale, cover crop seeds are one of the cheapest fertilizer inputs you can buy. So experiment! If you've never planted a cover crop before, you may want to start with an easy project, like seeding a garden bed in the fall after it has been harvested and cleaned up. Let the cover crop grow throughout the winter, and just till it in before spring planting. Rape, rye, and oats are all good crops for winter soil cover. If you're getting a late start, rye is probably your best choice because it will germinate and grow even in chilly 40°F weather.

Deciding on a Cover Crop

If you've never tried using cover crops, you may have no idea which crops to use. Two basic choices you'll make are whether to use a legume such as clover or a nonlegume like buckwheat and whether to plant a perennial crop or an annual crop. Perennial cover crops are deep rooting, which helps to improve soil structure, but are slow to establish and to start contributing nutrients to the soil.

One advantage of using legumes is that they add nitrogen to the soil through nitrogen fixation. However, perennial legumes are slow to start fixing nitrogen. If you're planning to let the crop grow through a whole growing season so that's it's truly a source of green manure, planting a perennial legume in fall makes sense. But if you're just planting a crop in early spring to cover the garden until you till and plant vegetables in late spring, a quick-growing annual would be a good choice.

Here are some guidelines for making a crop choice. Just look for the heading that describes the area where you want to plant your cover crop for information on what you should choose. For more information about seeding rates and cultural requirements for these crops, see "Cover Crop Requirements" on page 46.

Heavy soils. Crops that can handle heavy, poorly drained soils include alsike clover, berseem clover, white clover, 'Yarloop' subterranean clover, soybeans, and sunflowers.

Compacted soil. You might want to try planting a deep-rooted crop to improve structure and drainage. Your choices include buckwheat, rape, sunflowers, alfalfa, and most clovers.

Dry soil. Legumes that work well in dry soil are black medic and yellow sweet clover.

Acid soil. Alsike clover and hairy vetch are acid-tolerant legumes.

Shady sites. Subterranean clover and white clover are two legumes that will tolerate shade.

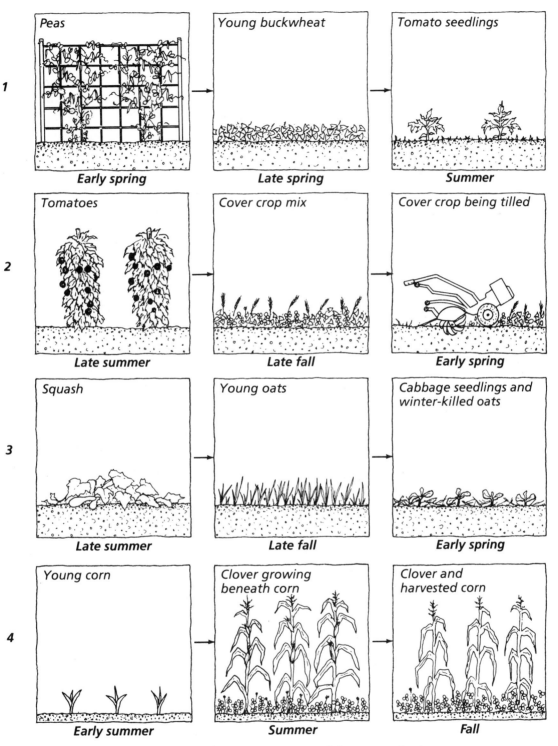

Plant cover crops to fill "holes" in the growing season (1), to cover beds over winter (2 and 3), or under crops as a living mulch (4).

Pathways. Subterranean clover and white clover are good legumes to plant in pathways because they handle foot and equipment traffic well. Subterranean clover is also easy to manage in small areas.

Orchards. Sweet clover, berseem clover, and buckwheat work well in the aisles between rows of fruit trees.

Vegetable gardens. Try planting berseem clover, fava beans, or soybeans in fall and planting transplants directly into the winter-killed mulch without tilling it.

Weedy areas. Red clover, subterranean clover, soybeans, buckwheat, rape, Sudan grass, and sunflowers are good weed-suppressing crops. Hairy vetch competes well with grass.

Nutrient-deficient areas. You can use a cover crop to help bolster particular nutrient levels. For example, buckwheat is a good source of phosphorus and sunflowers are a source of boron.

Planting Cover Crops

If possible, sow seeds for a cover crop when rain is forecast. The stand will not establish well if the soil surface dries during the germination period. Before sowing seeds, remove all crop residues and rake the soil free of clumps.

If you're planting a legume, inoculate the soil with the species-specific bacteria that associate with the root and fix atmospheric nitrogen. You can order bacterial inoculants from your seed supplier. Make sure you use the correct inoculant for the cover crop you choose.

You can sow seeds with a manually powered seeder that consists of a bag or reservoir for holding seeds connected to a crank-operated seed broadcaster. For small areas, try broadcasting seeds by hand. If you're sowing less than 1 pound of seed per 1,000 square feet,

mix the seeds with fine sand, organic fertilizer, or screened soil before spreading. When sowing fine seeds by hand, rake the seedbed afterward to cover the seeds. Larger-seeded crops, such as Austrian peas or soybeans, should be covered with ¼ to ½ inch of soil.

After seeding, tamp the soil with the back

COVER CROP CAVEATS

Just as some crops are the best choice for heavy soils or dry soils, there are some worst choices of cover crops for certain situations. Here are five examples of when certain crops are a poor choice:

1. Alfalfa, black medic, sweet clover, and sunflowers do not grow well in acid soil.

2. Alfalfa and crimson clover can carry diseases that will infect tomatoes.

3. Some cover crops are vigorous growers that can overrun beds and narrow rows. Avoid these in small gardens: alfalfa, sweet clover, hairy vetch, alsike clover, berseem clover, crimson clover, and red clover.

4. Residues of some cover crops, such as hairy vetch, contain substances that can inhibit growth of other plants. Plant hairy vetch 8 to 12 inches from any of your vegetables or fruits to avoid problems. For crops of buckwheat, rye, and Sudan grass, be sure to wait three to five weeks after tilling or mowing before planting your fruits or vegetables.

5. Some crops grow so tall they can become nearly impossible to mow or till in. Buckwheat can reach 5 feet; sunflowers can grow as tall as 10 feet.

of a hoe or spade to ensure good contact between soil and seed. You can cover the newly seeded area with loose straw or grass clippings to help prevent drying. For large plots (1 acre or more), a small seed drill pulled by a farm or garden tractor will plant and cover the seeds in one pass.

If you have to kill off a cover crop before planting your food crops, try mowing it severely, tilling it under, or solarizing the plot on which it's growing. The illustration on page 176 shows how to solarize soil. To solarize a cover crop, mow it as short as possible, leave the clippings in place, and stretch the plastic tightly over the clippings. This method probably will not kill the crop if spring temperatures are cool, with night temperatures in the 30°F range.

Keep in mind that after you till the cover crop, your soil microbes intensely attack this rich plant material. There is a lag time of at least two weeks during which nitrogen and phosphorus will be tied up by the microbes as they reproduce and process the residues. So wait two to four weeks after mowing or tilling your cover crop before planting main crops.

Managing Living Mulch

If you plant a cover crop as a living mulch among your food crops, plan to manage it throughout the growing season. Otherwise, the cover crop can outcompete your food crop for nutrients and water. Mowing helps keep vigorous cover crops manageable because it decreases their water uptake and reduces their competitive ability. Keep the mowed residues moist for at least five to seven weeks so that it will quickly decompose.

If your living mulch seems to be threatening to grow out of control, try tilling it lightly. If possible, make a quick pass with a rotary tiller over the surface of the cover crop. Do not let the tiller tines go into the soil more than 1 or 2 inches.

If you can't till or don't want to till, try hand-raking the cover crop vigorously until you can see exposed soil. Research at Cornell University in New York indicates that disturbing some legume cover crops by using light tillage is most successful during July.

USING FERTILIZERS

Fertilizer is icing on the cake for an organic soil. If your soil management program includes evaluating your soil, adjusting pH, adding compost, mulching, and covercropping, then your soil may be such a fine-quality cake that your plants will never miss the fertilizer icing. But if you haven't had time to prepare your soil thoroughly before planting, adding fertilizers can be good insurance for a healthy harvest.

Preblended Fertilizer

The simplest way to fertilize is to buy a bag of commercial preblended fertilizer and apply it according to label instructions. Many commercial organic fertilizers are available on the market. If you buy commercial fertilizer mixes, make sure the nitrogen, phosphorus, and potassium are balanced in a ratio of 1:1:1 or 2:1:1. It is easy to check because all fertilizers should have the ratio of percentage of nitrogen (N), phosphorus (P), and potassium (K)—the NPK ratio—listed on the label. Also check that all of the ingredients are organic, or check to see if the fertilizer is listed as certified organic. Commercial organic growers must adhere to standards for acceptable fertilizer materials. Reputable dealers and mail-order companies should be able to tell you whether their fertilizers comply with those standards.

Cover Crop Requirements

Planting cover crops, also called green manure crops, is a great way to improve soil structure and organic matter content. The following table is the result of many years of trials in many regions of the country by a very successful organic grower and researcher. This is not an exclusive, unchangeable list—it's just a guideline. Every individual microclimate, soil, management program, and year will change the behavior of plants slightly—so use this table as a starting point, and modify your choices as you find what works for you. Use this table to check the hardiness, soil requirements, and seeding rates of crops you may want to use. Keep in mind that all cover crops do best when soil pH is maintained above 6.0.

COMMON NAME	TYPE OF PLANT	SOIL REQUIREMENTS	SEEDING RATE	WHEN TO SOW	HOW TO MANAGE
LEGUMES					
Alfalfa	Very hardy perennial	Neutral-to-slightly alkaline, well-drained, loamy soil	½–1.0 oz. per 100 sq. ft.	Spring or late summer	Mow close.
Black medic	Hardy perennial	Neutral-to-alkaline, well-drained (even dry), loamy soil	¾–1.0 oz. per 100 sq. ft.	Early fall or spring	Mow only 1–3 times early in the season.
Clover, alsike	Hardy perennial	Slightly acid-to-neutral, well-drained, loamy soil	¼–½ oz. per 100 sq. ft.	Spring through late summer	Mow.
Clover, berseem	Tender winter annual	Alkaline-to-acid, well-drained soil	¾–1.0 oz. per 100 sq. ft.	Late summer	Keep mowed. Let winter-kill.
Clover, crimson	Hardy winter annual	Slightly acid-to-neutral, well-drained, loamy soil	¾–1.5 oz. per 100 sq. ft.	Late summer through fall or early spring	Mow.
Clover, red	Hardy perennial	Slightly acid-to-neutral, well-drained soil	½–¾ oz. per 100 sq. ft.	Late summer or spring	Mow, or lightly till top 1"–2" of soil.
Clover, subterranean	Semihardy winter annual	Slightly acid-to-neutral, well-drained soil	1.0–1.5 oz. per 100 sq. ft.	Late summer or spring	Mow.
Clover, white (Dutch)	Hardy perennial	Slightly acid-to-neutral, well-drained, loamy soil	½–1.0 oz. per 100 sq. ft.	Late summer or early spring	Mow.

COMMON NAME	TYPE OF PLANT	SOIL REQUIREMENTS	SEEDING RATE	WHEN TO SOW	HOW TO MANAGE
Fava bean	Tender annual	Slightly acid-to-neutral, well-drained, loamy soil	3.0–5.0 oz. per 100 sq. ft.	Spring through late summer	Let winter-kill; mow or till under at flowering.
Pea, Australian winter and field	Semihardy annual	Acid-to-neutral, well-drained soil	2.0–3.0 oz. per 100 sq. ft.	Spring or late summer	Mow or till before seed production.
Soybean	Tender annual	Slightly acid-to-neutral, heavy, wet soil	3.0–5.0 oz. per 100 sq. ft.	Late spring through midsummer	Let winter-kill for mulch; mow or till before full bloom.
Sweet clover, white, yellow, or annual	Hardy perennial	Neutral soil; wide variety of types	½–¾ oz. per 100 sq. ft.	Spring	Mow, then till.
Vetch, hairy	Hardy winter annual	Neutral-to-acid soil; wide variety of types	1.5–3.0 oz. per 100 sq. ft.	Spring or late summer through early fall	Mow when flowering starts and then till.

NONLEGUMES

COMMON NAME	TYPE OF PLANT	SOIL REQUIREMENTS	SEEDING RATE	WHEN TO SOW	HOW TO MANAGE
Buckwheat	Tender annual	Variable pH levels; variable soil types	3.0–5.0 oz. per 100 sq. ft.	Late spring through early fall	Till before seed production, or mow then till.
Rape	Tender annual	Acid-to-neutral loam	½–¾ oz. per 100 sq. ft.	Spring through fall	Till.
Spring oats	Tender annual	Variable pH levels; variable soil types	3.0–5.0 oz. per 100 sq. ft.	Spring through summer	Till, or mow then till before seeds harden.
Sudan grass	Tender annual	Variable pH levels; variable soil types	1.5–3.0 oz. per 100 sq. ft.	Late spring through early summer	Till, or mow then till, or remove tops for mulch and till stubble.
Sunflower	Tender annual	Neutral-to-alkaline pH levels; variable soil types	6"–8" apart	Late spring through summer	Till, or mow then till before seeds form.

Making Your Own Blend

With a little time and effort, you can blend your own organic fertilizer. This can save you money, and you can adjust your mix to suit your soils and crops.

If you're going to make your own fertilizer blend, it's important to evaluate your soil fertility level first. See the table "Rating Soil Fertility" on page 31 for instructions. Then, choose from the recipes in "Home-Mixed Fertilizer" on this page.

Using Specific Amendments

Experienced gardeners may want to experiment with giving particular crops a specific boost of a particular nutrient. For example, you may want to give your tomatoes or peppers a slight potassium boost.

Use your soil test results as a guide in determining whether to add fertilizers. The evaluation from the laboratory may suggest amendments and amounts to apply. Also, you can compare your soil test results to the values given in "Rating Soil Fertility" on page 31 to see whether you need to boost levels of nitrogen, phosphorus, and potassium. You can also read nutrient deficiency symptoms in your plants. See "Troubleshooting Plant Nutrient Deficiencies" on page 175 for a general guide to common nutrient deficiency symptoms. Keep in mind that deficiency symptoms can look similar to those of insect or disease problems. Make a careful diagnosis before you apply amendments because an overdose of some amendments can create new problems.

The table "Fertilizer Options" on page 50 lists many common organic soil amendments and their content of specific nutrients. Keep in mind that converting percentages and NPK ratios to pounds is simple. For example, if an amendment contains 5 percent magnesium,

---

HOME-MIXED FERTILIZER

Whip up a batch of balanced fertilizer for your garden. A wheelbarrow makes a convenient mixing bowl. The mix you make will depend on your soil fertility level, which you can deduce by following the directions in the table "Rating Soil Fertility" on page 31. The amounts listed below will make enough to fertilize 100 square feet.

Low-fertility soil. Combine 5 pounds of alfalfa or fish meal, 5½ pounds of rock phosphate, 1 pound of kelp, and 3 pounds of greensand.

Medium-fertility soil. Combine 3 pounds of alfalfa or fish meal, 3½ pounds of rock phosphate, 1 pound of kelp, and 1½ pounds of greensand.

High-fertility soil. Combine 2 pounds of alfalfa meal or fish meal, 2½ pounds of rock phosphate, and 1 pound of kelp.

If you have a hard time getting alfalfa meal, just substitute Litter Green—the green "all-natural" catbox filler—it's almost half pure alfalfa.

---

then 100 pounds of that amendment contains 5 pounds of magnesium.

If you're not comfortable making your own choices and calculations, you can refer to "Customized Soil Care," beginning on page 56. This section gives you complete soil and fertilizer management programs for fruiting vegetable crops, root crops, leafy crops, tree fruits, and small fruits.

Applying Fertilizers

Once you've decided which fertilizer or amendment to use, applying it should be easy.

You can sprinkle dry fertilizers over the soil surface and till or dig them in before planting. You can also apply fertilizers during the growing season or in the fall. For nuts-and-bolts instructions on how to apply fertilizers, see "Fertilizing 101" on page 126.

SOIL PREPARATION

Many gardeners may skip straight from selecting their site to revving up the tiller. But as we've learned, there is a crucial evaluation and planning process to go through before we're ready to start digging. And since you have invested time and care in planning your soil improvement program, take some care in how you physically work your soil as well. The way we handle our soil affects its structure, its ability to provide nutrition and water to our plants, and its long-term productivity.

Tilling and Digging

A tally of tilling tools would include a rotary tiller, a shovel or spade, a spading fork, a broadfork, a hoe, and a heavy rake. If your soil has good tilth (crumbles between your fingers) and is light (you can dig a shovelful of it with little effort), you may need to till only the top 2 to 4 inches for all but deep-rooted crops, such as tomatoes, sweet corn, root crops, and fruit trees. If your soil is hard to dig, using deep digging techniques to loosen the top 2 feet of soil often improves plant growth.

For light tillage, you can use a rotary tiller, heavy rake, hoe, or shovel. For deep tillage, try a broadfork, which is illustrated on this page. Broadforks are available from specialty garden supply catalogs. You can also work the soil deeply with a shovel or rotary tiller. Remember that rotary tillers tend to pulverize soil.

The result over time can be soil compaction and a loss of soil structure. As your soil improves, you may find that you can replace some of your deep tilling with deep-rooted cover crops such as buckwheat, sunflowers, or alfalfa. (See "Managing Cover Crops" on page 41 for more information.)

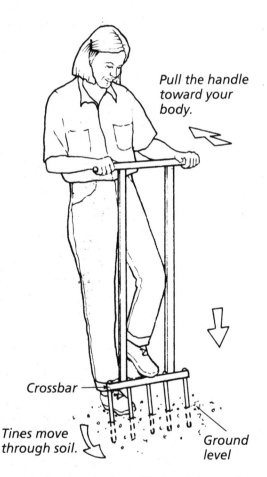

Pull the handle toward your body.

Crossbar

Tines move through soil.

Ground level

The design for the broadfork originates from Holland, where soils are deep and heavy and require deep cultivation to keep them open. The tines of a broadfork plunge down almost 1 foot deep when you step on the crossbar, and they cut through the soil as you rock the tool back.

Fertilizer Options

There is a surprisingly large choice of organic fertilizers available to home gardeners. Some are free for the taking on your property; others are available from garden supply centers. Use this table to select amendments that have the characteristics you need. The table lists the NPK ratio and the sulfur, magnesium, and calcium content. It also indicates whether or not the fertilizer supplies micronutrients. For materials that you might incorporate in bulk or include in compost, the carbon-to-nitrogen ratio is included. The table also includes information on whether nutrients are slowly or rapidly available and whether there are any precautions in using a particular amendment.

AMENDMENT	NPK RATIO	OTHER NUTRIENTS	C/N RATIO	COMMENTS
Alfalfa hay	2.6–0.6–2.2	0.3% sulfur; 1.0% calcium; 0.02% magnesium; micronutrients	16	Well-balanced, slowly available. Contains growth stimulants.
Alfalfa meal or alfalfa pellets	2.7–0.5–2.8	0.2% sulfur; micronutrients	15	Well-balanced, more rapidly available than alfalfa hay. Contains growth stimulants.
Blood meal	13.0–2.0–0	Not a significant source of other nutrients	3	Rapidly available nitrogen. Stimulates microbes.
Bonemeal	3.0–2.0–0.5	24% calcium	–	Rapidly available phosphorus source. Mildly increases pH.
Compost (dry, commercial)	1.0–0.8–1.0	0.4% sulfur; 0.2% calcium; 0.1% magnesium; micronutrients	10–17	Balanced, slow release. Good choice for busy gardener.
Compost (homemade)	1.0–0.5–1.0 to 2.0–1.0–2.0	0.4% sulfur; 0.2% calcium; 0.1% magnesium; micronutrients	10–17	Balanced, slow release.
Cottonseed meal	6.0–2.0–2.0	Not a significant source of other nutrients	7	Rapidly available nitrogen source. May contain pesticides.
Eggshells	1.2–0.4–0.1	0.4% calcium; micronutrients	–	Should be crushed. Good compost addition.

AMENDMENT	NPK RATIO	OTHER NUTRIENTS	C/N RATIO	COMMENTS
Epsom salts	0–0–0	13.0% sulfur; 10.0% magnesium	–	Rapidly available magnesium and sulfur source.
Feather meal	11.0–0–0	Not a significant source of other nutrients	4	Rapidly available nitrogen source.
Fish emulsion	5.0–2.0–2.0	5% sulfur	4	Rapidly available nitrogen source.
Fish meal	10.0–4.0–4.0	Not a significant source of other nutrients	4	Rapidly available nitrogen source.
Granite meal	0–4.0–0	Micronutrients	–	Very slow release of phosphorus. Use to build soil reserves.
Grass clippings (fresh)	0.7–0.3–0.8	0.1% sulfur; 0.2% calcium; 0.1% magnesium; micronutrients	33	Balanced, slow release.
Greensand	0–0–7.0	Micronutrients	–	Very slowly available source of potassium. Use to build reserves.
Gypsum	0–0–0	17.0% sulfur; 22.0% calcium	–	Slowly available source of sulfur and calcium. Does not affect pH. Improves alkaline soil structure. Increases plant growth in acid soils.
Kelp meal	1.0–0.2–2.0	3.0% sulfur; micronutrients	–	Slow release of potassium and micronutrients. Contains growth stimulants.
Lime, oystershell	0–0–0	96.0% calcium; 1.0% magnesium	–	Slow release of calcium. Used to increase pH.
Limestone (dolomitic)	0–0–0	51.0% calcium; 40.0% magnesium	–	Slow release of calcium and magnesium. Used to increase pH.

(continued)

Fertilizer Options—Continued

AMENDMENT	NPK RATIO	OTHER NUTRIENTS	C/N RATIO	COMMENTS
Limestone (high-calcium)	0–0–0	65.0–80.0% calcium; 3.0–15.0% magnesium	—	Slow release of calcium. Used to increase pH.
Manure, cow (dry)	2.0–1.0–2.4	0.5% sulfur; 0.2% calcium; micronutrients	18	Best when composted.
Manure, horse	2.0–1.0–2.5	1.0% sulfur; 0.2% calcium; micronutrients	22	Slow release when dry; rapid release when fresh.
Manure, poultry (dry)	4.0–3.0–1.0	0.2% sulfur; 2.0% calcium; 0.3% magnesium	7	Very rapidly available nitrogen and phosphorus. Should be composted; fresh manure will burn plants.
Oak leaves	0.8–0.4–0.1	Micronutrients	Variable	Very slow release. Improves soil structure.
Orchard grass (hay)	2.0–0.6–2.7	0.3% sulfur	24	Balanced, slow release. May need rapidly available nitrogen source added.
Rock phosphate (hard rock)	0–30.0–0	33.0% calcium; micronutrients	—	Slowly available phosphorus and calcium. Will increase pH. Used to build reserves.
Sawdust	0.2–0.2–0.3	Not a significant source of other nutrients	Very high	Use only when well-rotted. Add a rapidly available nitrogen source. Good soil conditioner and mulch for blueberries.
Soybean meal	6.0–1.0–2.0	0.8% magnesium; micronutrients	7	Rapidly available nitrogen.
Sulfur (flowers)	0–0–0	99.5% sulfur	—	Used to lower high pH.
Sul-Po-Mag	0–0–22.0	19.0% sulfur; 10.0% magnesium	—	Rapidly available potassium and magnesium. Don't use with dolomitic lime.

AMENDMENT	NPK RATIO	OTHER NUTRIENTS	C/N RATIO	COMMENTS
Weeds (fresh)	2.4–0.8–3.8	2.3% calcium; micro-nutrients	17	Balanced, slow release.
Wheat straw	0.6–0.2–1.0	0.2% sulfur; 0.2% calcium; 0.05% magnesium; micronutrients	78	Very slow release. Used to improve soil structure. Should be applied with a rapidly available nitrogen source.
Wood ashes (leached)	0–1.6–5.0	35.0% calcium; micro-nutrients	–	Low phosphorus content, but rapidly available. Good source of potassium and calcium. Will increase pH. Can injure microorganisms. Do not use more than ½–¾ lb. per 100 sq. ft.
Wood ashes (unleached)	0–1.7–7.0	35.0% calcium; micro-nutrients	–	Low phosphorus content, but rapidly available. Good source of potassium and calcium. Will increase pH. Can injure microorganisms. Do not use more than ½–¾ lb. per 100 sq. ft.
Wood chips (deciduous)	0–0.2–2.0 to 0–1.0–3.0	Not a significant source of other nutrients	Very high	Very slow release. Do not apply without a rapidly available nitrogen source. Used to improve soil structure. May take more than one year to decompose.
Worm castings (Biocast)	0.5–0.5–0.3	Micronutrients	–	Excellent for improving soil structure.

To Till or Not to Till

As soon as those warm breezes blow in the spring, we get that urge to till. There's something about freshly worked soil that refreshes our housebound minds and bodies. Control your impulses! Tilling is *not* always the best soil management choice. Keep in mind that tillage decreases soil organic matter content. Disturbing the soil kills many types of fungi that are important in nutrient cycling. And if you till when the soil is too wet or too dry, you may drastically affect its structure, leaving yourself a garden bed of tough clods or a hard, crusted surface.

On the positive side, tillage increases soil aeration and results in a flush of biological activity. It controls weeds, warms cool soils, and dries out wet soils. Deep digging can break up compaction and mix soil layers, improve water drainage, and extend crop rooting depth, thus increasing the range of nutrients available to plant roots.

You will want to till if you are breaking sod to start a new garden, if you're incorporating a cover crop or other residue into the soil, or if you're preparing a seedbed for small seeds like lettuce. Just as you rotate crops in your garden, try to rotate the areas you till annually. Disturb the soil as little as possible, and leave islands of undisturbed areas even when you do till. These islands will be a haven for microorganisms, earthworms, and beneficial insects whose habits are disturbed by tilling.

Double Digging

Double digging is a well-established method of deep digging. When you double dig, you remove the topsoil from a garden bed, loosen the soil layer below the topsoil, and then restore the topsoil layer. During the process, you can incorporate organic matter into the soil. Double digging your beds will raise them about 3 to 4 inches because it thoroughly loosens and aerates the soil.

Here's how to double dig a bed, as shown in the illustration on the opposite page:

1. Several days in advance, mark off the area you plan to dig, and soak the soil with water. A few days later, remove weeds or sod, and loosen the top 1 foot of soil with a spading fork.

2. The next day, begin digging, starting from one end of the marked area. With a shovel or spade, dig a 1-foot-wide, 1-foot-deep trench. Pile the topsoil from that trench onto a ground cloth or into a garden cart.

3. To loosen the exposed subsoil, stick your spading fork deeply into the soil and twist and wiggle the fork to loosen up the clumps. Spread a shovelful of organic matter over the surface of the exposed subsoil.

4. Slide the topsoil from the next 1-foot section of the bed onto the subsoil in the first trench. Loosen the subsoil in the second trench with the spading fork and spread a shovelful of organic matter over the exposed subsoil.

5. Continue down the bed, repeating Step 4 until you reach the end of the bed.

6. Use the reserved topsoil from the first trench to fill in the last trench.

7. Spread compost or other organic matter over the entire bed, and use a spading fork to work it into the top 4 to 6 inches of the soil.

Making Raised Beds

Making raised beds can be the finishing touch for your soil preparation. While your crops should perform beautifully in ground-level beds in a well-managed organic soil, they may do even better in raised beds. Raised beds increase soil aeration and drainage. Crops produce better because they grow in deep, loose, fertile soil that is never walked upon. And you can grow twice as many crops in the same space: In a row garden, the crops occupy only one-third of the garden area, and the paths, two-thirds. In a raised-bed garden, the proportions are reversed.

You can make raised beds by double digging as described in "Double Digging" on the opposite page. Or, if you have plenty of compost, you can build beds in a less labor-intensive manner. Figure out your desired bed size or sizes. Beds can be any length but should not be more than 4 to 5 feet wide, depending on how far you can comfortably reach to tend the middle of the bed. Mark the bed locations with string or corner stones. Spread a layer of compost where the bed will be. One inch is enough if your soil is very fertile, but you can use up to 8 inches if you have the compost to spare. If your soil isn't very fertile, try to find enough compost to make at least a 6-inch layer. Then, shovel or rake the top few inches of soil from the pathways onto the top of the beds. You will be left with raised beds and lowered walkways. You can also make raised beds by building wooden borders or by placing hay or straw bales around bed borders, then filling in the beds with a mixture of compost and soil.

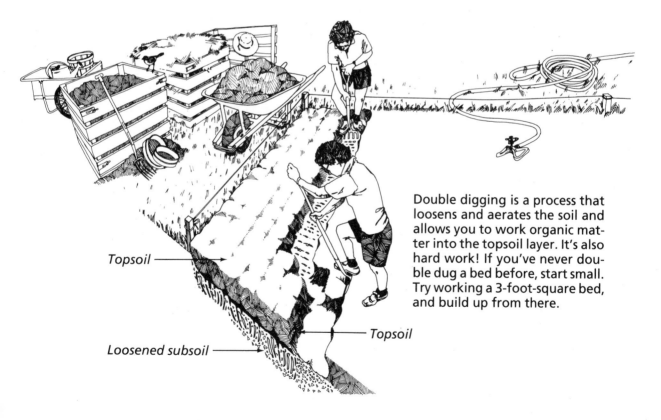

Topsoil

Topsoil

Loosened subsoil

Double digging is a process that loosens and aerates the soil and allows you to work organic matter into the topsoil layer. It's also hard work! If you've never double dug a bed before, start small. Try working a 3-foot-square bed, and build up from there.

CUSTOMIZED SOIL CARE

If you balance your soil pH, build its organic matter content with a range of organic materials, and work it carefully to preserve its structure, your fruits and vegetables should generally produce well. When you're ready for the next step beyond, you may want to try custom soil preparation and enrichment to suit the nutrient needs of a specific crop or group of crops.

The following five custom-care programs are designed to give you maximum yields. Vegetables are grouped according to the part harvested: fruits, leaves, or roots. Fruits are divided by growth habit: fruits that grow on trees (tree fruits) and fruits that grow on bushes and vines (small fruits).

Throughout these instructions, recommendations are given for high-fertility, medium-fertility, and low-fertility soils. To evaluate the fertility of your soil, refer to "Rating Soil Fertility" on page 31. Feel free to experiment with substituting ammendments that are common in your area. These recipes have been tested and work well in many regions of the country, but they are by no means the only option. ✳

CUSTOM CARE FOR ROOT CROPS

Root crops such as beets, carrots, potatoes, and turnips need a soil with balanced amounts of nitrogen, phosphorus, and potassium. If you'd like to specialize your care of root crops, try planting them after a fall-planted cover crop. Throughout the season, the clippings from the cover-cropped paths provide the perfect organic mulch for your crops.

Here's how to set up a strip-crop system:

1. In the fall, plant deep-rooted legumes to "plow" the soil. Try red clover, crimson clover, biennial sweet clover, or white clover. (See "Planting Cover Crops" on page 44 for instructions.)

2. In the spring, after your cover crop has grown 6 to 8 inches, mow it as short as possible.

Leave the residue on the soil surface for one to two weeks.

3. Apply compost and fertilizers based on your soil's fertility level. Use the amounts listed in the table "Fertilizing Root Crops" on the opposite page. Apply compost before you put on the fertilizers. A 30-gallon garbage can will hold about 40 pounds of compost. Mix

the powders in a large container and sprinkle them over the area by hand.

4. Till or dig residues under deeply (about 1 foot). If you do not have any established beds, try tilling the residues under in 2- to 4-foot-wide beds, leaving strips of your cover crop undisturbed between the beds to serve as pathways.

5. Plant root crops in the beds.

6. If your paths are planted with the cover crop, keep the strips mowed (one to four times a month, depending on your climate). Mulch the plants in the beds with the cover crop clippings each time you mow.

Busy gardeners with no time to compost or plant cover crops can still encourage best growth of root crops by applying mixed fertilizers as listed in the table "Fertilizing Root Crops" below. Spread the powders by hand over the soil before tilling or digging in the spring.

Potatoes seem to do well with the addition of gypsum. Many commercial growers swear by it. Add 5 pounds of gypsum per 100 square feet if your soil test levels of calcium and sulfur are low (less than 5 to 6 parts per million, or ppm, for sulfur and less than 600 ppm for calcium).

Fertilizing Root Crops

With cover crops and compost. If you have planted a cover crop and will apply compost, apply the following amounts of materials per 100 square feet, depending on your soil type.

HIGH-FERTILITY	MEDIUM-FERTILITY	LOW-FERTILITY
40 lb. compost	100 lb. compost	250 lb. compost
0.5 lb. bonemeal	1 lb. bonemeal	2 lb. bonemeal
5 lb. soybean meal	15 lb. soybean meal	25 lb. soybean meal
4 lb. rock phosphate	8 lb. rock phosphate	15 lb. rock phosphate
2 lb. kelp	2 lb. kelp	10 lb. kelp

Without cover crops and compost. If you have not planted a cover crop and don't have compost available to spread, apply the following amounts of materials per 100 square feet, depending on your soil type.

HIGH-FERTILITY	MEDIUM-FERTILITY	LOW-FERTILITY
0.5 lb. bonemeal	1 lb. bonemeal	2 lb. bonemeal
15 lb. soybean meal	25 lb. soybean meal	50 lb. soybean meal
8 lb. rock phosphate	15 lb. rock phosphate	25 lb. rock phosphate
5 lb. kelp	8 lb. kelp	15 lb. kelp

CUSTOM CARE FOR FRUIT CROPS

Some vegetables are, botanically speaking, fruits. These include corn, cucumbers, peppers, squash, and tomatoes. Other crops have similar nutrient requirements, even though we harvest the flower or other plant part. These include broccoli, brussels sprouts, cabbage, and cauliflower. In many areas, combining an off-season cover crop with black plastic mulch during the growing season works well.

Our goal in managing soil fertility for these vegetables is to provide balanced nitrogen, phosphorus, and potassium levels (giving a slight edge to potassium) and a good supply of micronutrients.

The best time to plant a cover crop to precede your fruiting vegetables is in the fall. Good cover crop choices for fall planting include hairy vetch, white clover, alsike clover, or subterranean clover (winter kills this in cooler climates). If you don't get around to starting the cover crop until spring, sow subterranean clover, white clover, berseem clover, or black medic. See "Planting Cover Crops" on page 44 for instructions and "Cover Crop Requirements" on page 46 for seeding rates.

Be sure to keep your fall-planted cover crop under control. Mow it whenever it reaches 6 to 8 inches. Two to three weeks before you plan to plant your vegetables, mow your cover crop very short. Use the lowest setting on your lawn mower.

If you do not have established beds, lay out beds 2 to 4 feet wide one to two weeks before planting. If you have compost available to apply, spread it evenly over the beds now. Then till the compost and cover crops lightly, just 1 to 2 inches deep. If your spring-planted cover crop grew slowly and is less than 3 inches tall when you mow it, you can skip tilling it in at this point.

At planting time, till or dig the beds to approximately 1 foot deep. Leave the cover crop growing undisturbed in the pathways between the beds. Add soil or a mix of soil and well-decomposed compost to raise the beds 6 to 8 inches above ground level. Cover the beds with black plastic for tomatoes, peppers, squash, cucumbers, and melons. Use flat rows or beds for cabbage-family crops. Mulch the younger plants with a 4- to 6-inch layer of legume hay as soon as you transplant them.

Fertilize with alfalfa meal or with a kelp/alfalfa meal mix. If you're using black plastic, just apply the fertilizer directly to the bed surfaces before laying the plastic. If you're not using plastic, rake the fertilizers into the top few inches of soil in the beds. See the table "Fertilizing Fruit Crops" on the opposite page for amounts of compost and fertilizers to add based on your soil's fertility level.

When transplants are set, water them in with compost tea and kelp (2 tablespoons of kelp per 1 gallon of compost tea). If you have low-fertility soil, you might also want to add magnesium as an Epsom salt spray when first blooms appear (1 tablespoon of Epsom salts per gallon of water).

You don't have to use black plastic on warm-season crops. However, harvests are usu-ally delayed without black plastic, especially if you use organic mulch around the plants. Or-ganic mulch keeps soil temperatures cooler, so wait until the soil has warmed up before you ap-ply it. Using organic mulches may increase the incidence of mildew in your cucumbers.

Fertilizing Fruit Crops

With cover crops and compost. If you preceded your vegetables with a cover crop, apply the following amounts of compost and alfalfa meal per 100 square feet, depending on your soil type.

HIGH-FERTILITY	MEDIUM-FERTILITY	LOW-FERTILITY
40 lb. compost	100 lb. compost	200–250 lb. compost
2–3 lb. alfalfa meal	5–10 lb. alfalfa meal	10–20 lb. alfalfa meal

Without cover crops. If you don't precede your vegetables with a cover crop, you can increase the amount of compost you use to add an equivalent amount of organic matter. Apply the following amounts of compost and alfalfa meal per 100 square feet, depending on your soil type.

HIGH-FERTILITY	MEDIUM-FERTILITY	LOW-FERTILITY
100 lb. compost	100–200 lb. compost	300–400 lb. compost
2–3 lb. alfalfa meal	5–10 lb. alfalfa meal	10–20 lb. alfalfa meal

Without cover crops and compost. If you are a busy gardener with no time to compost or tend cover crops, try applying the following mix per 100 square feet. If you are growing peppers or if your phosphorus levels are low, add 10 lb. of bonemeal to the mix, depending on your soil type.

HIGH-FERTILITY	MEDIUM-FERTILITY	LOW-FERTILITY
25 lb. alfalfa meal	50 lb. alfalfa meal	100 lb. alfalfa meal
5 lb. kelp	10 lb. kelp	25 lb. kelp

CUSTOM CARE FOR LEAFY CROPS

Lettuce, spinach, chard, and other greens from which we harvest leaves need a good balance of phosphorus, potassium, micronutrients, and nitrogen levels. They respond well in soil prepared with compost and fertilizer. You can undersow leaf crops with a legume, which will enrich the soil and serve as living mulch for a crop that follows the leaf crop.

Start by spreading compost, using amounts listed in the table "Fertilizing Leafy Crops" below, and till or dig it into the soil. If you do not already have estblished beds, build 6- to 8-inch-high beds. Sprinkle fertilizer (see the same table for the fertilizer recipe) on the top of each bed and rake it to a depth of 2 to 3 inches. You can immediately sow seeds. If you are planting transplants, wait one to three days after moistening the fertilizer before planting. Weed seed-grown greens scrupulously to prevent competition for water, light, and nutrients.

When your greens are 3 to 4 inches tall, you can undersow them with a legume to prepare for your next crop. To do this, just scatter the legume seeds between your plants. Try fast-growing, shade-tolerant clovers, such as subterranean clover.

Fertilizing Leafy Crops

With compost. If you are fertilizing with compost, apply the following amounts of materials per 100 square feet, depending on your soil type.

HIGH-FERTILITY	MEDIUM-FERTILITY	LOW-FERTILITY
40 lb. compost	100 lb. compost	200 lb. compost
1 lb. blood meal	3 lb. blood meal	5 lb. blood meal
3 lb. fish meal	5 lb. fish meal	10 lb. fish meal
3 lb. kelp	5 lb. kelp	10 lb. kelp

Without compost. If you don't have compost, apply the following materials per 100 square feet, depending on your soil type.

HIGH-FERTILITY	MEDIUM-FERTILITY	LOW-FERTILITY
1 lb. blood meal	3 lb. blood meal	5 lb. blood meal
6.75 lb. fish meal	10.6 lb. fish meal	21.25 lb. fish meal
4.25 lb. kelp	6.9 lb. kelp	13.75 lb. kelp
5 lb. rock phosphate	7.5 lb. rock phosphate	15 lb. rock phosphate

CUSTOM CARE FOR TREE FRUITS

Fruit trees such as apples, pears, peaches, cherries, and plums need a soil with rapid nitrogen release and balanced slow-release phosphorus, potassium, and micronutrients. Preparing the soil well in advance by planting a cover crop is crucial to success in growing fruit trees organically.

With fruit trees it's important to begin your preparations one full year before you want to plant. Gardeners in warm regions often plant fruit trees in fall, while northern gardeners plant in spring. Depending on your planned planting time, plant a cover crop in the spring or the fall of the preceding year. White sweet clover or hairy vetch are good choices. You'll have to mow the cover crop several times during the preparation year. Cut it whenever it grows more than 8 to 10 inches tall. Let the residue remain on the surface. Two weeks before planting, mow the cover crop very short. Allow the residue to dry out for two or three days, then till it in.

At planting time, soak your tree roots in compost tea, then dust with a mix of 1 cup of kelp and 1 cup of bonemeal. Also, add 1 cup of blood meal, 1 cup of kelp, and 1 gallon of compost to the bottom of each planting hole. Throw 1 inch of soil on top of this mix, then plant the tree. Immediately mulch with a 4-foot diameter circle of legume hay. Mulching will improve water availability. It also increases soil levels of nitrogen, phosphorus, potassium, magnesium, and calcium in the top 20 inches of soil.

After planting, sow a cover crop of fava beans, subterranean clover, or buckwheat between the mulched areas if you are planting more than one tree. Your goal is to have a crop that does not compete vigorously in spring, when trees need nitrogen for vegetative growth and fruit set. Instead it should grow and compete in fall, because high nitrogen levels are detrimental to fruit development and coloring as well as to winter hardiness development. Buckwheat and fava beans, and—in cooler climates—subterranean clover, will winter-kill and provide a dead mulch to be replanted each season.

You can plant a permanent living mulch for your fruit trees instead after the first year of growth in the aisles between the trees. Don't use deep rooters (such as alfalfa or deep-rooted, vigorous clovers and sweet clovers). These will compete for water. Keep your cover crop mowed short in the spring, especially around bloom time. Cover crop blooms may distract bees that should be pollinating the trees. If nematodes are a problem, avoid using legume species, since these have been reported to host pest nematode species. Instead, try bahia grass—which decreases pest nematode populations in peach trees.

If brown rot is a problem in your area, keep in mind that living mulches may increase humidity in orchards and, thus, the potential for brown rot infection.

The final aspect of custom care for fruit

trees is to manage your mulch. Renew the legume mulch yearly during late fall, increasing the size of the mulched circle so that it is just wider than the tips of the branches. Apply a fast-acting nitrogen source such as blood meal to the mulch around your young trees each spring. Mature trees should be fine with a yearly compost addition to the mulch.

Researchers report that fertilizer applications are more effective in a mulched, rather than bare-ground, orchard. In fact, in a high-fertility soil, a managed cover crop or annual mulch addition may be all the fertilization a mature fruit tree needs.

CUSTOM CARE FOR SMALL FRUITS

Blueberries, raspberries, blackberries, strawberries, and other small fruits grow best in soil that slowly releases balanced amounts of nitrogen, phosphorus, potassium, and micronutrients. Careful soil preparation before planting and use of a living mulch between rows of plants should give you bountiful berries for years to come.

Just as for tree fruits, use a deep-rooting green manure the season before planting and manage it similarly. After tilling in the green manure, spread fertilizers ten days to two weeks before planting as directed in the table "Fertilizing Small Fruits" below. On planting day, soak roots in compost tea. Before setting plants in place, dust the roots of each plant with 1 cup of bonemeal and 1 cup of kelp. Mulch right after planting with legume hay. Plant subterranean clover, white clover, or hairy vetch in the paths between rows as a living mulch and keep it mowed. Reapply mulch yearly.

Blueberries require special attention to pH levels; see the Blueberry entry on page 304 for pH amendment and planting instructions.

Fertilizing Small Fruits

Apply the following fertilizers per 100 square feet before planting, depending on your soil type.

HIGH-FERTILITY	MEDIUM-FERTILITY	LOW-FERTILITY
25 lb. alfalfa meal	50 lb. alfalfa meal	100 lb. alfalfa meal
1 lb. kelp	3 lb. kelp	5 lb. kelp
50 lb. compost	100 lb. compost	200 lb. compost

3 PLANNING AND RECORD KEEPING

Choosing Plants, Laying Out Your Garden, and Managing Garden Records

Managing a garden is like directing a play. First, you have to set the stage with good soil, then choose the plants that you want to see perform there. The main difference is that at the height of the season, you'll have many scenes going on at the same time—you'll have seedlings just starting out, plants coming into full flower, and fruits ripening and getting ready for harvest. Getting the timing right takes planning and practice. You need to know not only what crops you'll use but also when to have the garden ready for them, how much to plant, and when they'll be ready for harvesting. A good plan will help you do all of these things and more. For one thing, a good plan will help you spread out the harvest as much as possible. That means you won't end up overloaded with produce one week and without any the next. You can also plan crops that come all at once, making it convenient to freeze or can for the winter months.

In a sense, each garden you plant and harvest is a rehearsal for the next one—and with rehearsal, performance improves! That's where record keeping comes in. Garden records will help you build on your experience from year to year. The notes you keep each year on crops you liked and didn't like, insects and diseases that threatened your harvest, weather, and so forth will help you manage next year's garden that much better.

In the pages that follow, you'll find information on planning your vegetable garden and suggestions for how to plan for perennial crops like asparagus, small fruits, and tree fruits. You'll also find tips on starting your own garden record-keeping system.

PLANNING FUNDAMENTALS

Planning the garden is one of the off-season's most pleasurable tasks, but it's much more than an armchair exercise designed to keep you busy while the soil rests. It also involves more than looking through seed catalogs and picking what to grow. True, a good plan will help you pick what crops to plant, but it will also help you schedule planting times, use your garden space efficiently, rotate crops to build the soil and prevent disease problems, and spread out the harvest.

A clear, well-thought-out garden plan is the key to a successful and bountiful garden. That's because a plan lets you use your garden space to its fullest. Rather than planting one crop a season and letting the garden fill up with weeds after that, you'll be scheduling two, three, or more plantings each year, so one crop follows another. Just as important, careful planning helps minimize problems during the season—such as weeds and overcrowded, sickly plants. A good garden plan also makes it easier to keep track of the many details of planting, cultivation, and soil care that are too easily forgotten in the busy season.

Getting the Size Right

Once you've selected the best site for your garden, deciding on the best size is next. (For information on site selection, see "Selecting the Best Site" on pages 6 and 7.) The site you've selected may dictate garden size to some extent. Another important consideration in deciding on the size of your garden is how much *time* you want to devote to it. If you're not sure, start small. You'll be much happier with a small garden that's well cared for than a large, unmanageable one that's not. Keep in mind that a small garden that's thoughtfully planned and tended can yield as much as a carelessly planned one many times its size.

Trying to cram too many plants into too little space is another common error that inevitably leads to poorly developed plants and low yields. If you're determined to grow all of your favorite vegetables, be realistic and plan enough space for each crop. Intensive planting, interplanting, and succession planting, described later in this chapter, are great techniques that will help you get more out of your garden than you ever thought possible, without skimping on space plants need to grow.

If space is at a premium, there are a variety of options to consider. A vegetable garden doesn't have to be rectangular to be successful! Perhaps a long, narrow plot running along a fence in the backyard would fit best. Consider an L-shaped or even a triangular plot in a corner of the yard, if that suits your particular circumstances.

Another option is to reserve the garden proper for salad greens, root vegetables, and other crops that can be planted intensively, and to grow some larger plants—like summer squash, eggplants, and tomatoes—in containers elsewhere in the yard. See Chapter 9 for more on growing vegetables in containers. You can also grow space-hungry crops like sweet corn, winter squash, or melons in plots away from the main garden. For design options, see the seven garden themes in Chapter 10.

Sunlight and Angle

Whatever the size of your garden, you need to know how the sun strikes it before you start penciling in crops on a plan. If trees, fences or buildings reduce the amount of sunlight that part of the garden receives, plan to put shade-tolerant crops there and save the sunniest areas for sun-loving crops.

Once you've figured out how the sun hits your site, decide how to orient your rows or beds. If you orient them from east to west, your plants will get maximum light, and you won't have to worry about tall plants shading out their shorter neighbors. Beds oriented on a north-south axis give you the option of sheltering small patches of lettuce or other tender crops in the shade cast by tall or trellised crops.

Garden Layout: Rows or Beds?

In a bygone era, when large gardens were a virtual necessity, almost all crops were planted in single rows. Many still think of a garden as a series of tidy rows of vegetables, each marked with a seed packet impaled on a stick. But planting in single rows isn't necessarily most efficient. Since you need space on either side of the row to cultivate and harvest the crop, most of the garden ends up as workspace for the gardener, not growing space for plants. That's where garden beds come in. Beds increase production because they devote garden space to plants, not paths. They also allow you to plant intensively, so you get the highest yield in the least amount of space. The illustration on page 66 gives an example of just how efficient growing crops in beds really is. The plant entries in Part 2 provide spacing instructions for both row and bed planting.

Another advantage of planting intensively in beds is that the plants shade the soil as they grow, holding moisture in the soil and shading out weeds. Bush peas and beans planted in beds also support each other, which helps keep their pods out of the dirt and away from mold spores.

Bed planting also lends itself to interplanting—the technique of planting two different crops in the same bed. For example, you could drop a lettuce transplant between each cabbage plant in the example on page 66. The lettuce will be harvested before the slower-growing cabbage needs the space. One bed, one planting, two crops. That's using your

head, and your garden space. For more on interplanting, see "Two Crops in One" on page 70.

If you have a large garden or use mechanized equipment, it's still most efficient to grow some crops in rows. Potatoes, for example, are much easier to grow if the soil can be thrown up on either side of the plants.

While you're thinking general layout, don't forget to think vertically. Train crops like climbing peas or cucumbers to a trellis or other support. Trellised crops are best grown in conventional rows. Tall cultivars of edible-podded peas are typically more prolific over a longer period of time than bush pea cultivars. A trellised row of peas may give you better yield than the same amount of bed space devoted to bush peas—and they're easier to pick.

When you plan your trellises, keep the angle of the sun in mind. Trellised plants will cast shade, which may be desirable for some crops but not others.

DECIDING WHAT TO GROW

Once you've decided whether to use beds, rows, or some combination of the two, make a rough sketch of your garden. It needn't be precisely to scale, but it should tell you how many beds or rows you have to work with. Don't forget to include pathways between beds or rows. They should be wide enough to be comfortable for you to work in—1½ feet is a common width. If you're using a tiller to cultivate, make sure it fits between the beds.

Now it's time to start thinking about what to plant. This could take some time and probably should include some family consultation. Everybody likes salad? Okay. Start a list and write on it lettuce, spinach, radishes, or whatever salad ingredients you favor.

Green beans? Yes. Cucumbers? Sure. Broccoli? In moderation. Tomatoes? But of course. Eggplant? Not on your life. (This last comment comes from the kids, but if you love eggplant list it anyway.)

If your space is really limited, then it will help for you to rank the crops in order of most to least coveted, in case something doesn't fit. Don't worry about picking particular cultivars of lettuce or beans just yet. You should

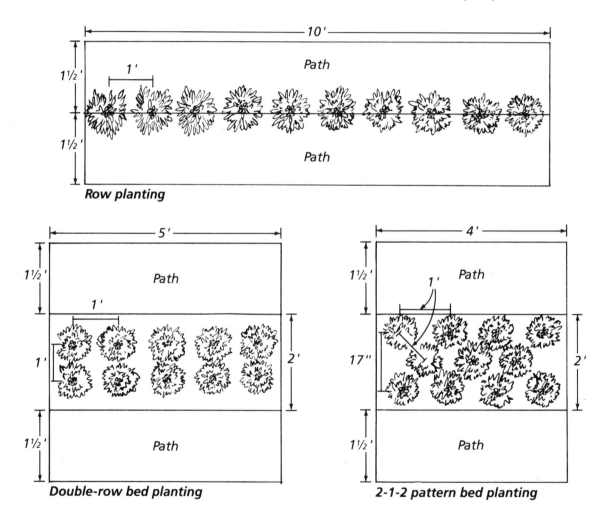

Row planting

Double-row bed planting

2-1-2 pattern bed planting

Planting intensively and planting in beds rather than in single rows can pay big dividends. For example, you can plant small-heading cabbage cultivars 1 foot apart. In a traditional row planting, that translates to 10 cabbages in 30 square feet of garden. In a 2-foot-wide bed, the same 10 cabbages take up only 25 square feet of garden space. And by planting in a 2-1-2 pattern, 11 heads will fit nicely in only 20 square feet.

save that for after you've decided how you're going to schedule and plant your crops. For more on selecting cultivars, see "Selecting Plants" on page 79.

Which Crop When?

Keep in mind that a well-planned garden makes use of space *and* growing season, so you're not going to plant everything on your list at once. Your plan will take into account how quickly a crop will mature and be harvested and what might be planted after it to keep the harvest coming. For example, the space that yielded lettuce in the spring may produce cucumbers in the summer and radishes in the fall. Early-summer's green-bean bed may be fall's broccoli bed.

Planning the succession of your crops will depend on your climate and the length of your growing season. For basic information about how climate factors affect when and what you'll plant, you may want to review "Climate and the Gardener" on page 91.

A good first step is to take your list of crops and divide it into three groups according to general planting season: frost-hardy plants, warm-weather plants, and cool-weather plants. Then you'll have a good start on a rough planting schedule. For information on timing individual crops, see the plant entries in Part 2.

Frost-Hardy Crops

Frost-hardy crops are the first crops you'll plant, and they will provide you with your first harvest. These crops tolerate the cold soil and occasional frosts of early spring. In fact, many will grow and be harvested before it's safe to set out tender plants like tomatoes. Take advan-

tage of these crops—they'll greatly increase the yield of your garden. Frost-hardy crops include:

- Leafy crops: Kale, lettuce, spinach, Swiss chard
- Root crops: Beets, carrots, onions, potatoes, radishes, and turnips
- Broccoli and cauliflower
- Peas

To cut down on early-season maintenance, group plantings of frost-hardy crops in one section of the garden, especially if you have a fairly large plot. That way you don't have to till and rake the entire garden at once. Besides, the first flush of annual weeds probably will have germinated by the time it's safe to plant warm-weather crops, and you'd have to prepare the soil all over again.

Warm-Weather Crops

Whether planted as seeds or transplants, warm-weather crops can go into the garden anytime after the last expected frost date. These crops do best if you wait for the soil to warm up before planting. Earlier planting generally means an earlier harvest, but waiting for thoroughly settled weather usually results in greater yield. A good compromise is to plan a small early planting and a larger later one. Warm-weather crops include:

- Eggplant, tomatoes, and peppers
- Summer squash
- Lima beans and snap beans
- Cucumbers and melons
- Sweet potatoes
- Corn

When you plan, take into account that some warm-weather crops lend themselves to vertical growing, which can save both space and weeding work. Cucumbers can be trained to trellises, and pole snap beans can be grown on stakes or strings. Tomatoes grown on stakes or in cages require far less space than tomatoes allowed to sprawl on the ground, and the fruit is better protected from sunscald, insects, and molds.

Cool-Weather Crops

For many gardeners, the late season—from late summer into fall—is the most productive part of the year. Many crops that thrive in the spring actually do better in the fall, when the days are growing shorter and cooler rather than longer and warmer. Another fall-planting advantage is that many of the most ferocious annual weeds become docile in the autumn, reducing weeding chores. Here are some cool-weather crops to consider:

- Leafy crops: Collards, kale and lettuce
- Root crops: Beets, carrots, and turnips (These can be harvested well into winter.)
- Broccoli, cauliflower, and kohlrabi
- Peas
- Celery, leeks, and parsnips (These are planted with warm-weather crops but require a long season to mature.)
- Garlic and shallots (These are planted in fall and harvested the following summer.)
- Spinach (This is planted in fall and overwintered to provide the earliest spring greens.)

If you want to reap the benefits of the late season, you'll have to plan for it. It's often hard to find vegetable transplants in midsummer, so you'll have to grow your own unless you live near an exceptional garden center.

How Much to Plant?

Now you know what you'll be planting and approximately when you'll plant it. The next question is how much to plant, which will depend largely on your family's eating habits. For example, if a green salad is on the menu almost every day, you'll probably want plenty of lettuce. If you have salad once a week, a few plants are enough.

Here's a general rule to keep in mind while you're deciding what to plant: The faster a crop matures, the more quickly it becomes overmature and the greater the chance that part of the crop will be wasted. For this reason, fast-maturing crops like lettuce, bush snap beans, and cucumbers are good candidates for succession plantings. Warm-weather crops like summer squash pose a different kind of problem. Many can be real space-hogs, requiring a considerable amount of garden space and occupying it for months. Fortunately, they generally bear so prolifically you needn't plant them in large numbers.

Incorporating sweet corn in a plan takes special consideration for a couple of reasons. It matures and passes its prime quickly, so it's best to plan a series of small succession plantings. It's also wind pollinated, so you need to plant it in blocks or beds with enough plants in each planting to ensure proper pollination, otherwise you'll end up with "snaggle-toothed" ears with great gaps where sweet kernels should be. (See the Corn entry on page 334 for details.)

You'll find recommendations for ways to spread out the harvest, proper spacing guidelines, and suggestions on how much to plant in the plant entries in Part 2. For more on succession planting, see "Succession Planting—Crop After Crop" on page 72.

❦ REGIONAL REALITIES ❦

PLAN FOR LOCAL WEATHER PATTERNS

To get you started thinking about regional weather patterns, here are some general guidelines. Look for the pattern that most closely describes the weather in your area.

Cold winters and hot, humid summers. In the northeast, mid-Atlantic, and north-central states, the outdoor gardening season begins several weeks before the last expected spring frost. In the North, plant quick-maturing cultivars for summer crops and pay careful attention to hardiness of perennial crops. In all areas, look for cultivars that are resistant to molds and mildews. The late season extends several weeks after the first fall frost and is ideal for cool-weather crops; it extends even longer for very hardy vegetables or those grown under cover.

Cold winters and hot, dry summers. In the mountain states, south-central states, and higher elevations of the Southwest and West the outdoor gardening season begins shortly before the last frost. Early crops may need protection from occasional heavy snows late in the season. Plant quick-maturing cultivars in mountain states. Protect heat-loving plants if nighttime temperatures are quite cool—even in the height of summer. Mulch cool-weather crops to keep roots cool in the heat of the day. Look for cultivars that can withstand temperature extremes.

Mild winters and cool, humid summers. In the Pacific Northwest, where this type of weather is typical, frost-hardy and cool-weather crops can be grown year-round, but growing warm-weather crops is a challenge. Choose quick-maturing cultivars, and cultivars with resistance to mildews and molds. Crops with high heat requirements, like lima beans, may not do well, but the long, cool springs favor substitutes like fava beans.

Mild winters and hot, humid summers. In the Southeast and coastal areas of the southwestern states, winters are mild enough to grow even warm-weather crops. Grow cool-weather crops in the late fall and winter months. To extend the harvest, protect cool-weather crops from the sun with shade cloth as temperatures rise in the spring. Look for warm-weather crops that are resistant to mildews and molds. Look for cool-weather crops that are heat-resistant. Choose perennial crops carefully. Rhubarb, asparagus, and many fruit trees require winter chilling, which your climate may not provide.

Mild winters and hot, dry summers. In the deserts of the Southwest and West, cool-weather crops are best grown in late fall and winter. In this region, gardeners can set out warm-weather crops while northern gardeners are still-ing waiting out the winter. Heat tolerance is critical; look for crops and cultivars that can stand up to scorching weather. The extreme heat, low humidity, and desert winds can sap moisture from plants. Mulch plants to conserve moisture. Consider using sunken beds—the reverse of raised beds—to help conserve moisture and protect crops.

GETTING THE MOST FROM YOUR GARDEN

The ideal food garden is the one that seems inexhaustible—yielding up vegetables for the dinner table and succulent greens for the salad bowl day in and day out. It also provides produce to tuck away for the winter. Such a garden utopia is quite possible, but it takes forethought. A few gardening tricks come in handy, too. Interplanting, succession planting, and crop rotation are the keys to planning a garden that provides a continuous harvest.

Two Crops in One

Interplanting—planting two crops together in the same row or bed—is an easy way to make the most of your garden space. We've already considered interplanting lettuce and cabbage seedlings in the early-spring garden. This combination works because cabbages take a minimum of 60 days to mature from transplants; lettuce seedlings take only about 30 days. That means the lettuce is ready for harvest about the time the cabbages are ready to take over the space. This same trick also works with broccoli, kale, or any other nonvining crop with a longer growing season than lettuce.

In fact, almost any small, fast-maturing crop is a good candidate for interplanting with larger, slower-growing crops. It's a great way to sneak in small plantings of things like radishes and baby turnips that you want to have on hand but not in large quantities. Just be sure you plant the quick-maturing crop at the same time as the slower one. That way, it will be out of the way before the later crop needs the space. Otherwise, both crops will suffer.

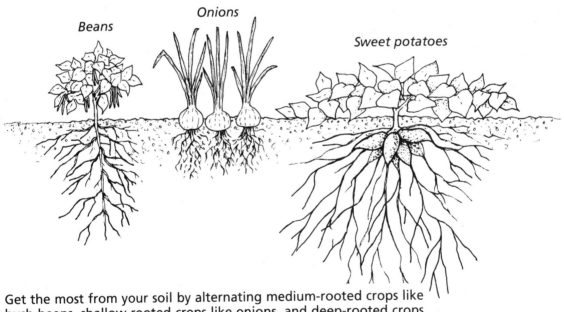

Beans   *Onions*   *Sweet potatoes*

Get the most from your soil by alternating medium-rooted crops like bush beans, shallow-rooted crops like onions, and deep-rooted crops like sweet potatoes. This minimizes competition for water and nutrients among closely planted crops.

Another consideration is how the crops you interplant will get along underground. For example, if you've planted several crops with spreading shallow root systems all together, you'll be making less effective use of your garden space than if you grouped shallow- and deep-rooted crops, as shown in the illustration on the opposite page.

There are other ways to use interplanting to maximize your harvest. Some gardeners use it to take advantage of two crops' differing use of soil nutrients. Our pioneer forebearers routinely planted pole beans with corn. Not only do the beans find cornstalks nice to climb on, but they also fix nitrogen, which helps out the corn, which is a heavy feeder.

You can also use interplanting to create microclimates for crops. For example, let's say you've decided to trellis cucumbers down the middle of a 2-foot-wide garden bed. That leaves plenty of space on either side for additional crops—maybe carrots on the side facing the afternoon sun and lettuce on the other side. The lettuce will benefit from the afternoon shade cast by the trellises. For more ideas on interplanting, see "Ideas for Interplanting" on this page.

Good Companions

Planting marigolds and herbs in the vegetable garden to confuse or repel plant pests is an age-old example of one type of intercropping—companion planting. Modern research substantiates the effectiveness of some companion plants in repelling pests or attracting pest predators and parasites. However, the mechanisms that cause a plant to repel or attract pests remain largely unverified, and many companion planting practices continue to combine folklore and fact. See "Interplant- ing with Companion Plants" on page 72 for combinations you might want to incorporate in your garden plan.

IDEAS FOR INTERPLANTING

A favorite trick of early market gardeners was interplanting—or companion cropping, as it was known then. Ralph L. Watts, professor of horticulture at Pennsylvania State College, outlined some suggestions in his 1911 classic *Vegetable Gardening* that are as useful today as they were then.

Lettuce and beets. Sow or transplant lettuce in rows 1 foot apart, then sow a row of beets down the middle. When the lettuce is harvested, reseed with beets. When the beets are harvested, replant with lettuce. Alternate crops all season long. You can substitute any quick-maturing root crop like carrots or radishes for the beets.

Beans and strawberries. Plant strawberries in early spring and then seed bush beans on either side after the last expected frost. After harvesting the beans, work the residue into the soil to enrich it just as the strawberries are setting runners for next year's crop.

Tomatoes and peas. Sow double rows of bush peas in early spring, with 2 feet between the rows. After the last expected frost, set tomatoes between the rows of peas. Once the peas are harvested, draw the dry vines up around the tomatoes as mulch. Let the tomatoes take over the space. This is a good scheme for large gardens where tomatoes will be allowed to sprawl.

Succession Planting— Crop After Crop

By far the best way to ensure a long harvest is to make double or even triple use of as much space as possible. That means succession planting. Succession planting is possible and practical because many crops only need to occupy space in the garden for a few scant weeks before they're ready to harvest. You can turn that same space over to a second crop and, depending on the length of the season and the crops you're growing, even a third. The illustration on the opposite page shows simple succession plantings in a single garden bed from early spring through summer. After harvest, a spring crop of potatoes can be followed with summer crops of beans and turnips. It's also possible to get a jump on a fall crop of pumpkins by interplanting them with kohlrabi as the kohlrabi is harvested.

For fast-maturing crops like cucumbers

INTERPLANTING WITH COMPANION PLANTS

Try some of these companion planting suggestions in your own garden to see how they work for you. If you want to test their performance more scientifically, try growing crop plants both with and without their companions in separate beds. Record your results so you can use successful combinations again next year.

1. French marigolds (*Tagetes patula*) confuse or deter pests because of their aromatic foliage. Plant them throughout the vegetable garden. Their roots also emit a substance that eliminates nematodes in the immediate area.

2. Rue (*Ruta graveolens*) repels Japanese beetles. Grow it as a garden border or scatter leaf clippings near beetle-infested crops. (Beware, though—rue foliage gives some people a poison-ivy-like rash.)

3. Interplant sweet basil with vegetables, or chop and scatter the leaves to repel aphids, mosquitoes, and mites.

4. Plant basil among your tomatoes to control tomato hornworms.

5. Combine thyme or tomatoes with cabbage plantings to control cabbage maggots, white cabbage butterflies, and imported cabbageworms.

6. Sow catnip by eggplant to deter flea beetles.

7. Set onions in rows with carrots to control rust flies and some nematodes.

8. Grow horseradish with potatoes to repel Colorado potato beetles.

9. Grow radishes or nasturtiums with your cucumbers for cucumber beetle control.

You can also interplant your garden with flowers that will attract beneficial insects. These companion plants provide beneficials with shelter and food during some or all of their life cycle. Try herbs such as fennel, dill, anise, parsley, and coriander; also plant some daisy-family members such as sunflowers, zinnias, asters, gazanias, and calendulas.

and sweet corn, which reach their peak quickly but go downhill just as fast, succession planting is the only way to ensure continuous harvest. But succession planting is useful for other vegetables as well. In areas plagued by the bacterial wilt spread by cucumber beetles, a second planting of summer squash and cucumbers, three to four weeks after the first, will generally begin bearing about the time that the first planting begins to decline. A third planting a month later often escapes the wilt altogether and bears right up until frost.

With a little attention to each crop's favorite growing climate, its speed of maturity, and its space requirements, you can orchestrate a season-long bounty from even a modest garden. The illustration below shows what the possibilities are for just one garden bed from early spring to fall. Frost-hardy crops like spinach and carrots are replaced in late spring with warm-weather ones like tomatoes and cucumbers. Cool-weather crops like Chinese cabbage and lettuce are moved into the garden to extend the harvest into fall.

Garden Rotations

Crop rotation is another all-important ingredient of any good garden plan. Rotating

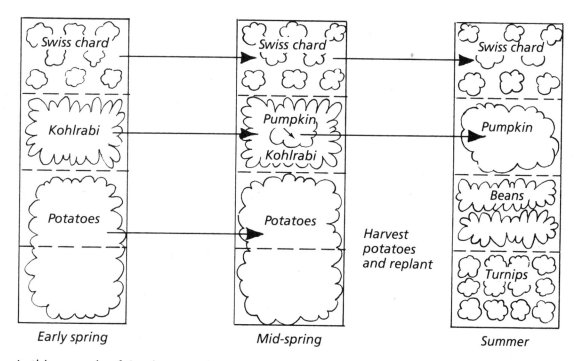

Early spring   Mid-spring   Summer

In this example of simple succession, spring potatoes are followed after harvest by beans and turnips. The kohlrabi and pumpkins illustrate a slightly different technique. As the kohlrabi are harvested in mid-spring, pumpkins are seeded in between the plants. The kohlrabi will be fully harvested once the pumpkins need the space. Swiss chard regrows after cutting and can be harvested all summer.

crops so you don't grow heavy-feeding crops in the same spot year after year helps manage soil fertility. Rotating the placement of crops that belong to the same botanical family also helps avoid or reduce problems with soilborne diseases and some soil-dwelling insects.

Crop rotation works to keep nutrients balanced because plants affect soil differently. For example, fruiting crops, like broccoli, corn, and tomatoes, are heavy feeders that rapidly use up nitrogen. Root vegetables, like carrots and beets, are light feeders. Peas, beans, and other legumes supply some of their own nitrogen needs through nitrogen fixation, but they need lots of phosphorus. To keep soil nutri-

ents balanced, avoid planting the same type of crop (leafy, fruiting, root, or legume) in the same place two years in a row. The illustration on pages 76 and 77 gives more information about rotating to help maximize soil resources. If you're not sure which grouping a particular crop belongs to, refer to the custom care regimes in "Customized Soil Care," beginning on page 56, which list vegetables that belong to the fruit, root, and leafy crop categories. A good general rotation to follow is: first year, fruit crops; second year, root crops; third year, leafy crops. For example, the year after planting tomatoes, you could plant carrots or radishes, and the following year, lettuce.

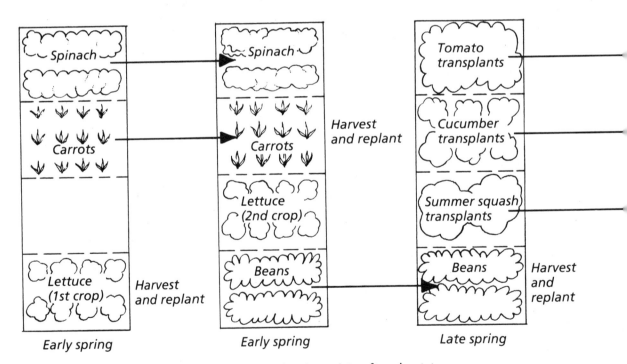

For a more complex series of succession plantings, it's often best to draw the same bed in each season. That way it's easy to keep track of when crops are planted and harvested. This plan accommodates 12 crops in a single year—an extremely efficient use of garden space.

∿ TRICKS OF THE TRADE ∿

EXTRA-EARLY LETTUCE

Market gardener Sylvia Ehrhardt of Ehrhardt Organic Farm in Maryland does her first *and* second lettuce planting at once—as early as late January.

After seeding lettuce, she covers the bed with floating row cover and black plastic mulch, both held down with bricks. When the lettuce germinates, she removes the black plastic but leaves the row cover in place. As the lettuce grows, she uses thinnings as transplants in a second lettuce bed.

Rotating crops also helps prevent many diseases and pests that are host-specific, meaning they attack only a certain plant or family of plants. Although in a small garden it can be difficult, try to avoid planting the same plants, or ones in the same family, in the same location year after year. For more on rotating crops, see the illustration on pages 76 and 77. Individual plant entries in Part 2 also have crop rotation recommendations.

"Rotating Vegetable Families" on page 78 lists botanical families and the common crops that belong to each family. Keep in mind that rotating botanical families doesn't always jibe

(continued on page 78)

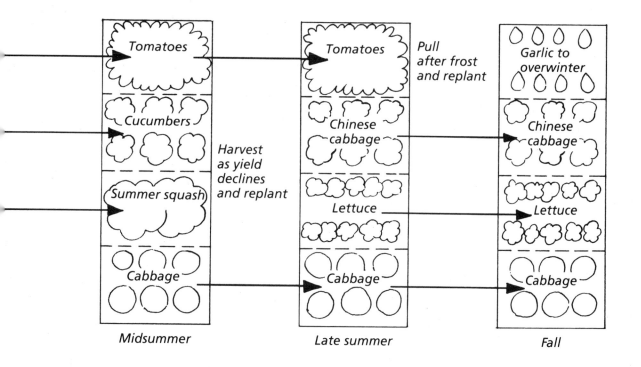

Midsummer Late summer Fall

EASY CROP ROTATION

Crop rotation balances soil nutrients and cuts down on disease. When planning rotations, think of your crops as members of one of four basic groups: fruit crops, leaf crops, root crops, and legumes. Within each group you'll find members of certain botanical families. Members of a family generally have similar flowers. Here's how some common crops fit in the rotation scheme shown below:

Fruit crops. This group includes tomatoes, peppers, and eggplant; corn and other grains; broccoli and other flower or flower-bud vegetables; and squash family crops such as melons, cucumbers, pumpkins, and squash.

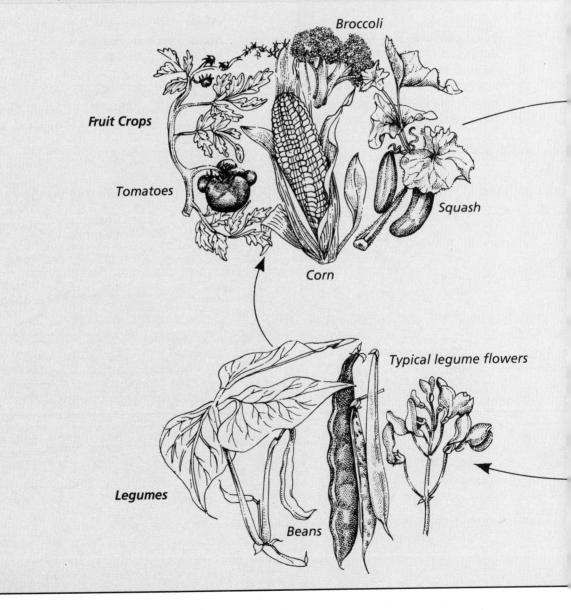

Broccoli

Fruit Crops

Tomatoes

Squash

Corn

Typical legume flowers

Legumes

Beans

Leaf crops. This group includes lettuce; spinach family members such as spinach and chard; leafy members of the cabbage family such as cabbage and kale.

Root crops. This group includes carrots, beets, potatoes, onions, garlic, and other root, bulb, and tuber-producing vegetables.

Legumes. This group includes peas, beans, and cover crops such as clover and alfalfa.

Plan your rotations to follow a fruit—leaf—root succession. Fit legumes in anywhere. In this scheme, they precede the fruit crops group.

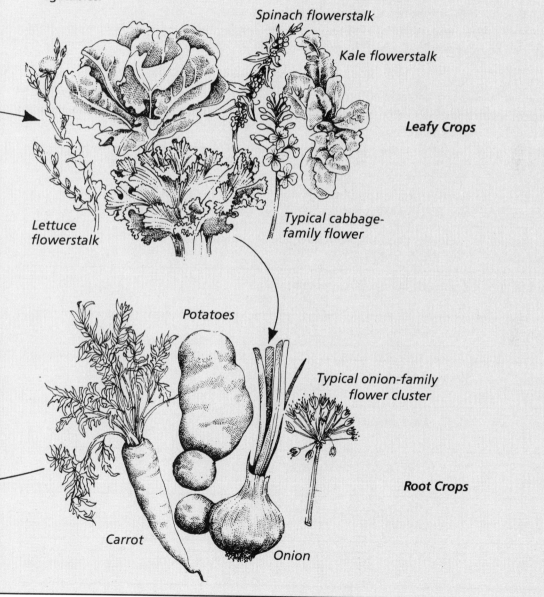

Spinach flowerstalk

Kale flowerstalk

Leafy Crops

Lettuce flowerstalk

Typical cabbage-family flower

Potatoes

Typical onion-family flower cluster

Root Crops

Carrot

Onion

with rotating for soil needs. For example, tomatoes are a fruit crop and potatoes are a root crop, and fruit-root is a good order of rotation. However, it's *not* a good idea to follow tomatoes with potatoes, because both of them belong to the tomato family (Solanaceae) and are susceptible to some of the same diseases.

You can also use cover crops in a rotation plan to discourage specific types of pests and improve soil. For example, beetle grubs thrive among most vegetables but not in soil planted in buckwheat or clover. A season of either crop can greatly reduce grub populations.

Here are three other general rules to fall back on if you're having trouble making your rotations work:

Rotating Vegetable Families

Susceptibility to pests and diseases runs in plant families. Leave at least two and preferably three or more years between the times you plant members of the same crop family in an area of your garden. Here are the seven family groups most often planted in vegetable gardens and the common crops that belong in each.

FAMILY NAME	COMMON CROPS
Cabbage family Cruciferae	Broccoli, brussels sprouts, cabbage, cauliflower, collards, kale, kohlrabi, radishes, rutabagas, turnips
Cucumber family Cucurbitaceae	Cucumbers, melons, pumpkins, squash, watermelons
Goosefoot family Chenopodiaceae	Amaranth, beets, chard, spinach
Grass family Gramineae	Corn, oats, rye, wheat
Lettuce family Compositae	Endive, Jerusalem artichoke, lettuce, sunflower
Onion family Liliaceae	Garlic, leeks, onions
Parsley family Umbelliferae	Carrots, celery, dill, fennel, parsley, parsnip
Pea family Leguminosae	Beans, clovers, peanuts, peas, vetches
Tomato family Solanaceae	Eggplant, peppers, potatoes, tomatoes

1. When in doubt, precede or follow any crops with a legume or cover crop.

2. Squash is a good preceding crop for root crops because squash help reduce weed problems, especially if they're planted in black plastic mulch.

3. Corn is a good preceding crop for potatoes.

Lengthy rotations are sometimes necessary to control chronic soilborne problems. Bean anthracnose fungus can persist in soil for three years, so a four-year rotation is needed to keep the disease at bay. The same holds true for such fungal diseases as Fusarium wilt and Verticillium wilt. A few problems, such as club root, persist in the soil for even longer, so rotation is less useful for controlling them.

Selecting Plants

Whether you love leafing through the seed catalogs that fill your mailbox each winter or spinning the seed racks and touring the transplants at your local garden center, picking the plants to grow is something to look forward to. Flavor, hardiness, disease resistance, plant habit, yield, fruit type, and days to maturity all come into play as you weigh your choices. For the most productive garden, you'll also want to consider when you're going to plant and how your choice of cultivars can help you extend the harvest. Here are some factors to keep in mind as you select the plants you'll grow.

Which Season Is Best?

Many cultivars have characteristics that make them especially suited for growing in certain seasons. Let's use lettuce as an example. If you look at the illustration on pages 74 and 75, you'll see two lettuce plantings scheduled in early spring and another in late summer to fall. Although you could probably sow all three of them with a packet or two of the same type of lettuce, that's probably not a good idea. For one thing, your family may tire of eating the same lettuce week in and week out. But more to the point, some lettuce cultivars, like the old favorite 'Black-Seeded Simpson', are ideally suited to the early spring. They germinate quickly in cold soil and grow fast, but they may fail to germinate in warm soil and bolt quickly in hot weather.

If you live in an area where spring temperatures can be quite warm, you may get better results with a cultivar that has better heat resistance—maybe 'Buttercrunch' or 'Red Sails'. For the late summer planting, you'll need a lettuce that can stand up to the approaching cold weather. That calls for a sturdy, thick-leaved cultivar, like 'Winter Density'. Most seed catalogs list such virtues among the cultivars they offer.

Days to Maturity

Catalog descriptions also generally include the number of days it will take a cultivar to mature. This figure is only approximate and will vary considerably depending on planting date and weather conditions. Nevertheless, it is an important piece of information.

Choosing cultivars that mature at different times can help assure a continuous, manageable harvest. For example, if your goal is a steady, season-long supply of tomatoes, you probably don't want to grow just one type of tomato. Instead, you probably want to plant a few different ones. Consider a plant or two of a fast-maturing cultivar (usually described as early or extra-early, 'Early Girl' is one example) for a supply of tomatoes early in the season. You could plant a long-bearing cultivar for the main crop and a late-maturing one to take over when the main-season plants have begun to fade.

Knowing how quickly a crop is likely to mature will also help you plan for follow-up crops on the same ground. Take the early spring sowing of 'Black-Seeded Simpson' in the example on page 79. It matures in 45 days, leaving plenty of time to follow it with a crop of beans later in the spring. 'Buttercrunch', on the other hand, matures in 75 days and would delay the bean crop too far into the spring.

Remember that the days-to-maturity figure in seed catalogs refers to number of days from seed for crops that are normally direct-seeded, like carrots and snap beans, and to number of days from transplant for crops that are normally put in as plants, like tomatoes and eggplant.

Dwarf or Full-Size Plants?

Plant breeders have worked diligently to tame the sprawling habits of some popular garden vegetables, resulting in compact cultivars that are more in scale with small gardens. There are now bush-type cucumbers, runnerless winter squashes, and tomatoes small enough to grow in pots. Of even older lineage are bush beans and bush peas, developed to free commercial growers (and home gardeners) of the labor needed to erect trellises.

These compact cultivars make it possible to grow crops that might otherwise have to be omitted for lack of space. They're also often faster to mature than their full-size brethren, which makes them useful as quick "fill-in" crops in larger gardens.

There are some disadvantages to be considered. Yield is one. It stands to reason that a small plant will produce less than a large one.

Dwarf plants also tend to produce their crop all at once, giving the gardener a week or two of good harvests and then nothing. But planting a series of small succession crops is one way to spread out the yield, and several smaller harvests may be just what your family wants.

In many cases, you can use a little ingenuity to get the yield of full-size plants without taking up too much space. The most common technique is trellising, which is really not much work if you know a few shortcuts. You can even make that trellis do double duty if you plan to grow peas on it in the spring and pole beans or cucumbers in the summer. For lots of good ideas on trellis styles, see "Trellising" on page 133.

Regionally Adapted Cultivars

Just as some cultivars are best suited to a particular season, some are best suited to particular areas of the country. If, for example, you live in an area where springs are brief and summer heat sets in suddenly, you will need a broccoli cultivar that matures quickly and can withstand a few hot days without going to flower. If your area has long, cool springs and mild summers, you may care little about heat resistance in broccoli but want a cultivar that produces lots of tasty sideshoots after the main head is cut.

Northerners want tomatoes that set fruit in chilly temperatures; southerners want theirs to set fruit when it's scorching hot. There are cultivars to fit both situations, and many other climatic peculiarities.

Choosing a cultivar that is suited to your region and climate will help ensure healthy plants and good yields. It is, in fact, one of your first defenses against pests and disease. Trying to grow and produce in unfavorable conditions can weaken a plant and make it vulnerable to attack. Moreover, many regionally adapted cultivars have been selected for their resistance to the most common diseases in the area.

The best way to identify adapted cultivars is to ask around. Question your local extension agent, a local garden club, or a gardening neighbor. Seed catalogs that cater to specific regions of the country also are a good source of adapted cultivars.

PUTTING A PLAN ON PAPER

Now that you've considered planting systems, crop rotation, and, most important, what plants you want to grow, it's time to draft a garden plan. To do this, you'll need your list of plants, any seed packets you already have purchased, a calendar, pencils, and something to write in—a three-ring binder with both lined and graph paper is ideal because you can also use it for your garden records throughout the season. A standard wall calendar is fine, or you might want to use some kind of appointment calendar that you can reserve exclusively for all of your garden-related information. You'll also need the rough sketch of your garden, which indicates how much space you have available for planting. Finally, you'll need to know the expected last spring and first fall frost dates for your area so you can schedule crops accordingly. You can get both of these

Drawing a garden plan is more than just deciding what to plant where. Keep your seed and plant catalogs and seed packets on hand so you can figure out how much space to devote to each crop. To plan succession plantings, you'll need to know days to maturity and ideal planting times for all of your crops.

dates from an almanac or by calling your local extension agent.

Start by adding some more information to your list of plants, which you'll probably want to keep in your notebook to refer to throughout the year. After each plant, list days to maturity, ideal spacing, how much you want to plant, and about when you want to plant it. (Use the plant entries in Part 2 and/or your seed packets to get this information.) Finally, list cropping techniques you'd like to try with each crop such as interplanting, succession plantings, and any special crop rotation notes you don't want to forget. (You'll find this information in the plant entries in Part 2 as well.)

Now you have all of the details you need to start penciling in crops on your plan. Start by calculating about how much space you'll need for each of the crops you want to grow. For example: You want 100 carrots. If you broadcast the seeds and thin the plants to be 3 to 4 inches apart each way, you can grow 9 to 12 carrots per square foot. So if your beds are 4 feet wide, you'll need to allot 3 linear feet of bed space. If you grow carrots in rows and thin them to 3 inches apart, you'll need a 25-foot row.

What do you do if you want room for radishes but don't want to fill up another bed? Try an old-timers' trick of seeding a few radishes with the carrots. They'll germinate quickly—helping to mark the carrot rows before the carrots come up—and will be harvested well ahead of the carrots.

Once you've finished filling in the spring crops, start scheduling the summer ones. Planting dates for these crops will be based on weather conditions in your area and when the harvest is finished for the first crops of the year. As you work, jot notes about planting

dates for specific crops on your calendar. You'll also want to jot down whether you'll need seeds or transplants, when to start looking for flowers or fruit, and problems you think might crop up. For example, you may want to anticipate how you're going to protect transplants of fall cool-season crops from hot afternoon temperatures of late summer.

Drawing It to Scale

Many gardeners like to draw a final version of their garden plan to scale on graph paper. That way, it's possible to record a fair amount of detail, including how many rows go on a bed, how crops will be placed to make maximum use of garden space, and interplantings you're going to try. You can list follow-up crops on the plan itself—maybe in a different color—or on a separate sheet of paper.

The illustration on pages 74 and 75 shows another option. In that case, there's a new outline of the bed each time any crop in the bed is harvested and changed. The end result is a succession of drawings of what the bed will look like at key points in the season.

If you want to get really fancy, you can use transparent overlays to show how the garden is intended to progress through the season. Just be sure that whatever you do is clear and understandable.

Keep your final plan together with the list of cultivars of each crop you planted. It's an important part of your garden records. Otherwise, you won't remember the details of which lettuce performed and tasted best or what tomatoes you'd rather not plant next year.

As you use your plan throughout the year, remember that the best-laid plans are subject to change. It may be too hot and dry to plant lettuce at the time you figured on getting in your third seeding. The kids may decide they hate broccoli, forcing you to scale back your fall planting. Cool weather may slow maturity in one crop or another, making its bed unavailable for a scheduled follow-up planting. All of that is part of the creative challenge of gardening, so be prepared to be flexible.

Making a Schedule

The notes you made on your calendar about when crops are scheduled to go into the garden are the beginnings of your planting schedule. On crops that will be grown from seeds sown directly in the garden, such as spinach and carrots, all you need is a planting date reminder on your calendar. Although the weather will play a big role in dictating when the earliest direct-seeded crops go into the garden, a note on your calendar will remind you when to start looking for a window of opportunity.

Other crops—tomatoes and cucumbers, for example—will be put in as transplants, which you'll need to have ready for planting when the garden is ready for them. That requires a little more timing. In the spring, when garden centers are bursting with vegetable transplants, you may be able to go out and buy what you need, but the selection of cultivars is limited. If you want to grow anything but the standard, mass-produced cultivars, you'll have to grow your own. Moreover, most garden centers are still geared toward a once-a-year vegetable planting season. So for mid-season and late-season transplants, you may have no choice but to grow your own. You'll find complete instructions for starting seeds and raising transplants indoors in "Planting Seeds Indoors" on page 102.

To make a schedule to grow your own transplants, use the plant entries in Part 2 and/or your seed packets, and work back from the date you expect to transplant to the garden. For example, cucumbers need to be started indoors three weeks before they are transplanted. If your last expected spring frost is around May 1, that means you'll want to sow your cucumbers around April 10. Jot the sowing date for cucumbers on your calendar and move on to the next transplanted crop—tomatoes, say. Keep in mind that the weather will undoubtedly affect your transplant schedule as well. If you're having an unusually cool spring, you may not be able to transplant your cucumbers when you expect to.

In general, the more intensively a garden is planted, the more sense it makes to use transplants wherever possible. You will get a faster crop from transplants without tying up bed space any longer than necessary. In large gardens, where space is not critical, using transplants can minimize weeding and thinning chores. It is much easier to cultivate a 20-foot-long bed of 4-inch-tall broccoli plants than to thin and weed the same bed filled with tiny broccoli seedlings.

Once you have a drawing of your garden, a list of cultivars, and a schedule, you're ready to go. You have a plan.

PLANNING FOR PERENNIAL CROPS

Planning a vegetable garden is an annual exercise, allowing plenty of flexibility from year to year—and even from season to season. On the other hand, perennial crops like fruit trees, asparagus, berry bushes, and grapes will occupy the same space for many years. Many of these plants will also attain great size, becoming part of the home landscape.

Planning for perennial crops is similar to planning for annual vegetables: You still need to consider sun and soil and allow for adequate space. But you also will want to consider aesthetics. An apple tree in bloom is beautiful and sweetly scented. You may want to plant it where you can see it and enjoy its fragrance. Or you may want to use the dramatic foliage of rhubarb as part of your perennial flower garden. Here are some factors to consider when planning for perennial fruit, berry, and nut crops. For more information on any particular plant, see its plant entry in Part 2.

Fruit and Nut Trees

There are lots of options to consider when it comes to selecting fruit and nut trees for home gardens. Now that many dwarf or semidwarf fruit trees are widely available, it's possible to accommodate a few fruit trees in even relatively small gardens. Even a large suburban lot rarely has space for more than a few standard (full-size) apple trees, for example, which can grow 30 feet tall and spread their branches just as wide. That means one standard apple tree occupies a space that would accommodate a small orchard of dwarf trees.

Since dwarf and semidwarf cultivars are created by grafting standard cultivars onto dwarfing rootstocks, you have just as wide a choice of cultivars as you would if you were planting a standard tree. A 'Northern Spy' apple is the same whether you pick it from a standard tree or a semidwarf or dwarf one. Plus, the smaller-size fruit trees are easier to prune, pick, and treat for diseases and insects. They also bear their fruit at a younger age than standard trees.

One disadvantage is that some trees grown on dwarfing rootstocks, especially stone fruits like peaches and nectarines, are shorter-lived than standard trees.

Pecan and walnut trees can easily grow more than 100 feet tall, which means they may not fit comfortably in many yards. But there are nut trees suitable for small spaces, such as Chinese chestnut, which rarely tops 20 feet. Almonds grow to 30 feet. Filberts or hazelnuts are bushy trees that can be trained as a hedge.

Think carefully about the mature size of the tree or trees you intend to plant. Each will need enough space to stretch its limbs, free of encumbrances such as buildings or adjacent trees. The trees will cast shade eventually; make sure that you don't inadvertently shade out your vegetable garden or sunny flower border.

As a general rule, plant trees about as far apart as their mature height. For avocados and standard apple, pear, cherry, and citrus trees, that means a minimum of 25 to 30 feet between trees. Standard peach, nectarine, and apricot trees, which can be kept in bounds by careful pruning, can go as close as 20 feet apart. Dwarfed trees may go closer still—12 feet apart. See the individual plant entries in Part 2 for the specific planting distances for the trees you wish to grow.

A north-facing slope or northern exposure is ideal for all fruit and nut trees, as it will tend to delay bloom in the spring and prevent blossoms from being damaged by late frosts. Avoid excessively windy areas if possible, or plan to stake the trees to prevent wind damage. You may need a sheltered location if you are growing a tender tree, like an almond or Japanese plum, at the edge of or outside of its climate zone.

Pick a Pollinator

Whether you choose standard or dwarf trees, be mindful that many fruit trees require a second tree of the same or another cultivar to pollinate them. Sweet cherries, pears, Japanese plums, most apples, some apricots, and some avocados need pollinators. Peaches, nectarines, tart cherries, some European plums, and most citrus trees will set fruit without a second tree as a pollinator.

Because trees differ in blossoming time and amount of viable pollen produced, it's important to choose cultivars carefully. If you plant two trees that either don't bloom at the same time or don't produce enough pollen, you may not end up with good fruit set. Mail-order catalogs that sell fruit trees will suggest good pollinators for all of the trees that they sell that need a pollinator. Pay attention to their recommendations and choose accordingly. If you're planning to buy from a local nursery, avoid ones that can't, or won't, provide information on the best pollinators. Or take a catalog or two along with you and go it alone.

Pecan and walnut trees also require a partner for pollination. Because of their size, that may rule out pecan and walnut growing for growers with small lots (unless, of course, you can persuade your neighbors to plant one in *their* yard).

Plan Your Planting

In cold climates, fruit and nut trees are best planted in the spring; gardeners in more southerly areas can plant in the fall. Your trees, especially fruit trees, will get a real head start if you get their new quarters ready well ahead of time. And since they'll be growing in the same site for many years, it pays to take extra care to prepare the site and plant them properly.

Soil tests are critical. Fruit trees won't require much nitrogen to start, but they need plenty of calcium, magnesium, and potassium, as well as adequate levels of micronutrients such as iron. Stone fruits are particularly sensitive to boron deficiency. Correct any deficiencies ahead of time. Next, make sure the top 1 foot or so of soil is loose and rich in organic matter throughout the tree's eventual root zone. Imagine the tree fully grown, and work organic matter into the soil all the way out to where the branch tips will end. The most active feeder roots will be in that area. You can maintain humus levels with mulch or cover crops after your tree is planted and growing. For more on preparing the soil and managing fertility for fruit and nut trees, see "Custom Care for Tree Fruits" on page 61.

Shrubs, Vines, and Brambles

You can plan to include many berry-bearing shrubs and vines as ornamentals in your landscape. Fruiting shrubs such as blueberries, elderberries, currants, and gooseberries add food for the table, but they're also quite attractive, especially when laden with berries. Elderberries are lovely in flower, and many blueberry cultivars have brilliant autumn foliage and striking red branches in winter. If grown over an arbor or pergola, fruiting vines like grapes and kiwis can do double duty—they'll provide both food and shade. Because of their thorny stems, most brambles, like raspberries and blackberries, are best planted in an out-of-the-way part of the yard.

Fruiting shrubs and vines all are prolific fruiters, so even a single plant will provide a worthwhile harvest. But like many fruit trees, they benefit from cross-pollination. If you have the space, a little group of two or three will produce more fruit per plant than a single specimen. Bramble crops also bear heavily, and a relatively small but carefully managed planting will bear a good crop of berries. See the Brambles entry on page 306 for more information on growing raspberries, blackberries, and their kin.

Some fruiting shrubs can get quite large: Elderberries and highbush blueberries will grow 6 to 12 feet tall. Rabbiteye blueberries, which are best for southern gardens, can get as tall as 25 feet. There are some dwarf, also called mid-high, blueberry cultivars; one called 'Top Hat' is small enough for containers. Currants will top out at 4 to 7 feet but can spread as wide. The slightly more diminuitive gooseberry ranges from 3 to 6 feet tall and as wide.

Fruiting shrubs, vines, and brambles all prefer well-drained soil in full sun, although elderberry and gooseberry will tolerate a little shade. Avoid putting brambles where the air can't circulate freely around them, such as against walls or buildings. Both foliage and berries are susceptible to fungal diseases and molds; good air circulation will help hold down problems. For blueberries, pay careful attention to soil pH. Blueberries require acidic soil, from 4.5 to 5.2, and will not survive a pH much above 6.0 or 6.2. The soil must also be moist, so plan to mulch blueberries heavily and don't plant them out of reach of the garden hose.

In some areas, there are restrictions against planting members of the *Ribes* genus, which includes gooseberries and currants, because of their role as host to a rust disease that affects white pine trees. Even if no restrictions apply in your area, be sure you plant these shrubs well away from any white pines in your own yard, or plant only rust-resistant cultivars.

Whether you're planting fruiting shrubs, vines, or brambles, it pays to get rid of any sod or weeds before you plant. Dig up or till the area, adding as much organic matter as possible, and keep it well-cultivated or heavily mulched for a season. This will also give you plenty of time to test the soil, adjust the pH if necessary, and add any soil nutrients that may be in short supply. For vines and brambles, you'll also need to erect a trellis. Although some brambles grow erect, all benefit from at least light support. Trellising also keeps the bramble bed tidier and makes picking easier. Before you plant either vines or brambles, know what kind of trellis you will install. For recommendations on trellising both of these crops, see "Trellising" on page 133.

Strawberries

Almost as soon as you decide where to put the strawberry bed, you need to decide where to put the next one. That's not just because you can never get enough strawberries, although it's a consideration. Strawberry plantings eventually decline, and the plants are subject to a variety of root diseases. Changing the location of your strawberry patch every few years is the best way to maintain a healthy and productive planting.

Strawberries need a sunny spot that has good drainage and is free of troublesome weeds and grasses. If you plan and prepare the site in the summer and fall, you can plant strawberries in the spring. (Southern gardeners can plant in the fall as well). If your soil is heavy or tends to stay wet, plan to grow strawberries in raised beds. Planting boxes constructed of untreated wood or metal strips work well, too, but build these ahead of time so they are ready by planting time.

Perennial Vegetables

Rhubarb and asparagus are perhaps the best-known perennial vegetables. Rhubarb may be divided and moved every few years, but asparagus will be in the same soil for two decades or more, so it pays to plan its spot carefully.

Asparagus likes sun and light, very rich soil; a southern exposure will encourage earlier crops. It's essential to eliminate perennial weeds and grasses before planting. Mulching helps control weeds in asparagus beds, but too-heavy mulch can deform the emerging spears, so get a handle on weeds before you plant.

Rhubarb is often relegated to some out-of-the-way spot, where it produces its crisp, tart stalks in the spring and then is forgotten until the next year. But its huge, red-tinged leaves are quite beautiful all year if the flower-stalks are removed and the plant is kept watered. Consider a more prominent spot for this striking plant. A single specimen in a sunny, well-drained spot will usually provide plenty of stalks for fresh-baked pies and sauces. Plant several if you intend to freeze or can some.

Artichokes and cardoon, both members of the thistle family, are less widely grown perennial vegetables. Both need sun but like to be shaded on hot afternoons. Cardoon is the hardier of the two; artichokes may fail to survive winters north of Zone 7, even with winter protection. If started early enough, however, it will produce a crop as an annual.

Artichokes can be grown from root divisions. But divisions are rarely available out-side the commercial growing areas of California and Florida, so count on starting plants from seeds at least six weeks before the last frost.

Perennial Herbs

While annual herbs like sweet basil and dill are often grown right in the vegetable garden, don't forget to plan for some more permanent herb plantings. A sunny, well-drained spot that's convenient to the kitchen is ideal for perennial culinary herbs like sage, thyme, oregano, and chives. And while you're at it, include some annuals and biennials like parsley as well. That way you can easily pop out into the garden whenever you need a sprig of oregano to add to the spaghetti sauce or some chives to sprinkle on a baked potato.

If you'd like to grow any of the mints, keep in mind that they can spread aggressively. Select an out-of-the-way site where they can wander at will, or plant them in large, bottomless buckets that have been sunk in the garden. Leave the rims an inch or two above the soil, and clip off any stems that begin to wander.

KEEPING RECORDS

Good records are invaluable to gardeners who are serious about their soil, their crops, and their time. They're also essential to a successful organic garden. Knowing what went wrong one year will help you avoid making the same mistake the next. Records will also help you build on the previous year's successes. You'll have a record of an additional sidedressing of compost that really boosted broccoli yields or a trellising trick that saved hours of work. You may think you'll remember all of this without bothering to write it down, but you'd be surprised how many useful lessons you will end up learning a second time, simply because you forgot.

Some gardeners keep a loose-leaf notebook or notepad with their gardening supplies, where it is handy for jotting down observations and thoughts. Others use a calender (the one that is already sprinkled with reminders about when to seed the eggplant and fall cabbage).

Your records can be as formal or informal as you choose, but try to keep them up-to-date. A good method is to take a once-a-week walk through the garden, not for the purpose of doing any weeding or harvesting, but just to observe, smell, and touch. You will notice more details when you're not there to do any work, and it can be one of the most pleasurable times you spend in the garden.

Rotation Records

Year-to-year and even season-to-season records on what crops you planted where are essential for rotating crops successfully. Your reward will be better use of soil nutrients, healthier plants, and reduced problems with diseases and insects.

Weather Records

Many gardeners find it useful to record general weather conditions, like frost dates, rainfall amounts, and unusually cool, hot, wet, or dry periods. Every garden has its own "microclimate," which can be either harsher or more benign than the climate around it. Frost, in particular, is a capricious phenomenon. Your neighbor's thermometer may record a tomato-blackening 30°F while your own plants, tucked in a sheltered spot, escape unscathed at 35°F. Keeping records will help you understand your garden's peculiar climate, which in

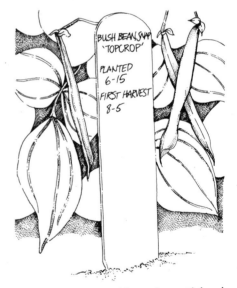

For on-the-spot record keeping, stick a large plastic label by each crop row or in each bed section where there's a different crop or cultivar. Jot down dates of planting, thinning, pest control treatments, and harvest on the labels as you work in the garden.

turn will help you determine the best time to plant certain crops and more accurately gauge the length of your growing season.

Keeping track of general weather conditions also can help you anticipate outbreaks of disease, like scab on apple trees, or insect pests. Spider mites, for example, are more troublesome in hot, dry weather. Accurate rainfall records will help you determine when and how much to irrigate, neither stressing plants nor wasting water.

Soil-Care Records

Your records also should include notes on any soil amendments you added, such as lime or sulfur to correct pH, rock powders, compost, fertilizers, tilled-in green manures, and so forth. You can use this information to fine-tune your planting scheme, putting heavier-feeding plants in areas that received the most compost, for example, or keeping carrots out of beds that just got a nitrogen boost.

Good notes also will help you identify problems like soil deficiencies. Say, for example, that you noted during the year that many of your cabbage-family crops, like Chinese cabbage and broccoli, had brownish cores or hollow stalks. A little wintertime reading will identify this as a potential boron deficiency, which you will need to take steps to correct.

Pest and Disease Records

Jotting down notes about insect populations will give you a better sense of how nature is operating in your garden and when—and if—you need to intercede. If you note when the first cabbage butterfly was seen, for example, you know you should start checking for signs of cabbageworm damage in 7 to 10 days. If you notice a great many ladybug larvae in your plants, you know you needn't bother to

✦ MAKE YOUR OWN ✦

WEATHER STATION

It's easy to make a simple weather station for recording temperature and rainfall in your garden. Mount a thermometer that records minimum and maximum temperatures on a wooden post with a small platform on the top. To make a rain gauge, cut the top one-third off of a half-liter plastic bottle, insert it upside down into the bottom two-thirds, and seal the joint with waterproof tape. With a permanent marker, draw lines at ¼-inch intervals on the outside of the bottle. Pour enough water into the gauge so that the water line is above the opaque bottom. Visit your weather station daily to record the minimum and maximum temperatures and any rainfall. After a rain, record how far the water has risen from the pre-rain level. Occasionally pour out excess water to bring the level down to your starting point.

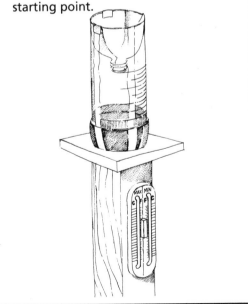

do anything about the aphids that you also see there.

You should also note the appearance and characteristics of any unfamiliar insects or plant abnormalities. If you don't have time to identify these right away, your notes will help you figure out later if you are dealing with an insect enemy or friend, or if your plants are suffering from a nutrient deficiency or a disease.

Knowing when to expect problems makes it much easier to deal with them before they become crises. For example, your garden notes of previous years might mention that the Japanese beetles emerged the first week of June. Forewarned is forearmed. By the end of May, you are ready with pheromone traps, row cover, or whatever means you have chosen to protect against beetle damage.

Harvest and Yield Records

If you make a note of when each crop was planted and when it matured, you can com-pare that to the seed catalog's days-to-maturity figure and get a better sense of when to expect crops to mature in your garden. This will help you plan next year's garden with cultivars that mature when you want them to.

Your records will also help you choose the best cultivars for your garden. You certainly don't have to count every bean your plants produced, but you will want to take note if the cultivar you planted yielded well or seemed unusually prone (or unusually resistant) to disease. Although most gardeners consider notes on yield to be the least critical of their records, such records can be useful. If you have notes on how many pints of frozen beans you put away or how many quarts of sauce your eight 'Roma' tomato plants yielded, you can adjust your plantings in subsequent years to produce more or less. During the off-season, it's also just enjoyable to be able to reflect on the wealth of good things that came out of your food garden.

4

PLANTING
Starting Vegetable Seeds and Plants, Perennial Crops, and Fruit Trees

Planting is a little bit like the "spring training" of gardening. It's time to warm up and begin a new season of harvest that will be even better than the last.

Whether you're starting seeds indoors in late winter, putting transplants directly in your garden after the last expected spring frost, or planting young fruit trees in the fall, both timing and technique are crucial in getting things off to a good start. This chapter explains how to decide on the right times to plant based on your climate. It also provides detailed instructions for starting seeds indoors and out and for raising and planting transplants. Finally, it covers techniques for planting perennial crops such as herbs, perennial vegetables, fruit trees, berry bushes, vines, and brambles.

CLIMATE AND THE GARDENER

When you planned your garden, you probably set an approximate schedule for planting seeds, transplants, and perennials. (If you don't yet have a garden plan, see Chapter 3 for instructions on making one.) But the realities of your other commitments and day-to-day weather patterns are the factors that will determine when you actually do your planting. The words "first day of spring" on your calendar won't melt away the mountains of snow covering your garden on March 20. Nor will temperatures in the 90s wait politely for June's summer solstice before descending upon the South. You may not always be able to predict how your weather will behave, but studying your climate will go a long way toward helping you judge when to plant your garden.

Know Your Climate

If you're new to gardening or if you've just moved, you may not know enough about your local climate to decide when to plant particular crops. Start by defining your garden in the broad terms of your region. This would be a large general area, such as the Northeast or the Deep South. From region to region, and within regions, there are differences in average daily temperatures and annual precipitation and in dates of last spring and first fall frosts. By selecting plants that are known to survive (and thrive) in your region's climate, you give your garden a strong foundation for success. Crop seasons and hardiness zone ratings are two guidelines gardeners use to match plants to place. To find out what hardiness zone you live in, consult the map on page 506.

Crop Seasons

The weather associated with the four seasons occurs at different times of the year in different climates. Winter in the Deep South may resemble the cool, moist conditions of fall and spring in northern states. And a northern summer may offer little of the southern warmth that heat-loving crops need. In general, ebb and flow of the planting seasons follows one of four seasonal patterns, as shown on the opposite page. Deciding which general pattern your area fits into can help you decide when to plant your crops.

Gardeners group crops by the seasons in which those plants thrive. In general, crops are described as cool-season, warm-weather, or hot-weather crops.

Cool-season crops, such as peas, radishes, and cabbage, enjoy cool, moist weather. These crops are cold- and frost-resistant to 40°F and you can plant them as early as several weeks before the last expected frost date for your area. Their ability to withstand cool temperatures and light frosts makes them equally at home in a fall garden when cold has chased away the summer crops. Cool-season crops also succeed in winter gardens in some south-

ern states and in summer gardens in the far North.

Warm-weather plants, such as corn, potatoes, and beans, prefer air temperatures of 50°F or more. Plant them outdoors just after the last spring frost is expected—late spring in the North and late winter to early spring in the South. Hot-weather crops, such as eggplant, okra, and lima beans, won't tolerate frost or cold soil. Wait three weeks after the last expected spring frost before planting these.

If you're not sure when to plant cool-, warm-, and hot-season crops in your area, see "Easy Crops by Region and Season" on page 503. You'll find 11 different regions, with lists of crops and suggested planting times for each region.

Hardiness

Hardiness describes a plant's ability to survive a particular climate. In most cases, hardiness denotes tolerance of low winter temperatures. True hardiness, however, includes the ability to endure all of the conditions—heat, cold, moisture, drought, and everything in between—peculiar to a particular climate. Since annual crops are grown at times when the weather suits their needs, discussions of hardiness usually involve perennial plants such as fruit trees and strawberries.

The USDA Plant Hardiness Zone Map, updated in 1990, divides the United States and southern Canada into 11 climatic zones, based on the average annual minimum temperature for each zone. Zone 1 is the northernmost, coldest region, and Zone 11 is the warmest and farthest to the south. If you garden in Zone 5, a plant labeled for Zones 4 through 7 should do fine in your area. But a plant identified as "suitable for Zones 6 to 9" might not fare as well, unless you give it extra winter protection.

Each perennial plant entry in Part 2 lists hardiness zones that correspond to the USDA Plant Hardiness Zone Map on page 506. Use the zone ratings to select plants that will be hardy in your area. Keep in mind, though, that hardiness zones don't have fixed boundaries. Factors such as altitude and exposure may make your garden warmer or cooler than the surrounding area.

Other Climatic Concerns

Freezing temperatures, particularly those that arrive unexpectedly, pose obvious hazards for many crops. But less extreme climatic conditions deserve your attention, too. Seeds germinate and plants grow, bloom, bear fruit, and die in response to both air and soil temperatures and any temperature fluctuations. Anticipating your crops' reactions to expected and unexpected temperature changes can help you time planting, pruning, harvesting, and protection.

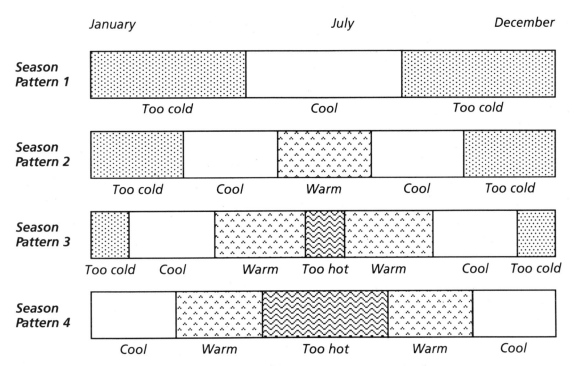

The length and timing of the growing season changes considerably as you travel from areas like northern New England and Minnesota (Pattern 1) to areas like southern Florida and Texas (Pattern 4). In Pattern 1 areas, it may be difficult to coax enough growth from warm- and hot-weather crops to reap a good harvest. In Pattern 4 areas, there's a midsummer period when high temperatures, rather than cold, limit what will grow successfully.

Consider Air Temperature

Once any plant sprouts up out of the soil, air temperatures begin to affect its growth. Warm-season vegetables, such as snap beans, are easily damaged by sudden cold. When the temperature drops to 42°F, bean pods become pitted and russeted. At 32°F or below, the bean plant's growing tip dies. Cold temperatures also have effects on cold-tolerant vegetables. For example, cabbage plants are more likely to bolt if they've been exposed to cold periods (below 50°F) of ten days or longer during their early days in the garden.

Hot weather presents problems, too. Temperatures above 75°F take their toll on cool-season crops. Cabbage transplants grow tall and spindly, and garden pea pods turn tough and woody.

Perennial crops must deal with the cold of winter and the danger of spring frosts. To prevent winter damage, try to match your plants to your hardiness zone. Spring frosts can damage your plants regardless of how hardy they may be in midwinter. Once the flower buds start to swell, they become quite vulnerable to even a light frost. You can help prevent spring frost damage to tree fruits and berries by avoiding frost pockets when you select a planting site. Frost pockets include areas at the bottom of a slope (even an almost imperceptible slope) where frosty air may collect on spring and fall nights. If you have a hilly landscape, place your frost-susceptible perennials about halfway up north- or east-facing slopes. They'll be less likely to bud and bloom too early in the spring.

Also try to avoid planting on a site that will be subject to strong winds because wind can contribute to winter damage by dehydrating the plants. Plant where a building or windbreak provides some relief from wind. If your entire yard is open and windswept, see "Winning Ways for Windy Sites" on page 116 for ways to give your plants a break from the gales.

While late-spring frosts can wreak havoc on tender fruit tree buds, those same buds do not form properly without temperatures below 45°F during the winter months. This required exposure to cold is referred to as a tree's chill hours and is very specific for certain fruit tree cultivars. Low-chill cultivars, for example, need fewer hours of low temperatures and will bloom and fruit even in very southern zones. Northern cultivars require longer cold periods; this delays their bloom in the spring and reduces injury from late frosts. Take advantage of fruit trees' natural responses to temperature by planting cultivars with chilling requirements similar to your region's average annual chill hours. Buy trees from a local nursery, or check with your local extension office to find out what your local chill hours usually amount to and what cultivars match that number.

Track Jack Frost

Two bits of local weather data are essential for every gardener: the average date of the last spring frost and the average date of the first fall frost. Two common sources of this information are your county's Cooperative Extension Service and the National Weather Service. Check the government listings in your telephone book to locate these organizations; the National Weather Service may also be associated with a nearby airport. Your local newspaper or cable television station may also provide garden-related weather data. Use local and regional statistics as a guide when planting, but keep your own annual records, too. Your garden's exposure and elevation may place it in a microclimate with a longer or shorter growing season than that of the surrounding area.

In spring, wait until after the last expected frost to plant tender seeds and hardened-off transplants. You can continue planting until expected crop harvest dates approach the date of the first expected fall frost. Fall's first frosts are usually light warnings that colder weather is near. A light frost occurs when the air temperature drops below 32°F (water's freezing point) and below the dew point (the temperature at which water condenses) for a short time. A light frost may injure cold-sensitive plants such as cucumbers or basil, but it rarely kills them. During a hard frost, the temperature stays above the dew point but falls to 28°F (the temperature at which most plant cells freeze) or below for several hours. This usually results in damage or death to all but the hardiest garden crops.

Remember Soil Temperature

Soil temperature influences seed germination, plant growth, and the ability of perennial plants to overwinter successfully. Like air temperature, it also fluctuates daily and seasonally. Unlike air temperature, soil temperature changes slowly. The air and water trapped between soil particles help to insulate the soil from the more dramatic temperature changes of the surrounding climate.

In early spring, this moderating effect can keep seeds from germinating too soon and suffering the ill effects of fickle spring weather. Later, cooler-than-air soil keeps cool-season crops going when summer begins to heat up. In fall, the soil retains summer's warmth long enough to let annual crops complete their life cycles, while gently guiding perennials into dormancy. You can use a soil or compost thermometer to monitor your garden's tempera-

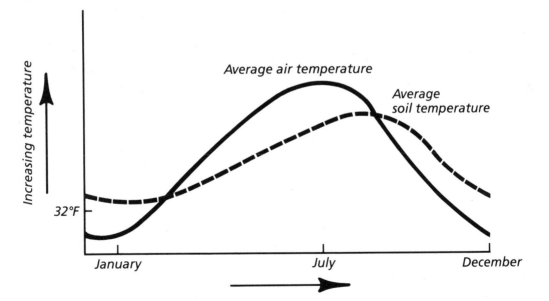

Over the course of a year, changes in soil temperature lag behind those of air temperature, and they are more gradual.

ture daily prior to and during spring planting. For directions on how to use one, see "Take Your Soil's Temperature" below.

SEEDS, BULBS, AND TUBERS

Planting seeds, bulbs, and tubers directly into the soil is gardening the way nature does it. It's a simple and satisfying process that doesn't require anything beyond some simple tools and a well-prepared seedbed.

Sowing Seeds Outdoors

When it's time to stock up on seed supplies, check with other gardeners in your area or with your local Cooperative Extension Service to find out which crops and cultivars perform the best. Buy from suppliers whose products most closely meet your needs and interests. Gardeners in the North and the South, for example, will find specialty garden catalogs that focus on cultivars for their region. Some seed companies specialize in a particular crop, such as tomatoes, or in a group of related crops, like salad crops or heirloom seeds.

Package sizes vary among seed suppliers. If you're unsure about how much seed to buy, start with the smallest packet. After a season's trial, you can adjust your order size accordingly.

Here are some pointers to get you off to a great start.

Set your calendar. Mark the date of the last expected spring frost on your garden calendar. Count backward from that date for crops you can sow before the last frost. Count forward to figure planting dates after the last spring frost.

Take your soil's temperature. To time your planting more accurately, use a soil or compost thermometer (available from garden suppliers) to monitor changes in soil temperature. Starting at least one week before you expect to plant seeds outdoors, keep a daily record of soil temperature. To take soil temperature, brush away any surface litter or mulch residues and insert the thermometer to a depth of 3 inches. Every five days, add up your daily

---

CHECK SEED VIABILITY

If you're like most gardeners, you have a collection of half-full and even unopened seed packets from previous seasons. Will they germinate? Or should you buy new seeds just to be safe? Most seeds are still viable the year after the date on the packet. Pea, bean, and squash seeds can last three years; peppers and tomatoes four years; and cabbages five years. Buy fresh corn, onion, and parsnip seeds each year.

The best way to decide whether to plant old seeds or buy fresh ones is to do a germination test. Here's how: Write the name of the cultivar on a paper towel and moisten it with water. Count out at least ten seeds and place them on the towel. Roll it up and put it in a plastic bag. Put the plastic bag in a warm (about 70°F) place. Check daily for germination. (Use the days to germination from the packet as a guide.) When the seeds have sprouted, count the sprouts and divide by the number of seeds you started with to get the germination rate or percent. Write the new germination rate on the packet. If it's low, buy new seeds, or plant the old seeds a little thicker to compensate for the lower germination.

readings and divide by 5 to determine the average temperature. When the average soil temperature over a five-day period reaches 45° to 60°F, plant cool-season crops. Sow warm-weather seeds when soil temperatures are between 65° and 80°F. Wait until the soil is consistently between 75° and 90°F before you plant hot-weather crops, which germinate best at 80° to 90°F.

Plants in and around your home landscape can provide other clues about garden timing. Read "Planting by Nature's Signs" on this page to learn how to interpret plant signals.

Make your seedbed. Prepare a welcoming environment for your fruits- and vegetables-to-be. See "Soil Preparation" on page 49 for directions on getting your site ready for seeding. First, till or turn the earth with a spade or garden fork. Then, to prepare a fine seedbed, rake the soil to a fine tilth, breaking up clods and removing stones and weeds. (If you do the tilling or digging in fall, you'll be one step ahead come spring.)

Prepare the seeds. Presprouting, scarifying, and stratifying are some of the seed preparation techniques that will enhance seed germination and seedling vigor. You'll find recommendations for seed preparation techniques in the individual plant entries in Part 2.

Presprouting is especially effective for crops that require warm soil to germinate, such as melons and squash. To presprout, roll the seeds in a damp paper or cloth towel, then place the towel in an open plastic bag. Put the bag in a warm spot, like the top of a refrigerator, and check for signs of sprouting every two to three days. Plant the seeds as soon as they sprout, handling them gently to avoid crushing the delicate roots.

Scarifying hard-coated seeds, such as okra, just before planting speeds germination. Scar-

PLANTING BY NATURE'S SIGNS

Let common landscape and native plants tell you when it's time to sow seeds, move transplants outdoors, or watch for pests. This method of garden timekeeping uses phenology—the study of the timing of biological events, such as buds opening, and their relationships to climate and to one another.

Each year, both plants and pests develop in a predictable sequence that follows local weather patterns. Keep your own record of wild and cultivated plant development, and note how it coincides with soil temperature and weather data. Some gardeners plant nasturtiums when the lilacs bloom. And when bearded irises bloom, it's time to plant cucumbers. Identify signals that mark the passage of time in your home landscape. Record the date when each occurs and the accompanying weather conditions. After a few seasons, the plants, insects, and wildlife around your home will help remind you when it's time to tend to your garden tasks.

ification means lightly damaging the seed coat. You can use a file, or you can rub the seeds between sheets of medium- to coarse-grit sandpaper. The illustration on page 98 shows a quick way to scarify seeds.

Still other seeds need to be stratified—exposed to a cool, moist period—to break dormancy. Seeds of woody shrubs and trees that grow in climates with cold winters often require stratifying before they'll germinate. To stratify seeds, put them in damp sphagnum moss or vermiculite and keep them in a cold

One way to scarify hard-coated seeds is to place them in a jar lined with coarse sandpaper and shake until the seed coats wear down.

place (34° to 40°F) for one to four months.

To help discourage seedling diseases such as damping-off, some gardeners soak seeds in a weak bleach solution (4 parts water to 1 part bleach) or in compost tea for 15 to 20 minutes just before planting. (See "Using Liquid Fertilizers" on page 128 for directions on making compost tea.)

Seeding Techniques

This is the moment you've been preparing for! Since some seeds are finicky about light, temperature, spacing, and moisture, check the individual plant entries in Part 2 for sowing specifics. When in doubt about depth, follow this rule of thumb: Cover seeds with soil to a depth no more than three times their diameter.

Be sure to consult your garden plan as you plant. Are you leaving enough space between plants and between rows? Do you need to install trellises or other supports? The size of the seeds and the quantity that you want to plant will influence how you choose to get them from packet to soil. Here are some of your choices.

Furrow vs. broadcast. It's easy enough to plunk bean seeds one by one into your garden's rows. But whether your plan calls for sowing in rows or planting intensively in beds, the single-plunk method is a recipe for tedium when you're sowing small seeds like carrots or lettuce. Lightly broadcast fine seeds over the tops of beds, or sprinkle them into furrows. See the top illustration on the opposite page for a foolproof way to make straight furrows.

Spacing. Whether you're sowing in rows or blocks, it's important to get the spacing right. Proper spacing reduces thinning chores later on and ensures that seedlings will get a good, healthy start in life. You can sow by placing single seeds at the right spacing or by gently tapping seeds from a hole torn in the packet. Carry a stick, marked at 3- to 6-inch intervals, to help you get seed spacing right. Mixing fine seeds, like carrots, with 3 or 4 parts dry sand is a good way to make them easier to see and to sow evenly; just scatter the mix evenly over the row or bed. For another technique for getting the spacing right, see the bottom illustration on the opposite page and "Make Your Own: Seed Tapes" on page 100.

Pipe seeding. One good way to improve on the single-plunk method—and save your back at the same time—is to use a simple length of pipe so you can stand up and sow. Choose any kind of lightweight tubing, such as PVC pipe. Make sure that it's long enough to reach the row while you're standing upright and that the pipe's diameter is large enough to let seeds pass through easily. Use a permanent marker to mark 1-inch intervals at the soil end of your pipe and—voilà!—it's an instant planting-depth checker, too. To use your "pipe-dream planter," hold one end and position the

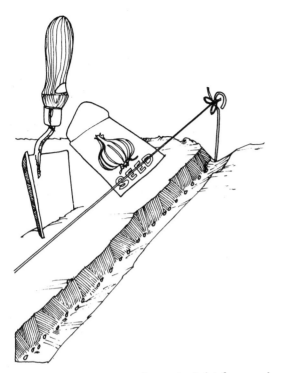

The easiest way to make a straight furrow is to pull the blade of a hoe or trowel along a length of twine strung between stakes at both ends of the row. After you sow, use a hoe or the back of a rake to push or pull the soil over the seeds.

seeds are deposited in the soil at the correct depth and spacing. Precision, of course, depends on the seeder's quality. When shopping for a seeder, look for these features: a suitable assortment of seed plates (for different sizes of seeds), an attachment for making a planting furrow in the row, adjustable planting depth, and a marker for the following row.

Whichever method you use, after sowing, use a rake to push or pull the soil back over the seeds to the right depth. Then gently firm the soil with your rake. Some seeds, such as dill, require light to germinate. Sprinkle them over a prepared seedbed, then use your rake to gently press the seeds in place.

Before leaving the garden, be sure to record what, where, and when you planted by marking your rows with labeled stakes. This way

other end in the row. Send seeds down the pipe one at a time, dragging the end through the row so you can direct seeds right where you want them for the correct spacing.

Mechanical seeders. Mechanical seeders can be real time and energy savers if you have a large garden. These handy gadgets sow straighter rows with more precise seed spacing than planting by hand. And there's less thinning to do when your seeds come up. Planting with a mechanical seeder is as simple as selecting and installing the right seed plate, filling the seed reservoir, then pushing the machine down the row. With a clickety-clack,

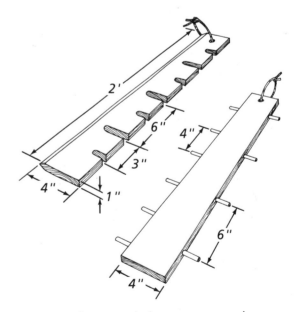

Homemade spacers help you space seeds more evenly at planting time and reduce thinning chores later on. You can sow seeds right into the slots of a notched spacer; wooden dowels make a spacer into a premeasured dibble.

✦ MAKE YOUR OWN ✦

SEED TAPES

Seed tapes are a handy way to sow seeds quickly during the busy planting season. But commercial seed tapes are expensive and offer a limited cultivar selection. Follow these steps to make your own seed tapes, using any small seeds, such as lettuce and carrots, that you want to direct-sow in your garden:

1. In a small saucepan, dissolve 1 tablespoon of cornstarch in 1 cup of cold water. Cook over medium heat, stirring constantly to prevent it from becoming lumpy. Once the mixture boils and turns translucent and gel-like, remove the saucepan from the heat, and let it cool to room temperature.

2. Tear off 4- to 5-foot-long sections of paper towels. Leave the towels attached to each other, and cut them into long strips that are ½ to ¾ inch wide.

3. Check the seed packet for the correct spacing for the seeds you're putting on your tape.

4. Mix the seeds and cornstarch mixture together in a plastic sandwich bag. Note: One teaspoon of cornstarch mixture and ¼ teaspoon of small seeds will cover 15'–20' of seed tape. Cut a small hole in one corner of the bag, and squeeze dots of seed-and-cornstarch mixture onto the paper towel strips, leaving the correct amount of space between them. It may take practice to get just one seed to come out with each dot of mixture. Don't let the seed-and-cornstarch mixture sit before making the tapes, or the seeds will become too moist and may sprout.

5. Let the finished seed tapes dry, label them, roll them up, and store them in a plastic bag for use this growing season.

6. At planting time, dig furrows of the appropriate depth, unroll a seed tape, place it in a furrow, and cover it with soil. The cornstarch and paper towels will decompose, and the seeds will sprout evenly spaced along the row.

you won't make the mistake of planting the same row twice.

Watering. Seeds need moisture for speedy, uniform germination. Most garden soil is sufficiently cool and moist during spring planting to make watering unnecessary. But if you plant during a dry spell, you may need to irrigate. Keep the soil evenly moist at least until stems and leaves emerge. Use a fine mist attachment on your hose or watering can to minimize the movement of soil and seeds before they've sprouted. Encourage quick, uniform seed germination in hot, dry weather by covering rows with wooden boards. The boards help hold soil moisture where it's needed. Lift the boards each day to check for sprouting; remove them at the first sign of seedlings. Floating row cover or recycled burlap bags laid on the soil surface provide similar moisture protection.

Planting Bulbs and Tubers

Most of the rules for planting seeds also apply when you're planting bulbs—such as onion sets or garlic cloves—or tubers—such as potatoes. You generally sow them in furrows but plant them more deeply than seeds. Plant bulbs to a depth three to four times their height. Potato tubers need 4 to 5 inches of soil on top. See the plant entries in Part 2 for the planting depth of the bulb or tuber that you want to grow.

One alternative to digging deep furrows for planting potatoes is to lay the tubers on the soil surface and cover them with 4 inches of coarse mulch, such as straw.

Aftercare

Once your tiny seedlings begin appearing above the soil, you'll need to protect them from extreme temperatures, animals, and insect pests, as well as promote vigorous growth.

Plastic row cover provides several degrees of protection against chilly nights. Floating row cover offers protection from wind and pests but provides less cold protection than plastic. Use shade cloth to give summer sowings protection from the sun. If a sudden cold snap threatens, cover small plants with cloches.

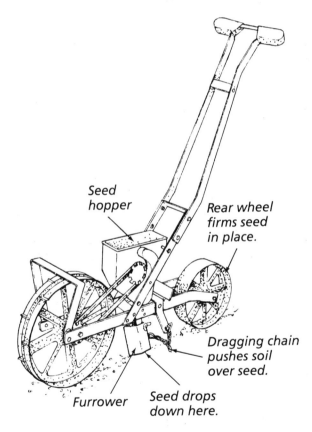

Seed hopper

Rear wheel firms seed in place.

Dragging chain pushes soil over seed.

Furrower

Seed drops down here.

Using a mechanical seeder to plant rows of seeds can cut your seeding time in half. As you push the seeder through prepared soil, seeds drop at the proper depth and spacing and are covered with soil.

See "Season Extension Techniques" on page 209 for more information on using plant covers to protect your garden.

Once new plants pop up, make sure they have room to grow. Plan to thin seedlings early. The idea is to pull the extras (called thinnings), or cut them off at ground level, leaving the rest at the proper plant spacing. When you're finished, tamp down any loosened soil. Some gardeners choose to thin edible seedlings, such as lettuce or radishes, a little bit each week, bringing the thinnings indoors as an early harvest.

Keep an eye on soil moisture, too. Young seedlings are very susceptible to water stress and wilting. Your goal is to keep the soil around their young roots constantly moist. See "Watering 101" on page 117 to learn more about when and how much to water.

PLANTING SEEDS INDOORS

It's a snap to buy ready-to-plant transplants, tuck them into garden soil, and create an instant garden. But with a little more effort on your part, you can grow your own transplants and gain a lot more control over what goes into your garden. Producing your own transplants frees you from the limited plant selection that most garden centers offer because you can choose from a wider selection when you buy seeds. You'll also know that your transplants are pest- and pesticide-free.

Starting your own seedlings indoors gives you a jump on the growing season, too. It also lets you protect vulnerable seedlings from early pests, soilborne diseases, and unpredictable weather. At a time when seedlings need lots of attention, you can lavish your indoor crops with care and give your plants a healthy start.

Starting Right

When starting seedlings, timing is critical. Your goal is to have healthy, hardy plants as soon as outdoor conditions—such as soil and air temperature—are right for transplanting. Plant too early, and your seedlings will grow tall and spindly, run out of plant nutrients, or form a mass of tangled roots. Start too late, and you'll lose gardening time. Refer to the plant entries in Part 2 for specific information on timing, planting depth, and germination temperature. If starting transplants is new for you, you may want to refer to "The Seeds of Success" below for suggestions on good crops to start with.

Choosing containers. You can start transplants in just about any container with enough room for root growth and several holes for water drainage.

If your sunny space is limited to narrow

THE SEEDS OF SUCCESS

If you've never started your own transplants before, choose seeds that are easy to germinate and seedlings that withstand transplanting well. You'll see it's easy to sow the seeds of your own success! Try sowing some of these easy seeds indoors:

Basil	Leeks
Broccoli	Lettuce
Brussels sprouts	Okra
Cabbage	Onions
Cabbage, Chinese	Peppers
Cauliflower	Radicchio
Celery	Tomatoes
Chives	Tomatillos

windowsills, choose small, individual pots. Recycled containers, such as milk cartons or plastic cups, are inexpensive but awkward when space is at a premium. Remember to put something, such as recycled baking sheets or saucers, under your containers to catch drainage when you water.

When your garden plans outgrow the windowsill, a few pieces of specialized growing equipment will serve you well. Add plant growth or fluorescent lights, flats, and trays to your collection of gardening tools. Plastic and Styrofoam containers come in a wide variety of shapes and sizes, and they're versatile enough to use under lights, in the greenhouse, and in hotbeds and cold frames. They're expensive, but with care you can use them for several years. Or fill your flats and trays with peat pots or pellets, and plant them out, pot and all. See "Make Your Own: Soil Blocks" on page 104 to learn about soil blocks, another potless method.

Seed-starting mixes. A good seed-starting medium helps to physically support seedlings and holds adequate amounts of moisture and air. Seed-starting mediums should also be free of weed seeds, pathogens, and environmental pollutants. (See "Make a Clean Start" on this page for information on how to prevent pathogens from ruining your crop of seedlings.) You can buy a seed-starting medium, but preparing your own is simple and inexpensive. Here are two basic recipes for preparing your own seed-starting mix:

1. Mix together equal parts of two or more of the following: vermiculite, milled sphagnum moss, peat moss, perlite, screened and pasteurized garden soil, or screened compost.
2. Combine 1 to 2 parts commercial potting soil or pasteurized garden soil, 1 part

---

MAKE A CLEAN START

You're unlikely to see any plant pathogens during a preplanting inspection of your seed-starting equipment—most of these troublemakers are microscopic. But if your containers and potting mix aren't clean, you can be sure that pathogenic critters are there. As part of your indoor planting routine, sterilize recycled flats and pots and pasteurize any garden soil you plan to add to your potting mix. Don't pasteurize compost, however—its healthy population of microorganisms can actually protect your seedlings from disease. Here's how to pasteurize your containers and soil to get off to a clean start.

Containers. Dip wooden or plastic containers in a 10 percent bleach solution (1 cup of bleach to 9 cups of water). Rinse, then allow them to air dry.

Soil. Preheat a conventional oven to 200°F. Place moist soil in a covered, shallow pan. Insert a meat thermometer into the soil. Once the soil temperature reaches 140°F, set a timer for 30 minutes, the time required for pasteurization. Don't let the temperature go above 180°F or you'll kill the beneficial microorganisms in the soil. Let the soil cool before using. Store in a covered container.

---

perlite or builder's sand, and 1 part screened compost.

Plan to transfer your seedings from the sterile starting mix to a nutrient-rich potting medium once they've formed true leaves. Or water them weekly with a fish emulsion or kelp solution.

Pretreating seeds. You can improve germination by preplanting treatments such as soaking seeds or exposing them to cold temperatures. Check the plant entries in Part 2 for specific directions, and read "Prepare the Seeds" on page 97 for more information.

How to Plant

Unless you have neighbors and friends to share extra seedlings with, don't automati-

---

✦ MAKE YOUR OWN ✦

SOIL BLOCKS

Soil blocks are homemade cubes of moistened soil used for starting seedlings without the walls—or the expense—of pots. To make your own soil blocks, you'll need to buy a block-making press, or blocker, available from most garden suppliers. The resulting cubes range in size from ¾ inch to 4 inches wide. Smaller blocks take up less space, but seedlings quickly outgrow them. You can start seeds in small blocks, then pot on to larger ones.

To prepare the soil block mix, follow the instructions that come with your press. You can add compost, worm castings, or other organic materials to the mix, but you'll need at least 50 percent peat moss to hold the block shape. Moisten the mix to the consis-

tency of a paste, using about 1 part water to 3 parts mix. Pack the press with the wet mix, then eject the blocks onto a tray or flat.

Plant seeds in the block center. Since peat is hard to rewet once it dries out, keep the blocks moist as you sow. Once your seeds germinate, the roots will hold the blocks together. (Until then, a flat-sided grain scoop is a handy tool for picking up and moving several blocks at a time.) Transplant blocks out, or pot on to larger blocks.

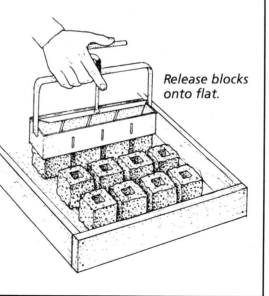

Release blocks onto flat.

Press blocker into mix.

cally sow entire packets of all of the seeds you're planning to grow. Unless the germination rate is low or the seeds are over one year old, count on getting one plant from each seed you sow. (Check the germination rate and the freshness date on each seed packet.) Figure out how many plants you want for your garden, then start that number of seeds, plus a couple of extras for insurance. Check individual plant entries in Part 2 for suggestions on how much of each crop to start.

Fill your containers with moistened starting mix, and prepare waterproof labels with the cultivar name and date of planting. If you need just a few plants, sow seeds in individual pots or other small containers. Plant several seeds, then thin out all but the most vigorous seedling in each pot.

If your plans call for several dozen plants, you can start the seedlings in open flats and transplant them to individual pots later. Broadcast seeds over the soil surface, leaving about ½ inch between seeds. Or, to separate cultivars within a tray, sow them in miniature furrows formed with a trowel. You can also sow seeds directly in individual cells or blocks.

PLANTS IN A PINCH

For some crops, planting more than one seed per cell or block is an easy way to harvest vegetables by the bunch. Instead of planting one seed per cell, sow a pinch. When it's time to transplant outdoors, treat the clump as one plant, allowing enough room for your hoe to pass easily between clumps. Vegetables like beets and onions will keep their usual round shapes, pushing each other aside as they grow. To plant instant bunches of beets, bulb onions, radishes, leeks, turnips, and kohlrabi, sow 3 to 6 seeds per cell or block. Sow 10 to 12 seeds for instant bunches of scallions. At harvest time, gather the entire clump with one pull.

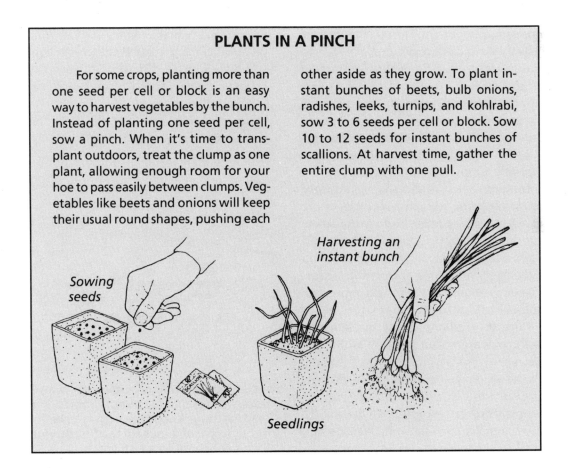

Sowing seeds

Harvesting an instant bunch

Seedlings

Aftercare

Once the seeds are sown, it's time to be patient. Monitor the planting environment to ensure the best growing conditions.

Temperature. Most vegetable seeds germinate best when the soil temperature is between 75° and 90°F. Warming the soil to this temperature range with bottom heat is much more efficient than warming an entire room. Use electric heating cables or mats under your containers to warm the planting medium. Or set pots and flats in a warm spot, such as the top of a refrigerator or water heater, until sprouts appear.

Once seedlings emerge, air temperature becomes more important. Most seedlings grow well in daytime air temperatures of 60° to 75°F, with a drop of 10°F at night. Cool-season vegetables, such as lettuce and cabbage, tolerate lower air temperatures, but cold-sensitive seedlings, such as tomatoes, may be damaged if temperatures fall below 45°F. Air temperatures above 75°F tend to promote weak seedling growth.

Moisture. Seeds need a steady supply of water to soften the seed coat and trigger the hormonal changes associated with germination. Monitor moisture by pressing your finger into the soil surface. The medium should be damp but not soggy. When it's time to water, heat-loving plants, such as peppers, will appreciate a drink of tepid, not cold, water.

Water tiny seedlings with a very fine mist to avoid compacting the soil or washing the seedlings away. Provide moisture above ground, too—most seedlings prefer 50 to 70 percent relative humidity. Humidity above 70 percent makes plants more susceptible to disease. To increase humidity, cover flats with plastic wrap. Don't allow it to touch the leaves; frames fash- ioned of bent wire coat hangers make a good support for the wrap. Or you can use rigid plastic germination covers to increase humidity. Set pots on pebbles in trays with 1 inch or so of water in the bottom to increase humidity.

Light. Once seedlings emerge, they need 12 to 16 hours of light each day. While the best light is outdoors or in a greenhouse, windowsills or plant growth lights make good substitutes in cold weather.

If possible, put your seedlings in a south-facing window for the best light quality. You can increase window space by installing wide shelves under the sill or pushing a small table closer to the window. If poor light quality or inaccessibility makes windowsill growing impractical, don't despair. Plant growth lights let you raise your seedlings in any location you choose. Ordinary cool-white fluorescent tubes work as well as the more expensive plant growth lights, and they use little electricity. Set an inexpensive electric timer to automatically turn

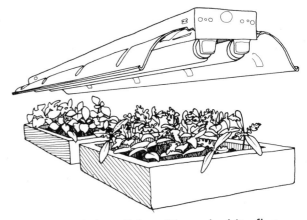

A standard shop light with cool-white fluorescent tubes provides ample light for indoor seed starting. Keep tubes no farther than 3 inches from seedlings for the first few weeks, then raise them to 4 to 6 inches.

the lights on and off, giving the plants a 16-hour "day" and an 8-hour "night."

Fertilizing. When seedlings first emerge, they live on nutrients stored in the seed or seed leaves. Once true leaves develop, the young plants need an outside nutrient source. At least once a week, water seedlings growing in a sterile planting medium (free of soil or compost) with a weak solution of compost tea or with fish emulsion. (See "Using Liquid Fertilizers" on page 128 for directions on making compost tea.) Soil- or compost-based growing media should provide sufficient nutrients for plants like lettuce that are moved outdoors in a matter of several weeks. If seedlings stand in pots or trays much longer and leaves begin looking pale, water with a full-strength solution every other week.

Thinning. Sow thickly; thin quickly! Thinning promotes quick growth and air circulation, making plants less susceptible to disease. Any open flats of seedlings that remain in the flat until planting outdoors—onions and leeks, for example—should be thinned to stand about 1 inch apart. Unless you're planting instant bunches (see "Plants in a Pinch" on page 105), thin packs to one plant per cell. Thin by gently pulling the extra seedlings out one by one, or use cuticle scissors to snip them off at soil level.

Potting On

You can start hundreds of seedlings in plug trays, soil blocks, small cells, or open flats in a fairly small space, lavishing them with the attention they need to germinate. Once they're up, potting on—transplanting into larger containers—offers several advantages. Potting on prunes the roots, encouraging the plant to produce a bushier root system. It also gives you a chance to examine seedlings and rogue out the weakest individuals. The best time to pot on most seedlings is when they have developed one or two true leaves.

When you pot on your seedlings, you can tailor the nutrients in the planting medium to keep them well-nourished until it's time to plant them in your garden. Combine the following ingredients to make a good general-purpose seedling mix:

1 part compost
1 part sphagnum peat moss
1 part vermiculite

To every cubic foot (roughly 6 gallons) of this mix, add:

¼ cup of bonemeal
¼ cup of kelp meal
⅛ cup of blood meal

To pot on, assemble your tools, containers, and medium at a location where you can make a little mess. Fill each container with moistened potting medium, tap it so the medium settles, then use a pencil or your finger to make a hole in the medium large enough for the new seedling's roots. If you're moving seedlings from an open, undivided flat, use a teaspoon or Popsicle stick to dig out and transfer seedlings one at a time. Tap out seedlings started in single cells. Place each seedling in a larger pot and use your fingers to firm the soil around the roots. Water your newly transplanted seedlings thoroughly before setting them in a shady spot for a day or two. After that, return the seedlings to sunny or lighted conditions to continue growing until it's time to plant them out in the garden.

TRANSPLANT TIME

Starting your gardening season with transplants is like starting a race with a lead on your competition. Heat-loving, long-season vegetables, such as peppers and tomatoes, need a head start where growing seasons are short. Gardeners who want to harvest early lettuce will start the season with transplants, then sow later plantings directly outdoors as the soil warms. To figure out the best time to plant transplants outdoors, see "Making a Schedule" on page 83. Check the individual plant entries in Part 2 for specific transplanting instructions.

Starting Right

You can grow your own transplants or buy them from a local nursery or garden center. If you choose the latter route, follow these guidelines when shopping for plants:

• Look for plants with lush, bushy growth and strong stems.
• Allow one plant per pot or cell, except for

A TRANSPLANT TROUBLESHOOTER

Few things are more frustrating than a flat of seedlings that fails to flourish under your care. Fresh seeds, a sterile growing medium, and adequate light, moisture, warmth, and humidity should add up to healthy seedlings. But what if no seedlings appear or, worse yet, your crop seems fine, then begins to die? Do your best to prevent problems when you plant, and use the following information to troubleshoot if a problem threatens your carefully tended crop.

Low or no germination. When a flat fails to fill with seedlings after ample time has passed, suspect one or more of these limits to germination: temperatures were too low or too high, planting depth was improper, seeds were old, or soil was allowed to dry out. Resow your crop or modify conditions and wait a little longer.

Seedlings fall over. You can't cure the distressing effects of damping-off, which can level a whole crop at the soil line. But you can take the following steps to prevent it: Sterilize recycled containers, thin to promote air circulation, and pasteurize soil added to the planting mix as described in "Make a Clean Start" on page 103.

Leggy seedlings. Tall, leggy stems mean seedlings are struggling to get enough light or are too crowded. Supplement windowsill lighting with plant growth lights, lower plant growth lights closer to your seedlings, and/or thin crowded seedlings. Plant leggy seedlings deeper than usual when transplanting them.

Discolored leaves. If your seedlings outgrow the nutrients stored in their seeds and seed leaves, their foliage may turn yellow, red, bronze, brown, or purple, depending on the nutrient(s) they lack. Water with fish emulsion or compost tea once true leaves develop.

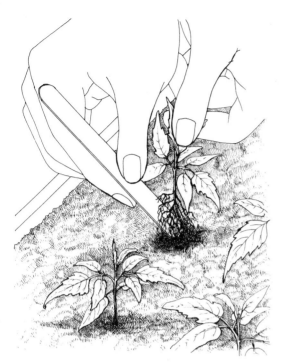

Use a teaspoon or Popsicle stick to prick out seedlings. Handle them gently, holding onto a leaf and supporting the roots from beneath. Avoid grasping easily crushed stems or delicate growing tips.

plants, like chives, that are sold by the clump.
• Reject plants with signs of insect damage or disease.
• Avoid large and overgrown plants; smaller plants will survive the transition best.

Hardening Off

Whether you've grown your own transplants or are starting with purchased ones, you'll need to harden them off in preparation for the rigors of the garden. Sudden exposure to extremes of temperature, direct sunlight, strong winds, and fickle spring weather can shock young plants and slow their growth.

Hardening off helps them make a smooth transition from indoors to outdoors.

Start the hardening-off process one to two weeks before transplanting outdoors by watering less frequently, stopping plant feedings, and lowering the air temperature by several degrees. For plants growing in open, undivided flats, use a knife to "block" them by cutting between seedlings. This severs roots, stimulates individual root growth, and makes it easier to untangle roots at transplant time.

After one week, move plants outdoors each day for several hours during the warmest part of the day. Leave them in partial shade—under a picnic table, for example—but away from strong winds, then bring them back indoors overnight. Gradually increase the time they're left outdoors. If you are away from home during the day, try short exposures early in the morning and again in the evening.

Planting Out

To get your plants off to the best start, water them thoroughly before you transplant. Some gardeners make it a practice to soak plants with compost tea or a weak solution of fish emulsion before planting. You can soak the potted seedlings in a shallow tray of liquid fertilizer for 15 to 20 minutes before planting. (See "Using Liquid Fertilizers" on page 128 for directions on making compost tea.)

To pop a transplant from its container, turn the pot upside down and tap on its bottom. Use your hand, with your fingers on either side of the plant's stem, to support the root ball as it slides out. Gently squeeze out plants growing in individual cells. For an extra boost, just before planting, dust the roots with fertilizer powders, such as blood meal, bonemeal, or granite dust, or add a generous handful of them to the planting hole. Use a trowel or other hand tool to make a planting hole slightly wider than the root ball. Place the plant in the hole, gently spreading out any roots that are wrapped into a ball. Firm the soil around each plant, leaving a saucerlike depression to hold water. Be sure the garden soil fully covers the block of potting mix around the roots. For plants like broccoli and tomatoes, which have a bare stem, it's wise to set the root ball ½ inch or more below the soil surface. For plants like lettuce, which has many leaves at the stem base, set the base at soil level to reduce later problems with stem rots.

If your plants are in peat pots, tear away the collar that extends above the soil in each pot and use your finger to poke holes in the bottom, before setting the plant and pot into the garden.

When you're finished setting out your transplants, sprinkle the soil around each one with at least 1 quart of water.

REDUCE TRANSPLANT SHOCK

Antitranspirants are commercial products that are sprayed on plant surfaces to help lower the rate of plant transpiration—water loss through the leaves and stem. You can use antitranspirants, such as Wilt-Pruf, to reduce the shock of transplanting. They are especially useful when adverse environmental conditions, like hot, sunny, and/or windy days, greet tender transplants.

For best results, spray your transplants with an antitranspirant two to three hours before planting out. Avoid spraying drought-stressed plants. Follow label instructions for application rates.

As an added benefit, studies indicate that antitranspirants also may protect plants from some fungal infections, although they are not registered for use as fungicides.

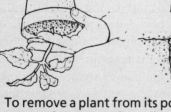

To remove a plant from its pot, invert the pot and tap it with your hand or a tool. Support the soil around the plant with your other hand. Set the root ball into the hole and spread the roots out evenly. Refill the hole and firm the soil, forming a slight basin to catch water.

Aftercare

Transplants need extra attention for the first one to two weeks after transplanting. Your goal is to protect them from extremes of sunlight, drought, heat, cold, and wind, as well as from pests and diseases.

Keep track of rainfall, and be ready to water whenever the soil begins to dry out. See "Watering 101" on page 117 for specific guidelines on when and how much to water. Provide shade on bright days by covering plants with overturned bushel baskets or with burlap or shade cloth supported on wire hoops over the row. To protect plants from wind, use any kind of barrier that's handy: cloches made from half-gallon milk jugs with their bottoms cut away or large, open-ended juice cans sunk into the soil. Plastic and fabric row covers (available at garden suppliers) are good for pulling over your plants on cold days and nights. A deep mulch of bulky organic materials, like straw, can also help protect plants from wind. Remove protective barriers when plants show signs of new growth and when variable spring weather gives way to more stable summer conditions. See Chapter 5 to learn how to water, feed, and train plants during the growing season.

PERENNIAL CROPS

Perennial crops include fruit and nut trees, berry bushes, brambles, vines, and a variety of herbaceous plants such as asparagus, horseradish, strawberries, and many of the herbs. Because they remain in the same location for anywhere from a few years to many years, it pays to plan carefully for perennial crops and to take time to select the best site for them. It's also important to select cultivars carefully:

While you can experiment with an unusual annual vegetable for a season, that's not really a practical option for long-lived trees, shrubs, and vines. Before you order perennial plants or choose a site, read "Planning for Perennial Crops" on page 83. Also be sure to read the individual plant entries in Part 2 for any of the perennial crops you're considering.

When to Plant

Garden centers, nurseries, and mail-order outlets generally sell perennial crops as either dormant bareroot plants or actively growing potted plants. All plants, especially bareroot perennials, appreciate a period of rest after transplanting. That's why most experts recommend planting during a cool spell or season. Cool-weather planting gives plants a chance to settle in and become established below ground before they have to begin active growth above ground. For this reason, plant dormant, bareroot plants such as apples, grapevines, or asparagus crowns in early spring in northern gardens. In southern gardens in Zones 7 and 8, plant in fall. Plant in winter in Zones 9 and 10.

You can plant actively growing, potted perennials anytime during the growing season—they'll begin taking up water and nutrients immediately. The best time to plant most herbs and other perennial crops is in spring or fall because the plants will have time to settle in before having to contend with summertime drought and heat. If the plants you buy were raised in a greenhouse, protect them from frost and other environmental extremes until they're acclimated to their new homes. You can harden them off just like vegetable transplants. See "Hardening Off" on page 109 for directions. Check the individual plant entries in Part 2 for specific planting times for individual crops.

Where to Buy

You'll probably find the best selection of plants to choose from in mail-order catalogs. Local garden centers, however, offer you the chance to see what you're getting before you buy, they're just around the corner, and they may offer plants suited for your particular location.

When buying plants, look for healthy foliage, strong stems, and stocky root systems. Avoid plants with signs of pest problems—chewed leaves, insect excrement, eggs, or webs—and reject bareroot plants with exposed, dry roots. Dormant plants should be just that: There should be no signs of new root growth. Trees should have straight trunks, widely spaced branches, and plump buds. Shrubs and vines should have firm canes, branches, and stems. Potted plants should show healthy new growth.

When ordering plants by mail, read plant descriptions carefully, and match your selections to your environment and hardiness zone. Most companies will ship at the proper planting time, but you may have to specify a date. Once plants arrive, inspect them for damage, following the guidelines above. You can expect a few broken leaves, but return plants that arrive with broken stems or dry roots. Most reputable mail-order suppliers guarantee their plants against losses in shipping.

When you're ordering, keep in mind that it's best to prepare the site and soil *before* you buy. For information on preparing planting sites, see "Soil Preparation" on page 49.

How to Plant

Planting procedures differ slightly depending on whether you're starting with potted plants or bareroot ones. Here are some guidelines to go by.

Bareroot Plants

For best results, plant bareroot trees, shrubs, and vines immediately. If you can't, remove the packaging and place plants in a bucket of water for up to two days. Bareroot plants such as strawberries can remain in moist packing material in the refrigerator for several days, at the most, but immediate planting is best. If you must hold bareroot plants for longer than a day or two, keep the roots moist by heeling them in. Dig a trench with one vertical and one slanted side in a spot sheltered from direct sun and wind. Lay bareroot plants against the slanted side, and cover the roots with soil. Uncover and move to a permanent position while the plant is still dormant.

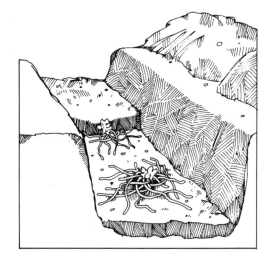

Bareroot perennials, like these asparagus roots, can be planted in a trench rather than in individual holes to save time. Make the trench wide enough so you can spread the roots out in all directions. Check the individual plant entries in Part 2 to find out how far apart plants should be spaced and at what level the crown, or growing point, of the plant needs to be.

At planting time, shorten lanky roots to 1½ feet and trim dead or injured roots back to healthy tissue. Soak the roots in a bucket of water or compost tea for a few hours before planting. (See "Using Liquid Fertilizers" on page 128 for directions on making compost tea.) For an extra boost, dust the roots with a mixture of 2 cups of powdered kelp and 1 cup of bonemeal just before you plant.

If possible, till up an area five times the diameter of the root ball or, at the very least, aerate the surrounding soil with a spading fork. Dig a planting hole deep and wide enough to accommodate the roots. Roughen the sides and bottom of the planting hole with your spade so the roots can penetrate the surrounding soil.

Build a mound of soil on the bottom of the hole to spread the plant's roots over. Make it high enough so your plant will stand slightly higher than it grew in the nursery (indicated by the old soil line on the stem or trunk) to allow for settling. Make sure the graft union of a dwarf or semidwarf tree is higher than ground level, as shown in the illustration on this page. Place your plant atop the mound, spread out its roots, and backfill with soil. After you have filled the hole, build up a shallow rim of soil 2 feet from the base of the plant to form a catch basin for water.

Potted Plants

Potted plants offer a little more freedom in terms of planting time. If necessary, you can hold them in a shady spot, protected from wind, until you have time to transfer them to your garden. Water regularly, and plant them out before they outgrow their containers.

Just before planting, drench the soil of container plants with compost tea or fish emulsion. Or give them foliar applications of liquid

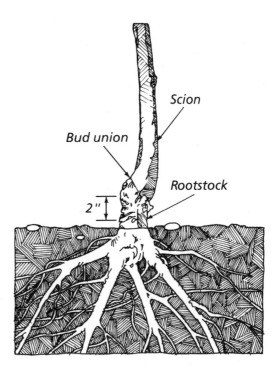

A fruit tree's rootstock dictates the proper depth for planting. Plant standard (ungrafted) trees at the same depth or slightly deeper than they grew in the nursery. Set budded or grafted semidwarf or dwarf trees with the bud union 2 inches above the soil level.

kelp. To plant a potted herbaceous perennial, remove the plant from its container. Turn it upside down, supporting the soil surface with one hand. Use the other hand or a tool to tap the pot's bottom, freeing the plant from the pot. You can lay a large potted plant on its side, then gently work the plant out, but avoid tugging on the stem. Also prune off any damaged or broken roots from plants before planting. If the plant's roots are tightly twisted, you can use a sharp knife to slice through the root ball at several points. The roots of a healthy plant should separate easily in your hands.

Dig a hole as deep as the container and

slightly wider. At the bottom of the hole, form a small mound of soil and place the plant over the mound so the crown is at soil level. Use your fingers to separate and spread the roots over the mound. Hold the plant in place while refilling the hole, then firm the soil and add several quarts of water. Apply 3 to 4 inches of organic mulch, such as straw or compost, to help retain moisture, regulate soil temperature, and control weeds.

Aftercare

Protect your new plants from environmental extremes for several weeks after planting. Use overturned bushel baskets or burlap covers to shield them from full sun and strong winds. (Support and anchor coverings so they don't rest on top of your plants.)

It's important to maintain even soil moisture around new perennials in their first year. When you water them, add enough water to soak the entire root system and encourage deep root growth. Shallow watering encourages shallow rooting. An organic mulch 3 to 4 inches deep will help conserve water, regulate soil temperature, and keep weeds down. For more information on watering, see "Watering 101" on page 117.

5 CARING FOR YOUR CROPS

Watering, Feeding, and Training Your Plants

The apple trees have tiny fruits for the first time, the corn reaches waist height, and the green tomatoes at the base of the plants are finally starting to turn red. While sky divers and mountain climbers might find it hard to understand, these are the events that give gardeners a thrill. Dozens of minor triumphs mark the progress of the gardening season. As we water, feed, and train our plants, we're rewarded with the delight of seeing them happily growing and producing delicious rewards. But the work required to water and feed can be less than delightful. No one likes dragging a heavy hose around on a hot, sunny day. In this chapter, you'll find lots of ways to reduce the time you spend watering, fertilizing, staking, and pruning, leaving you more time to enjoy a simple garden stroll.

CARE BASICS

Once your little green friends are off and growing, you have five primary jobs in helping them face the challenges of producing a crop: weather tamer, crowd controller, nutritionist, personal trainer, and pest patrol officer.

Weather tamer. Your first concern is protecting your tender youngsters from the whims of the weather. Since Mother Nature never seems to make it rain according to a perfect schedule, you'll have to add water and/or keep it from sneaking away by mulching. You'll find out how and when to water in this chapter. For information on mulches, see "Mulching" on page 35.

Gardeners in areas with frequent strong winds will need to protect trees and gardens from the gales. See "Winning Ways for Windy Sites" on page 116 for some ideas.

Torrential rains and hail can do ugly things to succulent young leaves. You may be able to reduce damage by covering plants with floating row cover or lath frames when storms are predicted. If hail or crushing rain does hit your garden, don't declare it dead immediately. While your plants may be set back, most of them probably will recover. Applying liquid plant food is a good first-aid measure.

In areas with cold winters, use cold frames and cloches to extend the growing season in spring and fall and other techniques to protect perennials during the winter cold or spring frosts. Chapter 8 gives you a full rundown of season extension devices and ways to provide winter protection.

Crowd controller. Once you've dealt with Mother Nature, your next concern is giving

---

WINNING WAYS FOR WINDY SITES

The Great Plains is notorious for its nearly perpetual wind, but exposed sites anywhere can make you feel as if you were gardening in a wind tunnel. Here are four ways to deal with windy sites:

1. Plant short, stocky cultivars.
2. Protect transplants with sturdy hotcaps or pieces of board stuck into the ground. Floating row cover also works, but be sure to anchor it well.
3. Choose substantial stakes or cages, and anchor them well to prevent them from blowing over. But choose stakes with a bit of flexibility, such as wood or bamboo, or wire fencing so they can flex slightly in the wind with the plant.
4. Grow a windbreak. Shrubs, corn, or asparagus all work well. Or build an instant windbreak. Solid fences are not good windbreaks—they cause turbulence. Choose something like burlap or snow fence that lets some wind through.

---

each plant some elbowroom. Follow standard spacing guidelines. (You'll find them listed on seed packets, or you can refer to the plant entries in Part 2.) Thin out some of the plants themselves so that the remaining ones are spaced as recommended. Remove weeds by pulling or cultivating, or apply mulch around the crop to suppress them. See "Weeds" on page 174 for ways to weed and weed control ideas. You'll find information on mulching in "Mulching" on page 35.

Nutritionist. If you prepared the soil well before planting, your crops will have plenty of food to live on. Most annuals will thrive right through harvest without any additional feeding. A few may benefit from an extra boost of fertilizer during the season. Perennial crops usually need an annual refueling to replace what they have used. You'll find out how to serve up light snacks, liquid pick-me-ups, and full meals for your plants in this chapter.

Personal trainer. No, you don't need to take them to the gym, but you may need to gently sculpt and/or provide support for your plants. Some, such as lettuce or corn, don't require this at all. Others, such as apples and grapes, need attention year after year. You may need to pinch, thin fruits, or prune; spread branches; and/or install stakes and trellises. This chapter gives you the nitty-gritty details you'll need to plan a fitness program for your plants.

Pest patrol officer. Insects, diseases, and animals can threaten the health and harvest of your garden. Taking an active preventive stance is the best way to fight pests. Chapter 6 gives the full rundown on measures to keep pests from attacking your plants and on organic methods for controlling pest problems.

WATERING 101

Do you live in the ideal climate where you get just enough rain just when your plants need it? Of course not! One of our fundamental gardening jobs is to add water as needed when the weather doesn't cooperate.

But monitoring the weather isn't all we have to do. We also have to evaluate how our soil and gardening practices affect the water needs of our plants. Good gardeners know that soil texture and structure have an effect on how much water is available to plants. Sandy soils lose water rapidly, while clayey soils can hold water *too* well. While you can't change your soil's texture, you can change its structure. Adding organic matter helps sandy soils hold water and helps clayey soils drain better. Adding compost and other organic materials or planting cover crops are some of the best ways to boost organic matter content. See Chapter 2 for complete instructions on these techniques.

Maintaining Even Moisture

There are two ends to the soil water spectrum: drought and flooding. Both are harmful to plants and soil life. Dry soil stresses plants by tying up nutrients, killing delicate root tips, and depleting the water in the plant itself. Soggy soil drowns or suffocates the plant and damages or kills root tips. Even short periods of dry or flooded soil conditions cause long-term stress to the plant. Ideally, the soil should stay *evenly moist at all times*.

Your goal in watering is to keep the top foot or two of the soil moist, but not wet, at all times. Research shows that frequent, short waterings that *maintain* the ideal soil moisture

are the best way to maximize growth and productivity. Note the word maintain—light waterings on dried-out soil are worse than no watering at all. Light waterings on dry soil encourage root growth only in the top few inches of the soil, rather than deep down into the soil. Plants with only shallow roots are far more susceptible to the slightest drought and are more dependent on you for water. They are also less able to absorb nutrients and are more prone to blowing over in high winds. So don't make extra work for yourself: Water frequently and keep the soil evenly moist.

Deciding When and How Much to Water

Southern California gets no appreciable rain from May through September. Gardeners there and in other dry regions can assume that consistent watering every day is the best way to maintain even soil moisture in their gardens. Other watering schedules such as one, two, or three times per week will work, but daily watering will give you the best results.

However, in most areas of the country, it does rain during the growing season but not at regular or predictable intervals. In these areas, figuring out the when and how much can be tricky.

Obviously, you won't need to water during or just after a heavy rain. But after that rain, you can't hold off watering until your plants start to wilt, or they'll already have suffered damage. What can you do? One of three things:

1. You can rely on the general "Watering by Rule of Thumb" on page 118.

2. You can feel the soil periodically to see if it's getting dry, as described in "Watering by Feeling Soil Moistness" on this page.

3. For a more accurate approach to watering, do some simple math to estimate how much supplemental water is needed to replace water lost from the soil, as described in "Watering by Replacement" on the opposite page.

Watering by Rule of Thumb

Some gardening literature gives general guidelines for watering such as "1 inch per week." There is a fatal flaw in any universal watering guideline—no one rate can work for all climates and all seasons. That 1 inch may be just right on a pleasant day in June. But it may be too much on a cool April day and way too little on a hot, dry day in August. If you live in a moderate climate and get rain a few times a week, your garden will do moderately well if you rely on the rule-of-thumb method. But if it's hot and dry for more than three or four days, your plants will suffer.

Making it work. If you plan to water by the rule-of-thumb method, keep track of how much rain falls on your garden with a rain gauge. To make your own rain gauge, see the illustration on page 89. Subtract the total rainfall each week from 1 inch (or whatever rule-of-thumb amount you decide to use), and add that amount of water to your garden.

How do you convert inches of water to the gallons of water coming out of your watering can or hose? To make a rough conversion, multiply the inches you want to add by the total square feet of the area you're watering. Then divide that number by 2.

Here's an example: If your garden is 20 × 40 feet, you want to give it 1 inch of water per week, and your rain gauge caught ¼ inch of rain this week.

1. Subtract inches of rain received from the rule-of-thumb amount, in this case 1 inch:

$$1 - \frac{1}{4} = \frac{3}{4} \text{ inch}$$

2. Calculate the garden area in square feet by multiplying length times width:

$$20 \times 40 = 800 \text{ square feet}$$

3. Multiply inches of water from Step 1 by square feet from Step 2 and divide by 2 to convert to gallons:

$$\frac{3}{4} \times 800 = 600$$
$$600 \div 2 = 300 \text{ gallons}$$

So you need to add 300 gallons of water to your garden. See "Watering Methods" on page 121 to find out how you measure water as you add it.

Watering by Feeling Soil Moistness

Judging when to water by feeling your soil is more accurate than following an arbitrary rule of thumb. The answer to when you need to water is waiting to be "read" in the soil.

Making it work. Here's how to read soil moisture: Wait for one or two dry days after a rainy day. Pull back any mulch around your plants and dig down 2 to 6 inches. Use your hands and gently make a fist-size ball of soil from the bottom of the hole. If the ball holds together, your soil still has plenty of moisture. Refill the hole and replace the mulch, then test the soil again in another day or so. If it falls apart when you pat it gently, it's time for you to water.

Unfortunately, a ball of soil isn't a crystal ball, and you can't magically tell how much water your soil needs with this method. You'll need to determine that from trial and error.

Add water (keeping track of how much you add or how long it takes) and feel the soil again the next day. If it feels sticky, it's too wet—you added too much. Try less water next time. If it's drier than the day before, you were too stingy—try a little more. Ideally, it will feel just the same as it did the day before—then you'll know you've added the right amount. Keep records and you'll eventually have a good idea of how much to add and how soon it will be needed.

Watering by Replacement

This method combines feeling how moist the soil is and evaluating your weather conditions. It tells you both *when* to water and *exactly how much* to add.

To understand this method, you need to think a bit about how your soil loses the water that falls on it. Some evaporates from the surface of the soil. Also, plant roots absorb water from the soil. They use some for their growth and development, but most is lost through their leaf surfaces, a process that is called transpiration. Scientists can measure both of these types of water loss from soil: they call it the evapotranspiration (ET) rate. It's a fancy word, but the idea is simple: The evapotranspiration rate gives you an idea of how quickly your soil is losing water. The ET rate takes average temperature, wind speed, humidity, precipitation, and the percentage of ground covered by foliage into account. ET rates are given in inches (or millimeters) per unit of time (day, week, or month).

The ET rate varies considerably by season and from climate to climate. A few practical examples make this easy to understand. On a cool day in March, your soil won't lose much water via surface evaporation. Plants are dormant or growing very slowly and aren't taking up appreciable water. So the rate of water loss—the ET rate—is very low. But on a hot, dry, windy day in August, evaporation from the soil surface may be quite high (if the soil isn't covered by dense plant growth). Plants will also be taking up and losing a lot of water in these conditions. So the overall ET rate will be high.

Making it work. The "Watering Guide" table on page 120 will help guide you in figuring out the ET rate under various conditions in your area. If you live in an arid climate, the Cooperative Extension Service or your local water district's water conservation department can tell you your average monthly ET rates.

Using ET rates to gauge the amount to water is simple in arid regions because there is virtually no rain during most of the gardening season. Just add the daily ET rate's worth of water back into your garden every day.

In areas that do get rain, use the method described in "Watering by Feeling Soil Moistness" on the opposite page to decide when to start watering after it rains. When the feel is right, start adding the ET rate's worth every day until the next rain.

Here's an example to demonstrate how easy it is to use the ET rate to find out how much to water: It's a humid, 75°F day, your garden is 800 square feet, and when you dig 6 inches below the surface and make a ball of soil, it falls apart—so you know you need to water.

1. Go to the "Watering Guide" table on page 120 and find the daily ET rate for 75°F and humid. The table tells you it's 0.20 inches.

2. Next to the ET rate, you'll find gallons per 100 square feet already calculated for you; in this case, 10.87 gallons per 100 square feet.

3. Multiply the area of your garden by the gallons per 100 square feet and divide by 100

to find out the total gallons you need to add:

$$800 \times 10.87 \div 100 = 86.96 \text{ gallons.}$$

So you need to add roughly 87 gallons of water to your garden per day. If you water every so many days, multiply 87 by the number of days to find out how much to add at each watering. See "Watering Methods" on the opposite page to find out how you measure water as you add it.

Watering to equal the ET rate is a good starting point. But often, especially in well-drained soil, you can apply even more water than the ET rate to encourage more growth and harvest. Or, if your water supply is limited, you'll have to back off on the amount suggested by the ET rate.

While it's best to water on every rainless day, your schedule may say otherwise. If you can't water every day, try to water every two or three days. Just multiply the daily ET rate by the number of days and add that amount. Be

Watering Guide

One measurement of the amount of water lost from your soil is the evapotransporation, or ET, rate. This table lists estimated ET rates based on temperature and humidity. If you live in a very windy place, you may want to use the next-higher rate to compensate for the additional water loss due to wind.

CLIMATE	AVERAGE HIGH TEMPERATURE (°F)	DAILY ET IN INCHES	DAILY GALLONS (PER 100 SQ. FT.)	WEEKLY ET IN INCHES	WEEKLY GALLONS (PER 100 SQ. FT.)
Cool, humid	Under 70	0.10	4.65	0.70	32.20
Cool, dry	Under 70	0.15	7.73	1.05	54.11
Moderate, humid	70–80	0.20	10.87	1.40	76.09
Moderate, dry	70–80	0.25	13.59	1.75	95.13
Warm, humid	80–100	0.30	16.31	2.10	114.17
Warm, dry	80–100	0.35	19.03	2.45	133.21
Hot, humid	Over 100	0.40	23.03	2.80	161.21
Hot, dry	Over 100	0.45	26.90	3.15	188.30

aware, however, that the longer between waterings, the more often the soil moisture will be less than ideal. If it's cool, this probably won't have much effect on your garden. But during a hot, dry period, water stress can make your plants more prone to insect and disease problems, reduce fruit set, and/or stunt growth.

Watering Methods

Watering methods range from the basic watering can to complex built-in irrigation systems with sophisticated timers or moisture sensors. You need to choose a method that suits your climate, soil characteristics, and crops. Ideally, your watering system should do three things:

1. It should put the water into the soil near the roots where it is needed, not just near the soil surface or near the plant's stem and not in the rows where it will just water the weeds.

2. It should keep water off of the foliage. (Wet leaves may encourage disease.)

3. It should prevent water from evaporating into the air or running off over the surface of the soil.

You'll choose between hand-watering, sprinklers, and drip irrigation, or some combination of these methods. Here are the pros and cons of each method.

Hand-Watering

Watering your plants with a watering can or hose is the least complicated method—equipment-wise. It isn't easiest in the long run, however. Unless you have a very small garden and lots of water, time, and energy, you will probably want to keep hand-watering to a minimum.

When you do hand-water, use a water breaker or "rose" to divide the water flow into a gentle sprinkle that will soak into the ground and not disturb your plants. Stand close to the plant you are watering so you can direct the water at the soil under the plant rather than at the leaves.

Making it work. When you water with a hose, it's difficult to know how much water you are actually adding to your garden. If your water pressure is reasonably constant, you can calibrate your hose using a 5-gallon bucket and a stopwatch. Just time how long it takes to fill the bucket, and you'll know the rate of delivery. Use that number to figure out how long you should water an area of a given size. Remember to spread the water evenly over the whole area.

For example, if it takes you 1 minute to fill the bucket, your hose delivers water at the rate of 5 gallons per minute. If you need to apply 100 gallons of water to your garden, you will need to water it for 20 minutes. If you want to be more precise, you can buy an in-line meter that tells you how much you've applied as you water.

Sprinklers

Sprinklers take much of the hands-on tedium out of watering. But most sprinklers are wasteful of water and soak the plants' foliage liberally. Traditional oscillating sprinklers and rotating impact sprinklers cover a very large area with a huge volume of water and very large droplets. They deliver water faster than the ground can absorb it, causing the excess to run off over the surface. And the size and velocity of the droplets can pummel young seedlings and batter older plants.

Such sprinklers may be appropriate for tasks such as keeping seedbeds moist for short periods of time. Choose one that breaks up the water into fine drops, set it to sprinkle only the area in question, and make sure you aren't causing runoff. Try putting it on a timer to run only 10 or 20 minutes out of each hour so the water will have time to soak into the soil and not run off over the surface. See "Making It Work" on page 121 for how to tell how much water you are applying.

Drip Irrigation

Drip irrigation slowly moistens the soil without flooding very many of the tiny pore spaces. You can tell exactly how much water you are putting on in a given time—something that is hard to do with a hose or a sprinkler. You can also be sure it's distributed evenly over the entire area.

Drip irrigation is the ideal way to water all gardens, not just drought-stricken western gardens. It produces the most prolific growth and can greatly increase your harvest, no matter what climate you live in. During a drought, it can make the difference between having a crop and having no crop at all.

There are three types of drip irrigation: porous pipes that leak all along their length, tubing with discrete holes or emitters every so many inches, and tubing that you plug individual emitters into only where you need them. Each type has advantages and disadvantages.

Porous pipes. Porous pipes "leak" water all along their length. They are fine for short distances (100 to 200 feet or so) and reasonably level yards. Longer lengths tend to let out more water near the tap and less at the far end. Sloped sites will get more water at the lowest point. Both situations mean that some plants will get overwatered while others get underwatered. They may also emit water too fast for the soil to absorb. Porous pipes can be a good choice for small, level gardens. Porous pipe works best if your water is chlorinated, as the clorine will prevent slime from forming inside the pipe and clogging the pores.

Tubing with regularly spaced holes or emitters. There are a number of types of drip irrigation tubing available that come ready-made with discreet openings every few inches to every few feet. There are three basic levels of sophistication. The most basic is just a hose with holes drilled at regular intervals. It shares the disadvantage of porous pipe, plus the holes get clogged easily. Clogged holes kill plants, so you'd best steer clear of this type.

The next level of irrigation tubing has more complicated innards. The innards ensure that the same amount of water will come out of each hole no matter how far it is from the tap (up to 400 feet or so) or how far above or below the tap. The holes are also designed to resist clogging. This type is often referred to as T-tape.

The Cadillac of irrigation tubing is in-line emitter tubing. It has emitters preinstalled at regular intervals.

T-tape or in-line emitter tubing are your best bets for most of your plantings. If you aren't sure what you are buying at the garden center, look for an experienced employee to help you. There are also very good mail-order catalogs that spell out exactly what is what.

No matter which type you use, each hole or emitter forms a "wet spot" beneath the soil's surface. The shape and width of the wet spot depends on your soil type. In clay soil, water spreads into flattened, beet-shaped moist areas; space emitters 1½ to 2 feet apart for complete coverage. In loam soil, water spreads into round, radish-shaped moist areas; space emitters 1 to 1½ feet apart for complete coverage. In sandy soil, water spreads very little and forms carrot-

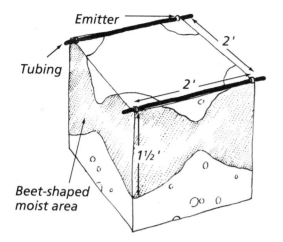

Water dripping onto the soil spreads out to form a round spot. As it sinks down into the soil, it continues to spread sideways. The shape of the wet spot varies according to the type of soil. In this clay soil, the spots are beet shaped.

shaped moist areas; space emitters 6 to 12 inches apart for complete coverage. The illustration above shows the wetting pattern in clay soil.

Choose tubing with an emitter or hole spacing and individual emitter or hole rating (the quantity of water each emitter releases over a certain period of time) that matches your soil type. Between 6 and 12 inches apart with 2-gallon-per-hour (gph) emitters is good for sandy soil. Emitters that are between 1½ and 2 feet apart with a rate of 0.5 gph is better for heavy clay soils. Lay lengths of drip tubing parallel to each other so that the entire root zone will be watered. Space the rows of tubing the same distance apart as the distance between the emitters as shown in the illustration below. For example, a 3-foot-wide bed with loamy or clayey soil needs two lengths of tubing; if the soil is sandy, the bed would need three lengths.

A 4-foot-wide bed needs three lengths in a clay loam or four lengths in sandy soil.

Individual emitters. Individual emitters are inserted into solid tubing where you need them. They may release water right at the main tube or at the end of a section of spaghetti tubing. Such systems work well for widely spaced shrubs and containers. Choose emitters rated from 2 gph for very sandy soil to 0.5 gph for clay soil.

Designing your system. You can use any combination of the three types of drip watering systems to suit your plantings if you put them on separate lines so you can run each type separately. You'll want to include a water filter at the tap end of the entire system to protect it from clogs. You'll also want to include a back-flow preventer (to prevent water and crud from being forced back into the tap)—these are required by law in many areas. Other

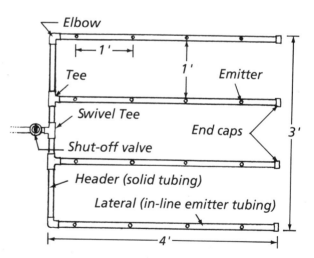

Drip irrigation systems are easy to manage if you include individual shut-off valves for each section. The swivel tee included in this simple emitter system makes it easy to lift the assembly out of the way so you can till the bed.

options you may include are a pressure regulator and/or a timer. Many garden centers and garden supply catalogs sell starter-system kits and individual components. It's not difficult to design and install a system to meet your needs. See "Drip Talk" below to help you get started.

Cover the system with a thin layer of mulch. This hides the tubing until the foliage grows up and protects the plastic from harmful ultraviolet rays so it will last longer.

Making it work. Once you've decided how many gallons of water you want to add, it's easy to calculate how long to run each section of your system to get that amount.

First, find out how many gallons of water each section of the system provides per hour.

• For leaky pipe, multiply the rating (gph per foot) by the total length.

• For T-tape, multiply the total length of tubing by the rating (usually given in gph per 100 feet) and divide by 100.

• For in-line emitter tubing, multiply the total length of tubing by the number of emitters per foot, then multiply the total by the emitter rating (usually given in gph).

• For inserted emitter systems, count the individual emitters and multiply the total by the emitter rating.

Once you know how many gph your whole system or section delivers, just divide the amount of water you want to deliver by the gph to get the run time.

DRIP TALK

Drip irrigation jargon can jumble your thinking. Here are a few definitions to make designing and buying a drip system easier:

Tubing (hoses) are flexible plastic pipes that water moves through. Tubing comes in various sizes; tubing that's ½ inch in diameter is usually used for main lines. Smaller tubing (¼ inch in diameter or less) is used to supply individual emitters and may be called spaghetti tubing.

Emitters (drippers) are openings in tubing where water comes out.

Connectors (tee, elbow, or straight) are fittings that connect sections of tubing. They hold the tubing in different ways; connectors can be barbed, wire-on, compression, or threaded types. Threaded fittings are described as either "fht" or "mht." Fht fittings are female

fittings; they are threaded on the inside. Mht fittings are male; they are threaded on the outside.

Swivel connectors are connectors that allow one or more of the arms of the joint to twist without leaking.

Shut-off valves are on-off switches that let you turn off part of the system. Ball valves are one of the most reliable types.

Pressure or flow regulator is the apparatus that controls the pressure of the water (expressed in PSI, or pounds per square inch) or the amount of water (expressed in gph, or gallons per hour) that flows into the system.

Anti-siphon device (backflow preventer) is the apparatus that keeps the water or water plus fertilizer from flowing back into the tap and the house water supply.

Match System to Plants

You'll want to tailor your watering system to the root spread of the plants you're watering. With annuals, you can figure on watering the area of the bed or one row width. Perennials are larger and many have quite extensive root zones. Here are some guidelines on where to apply water to perennials.

Drip Irrigation for Small Perennials

Water small perennials such as strawberries, rhubarb, herbs, brambles, and other berry bushes the same ways you water annual crops. A single length of in-line emitter tubing will usually work fine for a narrow row. Two parallel lengths work better in sandy soil and in wide beds. Place the tubing at least a few inches away from the crowns or the stems to help prevent root rot. Individual emitters are more efficient if plants are widely spaced.

Drip Irrigation for Trees

The roots of most trees and large shrubs spread much farther than their branches. In heavy clay soil, roots spread half again as wide as the branches. Sandy soils offer much less resistance to roots, and the roots will often grow three times wider than the branches above. See the illustration on page 126 for a bird's-eye view of how far the roots of some trees can spread beyond their drip line (a circle at ground level that corresponds to the farthest extent of the tree's branches).

Keep in mind that roots are not created equal when it comes to taking up water. The older roots of perennial plants, much like older branches, have a barklike covering that protects the root but can't produce water-absorbing root hairs. The roots responsible for absorbing water and nutrients are the very young,

LOW-TECH DRIP WATERING

You can get the benefits of drip irrigation without the expense of installing any tubing. Try punching a few pencil-lead-size holes in the bottom of a 1-gallon plastic jug and planting it next to a seedling, leaving only the neck of the jug exposed. Fill the jug with water. The water will slowly seep out to the plant's roots. For a portable system, set the jug on the surface of the soil over a plant's roots. Fill it up and the water will soak slowly into the soil. For a newly planted tree, place a ring of perforated jugs on the soil above the tree's roots.

tiny root hairs found near the tips of new roots. In fact, a scientific study of a ten-year-old apple tree showed that the older roots within 4½ feet of the trunk absorbed less than 10 percent of all of the water and nutrients absorbed by the entire root system. Ninety percent was absorbed by the younger roots near and outside the drip line! So when you water your trees, you need to apply most of the water away from the trunk and well out past the drip line.

You can water a tree by laying parallel rows of in-line emitter tubing over the entire area of the tree's root zone. See the bottom illustration on page 123 for a rectangular setup. Another layout option is concentric rings of in-line emitter tubing. One ring at or just beyond the drip line will work for a small tree. As the tree grows, add larger rings of in-line emitter tubing to water expanding roots. Existing large trees need many rings. For spacing between emitters and between lines, see "Tubing with

Regularly Spaced Holes or Emitters" on page 122. Keep the tubing in place by pinning it down every 4 to 6 feet with a U-shaped pin. Cover it with an attractive mulch.

FERTILIZING 101

If you faithfully improved your soil before planting, feeding your crops during the season will be a simple task. (See Chapter 2 for information on how to evaluate and amend your soil prior to planting.) Your annual crops won't need more than a light snack, if that, before they're harvested. Perennial crops are a different story. You'll probably need to serve them a meal or two every year.

A word of caution: Plants that overeat don't get fat—but they may bear less fruit or have more pest problems than those that dine more modestly. Nitrogen especially can cause problems. See "The Limits of Nitrogen" on the opposite page for more details on the effect of

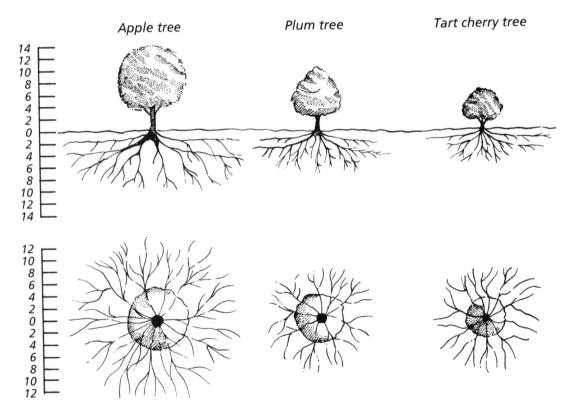

(distance in feet)

Contrary to popular opinion, tree roots don't go as deep as the branches are tall. The roots also extend two to three times farther sideways than the branches do. Be sure to put water and plant food all the way out to the edges of the root zone for maximum benefit.

THE LIMITS OF NITROGEN

When in doubt, many gardeners reach for water and a high-nitrogen fertilizer, such as manure or blood meal, to "cure" ailing plants. This may do more harm than good. A plant will readily absorb diluted nitrogen, even in excess of its needs. The surplus nitrogen makes the plant produce large, succulent leaves and long, soft shoots instead of fruit—and succulent foliage is an invitation to problems. Aphids, for example, love succulent new growth and flock to it in hoards. Fruit on overfed trees is also more prone to brown rot.

excess nitrogen. The two keys to feeding your garden properly are:

1. Enrich the soil properly before planting.
2. Watch your plants and give them only what they need as they grow.

There are three ways to feed your plants: Spreading (or mixing in) solid fertilizer, pouring liquid fertilizer on the soil, and spraying liquid fertilizer on the plants' leaves. Solid fertilizers are used before planting and applied yearly as long-term food for perennial plants. Liquid fertilizer drenches and sprays are used to give doses of nutrients to growing plants when they need them.

Using Solid Fertilizers

Solid fertilizers are solid food for your soil microherd. They chew it up slowly and steadily and provide your plants with nutrients over months or even years. The only nutrient

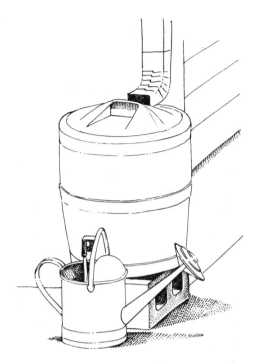

It's not hard to save rain for a sunny day. If your house has downspouts, you can just run one into a barrel. A spigot near the bottom of the barrel makes it easy to fill your watering can.

that is available immediately from solid fertilizer is nitrogen because it is readily soluble and doesn't need to be worked on by the microherd.

What to Use

You can use any of the organic fertilizers described in the "Fertilizer Options" table on page 50. Some, such as rock phosphate, contain a single nutrient. Others, such as compost, contain a blend of many nutrients. You can even mix your own blend or purchase a preblended organic fertilizer. See "Home-Mixed Fertilizer" on page 48 for some all-purpose fertilizer recipes or see "Customized Soil Care," beginning on page 56, for crop-customized recipes.

How to Apply Solid Fertilizer

There are two general ways to use solid fertilizers on established plants: topdressing and side-dressing.

Top-dressing. Top-dressing (or broadcasting) is the most common way of applying solid fertilizers. Sprinkle the fertilizer evenly over the entire bed or root zone by hand or with a spreader. (Pull back any mulch first so you can spread the fertilizer on the surface of the soil.) Then work the fertilizer into the top few inches of soil with a rake or spading fork. Working the fertilizer into the soil is especially important if you get little rain and use drip irrigation. Replace or renew your mulch when you're done.

Side-dressing. To side-dress, spread the fertilizer in a band along the row of plants. Side-dressing is used to fertilize annual crops during the growing season. Don't put the fertilizer right next to the stem—put it just beyond the drip line, where the roots are the most active. Then work it into the soil as for top-dressing. In general, top-dressing the whole area will give you better results than side-dressing will, but side-dressing will save you time and effort.

Using Liquid Fertilizers

Liquid fertilizers are quick food for plants. They provide a boost of available nutrients right away, sort of like an instant breakfast drink. Liquid fertilizers are especially useful when soil is cool and your microherd isn't converting solid fertilizer to plant food very fast. They are also useful for watering-in new plants.

What to Use

Compost tea, kelp fertilizer, and fish fertilizer are three common liquid fertilizers.

Compost tea. Compost tea is the perfect drink for your garden. It provides a balanced cocktail of nutrients, without overdoing any of them, and you can make it from scratch right in your own garden. Just fill a burlap or coarsely woven sack with finished compost, tie it shut at the top, plop it in a bucket or barrel of water, and let it "brew" for a few days. Dilute the resulting extract with water until it is the color of weak tea and use it freely. If you have some well-rotted manure, you can substitute it for the compost to make manure tea.

Kelp fertilizer. Kelp contains a wide range of trace elements and a good dose of potassium. Most kelp products contain some nitrogen and phosphorus; you'll need to read the label to find out how much. Kelp is sometimes sold as seaweed or kelp meal.

Kelp is available as a liquid (extract) or a powdered concentrate (meal). The powdered concentrate keeps longer after opening and doesn't have the chemical stabilizers or preservatives found in some liquids. The liquids are easier to mix with water, though. Dilute kelp extract or mix kelp meal with water according to the instructions on the label.

Fish fertilizer. Fish fertilizer is a good source of nitrogen. It also contains a few trace elements and may contain some phosphorus and potassium. Since kelp is noticeably lacking in nitrogen, fish fertilizer makes a good complement to kelp fertilizer. You can mix these two fertilizers yourself (equal parts) or buy them already mixed.

Fish fertilizer comes as a liquid concentrate (emulsion) or as a powder (meal). Dilute fish emulsion or mix fish meal with water according to the instructions on the label.

How to Apply Liquid Fertilizer

Feeding and watering your plants at the same time sounds like a dream come true. You can—it's called fertigating. Just use properly diluted liquid fertilizer instead of water once every two weeks as part of your regular watering program. On a small scale, just use diluted liquid fertilizer in your watering can.

For hose or sprinkler fertigation, you can use a siphon attachment. Just screw the siphon into your system between the tap and the hose and drop the intake tube into a bucket of concentrated liquid fertilizer. (The siphon will come with directions that tell you how much it dilutes your stock fertilizer.)

You can also fertigate with your drip system. Unfortunately, siphon attachments may not work reliably with the low flow rate of many drip systems. You'll need to spend a bit more and get either a proportioner or a fertilizer injector that isn't dependent on a high rate of flow or high water pressure.

Organic fertilizers often contain small particles that can cause clogged emitters, so be sure to filter any liquid fertilizer very carefully before introducing it to your irrigation system. Avoid using fish fertilizer with a drip system; it has a bad reputation for clogging drip systems. When you're finished feeding, flush the system clean by running clear water through it for a few minutes.

Using Foliar Sprays

Foliar sprays are like intravenous nutrition for plants. They don't make a steady diet, but they can work miracles if deficiencies threaten your plants' health. Deficiencies often show up as discolored leaves or stunted new growth. You'll find a list of deficiency symptoms in the "Troubleshooting Plant Nutrient Deficiencies" table on page 175. When you foliar-feed, your plants absorb the diluted liquid fertilizers directly through their leaf surfaces.

What to Use

The most frequently used foliar fertilizers are compost tea, kelp fertilizer, fish fertilizer, and chelated trace elements.

Compost tea. Compost tea is a good general-purpose foliar fertilizer. It helps plants resist diseases by enhancing overall plant health. There seems to be an additional benefit: Evidently, the microorganisms in the compost, or the compounds they produce, help suppress the growth of diseases like powdery mildew and Botrytis. Spray affected plants every three or four days. See "Compost Tea" on the opposite page for brewing instructions.

Kelp fertilizer. Kelp is particularly good at absorbing and concentrating many of the ocean's trace elements or micronutrients. It is helpful in correcting trace element deficiencies. See "Kelp Fertilizer" on the opposite page for more information. In addition to nutrients, kelp contains growth regulators. These naturally occurring compounds stimulate and regulate plant growth and flower formation. While scientists don't know exactly how it works, it's clear that kelp sprays improve plant growth and increase yields. Spray at least once a month for maximum results.

Fish fertilizer. Fish fertilizer is principally used to remedy nitrogen deficiencies during the growing season. See "Fish Fertilizer" on page 128 for details.

Chelated nutrient sprays. Chelation is a biochemical process that bonds metal ions to larger organic molecules. It occurs naturally as organic matter decomposes. Chelated trace minerals are readily absorbed by plants. Commercial chelated mineral sprays are especially useful for combating iron, calcium, and boron deficiencies. If you can't find them locally, order them from one of the garden suppliers listed on page 509.

How to Apply Foliar Spray

Always dilute foliar fertilizers according to the label instructions. Add ¼ teaspoon (no more) of vegetable oil or liquid soap to each gallon of spray to help it stick to the leaves.

Strain your spray before or as you pour it into your sprayer. The illustration below shows how to use panty hose to strain your spray. Not only are the smallest particles the easiest for the plants' leaves to absorb, but also big particles clog sprayer nozzles. Any sprayer or mister will work (unless it was used for herbicides in the past). Adjust it to emit as fine a mist as possible.

Spray in the early morning and early evening when the leaves are actively respiring. If the plant is showing any signs of disease, especially a water-stimulated disease such as blight, mildew, or fungus, spray in the morning so you don't worsen the disease. Spray both the upper and lower surfaces of the leaves until the spray starts dripping off of the leaf edges. If it rains within a day, respray.

Apply foliar sprays to fruiting plants at bloom, fruit set, and during the final stages of ripening or apply once a month. Leafy plants may benefit from sprays every two weeks or

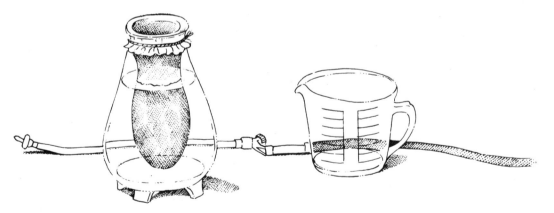

You can strain your spray solution as you pour it into the tank. Poke two layers of panty hose or cheesecloth into the open tank, tie them securely to the tank's neck, and pour the mixture through the panty hose or cheesecloth strainer. Remove the strainer and residue and close the sprayer. Rinse the strainer for the next tankful.

so. If you are spraying to correct a specific deficiency, spray when you see the first signs of nutritional deficiency. If you know a certain area is prone to a nutrient deficiency, start spraying early in the spring, before any visible symptoms appear, and repeat once a month.

Match Method to Plants

You'll want to tailor your feeding to match your plants. Annuals will benefit from some liquid or foliar food early in the season. Heavy-feeding annuals such as corn may benefit from a side-dressing of compost during the season. See the plant entries in Part 2 for recommendations for the crops you're interested in.

Since perennials grow in the same spot for many years, they count on you to deliver their meals. Here are some general recommendations for specific types of perennials.

Perennial plants. Perennials such as strawberries, rhubarb, and artichokes are heavy feeders; you'll want to give them a generous helping of solid fertilizer every year.

Bushes and brambles. Berries are moderate feeders. See "Custom Care for Small Fruits" on page 62 for suggestions on getting your berries off to a good start. Once plants are established, they'll need a snack every year.

Trees and vines. Trees and vines are light feeders. See "Custom Care for Tree Fruits" on page 61 for suggestions on getting your trees and vines off to a good start.

Because established trees and vines have such extensive root systems, they can usually get all of the nutrients they require from a cover crop or organic mulch. The length of the new growth that a tree puts out each year is a good way to gauge if a tree needs a little extra chow.

TRAINING 101

Training can make life easier for your plants, or it can make managing them easier for you. Here are five reasons for training plants:

1. Training opens up the plant to let in light, air, and gardeners. More light helps fruit ripen evenly. Air movement and sunlight encourage the leaves and fruit to dry off as rapidly as possible, which can reduce disease problems. You'll also be able to see and reach ripe fruits as well as monitor and treat problems as they develop.

2. Training makes a strong framework from the plant itself or by adding supports that can bear the weight of heavy crops of fruit.

3. Training reduces the number of fruit buds. This reduces the need for summer fruit thinning and increases the size of each individual fruit, encourages complete ripening, and prevents branch breakage from heavy crops.

4. Training limits the size of the plant to allow you to reach the fruit or to save precious garden space.

5. Training keeps the plant off the ground to protect it from soilborne problems.

The longer a plant's life span, the more important it is to train it. Many annual plants need little if any training. Many gardeners train annual vegetables like tomatoes and beans in order to make harvesting easier or to lessen the chance of disease outbreaks by improving air circulation around the plants.

Plants that have perennial roots but short-lived tops such as strawberries need no more training than annual crops. Vines and trees usually need quite a bit of training to develop a strong framework and stay productive.

To train your plants, follow these steps:

1. Add external supports if they're needed. This is the least disruptive training method.

2. Bend or redirect the plant to strengthen it, slow its growth, and make it more open. Redirecting branches works with the plant, and doesn't involve making cuts where diseases can enter.

3. If branch spreading doesn't do the entire job, prune parts of the plant. If pruning is required, don't put it off. A few cuts during the first years are far more effective than lots of cuts later. They disrupt the tree's natural processes less and heal faster.

Sturdy Supports

Busy gardeners may be tempted to skimp on providing plant supports, but time spent installing supports early in the life of the plant will save you time and headaches down the road. Supports fall into one of three general categories: stakes, cages, and trellises. Many food plants need the help of one of them to stand up tall and proud under a heavy harvest. While some plants will yield just fine sprawled along the ground, they take up lots of space. Plants that touch the ground are more susceptible to soilborne diseases and insect pests. They're also susceptible to that dreaded scourge, gardener's foot—the flattening experience of getting stepped on. Most important, good plant supports save your time and make caring for your plants and picking their bounty more pleasurable.

You can use everything from branch trimmings to PVC pipe and acrylic twine to support your plants. What you use will depend on your tastes, the needs of your plants, and what's available. Choose supports tall enough

Single stakes make good supports for bushy crops like tomatoes or vining crops like pole beans. You can also use 2- to 3-foot-long pieces of well-branched brush to support closely planted crops such as peas.

and strong enough to support the entire mature plant even when it is wet, windblown, and loaded with fruit. Insert the supports firmly into the ground so they won't fall over. Plants on slightly flexible supports are more forgiving than those on rigid ones.

Staking

Staking annuals is a single-season affair, but staking dwarf fruit trees and brambles may involve planning for something more permanent. Here are some options.

Temporary stakes. Some annual vegetables such as peppers and eggplant need staking to stand up under their load of fruit. Choose untreated wood or bamboo for natural flexibility. Insert stakes when plants are very young to avoid injuring roots. Loosely tie plants to stakes with soft twine or strips of cloth every 8 to 12 inches. Beans and other naturally twining plants won't need to be tied once they get started up, as shown in the illustration on the opposite page. Wood or bamboo stakes will last for a few seasons.

Permanent stakes. Fruit trees on very dwarfing rootstocks may need permanent stakes to compensate for their small root systems. Stakes are also used for some brambles. Metal fence posts inserted at planting are a good choice. Choose a post long enough so that you can bury about one-third of it and still have enough height to support your plant. A 6-foot-long post (2 feet in the ground and 4 feet above ground) will serve a very dwarf tree or a black raspberry plant. A 7- or 8-foot-long post is better for a semidwarf tree.

Caging

If you loop a few stakes together with string, you form a cage. Or wrap a length of wire fencing into a tube—the best-known exam-

---

NONTOXIC WOOD PRESERVATIVE

As gardeners, we like to use wood for stakes and trellises. But wood plus soil moisture equals rot. Preservatives or naturally rot-resistant woods are the answer. Rot-resistant woods tend to be rather expensive. Avoid commercially pressure-treated wood because it contains arsenic-based compounds. Buy borax-treated wood or try this paint-on preservative developed by the USDA's Forest Products Laboratory:

1 ounce of paraffin wax
1 gallon less 1⅔ cups of turpentine
1½ cups of boiled linseed oil

Melt the wax over water in a double boiler (not over a direct flame). In another container, vigorously stir the turpentine while slowly pouring in the melted wax. Add the linseed oil and stir thoroughly. Dip untreated wood in the mixture for 3 minutes or brush on a heavy coat.

---

ple is the tomato cage. Put up your cages when the plants are very small. Beware of the weak cages sold at bargain stores; they don't have long enough "feet" to hold them up. Install them with a sturdy stake. Cages give plants more room to grow than stakes do and they release you from having to tie the plants up. Remove and clean cages in the fall. Metal cages last for many years.

Trellising

Trellises run the gamut from a temporary structure made with a few sticks and a bit of string to a permanent arbor shading your patio.

Temporary trellises. You can grow annual vines and sprawling crops on trellises. Every so often, you'll need to tie plants with long, floppy growth such as sweet potatoes and indeterminate tomatoes to the trellis. Twining vines such as beans spiral around supports as they grow. They prefer single vertical wires or strings to wrap around. Plants such as peas and cucumbers have special slender, leafless tendrils that curl tightly around supports. They prefer a mesh or netting trellis.

The illustration below shows two common temporary trellis styles. Both types can be removed at the end of the season and then installed somewhere else the following year. To save storage space during the winter months, hinge your trellises so they can fold up flat, or design the joints to come apart.

Permanent trellises. Ideally, a trellis should last as long as the plant it is supporting. Use sturdy, long-lasting materials and put them together with rustproof screws or bolts rather than nails.

Choose a naturally rot-resistant wood such as cedar (the heartwood is the rot-resistant part), or paint untreated wood with a nontoxic preservative. You can buy a commercial product or make your own. See "Nontoxic Wood Preservative" on page 133. Metal, fiberglass, concrete, and even recycled plastic trellises and components are also available.

Use synthetic baling twine or 12- to 14-gauge galvanized or high-tensile fence wire to string your trellis. Synthetic baling twine is by far the easiest to work with.

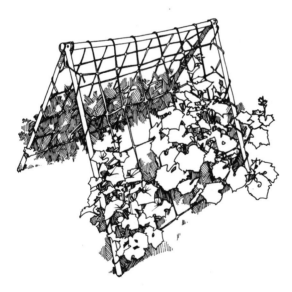

Plastic or wire netting trellises are strong and last for years. Biodegradable string or netting can be cut off and composted right along with the plant residues, which saves time after harvest.

Building a permanent trellis isn't difficult, but it does require some basic construction tools, such as saws and drills, and know-how. If you're a do-it-yourselfer, you may already have all of the tools and knowledge you need. If you're a beginner or if you want step-by-step trellis-building instructions, refer to "Sources" on page 507 for titles of books that offer detailed information on trellis construction.

Here are some trellising suggestions for different types of plants.

Annual crops. While most gardeners grow annuals on temporary trellises, annual crops also grow well on permanent trellises. If you choose to use a permanent trellis for a specific annual, pay careful attention to building the soil before you plant each year. Also, be sure to clean up residues at season's end each year to prevent a buildup of pest organisms.

Brambles. Blackberries and raspberries are easier to deal with and are more productive if they are supported. Individual posts (one per plant) work well for black raspberries. Red raspberries spread to form a continuous row and are better suited to a trellis. Trellis options range from a single row of posts with

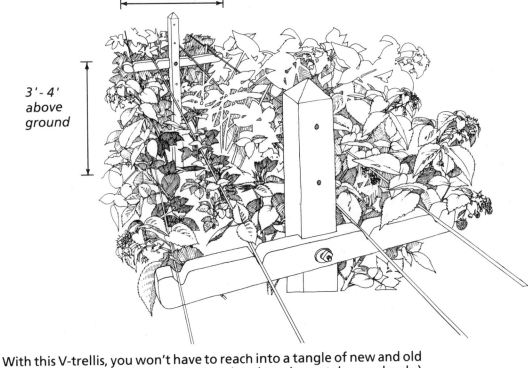

3' wide

3'- 4' above ground

With this V-trellis, you won't have to reach into a tangle of new and old bramble canes to pick the fruit. Notches (or, alternately, cup hooks) hold two lengthwise wires near the ends of the crossbars and two more wires near the post. After pruning in early spring, tie the fruiting canes to the outer wires to form a V. The new canes grow straight up between the spread fruiting canes. Tuck them between the center wires as they grow.

wire to a more complex arrangement of posts with crossbars and wire. One trellis option is pictured on page 135. Blackberries are the heftiest brambles and need a large, strong trellis.

Grapes. Grapevines grow well on arbors or along post-and-wire trellises. See the illustration below for one trellis design.

Shaping and Guiding Plants

Your plants will often grow in directions or shapes that are not exactly what you had in mind. When they do, you can gently guide them or fasten them to their stakes or trellises to keep them in line. With fruit trees, there are several ingenious ways to keep branches spread so that the trees keep a desirable form.

Guiding Annuals

Help vining annuals get started on a trellis by simply putting the shoot or branch against the support. If necessary, tie it loosely with strips of soft cloth or coarse twine until it takes hold. Nonvining plants need to be tied to their supports every foot or so.

Adjusting Perennials, Vines, and Trees

Woody perennials are harder to redirect but they will hold their new shape once it sets or hardens. Shrubs and nut trees are mostly self-shaping. Vines are shaped by pruning and by positioning them along the trellis they have to grow on.

Spreading fruit tree branches. Fruit trees develop stronger frameworks and bear more

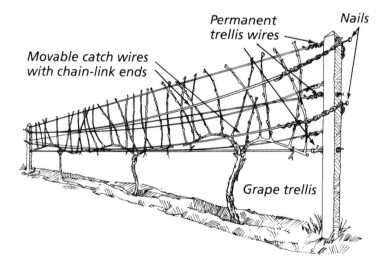

Movable catch wires with chain-link ends

Permanent trellis wires

Nails

Grape trellis

Grape shoots climb up the permanent wires of this trellis or they can be woven through. Attaching a catch wire on either side of the trellis will save you lots of time because catch wires act like a big rubber band around the trellis that holds the growing canes in an upright position so you don't have to tie them up. Drop the catch wires during winter pruning. When new growth is 2 feet long, raise the catch wires to the lowest nails to keep the shoots pointing up. As the shoots grow, raise the catch wires to the higher nails or use a second set of wires.

fruit if you direct their shape as they grow. Careful shaping also reduces the amount of pruning you'll need to do and helps the tree produce a crop sooner.

The strongest and most fruitful angle for a branch to be attached to the trunk is between 45 and 60 degrees. Branches with narrower angles break off easily because the joint is weak. Branches with wider angles bend too far under a load of fruit and won't bear much the following season. Read "How a Tree Works" on page 142 for more details on how the angle affects the growth and development of the branch.

As new side branches grow, keep an eye on the angle of growth. If any sideshoots begin to grow too vertically, you must reshape their growth early in the season. To judge whether

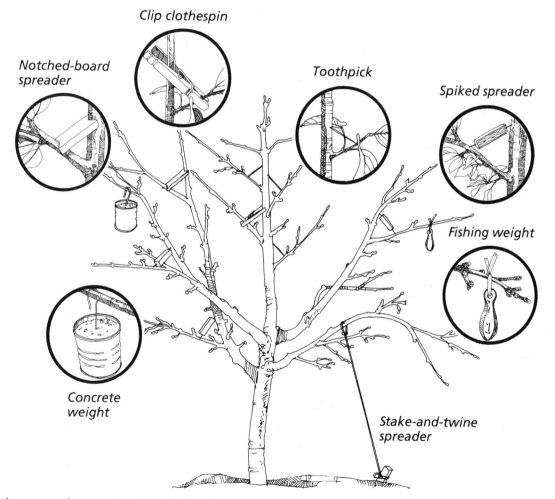

Using spreaders and weights helps branches to form strong attachments to their trunk and lets you redirect branch growth to form the desired tree shape.

shoots are growing at a good angle, place your forefinger into the crotch formed by the shoot and the trunk. If you see light below your finger, the angle is too narrow and the shoot needs spreading. If your finger nestles snugly between shoot and trunk, the angle is wide enough.

If you have a crotch angle that needs widening, you can insert things such as toothpicks or strips of wood to spread branches or you can hang weights from the branches to pull them down into the proper position. Both methods are shown in the illustration on page 137. Round toothpicks make good spreaders for young shoots. Insert one end of a round toothpick into the trunk 2 inches above the base of the shoot, spread the shoot slightly beyond the final 45- to 60-degree angle, and insert the other end of the toothpick into the bark of the shoot. You can also clip a clothespin to the trunk just above a young shoot to spread it, as shown on page 137. Several clothespins clipped near the end of the new growth will act as a weight.

Larger or hardened branches need larger spreaders. Use strips of wood with a V-notch in each end for large branches. Make spiked spreaders by tapping an eightpenny (8d) galvanized finishing nail into each end of a length of 1 × 1 and clipping off the nail head at a steep angle with heavy-gauge wire cutters.

To open up the crotch angle of an older branch, you can pound a stake into the ground and tie a piece of twine to it, then tie the other end of the twine to the branch to pull it to the desired angle. Use a knot that you can untie, and bring the branch down gradually over a few weeks.

Anything from fishing weights to large rocks will work as weights. Try filling small tin cans with concrete and inserting an S-hook of coat hanger wire into the center of the concrete while it is soft. When the concrete dries, hang the can by the S-hook from the branch you want to spread.

Pruning

Many gardeners find it hard to cut their plants for fear of hurting them. Judicious pinching and pruning actually help your plants, so please do it.

Pinching

Pinching is just pruning done with your bare fingers. You can pinch off the tip of the main shoot to make a plant grow more side branches. Or pinch off the side branches to make the plant grow tall and straight, and concentrate on growing a few large fruits. Pinch shoots off right above a leaf or flush with a main stem. Do your pinching on a dry day to help minimize disease problems. Pinching out

Keep rambunctious tomato plants in bounds by pinching off the sideshoots that form in the crotches of the leaves and main stem. Just pinch them off or rub them away with your fingers.

a sideshoot on a tomato plant is illustrated on the opposite page.

Thinning Fruit

Thinning fruit is another type of hands-on pruning. It is done for two reasons: to let new plants concentrate on making roots and branches for the first few years and to increase the quality of the harvested fruits on established plants.

New plants. Many fruits including strawberries, grapes, and apples will yield better in the long run if they don't have to try to ripen any fruit during the first season or two. You need to pick off *all* of the flowers or strip off the immature fruits before they get bigger than a jelly bean. This is a difficult task for many gardeners: After all, your ultimate goal is fruit. But your plants need time to grow roots and branches before they start concentrating on fruit. Grit your teeth and do it anyway.

Established plants. In a good year, some of your trees will set far more fruit than they can really handle. Large-fruited trees such as apples and peaches are more likely to over-bear than small-fruited trees such as cherries are. When you prune, you reduce the problem by removing some of the fruit buds before they have a chance to bloom. But often you'll still need to remove some of the little green fruits when they are about the size of a jelly bean. Refer to the plant entries in Part 2 for specific thinning recommendations for individual crops.

Pruning Perennials and Shrubs

Pruning is a mix of art and science. It isn't difficult to do—just go slowly and think about the effect each cut will have on the plant. And relax: Plants recover from most mistakes.

Asparagus, strawberries, and rhubarb. Plants such as asparagus, strawberries, and rhubarb have perennial roots but annual tops. Cut off and clear away the dead asparagus and rhubarb tops during the winter. See the Strawberry entry for when and how to remove the spent tops.

Brambles. Bramble roots are perennial but the canes live for only two growing seasons. Each individual cane dies after bearing its summer crop of berries. After the first year, the patch will have a mix of fruiting canes and juvenile canes—so pruning brambles often involves selectively pruning the stand to remove the canes that have borne fruit and are going to die.

Fall, or everbearing, raspberries are the simplest brambles to prune. Most gardeners cut all of the canes off at ground level during the winter and harvest just the fall crop of berries. You can let the fall-fruiting canes overwinter and bear a second but much smaller crop of berries the next summer. If you choose the second option, prune them just like summer raspberries.

Prune summer red raspberries and blackberries the same way. Cut the fruit-bearing canes off at ground level in midsummer as soon as all of their berries have been picked. You can wait until the following winter, but it is harder to tell which canes to remove. You may also have more cane disease problems because the dying canes are weaker and more susceptible to invasion. During the winter, cut slender or bent canes off at ground level to leave two to four sturdy canes per foot of row. Avoid removing the tips of the canes, since that is where next summer's fruit is waiting. The illustration on page 140 shows a before-and-after pruning view of summer-bearing red raspberries in the winter.

Black raspberries need slightly more pruning than red raspberries. In the summer when the new canes are 2½ to 3 feet tall, pinch off the tips. This encourages lots of branches to grow, and gives you more berries next season. As with other brambles, cut out the fruited canes when the berries are finished. During the winter, trim back the side branches to 1 foot long. Cut out small or misshapen canes to leave six to nine sturdy canes per plant.

Blueberries. Shrubs such as blueberries need little pruning. Each winter, remove any branches growing close to the ground. After the plants are three to four years old, you'll also need to cut off some of the oldest branches at or near ground level to encourage new, fruitful branches to grow. See the individual plant entries in Part 2 for specific information.

Pruning Perennial Vines

Vines seem to be destined by nature to take over the world. They need lots of pruning to stay fruitful and a manageable size.

Cane pruning and spur pruning are the two basic pruning methods used for grapes. There are numerous variations—many endowed with mysterious names such as 'Four-Arm Kniffen', 'Geneva Double Curtain', and 'Modified Chautaugua'—but don't let that throw you; they all boil down to the two basic methods. Most grape cultivars can be pruned either way with good results. A few cultivars will be more productive with one or the other depending on where they tend to bear fruit. Check with your supplier for guidance.

First and second years. No matter how you plan to train your grapevine, the steps you take during the first and second years of growth are the same. The first summer, let your vine grow so it can develop a strong root system. That winter, choose the sturdiest shoot and cut off all of the others. Then cut the remaining shoot back to just two buds.

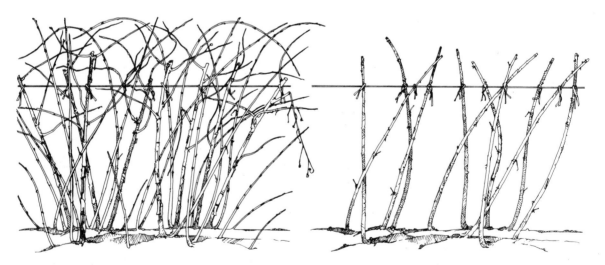

Prune summer-bearing raspberries in late winter or early spring. Cut off spent fruiting canes at ground level. Cut off skinny or crooked canes and canes outside the row. Thin remaining canes to two to four per foot of row. Don't cut off the cane tips unless they are winter-killed.

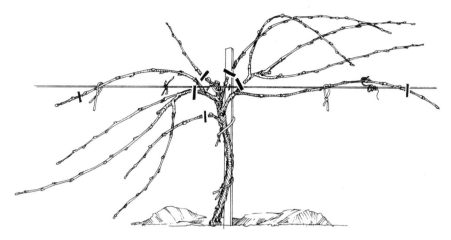

After three years of training, pruning cane-pruned vines involves select-ing new shoots for future growth and cutting back the fruiting canes to about ten buds.

The second summer, train the strongest shoot up a stake or string to a trellis, as shown in the illustrations on the opposite page. Pinch off the growing tip when it reaches the height you want the horizontal arms to be. This will stimulate branches to grow. The second winter, select two sturdy, pencil-size canes and firmly tie them to the trellis wire using twist ties or rot-resistant twine. Rub off buds to leave one every 4 to 5 inches, and shorten the canes to leave just ten buds on each. Remove all other canes.

Third year. The illustration above shows a vine after three growing seasons. Select a pencil-size shoot near the base of each of the previous season's canes or the main trunk and remove all other canes. Shorten the canes to ten buds and tie them to the trellis wire. Cane-pruned vines will be pruned this way every year from now on. You may want to leave a few more buds as the vines get older. Spur-pruned vines follow a different course of pruning be-ginning in the fourth year.

Fourth year. The illustration at right shows a spur-pruned vine after four growing seasons. Leave the canes you selected last win-ter tied to the trellis wires and shorten each shoot to two-bud spurs. Every year thereafter, select a pencil-size shoot near the base of each spur and remove the others. Then cut each back to leave two buds per spur.

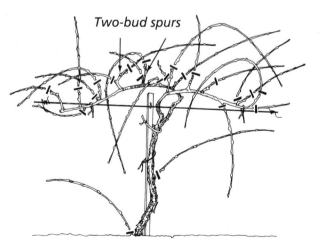

Two-bud spurs

Leave the main arms of a spur-pruned vine unpruned. Shorten shoots to a two-bud spur each winter.

Pruning Trees

Before you start to train your trees, it helps to understand what controls a tree's growth. Then you will know what effect each pruning cut you make or branch spreader you use will have on the tree.

How a tree works. Like a fast-growing teenager, a tree's growth is fueled and directed by hormones and food. But a tree's food comes from the sun, not mountains of groceries.

The controlling hormones (or growth reg-ulators) are made by the apical (or topmost) bud on each shoot or branch. The growth regulator signal travels down the shoot and prevents the undeveloped buds in the crotch of each leaf stem from growing into a side-shoot or a flower bud. The strength of the signal fades as it gets farther away, so side branches and fruit buds can start to grow to-ward the base of the shoot. If you cut off the apical bud, the "sleeping" buds below burst into growth. Eventually, the tip bud of the fastest-growing shoot becomes the new domi-nant apical bud. This control scheme is known as apical dominance.

The angle of the shoot also influences how strong the apical dominance signal is. If the shoot is pointing straight up, the signal is very strong. A strong signal makes the shoot grow fast, with long spaces between leaves and buds. A strong signal also makes for few

Unweighted branch

Nonfruitful area   *Fruitful area*

Weighted branch

Weight

The direction that a shoot grows in affects how fast and how far it grows. A shoot allowed to grow straight up will do so with a vengeance. Only a few branches will form near the base and few flower buds will develop. If that same shoot is weighted early in the growing season, it will be shorter and nearly every bud will grow into a branch or flower bud.

branches and little fruit. If the shoot is horizontal, the apical bud stops growing and the apical dominance signal is very weak. The undeveloped buds burst and grow into strong vertical shoots. This causes the formation of lots of branches but, again, little fruit. The best angle for fruit-bud development is somewhere between vertical and horizontal—between 45 and 60 degrees. In this range, branches grow slowly, some side branches can develop, and lots of fruit buds form. The illustrations on the opposite page show what will happen to the same shoot depending on what angle it is allowed to grow at.

Working with your tree. Now that you know how the tree regulates its own growth, let's look at what you can do to work with it. The best first step you can take is to change the angle of the branches to promote good tree form. See "Spreading Fruit Tree Branches" on page 136 for ways to do so.

You'll probably also have to do some pruning to get the best possible trees. When you prune, you cut off a shoot or branch either at the base or somewhere in the middle. If you cut at the base of a shoot, you've made a thinning cut. A thinning cut removes an entire shoot where it meets the trunk or a larger branch. This type of cut doesn't upset the apical dominance much and has less effect on the "sleeping" buds near the cut.

A cut made in the middle of a shoot is a heading cut. A heading cut removes the source of the apical dominance signal for that shoot. Once that signal is removed, the "sleeping" buds below the cut burst into life and grow

Thinning cuts

Heading cuts

A thinning cut (*left*) removes an entire twig or branch and causes limited regrowth. Thinning cuts are good for shaping a tree or opening it up to light and air. A heading cut (*right*) removes only part of a twig or branch. Regrowth is extensive as many of the buds just below the cut wake up and grow. Heading cuts are a good way to stimulate sideshoot development.

THE SEASON OF PRUNING

One outdated pruning rule is that fruit trees can be pruned only in the dormant season. Fruit and nut trees can be pruned in both winter and summer, and understanding the benefits and effects of winter and summer pruning expands your options.

Dormant or Winter Pruning

Dormant pruning is done in late winter or very early spring, before flowers or leaves open. Delayed dormant pruning is done while the flowers are open or just fading. Both types of dormant pruning stimulate the growth of new vegetative shoots.

Here are the best uses of dormant or delayed-dormant pruning.

Encouraging vigorous growth. Use heading cuts on young trees to stimulate branching and fill out the canopy. This helps in establishing a strong tree framework.

Forcing new branches. To stimulate the growth of new, fruitful branches on older trees, head back a limb or trunk to a point just above where you want a new branch.

Summer Pruning

Summer pruning does not make trees "bleed" to death. Cuts made on actively growing trees actually callus over faster than cuts made during the dormant season do. The callus tissue not only resists sprouting new shoots the following spring but also protects the tree from invading diseases.

Judicious summer pruning has a somewhat dwarfing effect. It also increases flower-bud development by opening up the canopy and letting the sunlight in.

Summer-prune after the initial flurry of spring growth. Early to mid-summer pruning is more dwarfing; mid- to late-summer pruning is less dwarfing. Don't prune after late August or early September if you get cold winters, or the new growth may be killed back by severe cold.

Here are the things that summer pruning is best for.

Thinning out crowded branches. To do so, remove the top shoot of narrow-angled, double shoots.

Removing watersprouts. Thin out long, vertical shoots, sometimes called watersprouts, in midsummer. Weight the remaining shoots to slow them down and make them branch.

Removing suckers. Suckers grow from the roots or trunk base. Rub them off when you see them. Check in midsummer and cut them off flush to the trunk. If they're growing out of the soil, yank them out or dig down and cut them off of the root.

Reclaiming abandoned trees. Thin out one-third of the excess growth per season over three years. Use dormant pruning to stimulate new growth, if needed. Weight well-placed watersprouts to slow them down and turn them into branches.

into a bunch of vigorous sideshoots. Heading and thinning cuts are illustrated on page 143.

No matter which type of cut you make, use a clean, sharp pair of pruners or pruning saw. Bypass pruners make a cleaner cut than anvil pruners that crush the wood next to the cut. Prune on a dry day to help minimize the chance of infection.

Pruning at planting time. If your new tree already has well-spaced side branches, you may choose to preserve them. Otherwise, prune back the trunk to just above where you want the lowest branches to be. Between 2 and 3 feet is usually recommended. There is no horticultural law that says you can't have the bottom branches lower or higher than that, however. See "Nonstandard Trees" on this page for two other options.

Pruning for shape and fruit. When you plant a new tree, your job for the first few years is to select and shape the major branches that will remain for the tree's entire life. Once the basic framework is in place, you'll work on encouraging fruit production and maintaining the shape of the tree.

Remember to spread your tree's branches to achieve the desired shape before you resort to pruning. Many fruit trees will still need a good deal of pruning even after spreading. Nut trees, in general, need less. You'll find guidelines for specific types of trees in the plant entries in Part 2.

There are two basic pruning shapes for fruit trees: open center and central leader. There are also slight modifications of each style referred to as delayed open center and modified central leader. The plant entries in Part 2 recommend which shape to use for each type of fruit tree.

NONSTANDARD TREES

If you're daring, you may want to experiment with these alternatives to conventional pruning. These techniques are somewhat experimental, so be prepared to have a less than 100 percent success rate.

Bush Trees

If you cover the ground underneath your tree with permanent mulch, you won't need to cultivate or mow under it. So why not make the tree double as the mulch cover? To do so, at planting, cut the trunk off about 6 to 12 inches above the graft. This will stimulate side branching close to ground level.

Bush trees are stronger and more wind-resistant than conventional trees. It's also easy to harvest fruit from these short plants. Bush trees are not a good choice if you have problems with summer humidity and disease, slugs, or animal pests.

Tall Trees

Fruit trees make fine shade trees if you prune the tree so that the first branches are high enough to walk under. Taller trees may also escape deer damage or low-lying frost. To make an elevated fruit tree, cut off any branches that your newly planted tree may have. Rub off any side branches that form until the young trunk is as tall as you need it to be. Just remember that you'll need to spend time on a ladder to care for the tree and pick the fruit if you prune this way.

Open center. Open center trees are shaped like a vase. Use open center training for stone fruits such as peaches that bear fruit on one-year-old wood; you can train full-size apples and pears this way. Pruning tasks are divided between winter and summer during the first three to four years of the tree's life. After that, you'll do the majority of the pruning in the summer unless you need to stimulate new sideshoots.

Follow these four steps to form an open center tree:

1. Cut the main trunk of the newly planted tree back to 2 to 2½ feet and head back any side branches by one-third to one-half of their length.

Step 1

2. During the growing season, when the new growth reaches 1 to 1½ feet long, choose four main branches that emerge in different directions and are separated along the trunk by about 4 to 8 inches. Cut off all other branches and cut off the main trunk just above the top branch. You may choose to leave the main trunk for an extra season to let it shade the center of the tree—if you do, you'll be making a delayed open center tree. Shorten branches by about one-third of their length to encourage branching. Spread branches as needed. See the illustration on page 137 for ideas.

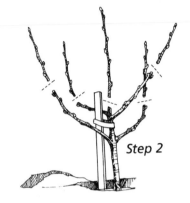

Step 2

3. In the third and fourth years, use late-winter or early-spring heading cuts to encourage plenty of smaller side branches. Use a limited number of summer thinning cuts to help shape the framework of the tree.

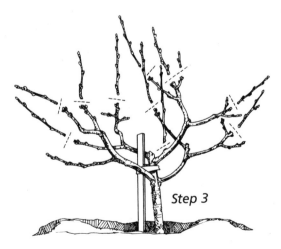

Step 3

4. From the fifth year on, prune in late winter. For fruits such as peaches, thin out about half of the branches by about half of their total length. This will encourage younger wood to take their place. Use winter pruning for apples only if you need to stimulate new growth and head back no more than one-quarter of the branches per year. Use summer thinning cuts to remove overly crowded or short and weak branches.

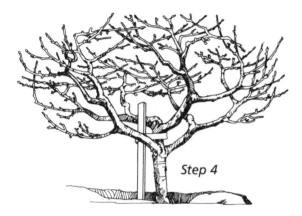

Step 4

Central leader. Central leader trees are shaped much like Christmas trees. Trees such as semidwarf apples and pears are trained by this method. Pruning tasks are divided between winter and summer during the first three to five years of the tree's life. After that, you'll do the majority of the pruning in the summer.

Follow these five steps to form a central leader tree:

1. Cut the main trunk of the newly planted tree back to 2 to 2½ feet and head back any side branches by one-third to one-half their length.

Step 1

2. During the growing season, when the new growth reaches 1 to 1½ feet, choose three or four main branches that emerge in different directions and are separated along the trunk by about 4 to 8 inches. Cut off all other branches. Leave the central leader (main trunk) alone. Spread branches as needed. See the illustration on page 137 for ideas.

Step 2

3. The next winter or early spring, use thinning cuts to remove any new shoots that are growing at a narrow angle and competing with the central leader. Also remove or weight any vertical side branches. Head back each branch tip by one-third to one-half to encourage side branch formation. If the central leader is very tall, you may choose to make a modified central leader tree by heading back the

leader by one-third to one-half.

When the new growth is 1 to 1½ feet long that growing season, choose another "layer" of three or four main branches about 1½ feet above the previous branches and cut off any other new branches. The main branches should be placed in a spiral pattern up the trunk so each will be in full sun.

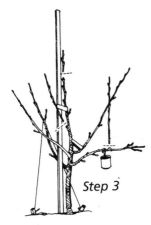

Step 3

4. Repeat Step 3 for the following few years. Each summer, your effort will focus on choosing and spreading the newest layer of main branches. If you did your job last year, the older layers will already be positioned for good fruiting.

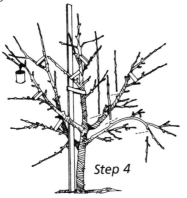

Step 4

5. Once the main shape of the tree is complete, usually after four or five years or so, use summer thinning cuts to keep the tree open to the air and sunshine. Remove dead wood and remove or weight vertical shoots at any time during the year. Once the tree starts to bear, the fruit will weigh the branches down for you, causing more fruiting. Use thinning cuts to remove the nose-diving branch tips if they get shaded. Use winter pruning only if you want to force new branches to fill an empty spot in the tree.

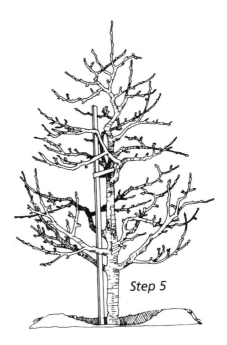

Step 5

A final note on pruning. With a little patience and care, you can prune your tree like an expert. Walk around the tree as you work to get a better view. Envision how it will look without that branch *before* cutting it. And remember: Trees are very forgiving.

6 PREVENTING AND CONTROLLING PROBLEMS

Minimizing Problems with Weeds, Diseases, Insects, and Animals

When it comes to your own health, the old saying "An ounce of prevention is worth a pound of cure" rings true. If you eat right, drink lots of fluids, and generally take care of yourself, you can avoid getting sick.

The same is true for your garden's health: It's easier to provide your garden with the conditions it needs to be healthy than it is to rescue it once it is in the clutches of a problem. For example, you can either eliminate weed seedlings early in the season or ignore them until you have trouble finding the rows of vegetables in the sea of weeds. You can hang one trap early in the season and catch adult insect pests, or you can let them reproduce, leaving you to face hoards of plant-chewing larvae later in the season.

In the real world of gardening, most of us fall somewhere between the above examples. We pull weeds, but maybe not as early as we should. We try to prevent pest problems, but we don't always know how or we might not get to it as soon as we should.

In this chapter, you'll learn how you can use a system called Organic Pest Management (OPM) to organize your preventive fight against garden pests. You'll learn about building pest-preventing practices into your garden planning, soil preparation, planting, and routine garden care. You'll also find specific information on how and when to use safe, organic preventive controls such as insect traps and barriers. Throughout the chapter, look for the "On Target" features, which give quick tips for applying principles to specific types of problem prevention, as well as short, specific examples that illustrate OPM principles.

As your understanding of the principles of OPM increases, and you build your repertoire of specific techniques, you'll find that worrying about pests takes less and less of your gardening time. To help you build a base of knowledge and to help when you need to troubleshoot a problem, we've included quick-reference tables, beginning on page 175. They identify the most common insects and diseases that damage fruits and vegetables, and they tell you how to prevent and control them.

INTRODUCING OPM

Organic Pest Management (OPM) involves making a plan of action that includes organic soil building, proper plant care, and preventive controls. The key word here is management. You need to see the big picture. You're not trying to destroy every creeping, crawling, sliming, or flying creature in your garden or orchard. Instead, OPM emphasizes creating a diverse natural system where pest problems are regulated naturally. In fact, you'll find that your best ally in the garden is nature itself.

When you use an OPM approach, you rely heavily on cultural controls—steps you can take as you plant and care for your garden that make it less hospitable to pests. These include things like choosing cultivars resistant to diseases that are prevalent in your area, cleaning diseased or insect-infected plants out of your garden, and rotating crops.

You'll also take advantage of ingenious barriers and traps that keep pests away from your plants. These range from an old-fashioned garden fence to new-on-the-market pheromone mating disrupters.

With OPM, pesticidal sprays, even organically acceptable ones like rotenone or insecticidal soap, become your last resort. You'll use them mainly when a pest threatens to damage your crop so severely that if you don't spray, you will have to sacrifice your harvest.

Applying OPM in Your Garden

You're probably wondering how you can make a preventive approach to pest control a reality. You do it by translating the concepts of OPM into specific actions that make sense for your garden. Here's an overview of the steps to take:

1. Find out what pest problems are common in your area. Your four areas of concern are weeds, diseases, insects (and other small pests like slugs and mites that aren't insects), and animals. If you've been gardening for a while in one area, you can probably write up a common pest list based on your own experience. If you're new to gardening or new to your area, talk to other gardeners in your neighborhood. Ask about their most common garden problems and how they deal with them organically. For information on pests common to your area, consult your nearest Cooperative Extension Service office. While extension offices aren't always fully informed about organically acceptable pest controls, they are the best source of information on soils, local conditions, and recommended cultivars.

2. Gather information on pest prevention. Once you have a list of specific pests and problems, take some time to learn about how to prevent them. Information—not insecticides—is your best weapon against pests. Many of the plant entries in Part 2 have a section called "Problem Prevention" that lists specific tactics for specific crops. You can also refer to the tables "Troubleshooting Plant Nutrient Deficiencies" (page 175), "Troubleshooting Fruit and Vegetable Diseases" (page 178), and "Troubleshooting Fruit and Vegetable Pests" (page 182) for problem-specific prevention and control suggestions.

In the case of insects and diseases, it's helpful to learn about a pest's life cycle. From that, you can determine its weaknesses and figure out how to exploit them. For example, apple maggot flies have to lay eggs on young apples so that the larvae have a food source when they hatch. If you hang apple-size red balls coated with a sticky substance in your apple trees, you'll trick most of the moths into landing there to lay eggs. Once there, they stick and die, and no apple maggots tunnel into your apples. You'll find names of some in-depth references on insect and disease pests in "Recommended Reading," beginning on page 511.

3. Make a list of supplies you need. For example, if you want to make apple maggot traps, you'll need red balls (or balls and red paint), sticky coating, and a paintbrush. Many of the supplies you need aren't easily available from garden centers. You'll have to do some mail-order shopping from businesses that stock organic gardening supplies. You'll find several companies listed in "Sources," beginning on page 507.

4. Start a crop rotation system in the vegetable garden. You may think that crop rotation is too much trouble to bother with. But crop rotation is a cornerstone of an OPM plan. Over time, your soil quality will be better if you rotate crops. Better soil means healthier crops, and strong plants are more resistant to attack by insects and diseases, and they compete better with weeds.

Also, rotation disrupts weed, insect, and disease cycles. If you grow tomatoes year after year in the same spot, the pests that feed on them and the disease organisms that infect them have a constant supply of what they need. But if you mix up the types of crops you plant in any given bed, it's harder for the pests to find their host. The number of pests that survive from year to year to trouble your crops will be fewer. For details on how to rotate crops, refer to "Garden Rotations" on page 73.

5. Put reminders on your calendar. You may not be used to thinking about pests when there's not a pest in sight. If you're going to plant cabbage and broccoli transplants, are you anticipating nocturnal raids by slugs or cutworms? If so, write down "Cutworm collars!" and "Slug traps!" on your calendar next to your projected planting dates. Throughout the season, make similar notes concerning various pest problems.

6. Keep an eye on your garden. Inevitably, some problems will develop in your garden. The sooner you spot them, the more likely you'll be to have time to remedy them. For example, most plant diseases can't be "cured." If you find a plant or two that looks sickly, chances are you should pull it up and throw it away before the infection spreads to the rest of the crop.

7. When problems occur, remember that pesticides are your last resort. Crops can withstand a surprising amount of damage and still produce a harvest. And some pest damage is mostly cosmetic. Don't make a hasty decision to spray. Even organically acceptable pesticides can have some harmful side effects on people who come in contact with them or on beneficial organisms that live in and around your plants.

PREVENTION PAYS

The lion's share of successful Organic Pest Management (OPM) is simply good, old-fashioned common sense and good housekeeping. In formal terms, this aspect of OPM is called using cultural controls. In plain terms, it means "Take good care of your soil and plants, and your garden will be healthier and have fewer problems with insects, diseases, and weeds."

Selecting Plants

You can prevent or reduce many pest problems by selecting crops that are suited to your local growing conditions. Whenever possible, select cultivars that are resistant to severe problems that are common in your area. If no resistant cultivars are available, you'll have to decide whether to risk problems or plant a different crop instead. And, of course, make sure the actual plants and seeds you buy are vigorous and pest-free.

Built-In Resistance

Plants vary in their ability to resist or tolerate harsh growing conditions, pests, and diseases. Some cultivars do well over a wide range of conditions. One indicator of such cultivars is the All-America Selections (AAS) shield on a seed packet. Cultivars are evaluated in test gardens all over the country, and the best cultivars are selected as AAS winners.

Another way to choose cultivars that will do well in your area, although not necessarily nationwide, is to select them from small seed companies and nurseries that specialize in cultivars that are adapted to your local growing conditions.

Sometimes it's easy to tell from catalog descriptions whether a cultivar is resistant to a particular problem. For example, tomato cultivars with a VF after their name are resistant to Verticillium (V) and Fusarium (F) wilt.

More often, however, you'll need to read between the lines to evaluate resistance. For example, how can you tell which corn cultivars are more resistant to damage by birds? Cultivars with tight husks are less attractive to birds than ones that gap open and show the end of the ear. Once you know this, you can

---

➥ ON TARGET

BUYING PLANTS WITH BUILT-IN RESISTANCE

Here are a few examples of how you can use built-in resistance to battle specific types of problems.

Weeds. Choose vigorous, fast-growing crops if you have a weedy site. Plant transplants whenever possible, and skip slow-to-start crops like carrots.

Diseases. Choose cultivars that resist the problem disease or choose cultivars that don't appeal to the insect that spreads the disease. Plant Verticillium-resistant tomatoes.

Insects and tiny pests. Choose plants or cultivars that are less attractive to problem pests. Silver-leaved squashes are less attractive to aphids than green-leaved ones are.

Animals. Avoid planting crops that you'll need an armed guard to protect. Plant yellow cherries instead of red to deter thieving birds.

---

look for cultivars described as having tight husks or good husk cover.

Buyer Beware

One infected or infested plant can spread a problem to many other plants in your garden. Here are four things to keep in mind when acquiring new plants:

1. Select healthy-looking plants. If in doubt, don't buy it. See the illustration on page 13 for more information on how to select healthy transplants.

2. Inspect gift plants with equal care. Graciously decline or discreetly dispose of suspicious gift plants.

3. Buy certified disease-free plants and seeds from reputable distributors whenever possible.

4. Don't fall for unbelievably cheap deals. It really is true that you get what you pay for.

Improving Your Site

Even the healthiest, most problem-resistant plants will languish and die if they are planted in an unfavorable environment. Your choice of a site and how you choose to develop that site are critical to your gardening success.

> **ON TARGET**
>
> **BUYING HEALTHY PLANTS**
>
> Here are a few examples of how you can use careful shopping to avoid specific types of problems.
>
> **Weeds.** Avoid buying weeds or weed seeds with your plants or seeds. When you buy container stock, avoid plants in very weedy containers; bare-root stock won't carry weeds or weed seeds. Look for vegetable seeds that are certified to be weed-free.
>
> **Diseases.** Avoid plants that are diseased or even sickly looking. Watch for clues such as white mold or blotches on leaves, missing leaves, withered branches, and lesions or abnormal tissue on stems.
>
> **Insects and tiny pests.** Avoid plants that show signs of insect damage. These may include holes in leaves, tiny dots on leaves, insect eggs, or borer holes.

A successful food gardening site has full or almost full sun, good drainage, and sufficient water. The better the site you choose, the fewer problems you will have to deal with later. "Selecting the Best Site" on pages 6 and 7 describes the factors you should consider when selecting a site.

You can also take steps to make the site you choose less inviting to pests and more inviting to the insects and other creatures that eat garden pests. Begin by planting a wide variety of crops. Choose more than one cultivar of each major crop if you can. Mix different types of plants together rather than grouping all of the lettuces in one bed and all of the onions in another, for example. Mixed groupings of crops slow down pests because it literally takes the pests longer to find their favored host. For more ideas on attracting beneficial insects to your garden, see the illustration on page 154.

Plants that attract and provide homes and food for beneficial insects include sage, nasturtium, hyssop, mint, lemon balm, tansy, chamomile, tarragon, thyme, savory, and borage. Even patches of weeds can provide homes for beneficials. Just be sure to remove them before they set seed. Odoriferous plants such as garlic and marigolds may actually repel some insect pests.

You can increase the beneficial insect population in your garden still further by using commercial lures or by releasing purchased insects. See "Hiring Garden Helpers" on page 157 for more details. And don't forget to encourage the larger beneficial creatures such as birds and toads. Bats, spiders, and snakes also eat pests. The best thing you can do for these creatures is provide food, water, and a safe place for them to raise families. Here's how.

Bats. Buy or make wooden bat houses as shown in the illustration on the opposite page. Mount it on the east or southeast side of a building 15 to 20 feet off the ground.

Birds. Put out a variety of styles of bird feeders, and also let your garden feed the birds. Grow sunflowers, wheat, or millet for them, and let late-maturing vegetables go to seed. Put out a birdbath and bird houses.

Snakes. It's your choice whether you feel

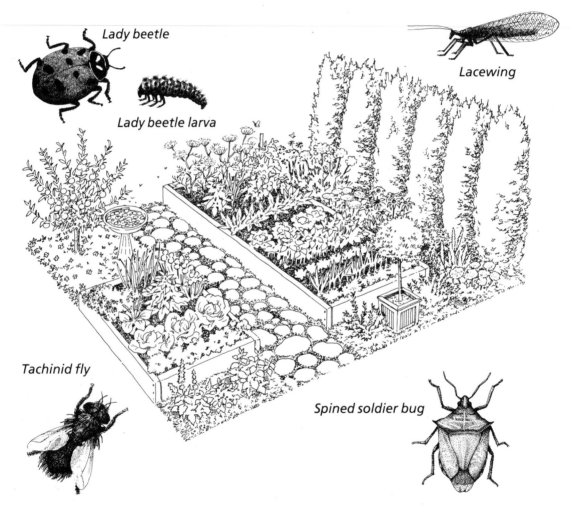

Lady beetle

Lacewing

Lady beetle larva

Tachinid fly

Spined soldier bug

To attract tachinid flies and lady beetles, plant small-flowered herbs and flowers and let some weeds grow in and around your food garden. Delicate lacewings can drink from a "bug bath" made from a birdbath filled with stones, which serve as landing sites for the tiny insects. Spined soldier bugs will take cover among herbs and perennials; permanent pathways and mulched areas also provide shelter for some types of beneficials.

comfortable having snakes around your yard. Keep in mind that snakes don't seek people out to bite (most only bite if they are handled or stepped on); their prey is generally insects and rodents. Snakes will take cover under mulch or under piles of wood or brush, so if you don't want them around, keep your yard tidy.

Spiders. One of the best ways to attract pest-catching spiders to your garden is to lay coarse mulch, such as straw, around your plants. Many people fear spiders, but keep in mind that of all the species of spiders in the United States, only two (the black widow and the brown recluse) have enough venom to cause serious harm to humans.

Toads. Make a toad house by digging a shallow depression in the garden and covering it loosely with boards. Or break a small "doorway" in the side of a clay flowerpot, and set it upside down in the garden. Place a plant

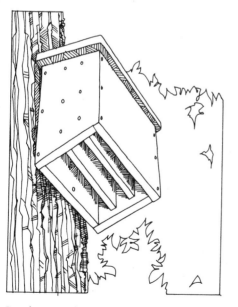

Bat houses have an entrance at the bottom and interior vertical partitions where the bats can roost.

saucer at ground level and fill it with water for your toad friends. Locate the saucer near rocks or plants so the toad can get cover.

Providing Optimum Care

Your goal as an organic food gardener should be to provide the best possible conditions for your plants. Give them every advantage by providing plenty of food, water, and sunlight. Perfect plant care starts with treating your soil with tender loving care.

Soil care. The success or failure of your organic food garden may depend more upon how you take care of your soil than any other single factor. Chapter 2 describes how to evaluate, enrich, and prepare your soil. Work to improve your soil every year. Keep in mind that tilling and planting cover crops the year before you plan to plant will help reduce subsequent weed problems. Also, solarizing the soil by covering a dormant seedbed with plastic sheeting the year before planting is an effective weed-preventing technique. (For step-by-step soil solarization instructions, see "Soil Solarization" on page 176.)

Planting. Planting is one of the gardener's most critical jobs in the garden season. Planting correctly gets your plants off to the best possible start. Review planting guidelines for seeds, bulbs, tubers, and perennial trees and shrubs in Chapter 4 before you plant. Try putting some damage-preventing measures in place at planting time. For example, cover rows of seeds or transplants with floating row cover to keep out insects that attack delicate seedlings or that spread disease organisms as they feed. Put rabbit guards around fruit tree trunks to prevent damage by rabbits, mice, and other chewing animals.

Seasonal care. Preventing water and nutrient stress during the growing season not only will boost your eventual yields but also will prevent pests from getting a foothold on your plants. You've probably seen a weak plant quickly succumb to insect damage or disease while healthier plants nearby continue to grow despite some insect feeding or disease symptoms. See Chapter 5 for complete instructions on knowing when and how to water and feed your plants to keep them growing strongly. Foliar feeding plants with kelp or compost tea is one step you can take to keep your plants extra-healthy and possibly confer some disease resistance.

Harvesting. Once you've gotten your crops through the season, don't let careless harvesting ruin your bounty. A little bruise or cut can seriously shorten the storage life of apples, potatoes, and many other crops. Overmature crops will also spoil more quickly than crops picked on time. See Chapter 7 and the plant entries in Part 2 for more information on how and when to harvest. Take the time to separate damaged produce from your harvest, and quickly use it fresh.

Dormant-season care. What you do in preparation for the dormant season sets the groundwork for the problem-free growing season to follow. You should clean your garden and store garden tools as thoroughly as if you were tidying up your kitchen after a big meal. Refer to your records of the season that has just passed, review any problems, and plan ahead so that they are not repeated the following season. See "Garden Cleanup" on page 207 for a full listing of important chores to close the growing season. The off-season is also the time for pruning and training many perennial crops to improve next season's fruit. You'll find pruning and training directions in "Training 101" on page 131. You'll also find specific suggestions for dormant-season care and pruning of specific plants in the plant entries in Part 2.

FIGHTING THE KNOWN ENEMIES

Being the best gardener you can be is a critical first step in preventing problems; your second step is to be an informed and prepared gardener. As an organic pest manager, it's important to learn about the specific insects and diseases that may attack the crops you grow. Many effective organic controls are preventives—they work well if you do them before the problems occur but not as well once the problem is happening. So pest control involves planning ahead for problems that you can make an educated guess you'll get. For example, if Mexican bean beetles devoured your young bean plants last season, chances are they'll be back this season, and in larger numbers. Don't just wait for them to show up. You can order spined soldier bugs and release them in your garden, or if your planting is small, cover your plants securely with floating row cover to keep the bean beetles out.

Here is the three-step process for dealing with whatever enemies have set up camp in your garden:

1. Identify your competition. If you're new to gardening or are gardening in a new area, talk with your neighbors and other gardeners from around your area. Join a local garden club. Read the gardening column in your local newspaper. Pick the brains and bookshelves at your local Cooperative Extension Service office.

Keep the long term in mind, too. Buy a notebook and keep a diary about events in and around your garden. You might record soil temperature, weather, and what plants are budding or flowering when you see the first bean beetle or plum curculio scar. Write down what insects or diseases hit each plant or at least what they look like. These notes will help you remember problems in following years when you're making garden plans.

2. Find the weaknesses. Now that you've identified some of the common problems you may encounter, do a little detective work on each one. Write the name and description of each pest or problem on a 5 × 7-inch index card and list what plant or plants you find it on. Also note when it first appeared.

Now see what you can find out about each pest or problem and write it all down on its card. Learn the pests' life cycles, where they hang out, their strengths and their vulnerable times, and their likes and dislikes. Write down what controls are effective and when they need to be done. This chapter is a good place to start finding this information. The more you learn the better. Because everything you learn can—and will—be used against them.

3. Develop a plan. Once you have identified your plants' particular problems and discovered their weaknesses, you can plan effective strategies to short-circuit them. Write your plan down and try it next season. Record your results and fine-tune the plan. Your plan will include a mix of strategies. Some will be aimed at only one pest—such as using cutworm collars to stop cutworms. Others, such as applying floating row cover, will help prevent several pest problems in one step.

Hiring Garden Helpers

There are multitudes of helpers waiting to pitch in for you in the garden, and all they ask in exchange is room and board. These include beneficial microorganisms, beneficial nematodes, beneficial insects, and beneficial animals. You'll want to take steps to make your garden attractive to these creatures, and you may actually want to buy and release specific garden helpers.

Beneficial Microorganisms

Beneficial bacteria, fungi, viruses, and other microorganisms can work wonders for you. Some make pests sick or outcompete pest microorganisms. You'll find details on them in "Biological Controls" on page 167.

Other microorganisms help out by enhancing plant growth. Soil microorganisms work to process organic matter into nutrients that your plants need. See "Living Organisms" on page 23 for more information. One important commercial product is nitrogen-fixing bacteria to inoculate legumes to promote better growth and increased nitrogen fixation.

Beneficial Nematodes

Nematodes are microscopic worms. They are so small that they can swim freely in the film of moisture surrounding soil particles and plant roots. The name may bring horrible thoughts of root knot nematode damage to your mind. However, the majority of nematodes actually help gardeners. Some of them feed on the harmful nematodes that attack plants. Others parasitize pest insect larvae.

Beneficial nematodes are available commercially. They control hundreds of soil-dwelling pests including cutworms, onion maggots, and the soil-dwelling stage of many other pests. Apply according to label instructions. Beneficial nematodes can also be syringed into borer holes or the tips of corn ears to control munching larvae there.

➡ ON TARGET

HIRING GARDEN HELPERS

Here are a few examples of how you can use garden helpers to battle specific types of problems.

Diseases. Beneficial insects and animals can help to control the insect vectors that transmit diseases.

Insects and tiny pests. Many beneficial animals and insects eat pest insects and other small pests. In unsprayed fruit tree plantings, predatory mites usually provide all of the control needed for pest mites.

Animals. Cats and snakes eat mice and voles, while dogs repel deer.

Beneficial Insects

You may have heard that the only good bug is a dead bug, but it's not true. Many insects are neutral, and quite a few actually *help* gardeners. Beneficial insects fight pest insects for you. Some are native to your garden and need only be encouraged. Others can be purchased and released to fight specific pests. See "Improving Your Site" on page 153 for general ways to encourage and attract beneficial insects.

You may also want to buy and release beneficial insects to combat specific pest problems. There are several species of beneficial insects available through mail-order catalogs. Some are more effective than others for controlling pests in home gardens. Some are effective only in greenhouses or when released on a community-wide basis. Here are some that are effective when released in home gardens:

• Aphid midge larvae attack aphids and suck out their body fluids. You can buy the cocoons and spread them around your garden.

• Lacewing larvae prey on a range of insect pests, including aphids and scales. You can buy lacewing eggs and scatter them about your garden.

• Mealybug destroyer adults and larvae eat mealybugs on citrus and grapes.

Beneficial Birds and Animals

While gardeners have little control over wild animals, many can be beneficial in the garden. See "Improving Your Site" on page 153 for ways to attract and encourage pest-eating birds, bats, toads, and other wild animals. You can also hire domesticated creatures to help you fight weeds, insects, and animal pests. Your cat may be a rodent-catcher extraordinaire, and the mere presence of a dog may make many furry critters look for their dinner elsewhere.

If you keep poultry, you can get double duty out of your two-legged friends while they earn their own snacks. Chickens like to eat insects, and while they scratch too much to be loose in a vegetable garden, they do well in runs or under fruit trees. You can also buy breeds of geese that will eat weeds, but they need to be carefully managed, or they may eat your crops, too.

Hands-Off Tactics

What's the best way to keep pests from feasting on the fruits of your labor? Trick them or trap them! Scare them or shock them! Or just slam the door in their faces. Here are some specific strategies.

Pheromones

When a female insect is ready to mate, she emits a species-specific chemical signal to tell potential mates where she is. Males of the same species can detect these pheromones from great distances and use them to home in on the female. Gardeners can take advantage of this system by flooding their gardens with specific pest pheromones. The males will wander about in confusion and never locate females. Since frustrated females lay no eggs, that leaves plants free from munching offspring. This is known as mating disruption.

Mating disruption products are available for codling moths, grape berry moths, and other pests. To use them, twist the pheromone dispensers, which look like plastic twist ties, onto trees just as the buds swell in the spring. The technology is recommended for a minimum of 5 acres but is worth trying for smaller areas. Try applying lures over a wider area than your trees fill.

Pheromones are also used to bait traps. See "Pheromone Traps" on page 167 for information on pheromone-baited traps.

Repellents

Offend a pest's senses (taste, smell, sight, hearing, and touch) and they will make themselves scarce. Scare them by imitating their predators and they'll leave even faster. Here are some ideas.

Smells and tastes. Insects and animals have flavor likes and dislikes just as we do. If you make a plant taste or smell like something yucky, the moochers will munch elsewhere. Use commercial repellents or experiment with making your own. Smells that say "Danger! Predator alert!" will make animals skedaddle. You can buy things like fox urine concentrate or rely on domestic predator scents such as dog, cat, and human. Red pepper, garlic, and other aromatic herbs repel various insects and animals. See "Make Your Own: Pesticides" on page 172 for sample recipes. Also see "Make Your Own: Repellents" on this page for bad-tasting and smelly things to try.

Sights and sounds. Sights and sounds work best when they are intermittent and move around from place to place. Birds and animals quickly learn to ignore things that stay the same. You can buy shiny balloons and streamers or fake snakes, hawks, and owls; or you can make your own scare devices to frighten birds and make them think their worst enemy is about to gobble them up. Whatever you use, put them out just before you expect problems, and move them from place to place at least every two days.

Aluminum foil mulch confuses aphids: Evidently they can't tell which way is up to the sky and which way is down to dinner. Use it under susceptible crops to prevent invaders.

Touch. If you have problems with crop-nabbing birds, try smearing potential roosts with sticky coating. It won't hurt the birds, and it can keep them from eating your harvest.

Barriers

If you don't want someone to come into your house, you close the door. Give nonflying garden pests the same treatment. Build a continuous, pest-proof wall around your garden or plant and they just won't be able to get in.

Barriers and fences range from a band of diatomaceous earth to a 6-foot-high fence of welded wire. Here are some of your barrier options.

Scratchy bands. You can ward off soft-bellied, creeping critters like slugs and snails

---

✦ Make Your Own ✦

REPELLENTS

Keep animal pests and insect pests at bay with these evil-smelling and bad-tasting tricks.

Tastes and Smells

Soap—the cheapest, smelliest deodorant soap you can buy—is a good animal repellent. Drill holes through bars (wrapper and all) and hang them at about chest height every 5 to 10 feet around your garden.

Human hair (get it from a barber), dog and cat droppings, or used cat litter can be put in small bags and hung around your garden, too. Walk your dog and encourage him to mark his territory. Or use a squirt bottle full of human urine to mark it yourself.

Make your own anti-deer spray by mixing 1 egg per quart of water. Spray plants liberally and repeat after rain.

Sights and Sounds

Aluminum pie pans and shiny pinwheels help repel birds. Hang them from stakes so they flash in the breeze and relocate them every day or two so birds won't get used to them.

Discourage nocturnal visitors by leaving a radio or some blinking lights on at night in the garden. Better still, use a motion detector to switch them on when anything approaches.

Strawberry-pecking birds may get disgusted and go elsewhere if you paint some strawberry-size rocks red and sprinkle them around your patch just before the real berries get ripe.

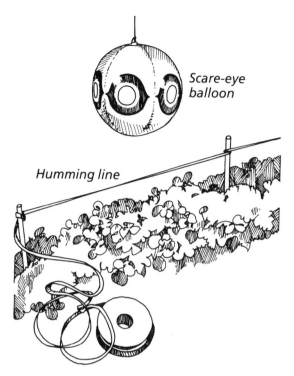

Scare-eye balloon

Humming line

Scare-eye balloons startle birds because the shape on the balloon resembles the eyes of birds of prey. A humming line made of very thin nylon, strung in a garden, makes a humming noise heard by birds but not humans.

by spreading a band of wood ashes, diatomaceous earth, talc, lime, or crushed eggshells around plants or garden beds. The sharp dusts scratch insects and cause them to die of dehydration.

Tree bands. Tree bands are effective repellents against snails, slugs, ants, gypsy moth caterpillars, and other pests that can't fly. Wrap a 15-inch-wide piece of burlap around a tree trunk, tie it in the middle with string, and then fold the top of it down over the string. You can also buy slippery tape and wrap it around tree trunks—

crawling insects can't get a foothold on it.

Cutworm collars. Cardboard tubes placed around plant stems ward off cutworms. Cut a $2\frac{1}{2} \times 8$-inch strip of lightweight cardboard, overlap the short ends to form a circle, and staple or tape it. Slip the collar over a transplant and press it 1 inch into the soil.

Copper strips. For an excellent permanent barrier against slugs and snails, fasten strips of copper sheet metal around the edges of garden beds or the legs of greenhouse benches, as shown in the illustration on page 162.

➨ ON TARGET

USING HANDS-OFF TACTICS

Here are a few examples of how you can use barriers or repellents to battle specific types of problems.

Weeds. Black plastic mulch or a heavy layer of organic mulch can block sunlight from young weeds, killing them off before they become a problem.

Diseases. Antitranspirants can help prevent infection by forming a thick barrier on leaves. Row covers keep out disease-carrying insects.

Insects and tiny pests. Floating row cover keeps a wide variety of insect pests away from your plants. You can also custom-design barriers like tar-paper squares to keep cabbage root flies from laying eggs at the base of cabbage-family plants.

Animals. Fencing and repellents are the best recourse for keeping animal pests away from your crops. Using repellents is faster and cheaper, but erecting a fence is a more permanent and effective measure.

Aboveground fences. When using welded or so-called woven wire fencing, be sure to get the kind with wires closer together in the bottom half of the fence to discourage smaller animals from crawling through the fence. Chicken wire also works well. Climbing raccoons can be stopped by leaving the top foot of wire unattached. When they reach the unattached portion, their weight will pull the fence back and they will drop back to the ground outside of your garden.

Underground fences. You can extend your fence below ground level to stop animals from tunneling underneath it, as shown in the illustration on the opposite page. Burrowing animals such as moles, gophers, and woodchucks can be excluded from garden areas by filling a ditch with sharp crushed rock and/or lining

Encircle a strawberry bed with a copper barrier to keep out snails and slugs. Bury a 3- to 4-inch-wide copper strip around the bed, with 2 to 3 inches of copper exposed. Bend the top ½ inch of the strip outward at a right angle to form a lip.

the bottom and garden side with ½-inch hardware cloth. Make the trench a foot or more deep and up to 3 feet wide to stop determined woodchucks. Gophers can be foiled with a 2-foot-deep, 6-inch-wide trench.

Electrified fences. The most effective fences are electrified. They provide a sharp electric jolt that does not injure animals but quickly convinces them that whatever is on the other side of the fence is not worth it. Control small critters by adding a single strand about 6 inches outside of your existing fence and 4 to 6 inches off the ground. For deer control, put the single strand 3 feet outside of the existing fence and 2 feet off the ground. To make sure deer make contact with the wire and get the "keep out" message, put aluminum foil flaps smeared with peanut butter here and there along the electrified wire. Be sure to read the manufacturer's instructions carefully and completely before installing any electric fence.

Antitranspirants. Antitranspirants are commercial products that are designed to block water loss from leaves. You can use them to seal leaves against diseases such as powdery mildew. Apply them according to label instructions.

Root fly squares. Cut 8-inch squares of tar paper and make an X-cut in the center. Slip one over each young cabbage-family plant and press it gently against the stem and the soil. This prevents cabbage root flies from laying their eggs on the soil near the roots.

Floating row covers. Floating row covers do a dandy job of keeping unsavory characters such as Mexican bean beetles, flea beetles, carrot rust flies, and disease-carrying insects away from your plants. They even exclude birds and animals to some extent. Spread them loosely over the bed right after you seed or transplant and seal the edges with soil for complete protection. They are so light they "float" right on the plants and don't require any frame to hold them up. You can leave crops that don't flower, such as onions and carrots, covered all season. Plants that require pollination must be uncovered when flowering begins or they must be hand-pollinated. In hot-summer areas you may need to remove covers to prevent heat damage in midsummer.

Netting. Netting can keep birds from making off with your edibles. Drape it directly over your plants or stretch it over a frame. Draped netting can be awkward to handle, fruit may be knocked off as you uncover it, and robbers may reach through it where it touches the goodies. But it's a quick solution, and it works well for things that are harvested all at once. Netting-covered frames may be a better choice for crops that are harvested over a long period. Either way, make sure to leave no gaps. No matter how tightly you secure netting, one or two birds always seem to manage to get inside. Sometimes birds get tangled in the netting and die, so check netted plants regularly to let out captives and check for gaps.

Paper bags. You can protect individual fruits or clusters from codling moths and birds with small paper bags. Tie the bags securely around the stem.

Hands-On Tactics

Two of the best gardening tools ever created are your own two hands. With them, you can remove many insects, weeds, or diseased plants and prevent a lot of problems from

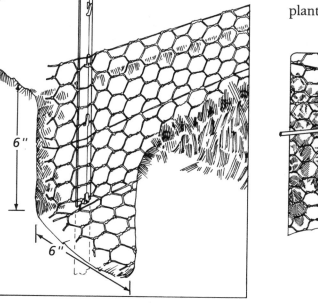

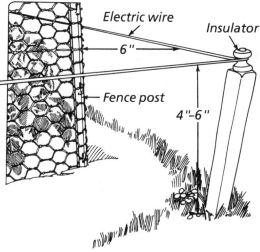

Keep burrowing animals out of the garden with a fence that's both above and below ground. Dig a trench 6 inches deep and 6 inches wide around the garden where your fence posts will be. Line it with chicken wire *(left)*. Another fence enhancer is a low single-strand electric fence set up 6 inches outside your chicken-wire fence *(right)*.

getting worse. With a few basic tools in your hands, there is almost no limit to what you can do. Here are some hands-on controls.

Handpicking. Insects that don't move quickly can be squashed between your thumb and forefinger. (Use gloves if you're squeamish.) Or you can pluck them off into a can of soapy water. Pick off moldy or rotten fruits to keep the scourge from spreading to other fruits. Pull up the entire plant and destroy it if a disease has overrun it, especially if you suspect the disease is viral in nature. Weeds are also good candidates for hand-removal.

Vacuuming. Hand-held vacuums are good for automatic handpicking of insects. Remember to empty the vacuumed pests into a bucket of soapy water to kill them, or they may simply crawl out of the vacuum and find their way back to your plants.

Shaking. Certain insect pests such as beetles are hard to handpick because they play possum and drop to the ground at more than the slightest movement of the plant. Take advantage of this weakness by spreading an old sheet or cardboard tray under the plant, then shaking the plant until the pests drop off. Carefully empty them into a container of soapy water to kill them.

A few diseases such as blueberry mummy berry are quite sensitive to shaking at specific stages in their life cycle. If you stir up the mulch or soil surface in early spring, you can prevent spore formation and stop the disease in its tracks.

Pruning. Pruning is just an extension of handpicking. Cut off and destroy diseased leaves and branches to keep the disease from spreading. Cut out tent caterpillar nests and destroy them, worms and all. You can also prune to open up the plants and let more air and sunshine in to reduce disease problems.

Mowing. Mowing is like wholesale pruning. You can use it to control many weeds. A single mowing just as the plants begin to flower will kill some annual weeds. Perennial weeds are more tenacious and must be mown repeatedly close to the ground to kill them.

Digging. Dig out stubborn perennial weeds

➥ ON TARGET

USING HANDS-ON TACTICS

Here are a few examples of how you can use hand-to-hand combat to battle specific types of problems.

Weeds. Hand-pulling of weeds is best for small areas, especially close to plants. Hoeing is most effective on larger areas. Destroy weeds before they set seed, since just one weed can produce up to 250,000 seeds. Any weed can be mown, but be careful not to till perennial weeds, such as quack grass, which regrow from small sections of root. To prevent a big problem later in the season, cultivate when weeds first start to appear.

Diseases. Prune out infected areas or pull up diseased plants. Destroy all diseased material by incorporating it in a hot compost pile, burning it, burying it, or sealing it in bags for disposal with household trash.

Insects and tiny pests. Handpicking, vacuuming, and shaking are your hands-on options for dealing with insect pests. Handpick gypsy moth eggs from tree trunks, tomato hornworms and other large caterpillars, and even slugs in nighttime raids. Shaking is a favored tactic for fighting plum curculios on fruit trees.

and terminally ill plants. Tilling can kill weeds, but *don't* do it to those perennial weeds that spread underground! Tilling can also expose insect pests to winter's killing frosts and bury diseased plant material where it won't cause further damage.

Traps

Traps come in all shapes, sizes, and colors. Most traps have two components: a lure and a detaining device. Lures may work by sight (color and/or shape or light) and/or smell, such as a food or sex scent (pheromone). A few traps use your plant as the lure. Detaining devices may be sticky surfaces, one-way entrances, triggered doors, or triggered killing mechanisms. You can use traps in two basic ways: to monitor pests or to control pests.

Monitor traps don't provide effective control. They do give you early warning of upcoming problems, and they help you to time releases of beneficial insects or sprays of botanical poisons.

Control traps take the pests out of action. Note: If your traps are catching lots of the pest but new damage does not decrease, you'll have to take additional steps. You may even decide that your traps are attracting more pests than they are catching. Japanese beetle traps are a prime example. One beetle trap is often worse than no trap at all. Use them only if you can combine your efforts with neighbors to cover a large area with traps, using at least 12 traps per acre.

Sticky band traps. Sticky band traps use the plant as a lure and a sticky substance like Tangle-Trap as the detaining device. They work for nonflying, nonhopping pests. Use them on greenhouse table legs to stop pesky aphid-bearing ants and on tree trunks to stop codling moth larvae in their tracks. *Caution:* Don't put the sticky coating directly on a tree trunk;

> ➡ **ON TARGET**
>
> ### USING TRAPS
>
> Here are a few examples of how you can use traps to battle specific types of problems.
>
> **Diseases.** Traps don't stop disease organisms directly, but they are effective monitors for aphids and thrips, which are vectors of many plant diseases.
>
> **Insects and tiny pests.** Traps are effective controls for apple maggots, cherry fruit flies, peachtree borers, codling moths, slugs, and some other pests. You can also use traps as monitors for aphids, thrips, and Japanese beetles.
>
> **Animals.** Live traps let you safely capture and remove crop-destroying animals, such as stubborn woodchucks, without harming the animal.

---

wrap plastic kitchen wrap around the trunk and put the coating on that.

Flat, colored, sticky traps. Yellow sticky traps like the one illustrated on page 167 attract whiteflies, aphids, leafhoppers, pear psyllas, and many other flying pests. To control cucumber beetles, staple a cotton ball on each trap and soak it with allspice, bay, or clove oil. To control cherry fruit flies, hang an apple maggot lure or a small uncapped bottle of 1 part water and 1 part household ammonia from the bottom of the trap. Blue traps work to monitor for thrips. White traps catch flea beetles and tarnished plant bugs.

You can buy commercial traps or make your own. See "Make Your Own: Insect Traps" on page 166 for instructions. Cover traps with plastic kitchen wrap (for easy cleanup) and coat them with sticky coating. (Ignore this step if the trap is already coated with a sticky substance.) Hang or staple traps to stakes in the problem area just above the plants or within trees. Renew the sticky coating as needed. At the end of the season, remove the plastic wrap and store the traps.

Fruit-shaped, colored, sticky traps. Pests that attack fruit look for fruit-shaped objects to eat or lay eggs on. You can fool them with traps that appear to be fruit. Red spheres like the one on the opposite page trap apple maggots. Buy commercial traps or paint apple-size balls an apple-red color. Cover them with plastic kitchen wrap (for easy cleanup) and coat them with sticky coating. Hang traps in trees. Renew the sticky coating as needed. At the end of the season, remove the plastic wrap and store the traps. Apple-scented lures or perfume may increase the traps' effectiveness. Apple-green spheres work for plum cucurlio. See the plant entries in Part 2 for specifics on how to use these traps on particular crops.

Food-scented traps. Many pests follow their noses to food; invite them over for a fatal snack. Try these traps:

1. Use cubes of carrot or potato on skewers to catch wireworms. Bury them a few inches deep in the soil with the skewer sticking out. Every few days, pull them up and destroy the wireworms by putting them in a bucket of soapy water or by squashing them.

2. Slugs like yeast. Mix yeast and molasses with water and fill small plastic containers set into the soil to trap and drown them. Cover traps to keep rain out, but be sure to leave a small opening in the cover or the side of the container so the slugs can still get in.

3. Use half of a melon rind to catch picnic beetles. Just fill the rind with soapy water and set it near ripening fruit crops.

✦ MAKE YOUR OWN ✦

INSECT TRAPS

Here are some traps and trap components you can make at home.

Sticky Coating

Mix equal parts of petroleum jelly or mineral oil and liquid dish soap for an inexpensive and easy-to-remove sticky trap coating.

Sticky Rectangles

Paint rectangles of ¼-inch plywood or stiff plastic (such as bleach bottles) with yellow, bright white, or royal blue, depending on the insect you hope to trap. Rustoleum "Federal Safety Yellow #659" and Day-Glo Colors "Saturn Yellow" are the right yellow for traps.

Cherry Fruit Fly Trap

Paint the top half of a 2-liter plastic soda bottle with one of the yellows mentioned in "Sticky Rectangles" above. Fill the bottle with equal parts of water and household ammonia. Add a few drops of liquid soap. Hang the bottle in the tree, and empty and renew weekly.

Pheromone Lure Trap

Cut three large holes in the upper half of the sides of a 1-quart plastic yogurt container. Line the lid with cardboard or cover it with duct tape to shade the lure. Fasten the container to a sturdy stake or give it a wire handle to hang from. Tape a pheromone lure to the inside of the lid. Fill the bottom of the container with soapy water, snap on the lid, and insert the stake into the ground or hang the trap from a tree. Refill water or refresh lure as needed.

Trap crops. You can also plant treats for your pests with the sole purpose of destroying the plants once the pests have moved in for the feast. A few elderly sprouting onions planted along with your onion seeds will be far more attractive to hungry onion maggots. In two weeks, pull and destroy the trap onions and their inhabitants.

Pheromone traps. Insect sex scents, or pheromones, make effective lures for male insects. If you catch all the males, the females will go unmated and lay no eggs. Pest-specific lures are available for many insects including peachtree borers, codling moths, oriental fruit moths, and corn pests. They are usually paired with a container with a sticky interior that traps the lured pests. Purchase disposable cardboard traps, such as the wing trap shown on this page, or make your own traps and bait them with commercial lures. See "Make Your Own: Insect Traps" on the opposite page for instructions. Refer to the plant entries in Part 2 for information on how many traps to use.

Trigger traps. Small and medium-size animal pests are candidates for trapping. Trigger traps range from the familiar mouse-size snap trap to coon- or even bear-size live traps. You must be prepared to deal with your captive if you choose a live trap. (Leave the bear trapping to professionals, please.) See "Animal Pests" on page 191 for a roundup of ideas to make animal pests keep their distance.

Light traps. Ultraviolet-light traps, sometimes referred to as bug zappers, attract many insects, good and bad. They can be useful in dealing with codling moths and corn pests. Use them only for limited periods of time and only from 11:00 P.M. to 3:00 A.M. (put them on a timer) to reduce the number of beneficial insects lured to untimely death.

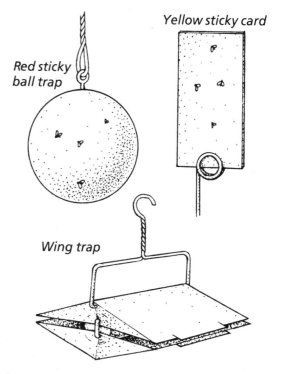

Red sticky ball trap

Yellow sticky card

Wing trap

Insect traps can serve as controls or as monitors of emerging pest problems. Yellow sticky cards are useful for monitoring aphids, red sticky ball traps are an effective control for apple maggots, and wing traps, which house pheromone lures, are available for several different pests, including codling moths.

Biological Controls

Biological controls have few, if any, of the drawbacks of chemicals. They take advantage of pest diseases or other natural control methods. Most only affect specific pests and are harmless to nontarget organisms. This is an area of active research, with new controls being developed every year.

Making Pests Sick

Pests get sick due to infection by a variety of bacteria, fungi, viruses, and other microorganisms. You'll find that commercial products containing beneficial organisms are an excellent way to control pests. While these products are nontoxic to nontarget insects and to humans and other mammals, don't use them indiscriminately. The possibility exists that pests constantly exposed to these biocontrols will develop resistance.

***Bacillus thuringiensis* (BT).** BT is one of the best-known biocontrols. The bacterium paralyzes the stomachs of susceptible pests that eat it and causes death by starvation. *B.t.* var. *kurstaki* (BTK) kills many caterpillars including cabbage loopers, cabbageworms, and hornworms. *B.t.* var. *san diego* (BTSD) kills small Colorado potato beetle larvae. *B.t.* var. *israelensis* (BTI) controls mosquitoes, black flies, and fungus gnats. Unless the label specifies which strain it contains, you may assume it is BTK. BTs come as a powder, granule, or liquid for dusting and spraying. Add up to 1 teaspoon of soap per gallon of BT spray to help the spray stick. Add 1 tablespoon of molasses per gallon to encourage insects to feed on sprayed foliage and thereby ingest the bacteria.

Milky disease spores. *Bacillus popilliae* and *B. lentimorbus* bacteria, also called milky disease spores, infect Japanese beetle grubs. Dust the powder on turf areas according to the label directions. Milky disease reduces beetle populations in subsequent years if a large area (several acres) is treated.

Nosema locustae. *N. locustae* is a protozoan that infects most grasshoppers when they eat it. Infected grasshoppers stop feeding after a while and may die or fail to reproduce. Spread *N. locustae* according to label directions in early summer when you first see grasshoppers.

Outcompeting Pests

Some biocontrols work by outcompeting or inhibiting the growth of a pest rather than sickening or killing it outright.

Agrobacterium radiobacter. This type of bacteria prevents crown gall infection by producing antibodies that inhibit its cousin—crown gall bacteria. Use it as a root dip at planting or as a soil drench to prevent infection of wounds. It won't cure existing crown gall infections. Galltrol and Norbac 84-C are two brand names.

Gliocladium virens. This soil-dwelling fungus is used to control damping-off of seedlings in greenhouses and seedbeds. Apply according to label directions.

➥ ON TARGET

USING BIOCONTROLS

Here are a few examples of how you can use biocontrols to battle specific types of problems.

Weeds. Some plants secrete substances that inhibit the growth of weeds. For example, a thin mulch of rye or Sudan grass can suppress the growth of weed seedlings.

Diseases. There are beneficial organisms that secrete antibiotics that are toxic to other microbes. One fungus sold as Galltrol-A and Norback 84-C is antagonistic to the fungi that cause crown gall diseases of fruit and nut trees.

Insects. Biocontrol options for controlling insects range from releasing beneficial insects like lacewings to spraying *Bacillus thuringiensis* on plants that are under attack by chewing caterpillars.

Botanical Herbicides

Many plants produce chemical compounds that inhibit the growth of certain other plants. This is known as allelopathy. There are no ready-to-apply extracts, but you can make use of them by growing the plants themselves. Here are some of the more widely recognized plants with potentially useful herbicides:

• A number of cover crops are allelopathic to weeds. See "Weedy Areas" on page 44 for a list. Rye and Sudan grass are especially effective as a thin mulch around transplants, where they suppress weed seedlings until the transplants get a good start.
• Sweet potatoes can be used to chase out yellow nut sedge, a troublesome perennial weed, and perhaps some other weeds, too.

Plant and Animal By-Products

These biocontrols aren't living organisms; they are biological compounds produced by animals or microorganisms as part of their self-defense mechanisms. Some of these compounds can be synthesized in laboratories. Whether these products should be considered acceptable for use by organic gardeners is a gray area. You'll have to make your own decision whether you think these materials are "natural" enough to meet your standards.

Streptomycin and avermectins. A common soil bacterium, *Streptomyces avermitilis,* is the source of this antibiotic. It is also the source of biological insecticides called avermectins. Streptomycin is the most effective product for controlling fire blight bacteria, and it may even be labeled "fire blight spray." It is also effective on bacterial leaf spot. Apply according to label directions.

Chitin. Ground-up shellfish shells are a potent nematicide. The active ingredient is a

---

✦ MAKE YOUR OWN ✦

BIOCONTROLS

Gardeners are born experimenters. Here are two potentially powerful sprays you can make from scratch.

Bug Juice
Some insects won't feed on plants where there are dead members of their own species present. Enterprising gardeners take advantage of this and of disease-causing organisms that may be present in the bodies of pest insects. They collect a handful of the pest (sick, sluggish ones, if possible), liquefy them in a blender, and spray the resulting extract back on the plants. This spray works to control some pest problems some of the time. If you try it, be sure to protect yourself from possible hazards (toxins in the insects that could cause allergic reactions or bacteria that could infect you). Don't use a blender that you use for food. Wear a dust mask when you spray, and don't let the mixture get anywhere on your skin.

Compost Tea
Compost tea has disease-controlling properties. You can spray it on your plants to provide general insurance against disease problems. See "Using Liquid Fertilizers" on page 128 for instructions on making and using it.

---

protein complex called chitin. Apply 2½ pounds of ground shells per 100 square feet. Be sure to add a high-nitrogen amendment such as alfalfa meal at the same time, or the soil microbes won't be able to use the chitin. Repeat yearly.

Vitamin D. Rodents can't metabolize this vitamin properly, and eating it leads to fatal calcium buildup. It is harmless to other animals. Purchase prepared bait to control mice, voles, and rats.

Physical Pesticides

Not all pesticides are poisons. In fact, you bathe with two of them—soap and water. Unlike poisons, physical pesticides kill problem-causing organisms in other, often more subtle or indirect ways. For example, some compounds such as diatomaceous earth puncture an insect's skin. The insect then dies of dehydration. Soaps wash away an insect's protective coatings to the same end. Oils smother pests. Hydrogen peroxide burns up fungus spores much as its fizzing kills germs in a cut on your finger.

Use physical pesticides with care. While some physical pesticides are harmless to non-target organisms, others such as copper can be quite damaging to nontarget organisms and should be used only when absolutely necessary. Even something as innocuous as lime can cause you problems if you breathe the dust or get too much on your skin. See "Be Safe While You Spray" on page 189 for a general rundown on how to use sprays and dusts safely.

You probably have some of these materials in your kitchen or bathroom. Others are available at garden centers or from mail-order catalogs.

Water. A strong spray of water can knock bugs right off your plants and even physically injure soft-bodied insects such as aphids. Spider mites thrive in dry conditions, so spraying infestations once or twice a day can put a major dent in them. Boiling water is an effective weed killer for small areas.

Alcohol. Isopropyl (rubbing) alcohol controls a variety of pests including aphids, flea beetles, and thrips. Mix 1 to 2 cups of alcohol with 1 quart of water, and spray infested plants.

Baking soda. Baking soda (sodium bicarbonate) is a preventive fungicide that remains active until it is washed off by rain. It keeps fungal spores from getting started. It can even stop some fungal diseases, such as powdery mildew, after they're visibly attacking a plant. Dissolve 1 teaspoon of baking soda in 1 quart of warm water and add ¼ teaspoon of vegetable or other horticultural oil or liquid soap to help it stick. Let it cool and thoroughly spray susceptible or infected plants with it. Repeat weekly or after it rains.

Hydrogen peroxide. Hydrogen peroxide

➤ ON TARGET

USING PHYSICAL PESTICIDES

Here are a few examples of how you can use physical pesticides to battle specific types of problems.

Weeds. Soap-based herbicides will kill some young, tender weeds. They will also kill young crop plants, so always apply with caution and according to label directions.

Diseases. Water, baking soda, hydrogen peroxide, and oils are physical pesticides that work as preventive measures. Last resorts for existing disease problems are lime-sulfur and copper.

Insects and tiny pests. Soaps, oils, diatomaceous earth, lime, and water are physical pesticides that are effective against a wide range of pests. Spraying horticultural oil can be a very effective preventive measure for some tree fruit pests.

is a preventive fungicide that breaks down within minutes of application. Use it to combat a variety of diseases including peach leaf curl and early blight on tomatoes. Buy the 3 percent hydrogen peroxide from the drugstore and mix 1 to 2 teaspoons of it with 1 quart of water, and spray it on susceptible plants once a week. For best results, you'll need to start spraying before the disease gets going on the plants.

Soap. Soaps kill some bugs by washing off their protective coatings. Insecticidal soaps are specially formulated solutions of fatty acids. They are a contact insecticide that controls many soft-bodies insects such as aphids, leafhoppers, mites, and whiteflies. Mix and apply according to label directions. Insecticidal soap will not mix well with hard water. If you have hard water, use bottled drinking water instead. You can also use 1 to 3 teaspoons of household soap—not detergent—per gallon of water instead of insecticidal soap. The effectiveness of dish soap will vary from brand to brand, and even from bottle to bottle of the same brand.

Caution: If you apply a soap solution that is too concentrated or if plants are stressed by drought or heat, your plants may suffer damage. Cabbage-family crops are most susceptible to burns. Use a more dilute solution or spray a few leaves and wait a day or two to see what happens if you have any doubts.

Soap is useful as a spreader-sticker (something that makes a spray cover and stick to the leaves) for many other pesticide sprays. Use 1 teaspoon of soap per gallon of spray solution.

Different formulations of soaps, or fatty acids, are used as nonspecific weed killers. Spray soap-based herbicides according to label directions early in the morning on a hot, dry, sunny day. Strong sunlight is needed for these products to be effective. They work best on succulent young growth up to 5 inches tall. Maturing (flowering) or woody weeds may not be killed. Spray only unwanted vegetation, since such herbicides are nonselective. Avoid spraying in windy conditions.

Oil. Oils, both petroleum and vegetable, kill insect eggs and immature insects by smothering them. They may also poison or repel some insects. There are two kinds of petroleum oil sold for pest control: heavy, dormant oils and lighter, superior (or summer) oils. Heavy, dormant oils are sprayed on dormant trees and ornamentals to control overwintering stages of mites, scales, and aphids. Lighter, superior oils contain fewer plant-damaging impurities. They may be used on plants in full leaf. Apply according to label directions.

You can also use 1 tablespoon of plain vegetable oil and ¼ teaspoon of liquid soap per quart of water. Shake vigorously and spray.

Caution: Oil plus sulfur can damage plants. Don't use them within 30 days of each other.

Oil is useful as a spreader-sticker (something that makes a spray cover and stick to the leaves) for many other pesticide sprays. Use 1 teaspoon of oil per gallon of spray solution.

Diatomaceous earth (DE). DE is the fossilized shell remains of 20-million-year-old algae known as diatoms. Its microscopic, razor-sharp edges pierce soft-bodied pests, causing death by dehydration. DE controls pests such as aphids, leafhoppers, slugs, and thrips. DE is nontoxic to animals, but it is a respiratory irritant, so wear a mask when handling it. Buy natural-grade DE (not pool-grade—it doesn't control pests). Dust dew-wet plants or soil (for slugs) or mix it with water to make a thick slurry to paint on tree trunks. Repeat as needed.

Lime. Lime is ground-up limestone and is an important soil amendment. Because it is a caustic, alkaline substance, lime also makes a dandy insecticide (or at least an insect repellent) and probably has some fungicidal quality, too. Dust your plants with lime as often as needed to maintain a light dusting. Wear a mask when you do—it's not good to breathe. Wear protective clothing and wash lime off of your skin to keep it from burning you. Wood ashes are often used instead of lime.

Sulfur. Sulfur is a naturally occurring element. It is most effective as a preventive fungicide, literally burning fungal spores it touches. It controls diseases such as brown rot. It's gentle on large predacious insects, but it will kill small ones such as parasitic wasps. High concentrations of sulfur damage important soil microbes, so don't spray it directly on the soil. It is somewhat toxic to fish and animals, including humans. Apply according to label directions. Sulfur needs to be present on the leaves before the spores land and must be reapplied after rain or every week to 10 days.

Caution: In hot weather (above 80°F), sulfur is highly phytotoxic and will damage plants. Sulfur plus oil also damages growing plants. Do not use sulfur within one month of an oil spray.

Copper. Copper is a naturally occurring element. It is a powerful, nonspecific fungicide and herbicide. It is toxic to animals and beneficial insects. Copper is also toxic to plants, and repeated applications of it can stunt them. In addition, it damages beneficial soil organisms and accumulates in the soil. Compounds that combine copper with lime or sulfur are less toxic to plants and nontarget organisms. See "Lime-Sulfur and Bordeaux Mix" on the opposite page for information about combined sprays. Many organic gardeners prefer to use copper only as a last resort, if at all. If you do use it, avoid spraying it directly on

---

✦ MAKE YOUR OWN ✦

PESTICIDES

You can make concoctions that repel or damage pests from nettle, comfrey, or tomato leaves; ground hot peppers; or assorted herbs extracted in oil, water, or isopropyl (rubbing) alcohol. Devise your own recipe based on the materials you have on hand. Be sure to strain the extract through cheesecloth before mixing it with water and spraying, or it may clog your sprayer. Protect your skin and eyes from these mixtures because they can be very irritating.

Here are two make-your-own pesticide recipes that many gardeners have had success with.

Garlic

Garlic has antibiotic, antifungal, and insecticidal properties and it repels some pests. To make a garlic spray, soak 3 ounces of minced garlic in 2 teaspoons of mineral or vegetable oil for at least one day. Strain the oil and mix with 2 cups of water and 1 tablespoon of liquid soap. Mix 2 to 4 tablespoons of this concentrate with 1 quart of water, and spray plants thoroughly.

Horsetail

Horsetail (*Equisetum arvense*) is a common weed in many areas. Horsetail spray is used as a protectant fungicide. Boil ⅛ cup of dried horsetail with 1 gallon of water in a glass or stainless steel pot. Simmer for at least half an hour, cool, and strain. It keeps for one month in a closed jar. Mix ¾ cup of concentrate with 1 quart of water, and spray plants. Repeat weekly.

the soil. Apply copper according to label directions.

Lime-sulfur and bordeaux mix. Lime-sulfur is another name for a compound called calcium polysulfide. Bordeaux mix is a formulation of copper sulfate plus hydrated lime. They are protectant fungicides. Lime plus sulfur is more effective—and caustic—than either alone because it can actually penetrate leaves and kill recently germinated disease spores. Unfortunately, the combination is also more likely to damage growing plants. Use it only when more benign methods haven't worked. Both compounds are often used on dormant plants just before or just as the buds open, and they tend to be quite safe for plants at that stage. They control many diseases including anthracnose, bacterial leaf spots and wilts, fire blight, peach leaf curl, powdery mildew, and rust. Apply according to label directions. See "Sulfur" on the opposite page for two important cautions. Repeat in 10 to 14 days if necessary. Lime-sulfur mixed with water to make a thick slurry also makes a good paint for covering tree wounds.

Botanical Poisons

Botanical poisons are so named because they occur naturally in certain plants. In general, botanicals have fewer harmful side effects and break down more quickly in the environment than synthetic chemicals do. Botanical poisons *are* still poisons, however. They can be toxic to you or other living creatures. They should be used only for problems that cannot be kept to a tolerable level by other means. Treat botanical poisons with respect.

You may decide to include botanical poisons as part of your plan for dealing with specific known enemies. Plan to apply them only when the pest level reaches a predetermined level (such as four aphids per shoot tip) or when the plant reaches a specific growth stage. Avoid applying them as blanket preventives. For details on specific botanical poisons and application instructions, see "Using Botanical Poisons" on page 181.

TROUBLESHOOTING PROBLEMS

Suppose you didn't get your beneficial insects released in time. Now, Mexican bean beetles are ripping through your green beans like a four-alarm fire through a lumberyard. What do you do? Put out the fire, of course. Hit the problem as hard and as quickly as you can. This may mean anything from pulling up and composting the infected or infested plant to spraying it with botanical poisons.

Every gardener has to deal with a crisis like this now and again. The important follow-up step to take is to figure out what went wrong and what you can do differently next year to prevent the problem from getting out of hand again.

Diagnosing the Problem

While the symptoms of your plant's problems are easy to see, they may not be so easy to diagnose. Your plants can't tell you if the yellowing of their leaves is due to disease, insect feeding, lack of water, or a nutrient deficiency. Investigate carefully before you take action. Look for insects or insect eggs or excrement on damaged plants. If you don't find any, look for signs of disease organisms like molds or spore bodies on leaves. Consider whether symptoms are due to nutrient deficiencies. You'll find a key to common symptoms of nutrient deficiencies in the table "Troubleshooting Plant Nutrient Deficiencies" on page 175. You'll also find keys to common insects and diseases of fruits and vegetables in the tables "Troubleshooting Fruit and Vegetable Diseases" on page 178 and "Troubleshooting Fruit and Vegetable Pests" on page 182. These listings don't include *every* possible pest or problem you may encounter. If you feel you need more guidance, try taking a sample of the damaged plant to your local Cooperative Extension Service office for identification, or consult the reference texts on pest control listed in "Sources" on page 507.

Weeds

Weeds are an unpleasant fact of life in almost everyone's garden. If you're facing a weed problem now, remember that the sooner you tackle it the better. The bigger your weeds get, the more difficult they are to control. Once you solve your current weed crisis, get into the habit of a once-a-week weed patrol to cut your weed problem down to size. Using the right tools and techniques also will help to make weeding a manageable—maybe even enjoyable—task.

Weeding by Hand

Hand-pulling weeds is simple and effective. It's good for small areas and young or annual weeds such as purslane and lamb's-quarters. Using your hands allows you to weed with precision, an important skill when sorting the weeds from the seedlings. For notorious spreaders like ground ivy, the only choice for control is to patiently hand-pull the tops and sift through the soil to remove as many rhizomes as you can find.

Short-handled tools such as dandelion forks (sometimes known as asparagus knives), pronged cultivators, and mattocks are good for large, stubborn weeds, especially in close quarters such as among strawberry plants. You can also use a garden fork to pry up tough perennial weeds. Hand weeders come in all shapes, and everybody has a favorite. If one type feels awkward, try another.

If the weeds you pull haven't yet set seed, recycle them: Leave the weeds upside down on the soil to dry, then cover them with soil or mulch. If they have gone to seed, add them to the compost pile only if you keep the pile temperature high (at least 160°F). Otherwise the weed seeds will survive the composting process and you'll spread weed problems along with your finished compost. See "Fast Compost or Slow?" on page 41 for instructions on keeping a compost pile hot.

Hoeing

A hoe is the best tool for weeding larger areas quickly and cleanly. Use it to rid the vegetable garden of weeds that spring up between rows. When you hoe, slice or scrape just below the soil surface to sever weed tops from roots. Don't chop into the soil—you'll just bring up more weed seeds to germinate. Keep the hoe blade sharp. Hoeing kills most annual weeds, but many perennial weeds, such as dandelions, will grow back from their roots. Dig out these roots with a garden fork or spade.

In gardens with wide spaces between plant rows, you may be able to handle most of your weeding chores with a wheel hoe (an oscillating or stationary hoe blade mounted on a wheel with two long handles) or a rotary tiller. But keep in mind that while a tiller makes fast work of weeds, tilling can have detrimental effects on your soil structure and will bring up more weed seeds in the process. Also, tilling perennial weeds can chop their rhizomes into small pieces, each of which will then sprout into life, worsening your weed problem.

Troubleshooting Plant Nutrient Deficiencies

This table groups nutrient deficiency symptoms according to where symptoms are likely to show up first. It also suggests organic soil amendments and fertilizers you can use to help remedy deficiencies. You'll find out more about soil amendments in Chapter 2. For directions on applying these materials, see "Fertilizing 101" on page 126.

NUTRIENT	SYMPTOMS	SOURCES OF NUTRIENT
SYMPTOMS APPEAR FIRST ON OLDER OR LOWER LEAVES.		
Nitrogen	Lower leaves yellow. Overall plant light green. Growth stunted.	Alfalfa meal, blood meal, fish emulsion, fish meal, guano, soybean meal
Phosphorus	Foliage red, purple, or very dark green. Growth stunted.	Bonemeal, colloidal phosphate, rock phosphate
Potassium	Tips and edges of leaves yellow, then brown. Stems weak.	Granite meal, greensand, Sul-Po-Mag, wood ashes
Magnesium	Interveinal chlorosis. Growth stunted.	Epsom salts, dolomitic lime
Zinc	Interveinal chlorosis. Leaves thickened. Growth stunted.	Chelated spray, kelp extract, kelp meal
SYMPTOMS APPEAR FIRST ON YOUNGER OR UPPER LEAVES.		
Calcium	Buds and young leaves die back at tips.	Lime, gypsum, oyster shells
Iron	Interveinal chlorosis. Growth stunted.	Chelated spray, kelp extract, kelp meal
Sulfur	Young leaves light green overall. Growth stunted.	Flowers of sulfur, gypsum
Boron	Young leaves pale green at base and twisted. Buds die.	Borax, chelated spray
Copper	Young leaves pale and wilted with brown tips.	Kelp extract, kelp meal
Manganese	Interveinal chlorosis on young leaves with brown spots scattered through leaf.	Kelp extract, kelp meal
Molybdenum	Interveinal chlorosis. Growth stunted.	Kelp extract, kelp meal

Using Herbicides

In some cases, fatty-acid-based herbicides such as SharpShooter can help control weeds. These herbicides provide effective spot control for annual weeds, but perennial weeds will spring up anew from the unharmed roots. Some organic gardeners have traditionally relied on vinegar or salt to kill weeds. However, these substances will affect soil balance and can harm your garden plants as well. Only use them in areas where you don't want *any* plants to grow, such as between cracks in a patio.

Soil Solarization

For a long-term solution to a weed-plagued area, consider giving up on production for a while and solarizing it clean. Soil solarization is one of the most effective methods for ridding a site of weed seeds, as well as many insects and disease pathogens. The high heat and humidity produced by covering moist soil with clear plastic are lethal to most organisms.

In order to be effective, however, the procedure *must* be done properly, during the hottest months of the summer. Here's how to treat your soil with the sun's radiant energy:

1. Clear the area or bed of all existing plants and debris. If previously uncultivated, till the soil to a depth of about 1 foot. Break up any clods of dirt and rake the surface smooth.
2. Dig a 3- or 4-inch-deep trench around the area.
3. Water the soil thoroughly until it is literally soaking wet.
4. Before the soil has a chance to lose moisture, spread 1- to 4-mil clear (not black or colored) plastic film over the area and press it down so that it touches the soil. The plastic should extend into the trench on all sides.
5. Mound dirt over the plastic in the trench to seal off the edges.
6. Keep the soil covered for four to six weeks.

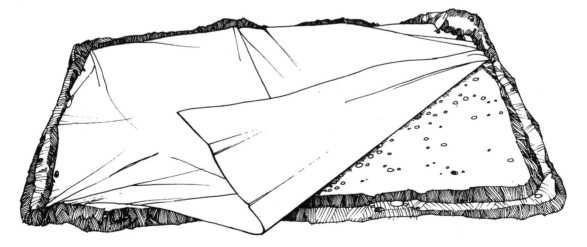

Heating the soil with solar energy trapped under a sheet of clear plastic—a process known as solarization—can kill weed seeds, disease organisms, and some insect pests. This process takes several weeks and only works in hot, clear weather.

Stale Seedbed

You can also control your weeds by repeated tilling. As with soil solarization, you'll lose part of a growing season with this method. Essentially, a stale seedbed is a plot that is tilled shallowly several times, as shown in the illustration below. The repeated tilling eventually wears down the reservoir of stored energy in perennial weed roots, as they are forced to resprout over and over again without getting a chance to grow. Annual weed seeds are turned up, germinate, and die after the next tilling.

Plan to do the tilling in the season when the weeds are worst. If your weeds are those that grow mainly in the spring, then leave the area crop-free during the spring season. If you have summer weed problems, try a summer-season stale seedbed, and likewise for fall weed problems.

Diseases

If you have mildly diseased vegetable plants, your best chance for salvaging a crop may be to give it tender loving care. Don't let the plants suffer water stress—but don't overwater, either,

(continued on page 180)

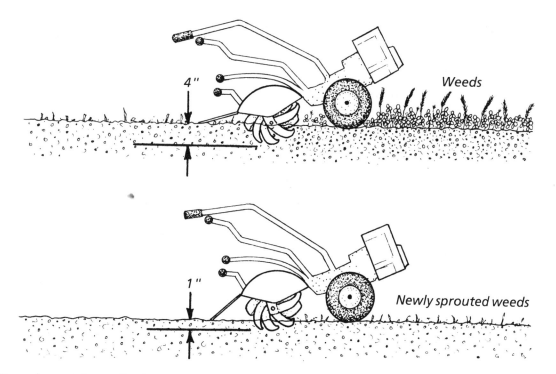

To make a stale seedbed, till about 4 inches deep. Then, every 2 weeks or so, till shallowly (about 1 inch deep). This technique eventually weakens and depletes the weed population in a weedy area so that it will be ready for planting a crop.

Troubleshooting Fruit and Vegetable Diseases

Home gardeners often have few options when it comes to fighting plant diseases. This table will help you decide what type of disease problem you have, and it offers some general suggestions to prevent recurrence of that problem. In some cases, there are some organically acceptable fungicides that can help prevent the spread of a disease.

DISEASE	SYMPTOMS	CONTROLS
Alternaria blight	Infected leaves develop brown to black spots that enlarge and develop concentric rings like a target. Heavily blighted leaves dry up and die. Sunken spots appear on fruits and tubers. Affects many vegetables and fruit trees. Known as early blight on tomato-family crops.	Plant resistant cultivars. Soak seeds in a disinfecting solution before planting. Dispose of infected annual crops. Use a 3-year rotation.
Anthracnose	Infected fruits and pods develop small, dark, sunken spots. Pinkish spore masses appear in the center of the spots in wet weather. Tomatoes, cucumbers, melons, and beans are often affected. Also a problem on raspberries and gooseberries, where symptoms appear as gray spots surrounded by red or purple margins on canes and leaves; sideshoots may wilt and entire canes may die.	Plant resistant cultivars. Using disease-free seeds and rotating crops may help prevent the problem. For cane plants, apply lime-sulfur spray just as leaf buds break in the spring. Remove and destroy severely infected plants.
Bacterial spot	Appears as small, dark spots on fruit tree leaves; centers dry and drop out, leaving shot holes. Small, sunken dark spots or cracks form on fruit. On cabbage-family crops, small brown or purple spots appear on leaves; leaves eventually turn yellow and die. Affects apricot, peach, and plum trees and cabbage-family crops.	Spray copper on fruit trees when buds open until temperatures reach 85°–90°F in wet weather. Check with supplier because some types burn leaves. Limit high-nitrogen fertilizers. Destroy infected vegetable plants. Use a 3-year crop rotation to reduce problems.
Brown rot	Flowers and new growth on infected trees wilt and decay. Developing or mature fruits show soft, brown spots that enlarge rapidly and may grow gray mold. Affects apricot, peach, and plum trees.	Remove and destroy dried fruits. Cultivate soil just before bloom. Cut out infected twigs. Spray sulfur during summer and lime-sulfur when trees are dormant.

DISEASE	SYMPTOMS	CONTROLS
Canker, perennial	Infection causes sunken, oozing cankers to form on trunk or twigs. May cause wilting or death of branches or trees. Affects apricot, cherry, peach, and plum trees.	Avoid mechanical injury: The fungus enters through wounds. Cut out cankers and paint wounds with a 1:1 mix of lime-sulfur and white latex paint.
Club root	Infected cabbage-family plants wilt during the heat of the day. Older leaves turn yellow and drop. Roots are distorted and swollen.	Select resistant cultivars, buy uninfected transplants, and follow a 3-year rotation.
Downy mildew	A white to purple downy growth forms on the undersides of leaves and along stems. Affects many fruit and vegetable crops.	Buy disease-free seeds and plants, follow a 3-year rotation, and remove and dispose of infected plants. On perennials such as grapes, remove and destroy badly infected leaves. Try sprays of bordeaux mix or other copper-based fungicides to reduce the spread of the disease.
Fire blight	Young, tender shoots on infected trees die back suddenly. Leaves turn brown or singed-looking and remain on the twig. Areas of bark may become water-soaked and ooze. Affects apple, pear, and quince trees.	Select resistant cultivars. Cut off blighted twigs at least 1' below decay on a dry day. Sanitize pruning tools between cuts. Limit high-nitrogen fertilizers.
Late blight	First symptom is water-soaked spots on lower leaves. Downy white growth appears on leaf undersides. In wet weather, plants will rot and die. Affects nightshade-family crops.	Dispose of all infected plants and tubers, presoak seeds in a disinfecting solution, and plant resistant cultivars. Sprays of bordeaux mix can help control outbreaks during wet weather.
Mosaic	A viral disease that causes mottled green and yellow foliage or veins. Leaves may be wrinkled or curled; growth may be stunted. Attacks beans, tomatoes, and many other crops.	Plant resistant cultivars. Mosaic is spread by insects, especially aphids and leafhoppers. Keep insects away from crops by covering them with floating row cover. Remove and destroy infected plants.

(continued)

Troubleshooting Fruit and Vegetable Diseases—Continued

DISEASE	SYMPTOMS	CONTROLS
Powdery mildew	Mildew forms a white to grayish powdery growth, usually on the upper surfaces of leaves. Leaves of severely infected plants turn brown and shrivel. Fruit ripens prematurely and has poor texture and flavor. Infects melons, cucumbers, apples, grapes, and many other crops.	Plant resistant cultivars whenever possible. Prune or stake plants to improve air circulation. Dispose of infected plants. Applying a 0.5% solution of baking soda (1 teaspoon of baking soda in 1 quart of water) may help to control the disease. Apply sulfur weekly to prevent infection of susceptible plants.
Rust	Infected plants develop reddish brown powdery spots on leaves and stems. Leaves turn yellow and growth is stunted. Different species of rust fungi infect apples, asparagus, beans, brambles, carrots, corn, onions, and other crops.	Provide good air circulation around plants. Remove and destroy seriously affected plants or plant parts. Starting early in the season, dust plants with sulfur to prevent infection or to keep mild infections from spreading. For bramble fruits, immediately destroy any infected plants and replant with resistant cultivars.
Wilt, Fusarium and Verticillium	Infected plants wilt and may turn yellow. Leaves may drop prematurely. Severely infected plants may die. Affects a wide range of fruits and vegetables, especially tomatoes, peppers, melons, strawberries, peaches, and cherries.	Select resistant cultivars when available. Crop rotation does not control these diseases well because so many crops are susceptible. Soil solarization before planting may help.

because wet conditions favor development of many fungal diseases. Try applying foliar sprays of kelp or compost tea to boost general plant health. With luck, you may still pull off the harvest.

If vegetable crops become severely diseased, your best course of action is to pull up the plants and get them out of your garden. They are just a reservoir of disease organisms that could infect other plants, and there are no organically acceptable cures. Bury the diseased crops deeply in the soil, put them in the center of a hot compost pile, burn them, or put them in sealed containers with your household trash.

In the case of diseased perennials, such as asparagus, rhubarb, berry vines, vines, and fruit trees, you may want to consider your spray options. While sprays won't magically fix the problem this season, they can help to contain it. For example, streptomycin sprays can halt the spread of fire blight. And in the following season, if you decide to use preventive spray tactics—in other words, to spray even before symptoms appear—you can have good success in warding off many disease problems. For more information on pesticides for disease control, see "Physical Pesticides" on page 170. You'll find recommendations for fighting some of the most common diseases of fruits and vegetables in the tables "Troubleshooting Fruit and Vegetable Diseases" on page 178 and "Troubleshooting Fruit and Vegetable Pests" on page 182.

Insects

Plants swarming with chewing caterpillars or beetles aren't good news, but it is good news that there is a range of organically acceptable controls for insect pests. They range from nontoxic substances like sprays of plain water to potent botanical poisons like rotenone. Always investigate and use less-invasive options first, and save botanical poisons for the last resort. See "Using Botanical Poisons" on this page for information on these controls.

There are a few biological controls that work fast enough to be a help in a pest emergency. The billions of worm-wrecking bacteria in *Bacillus thuringiensis* (BT) preparations can make fast work of leaf-riddling cabbageworms. See "Biological Controls" on page 167 for an overview of these measures.

Physical pesticides such as soap, diatomaceous earth, and even water are good for killing a wide range of insect pests on short notice. "Physical Pesticides" on page 170 gives you an idea of which types of problems can be controlled with physical pesticides. Once things

are under control, decide what you'll do next year to head off the problem before it happens.

Using Botanical Poisons

Botanical pesticides are naturally occurring, plant-based poisons. They need to be eaten or absorbed by a pest to be effective. They kill either outright or by preventing proper feeding or reproduction of the pest. Unfortunately, they are not pest-specific and can be quite damaging to nontarget organisms, including humans. Most do break down reasonably rapidly in the environment into harmless compounds.

Use botanical poisons only after you have exhausted all other options. Treat only the affected plants. When using them preventively for a specific, known problem, learn exactly when to use them for maximum effectiveness.

Use proper precautions to protect yourself when using any pesticide. Read and heed warning labels on product containers. See "Be Safe While You Spray" on page 189 for a general rundown on how to use sprays and dusts safely.

Citrus oil. The oil found in citrus peels is an insecticide. The active ingredients are linalool and d-limonene. Linalool is a nerve poison that kills insects on contact. Citrus oils are reasonably harmless to humans but may cause some animals to shake and salivate. Mix citrus oils with water per label directions, and spray infested plants thoroughly. Repeat every one to two weeks.

Neem. Neem, which comes from the neem tree, is a broad-spectrum insect repellent, growth regulator, and poison. As a spray, neem works against more than 200 insect pests, including Colorado potato beetles, leafminers,

(continued on page 189)

Troubleshooting Fruit and Vegetable Pests

While the most troublesome pests of home gardens vary from one region of North America to another, there are some well-recognized pests that plague gardens in most of the country.

Use this table to identify the insects and other related pests that are damaging your fruit and vegetable crops and to find out what your control options are.

PEST	DESCRIPTION AND CONTROL

Adults

APHIDS

These tiny, pear-shaped insects attack most edible crops. They suck plant sap, causing distorted foliage and dropped leaves. They excrete honeydew, which supports the growth of sooty mold.

Control: Avoid feeding too much nitrogen because fleshy growth attracts aphids. Spray plants with a strong stream of water to knock aphids off. Release beneficial insects such as lacewings or aphid midges. Spray severe infestations with insecticidal soap or superior oil.

APPLE MAGGOTS AND CODLING MOTHS

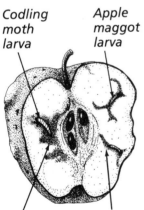

Codling moth larva   *Apple maggot larva*

Codling moth damage   *Apple maggot damage*

Apple maggot flies are ¼″ flies with yellow legs and transparent wings patterned with dark crosswise bands. Larvae are white maggots that tunnel through apples, blueberries, and plums.

Codling moth adults are gray-brown moths with a ¾″ wingspan; larvae are pink or creamy white caterpillars with brown heads that tunnel through apple, apricot, cherry, peach, pear, and plum fruits to the center.

Control: To limit apple maggot damage, collect and destroy dropped fruit daily until September and twice a month in fall. Hang apple maggot traps in trees from mid-June until harvest (1 trap per dwarf tree, 6 per standard tree). Plant clover groundcover to attract predatory beetles. Grow late-maturing cultivars.

To control codling moths, in early spring, scrape loose bark to remove overwintering cocoons, and spray dormant oil. Grow cover crops to attract native parasites and predators. Use pheromone traps to determine the main flight period for moths, then release parasitic *Trichogramma* wasps to attack eggs. Trap larvae in tree bands, and destroy them daily. In areas with severe infestations, spray ryania when 75% of petals have fallen, followed by three sprays at 1–2-week intervals.

PEST	DESCRIPTION AND CONTROL

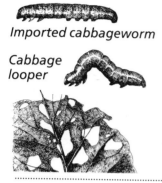

Imported cabbageworm

Cabbage looper

CABBAGE LOOPERS AND IMPORTED CABBAGEWORMS

Cabbage looper adults are gray moths. Larvae are smooth, green caterpillars with 2 lengthwise white lines.

Imported cabbageworm adults are white butterflies. Larvae are velvety green caterpillars. Larvae chew large holes in leaves of cabbage-family and other plants. They may kill plants.

Control: Cover plants with row cover. Handpick. Spray *Bacillus thuringiensis* var. *kurstaki* (BTK). Spray pyrethrins, ryania, and sabadilla for severe infestations.

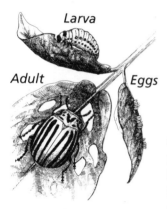

Larva

Adult   *Eggs*

COLORADO POTATO BEETLES

Adults are yellowish orange, ⅓″ beetles with black stripes on their wing covers and black spots on their thorax. Larvae are small, dark orange, humpbacked grubs. Eggs are bright yellow ovals found in clusters on leaf undersides. Both adults and larvae chew leaves of tomato-family plants.

Control: In spring, shake adults from plants onto a ground cloth in early morning. Dump beetles into soapy water. Attract native predators and parasites with pollen and nectar flowers. Mulch plants with deep straw layer. Cover plants with floating row cover until mid-season. Release 2–5 spined soldier bugs per square yard of plants. Apply parasitic nematodes to soil to attack larvae. Apply double-strength sprays of *Bacillus thuringiensis* var. *san diego* (BTSD) on larvae; spray weekly with pyrethrins, rotenone, ryania or neem.

Corn earworm

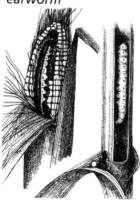

CORN EARWORMS AND EUROPEAN CORN BORERS

Corn earworm (tomato fruitworm) adults are tan moths. Larvae are 1″–2″ caterpillars of various colors.

European corn borer adults are brown moths. Larvae are small, beige caterpillars. Larvae feed on corn silks and burrow into ears. They may damage many other vegetables.

Control: Destroy infested crop debris. Apply *Bacillus thuringiensis* var. *kurstaki* (BTK). See the Corn entry for more details on effective control.

European corn borer

(continued)

Troubleshooting Fruit and Vegetable Pests—Continued

PEST	DESCRIPTION AND CONTROL

CUCUMBER BEETLES

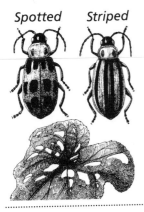

Spotted   *Striped*

Adults are ¼″ yellowish beetles with black spots or lengthwise stripes. Larvae are small, whitish grubs. Beetles chew flowers and leaves of squash-family and other plants. Larvae feed on corn or squash-family roots. Larvae and adults spread mosaic virus and bacterial wilt.

Control: Destroy infested crop residues. Treat soil with parasitic nematodes. Apply row cover before beetles appear to prevent transmission of mosaic virus and bacterial wilt (remove covers when female flowers appear or hand-pollinate flowers). Spray adults feeding in flowers with sabadilla or pyrethrins.

CUTWORMS

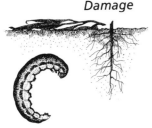

Damage

Larva

Adults are brown or gray moths. Larvae are fat, greasy, gray or dull-brown caterpillars with shiny heads. At night, caterpillars feed on stems of vegetable and flower seedlings and transplants near the soil line, severing them or completely consuming small seedlings.

Control: Put collars made of paper, cardboard, or plastic around transplant stems at planting, anchoring each collar half above and half below the soil line. One week before setting out plants, scatter moist bran mixed with *Bacillus thuringiensis* var. *kurstaki* (BTK) and molasses over the surface of beds. Apply parasitic nematodes to the soil. Dig around the base of damaged transplants in the morning and destroy larvae hiding below the soil surface. Set out transplants later in the season to avoid damage.

FLEA BEETLES

Adult

Adults are tiny, dark beetles that jump like fleas. Larvae are tiny, white grubs. Adults chew numerous small, round holes in the leaves of many crops. Larvae feed on roots. Plants may be stunted or killed. Adults may spread viral diseases.

Control: Delay planting to avoid peak populations. Cover seedlings with row cover. Treat the soil with parasitic nematodes. Spray with neem, pyrethrins, or sabadilla.

PEST	DESCRIPTION AND CONTROL

HORNWORMS

Adults are large, gray moths. Larvae are green caterpillars up to 4½″, with a red or black horn on the tail. Larvae eat leaves, stems, and fruits of nightshade-family plants.

Control: Handpick caterpillars from foliage. Attract native parasitic wasps. Spray *Bacillus thuringiensis* var. *kurstaki* (BTK) while caterpillars are still small.

Tobacco hornworm

JAPANESE BEETLES

Japanese beetle

Adults are metallic blue-green, ½″ beetles with bronze wing covers. Larvae are fat, dirty white grubs with brown heads. Adults eat flowers and skeletonize leaves of a broad range of plants. Larvae feed on roots of lawn grasses and garden plants.

Control: In early morning, shake beetles from plants onto a ground cloth and destroy. Cover plants with floating row cover. Apply milky disease (*Bacillus popilliae*) or parasitic nematodes to sod to kill larvae. Attract native species of parasitic wasps and flies. Organize a community-wide trapping program to reduce the adult beetle population. Spray plants attacked by beetles with ryania or rotenone.

White grub

LEAFHOPPERS

Adults are wedge-shaped, slender insects that jump rapidly into flight when disturbed. Nymphs are pale and wingless and, similar to the adults, hop rapidly when disturbed. Adults and nymphs suck juices from most fruit and vegetable crops. Their toxic saliva distorts and stunts plants. Fruits may be spotted with drops of excrement and honeydew.

Control: Wash nymphs from plants with stiff spray of water. Attract natural enemies (predatory flies and bugs and parasitic wasps). Spray with insecticidal soap, pyrethrins, rotenone, or sabadilla.

Adult

(continued)

Troubleshooting Fruit and Vegetable Pests—Continued

PEST	DESCRIPTION AND CONTROL

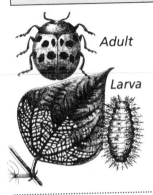

Adult

Larva

MEXICAN BEAN BEETLES

Adults are ¼″-long, yellowish brown beetles with 16 black spots. Larvae are yellowish orange. Both skeletonize bean leaves, chew pods, and may eventually kill plants.

Control: Plant beans early to avoid the main beetle population. Cover young plants with row cover. Handpick daily. Release spined solder bugs or parasitic wasps. Spray severe infestations with pyrethrins, sabadilla, or neem.

Larva

Larva
in fruit

Larva
in shoot

ORIENTAL FRUIT MOTHS

Adults are small, dark gray moths. Larvae are white to pinkish gray, ½″ caterpillars with a brown head. In spring, young larvae bore into green twigs of peach, almond, cherry, apple, pear, or other fruit trees, causing twig wilting and dieback. Later generations bore into fruits.

Control: Where possible, plant early-bearing peach and apricot cultivars that are harvested before midsummer. To destroy overwintering larvae, cultivate soil 4″ deep around trees in early spring. Attract native parasitic wasps and flies with flowering cover crops. Disrupt mating with pheromone patches applied to lower limbs of trees (1 patch per 4 trees). Spray summer oil to kill eggs and larvae. Spray ryania as a last resort.

Adult

PEACHTREE BORERS

Adults are blue-black, 1¼″ wasplike moths with narrow translucent wings. Larvae are white caterpillars with a dark brown head. Larvae bore beneath the bark of peach trees at the base and into the main roots near the surface. They also occasionally attack plum, prune, cherry, apricot, and nectarine trees.

Control: Maintain vigorous trees and avoid mechanical injury to trunks. Beginning in late summer and into fall, inspect tree trunks from 1′ or so above ground level to a few inches below ground level, digging away soil to expose the trunk area below the ground surface. Kill borers in exposed burrows by inserting a sharpened wire. In the fall and spring, cultivate soil around the base of the trunk to expose and destroy larvae and pupae. Attract native parasitic wasps and predators.

PEST	DESCRIPTION AND CONTROL

PLUM CUCURLIOS

Adult

Adults are brownish gray, ¼″ beetles, with warty, hard wing covers and a prominent snout. Larvae are plump, white grubs with brown heads. Adult curculios feed on petals, buds, and young fruits of plum trees. Females make a crescent-shaped cut in fruit skin to deposit an egg, scarring the fruit. Newly hatched larvae feed inside the fruit. Other susceptible fruits include apples, peaches, cherries, and apricots.

Control: Twice daily throughout growing season, knock beetles out of trees onto a ground cloth by hitting branches with padded stick. Gather and destroy beetles. Every other day, pick up and destroy all fallen fruit. Let chickens feed on dropped fruit. In areas where severe infestations occur, check developing fruits for egg scars twice a week. When the first fruit scars appear, apply a botanical pesticide containing pyrethrins, ryania, and rotenone, such as Triple Plus. Repeat in 7–10 days. Do not use a botanical pesticide before petals drop—it kills beneficial pollinators.

SLUGS AND SNAILS

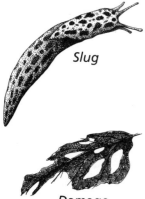

Slug

Damage

Adults are soft-bodied, wormlike animals. Slugs have no shells, and snails have coiled shells. Measuring ⅛″–1″, both slugs and snails leave a characteristic trail of mucus wherever they crawl. Both slugs and snails rasp large holes in foliage, stems, and bulbs. They feast on any tender plant or shrub and may demolish seedlings.

Control: Wrap copper strips around trunks of trees or shrubs, or use copper flashing as edging for garden beds. Trap slugs and snails under flowerpots or boards. Attract them with pieces of raw potato or cabbage leaves set out in the garden. Collect and destroy them every morning. Trap them in shallow pans of beer or fermenting liquids, buried with the container lip flush with the soil surface. To encourage predatory ground and rove beetles, maintain permanent walkways of clover, sod, or stone mulch. Protect seedlings with wide bands of cinders, wood ashes, or diatomaceous earth, renewed frequently.

(continued)

Troubleshooting Fruit and Vegetable Pests—Continued

PEST	DESCRIPTION AND CONTROL

Spider mite webbing

SPIDER MITES

Adults are minute, eight-legged mites with fine hairs on their body; most species spin fine webs. Nymphs are similar in appearance but are smaller than adults. Adults and nymphs suck plant juices from many food crops, ornamentals, and fruit trees. Early damage appears as yellow-specked areas on leaf undersides. Leaves may drop and fruit may be stunted. Webs may cover leaves and growing tips.

Control: Spray fruit trees with dormant oil to kill overwintering eggs. In the garden or greenhouse, rinse plants with water and mist them daily to suppress reproduction of mites. Release predatory mites *Metaseiulus occidentalis* on fruit trees and *Phytoseiulus persimilis* or similar species on vegetables, strawberries, and flowers. Spray insecticidal soap, pyrethrins, or neem. As a last resort, spray avermectins or rotenone.

Adult

SQUASH BUGS

Adults are brownish black, flat-backed, ½″ bugs. Nymphs are whitish green or gray when young, darkening as they mature, and similar in shape to adults. Eggs are shiny, yellow to brown ellipses in groups on leaf undersides. Both adults and nymphs suck plant juices of all squash-family crops, causing leaves and shoots to blacken and die back.

Control: Maintain vigorous plant growth. Handpick all stages from undersides of leaves. Support vines off of the ground on trellises. Attract native parasitic flies with pollen and nectar plants. Cover plants with floating row cover (and hand-pollinate flowers). Spray rotenone or sabadilla.

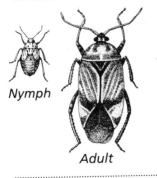

Nymph

Adult

TARNISHED PLANT BUGS

Adults are oval, light green to brown, mottled ¼″ bugs. Nymphs are yellow-green, wingless, and similar to adults in appearance. Adults and nymphs suck plant juices of most flowers, fruits, and vegetables, causing shoot and fruit distortion, bud drop, wilting, stunting, and dieback.

Control: Cover plants with floating row cover. Attract native predators with groundcovers and pollen plants. Try releases of minute pirate bugs. As a last resort, spray rotenone or sabadilla.

thrips, cabbage loopers, and aphids. It is also used as a soil drench against the soil stages of insects. Neem is thought to be mild on beneficial insects and of low toxicity to mammals. It's been used in human herbal medicine for centuries. Apply per label directions. Repeat after a week.

Pyrethrum. Pyrethrum is the dried and pulverized flowers of pyrethrum daisies. Pyrethrins are an extract of the natural active ingre-

dient. (Pyrethroids are synthetic, pyrethrum-like insecticides—avoid them.) Pyrethrins attack an insect's central nervous system and provide a quick knockdown. Pyrethrins are effective against many chewing and sucking insect pests including codling moths, Mexican bean beetles, and spider mites. At low doses, they may only stun insects, so keep an eye on them to make sure they stay "dead." Pyrethrins are moderately toxic to mammals and highly toxic to

BE SAFE WHILE YOU SPRAY

You've probably made the choice to raise fruits and vegetables organically because you're concerned about the quality of your health and of the environment. So on those occasions when you use materials that can have some harmful effects, take all of the precautions you can. Keep these points in mind:

• Store pesticides only in their original containers. Keep them tightly closed and away from food and out of reach of children.
• Read the labels before you use pesticides. Pesticides are labeled "Danger," "Warning," or "Caution," depending on their degree of toxicity. ("Danger" indicates the highest risk).
• Mix and apply pesticides exactly according to label directions. Measure carefully, and keep a set of measures just for mixing pesticides.
• Wear protective clothing when mixing, applying, and cleaning up. Wear long sleeves and long plants, rubber boots, rubber or other waterproof gloves, goggles, and a dust mask or respirator.

• Wash your skin, clothing, measures, and sprayers thoroughly when cleaning up.
• Stay out of treated areas until spray is dry or dust has settled.

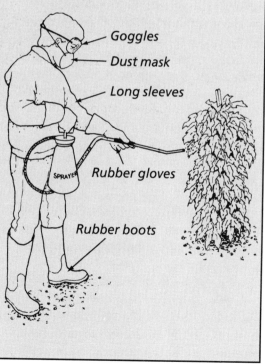

Goggles
Dust mask
Long sleeves
Rubber gloves
Rubber boots

BOGUS BOTANICALS

Some botanical poisons *don't* break down rapidly in the environment and are quite toxic to many nontarget organisms. For example, nicotine sulfate is extremely toxic to insects—and humans. It is absorbed by plant leaves and remains toxic and in the plant for weeks. (You can't wash it off.) Your best choice is to spray a safer botanical poison instead.

---

fish. Follow label directions for application. Two applications may be needed for complete control.

Quassia. *Quassia amara* is a Latin American tree. The wood and bark contain a poison that controls various insects including aphids, Colorado potato beetle larvae, and several types of flies. Since it was once used as a hops substitute in beer making, quassia is probably fairly safe for humans. Purchase chips or shavings (some natural-food stores carry them) and use them as a mulch. Or add ¼ cup of chips to 1 quart of water boiling water and let cool to make a sprayable solution. Spray plants as often as twice a week.

Rotenone. Rotenone, which can be extracted from several plant species, is a nonselective, slow-acting nerve poison that paralyzes insects after they eat it. It is highly toxic to most beetles, as well as birds, pigs, and fish. (In fact, rotenone was first used by South American native peoples for just that—killing fish.) Some people are highly allergic to it, too. Rotenone was once considered to be quite safe, but more recent evidence shows that it may have detrimental side effects on animals and humans. Some organic certification programs have

dropped it from lists of permitted substances; choose other botanical poisons instead whenever possible. If you do use rotenone, read the label carefully and wear a respirator (not a dusk mask) and protective clothing.

Ryania. Ryania comes from a tropical shrub of the same name. It is a broad-spectrum insecticide, but it works best on butterfly and moth larvae such as cabbageworms and corn earworms. It also controls many chewing and sucking insects including citrus thrips (add some molasses to it), Japanese beetles, and Mexican bean beetles. It is not as toxic to beneficial insects but is somewhat toxic to fish, animals, and humans. Spray or dust according to label directions. Usually two applications ten days apart will provide control.

Sabadilla. Sabadilla is a powder made from the seeds of a tropical lilylike plant. It provides excellent control of hard-to-control bugs such as Mexican bean beetles, cucumber beetles, squash bugs, tarnished plant bugs, and harlequin bugs. Toxicity is much lower than rotenone and pyrethrins, but it is toxic to honeybees, so don't use it while they are active. It causes violent allergic reactions in suscepti-

---

TEMPT PESTS WITH MOLASSES

Just as a spoonful of sugar helps the medicine go down, a spoonful of molasses helps the pesticide go down—right into the bellies of the pests that plague your plants. Just add molasses to insecticidal spray solutions. It attracts the insects and encourages them to eat more. The larger the quantity of a sprayed plant they eat, the faster they'll expire. Try adding 1 tablespoon of molasses per gallon of spray solution.

ble humans, so protect yourself when applying it. Spray or dust according to label directions. Strain before spraying, and shake tank while spraying. Weekly applications usually provide control.

Animal Pests

Whether you garden in the suburbs or in a rural area, you may find that animals and birds cause you more headaches than insect pests do. The trickiest part of coping with animal pests can be identifying the pest. Since many animals feed at dawn or dusk, you'll need to notice such signs as feeding patterns, tracks, tunnels, and excrement to figure out what culprit is invading your garden. For example, gnawed strawberries may be the work of birds, mice, or slugs. Controls that work for one pest may do nothing to stop another, so it's important to determine as best you can which pest is to blame before you act. Once you do decide, you need to act fast to prevent a complete crop loss.

Deterring Deer

An electric fence, and not necessarily a high one, is the most effective way to keep deer out. One design suitable for small areas uses two fences, an inner chicken-wire fence 4 feet high and a single-wire electric fence only 2½ feet off the ground and located 3 feet outside the chicken wire. Deer find it hard to jump the chicken-wire fence with the electrified wire in the way. If you prefer a conventional woven wire fence instead of going electric, construct one at least 8 feet high. A second outer fence about 3 feet high increases the effectiveness of a nonelectric fence because double obstacles confuse deer. If deer are nibbling on bushes or individual young fruit trees, consider enclosing the plants in woven wire fence cages. For a

ADDED PUNCH FOR PESTICIDES

Botanical pesticides are reasonably mild and break down rapidly. These are their good points—and their downfall. Often it would be nice if they were a *little* stronger or kept working a *little* longer. Pesticide manufacturers have found substances that help botanicals work longer and stronger. Unfortunately, these materials, called synergists, are not always naturally derived or harmless materials.

One of the most common synergists is piperonyl butoxide, or PBO. PBO is a synthetic substance that can cause damage to the nervous system of animals and humans when used frequently at high concentrations. Check labels of products you buy to see if PBO is listed as an ingredient so you can make an informed choice.

A better solution to the problem of too rapid breakdown is encapsulation. In encapsulation, the active ingredient is somehow enclosed in tiny packages to protect it from light and heat. One such product is MVP. MVP is made up of *Bacillus thuringiensis* (BT) encased in the empty cell walls of a harmless single-celled creature. Unprotected BT is no longer working after four days, while MVP retains its original potency after the same number of days and is still working after a whole week. This method involves biotechnology, but the result appears to be harmless and very useful.

This is an area of active research, and new products are being introduced every year. Check with your supplier to see what products are available.

slight deer problem, this is an inexpensive, effective solution.

Repellents such as bars of highly perfumed deodorant soap or sprays of red pepper and rotten eggs deter deer as long as the pressures of starvation or overpopulation don't force them to eat anything in sight. However, repellents are most effective as a preventive. If deer have already gotten a taste of your crops, anything less than a strong physical barrier may not keep them away long.

Repelling Rabbits

The best way to keep rabbits out of a garden is to erect a chicken-wire fence with mesh no larger than 1 inch. If you have an existing picket or woven wire fence, simply attach a 2-foot-wide strip of chicken wire to the bottom of the fence. Rabbits also sometimes burrow under a fence, so you may need to dig a trench and lay wire in it as well, as shown in the illustration on the left on page 163. If your soil is rocky, pile a 1-foot-wide border of small stones around the periphery of your fence to discourage burrowing. To protect young trees and shrubs from rabbits gnawing bark in the winter, erect cylinders made of ¼-inch hardware cloth; the cages should be 1½ feet to 2 feet high (higher if you live in an area with deep snowfall) and should be sunk 2 to 3 inches below the soil surface. This method is also effective in protecting trees from bark feeding by mice and voles.

Most repellents will deter rabbits, but they need to be replenished frequently and are best used as a preventive, not after an attack starts.

Banishing Birds

While birds eat insect pests, they also consume entire fruits or vegetables or will pick at your produce until it is damaged enough to be unappealing. Most bird controls involve making the area you wish to protect less appealing to birds or more difficult for them to feed in. The most effective control to protect bush and vine fruits and small fruit trees is to cover them with lightweight plastic netting. Cover row crops with floating row cover. You can also use a variety of commercial or homemade devices to frighten birds away from your crops. See "Sights and Sounds" on page 160 for more information.

7 GATHERING THE HARVEST

Getting and Keeping the Most from Your Garden

From apples to zucchini and from asparagus tips to potato tubers, the ultimate goal of a food garden is the harvest. Once you've coaxed every vegetable plant, berry bush, and fruit tree to its peak of productivity, it only makes sense to harvest and store each crop properly. Good harvesting and storage techniques ensure the best possible flavor and nutritional value. They also can allow you to enjoy weeks or even months of meals featuring homegrown fruits, vegetables, herbs, and grains.

HARVEST TIMING AND TOOLS

When the tomatoes are coming thick and fast and the zucchini are threatening to grow into Louisville Sluggers, success boils down to knowing three things: when to harvest, how to harvest, and what tools you need to do the job. The conditions that maximize flavor, nutrition, and storage length differ for each fruit and vegetable, although related crops generally can be handled similarly. You'll find crop-specific harvest hints in the table "Making Fresh Flavor Last" on page 202 and in the individual plant entries in Part 2.

Ready or Ripe?

Harvesting at the right time helps you bring fruits and vegetables to your kitchen at their flavorful best. The first rule of harvest timing is pick it when it's ready. Just remember that ready doesn't always mean ripe.

As a general rule, crops that you grow for their vegetative parts—leaves, stems, and roots—should be harvested when they are young, tender, and immature. Examples include basil, broccoli, lettuce, and radishes. If the edible part is truly a fruit—a seed-bearing structure such as a tomato or an apple—let it ripen on the plant before you pick. Compare the flavor of aging, weather-beaten lettuce to that of a juicy, red, just-picked tomato. Both are "ripe," but the lettuce had reached its sweet, tender best back when the tomato was a flavorless green golf ball.

There are, of course, exceptions to this guideline. Several of the "fruits" we call vegetables—summer squash, snap beans, and eggplant, for example—taste much better when plucked at a young age. And a few food crops such as nuts, grains, and dry beans are left on the plants until they are mature and almost completely dried. Harvesting these foods too soon can result in poor flavor and a short shelf life.

Since many garden crops are ready for harvest at about the same time, it pays to know which can wait and which can't. See "What's the Rush?" on this page for help in setting your harvest priorities.

If you suspect that a crop has passed its prime, let your taste buds make the call. A quick flavor check can help you decide if the harvest belongs in your kitchen or your compost pile. Better to face the disappointment of bitter lettuce before it reaches the salad than to waste your time picking and cleaning a barely edible crop.

Harvest Early and Often

Sun-warmed produce may be romantic, but warmth translates into a shortened storage life for your precious produce. The flavor and keeping quality of fruits and vegetables changes with the weather and even the time of day. Harvesting in the morning, just after the dew has dried, is best because your crops are cooler and have higher water content than during the heat of the day. Higher water content means crisper texture. And cool crops chill more quickly once refrigerated than sun-heated ones do, which saves energy and reduces spoilage.

Make weather part of your harvest plan, too, by remembering these tips:

• Cloudy and cool days offer many of the same advantages as early-morning picking, as long as you avoid times when plants are wet.
• Wait for dry weather to harvest grains, dry beans, and other crops that dry on the plants.
• Hard rains can beat down tender leaf crops and strong winds may topple tomato cages and shatter dried grains. If you know a storm

---

WHAT'S THE RUSH?

The bounty of a well-grown garden can induce harvest hysteria. Before you panic, prioritize your picking. While some crops deserve immediate attention, others tolerate a more relaxed harvest schedule. A few crops will endure near-neglect, for a limited time.

Big-rush crops. Peas, broccoli, cauliflower, cucumbers, summer squash, sweet corn, raspberries, and blackberries quickly pass their prime; pick them at the right time or you'll miss some of the garden's most delicate flavors.

Weekend crops. Harvest cabbage, leafy greens, melons, peppers, tomatoes, and apples every few days or only on weekends. Gather herb seeds like dill, fennel, and coriander before seed heads shatter.

No-rush crops. These won't wait forever, but you can hold out for good weather and a few spare hours to harvest and store carrots, dry beans and grains, onions, potatoes, winter squash, and pears. Pick leafy herbs as needed for fresh use or storage.

is coming, gather or protect crops that might be damaged.

• Frost predictions may spur you to either harvest or protect tender crops like tomatoes.

Don't forget that planning plays a part in a well-timed harvest. See "Succession Planting—Crop After Crop" on page 72 and the individual plant entries in Part 2 for tips on making sure your crops don't all ripen at once.

Get the Right Tools

Good tools will help you harvest your crops job safely, efficiently, and without damage to your vegetables and fruits. Here are some factors to consider when deciding what tools you'll need:

• What do you need to reach your crop? Is it in the top of a tree? Underground? In a briar patch?

• How big is your crop?

• Will it be ready for harvest all at once or over an extended period?

• How long/often will you pick?

• Is your crop fragile? Will rough handling reduce its quality for fresh eating or in storage?

Once you've considered what you need to get the job done, gather your tools of choice. Start with the basics. You can expand your collection over time as you gain experience. The items that follow range from essential to handy-to-have-around to occasionally necessary.

Your hands. Most fruits and vegetables are easy to pick by hand, but sometimes your hands need help to do the job right. For example, you can pull peppers and squash off of their plants, but pulling can damage the plants. Also, the fruits frequently snap off right where the stem is attached. The stem forms a natural

---

AVOID THE ITCH

The itch to garden can turn into the itch to scratch when you run afoul of natural plant defenses. Thorny brambles are an obvious hazard, but less-threatening plants also may cause you woe. Some gardeners get a rash from picking squash and okra; others scratch at the sight of tomatoes or beans.

Finding out what crops make you itch is mostly a matter of trial and error. Once you know which plants to avoid, it's easy to take precautions. Long sleeves help a lot, since inner arms tend to be more sensitive than palms or the backs of your arms. Long pants are equally useful when wading into the midst of an itchy or scratchy crop. Experienced okra pickers recommend gloves for protection from the tiny spines that cover okra. But for crops such as berries that are easily crushed by clumsy gloved fingers, try cutting finger holes in the toes of a pair of long cotton socks and slipping them over your arms. Or cut the first three fingers out of a long cotton glove.

---

barrier that seals juices in and microorganisms out. Loosing it can reduce storage life. Harvesting tools that let you cut instead of pull spare your plants for ongoing production. Don't jeopardize future harvests with careless handling; pick carefully, whether you're using your hands or one of the following "hand accessories."

Gloves. Some crops, including okra, raspberries, and blackberries, guard their fruits with thorns or other protective features that make gloves a desirable harvest tool. But ill-fitting gloves impede harvesting, and most gardeners prefer to pick without them. See "Avoid the Itch" on page 195 for other ways to escape an itchy, scratchy harvest.

Reach extenders. Whether your fruit trees are on dwarfing rootstocks or not, they'll inevitably bear fruits out of arm's reach. Clambering into a tree to gather fruit is a recipe for broken limbs—yours, the tree's, or both. It's worthwhile to invest in both a sturdy ladder and a long-handled fruit picker. A ladder lets you pick each fruit by hand but leaves you balanced precariously in the air, holding your harvest. The fruit picker keeps you securely on the ground while you maneuver its business end—a fruit-size wire basket with extended wire "fingers"—amid the branches. Choose a picker that has a plastic-coated basket with some sort of padding at its bottom to minimize bruising of your fruit.

A sharp knife. Make a good, sharp knife a part of your regular harvest equipment. Use it to cut heading vegetables, such as broccoli, cauliflower, cabbage, and lettuce. You can also use a knife or pruning shears to sever stems of winter squash and other crops that should be cut, not pulled, from the plant.

Clippers or pruning shears. Sawing through sometimes-woody stems with a knife grows tedious when you have a lot of harvesting to do. Sharp clippers make the job go more quickly when picking okra, peppers, pumpkins, and other squash-family members.

Scissors. Find a pair of scissors that fits your hand comfortably, and keep them sharpened for harvesting herbs and leafy greens. Wrap some rubber bands around the handle and use them to bundle up your herb harvests.

A fork, spade, or shovel. You'll need a digging tool to loosen the soil around root crops before you harvest. (Tugging on plant tops generally results in a handful of tops and

a small stub marking the vegetable's place in the soil.) Spading forks, spades, and shovels all work equally well to unearth carrots, onions, parsnips, peanuts, potatoes, radishes, and other subterranean crops; the trick is in the technique, not the tool. Consider where the roots are in relation to their aboveground tops and dig

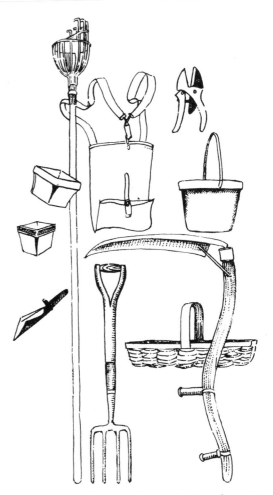

Start with the basics when selecting harvesting tools. A few simple containers, a sharp knife, and a shovel or fork for digging are probably all you need to begin with. Expand your collection as new needs arise or as your interest in owning unusual tools grows.

accordingly to minimize spearing and severing roots as you harvest.

A scythe. This age-old tool is just the thing for cutting your grain crops just above ground level. The scything motion is a little tricky, however, and it's important to sharpen the blade frequently as you work. For very small plantings, you can also use a machete.

An old sheet. Use an old sheet to hold grains or dried beans for threshing. Spread the sheet over a hard surface such as a patio or driveway, then pile cut plant parts on it. Fold up the sheet and beat or stomp on the bundle to shatter its contents. Open the sheet, remove barren stems, and repeat until you've removed most of the inedible plant material.

Containers. Unless you plan to eat your harvest on the spot, you'll need some kind of container to put it in. The ideal harvest container is sturdy yet lightweight, easy to carry, and reusable. It provides support and protection for your fruits and vegetables without slowing you down as you pick. Woven baskets are pretty, but the sharp interior edges may bruise tender fruits and vegetables like tomatoes. (To prevent bruising, line them with a towel or cloth.) Smooth-sided pails or soft cloth bags work better. A bucket is especially useful for berry picking; tie it around your waist with rope or a strip of cloth to free both hands for harvesting. Plastic bags work well for many crops but hold in heat and moisture, which can encourage spoilage.

HANDLING YOUR HARVEST

The time you've spent nurturing your crops can go to waste if you handle your harvest carelessly. The nifty toss that takes an apple from your hand to the basket 2 feet away leaves bruises that can spoil a whole bushel in storage.

And knowing whether to wash, wipe, cure, or chill a just-picked crop can add significantly to its storage life. Here are some handling guidelines to help you enjoy crops that taste better, produce more, and store longer.

Collect with Care

It just makes sense not to bruise the tomatoes or crush the cabbage. But it's just as important to handle your plants gently, too. Techniques that twist stems and tear off branches can bring your harvest to an untimely end and, in the case of perennial producers, can reduce future years' harvests.

Be gentle. Bruises, punctures, scrapes, and missing stems all provide opportunities for decay-causing microorganisms to gain access, which means a rotten mess in storage. Pick carefully. Place fruits and vegetables gently into containers. And don't stack soft crops like tomatoes so deeply that the fruits on the bottom get crushed.

Show your support. When harvesting tree fruits, tomatoes, or beans, use one hand to support the plant and the other one to pick.

Don't do dew. Avoid harvesting when your plants are wet from dew or rain. Many fungi and bacteria travel in water droplets, which busy gardeners can spread all too efficiently. With the exception of crops you plan to plunge into cooling water (such as leafy greens and cole crops), wait until crops are dry before you harvest.

Keep your cool. Fresh-picked food fades fast in the sun. The sooner you can cool your crop, the better it will taste and the longer it will last. All crops fare best when the time from harvest to curing or storage is kept to a minimum, but quick cooling, as described in "Post-Picking Procedures" on page 198, helps when delays are unavoidable.

Post-Picking Procedures

Many crops, including broccoli, cauliflower, and leafy vegetables such as lettuce, spinach, and kale, decline quickly if they're not cooled almost immediately after harvest. According to organic market gardener Miranda Smith, a refrigerator is fine for storing some crops but is too warm to cool them straight from the garden. Pick the crops listed above into cold (or even iced) water, then drain them and refrigerate them in ventilated plastic bags. You can cool a salad's worth of lettuce in a mixing bowl, or, for a larger harvest, bring a flat-bottomed tub or cooler full of cold water to the garden in a child's wagon. Change the water as necessary to keep it cool while you harvest.

Prompt cooling extends storage life for many crops, but the excess moisture can encourage disease organisms in storage. Snap beans and peas benefit from rapid cooling, but they often carry fungal spores. Don't wet these crops at harvest time if there is any sign of disease. Eat or preserve them as quickly as possible.

To Wash or Not to Wash?

A freshly washed harvest is as pretty as a picture, but washing isn't always good for storage life. Clinging soil doesn't usually cause problems, but introducing moisture at harvest time can—it invites rots and molds. Washing and scrubbing may also remove a crop's protective coating or damage its skin, breaking down its natural defenses against diseases.

Organic market gardener Miranda Smith recommends cleaning only those crops that you plan to use right away. Smith washes the soil from carrots only when she plans to take them to market—it makes their color better—

and wipes sale-bound squashes and melons with a damp cloth.

Gently brushing away excess soil is sufficient prestorage cleaning for most crops. Of course, washing winter squashes that are covered with wet mud isn't going to get them any wetter. For leafy crops and herbs, rinse away dust and grit the day before harvest by using overhead watering. Swish particularly gritty herbs in cold water and hang them in a shady spot to dry.

Commercial fruit growers wash apples, pears, peaches, and citrus crops in a mild chlorine bleach solution to inhibit disease problems in storage. You can do this, too. Gently dip them in a solution of 1 part bleach to 9 parts water. On the other hand, stow berries unwashed. Water clings to berries' soft, bumpy surfaces and quickly turns them into a fuzzy, gray mass in your refrigerator. Whether you brush, wash, dip, or leave it "dirty," make sure your harvest has dried off before you put it into storage, where excess moisture spells spoilage.

READY, SET, STORE

A well-prepared, carefully stored harvest stands a good chance of reaching your table tasting much as it would fresh from the garden. Whether you store crops whole, or freeze, preserve, or dry them, it pays to find out which storage conditions are best for the crops you want to save and prepare them accordingly.

Storing crops whole is an easy and age-old practice. But remember, one of the keys to successful storage is keeping your harvest in *conditions that you can easily maintain.* If a crop's whole storage requirements vary greatly from the conditions that normally exist around your home, consider other storage options. Is it more efficient to freeze, can, or dry the crop? Or is it something you should enjoy fresh and look forward to again next season? It's best to eat or process and preserve crops such as berries, snap beans, and tomatoes as soon as possible after harvest.

Here are some general tips to get you started storing. You'll find harvest tips, information on optimum storage conditions, and suggested preservation methods for major crops in "Making Fresh Flavor Last" on page 202. You'll also find harvest tips in the plant entries in Part 2.

Remove leafy greens from root crops. Leaves of root crops such as carrots and beets will continue to try to grow, robbing moisture and nutrients from the roots. Cut them off an inch above the root.

Cure before you store. Many crops, including potatoes, onions, sweet potatoes, and winter squashes, need to be cured before storage. See "Taking the Cure" on this page for information on curing crops.

Consider countertop storage. Crops such as tomatoes, peppers, and avocados continue to gain color and flavor at room temperature on a kitchen countertop. Some fruits—such as peaches and plums—also ripen at room temperature. Pears have better texture when ripened off the tree—they form fewer grit cells when harvested after they blush but before they're fully ripe. Remember that produce stored this way continue to ripen, so check your countertop crops often for signs of spoilage. Discard fruits such as peaches if they begin to shrivel and lose texture instead of ripen; they probably weren't mature enough when harvested.

Look for long keepers. With many crops, the time they will keep well—either under refrigeration or at room temperature—varies with cultivar. When you select new plants, look for plants described as good keepers.

TAKING THE CURE

A brief curing period enhances the storage life of garlic, nuts, onions, peanuts, potatoes, sweet potatoes, and winter squash. Curing lets the skin, shell, or rind dry and harden, protecting the inner flesh from outer contaminants. Here are tips on curing some favorite crops:

• Cure sweet potatoes and peanuts by washing them with water and then laying them out to dry in a single layer in a warm (80°F) place for two weeks.

• Wipe winter squash and pumpkins clean with a soft cloth, then cure them in a well-ventilated place at room temperature, for seven to ten days.

• Gently brush or wipe onions and garlic to remove soil, then allow them to air dry in a warm place for two weeks. Store braided or in net bags. Leave the papery outer skin intact—it contains chemicals that retard spoilage and sprouting.

• Protect potatoes from light to keep them from turning green and to prevent sprouting. Dry them in a dark place, at room temperature, for two weeks after digging.

• Remove the outer husks from nuts and cure them in a cool, dry, rodent-free area for one to three months.

Subterranean Storage

It's no surprise that root crops love root cellars. The steady, cool temperature of the surrounding soil mimics the conditions in which those crops formed. A root cellar makes use of the earth's temperature-moderating effects, giving you a storage facility that is cool in summer and colder but not freezing in winter—without the energy costs of refrigeration.

For best results, a root cellar must remain constantly cool, with an average temperature just a few degrees above freezing. High humidity without excessive moisture is also important. Ventilation with outside air enhances a root cellar by releasing crop-produced gases, such as carbon dioxide and ethylene, that cause increased ripening and rotting in storage. If you don't have room for a root cellar, consider a corner of an unheated basement or storm shelter.

Another option is to bury an insulated box, such as a cooler or the shell of an apartment-size refrigerator or freezer. (Before using a refrigerator, remove the motor, coils, and all door locks or latches, leaving a box with hinges and a lid.) Set the cooler or box on its back in the ground, with the lid at or just below ground level. Add a padlock on the lid as a safety precaution. Use it much as you would a root cellar. Loosely pack potatoes, carrots, and other root crops in slightly dampened sand or straw to store them. Insulate the lid with bales of straw or hay to prevent freezing. Such a structure lacks ventilation, so check stored crops frequently for spoilage.

An even simpler storage method for root crops is to leave them in the ground. You can harvest carrots and other root crops all winter if you mulch them heavily to keep the soil from freezing. Don't forget to mark them so you can find them in the snow. One drawback is that hungry rodents can dramatically reduce the success of this technique.

Some crops just don't belong in the root cellar. Nuts and onions need lower relative humidity than a root cellar can offer. And even in storage, fruits and vegetables continue some normal plant functions. One by-product of these functions is a gas called ethylene, which encourages ripening. In storage, it can build up and cause unwanted ripening and decay. Fruits, in particular, tend to produce ethylene. Root crops tend to sprout when exposed to it. When possible, store fruit crops and root crops separately and use good ventilation to reduce problems.

Fresh from the Fridge

Stash snap beans, peas, sweet corn, broccoli, cauliflower, leafy greens and herbs, summer squash, and berries in the refrigerator as quickly as possible after harvest. But keep in mind that refrigerated crops have a limited storage life—use or preserve them as quickly as possible. But keep in mind that your refrigerator is designed to *keep* foods cold, rather than cool them quickly. See "Post-Picking Procedures" on page 198 for ways to get crops cooled quickly.

Refrigeration slows down the metabolism of harvested produce, improving moisture retention and retarding spoilage. Most important, it safeguards foods' nutritional content. For example, refrigerated broccoli quickly loses its vitamin C, and folic acid levels fall when leafy crops linger without cooling. As kale and cabbage wilt, they lose large amounts of carotene.

Use ventilated plastic bags to maintain moisture levels of refrigerated produce, but don't seal them into a soupy bath. With delicate lettuces and herbs, try placing a damp paper towel in the bag to keep the produce moist but not soggy.

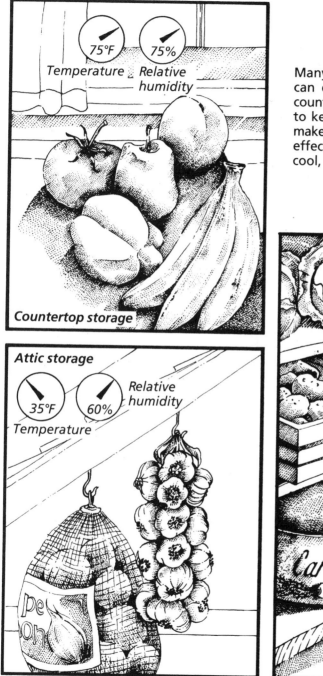

Countertop storage

75°F Temperature · 75% Relative humidity

Attic storage

35°F Temperature · 60% Relative humidity

Many crops keep well in conditions that you can easily maintain. Storing fruits on the countertop at room temperature allows them to keep ripening after harvest. Root cellars make use of the soil's temperature-moderating effects. An unheated attic or garage offers a cool, dry storage spot in the winter.

Temperature 35°F · 90% Relative humidity

Root cellar storage

Making Fresh Flavor Last

Good harvesting and storage techniques go hand in hand when it comes to bringing fruits and vegetables to your table at their best. The guidelines below include tips for harvesting your produce at its peak, optimum temperature and relative humidity (RH) for storage, and special considerations for best storage life.

CROP	HARVEST TIPS	STORAGE REQUIREMENTS	COMMENTS
Apples	Gather firm, well-flavored fruits with stems attached. Avoid bruising.	32°–38°F at 85%–90% RH	Keep away from root crops. Late-maturing cultivars store best—up to 8 months.
Beans, snap	Pick when pods are tender yet crisp, and seeds are one-quarter developed.	Refrigerate up to 5 days for fresh use. Good for freezing or pressure canning.	Use two hands when picking to avoid mangling plants.
Berries	Pick when fully colored and glossy.	Refrigerate immediately; use within 2 days or preserve. Wash just before using.	Best when fresh. Freeze or can whole fruits or fruit preserves.
Broccoli and cauliflower	Cut from plant when beads or curds are tight. Additional side-shoots may develop.	Wash, refrigerate, and use within 10 days.	Excellent for freezing. Rapid cooling at harvest preserves nutritional value.
Cabbage and brussels sprouts	Cut when heads are firm and full-size. In fall, cool weather improves flavor.	32°–40°F at 90% RH	Stored cabbage may create a strong odor. Use an outdoor storage pit when possible.
Carrots and beets	Dig after roots reach full-size. Lightly harvest young roots for fresh eating.	Mulch to store in the ground, or remove tops and hold at 34°F at 95% RH.	Pack in damp sawdust or similar material. Easy to overwinter in the ground in a box or pit.
Corn	Harvest when kernels are tender and plump and silks are dry.	Store in plastic bags in the refrigerator. Use within 2 days for best flavor.	Husk ears before storing to save space. Freeze or can surplus soon after picking.

CROP	HARVEST TIPS	STORAGE REQUIREMENTS	COMMENTS
Grains, dry beans, and other seeds	Gather when seeds rattle but before the pods begin to shatter. Thresh to remove pods and other material.	Heat seeds at 175°F for 10–15 minutes to kill pests; store in airtight containers. May also store in freezer.	Place a bay leaf or dried hot pepper in storage jars to discourage moths and weevils.
Grapes	Cut clusters on a cool day when fruit is firm and well-flavored.	Rinse, dry, and store in single-bunch layers at 40°F and 80% RH.	Best when fresh. Freeze or can whole fruits or fruit preserves.
Greens	Cut leaves from young plants, or cut whole heads when full-size.	Rinse and refrigerate immediately, loosely packed in plastic bags.	For best flavor, harvest in early morning after a cool night.
Melons	Signs of ripeness vary. Check rind color, aroma, and drying of stem.	Store at 55°–60°F for 7–10 days, or refrigerate.	Avoid harvesting too early. Melons with thick, hard rinds store longest.
Nuts	Gather as soon as they fall. Remove hulls (if present). Dry thoroughly.	Store in ventilated containers at 35°–45°F and 60%–70% RH. Freeze shelled nuts.	See the Chestnut and Peanut entries in Part 2 for special handling tips.
Onions, garlic, and shallots	Pull or dig 2 weeks or more after tops die back. Dry for 10 days.	Trim after drying. Store in ventilated bags at 40°F and 50%–60% RH.	A cool attic or garage is best for winter storage. Dry storage conditions are needed.
Peaches and other stone fruits	Judge ripeness by color, flavor, and ease with which fruit separates from stem.	Ripen at room temperature. Handle very gently at all times.	Refrigerate to stop ripening process. Best when fresh. Freeze or can whole fruits.
Pears	Lightened skin color, full-size, and mature seeds indicate ripeness.	Store at 34°F and 80%–90% RH. Ripen at room temperature.	Pick before fruits turn yellow. Tree-ripened pears have more grit cells.

(continued)

Making Fresh Flavor Last—Continued

CROP	HARVEST TIPS	STORAGE REQUIREMENTS	COMMENTS
Peas	Pick sweet and snap peas when pods are plump but before peas are touching one another inside the pods. Pick snow peas before peas start to swell.	Refrigerate promptly. Use as soon as possible, or freeze.	Peas become starchy very quickly. Pick often and use or preserve promptly.
Peppers	Harvest peppers when immature (usually green) or after they ripen and change color.	Refrigerate for up to 2 weeks in ventilated plastic bags. May be frozen or dried.	Ripe peppers are sweeter than immature peppers but tend to soften more rapidly.
Potatoes	Dig 2 weeks after vines wither. Break vines to make crop mature all at once.	Cure in the dark, then store in darkness at 38°–40°F and 90% RH.	Storage is easy for the first 2–3 months. After that, check often for spoilage.
Summer squash	Cut with stem attached when rind is thin and glossy. Best when picked young.	Wash gently and refrigerate for up to 2 weeks. Easy to freeze.	Harvest often to keep squash coming. Flowers are edible.
Sweet potatoes	Dig when tubers reach desired size. Wash gently, sort, and cure.	Store at 55°–60°F and 85%–90% RH.	Flavor, texture, and nutrition improve with curing.
Tomatoes, green	Pick when outer skins are light green and seeds are completely developed.	Ripen at room temperature, out of sunlight. Very immature fruits will not ripen.	Wrap in newspaper for short-term storage. Ripening slows or stops below 60°F.
Tomatoes, ripe	Gather when fruits are fully colored and have begun to soften.	Keep at room temperature until ready to eat, can, or freeze.	Refrigeration robs tomatoes of their full flavor and aroma.
Winter squash and pumpkins	Cut with stem attached when plants die back or before first freeze.	Wipe clean, cure, and store at 50°–55°F with good ventilation.	Cultivars with hard rinds store longest. Freeze cooked flesh.

Flavors Worth Preserving

If you're going to savor a taste of summer while the snow flies, freezing, canning, and drying are the best storage options for crops that don't store well whole for more than a couple of days.

Freezing

Assuming you have adequate freezer space, freezing is the fastest and easiest method of preserving your harvest. Most fruits and vegetables should be blanched in boiling water before freezing to stop enzyme activity and kill microorganisms. Otherwise, the texture and nutritional value can deteriorate even at freezing temperatures. Blanching times vary with the food being frozen; consult a good food-preservation book for specific directions. Some foods, such as blueberries and raspberries, are so delicate that they are frozen without blanching. Unblanched foods do not keep their quality in the freezer as long as blanched ones do.

Although they're traditionally stored dry, many herbs keep well in the freezer, too. Wash freshly harvested herbs and pat them dry. Chop them into pieces and pack them in labeled freezer bags. Or puree herbs with water or oil and pour the puree into ice cube trays for freezing; later, move the solid cubes to labeled freezer bags. Either method lets you add fresh-flavored herbs to recipes all winter long.

Canning

Boiling-water-bath canning is a relatively easy way to preserve naturally acidic foods like tomatoes. It's also good for foods preserved in brine (such as pickles) or syrup (such as fruit preserves, sweetened relishes, and chutneys). Most other garden crops must be canned in a pressure canner to adequately sterilize the food and seal the jars. Your local extension agent can supply you with up-to-date guidelines for safely canning your harvest.

Drying

Drying preserves crops by removing the moisture that spoilage organisms need to survive. A food dehydrator is a practical option for drying many fruits and vegetables. Most herbs, however, dry readily with little processing; simply hang them or lay them on screens in a dry, dark, well-ventilated spot. Fruits and vegetables hold their colors and flavors well if you pretreat them before drying. First, wash, core, peel, and slice or chop fresh foods. Make the pieces uniform in size so that they dry at the same rate. Thin slices dry quickly; bigger, thicker pieces take longer to dry.

To prevent light-colored fruits such as apples and peaches from darkening, soak slices for three to five minutes in orange, lemon, or pineapple juice or in ascorbic acid solution (1 tablespoon of ascorbic acid powder in 1 quart of water). Drain the fruit before transferring it to drying trays.

Blanch vegetables before you dry. Blanching times vary with the food being frozen; consult a good food-preservation book for specific directions. Spread them on drying trays. Store all dried foods in sealed, airtight containers.

8

ENDING AND EXTENDING THE SEASON

Preparing Your Garden for Winter and Stretching the Harvest Season

The first fall frost signals the end of the growing season for many gardeners—but it doesn't have to for you. With good planning, frost needn't bring an abrupt end to the gardening year. Instead, it can signal nothing more dramatic than a change in your gardening style and the crops you'll be harvesting. Plan from the start to use season extension devices like cold frames and row covers. With them, you can continue to bring fresh food from your garden to your table well into the fall and early winter. If you're ambitious, you could even find yourself becoming a year-round vegetable gardener.

Along with protecting crops from frost, most gardeners use fall to build their soils by covercropping or planting green manures. They also do some important preventive "gardenkeeping" chores to decrease future weed, pest, and disease problems. The end of the more active gardening season is also a good time to organize and repair garden tools and supplies, put a finishing touch on the season's

records, and sometimes get a start on spring planting.

In this chapter, you'll learn how to clean up your garden in fall. You'll also find hands-on information on extending the season, from using simple single-plant protectors to covering part or all of your garden with a plastic hoophouse. Last, you'll find an innovative calendar approach to season extension that helps you think ahead—something that's needed for you to get the most out of season extension techniques.

GARDEN CLEANUP

Good "gardenkeeping" is as important to a garden's health and well-being as housekeeping is to your family's. Fortunately, the effects of good gardenkeeping tend to last longer than those of housework. Done well, garden cleanups eliminate niches for overwintering pests and disease-causing organisms, decrease future weed populations, and increase gardening safety, convenience, and efficiency.

So when the days begin to shorten and you've picked most of what your garden has to offer, don't just close the gate and walk away. Garden cleanup really doesn't take long, and the benefits are many. Also, think how much happier you'll be in the flurry of next spring's planting if you don't have to pull down half-collapsed trellises and clear aside mushy plant remains to get at the soil. Here are some gardenkeeping chores to remember.

Remove plant debris. Healthy plant material should go right on the compost pile. (For instructions on making a compost pile, see "Making a Compost Pile" on page 38.) If you have crops that are diseased or pest-ridden or if you're clearing weeds that have gone to seed, burn them or dispose of them in sealed containers with your household trash.

Lift old plastic mulches and row covers. If they are still usable, hose them clean and hang them on a clothesline or spread them out on the lawn to dry. Then roll them up and store them until next season. To avoid future problems, do not save materials that were used to mulch or cover diseased plants.

Clean up the miscellaneous paraphernalia. Remove all pots, boards, bricks, and stakes that aren't in use. Scrub pots and dip them in a 10 percent bleach solution (1 part bleach to 9 parts water) to sanitize them. Scrape old soil off of stakes, boards, and bricks. If they were used near plants that showed symptoms of soilborne diseases or were infested with insects that bury eggs in soil, wash them with a 10 percent bleach solution before storing.

Pick up all tools. Scrape soil off tools and wash them in a 10 percent bleach solution. Sharpen any dull blades and fix any broken handles. Coat metal parts with mineral oil or recycled motor oil.

Patrol for weeds. Don't stop at the edge of the garden bed; walk your whole yard carrying a large bucket and a weeding tool. The seeds from weeds at the edge of your property can easily blow as far as the garden. If you can't pull or dig a stubborn perennial weed, cover it with a deep, light-obscuring mulch that you can leave in place over the next season.

Do therapeutic pruning. Once perennial trees and shrubs go dormant, check them for any disease problems and prune off diseased stems. Dip pruners in a 10 percent bleach solution between each cut; this may help prevent problems from spreading. Mulch perennials when the ground freezes.

Prepare perennial crops to withstand the winter. Plants such as strawberries, berry bushes, and fruit trees may need protection from winter cold, sunscald, and frost heaving (movement of soil caused by thawing and freezing). Protect fruit trees from sunscald by wrapping the trunk with a white plastic tree guard or by painting it up to the first branch with a mixture of 1 part white latex paint and 1 part water. Mulch a strawberry bed and the soil around young fruit trees after the soil freezes to prevent root damage from frost heaving. In very cold regions, bend berry canes to the ground and insulate them with straw to prevent cold damage to the buds, as shown in the illustration on the opposite page.

Sort your seeds. Most seeds remain viable for more than one growing season. Make a list of your leftover seeds, noting how much seed remains. Pack them in an airtight container and store them in a cool place until it's time to make up your seed order the following season. See "Check Seed Viability" on page 96 for how to test seeds for viability.

Complete your garden records. The best time to fill in blanks in your records left during those oh-so-busy weeks in summer is now, while your memory is fresh. By next spring, you'll be too involved in starting new plans and plants to have time for reconstructing old records.

SEASON EXTENSION TECHNIQUES

If you've ever started seeds inside or covered crops with a blanket or tarp to protect them from forecast frost, you've used season extension techniques! Any steps you take to push your gardening window beyond the traditional season is season extension. It's not hard to do, and the rewards can be great.

When and how to extend your season depends to some extent on where you live. In the Northeast and upper Midwest, the goal, of course, is to protect plants from cold spring and fall weather. Gardeners in the South or Southwest may have the opposite problem—they need to find ways to keep plants going despite too much heat.

Common season extenders used to protect crops from the cold include:

- Row covers
- Cold frames
- Hoophouses
- Cloches
- Hotbeds

Each of these devices has benefits and limitations. Few gardeners are satisfied to use only one or two of them. Instead, they use several, matching the devices to particular crops and environmental conditions. When you understand these principles, you can be creative and flexible with designs for your crop protection devices.

Row Covers

One of the easiest ways to extend the season is to cover rows of plants with some

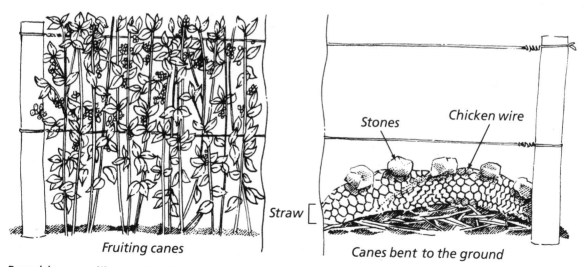

Fruiting canes

Straw

Stones   *Chicken wire*

Canes bent to the ground

Bramble crops like raspberries are hardy, but some may require winter protection in northern zones. Bend year-old canes to the ground, insulate them with a 6- to 8-inch layer of straw, cover the straw with chicken wire to hold it in place, and weight down the wire with stones.

type of insulating material. This helps plants in spring by giving them a somewhat warmer environment so they can get a faster start. In the fall, row covers protect against frosts that could injure plant tissues, and, again, a warmer microclimate around plants like tomatoes helps to ensure that fruits continue to ripen.

Floating Row Covers

Floating row covers made of spun-bonded synthetic fabric give about 4° to 6°F of frost protection. Rain or irrigation water penetrates them easily and air moves almost freely between the enclosed area and the outside. In the fall, use them over mature or nearly mature, rela-

SEASON EXTENSION CONCEPTS

Season extension technologies take advantage of basic laws of nature. Here's a short course on the theory of season extension.

Light energy becomes heat energy. As shown on the opposite page, on a sunny day light waves penetrate the glazing, or transparent covering, of a greenhouse or cold frame. The glazing also prevents reflected light waves from escaping. As the solid objects inside absorb light waves, they change into heat waves, warming the objects. Some heat reradiates into the surrounding enclosed air, heating it, too.

Warm air is trapped inside. As the air inside warms up, it heats the soil and solid objects, such as the jug of water shown on the opposite page. As the air warms up, it can hold more moisture. Plastic traps and holds heated air better than floating row cover material, and glass traps more than plastic. Wood framing retains more heat than metal or PVC pipes.

Some heat gradually escapes. The air inside is warmer than that outside and heats the glazing material. But the glazing gradually gives up some of its heat to the cooler outside air. As it does so, it absorbs more heat from the inside air. In turn, the inside air absorbs more heat from the soil and solid objects, such as the jug of water, it surrounds. The more objects to store heat, the longer the air inside will remain warmer than that outside. The effects of this heat loss are most dramatic at night or when the sun isn't shinning and the weather is cold and windy.

Condensation occurs as the air cools. As the inside air cools to its dewpoint, beads of water condense on the cool glazing and on the plants themselves. Excess moisture can cause disease problems if not dealt with.

Venting regulates heat, humidity, and air supply. Venting releases extra heat and humidity. It also lets in fresh air—air that contains new supplies of an essential "nutrient" for plants, carbon dioxide. Plants use carbon to make glucose, the sugar that is the building block for all plant parts.

tively hardy plants such as lettuce, spinach, broccoli, and peas.

Since crops don't overheat under row cover material in cool fall temperatures, save yourself anxiety by enclosing plants long before you expect frost. As in the spring, you can lay floating row cover directly over a crop, anchoring it with rocks, garden staples, or boards. However, because moisture doesn't evaporate quickly from leaves touching the polyester material in cool, humid air, fungus-susceptible plants sometimes suffer under floating row cover in the fall. To combat this problem, set the floating cover over wire hoops or drape it from

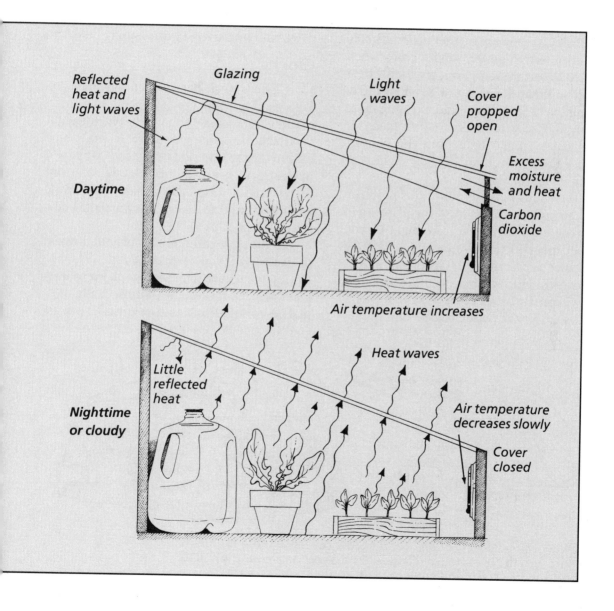

cables or over stakes. If you are using it over cables or stakes, use duct tape to connect two lengths of the material together to account for the extra height you'll need. Or put the edges together, fold them over about ½ inch, and staple through all four layers with a regular office stapler.

Plastic Covers

Plastic sheeting is another material many gardeners use to protect tender crops when the first frosts threaten. Plastic gives more frost protection than floating row cover material. But plastic holds both air and moisture more tightly, too, so you can't leave it in place for many days without running the risk of overheating the plants or increasing their susceptibility to fungal diseases.

There are two solutions to this problem. You can pull the plastic off of the plants each morning and put it back on each night. Or you can set up supports like you would for floating row cover, as described in "Floating Row Covers" on page 210. However, even with supports, you will need to provide an easy, efficient venting system for the plastic enclosures.

If you drape plastic over hoops to make a growing tunnel, you might want to use preslitted plastic. This material gives slightly more frost protection than floating row cover and, thanks to the slits, vents itself. To protect plants longer into the fall, just throw a second sheet of unslitted plastic over the slitted plastic tunnels when temperatures fall below 30°F at night. You can leave this second cover in place on cloudy days, but remove it on warm, sunny days.

Cloches

Cloches work like a personal greenhouse for a plant or small group of plants. The first cloches were glass bell jars—heavy, unventilated and breakable, but useful in extending the growing season. Today, you can buy paper or plastic cloches ready-made, or use a variety of household materials to make your own. Several types of cloches are shown in the illustration on page 214.

In the spring, set transplants out a week or two early if you cover each with a cloche. During the season, cloches can play a role as plant protectors, keeping out insect and animal pests. Be careful not to let enclosed plants

In fall, moisture collects under floating row covers. Disease problems can flare up if the cover touches leaves. Erect a wire arch over the bed to support the row cover and prevent plant contact.

Plastic sheeting draped over wire arches makes a protected microenvironment that can be several degrees warmer than the outside air. Tuck the plastic into the soil at the sides, and weight the ends with rocks.

overheat. In the fall, devise a jumbo-size cloche using a tomato cage and plastic sheeting, as described in "Tricks of the Trade: Simple Season Extenders" on page 216.

Cold Frames

Cold frames are enormously useful in spring and fall and, in many regions, can serve a purpose year-round. Depending on your design and climate, you can hold and harvest hardy crops in a cold frame through the winter, until you clear it for early-spring vegetables.

Cold frame designs are straightforward. As shown in the illustration on page 215, most cold frames have a slope from back to front to accommodate various crop sizes. If the glazing (the glass or plastic) slopes to the south, this design also lets in more light than level glazing. The back wall of a cold frame should be 1 to 1½ feet tall. If it's taller than that, air in the cold frame cools too much.

Painted plywood is the most practical building material to use. Wooden cold frames are durable, light enough to move around, and the easiest to operate. But if you want to get a feel for the system before committing yourself to the expense and time of building a wooden cold frame, try making an enclosure of cinder blocks or bales of hay. Cover it with old storm windows. This should provide enough protection for you to gain experience with off-season gardening. Chances are that you'll decide to build or buy a more permanent structure for the future.

Many people use old storm windows for glazing panels because they are so inexpensive and easy to locate. Other people make their own glazing panels, using tempered glass, fiberglass, or either rigid or flexible plastic. When using glass or a rigid plastic glazing material, it's important to enclose it in the framing so it can't slide out. If you have access to a router, use it to rout channels on both long sides of your frame. Then, slide the glazing into place, and secure it by nailing molding strips across both ends.

If the glazing material is lightweight, you may want to attach the panels to the back side of the cold frame with hinges. Hinges allow you to vent by propping the panel open without worrying that the wind will carry it away.

People who are home during the day can vent manually. Cut a 1-foot length of a 1 × 4 and notch it as shown in the illustration on the opposite page to hold the glazing panel at various levels. If you aren't home during the day or don't want to be tied to the cold frame's schedule, buy an automatic venting arm. This invention is filled with a substance that expands the arm as it heats, which raises the panel. The arm lifts only 20 pounds, so you may need two of them on a panel if you've used storm windows or if you've built with glass. If you have a large frame with several panels, you don't need to equip every panel. During cold but sunny weather, venting through

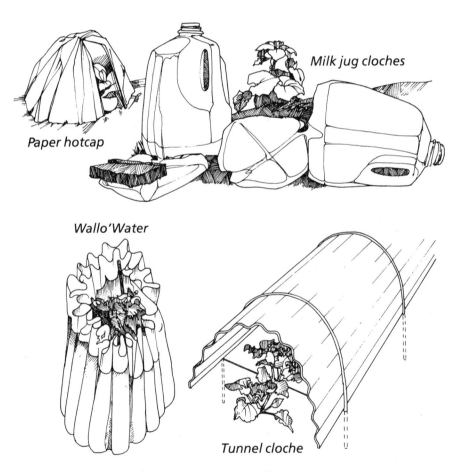

Milk jug cloches

Paper hotcap

Wallo'Water

Tunnel cloche

Commercial cloches, or plant protectors, include paraffin-treated paper hotcaps and Wallo'Waters. Make your own cloche by cutting off the bottom of a plastic milk jug. A tunnel cloche made of a 4-foot-long section of translucent corrugated fiberglass can protect several plants.

every other or every third panel is adequate. Suppliers for the venting arms are listed in "Sources" on page 507.

Hotbeds

Hotbeds are cold frames in which the soil is heated. Insulating the frame of the hotbed is certainly not necessary, but it can make economic sense, especially for northern growers. Rigid foam insulation is easy to sandwich between two layers of plywood or boards. Old blankets make good night covers over the glazing.

Hotbeds maintain slightly higher temperatures than cold frames but, like cold frames, they will overheat in bright sunshine. Install automatic venting arms or open the glazing on sunny days.

Fairly fresh manure with its bedding was once the only source of heat for a hotbed. Sandwiched between the subsoil and a layer of topsoil, fresh manure and bedding gives off heat as it decomposes over the winter. Today, it's more common to use electric heating cables than manure.

Cable-Heated Hotbeds

Electrified hotbeds are easy to assemble. Because the cables are thermostatically controlled, their heat is more consistent and predictable than that from decomposing manure. To construct a cable-heated hotbed:

1. Excavate the site of the hotbed to a depth of 8 to 12 inches, separating topsoil from subsoil as you dig.

In the spring, a cold frame is a good place for raising or hardening off transplants. In the summer, remove the glazed lid, shade the frame with lath, and use it for rooting cuttings of herbs and shrubs.

2. Cover the bottom of the excavated area with 1 or 2 inches of washed gravel.

3. Cover the gravel with fine-mesh metal screening.

4. Cover the screening with a 2-inch layer of washed sand.

5. Embed a heating cable in the sand. Use 6 feet of cable for every square foot of soil surface and space the cable lines 2 inches apart.

6. Place fine-mesh metal screening over the sand to prevent the cable from being pierced by stakes or tools you might stick into the soil in the hotbed.

7. Fill the area with 4 to 6 inches of good topsoil. (The subsoil that you removed in Step 1 can be used as fill for some other garden project or can be gradually mixed into your compost pile.)

Manure-Heated Hotbeds

Old-fashioned manure hotbeds work well and can be located anywhere because they don't require a source of electricity. So gardeners with access to manure may want to consider building one. Horse manure is the best choice for a hotbed, but cow manure will work. Avoid using poultry manure, even if it contains a great deal of bedding material. It is still so rich in nitrogen that it can burn roots or release lethal amounts of ammonia into the air.

To build a manure-heated hotbed, excavate the site to a depth of 10 to 18 inches,

---

✌ TRICKS OF THE TRADE ✌

SIMPLE SEASON EXTENDERS

When protecting plants from freezing is your theme, the number of variations you can create is nearly endless. Use your ingenuity in designing season extenders with simple materials. Here are some examples.

A cagey solution. Cold weather often arrives when your pepper plants are still loaded with ripening fruit. You can create a miniature greenhouse around the plant to keep temperatures warm enough to help the fruit finish ripening. To do so, put a tomato cage around the plant. Wrap the cage with clear plastic, and tape the overlap to hold it in place. Drape another piece of plastic over the top. For extra warming, put plastic or glass bottles or jars filled with water inside the cage.

An artistic touch. Painters' frames, available at any art supply store, make a nice enclosure for a tomato plant. You'll need five 3 × 3-foot frames to make a boxlike enclosure with a lid. Double-glaze the frames by stapling 4 to 6 mil plastic film to each side of the frame. Hinge one side of the enclosure for both venting and ease of picking. Use rectangular frames to make a lower, longer box that can cover a bed of mixed greens. Vent the frames by propping up one side with a stake or rock. Protect the plastic by storing the frames in a cool, dark area when they aren't in use.

Hoophouses

Hoophouses are greenhouse-size plastic tunnels. They are unheated and rely only on openings for ventilation. Growers who own them can't say enough good things about them.

One design for a hoophouse, from organic market gardeners Stewart Hoyt and Grace Gershuny in Vermont, uses a wooden base and arches of PVC pipe to support the plastic. Hoyt and Gershuny designed the hoophouse so they could easily move it from one area to another. It's also constructed to withstand the early-fall and late-winter, usually heavy snow-

separating topsoil from subsoil as you dig. Shovel in a 6- to 12-inch layer of fairly fresh manure mixed with bedding, and level it out. Cover the manure with 4 to 6 inches of the separated topsoil. There's no need to bother with sand or screening. Put the hotbed frame in place, water the hotbed well, and cover it with whatever you're using for a lid. Wait a few days for the hotbed to warm up, and then put seeds or transplants into it.

falls that are common in the "Northeast Kingdom." Here's how to make one like that shown in the illustration on this page.

1. Construct a rectangular base of 2 × 4's (standing on edge) of the size area you want to cover. A good starting size is 20 feet long and 10 feet wide.

2. Drill 3-inch deep, ½-inch-diameter holes every 4 feet along the top of each of the frame's long sides. Insert a 6- to 12-inch length of ½-inch-diameter rebar in each hole.

3. Cut lengths of 1½-inch hot-water PVC pipe long enough to arch from one long side piece of the frame to the other; pick the length that will give you the height hoophouse you want. A house that's 5 feet tall at the peak requires less material to construct, but one that's 7 feet at the peak will be more comfortable to work in. For a 10-foot-wide, 7-foot-high house, you will need pipes about 18½ feet long.

4. Fit one end of one of the PVC pipes over a piece of rebar and bend the pipe over so that you can slip the other end of it onto the rebar on the opposite side of the frame. Repeat Step 4 for each pipe arch.

5. Drill a ⅛-inch-diameter hole every 2 feet along each of the two end arches. Insert a ½-inch #10 sheet metal screw into each hole.

6. Use sturdy cable or wire to make a network on top of the pipes to help support the plastic. Tie one end of the cable to one of the end PVC pipes just below the lowest sheet metal screw. Stretch the cable up and over all of the other PVC arches to the opposite side and end of the frame. Tie the cable to that pipe just below the lowest sheet metal screw, pulling the cable as tight as you can.

7. Tie another cable to one of the end arches just below the next higher sheet metal

screw, stretch it up and over the frame, and tie it just below the next sheet metal screw at that end. Repeat Step 6 as many times as needed until you reach the last screw on the arches. When you finish, all of the cables will cross at the same point at the exact top and center of the frame.

8. Cover the frame with a single sheet of

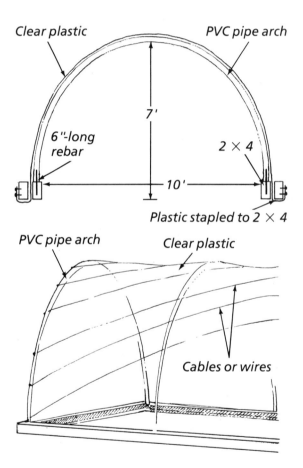

A plastic hoophouse can cover whole garden beds, allowing you to grow sizable quantities of food in the fall. If you build a cold frame inside the hoophouse, you can even continue to harvest greens and other hardy crops through the winter in many regions.

clear plastic. Anchor the edges of the sides by stapling the plastic to loose 2 × 4's, as shown in the illustration on the opposite page. You can close the ends of the hoophouse by leaving enough extra plastic to gather up like the end of a bread bag. Just twist the plastic closed at ground level and weight it with rocks or a heavy board. If you prefer, you can build more permanent end walls with doors for easy access.

If you live in an area that doesn't get heavy snows, you can probably space the cables farther apart than 2 feet. Hoyt takes the plastic down at the end of the season after a couple of snows and stores it until the following spring.

Gershuny and Hoyt have had great success producing peppers and tomatoes in the hoophouses. Their yields are much higher and their plants have fewer disease problems.

Hoophouses can be four-season devices, depending upon the climate and their sturdiness. In the North, for example, you can grow heat-loving crops all summer and fall under the plastic cover. By installing a hotbed, cold frame, and/or tunnels inside when the weather gets cool, you can harvest crops through the winter months. In spring, you'll be able to move flats from hotbed to cold frame to tunnel and finally outside as the weather warms.

Southern growers can use a hoophouse all year, too. But instead of leaving the plastic up during the summer, you can replace it with shade cloth to cool mid-season greens. Or if that seems to be too much trouble, you can use the pipes to support netting for climbing crops.

Greenhouses

Greenhouses are the best of all season extension devices. Depending on the design and accessories such as heaters and artificial lights, greenhouses allow you to garden all through the year. In a greenhouse with good lights and reliable heat, you can plant successive crops of greens, timing them to provide a steady source of fresh young salads. Many greenhouse owners start a few tomatoes and peppers in late December and early January. By coddling them, generally with bottom heat and extra lighting, the first fruits ripen just about the time you're transplanting seedlings into the garden.

The choice of spring transplants broadens as well. A heated and well-lit greenhouse allows you to raise slow-growing herbs and ornamentals to good transplant size by spring. The advantages are twofold—not only can you select species and cultivars that are either unavailable or prohibitively expensive at the local garden nurseries, but you can also be certain that they've never been sprayed with pesticides that you don't want to be exposed to.

Summer greenhouse management depends as much on your climate as it does on your crop preferences. In a hot, bright region, you might find the greenhouse more useful as a solar dryer than a growing area. In colder climates, greenhouses can ensure bountiful yields of heat-loving delicacies such as melons and seedless cucumbers, no matter what the outside weather. With enough space, you can also grow some fig trees or even a dwarf citrus or two.

In the fall, a greenhouse in almost any region can prolong the harvest season of tomatoes and other frost-sensitive crops. It's no wonder than that greenhouses head the wish lists of many a good gardener.

One major limitation for many gardeners who wish for a greenhouse is the cost. Greenhouse kits cost upward of $1,000. Building your own saves money but requires know-how.

Another important consideration is the requirement for successfully making use of a home greenhouse. Greenhouses do not manage themselves. Accessories—heaters, irrigation, ventilation fans, and lights—can be automated to minimize the amount of time you'll have to spend in the greenhouse on a daily basis. But even with these technological time-savers, you'll need to carefully monitor both the environment and pest and disease incidence.

Time is the most urgent requirement of a new greenhouse operation. If you've never run a greenhouse before, you'll need to spend some time learning how to operate it to provide an optimum environment for the plants you're growing, as well as how to control the various pests and pathogens that like a greenhouse environment as much as the plants do. "Recommended Reading" on page 511 lists good reference books to guide you through this adjustment.

Time requirements diminish with experience. You'll know, for example, whether an aphid population can be controlled by hand-squashing rather than insecticidal soap and what temperature settings are appropriate. However, even with this background, you'll still need to spend a few minutes every day in the greenhouse and devote a few days a month to jobs such as trellising, planting, and harvesting.

THE EXTENDER'S CALENDAR

Planning for season extension involves thinking about your garden in a new way. You'll be planting crops at times that you normally wouldn't consider planting them. Here, we present scheduling suggestions to help you get started on planting and harvesting crops beyond your standard gardening season. For some specific tips from expert gardeners in various regions, see "Regional Realities: Season Extension Stories" on page 222.

Start in Midsummer

If you're a beginning gardener, you may find that the easiest time to launch a plan of action for season extension is midsummer. By then, you'll have learned the basics of planting and garden care. If you plant some crops in midsummer, they'll grow without any protection at first. This will give you time to buy or find materials for making some simple season extension devices to protect them once cold weather arrives.

Planting for fall harvests usually begins in July or, if you live in a southern region, August. Planning for fall and winter crops should have begun before this, when you developed your yearly garden map and ordered your seeds. However, if you're like most gardeners, you'll have some seeds left over from spring planting to work with.

Scheduling is the key to good fall and early-winter production. As with starting spring plants, you will have to develop fall planting schedules in reference to your particular climate. Temperature is not your only concern, however. Light is equally important during this season when the daylength shortens and the light intensity weakens every day. Even in a warm environment, low light means that plants can't make the rapid growth they do during the spring. Here's what this means to your schedule:

1. Leafy crops planted in late summer and early fall will take at least two weeks longer to come to maturity than they do in the spring.

So, for example, a lettuce cultivar that normally requires 55 days to maturity could take about 70 days instead.

2. Crops may never grow as large as they do under high light and warm temperatures. Most root crops don't develop as large or succulent a root in low light, either. Your best strategy for summer-sown root crops may be to cover them with a heavy mulch and overwinter them for spring harvest.

3. You will also have to make sure to plant at the right time. To determine when to plant particular crops for fall harvest, follow the guidelines in the plant entries in Part 2. Also refer to "Managing Fall Crops" on page 224.

Summertime Seeding

Getting seeds to germinate in the summer garden is sometimes difficult. Garden soil may be too hot or too dry for these crops during the late summer and early autumn when they are planted. If you experience problems, use some market gardeners' tricks to get them going.

Let them soak. Seeds never appreciate a good soaking as much as they do when it's hot. Soak them anywhere from 8 to 16 hours before planting, in either chlorine-free water or a liquid kelp dilution. You can also presprout seeds by draining off the soaking water and then sandwiching the seeds between moistened paper towels for a couple of days. Check these seeds frequently and at the first sign of a root, plant them in prepared soil.

Start them inside. You can also start seeds in a seed-starting mix in flats indoors. (See "Planting Seeds Indoors" on page 102 for instructions on setting up seed flats.) But rather than keeping the flats artificially warm during germination and early growth, keep them cool and slightly shaded. This works well for crops that are easy to transplant, such as broccoli and cabbage.

Cover for coolness. Start crops that do not transplant well, such as bok choy and Chinese cabbage, where they will grow. Soak the soil thoroughly before seeding, seed in a slight depression, and cover the area to retain moisture. If the seeds can germinate in darkness, put a board over the row to hold in moisture and coolness well. Use moistened burlap or a light covering of straw mulch to cover seeds that need light, such as lettuce.

Make a shade tunnel. When temperatures are still too high for good growth of a crop such as spinach or late peas, erect a shade tunnel. Plastic shade cloth, burlap, and even thin bamboo shades are all useful summer crop protectors. Install these devices as you do plastic sheeting—over frames or tunnels, or tied to stakes. Lettuce, cabbage-family greens, and even violets for the salad bowl all appreciate the cooler temperatures this cover provides.

Cover Crop Considerations

While it's not technically season extension, covercropping is an off-season technique that you should start thinking about now. You can undersow fall crops with cover crop seeds. Covercropping also begins in late summer when you undersow fall crops. Continue covercropping through the fall as you harvest beds and growing areas. Keep two factors in mind as you covercrop: Most legumes require 40 days of warm weather to become established; and annual cover crops are more appropriate for areas where early-season crops will grow the next year. Use perennial cover crops in areas you plan for summer and late-season crops.

For complete information on choosing and planting cover crops, see "Managing Cover Crops" on page 41.

Fall Planting for the Future

Fall planting schedules include more than cover crops and winter vegetables. Fall is the best time to plant garlic and some perennial onion crops. Gardeners can also take advantage of lighter gardening schedules and plant quickly established perennial crops. Many people use fall to get a jump on spring planting, too.

🌿 REGIONAL REALITIES 🌿

SEASON EXTENSION STORIES

Growers across the country report eating from their gardens year-round, thanks to season extension technologies.

Pacific Northwest

Organic farming consultant Lynn Coody lives in Oregon, where winter temperatures are mild. She says she has harvested as many as 32 different crops during midwinter. Coody doesn't actually use many season extension technologies because of her cloudy, relatively warm, and usually rainy climate. If snow is predicted, she covers crops with floating row cover. She avoids plastic because it holds in too much moisture and leads to disease problems. Coody plants fall crops farther apart than the standard spacing and always uses raised beds.

Midwest

Organic farmer Richard de Wilde of Harmony Valley Farm in Wisconsin harvests fall and winter crops from a greenhouse, a hoophouse, cold frames, and plastic tunnels. He uses plastic tunnels inside a hoophouse so he can get to crops more easily. He also grows hardy crops like kale under tunnels directly in the field, but he explains that they are more work to harvest because he often has to dig through snow to reach them.

De Wilde has devised a way to use cover crops for extending the season. He interplants spinach and radishes with white clover and continues to harvest them until the first week of December.

He also plants oats and spinach simultaneously in the first week of September. The oats grow and eventually are killed by the cold. Their white stems reflect winter sunlight, which prevents the soil from thawing. The spinach overwinters better because it's not disturbed by alternate freezing and thawing of the soil.

Southwest

Organic market gardener Fred Hoover of Fre-Bar, Inc., farms near Phoenix, Arizona, where the worst of the winter brings a daytime temperature of 60°F, which drops to the 20s during the night. Hoover can grow hardy crops like kale and mustards for winter harvest without any cover. He also grows lettuce uncovered. He harvests it as baby lettuce, so it has little chance of being cold-damaged because of its short growing period.

Hoover does put covers over his winter herbs because he's found that otherwise they just lie dormant and don't make any new growth.

Onion-Family Crops

Garlic, multiplier onions, and top-setting onions are customarily planted in the fall, as described in "Friends and Relatives" on page 425. Timing is important for these plants. Your goal is to have the plants establish a good root system in the fall without sending up a green shoot. Planted too early, they produce top-

In July and August, Hoover has to protect all of his crops because temperatures commonly are over 100°F. Hoover uses shade cloth as much as possible.

Prize-winning gardener Lynn Tilton grows in Arizona, too, but 4,000 feet higher in altitude than Phoenix. In his area, the first frost hits about Thanksgiving time, and while February is usually frost-free, there can be frosts in March. In these unusual conditions, Tilton says he'd have to cover most crops other than root crops and hardy greens; however, Tilton usually uses the midwinter period for improving the soil and preparing it for planting, rather than doing much season extension. Since he can harvest two crops of peas, three crops of tomatoes, and several crops of corn each year, it's understandable that he likes a little time off.

Northeast

Veet Deha, an agricultural consultant with Crest Lane Designs in New York, gardens near Ithaca, where gardeners really do need season extension technologies to get much variety during the winter. Deha generally picks from the garden up until the end of December but finds that due to variable weather conditions, even gardening under cover is a gamble.

Deha likes plastic tunnels for winter crops such as kale and spinach. The temperatures in the tunnel may not be any higher than the surrounding air, but the crops don't get crushed by snow.

Deha usually overwinters some leeks for spring harvesting. She finds they require heavy mulching to prevent the soil from repeatedly freezing and thawing, which can cause the leeks to deteriorate badly.

Overwintered carrots are another crop Deha counts on for spring harvests. She piles bags of leaves on them before the soil freezes in the fall. If she can get the bags unstuck, she harvests them during the fairly predictable January thaw.

Corn salad is Deha's winter staple. She makes two plantings of corn salad every fall, one during the first week of September and the other ten days later. If she's going to put it under cover or in a hoophouse, she makes a planting every week through mid-October. She says it actually grows best in compacted soil. She actually straps boards on her feet (1 foot wide, 2 feet long, and ½ inch thick) and walks on the seedbed after planting the seeds to press them into the soil.

growth. Planted too late, they do not root well and may rot.

Asparagus

Asparagus yields just as quickly when planted in the fall as when planted in the spring. But with fall planting you don't plant in a trench and fill it gradually as the stalks grow. Instead, follow the relatively new advice of researchers and plant the crowns only 5 to 6 inches deep in soil that has been composted and generously supplied with rock phosphate or bonemeal. Mulch after the ground freezes. If you are planting a new "all-male" cultivar, you can harvest the plants very lightly for two weeks the following spring. Otherwise, wait until the next year, and harvest as advised in the Asparagus entry in Part 2.

MANAGING FALL CROPS

Hardy crops fall into several broad categories of treatment for fall, winter, and spring harvesting. Use the following guidelines for planning season extension techniques and harvesting schedules.

Super-Tough Crops

Each of these crops withstands light frosts and snow without losing quality. Cover for quality harvests through the winter.

Brussels sprouts	Endive
Cabbage	Kale
Chard	Radicchio
Chicory	Spinach

Moderately Tough Crops

Each of these crops is cold-hardy and will stand a little frost. However, their quality is better if protected from snow and temperatures below 30°F.

Arugula	Florence fennel
Beet greens	Lettuce
Bok choy	Mizuna
Broccoli	Mustard

Broccoli raab	Onion greens
Cauliflower	Parsley
Celery	Peas
Chinese cabbage	Turnip greens

Undercover Crops

Each of these crops can be held under cover or a mulch and harvested through the winter or in the spring.

Beets	Radishes
Carrots	Rutabagas
Daikons	Salsify
Leeks	Turnips
Parsnips	

Overwintering Crops

Each of these crops can overwinter under cover and make new growth in the spring. Cover with plastic tunnels or thick straw mulch, depending upon the severity of your winter climate.

Leeks	Onions
Lettuce	Parsley
(winter cultivars,	Spinach
young plants	
overwinter)	

Leafy Crops

Early salads make spring seem real. Many gardeners start spring crops early in cold frames or under plastic tunnels, but that's not the only way to get an early harvest. Two other methods are effective: wintering over a fall-planted crop and fall-seeding a spring salad bed.

Overwintering. To overwinter a crop, direct-seed lettuce, spinach, and other hardy annual leaf crops in mid-fall. Time the planting so crops have about six or seven leaves when heavy frosts arrive. Before they freeze, cover them with a heavy straw or shredded autumn leaf mulch. In early spring, pull the mulch aside to give them light and cover with plastic tunnels or floating row cover material.

Overwintered crops usually bolt quickly once the spring settles. Cut whole plants, rather than leaves, very early in the season.

Fall seeding. You can also seed your crop in late fall so that it will be in place to germinate at the earliest possible time in spring. This gives you a jump on the season because seeds often can germinate in early spring, but you can't sow them because the soil is too wet to be worked safely to make a seedbed.

Instead, prepare your seedbed in late fall. If you have lettuce plants that have gone to seed, just shake the seed heads over the seedbed. Or mix seeds from a seed packet with sand, and lightly scatter it over the seedbed.

Timing is important with this technique. You want to plant late enough in the year so that seeds will freeze rather than rot or germinate. After planting, mulch with a thick layer of straw or shredded leaves. In early spring, remove the mulch and cover with a floating row cover for an even earlier start. Lettuce, spinach, mustard, mizuna, and other hardy greens do well with this system.

Early-Spring Start-Up

Season extension technologies can be used for all spring crops, from the earliest spinach and peas to the latest melons and eggplant. Cultural techniques and concerns are not much different than in the fall, with one important difference: In the spring, you'll rarely have to worry about fungal disease. And you may find that you treasure your floating row covers as much for their insect pest protection as for their effect on temperature.

It takes a little experimenting to learn which devices you like best and how much earlier you can plant outside under cover. So start your first year with simple projects, like swathing tomato cages in plastic or putting out early broccoli transplants under hotcaps, and eventually work your way up to more ambitious projects.

One of the biggest boons season extension technologies can give is an increase in early-spring soil temperatures. Lay clear plastic sheeting over the soil several weeks before planting early crops. (If the soil is already covered with snow you don't need to shovel it off—just cover the soil, snow and all. The plastic will help melt the snow and then warm the soil.) Check the soil temperatures daily and you'll know when it's safe to plant the first covered peas and spinach.

Think Ahead

Advance planning will make all of your seasonal transitions easier. For example, if you want to try pushing for a late tomato harvest—say, up until Thanksgiving—you'll have to lay your plans for it during the spring. When you order seeds, you'll need to either get one long-season cultivar or order a short-season one and plant it late.

Set up your garden areas for season extension technologies when you plant, even if it's spring. Install the supports for plastic sheeting or other covers when you plant; this preparation makes late-season protection so easy that you won't put it off because you "couldn't get to it in time." Similarly, stockpile bricks or boards near the plants you'll be covering with tunnels in fall so the bricks and boards will be there when you need to anchor the tunnels.

9 GARDENING IN CONTAINERS
Growing Fruits, Vegetables, and Herbs in Pots and Planters

Whether you garden on a city rooftop or on a large suburban lot, container gardening can add a new dimension to your food garden. Even if you have ample space for growing fruits and vegetables, it's a great way to grow some of your favorite foods. Most herbs and a wide range of vegetables and dwarf fruit trees will thrive in containers. With a cluster of containers, you can grow a garden full of fruits, vegetables, and herbs right outside your door.

For plants that aren't hardy in your region, container culture may mean the difference between growing a favorite plant or not. For example, both rosemary and sweet bay are popular herbs that can be grown in containers. If they're not hardy in your region, you can grow them outdoors in summer and move them in when the weather gets cold in fall.

You also can use container culture to prolong your harvest. Whether you grow a few salad greens on your windowsill all winter long, pot up a few herbs to bring indoors at the end of the season, or have an elaborate indoor food garden with artificial light, container culture helps you keep your garden giving all year. All it takes to add this flexibility to your food garden is a few supplies and some easy gardening techniques.

For the most part, gardening in containers is much like gardening in a garden bed. Once you've selected containers and plants to grow in them, you will need to pay particular attention to the potting mix and fertilizers you use. For techniques like planting, pest and disease control, and basic care through the season, the information on in-ground gardening in Chapters 4, 5, and 6 applies. You'll also find information on container culture in the individual plant entries in Part 2.

SELECTING CONTAINERS

You can grow great fruits, vegetables, and herbs in almost any kind of container imaginable. Two things are important about the containers you select: They must have provision for adequate drainage, and they must hold enough potting medium for the crops you've selected to grow in them.

The containers you select also may depend on whether your garden is strictly utilitarian or designed to be ornamental as well. Other than that, anything goes. If you want to grow a thyme plant in an old olive oil can, that's fine—as long as you poke about four holes in the bottom of the can. Five-gallon buckets hold enough potting mix for a pepper or tomato plant. A galvanized washtub or half of a wooden barrel is just right for a bush squash or a small, bush or trellised melon plant.

Don't forget that you can combine several plants in a single container—a half-barrel planted with a handful of herbs or with salad greens and baby carrots, for example. Just be sure that all of the plants have adequate room. For a list of vegetable cultivars and recommended container sizes, see "Vegetables for Containers" on page 230.

Each type of container has merits and disadvantages. To help you decide what type to use for your plants, here are some guidelines on various types of containers.

Clay and terra-cotta. Clay and terra-cotta containers are attractive but breakable, and they are easily damaged by freezing and thawing. Because these materials "breathe," they require more frequent watering than plastic or fiberglass containers do.

Concrete. Cast concrete is long-lasting and comes in a range of sizes and styles. You

The sky's the limit when it comes to choosing containers. In addition to planters, window boxes, and pots made from a variety of materials, you can grow in packing crates, in bushel baskets, and right in holes punched in bags of store-bought potting soil. Just be sure each container has holes in the bottom for drainage.

can even make attractive ones yourself. Plain concrete is heavy, but concrete-and-fiberglass blends and concrete mixed with vermiculite or perlite are both much lighter.

Plastic and fiberglass. Plastic and fiberglass are lightweight, relatively inexpensive, and available in many sizes and shapes. Choose sturdy and somewhat flexible pots. Avoid thin, stiff pots—they become brittle with cold or age.

Wood. Wood is natural-looking and protects roots from rapid temperature swings. You can build wooden planters yourself. Choose naturally rot-resistant wood and protect it with paint or a nontoxic preservative. See "Nontoxic Wood Preservative" on page 133 for a recipe. (Don't use creosote, which is toxic to plants.) Molded wood-fiber containers are sturdy and inexpensive.

Metal. Metals are strong but they conduct heat, exposing roots to rapid temperature fluctuations. Line lead or lead-soldered containers with plastic.

Potted Fruits and Berries

Don't forget to include some dwarf fruit trees in your container garden. They'll do well, provided they have large enough containers. For best growth on dwarf apples, apricots, peaches, pears, and plums, select a container that is at least 2 feet wide and 3 feet deep. Blueberries and both sweet and sour cherries need ones that are at least 2 feet wide and 2 feet deep.

All strawberries do well in containers. They need to be spaced 1½ feet apart and grow in containers that are at least 8 inches deep. Brambles such as raspberries and blackberries will grow in containers but are not good subjects with their thorns and spreading habit.

POTTING MIXES FOR CONTAINERS

The potting mix you select for your container plants is important. A good potting mix should be well-aerated, highly nutritious, and moisture-retentive. It also needs to drain well. Since even the best garden soils don't behave like this when you put them in a pot, you have to buy a commercial potting mixture or make your own. See "Special Container Concerns" on page 233 for information on how gardening in containers differs from gardening in a conventional garden.

Whether you buy potting mix in a bag or make your own, you'll find that there are two general types of mixes: soilless mixes and soil-based ones. As their name suggests, soilless mixes don't contain any garden soil; soil-based ones do. Soilless mixes are made up of ingredients like peat, composted bark, perlite, and vermiculite that alone don't provide the nutrients plants need to grow. Many commercial soilless mixes contain chemical fertilizers to provide fertility. Soilless mixes that don't contain chemical fertilizers are fine in an organic garden, but the plants growing in them will need to be fertilized at least weekly with a weak solution of compost tea or fish emulsion. Today, compost-based soilless mixes are also available, as well as ones that have composted manure or other organic nutrient amendments added for fertility.

Soil-based mixes continue to be popular as well. The soil they contain provides a reservoir of nutrients, but, for best performance, plants growing in them should be fertilized regularly throughout the season.

When you buy a commercial potting mix,

(continued on page 232)

Vegetables for Containers

Two characteristics are important in choosing vegetable cultivars for containers: growing speed and size. In general, the faster and smaller the plant, the better it will grow in a container. Use these selections as suggestions and watch catalogs for new, container-size cultivars. An asterisk (*) after the container size indicates that the container will house more than one plant. Use normal spacing unless otherwise indicated. To interplant in containers, mix plants with different types of root systems; for example, mix lettuce with carrots or basil with tomatoes. For ideas, see "Ideas for Interplanting" on page 71 and "Interplanting with Companion Plants" on page 72. The container sizes in this table assume plants will be fertilized weekly.

PLANT	CULTIVARS	CONTAINER SIZE
Beans, bush	All cultivars, especially French filet types. Space 6″ apart.	1′ wide, 10″ deep*
Beans, climbing	Yard-long beans, scarlet runner beans	1′ wide, 1′ deep*
Beans, lima	'Bush Baby'	1′ wide, 10″ deep*
Beets	'Baby Canning', 'Little Ball', 'Spinel Baby Beets'	Dwarf cultivars: any width, 6″–8″ deep, allow about 2″ between plants. Standards: any width, 8–12″ deep, allow 4″ between plants.*
Broccoli	'Green Comet' (plant is only 12″–16″ tall but heads weigh about 1 lb. each)	8″–12″ wide, 20″ deep
Brussels sprouts	All cultivars, especially 'Rubine' (a 2½′–3′-tall red cultivar)	1′ wide, 18″–20″ deep
Cabbage	'Flash' (4″ across, weighs 1 lb.). 'Baby Head' and 'Dwarf Morden' are also small and mature rapidly.	8″–12″ wide, 1′ deep
Carrots	'Baby Finger Nantes', 'Gold Nugget', 'Kinko', 'Thumbelina', 'Tiny Sweet'. Space 2″ apart.	Round cultivars: any width, 6″ deep, allow about 2″ between plants. Standards: any width, 1–1½′ deep, allow about 2″ between plants.*
Cauliflower	'Early Snowball' and other fast-growing, small cultivars	1½′ wide, 2′–3′ deep

PLANT	CULTIVARS	CONTAINER SIZE
Chard	All cultivars	1'–1½' wide, 1'–1½' deep*
Chinese cabbage	All cultivars	1' wide, 20" deep
Corn	Small, quick-maturing cultivars. Grow at least 3 plants in each container, preferably in groups of 3 or more containers.	3' wide, 1' deep*
Cucumbers, pickling	Bush cultivars, including 'Lucky Strike'	8" wide, 1' deep
Cucumbers, slicing	Bush cultivars, including 'Bush Crop', 'Patio Pic', 'Salad Bush', 'Spacemaster'	8" wide, 1' deep
Eggplant	'Easter Egg' (small, white-fruited cultivar), 'Morden Midget'	1' wide, 1½' deep
Greens	All	Any width, 6"–8" deep. Check seed packets for spacing.
Lettuce	All cultivars	8" wide, 6"–8" deep
Muskmelons	'Burpee's Sugar Bush,' 'Minnesota Midget', 'New Hampshire Midget'	2'–3' wide, 2'–3' deep
Okra	'Green Best'	1' wide, 1'–1½' deep
Onions	All green onions do well in containers. Small, standard-size onions, such as 'Copra', 'Early Yellow Globe', 'South Redport'	Green onions: 6"–8" deep. Standards onions: 1'–1½' deep.*
Peas, edible-podded	Bush and compact cultivars, including 'Sugar Ann', 'Sugar Bon', 'Sugar Daddy'	1' wide, 1' deep*
Peas, green	'English Novella II', 'Little Marvel', and other small bush cultivars	1' wide, 1' deep*
Peppers	Most cultivars, sweet or hot, do well in containers. Try the small 'Canape', 'Jingle Bells', 'Pepper Pot', and 'Pimento'.	1' wide, 1'–1½' deep

(continued)

Vegetables for Containers—Continued

PLANT	CULTIVARS	CONTAINER SIZE
Potatoes	All cultivars	Use a container such as a wooden barrel, at least 3' deep, with 6"-diameter holes cut at intervals. Add soil as plants grow.*
Radishes	All cultivars except large winter types, such as 'Daikon'	5" wide, 6" deep*
Rhubarb	All cultivars	2' wide, 2'–3' deep
Spinach	All cultivars	6"–8" wide, 6"–8" deep*
Squash	Generally unsuitable, but bush cultivars will tolerate large containers if well-fertilized.	Tubs and half-barrels
Tomatoes	Most cultivars. Container cultivars include 'Micro-Tom', 'Patio', 'Pixie', 'Super Bush', 'Sweet 100', 'Tiny Tim', and 'Yellow Pear'.	Dwarf cultivars: 6"–8" wide, 1' deep. Standard cultivars: 2' wide, 1½'–3' deep
Turnips	All small cultivars	10"–12" wide, 1' deep*
Watermelons	Bush or dwarf cultivars	3' wide, 3' deep

it's a good idea to read the label so you know whether it's soilless or soil-based. You'll find more information on peat, perlite, vermiculite, and other ingredients in "Ingredients for Potting Mixes" on the opposite page, but now that "organic" is a commercial selling point, it's also important to look for what else is in the bag. Some products that depend on synthetic fertilizers for their main nutrient content are being marketed as organic simply because they contain peat moss or a small fraction of composted manure. You'll find information on organically acceptable ingredients in "Preblended Fertilizer" on page 45 and "Fertilizer Options" on page 50.

Despite the convenience of commercial potting mixes, many gardeners still prefer to make their own. Homemade mixes give several advantages. Because you are in charge of quality control, you can be certain that only the very best and most finished compost goes into the mix. You can also be certain about the quality and amount of other ingredients you add, and, finally, you can mix media for specific crops or uses. See "Make Your Own: Potting Mixes for Containers" on page 234 for several good recipes of both soilless and soil-based mixes.

Ingredients for Potting Mixes

Commercial potting mixes are made from a variety of materials that retain moisture, improve drainage, or add bulk to the mix.

You'll find some or all of the ingredients that follow on the labels of commercial mixes or in the recipes in "Make Your Own: Potting Mixes for Containers" on page 234.

Compost

Compost is an essential ingredient in organic mixes for containers. Good compost supplies nutrients through much of the growing season and holds supplemental nutrients well. It also maintains a slightly acid pH better

---

SPECIAL CONTAINER CONCERNS

Gardening in containers just isn't the same as gardening in a conventional vegetable garden. And that's not just because plant roots are confined to a smaller area than usual. Soil in a container works quite differently than garden soil. For one thing, there is no subsoil from which deep-rooted plants can draw nutrients. Populations of microorganisms and soil animals are smaller and less diverse, too, so soil compaction and aeration can be a problem.

Rain or irrigation water moves down through the soil in both the garden and in pots, but in garden soil, when the soil surface dries out, water from the lower depths can move upward as well. Plant roots in a garden can also reach deep into the soil to draw from that moisture reserve.

Container plants are more dependent on you to supply their needs than plants growing in the garden are. Be sure to start with a good potting medium and add water and fertilizer regularly for best yields from container food crops.

than mixes fortified with quick-release, synthetic fertilizers. Gardeners sometimes wonder if 100 percent compost—not mixed with any other ingredients—will work as a container medium. In most cases, the answer is no. Compost alone contains and holds a nutrient level that's too concentrated for most plants.

However, heavy feeders such as corn, cucumbers, and spinach prosper in mixes that contain a higher-than-normal proportion of compost.

The quality of the compost you use is very important. Use only completely finished compost that has been made from a variety of

---

✦ MAKE YOUR OWN ✦

POTTING MIXES FOR CONTAINERS

The recipes below are all intended for container planting. The first recipe is for a soilless mix and the rest are for soil-based mixes. If you are using garden soil in a container mix, the recipe will change depending on the type of soil you are using. For example, mixes based on sandy soils won't need as much drainage material as those based on clay soils. If you're using purchased topsoil, assess its texture using the technique described in "Feeling for Texture" on page 28.

Follow the appropriate recipe for your soil texture. Amend all of the following recipes (including the soilless one) with 1 handful of greensand, 1 handful of rock or colloidal phosphate, 1 handful of bonemeal, and a sprinkle of blood meal per bushel basket of mix.

. . . .

General-Purpose Soilless Growing Mix

3 parts compost
2 parts sphagnum peat moss
2 parts vermiculite
1 part perlite
1 part sand

Soil-Based Mix for Loamy Soils

2 parts soil
1 part compost
1 part peat moss
1 part perlite
1 part vermiculite

Soil-Based Mix for Very Sandy Soils

2 parts soil
2 parts compost
1 part peat moss or leaf mold
1 part vermiculite

Soil-Based Mix for Very Clayey Soils

2 parts soil
1 part compost
½ part sand
2 parts perlite
½ part vermiculite

organic materials. Otherwise, the nutrient supply may be unbalanced. For information on making compost and how to tell if it is finished, see "Making and Using Compost" on page 36.

Peat Moss

Peat is a time-honored ingredient in potting mixes. As far as your plants are concerned, it has wonderful qualities in a mix. It's primarily used to add bulk to mixes because it's relatively chemically inactive. It also holds moisture well, takes a long time to break down and suppresses disease organisms.

Peat humus is darker, heavier, and even more moisture-retentive than sphagnum peat moss. Because of its stickiness, peat humus is a common ingredient in mixes used to make soil blocks. (For information on making soil blocks, see "Make Your Own: Soil Blocks" on page 104.) The sticky quality of peat humus is a virtue in a soil block, but it can be a liability in all but the lightest, least compost- or clay-filled, container mixes.

Many gardeners are trying to move away from using peat because it is a mined material and takes so long to form that it is essentially a nonrenewable resource. Completely finished leaf mold and well-rotted hardwood are both possible alternatives. You can try substituting either of these materials for peat moss. But if you do so, understand that you may have some plant failures while you are experimenting. You will have to determine just how finished or rotted the leaf mold or hardwood should be, as well as juggle proportions of these materials in proportion to compost and the other ingredients of the mix. To be on the safe side, consider growing the majority of your plants in a mix with peat moss while you do this experimentation. Because so many gardeners are working on this problem, information

about consistently reliable mixes containing peat moss substitutes is only a few years away.

Perlite

Another natural product, perlite is a heat-expanded volcanic glass. It is chemically inert and sheds water better than any duck's back. This quality makes it a good choice for an aerating and drainage material. Exercise caution when using it in large quantities, though. Unless it's premoistened, its scratchy surfaces can irritate your eyes, ears, nose, and throat. (You can premoisten perlite by pouring water through a hole in an otherwise unopened bag. Let it soak for a few minutes and then poke a few holes in the bag to let the excess water flow out.) Perlite also has a tendency to migrate to the top of a mix over the course of a season. Algae may grow on this top covering, especially if humidity is high or plants are watered too frequently. If this happens, try to water less often but more thoroughly. You also can add a top layer of compost to the container, which will hide the algae-covered perlite and contribute new nutrient supplies as irrigation water drains through it. Because perlite is so lightweight, use it instead of sand in containers on rooftops or balconies or anywhere you want a slightly lighter mix.

Some commercial mixes contain polystyrene instead of perlite. It's best to avoid them because polystyrene doesn't belong in a compost pile, which is where most potting mixes end up after they've been used for a season or two. You also wouldn't want to incorporate used potting mix that contained polystyrene into your garden soil.

Sand

Washed builder's sand sheds water and is used primarily for its drainage characteristics.

But without some perlite, vermiculite, or peat moss in the mix, sand can contribute to soil compaction. It is extremely heavy and should never be used where weight is a consideration—on rooftop gardens, for example. (In such places, perlite is a better alternative for drainage.) Don't use the play sand for children's sandboxes in your potting mix. It's too fine and won't drain as well as coarse builder's sand.

Vermiculite

The thin layers of vermiculite, which is made from mica deposits, hold moisture in a potting mix. Like compost, vermiculite holds nutrients well. It also improves drainage and aeration. Root hairs will grow between the thin sheets of vermiculite particles in search of both water and nutrients.

Topsoil or Garden Soil

Soil-based mixes obviously contain soil, but don't dig up any old soil around your property to make your potting mixes. Clay soil, for example, can be a disaster in containers because it compacts easily and drains poorly, and garden soil often is chock-full of weed seeds and soilborne diseases or insect pests. You'll find recipes in "Make Your Own: Potting Mixes for Containers" on page 234 for mixes based on clay, sand, and loam soil, but unless you have a large number of containers to fill, you are probably better off leaving the soil in the garden. A good option is to buy bags of topsoil at a garden center.

Amendments in Container Mixes

If you're going to have a healthy container garden, it's important to start thinking about plant nutrition right from the start—when you select your potting mix. Potting mixes tend to become acidic before the plants have finished their growing season. Since pH levels below 6.0 affect nutrient availability, good mixes contain calcium-rich amendments, which help keep the pH from becoming too acidic. These amendments include bonemeal, rock or colloidal phosphate, ground basalt, and ground limestone. You'll find these included in the recipes in "Make Your Own: Potting Mixes for Containers" on page 234. You'll also find them in prepackaged mixes sold by responsible companies. For more information on managing pH, which is an essential part of managing plant nutrition, see "Keeping the Balance" on page 238.

Phosphorus deficiencies are quite common in container-grown plants. That's not because the mix doesn't contain phosphorus, but because it has become unavailable due to a too-acid pH or low microbial populations. One solution is to add a handful of kelp meal per bushel basket of soil mix. See "Fertilizing Container Plants" on the opposite page for other ways to add phosphorus and other nutrients.

Greensand is another popular potting mix amendment. This natural deposit is a good potassium source, and, even more important, it absorbs three times its weight in water and seems to stimulate mineral release and take-up. Like kelp meal, it is also an excellent source of trace minerals.

Here are some other amendments that are commonly added to enrich potting mixes with specific nutrients:

- Bloodmeal or alfalfa meal for nitrogen.
- Hardwood ashes for potassium.
- Worm castings for calcium and balanced trace elements.
- Rock powders, including granite and langbeinite (Sul-Po-Mag), for both major nutrients

and trace minerals, notably potassium, sulfur, and magnesium.

Use all of these amendments in moderation in a potting mix. For example, to 1 quart of mix, add no more than 1 teaspoon of blood meal, 1 tablespoon of hardwood ashes, 2 tablespoons of worm castings, and/or 1 tablespoon of rock powders.

Azomite (a hydrated sodium-calcium aluminosilicate) is an organically acceptable rock product that's new to the market. It contains high levels of potassium and trace elements. Use 1 tablespoon to every quart of growing or starting mix. For a complete rundown on organic soil amendments, see "Fertilizer Options" on page 50.

PLANTING IN CONTAINERS

Plant in containers as you would in the garden. While the bottoms of your containers must have drainage holes, it's not necessary to cover them with a layer of pot shards or gravel. A layer of shards or gravel doesn't improve drainage, and pot shards may actually block the drainage holes. Prevent soil from washing out by placing a layer of paper towel or newspaper over the holes before adding soil. If your container is too deep, you can put a layer of gravel or rocks in the bottom to reduce the amount of soil required. Where container weight is a problem, such as on rooftop gardens, you can use a layer of Styrofoam on the bottom, where it won't show.

It's a good idea to premoisten the potting mix before you plant. Wetting it down a day before you plant is best. You can do this in a plastic garbage can or a wheelbarrow, or you can fill the containers with dry mix and water them thoroughly afterward.

When planting trees and shrubs, trim off any circling roots and cover the root ball to the same level as it was set at the nursery. Firm the planter mixture gently and settle by watering thoroughly. Don't fill pots level to the top with soil mixture, but leave 1 or 2 inches of space for watering.

Keep in mind that potting mixes, especially soilless ones, can be hard to rewet if they're allowed to dry out completely. Try to keep the soil evenly moist throughout the season.

FERTILIZING CONTAINER PLANTS

If you're going to have a successful container garden, you'll need to plan a fertilization program for your plants. That's because container-grown plants tend to be nutrient stressed. The small volume of potting mix in which plants are growing is part of the problem. Nutrients also leach out of containers as water

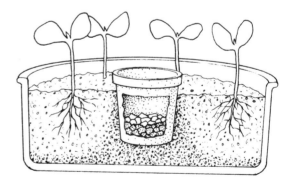

Try using a watering well to provide your container plants with an even supply of moisture. Just take an unglazed terra-cotta pot, plug the bottom hole with a cork, fill it with loose gravel, and sink it in a larger container. Keep the well filled with water, which will seep out slowly through the porous pot and keep the soil moist.

drains through the mix. In addition, pH levels that are either too high or too low will tie up nutrients and make them unavailable to plants. Inadequate drainage can also cause problems because it leads to inadequate leaching and a high soluble salt content, which in turn prevents roots from taking up enough water and nutrients.

There are three ways to deliver fertilizers to your container plants: fertigation, top-dressing, and foliar feeding.

Fertigation. Fertigation (fertilization and irrigation) is the term used for applying liquid fertilizers directly to the soil. The liquid fertilizers used to fertigate container plants include nutritionally complete substances such as compost tea as well as more specific fertilizers such as dilutions of liquid kelp, fish emulsion, Sul-Po-Mag, and Epsom salts. See "Using Liquid Fertilizers" on page 128 for directions for making a variety of liquid fertilizers. Although enormous variation is possible when fertilizing container plants, one suggestion can save you a great deal of trauma: When working in containers, use liquid fertilizers at *half* the recommended strength but *twice* as frequently.

Topdressing. Topdressing is a technique that's the same whether you're growing plants in containers or in the garden. For example, to give a potted tomato plant a boost, spread ¼ cup of Sul-Po-Mag on the soil surface when the first blossoms open. The nutrients will flow downward with irrigation water. Similarly, potted cucumbers prosper when 1 tablespoon of blood meal, mixed into a quart of compost, is spread around plants that have just begun to bloom. See "Fertilizer Options" on page 50 for information on fertilizers that can be used for topdressing.

Foliar feeding. Feeding a plant by spraying its leaves with a nutrient solution can mean the difference between a mediocre plant and one that is spectacular. Although plants don't absorb all of the necessary nutrients through their leaves, they will take up balanced quantities of trace elements and also make better use of available soil nutrients. You can't rely entirely on foliar feeding, but it is a valuable part of a good fertilizing program. As a bonus, weekly foliar feeding with some sprays—notably compost tea, nettle tea, equisetum tea, or liquid kelp—helps plants resist many diseases. For information on foliar feeding solutions and how to apply them, see "Using Foliar Sprays" on page 129.

Keeping the Balance

Good potting mixes maintain nutrient and pH balance long enough for short-season crops to mature to harvestable age. But if you have a crop in your containers for six months or more, the soil can develop a nutrient and pH imbalance. Here are some steps you can take to make sure that your potting mixes stay in balance.

Leach containers. To avoid nutrient imbalances, thoroughly leach containers with clear water once a month. Choose a bright day and run water through the soil until at least 1 cup of water comes out of a bucket, or until 1 quart comes out of a large, 3-foot-square container. Fertigate with compost tea or a kelp-and-fish-emulsion mixture the next time you water.

Check pH regularly. Check your soil pH with litmus paper once a month, starting in the third month of a mix's service. If the pH is too acidic (less than 6.0, unless you're growing blueberries), sprinkle limestone over the soil surface at the rate of 1 heaping tablespoon for a 5-gallon pot or a scant ⅛ cup for a half-barrel. Limestone won't react with the potting

QUICK-FEEDING FIXES

If you suspect that your container plants aren't getting the nutrients they need, here are some quick fixes for common nutrient deficiencies you may encounter. (See "Troubleshooting Plant Nutrient Deficiencies" on page 175 for descriptions of the symptoms of specific deficiencies.)

Boron. Dissolve 1 tablespoon of borax in 1 gallon of water and foliar-feed leaves when plants are about six weeks old. Do *not* water with this material! Excess boron is a toxin to plants and soil life. Apply only once in the life of a plant.

Calcium. Fertigate with an eggshell solution. To make it, collect approximately 24 eggshells, then crush them and put them in a food processor or blender with 2 cups of water. Process the mixture, stopping to scrape down the sides periodically, until you have a creamy white material without any recognizable shards of shell. Add 2 to 3 gallons of warm water. Stir repeatedly while fertigating.

Magnesium. Fertigate with an Epsom salt solution. To make it, pour 1 cup of boiling water over 1 tablespoon of Epsom salts and stir until the salts are dissolved. If the Epsom salts don't dissolve, add another cup of boiling water and try again. Combine this solution with enough water to make 1 gallon.

Nitrogen. Top-dress with compost. For a fast supply of nitrogen, fertigate with compost tea or fish emulsion. Or soak 1 ounce of blood meal in 1 cup of boiling water and mix with enough water to make 1 gallon; fertigate with this solution.

Phosphorus. Fertigate with a solution of fish emulsion.

Potassium. Fertigate with alfalfa or comfrey tea. To make either tea, soak 1 quart of freshly picked green leaves, packed into a burlap bag, in a gallon of water, covered, for two or three weeks. Strain and mix 1 part of this concentrate with 3 parts water for fertigating. Store in dark, cool conditions.

Sulfur. If you need sulfur, potassium, and magnesium, fertigate with Sul-Po-Mag tea, which is made exactly like the Epsom salts tea in "Magnesium" mentioned previously. If not, top-dress with compost to supply sulfur, or sprinkle tiny pinches of flowers of sulfur on the soil surface.

---

mix for several weeks, so you'll have to wait to find out if the pH has risen. Incidentally, high worm populations in the potting mix often prevent it from becoming acidic.

If the mix has become alkaline, common cider vinegar will come to the rescue. If the pH tests from 7.0 to 7.9, add 1 pint of cider vinegar, which contains 5 percent acetic acid, for a 5-gallon pot or ½ gallon for a half-barrel. Test a couple of inches below the soil surface in a week or so. Repeat the procedure if the pH is still too high.

Refurbish your mix. You could replace your potting mix between crops, but it's less expensive and easier to refurbish it. If drainage and moisture-holding qualities have been good, top off the container with a mixture of 2 parts compost plus 1 part vermiculite plus 1 part perlite. In cases where drainage and/or moisture-holding qualities weren't good, take this opportunity to readjust the mix. Dump it out and mix in either equal parts of compost and vermiculite to improve water-holding capacity or equal parts of compost plus perlite and/or sand to improve drainage.

ENDING AND EXTENDING THE SEASON

Don't forget to use season extension devices to extend the harvest from your container garden. Try erecting a plastic cage around the last of the tomatoes for fall protection, or cover midsummer lettuces with shade cloth to forestall their becoming bitter in the heat. You can also move containers from open, exposed locations to more protected ones as the season progresses.

Container gardens can be enjoyed for one season and discarded, or they can be designed to last for years. When designing permanent containers, remember that container-grown plants are less hardy because their roots are more exposed to air temperatures. Nonhardy plants will need to have winter protection, as shown in the illustration on this page, or will need to be moved to a sheltered space. The amount of protection required varies, of course. In many areas, dwarf fruit trees grown in containers need winter protection, for example. Moving them to a protected location outdoors and insulating the container may be all they require to weather the winter. Container-grown dwarf citrus trees, on the other hand, must be moved indoors where temperatures don't dip below 45°F. All of this goes to show it's a good idea to consider how heavy the container will be and to decide how you will move it before choosing a nonhardy plant.

INDOOR GARDENS

Windowsills aren't just for ornamentals anymore. Today, herbs, salad crops, and edible flower plants jostle for room at the brightest windows in the house. Light, temperature, and relative humidity are all concerns for windowsill gardeners. Grow your indoor food garden in the same potting mixes you'd use for an outdoor container garden. (See "Potting Mixes for Containers" on page 229 for details.) You

Container-grown trees need extra protection in the winter since their roots are less protected than they would be in the ground. Large garbage bags filled with leaves will provide extra insulation if piled around the pot.

can also use the fertilizing guidelines described in "Fertilizing Container Plants" on page 237 for planning a regular feeding schedule. Here are some basic care guidelines that will ensure your indoor food garden is a success.

Lighting

Most food crops need bright light to grow well indoors. In the winter, your best bets are plants that tolerate low light, because even a sunny south window doesn't provide the illumination of a sunny summer garden. Try growing winter cultivars of lettuce such as 'Winter Density' and 'Rouge d'Hiver'. Other greens tolerant of low light include spinach, corn salad, and orach. Thyme, rosemary, parsley, and cilantro all tolerate low light levels. You can also grow shade-loving edible flowers such as Johnny-jump-ups. During the summer, you can add many more plants to the list. Basil, leaf lettuces, and nasturtiums grow vigorously in a summer-bright window, while hanging baskets of cherry tomatoes may have to be restrained from coiling up the curtains.

Keep in mind that light intensity drops off rapidly as you move away from a window. If your plants aren't receiving enough light, they'll become elongated and pale. Or they may just fail to grow at all and drop their lower leaves.

To make the most of your sunny windows, add shelves or plant hangers to windows. You can augment the amount of light your plants receive as well. Near a window, the most unobstrusive method is with a standard-shaped plant growth light. Leave it burning for 12 hours at a stretch, during the day rather than at night. Small fluorescent fixtures work, too.

If you have container plants that you have moved indoors in the winter for protection, make sure to place them in the shade at first when you move them outdoors for the summer. Then gradually move them out into sunnier locations.

Temperature

Temperature is another concern because many homes are too warm at night for good plant growth. Most plants require a 10 to 15 degree differential in night and day temperatures. Nighttime temperatures of around 60°F are ideal for most plants—but chilly for most gardeners. High temperatures at night cause leggy growth; so does low light during the day. Plants such as rosemary and sweet bay, which just need to be kept from freezing, do best with winter temperatures that are quite cool. They can be kept at temperatures around 40°F.

Watering

Various factors including size of containers, season, rate of growth, light, and temperature will affect how much water each plant requires. Don't follow a strict schedule, because you may overwater or underwater. You also don't want to wait until the plant wilts to water it. Instead, check each pot by pushing your finger into the soil an inch or so and feeling for moistness before you water. If the top inch is dry, it's time to water. Avoid overwatering; if in doubt, wait.

Always water until water seeps out the bottom of the pot. Use pots with drainage holes and saucers, but never allow plants to sit in water. If the soil becomes very dry, it may shrink away from the pot sides, allowing water to run through rapidly without being absorbed. If this happens, add water slowly until the soil is saturated, or set the pot in a tub of water for a few minutes. Water will also run out rapidly if the plant is rootbound.

Humidity

Humidity is rarely high enough for plants on windowsills. The easiest solution is to set pots on trays filled with pebbles. Grouping several plants together increases humidity levels, as does a daily hand-misting in the morning. If the humidity is extremely low, enclose pots—pebble trays and all—in a sheet of clear plastic. Open the enclosure for an hour or so each morning to let in fresh air. If fungus strikes, dispense with the plastic covering and start misting them every time you pass them in the morning and early afternoon. Another option is to run an electric humidifier.

If you need to increase humidity around a plant growing in a hanging basket, try this florist's trick. Choose extra-large pots for your crops. But rather than completely filling them with a soil mix, pack a moistened layer of peat moss around the sides. Water this edging and let the soil mix draw moisture from it. Additional hand-misting may also be necessary.

Pests and Diseases

If you grow your plants in a good organic potting mix, give them the correct amount of water and light, and repot them regularly, you shouldn't have many insect or disease problems. It's a good idea to inspect your plants regularly, though, so that if a problem develops, you catch it early. Isolate plants you suspect are infected or infested. Yellowing or discolored leaves may mean disease or incorrect light levels or watering practices. Overwatering probably kills more houseplants than anything else

does. Double-check the plant's requirements, remove damaged areas, and watch for developments. Whatever treatment you use for any of these pests, repeat it several times to control later hatchings.

Damaged or deformed plants or sticky deposits may indicate insect problems. These pests are common on indoor plants:

Aphids. Aphids are $1/32$- to $1/8$-inch, translucent, pear-shaped insects. They may be many colors including white, green, and black. Sticky deposits of plant sap in growing tips may indicate aphid activity. Remove these soft-bodied, sucking insects by hand, wash them off with sprayed water, or spray with insecticidal soap.

Mealybugs. These insects look like $1/10$-inch tufts of white cotton. They are often found under leaves and in sheltered areas of stems. The immature stage can crawl, but adults are attached to the plant. Remove each insect with rubbing alcohol on a cotton swab, or spray with insecticidal soap.

Mites. Mites are tiny pests about the size of a grain of salt. You are likely to notice plant symptoms before you actually see the pests themselves. Leaves attacked by mites are stippled or mottled; flowers may be deformed. Wash plants with a hose or shower to remove pests, mist daily, and spray plants with insecticidal soap.

Whiteflies. These ubiquitous pests are about $1/16$-inch long. They fly around in a cloud whenever an infested plant is disturbed. Wipe crawling young off of the underside of leaves, vacuum up the flying white adults, spray with insecticidal soap, or place a yellow sticky trap on a stake in each pot to catch them.

10 SPECIALTY GARDENS

Seven Food-Garden Themes You Can Try

This season, add some spice to your gardening by starting a specialty garden. In this chapter, you'll find discussions of seven different types of gardens. Pick a new one each year, or use these ideas as stepping stones to creating your own unique garden. Perhaps you'd like to plant a salsa garden for spicy sauces, or a yellow or purple color theme garden, for example. The possibilities are endless!

Gardens for children. Make gardening a fun family activity by getting the kids involved, too. Give them a corner plot where they can plant a namesake pumpkin patch. If space is limited, try a half-barrel planter with a rainbow salad garden. Page 244.

Convenient container gardens. If you don't have the time or space for a full-size garden, grow a small container garden instead. Our designer shares the secret to getting a season-long harvest of fresh, tender salad greens from a simple patio planter. Page 246.

A side-yard garden. Don't let that space go to waste! Turn an unused sunny side yard into a beautiful, productive garden chock-full of fruits and flowers. Page 248.

A small-space fruit garden. You don't need a large property to enjoy the pleasures of homegrown fruit. This designer shows how even a small-space fruit garden can produce loads of delicious eating. Page 250.

A salad garden. Gardeners with limited growing area will appreciate this design—you'll be amazed at the quantity of vegetables you can raise in one easy-care plot! Page 252.

A tea garden. If you enjoy the pleasure of herbal teas, this tea garden is for you. It includes a wide variety of flavorful tea herbs, from delicately fruit-flavored chamomile to strong and spicy cinnamon basil. Page 254.

Edible landscaping. There's no reason you can't mix a combination of herbs, vegetables, and ornamentals all together in a glorious profusion of fruits and flowers. Expand your growing area throughout your yard by following these tips for developing an edible landscape. Page 256.

GARDENS FOR CHILDREN

By Sharon Lovejoy

The seeds for a gardener are sown early in life. Involving children in gardening is an easy and enjoyable way to teach them skills like patience and persistence that will last a lifetime. Gardens also help to develop children's natural interest in the world around them. Adult and young gardeners can share a sense of wonder about the whole growing process and experience the magic of watching tiny seeds grow into tasty fruits and pretty flowers.

Of course, not all gardens are child-friendly. Long, straight rows and regimented garden chores will not appeal to the creativity and freedom children crave. Kids love bright colors, interesting textures, nice smells, great tastes, and some immediate signs of growth.

To get your young gardeners off to a good beginning, start with one of the projects discussed below. Choose from a rainbow salad garden, a namesake pumpkin patch, or a luffa tepee. Any one is sure to bring a smile to the face of young and older gardeners alike.

Rainbow Salad Bowl

Kids don't need the frustration of a huge garden plot. A small, manageable garden can yield a rewarding amount of produce with a minimum of work. Half-barrels are great for children's gardens—they're easy to care for and hold a good quantity of plants at kid level. Look for a half-barrel that's about 2 feet in diameter. If it hasn't been done already, nail the metal hoops to the wooden staves and drill some drainage holes in the bottom.

A rainbow salad garden planted in a barrel will provide color and fast-growing action. For planting suggestions, check out "Seven Simple Plants to Try" on this page. Set up the

garden in a half-barrel that has drainage holes. Fill it with moist, loose, potting mix. (See "Make Your Own: Potting Mixes for Containers" on page 234 for recipes.)

Now the fun begins. Choose a large bowl for mixing, set it on your kitchen table, and let the kids add 1 or 2 cups of potting mix. Open the seed packets and sprinkle them into the soil; keep stirring the mix as you add the seeds. Pour the seed-and-soil mixture into an empty sugar shaker or Parmesan cheese shaker. Now let the kids shake the seeds over the barrel to their heart's content!

Provide a watering can and let them water

SEVEN SIMPLE PLANTS TO TRY

Colorful, dependable, fast-growing, and flavorful are key words to remember when choosing crops for children's gardens. Here are some ideas:

1. 'Easter Egg' radishes, in hues of pink, lavender, red, and white, are round and delightful.

2. Carrots are personality plants. Show kids the variety of shapes and sizes available, and let them pick a pack of their favorite.

3. Cress grows fast and is tasty in salads.

4. Nasturtiums are pretty and have edible flowers and leaves.

5. Chervil's light, licorice-parsley taste adds zip to a salad.

6. Lettuce comes in a wide range of textures and colors. Try 'Tom Thumb', which produces single-serving heads.

7. Tomatoes, in any shape or color, are a natural choice for kids. Let them choose a few for variety.

the surface to settle the seed-and-soil mixture. This is a good time to explain the "dry finger test" for future waterings, to avoid drowning the seedlings. Poke the tip of your finger into the soil and wiggle it around a little bit. If the top soil is dry, it's time to water; if it's moist, wait a day or two and test again.

Within a few days, fast growers like cress and radishes will poke through the soil. Kids can start harvesting tiny, Peter Rabbit–size veggies in less than a month.

Namesake Pumpkins

Giant or miniature, orange, red, white, or blue—pumpkins are one of the most beloved plants in a child's garden. Choose a sunny spot with humus-rich soil and allow plenty of room for the vines to spread. Plant the seeds, add water, and step back—pumpkins will ramble everywhere, providing loads of jack-o'-lanterns, pie filling, and yummy roasted seeds.

Add personality to the patch by creating namesake pumpkins. Let kids pick a green pumpkin and scratch their names into the soft skin with a nail. As the pumpkin grows, the name grows, too. At harvest time, your kids can pick their own personalized pumpkins.

Homegrown Sponges

Luffas, also known as sponge gourds, are a great garden project. These rambunctious vines produce loads of long, zucchini-like fruit. You can pick the young luffas and eat them steamed, stir-fried, or pickled. But what really make luffas special are the mature fruits. Inside, they produce a network of tough fibers that makes a unique, multipurpose sponge. Dishwashing isn't quite such a chore when kids can use their own homegrown sponges!

Fun with luffas starts in the garden. Find a flat, sunny spot and build a tepee of five to

What could be more fun to play in than a flower- or squash-covered tepee? Cover the poles with flowering climbers such as morning-glories or vining vegetables such as squash.

nine 6- to 10-foot-long poles. Use string to tie the poles together at the top, and then lace the free end of the string over and under the poles to create a sort of netting; remember to leave one section open as a door! When the ground is warm, let the kids plant luffa seeds at the base of their tepee. Within two weeks (providing the weather is warm), they'll see the green beginnings of their sponge tepee.

At the end of the season, pick all of the fruits and soak them in a bucket of water for a few days. Peel off the outer skin, and remove the pulp and seeds under a stream of running water. Dry the luffa sponges on a rack in the sun. Once they're dry, they're ready to use.

Sharon Lovejoy is the author of Sunflower Houses, *a book on gardening with children.*

CONVENIENT CONTAINER GARDENS

By Pam Peirce

Limited time or space (or both) is no reason to give up the pleasure of homegrown produce. Even if you have little or no yard, you can still grow some of your own food in containers. A single large tub can hold a variety of culinary herbs or perhaps a medley of salad greens. With a bit more space, you could grow larger vegetables, edible flowers, and maybe even a dwarf fruit tree or two.

Containers are easy to set up and even easier to care for. Since the rooting area is limited, regular watering and fertilizing are musts. But the height of the containers makes harvesting and maintenance easy, and weeds are usually not a problem. You'll find complete information on setting up and caring for container gardens in Chapter 9. But here I've given you some specific planting ideas that you can use directly or modify to fit your needs.

A Handy Herb Barrel

All you need for this plan is a wooden half-barrel filled with a container soil mix. (See "Make Your Own: Potting Mixes for Containers" on page 234 for recipes.) Look for a half-barrel that's about 2 feet in diameter. If it hasn't been done already, nail the metal hoops to the wooden staves and drill some drainage holes in the bottom.

I've included five of the herbs that I find useful in my kitchen. All of these can be harvested over an extended period. Flat-leaved Italian parsley has a better flavor than the curled type, and it is easier to chop. If it goes to seed, just replace it. Greek oregano and English thyme are familiar perennial herbs that produce over a long season—almost year-round

in warm climates. Replace them every few years if they become leggy and unattractive.

Other flavorful favorites of mine include garlic chives and Mexican tarragon. Garlic chives are larger than regular chives, with a flavor reflecting both chive and mild garlic. In summer, these perennial plants bear stems topped by white flowers. The flavor of Mexican tarragon is a bit less subtle than that of true French tarragon. But in our warm California climate, Mexican tarragon remains green in the winter while French tarragon goes dormant. Mexican tarragon is a short-lived perennial, living at least one full year and possibly two or three.

All of these herbs thrive in full sun and a well-drained soil mix. In cold climates, bring the Greek oregano and Mexican tarragon indoors for the winter. For more specific growing information, see the Chives, Oregano, Parsley, and Thyme entries in Part 2. You'll find more on Mexican tarragon on page 407.

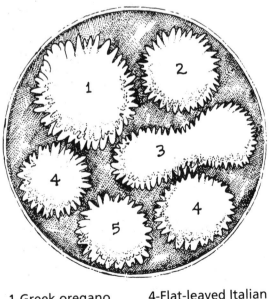

1-Greek oregano
2-Garlic chives
3-Mexican tarragon
4-Flat-leaved Italian parsley
5-English thyme

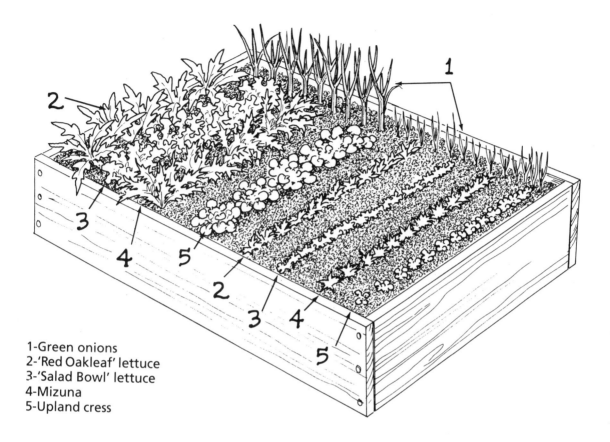

1-Green onions
2-'Red Oakleaf' lettuce
3-'Salad Bowl' lettuce
4-Mizuna
5-Upland cress

A Patio Planter Garden

One of the most productive crops for a small container food garden is lettuce. Combine it with other small, easy-to-grow crops to create a salad planter. Good choices are cilantro, arugula, upland cress, mizuna, green onions, and radishes. Use leafy, rather than heading, lettuce cultivars. I suggest starting with 'Oakleaf', 'Red Oakleaf', and 'Salad Bowl', but you should try several kinds and see which you like best.

The trick to salad growing is successive sowing—dividing your seeds into several smaller plantings a few weeks apart. That way, you'll have tender young produce throughout the season. If your planter provides 6 square feet or more of growing area, it will work well for successive sowings. Divide the space in half, and plant one half in lettuce and other salad fixings as desired. Then, when these crops are half-grown, plant the other half of the container the same way. When the second planting is half-grown, finish harvesting the first planting and sow a third planting there. Repeat as long as the days are usually cooler than 75°F and warmer than 45°F. For more detailed growing guidelines, see the Greens, Lettuce, and Onion entries in Part 2.

Pam Peirce is the author of Golden Gate Gardening, *a book on gardening in the Bay Area.*

A SIDE-YARD GARDEN

By Sally McCabe

Side yards are often the most underused part of a property, relegated to a boring strip of grass or some scraggly shrubbery. It can be challenging to make efficient use of that long, skinny space next to the house. But with some creative landscaping, it can be both pretty and productive.

Getting Started

Before you grab some seeds and start planting, there are a few things you'll need to consider. First, do you know what's underneath your site? Try digging down a foot or so to make sure you don't hit the foundation. Dwarf fruit trees grow best where the soil is at least 2 feet deep; most other plants can get by with 1 foot of soil. If your soil is shallow, consider building a raised bed. You'll probably also want to add lots of organic matter to build up the soil's fertility.

Consider the condition of the house, too. Inspect the surface of the wall. Is it going to need repairs or repainting in the next few years? How does the inside of the cellar wall look? Check it after a heavy rain or a good watering to see if any water is coming through. Make any repairs or improvements to the house before you plant anything permanent!

If you have an older house, lead paint could be a concern. Houses built before the early 1970s often have lead paint both inside and out. Since you're going to be growing food crops, it's a good idea to test the soil for lead contamination. To take a sample of your soil for testing, see "Collecting a Soil Sample" on page 29 for directions. Then call your local Cooperative Extension Service office for information on where to send it to be tested. If your soil contains lead, you should consider planting only fruiting crops or ornamentals, and mulching heavily to prevent raising dust.

Access to water is another important factor to think about. Walls and eaves can block much of the incoming rain, and a sunny, south-facing site will dry out quickly. Consider putting in a drip irrigation system. It wastes very little water, is low-maintenance once installed, and is easy to lay out in a long, narrow garden plot.

The Garden Design

To break up the space and add interest to the design, my plan calls for a large focal point at either end of the plot: a grape trellis and a semidwarf fruit tree. I broke the rest of the plot into 10-foot sections, with plantings in alternating vertical and horizontal lines. I also tried to mix in some rounded areas to help soften the lines. Because the space is so narrow, I devoted as little area as possible to paths. Remember, however, that everything should be within reach, and place your stepping stones or pavers accordingly. If your space is longer or shorter, you can use more or fewer 10-foot "rooms."

To get the most out of a small space like this, go for plants that are both attractive and edible. Besides the semidwarf fruit tree and grapevines, I've added an espaliered dwarf apple to give some height, as well as for its fruit and flowers. You could also plant an espaliered dwarf peach or pear tree, if you prefer. Grown flat against the wall on wires or hooks, your espaliered tree will extend about 1 foot out from the wall. The brightly colored fruits of hot peppers are quite showy, and a row of plants makes a tidy small hedge. To get even more color, look for special cultivars of common vegetables, like the red-podded 'Burgundy' okra or yellow-fruited 'Golden Bell' sweet peppers. Mix in some edible flowers like nasturtiums to add color to your garden and your meals. Fill the wide vertical rows with beets, carrots, onions, lettuce, spinach, and mixed oriental greens in spring. In summer, replace them with beans, basil, and Swiss chard, or second crops of beets, carrots, lettuce, spinach, and mixed oriental greens. For complete growing guidelines, see the individual plant entries in Part 2.

Sally McCabe is an education specialist at the Pennsylvania Horticultural Society in Philadelphia.

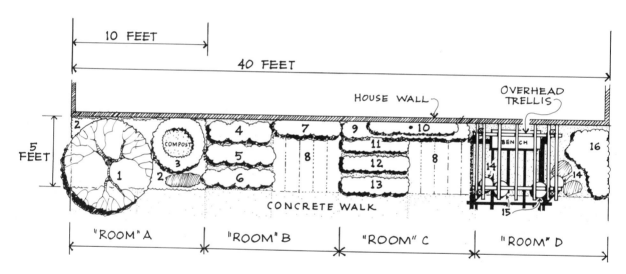

1-Semidwarf fruit tree
2-Groundcovers, such as thymes and mints
3-Squash growing up over the compost bin
4-Tomatoes
5-Eggplant
6-Hot-pepper hedge
7-Peas on trellis. (Replace with beans during hot weather.)

8-Rows of leafy crops and root crops
9-Strawberries interplanted with spring-flowering bulbs
10-Espaliered dwarf apple tree
11-'Burgundy' okra
12-Cabbage
13-Border of nasturtiums
14-Clematis

15-Grapes growing up over trellis
16-Squash interplanted with tall annual flowers

A SMALL-SPACE FRUIT GARDEN

By Lee Reich, Ph.D.

Fresh, organically grown fruit, harvested at its peak of ripeness, is a delectable luxury. This practical and productive garden, measuring only 15 × 30 feet, would add appeal to any landscape. It features an assortment of fruits that will keep you supplied almost non-stop throughout the growing season, with perhaps a surplus for preserving. For example, the four blueberry bushes alone could provide over 25 pounds of fruit once established.

The Garden Design

This design features a semiformal layout that creates an appealing garden that's also easy to manage. The small size of both the garden and the plants in it makes management easy—you need neither a ladder nor an abundance of time to care for the plants. The path that runs through the center of the garden makes it easy to reach into the beds to care for the plants, mulch, or weed. It also invites you in for a stroll past a sundial surrounded by mints or edible flowers and on to a bench shaded by a vine growing overhead on an arbor. The semiformal layout is for more than just appearance, too: You'll find it's easy to throw bird netting over fruits planted in rectangular blocks, should birds try to help themselves to too much of your harvest.

Getting Started

Most fruit plants need abundant light, so select a sunny location for this garden. Site the arbor at the north end of the garden so that it won't shade the rest of the planting. All of the plants in this garden will grow well in moderately fertile soil that is rich in organic matter. Since all will produce for many years in the same site, take extra care to prepare the soil properly before planting. For best results, evaluate the fertility of your soil using the information in Chapter 2. You'll also find recommendations for the care of both tree fruits and small fruits in "Custom Care for Tree Fruits" on page 61 and "Custom Care for Small Fruits" on page 62. See the individual plant entries in Part 2 for cultural information on the plants you choose to grow.

After you plant, protect the soil by blanketing the ground with a permanent organic mulch. To accent the paths, cover them with a mulch that visually contrasts the mulch beneath the plants. Consider wood chips or, for a more formal effect, light-colored gravel.

Picking the Plants

The plant list beneath the garden design illustration on the opposite page gives you suggestions for what to plant in each spot, but remember that you can tailor your planting to your region and your family's preferences. For example, if you aren't a big fan of grapes, grow hardy kiwi (plant a dwarf, self-fruitful cultivar such as 'Issai') or maypop instead. Or, if you live in the South, you may want to replace the currants with a carissa, or you might consider planting feijoa, strawberry guava, acerola, or pineapple in place of the highbush blueberries. When choosing your brambles, remember to consider the zone you live in. In Zones 3 to 5, try fall-bearing red raspberries; in Zones 5 to 7, mix red and black raspberries. In the South, consider dwarf papaya or try 'Baba Berry' red raspberry.

Before you plant, take some time to read about the individual fruit plants you'd like to include, and learn about the cultivars available.

Pest- and disease-resistant plants will help reduce maintenance; specific plant choices will depend on what pests are a problem in your region.

The spectrum of fruits in this garden provides months of fresh eating. Strawberry cultivars have been bred to grow almost everywhere in the country, and these fruits begin the season in spring. From then on, other fruits, such as brambles followed by grapes, carry the harvest on through the season. Whenever you're growing more than one plant of a particular fruit, plant more than one cultivar; this can spread out the harvest. It also allows for cross-pollination, which often results in both more and larger fruits.

If you'd like to add tree fruits to this design, you could replace the sundial with a genetic dwarf peach or a dwarf apple (grafted on an 'M.9' rootstock). Or widen the strawberry bed (number 7 on the plan) to 4 feet and plant two genetic dwarf peaches and two dwarf apples there. In the South, consider a dwarf citrus such as a blood orange.

Lee Reich, Ph.D., is the author of Uncommon Fruits Worthy of Attention *and* A Northeast Gardener's Year.

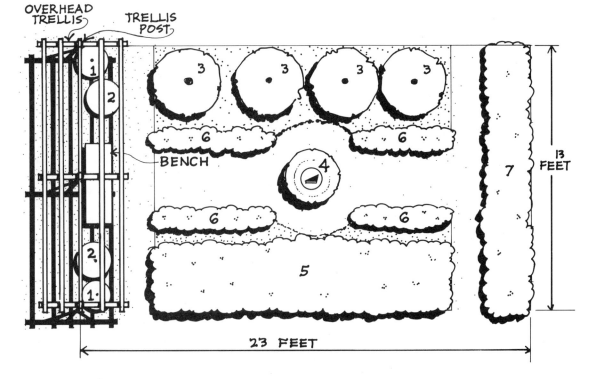

1-Grapevine growing up over trellis
2-Red, white, or black currant
3-Highbush blueberries
4-Sundial surrounded with mints or edible flowers
5-Brambles
6-Red- and yellow-fruited cultivars of Alpine strawberry
7-Strawberries or lowbush blueberries

A SALAD GARDEN

By Melody Aumiller

A salad garden close to your kitchen door will bring delicious, beautiful salads to your table all summer long. What could be better than picking a handful of fresh basil to make the pesto you're planning to serve with pasta for dinner? Or filling a salad bowl with a colorful mixture of greens garnished with edible flowers, all of which you grew yourself? A salad garden like this one will bring you months of pleasure and, of course, tasty, nutritious vegetables at your convenience. It's also an attractive garden that will add appeal to any yard, yet it's small enough to be a snap to maintain.

The Garden Design

The design is a 50-square-foot quarter circle, big enough to supply one salad lover or two moderate salad eaters all season. (The salad garden at the Rodale Institute Research Center yielded over 100 pounds of vegetables from April to late fall in a 50-square-foot area!) Both straight sides are 8 feet in length, and there is a trellis at the corner of the design with a 5-foot-long arm extending along each straight side.

If you'd like a larger garden, you can increase the size by doubling or tripling the design to form a half circle or three-quarter circle. Put paths between the quarters to allow you to reach everything without stepping on the soil. Stepping stones inside each quarter are attractive and practical. They eliminate muddy feet and reduce soil compaction. To vary and increase your harvest, you can replace the suggested plants with ones you'd like to try. Or, once you've harvested from the suggested plants, replace them with something different. For example, follow the peas with

cucumbers ('Lemon' or 'Early Perfection') or Malabar spinach. Or plant 'Rubra' fennel or cilantro in place of the dill. Swiss chard or kale can take the place of beets, cress can replace the radishes, and eggplant can be grown where the design says to plant cherry tomatoes.

Getting Started

Select a site for this garden that is both convenient to the kitchen and in full sun. All of the salad plants listed here grow best in rich, well-drained soil. Prepare the site thoroughly, as you would for any garden. Work in compost both when you prepare the soil and between crops to keep it in good condition. Raised beds are a good option for this design: They will improve drainage and add appeal to the design.

All of the salad plants suggested for this design are easy to grow and require fairly low maintenance. Keep the garden mulched with grass clippings or other organic material to help retain moisture and reduce weeds. For specific cultural information, see the individual plant entries in Part 2.

Picking the Plants

When picking plants for a salad garden, plant as wide a variety of ingredients as you can. Planting a garden of different tastes, colors, textures, and fragrances will enable you to create an endless variety of salads. In addition to attractive red and green lettuces and spinach—the mainstays of a mild basic salad—my design includes space for many other salad ingredients, including herbs, edible flowers, small-size vegetables, and some specialty crops such as mizuna, mesclun, and cress.

Since most of the fun of gardening is experimenting with new cultivars, use this design and the list that accompanies it as a chance to experiment. Keep your eyes open each winter for new salad plants in seed catalogs. For more ideas on plants that will add zest to your salads, see the individual crop entries in Part 2, including the Asian Specialties, Edible Flowers, Greens, Herbs and Spices, Italian Specialties, and Mex-

ican Specialties entries. For information on plants that don't have their own entry, look in the index for where more information can be found.

Melody Aumiller is an intern at the Rodale Institute Research Center in Pennsylvania.

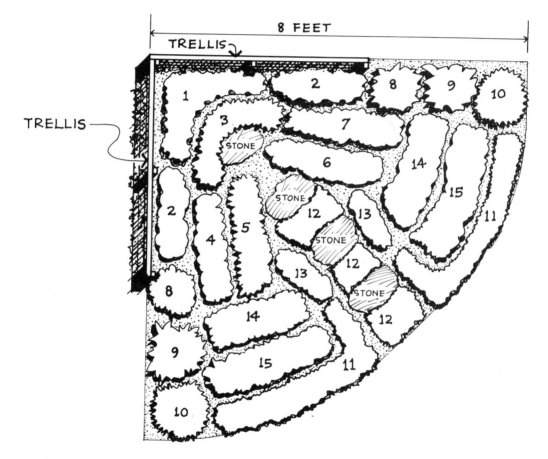

1-Peas growing up trellis	6-Radishes	13-Lemon or creeping thyme
2-Scarlet runner beans growing up trellis	7-Carrots	14-Basil or oregano
3-'Fernleaf' dill	8-Cherry tomatoes	15-Red or green leaf lettuce or red mustard
4-Beets	9-Sweet or hot peppers	
5-Green onions or bulb onions	10-Rosemary	
	11-Marigolds and/or pansies	
	12-Curly parsley and/or chives	

A TEA GARDEN
By Louise Hyde

There's no place like a garden for smoothing the edges of a rough day. And what could be more self-indulgent than sipping a cup of homegrown tea while relaxing in your own herbal tea garden? It's a completely luxurious feeling—enjoying the flavor of your herbs as you sit among them, smelling their scents and savoring their beauty.

I designed this garden to create a quiet and peaceful setting for relaxing each day. A very simple path leads to a comfortable bench in the center of the garden. On one side of the garden, a fence or house wall gives a sense of privacy, and, by midsummer, the taller plants on the adjoining side make a hedge for further seclusion.

Picking the Plants

The plants I chose for this tea garden have been my favorites for years. When we moved to our home in New Jersey, there was an old Damask rose bush out by the barn. Through the years, I've made rose petal tea to use as a base for a delicious punch. The petals are a lovely pink color with a heavenly old-rose scent and the tea tastes like the flowers smell. Moving this rose bush to the tea garden was a must.

Another of my favorite herbs is anise hyssop. The leaves give off a sweet licorice scent and the plant blooms from midsummer to frost with long spikes of lavender flowers. Use both the leaves and flowers for a very aromatic tea.

In this garden, I've included several other mint-family members that I find refreshing and invigorating. For hot tea, I enjoy spearmint. For a refreshing iced tea, try a blend of orange mint, spearmint, and lemon balm. Used alone, lemon balm gives a minty lemon flavor.

To my mind, the best of all of the lemony herbs is lemon verbena. Just a few leaves, used alone or in combination with another herb, give you a wonderful lemon tea. In all but the warmest climates, you'll need to bring this tender herb indoors for the winter.

Lavender is not often thought of as a tea plant, but small amounts of the flowers make a most aromatic tea or a good base for a punch. Cinnamon basil leaves make a very spicy tea, while the violet and alpine strawberry leaves produce a milder-flavored brew. The strawberry plants also reward you with small, flavor-packed berries all summer long.

Many of the herbs I've included in this garden have sentimental associations for me. My grandmother always grew bee balm—a beautiful flowering perennial that also makes a flavorful tea. Sage, thyme, catnip, and chamo-

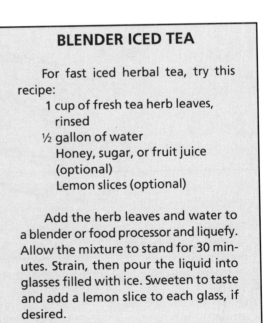

BLENDER ICED TEA

For fast iced herbal tea, try this recipe:

    1 cup of fresh tea herb leaves, rinsed
½ gallon of water
    Honey, sugar, or fruit juice (optional)
    Lemon slices (optional)

Add the herb leaves and water to a blender or food processor and liquefy. Allow the mixture to stand for 30 minutes. Strain, then pour the liquid into glasses filled with ice. Sweeten to taste and add a lemon slice to each glass, if desired.

mile were other favorite tea herbs. And what would an herb garden be without the soft, deliciously scented leaves of the old-fashioned rose geranium? Just one leaf is all you need to give a pot of regular tea that delicate rose flavor.

Since most of these herbs grow best in full sun, site the garden where it will get sun for most of the day. Your plants will need loose, well-drained soil. Prepare the site thoroughly, as you would for any garden, adding compost to keep the soil in good condition. To keep the mints from spreading out of control, surround each plant with a deep metal edging. Lemon balm can also be invasive if you let it go to seed; pinch it back frequently to prevent flower and seed formation. For more specific growing tips, see the Basil, Herbs and Spices, Mint, Sage, Strawberry, and Thyme entries in Part 2. The Tea entry, also in Part 2, discusses several other herbs that make wonderful tea and offers details on harvesting and storing plants for tea, as well as other tea recipes.

Louise Hyde is co-owner of Well-Sweep Herb Farm in New Jersey.

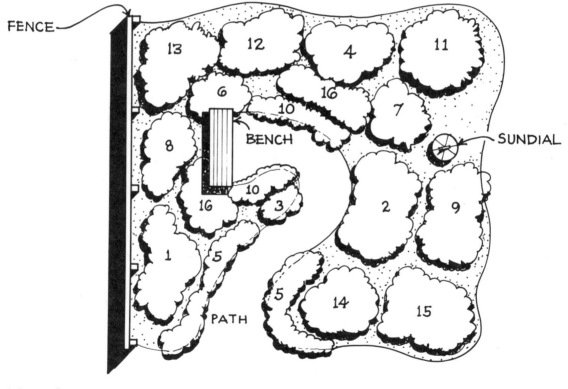

1-Damask rose
2-Rose geranium
3-Lemon verbena
4-Catnip

5-Alpine strawberry
6-Lemon balm
7-Chamomile
8-Anise hyssop

9-Garden sage
10-Common thyme
11-Spearmint
12-Orange mint

13-Bee balm
14-Cinnamon basil
15-'Hidcote' lavender
16-Sweet violet

EDIBLE LANDSCAPING

By Robert Kourik

If you don't have the time or space for a separate food garden, why not consider transforming your yard into an edible landscape? Many edible plants are also beautiful, and edible landscaping means taking advantage of both their ornamental *and* edible characteristics when you plan your garden. By including herbs, vegetables, fruits, and flowers in all of your landscape plantings, you can create a great-looking yard that also produces food for the table.

There are food-producing plants to satisfy every need in your landscape. Fruit and nut trees come in a wide range of sizes and shapes, provide shade, and may provide spring blooms and/or fall color. Berry-producing shrubs, such as blueberries and wild plums, also provide flowers and fall color. The blossoms of some annual and perennial flowers, such as nasturtiums and chives, are edible, too. (See the Edible Flowers entry in Part 2 for ideas on which ones to include in your landscape.) Many vegetables and herbs have interesting foliage and some have showy flowers or brightly colored fruit. Fruiting vines such as grapes, melons, and climbing beans will cover fences and trellises. Some edibles, such as creeping thyme and Alpine strawberries, make good groundcovers.

Getting Started

Since your yard probably already has many permanent plantings, creating an edible landscape generally is a gradual process that develops over time. Don't plan to redesign and uproot your whole yard overnight. Instead, look for ways to gradually transform existing plantings into an edible landscape. For example, you can add a small island bed of herbs, berries, vegetables, and edible flowers around the base of a small fruit tree. Keep in mind that an edible landscape is one in which *most* but not all of the plantings are food-producing plants.

If you need a new tree or shrub or want to remove an existing one that has died, consider planting a fruit or nut tree. A pecan, hickory, English walnut, or hazelnut (whatever is suitable for your climate) makes a nice large shade tree. A standard fruit tree is a good replacement for a medium-size tree. Very dwarf apples and genetic dwarf peaches or nectarines are so small that they can be used as shrubs in the landscape. Blueberries, figs, cornelian cherry, and shrub roses with edible hips such as rugosa roses also are suitable landscape shrubs.

Picking the Plants

Showy annual vegetables and a variety of herbs play all-important roles in any edible landscape. When you look through catalogs to order plants for spring planting, look for cultivars that have especially attractive leaves or flowers. Then add them to your garden to take advantage of their ornamental features. 'Dark Opal' basil, for example, has deep maroon foliage that can add color and interest to a planting of flowers and herbs. 'Lettuce Leaf' basil has exceptionally large, bold leaves.

There are many vegetables that make interesting or attractive additions to kitchen gardens, dooryard plantings, or flower beds. Consider trying plants such as 'Rubine Red' brussels sprouts, 'Ruby Red' Swiss chard, 'Purple Giant' cauliflower, 'Triple Curled' parsley, and 'Romanesco' broccoli. Various cultivars of artichokes, cabbage, cardoon, kale, lavender, leeks, marjoram, onions, rosemary, and sage feature foliage in shades of gray and blue. For red and pink shades, consider beets, red cabbage, pink cress, purple ornamental kale, red lettuces, and purple mustard.

Many herbs make fine groundcovers, including chives, garlic chives, oregano, prostrate rosemary, French tarragon, and culinary and lemon thyme. Creeping types of thyme and oregano are low-growing and work well planted between stepping stones, where they may be lightly stepped on, releasing their fragrance. Strawberries, especially Alpine strawberries, and burnet, which is a salad green, also make good groundcovers.

For partially shaded spots, try currants, daylilies, huckleberries, pawpaws, American persimmons, rhubarb, French sorrel, mints, Alpine strawberries, and violets. For more edible landscaping ideas, see the design for a circular herb garden below.

A Circular Herb Garden

A good way to get started in edible landscaping is to plant a small herb garden. This garden, which is only 8 feet across, surrounds a sundial but could just as easily be planted around a flagpole or lamppost. Where the design indicates just "perennial herbs," choose from whatever perennial herbs you like, such as lavender, oregano, tarragon, sage, or rosemary. Choose four, one for each site.

Robert Kourik is a free-lance writer, publisher, consultant, and landscape designer in Occidental, California. He is the author of Designing and Maintaining Your Edible Landscape Naturally *and* Drip Irrigation for Every Landscape and All Climates.

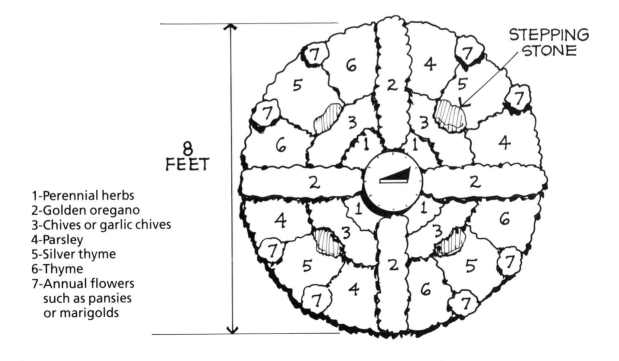

STEPPING STONE

8 FEET

1-Perennial herbs
2-Golden oregano
3-Chives or garlic chives
4-Parsley
5-Silver thyme
6-Thyme
7-Annual flowers
　such as pansies
　or marigolds

EDIBLE LANDSCAPING
MADE EASY

Here are some edible landscaping ideas to help you get started:

Start small. For example, try including some edibles with your annual flowers by accenting a flower bed with deep green rosettes of corn salad, small mounds of 'Spicy Globe' basil, or crinkly red leaf lettuce.

Add to existing beds. Plant perennial herbs and vegetables such as rhubarb, chives, or sage in your existing beds of perennial flowers. Make room by relocating or replacing existing plants.

Cut down on the grass. Replace grass with food-producing groundcovers in some areas. Alpine strawberries produce fruit all summer and tolerate light shade. Thyme and oregano are good groundcovers for full sun.

Grow up your fences. Make use of existing walls and fences or add new ones. Train dwarf fruit trees against them or use them to support raspberries, blackberries, or vegetables.

Plant a fruiting hedge. Bush cherries, wild plums, gooseberries, currants, hazelnuts, and highbush cranberries make good hedges. Tightly planted raspberries or blackberries create a living fence. Rugosa roses also make a lovely and intruder-resistant barrier.

Build an arbor or trellis. Grapes are traditional, but hardy kiwi would also be a good choice for a large arbor. Vegetables like cucumbers, melons, and beans work well, too, but some need special support for the fruit.

Add containers to your landscape. Many dwarf fruit trees are now available and can be grown in large tubs. You can grow dwarf citrus even in northern climates if you move them to a cool, sunny location indoors during the winter. Strawberry jars are good for strawberries or herbs.

Plant in a convenient spot. Place the salad greens and herbs as close to the kitchen as possible. During inclement weather, you can easily gather heaps of fresh greens and savory herbs.

Separate your salad fixings. The easiest-to-manage edible landscapes have a separate area for salad greens. Don't scatter them randomly throughout a flower border; they'll be hard to find at harvest time, and you won't notice when it's time to transplant or plant seeds to replace harvested plants.

Segregate your mass-production garden. Plant vegetables that take up a lot of room, are used in quantity for canning, and aren't particularly attractive away from the house. Or plant them behind an attractive hedge or a grape-covered trellis. Examples include paste tomatoes, eggplants, vining squash plants, potatoes, and corn.

Structure your space. Remember that the core of any good landscape design is its structure—walkways, arbors, stone walls, trellises, or wood-chip pathways. The more annual vegetables you have in your design, the more visually dominant the permanent structures should be.

Buy healthy plants. Make sure you choose as many relatively pest- and disease-free edible plants as possible.

11

SEED SAVING AND PROPAGATION
Multiplying Your Plants for Future Harvests

Once you've been bitten by the gardening bug, you'll want to grow more and more plants. Propagating your own plants is fun and practical. You save money because you're producing the plants instead of buying them. And you can be sure that the plants will be the type you expect—as long as you label them properly!

Saving seeds from your plants is an easy way to multiply most garden vegetables, many herbs, and some nut trees. To increase herbs or bush fruits such as currants, you can use division, layering, or cuttings. To propagate fruit trees and nut cultivars, grafting is the ideal method. Following, you'll find each of these methods covered in detail. For specific propagation tips for particular plants, check under "Propagation" in the plant entries in Part 2.

SAVING SEEDS FOR FUTURE CROPS

If you buy seeds to start your own vegetable and herb plants, you've probably noticed that you're paying more and more money each year for fewer seeds. You may have wondered if it would just be cheaper to buy the plants or produce that you want. But wait—did you know that it's easy to save and grow seeds from many of the plants you already have?

By growing and planting your own seeds, you'll gain a wonderful feeling of independence. The seeds haven't been treated with chemicals, and your plans won't be affected by the discontinuance of a favorite cultivar. By saving seeds from your best plants year after year, you can even produce crop strains that are particularly well-adapted to your needs and conditions.

Unfortunately, you can't raise all plants from seeds. Some, such as Jerusalem artichokes, do not bear seeds readily. And if you raise fruit tree and berry cultivars from seeds, their offspring seldom produce high-quality fruit. But many common vegetables and herbs, like lettuce, tomatoes, basil, and dill, are good candidates for home seed saving.

Botany 101

Before you go out scavenging for seeds, take a few minutes to review some basic botany. Knowing how seeds are formed will help you later on, when you're reading about more complicated matters like self- and cross-pollination.

First, remember that flowers generally contain both the male and female organs of plants. The male organs are a cluster of stemlike parts called stamens. The stamens carry pollen: a yellow, brownish, or reddish powder composed of male cells. The female organ is the pistil—a single stem that is usually longer than the stamens and is located in the center of the stamen cluster. At the pistil's base is the ovary, which contains female reproductive cells.

To produce a seed, a grain of pollen must reach the stigma, which is the sticky top of the pistil. Then it must move down the style, or pistil tube, and join a female cell in the ovary at the base. Bees and other insects transfer the pollen of most plants while collecting nectar, but wind moves the pollen between nut trees, corn, and other grains.

Plant Parenthood

How do you decide whether a particular plant would be a good "parent?" First, you need to know what its life cycle is: Is it annual, biennial, or perennial? Annual and perennial crops are generally easy to save seeds from. Biennials can be trickier.

You also need to find out whether the plant is stable, which means its seedlings will be similar to the parent plant, or if it is a hybrid. Seeds from hybrid plants produce seedlings that are quite different from each other—

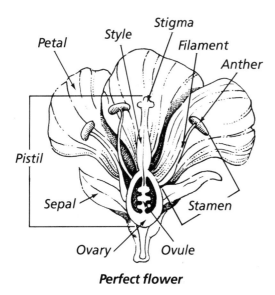

Perfect flower

A perfect flower (*top*) contains both male parts (stamens) and female parts (pistils). Imperfect flowers (*right*) lack either stamens or pistils. On some plants, such as squash, female flowers have a visible swelling (the ovary) at the base of the bloom.

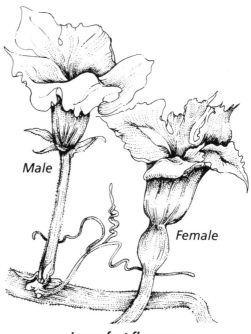

Imperfect flowers

and in most cases not as good as the parent. If you plan to save seeds, you'll want to stick with stable cultivars and avoid hybrids.

And last, it's important to know if the plant can pollinate itself, or if it needs a partner. This will determine how you arrange the crops in your garden. Different cultivars of self-pollinated crops can be close together and their seedlings will still look like the plant you got the seeds from. But if you grow cross-pollinated crops, you'll need to separate them with space or screens to avoid a genetic jumble.

Learn about Life Cycles

Annual plants grow, produce seeds, and die, all in the same year. Many vegetables and herbs, including lettuce, corn, borage, and cilantro, are annuals. Biennials don't flower and set seed until their second growing season. This group includes plants like beets, carrots, parsley, and kale. Perennials, such as asparagus, rhubarb, and sage, live and produce seeds each year for many years.

Annuals are generally the easiest plants to save seeds from. They are genetically pro-grammed to produce lots of seeds to ensure the survival of the species. Just plant the crop, let it go to flower, and then collect the seeds.

Many perennials are also simple to gather seeds from. Growing perennial crops from seeds is often a long-term prospect, though, since it can take a few years to get your first harvest. Some you can't grow from seeds. Named cul-tivars, like 'Crimson Red' rhubarb, generally don't produce seedlings that are just like the mother plant. And a few perennials, like French tarragon, rarely set seed. You'll need to propa-gate these perennials by cloning.

Biennials can be the most difficult plants to collect seeds from. Some biennials, such as parsnips, carrots, and beets, overwinter well in the garden if you mulch them heavily. In cold climates, though, you'll need to dig up most biennials, roots and all, and store them in leaves or sand in a cool root cellar. Replant them in the garden in spring, where they will flower and set seed.

Consider Pollination Patterns

Open-pollinated, cross-pollinated, self-pollinated, hybrid—the jargon of seed saving can be intimidating at first. But you don't need a Ph.D. to be a seed saver. Take a minute to review the explanations below, and you'll be on your way to making informed seed-saving plans.

Open-pollinated vs. hybrid crops. Most commercial seeds are from stable, open-pollinated crops. This means they consistently produce plants that are very similar. First-generation (F_1) hybrids are *not* stabilized. Seeds collected from F_1 plants will produce seed-lings that are unlike the parents.

Seed catalogs or packets usually indicate if you are buying hybrid seeds; look for the symbol F_1 behind the cultivar name or in the description. If there's no mention of the word hybrid, you're probably dealing with an open-pollinated crop.

To get reliable results from your seeds year after year, stick with collecting from open-pollinated plants. If you're adventurous and have lots of room in your garden, you can try planting seeds from a hybrid and see what you get. The resulting plants will likely be duds, or at least not as good as the plant you collected from. But every once in a while, you may spot a seedling with some particularly good traits, like bigger fruit or earlier ripening. You can try to preserve or improve on that genetic combi-nation by saving seeds from the best of these plants each year.

Self-pollinated crops. Remember our review of basic botany, and the different types of flowers? (If not, see "Botany 101" on page 260.) All self-pollinated crops have perfect flowers, which means they have both female and male parts. Each flower can be fertilized by pollen from itself or from another flower on the same plant. Since the mother plant usually fertilizes itself, its genetic material basically remains the same year after year. The resulting seeds will therefore produce plants that look just like the parent.

What does this mean in the garden? It means, for example, that you can plant bush peas and snow peas fairly close together in your garden without worrying that you'll have a genetic mix-up in the seeds you save from them. Beans, tomatoes, lettuce, endive, barley, oats, and wheat are other examples of crops that usually self-pollinate. These are all good candidates for beginning seed savers.

A note of warning, though: Just because plants are *usually* self-pollinated doesn't mean they are *always* self-pollinated. Sometimes wayward insects can transfer a bit of pollen from one cultivar to another, and the seeds from that flower will be different from all of the other seeds produced by that plant. To be on the safe side, separate rows of the same self-pollinated crops with a row of a different, fairly tall, crop. In the example above, for instance, a row of tomatoes or corn between the bush peas and snow peas would be good insurance against chance crosses. To virtually eliminate any chance of crossing for more susceptible plants like beans, separate different cultivars by about 150 feet.

Cross-pollinated crops. Most other crops you grow, including broccoli, cucumbers, and peppers (to name a few), are cross-pollinated. Cross-pollinated plants can have either per-

fect or imperfect flowers. Unlike self-pollinators, though, the flowers of cross-pollinators can be fertilized by pollen from a different plant in the same species or genus. The resulting seeds contain genetic material from each of the parent plants. Depending on the pollen source, the seedlings may look quite different from the plant that produced the seeds.

Here's an example: Let's say you're growing both 'Tendersweet' and 'Oxheart' carrots. The flowers of the 'Tendersweet' could be fertilized by pollen from another 'Tendersweet' plant or by pollen from the 'Oxheart' plants in the next bed. They could even be fertilized by pollen from the closely related Queen-Anne's-lace growing in the field across the street. If you saved seeds from your 'Tendersweet' plants, it's highly likely that the seedlings won't grow into the long, sweet roots you expect.

If you want seeds that come true from a cross-pollinated plant, you must ensure that no pollen from a different cultivar can reach its flowers. The easiest way to avoid mongrel seeds is to grow only one cultivar of each crop and be sure that your garden is several hundred feet away from your neighbor's. If you want to grow several different cultivars of the same crop, plant each kind at least 200 feet apart.

Squash, cucumbers, and melons need a half-mile or more between crops of the same species. For home gardeners, a more practical approach is to grow a few plants of the cultivar you want under row cover or insect-proof screens and pollinate them by hand. Or cover the flowers you plan to save seeds from with bags before they open, and dust the flowers with pollen from another flower from the same cultivar. This technique also works well for wind-pollinated crops like corn; just strip a bag over the ear to protect the silks.

Getting Started

Good candidates for your first seed-saving venture are self-pollinated annuals such as beans, lettuce, peas, and tomatoes. As you gain experience in seed saving, you may want to try more challenging crops like squash and melons.

Always choose your healthiest, most vigorous plants to save seeds from. Look for plants that have special characteristics, such as the earliest fruit or the best cold or heat tolerance. Selecting for special characteristics is an easy form of plant breeding. By propagating only the best plants each year, you'll gradually develop a crop strain uniquely adapted to your garden.

Harvesting Seeds

You've probably noticed seedpods forming on radish and asparagus plants or loose clusters of seeds on spinach and basil that somehow went to seed when your back was turned. The peas, corn, and beans we eat are seeds, and vegetable fruits, such as cucumbers, eggplant, melons, peppers, squash, and tomatoes, produce seeds hidden in their interiors.

Seeds that are borne in loose clusters are the fastest and easiest to harvest. Keep an eye on the plants until a few of the seeds begin to drop; then collect whole seed heads or clusters. If they are ripening unevenly, cover them with paper bags and fasten them with ties to trap seeds that fall early.

Seeds borne in pods, like beans and peas, take a bit more work to harvest and clean. Leave pods on the vines until they are overripe, but pull up vines before the pods open. Dry the vines on a rack, or tie them to a post outdoors if the weather is sunny. When the vines are dry, pick off the pods and shell them or thresh them by putting them in a pillowcase and beating the pillowcase with a stick.

Clean away the chaff by pouring the seeds from one container to another in a light breeze.

To save corn seeds, leave a few ears unpicked until the husks begin to get brown. Then pick and open them, but leave the husks attached. Use the husks to hang the corn in a warm, dry place. Shell the ears after the kernels turn hard and separate easily from the cob.

For fruit-type plants like cucumbers, let the fruits ripen on the plant until they're a bit past maturity. Then pick the fruits and remove the seeds. Be sure to get the seeds before the fruits start to spoil, otherwise the seeds will rot.

Tomato seeds need a bit of extra care. Pick the best ripe fruits to save. Cut each fruit open and squeeze out the seeds and juice into a bowl. Add some water—about half as much as the amount of tomato juice—and stir this mixture twice a day for three days. A thick layer of white or gray mold will form on the top. Add more water and stir vigorously. Pour off the mold and any floating debris and seeds; the good seeds will sink. Add more water and repeat the process until only clean seeds are left.

❧ TRICKS OF THE TRADE ❧

DUAL-PURPOSE PAPER

Want an easy way to dry and store your tomato seeds? Once you've soaked and cleaned the seeds, spread them thinly and evenly over a paper towel to dry. The dried seeds stick to the paper, which you roll up and store until late winter. At planting time, place the towel on a flat of seed-starting mix, cover it lightly with perlite, and keep the flat warm and watered. As the paper breaks down, the seeds sprout in a well-spaced fashion and need no thinning.

Drying and Storing Seeds

Drying seeds is a snap. An excellent way to dry large seeds, like peas and beans, is to spread them on a fine-mesh wire screen. Support the screen a few inches above a table or lay it over two sawhorses so air can circulate beneath it. Fine seeds dry well on a newspaper or paper towel. One to two weeks in a warm, airy place is usually long enough to dry your seeds.

Once the seeds are dry, brush away or screen out any debris. Put the clean seeds in containers labeled with the date and cultivar name. In most cases, it's best to store seeds in tightly closed containers to prevent them from reabsorbing moisture from the air. If they're not quite dry, though, they can turn moldy. When in doubt, store your seeds in paper envelopes, paper bags, or cloth bags. Store all seeds in a cool, dry, dark place until planting time.

PROPAGATION TECHNIQUES

While the successful cloning of humans and animals may lie somewhere in the future, people have been cloning plants for centuries. You don't need a laboratory full of test tubes or other fancy equipment—a spade, a knife, and pruning shears are the tools you'll use to duplicate many of the plants you already have through division, layering, and cuttings.

Division

Dividing one plant into two or more parts is an easy and dependable propagation technique. There are two ways to divide clump-type plants, like rhubarb, chives, and thyme. One is to thrust a sharp spade downward through the clump while it is still in the ground, dig up one or more portions of the plant, and transplant them. Or, instead, dig up the entire plant and cut the sections apart with a knife, clippers, or saw.

Certain bush fruits, such as currants, form offshoots—little plants around the mother plant. In early spring, chip off these little plants and move them to a new spot. Feel around in the soil by the offshoots first, though, and only separate offshoots that have roots.

Plants such as red raspberries, upright blackberries, and elderberries send up suckers from their roots. Suckers are similar to offshoots but may appear many feet from the parent. Digging up and transplanting them is an easy way to start new plants. Since suckers are not likely to have heavy roots, cut the tops back by about half when you plant them. This way, the new plants won't start life with more topgrowth than their meager root systems can support.

Early spring is generally the best time to divide. When dividing any plant, be sure there are roots and topgrowth on each portion that you split from the parent. Always plant the divisions immediately, before they dry out, and water them in well.

Layering

Layering is like fooling a plant into forming roots it doesn't really need. By bringing a plant stem into contact with the soil, you can induce it to take root. You then cut the rooted stem off of the mother plant and you have a little clone of the mother plant.

Small fruits such as grapes, gooseberries, wild blueberries, and currants are easy to propagate in one season by layering. When high-bush blueberries, serviceberries, filberts, and quince are layered, they form roots more slowly, often taking a year or more. Strawberry plants layer themselves naturally by forming runners.

Don't try to layer a grafted plant. The scion,

or top portion, of a grafted plant is a different cultivar than the rootstock, or the part from which the roots grow. The rootstock generally has important characteristics such as dwarfness or disease tolerance, which the scion does not have. The scion will take root if you layer it, but the new plant won't have the desirable qualities of the rootstock and may not grow well. Propagate grafted fruit trees and other plants by grafting.

You can layer nongrafted plants anytime, but roots form fastest in the spring. Choose a flexible, vigorous, low-growing shoot about as thick as a pencil. Gently bend the free end of the shoot down to the soil. Measure back about 9 inches from the shoot tip, and mark the spot where it touches the soil. Release the shoot and loosen the soil where you marked it. This will allow the roots from the layer to grow easily.

Remove the leaves from the part of the shoot that will be buried—6 to 12 inches behind the tip. To promote rooting, cut a shallow tongue about 9 inches back from the tip, and insert a toothpick to hold the tongue open. (Or, instead, scrape a bit of bark off the bottom of the stem.) Bend the branch down, and bury the prepared section about 1 inch deep. If needed, use a wire pin to anchor the shoot in the soil. Let the end of the shoot stick out in the air; stake it if it won't stay upright by itself. Mulch the buried part with leaves or grass clippings to conserve moisture. Water it occasionally to keep the soil evenly moist.

Black raspberries, dewberries, and boysenberries naturally form layers from their tips when their canes bend over and touch the soil. To get even more plants, bend over a few standing canes and cover their tips with soil. New plants will sprout and shoot up from the tips.

It's tempting to poke in the soil around a layered stem to see if you can spy new roots forming. Resist the urge. Wait a month or two. Then dig *carefully* around the layer to check for roots. If you don't see any roots, wait for another month and check again. When you are sure the layered stem is well-rooted, cut it from the parent plant 6 inches above the roots,

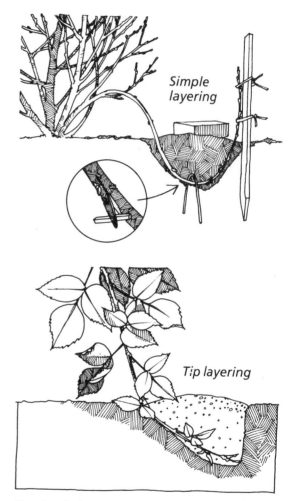

For simple layering (*top*), use a bent piece of wire to secure the stem. A brick or stone over the area also holds the stem down and retains soil moisture. Tip layers (*bottom*) usually stay in place on their own.

but don't dig it up. Leave it alone until the following spring. Then move it to its permanent location.

Cuttings

Cuttings are a bit trickier than layering, but in many cases, they're worth the trouble. Cuttings can root in a matter of weeks, as opposed to month for layers. And with cuttings, you can get dozens of babies from one parent plant; with layering, one or two per parent plant is the norm.

Most cuttings come from stems or branches. Hardwood cuttings are those taken from dormant wood; softwood cuttings come from growing wood in early summer. Some plants

will even regrow from small pieces of root. For details on root cuttings, see "Raising Fruits from Roots" on the opposite page.

Hardwood Cuttings

Currants, jostaberries, figs, and quinces start easily from hardwood cuttings. Grapes do, too, although you shouldn't use this method for grafted grapes; otherwise, you'll lose the beneficial effects of the grafted rootstock.

When the plant is dormant in late winter, cut pieces 8 to 10 inches long from the ends of the branches, and remove the tips. Some plants, such as quince, benefit from cuttings that have a bit of older wood at the base. (These are

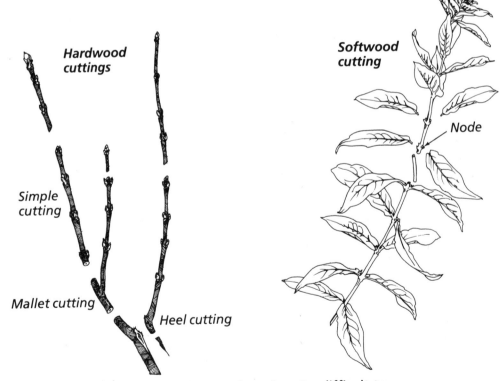

Take hardwood cuttings (*left*) from dormant branches. For difficult-to-root plants, try a heel or mallet cutting, with a piece of older wood at the base. Softwood cuttings (*right*) come from active growth.

RAISING FRUITS FROM ROOTS

You can start large numbers of plants such as raspberries and blackberries from root cuttings. Dig around the base of a healthy plant in late winter or early spring and look for pencil-thick roots. Collect a few of these roots by snipping them off with sharp pruning shears. Then replace the soil around the plant.

Cut the roots you've collected into pieces about 1 inch long. Plant them horizontally about ½ inch deep in light soil in early spring. After the plants start to grow, move each to a small pot filled with potting soil. Give them a dose of compost tea or other organic liquid fertilizer once a week for four weeks. As soon as roots fill the pot, transplant them to their permanent home.

known as heel or mallet cuttings.) Tie the stem pieces in bundles of the same cultivar, with all of the tops at one end. Label the bundles and bury them completely in barely moist vermiculite. Store in a cool place that doesn't freeze, such as a cellar or refrigerator. By spring, a thick, fleshy callus will form on the bottom end of each cutting.

As soon as the ground has thawed completely, prepare a nursery bed where the cuttings can take root. Choose an out-of-the way spot in the garden that gets morning sun, and loosen the soil to a depth of 8 to 10 inches. Before planting, dip the callused ends in commercial rooting hormone (available at your local garden center). Then plant the cuttings upright, setting the callused ends about 4 inches below the soil surface. Keep the soil evenly moist. After a few weeks, the cuttings should start to grow. Leave them in place until the following spring. Then move them to their permanent spot in the garden.

Softwood Cuttings

If you want to take cuttings during the growing season, you'll be working with softwood cuttings. Softwood cuttings are a good way to propagate nongrafted grapes, nearly all bush fruits, and many herbs, such as bay and rosemary. Blueberries, gooseberries, and serviceberries root best by this method.

Gather softwood cuttings in late spring or early summer when the plant is growing vigorously. Cut off pieces of new growth 5 to 6 inches long, with at least two nodes (leaf joints). Remove the bottom leaves. Set cuttings about 2 inches deep in pots or trays filled with sand or a mixture of half perlite and half vermiculite.

From this point on, your softwood cuttings will need a bit more babying than hardwood cuttings do. Because they come from actively growing tissue, softwood cuttings are much more prone to wilting. You'll need to provide a sheltered, humid environment to prevent this. Protect your cuttings by covering them with a clear plastic bag or plastic sheet. Make sure the plastic doesn't touch the cuttings—otherwise, the cuttings will tend to rot. Put the covered cuttings where they will get lots of indirect light (not direct sunlight), and keep the temperature from 70° to 75°F. Mist the cuttings with water often to keep the leaves and potting medium moist but not soggy.

Most plants will take three to four weeks to root. Topgrowth is a good but not infallible clue that the cuttings have rooted. To be sure, tug lightly on the cuttings. If they resist your pull, they're rooted. Or look at the bottom of the container to see if any roots are visible. For best results, transfer each cutting to an individual pot as soon as it roots. Plant them out in the garden in fall, or overwinter the potted cuttings in a cold frame and plant them in spring.

Grafting and Budding

Grafting is real garden magic. With a wave of your knife, you can transform a seedling tree into a named cultivar. With a little practice, it's easy!

Grafting—attaching a portion of one plant to another plant—is generally the method of choice for propagating named cultivars of fruit and hybrid nut trees. It works best on closely related plants (usually those in the same genus); don't try to graft stone fruits like peaches onto apples, or vice versa.

There are two types of grafting commonly used: cleft grafting and bud grafting.

Cleft Grafting

Cleft grafting involves inserting a scion (stem piece) of one plant into a cut made in the stem of another (the rootstock). It is used especially for apples, pears, and some nut trees. This method is one of the easiest ways to graft good fruit cultivars onto small fruit trees you find growing wild or raise from seeds.

Collect the scion wood in late spring, just before the buds start to swell. Cut 6- to 12-inch-long branch tips from the trees producing the fruit you want. Use only new wood that grew the previous year. Label the branch tips with the cultivar name. Wrap them in plastic, and store them in the refrigerator.

Select rootstocks based on special characteristics such as dwarfness or resistance to pests and/or disease. The plant entries in Part 2 will tell you the best rootstocks for many fruit trees, such as apples and peaches.

When the buds on the rootstock trees begin to swell and show a bit of green, it's time to graft. Take out the pieces of scion wood and put their bottom ends into a pail of water to keep them moist. Cut the top off of a rootstock seedling tree at a few inches above ground level, or, if you are grafting onto a larger tree, cut off the end of a limb. (Cleft grafting is most successful on trunks or limbs that are anywhere from the size of a pencil thickness to about 1 inch in diameter.) With a super-sharp knife, split the top of the rootstock or the end of the branch through the middle. Make the cut only deep enough to insert a scion.

Next, prepare the scion wood by cutting each branch tip into 2- to 3-inch pieces, discarding the very tip of the branch. For each piece you cut, make sure you keep track of which end is which. Make a slanted cut at the top of your scion pieces and a straight-across cut at the bottom of them. You'll want to do this because if you insert the tip end of the scion into the rootstock, your graft won't work. Each scion should have one or two buds, with one at the tip of the scion. Make two downward-sloping cuts at the bottom end of the scion to form a wedge shape.

Stick your knife blade in the slit on the rootstock or branch, and gently push the two sides apart. Insert the wedged end of the scion into the slit. Be careful to align, on one side, the thin, green cambium layer (the actively growing tissue) under the bark on both the scion and rootstock. When you've got the scion where you want it, take out the knife blade. The pressure of the split rootstock will hold the scion in place.

Cover the graft with grafting wax or a commercial tree paint to keep it from drying out. When all goes well, the scion buds will sprout and grow after a few weeks. If the scion takes longer to sprout than buds on the surrounding trees, don't be alarmed: This is normal.

Bud Grafting

In bud grafting (also known as budding), you transfer only one small bud, instead of a whole scion, to the rootstock tree. It is an easy way to propagate most tree fruits.

Budding is easier than cleft grafting because you don't need to line up cambium layers and grafting wax is unnecessary. And unlike cleft grafting, you can bud graft during the growing season, since you are working with live buds instead of dormant scions. Conditions are right for bud grafting when the sap is flowing and the bark slips (separates easily from the wood below). You can start bud grafting as early as June in the South and late July in the North. Bud graft anytime until the tree's new growth hardens and the sap stops flowing in late summer.

Start by collecting your bud wood. A day or two before you plan to bud graft, cut 8- to 15-inch-long stem pieces from the current year's growth of your desired plant. Put their bottom ends in a pail of water and set them in a shady spot. Pinch off the leaves, but leave a bit of each leaf stem to use as handles.

On the rootstock, as close to the ground as you can work, make a shallow, T-shaped cut through the bark to expose the green cambium layer attached to the wood beneath. Open the flaps of the T with your knife. Next, prepare the bud. Place the edge of your knife below a plump, healthy-looking bud on the bud wood. With a sliding, upward motion, cut out the bud and a small sliver of wood behind it. Make a horizontal cut just above the bud, to sever it from the bud wood.

Holding the bud patch by its stem handle, slip the bud behind the bark flaps of the T on

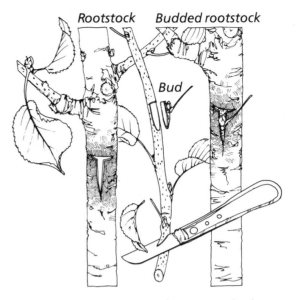

Make a shallow T-shaped cut near the base of the rootstock. Cut a bud from the desired plant and slip it into the cut on the rootstock.

the rootstock. Wrap tightly with a rubber budding strip or masking tape, being careful not to cover the bud itself.

Check the graft after a few weeks. If the bud is green and plump, you were successful; if it is brown and dry, try rebudding on a different part of the rootstock's stem. Leave healthy bud grafts alone until the following spring. Before the plant begins to grow, remove the wrapping and cut off the top of the rootstock tree on a slant just above the bud.

Aftercare for Grafted Plants

Suckers may sprout below the graft on a newly grafted tree. Don't procrastinate about cutting off these unwanted shoots: They'll quickly crowd out the good portion of the tree.

Don't feed the tree the first year unless it is growing poorly. The new shoots will grow rapidly without added nutrients. The second year, begin to fertilize as you normally would.

PART 2

THE HOME FOOD GARDEN

✳

A Practical Encyclopedia
of Vegetables, Fruits,
Herbs, and More

ALMOND

Prunus amygdalus. Rosaceae.
Deciduous tree. Zones 7–9.

The earliest blooming of all deciduous trees, almonds need a long, dry growing season. Depending on the cultivar, trees bloom in February or March; nuts ripen from August through October. Almond trees can grow up to 30' tall.

Crops are very susceptible to disease problems in humid areas and to blossom damage from late spring frosts. Because of these restrictions, about 99 percent of the domestic almond crop is grown in California's Sacramento and San Joaquin valleys.

Some almonds need a relatively frost-free location. The hardiest sweet almond cultivar is 'Titan'. Some hardy almonds are actually almond-peach hybrids. These hybrids may produce bitter kernels.

Site. Choose a warm site in full sun.

Soil. A fertile sandy loam with a pH from 6.0–7.0 is best, but almonds will tolerate heavier soils.

How much to plant. Only a few cultivars are self-fertile or partially self-fertile. For good pollination, most need to be planted near at least one tree of another cultivar that will bloom at the same time.

Spacing. For good pollination, plant trees no more than several hundred feet apart and no closer than 25' apart to avoid crowding.

Seasons to bearing. A budded or grafted tree will start bearing in three to four years and give full yields in eight to ten years.

Planting and growing. Plant as you would any young tree. For directions, see "Perennial Crops" on page 111. Water newly planted trees well for the first couple of days. Continue to water the trees regularly when weather is hot

and dry, and as needed in wintertime.

Almonds are fairly high users of nitrogen and will benefit from a leguminous cover crop or a mulch containing well-rotted animal manure or another nitrogen source. Leave the base of the tree clear when you mulch; don't let the mulch touch the trunk. Renew the mulch annually.

Prune lightly to remove old wood and promote new growth and air circulation. The best almond crops are on spurs that are five to seven years old.

To prevent damage by navel orangeworm or peach twig borer, harvest promptly and practice good winter sanitation. Remove any mummies (undeveloped nuts) from the tree or beneath it and destroy them.

Harvesting. When the hulls of the nuts are split open, spread a canvas beneath the tree and then gently knock the nuts down. Allow to dry on the ground for seven to ten days, then gather up and remove the hulls. (For an illustration of almonds, see page 416.) For long-term storage, shell the nuts and keep them in containers in the refrigerator or freezer. Nuts will keep for several months at room temperature but are vulnerable to attack by dry-storage pests such as the Indian meal moth.

Propagation. Most almond trees that you can buy are grafted. You can propagate them by budding or by whip-and-tongue, cleft, or bark grafts. Be sure to choose a rootstock that is appropriate for your climate. Bitter-almond rootstocks are drought-resistant. Peach rootstocks grow best with irrigation.

Friends and relatives. The so-called Chinese almond is simply any of a number of sweet-pitted apricot cultivars. See the Apricot entry for culture. ✳

APPLE

Malus pumila and other spp. Rosaceae.
Deciduous tree. Zones 3–9.

You can grow apples almost anywhere and, by choosing cultivars carefully, you can enjoy your own fresh apples through most of the year. You can also preserve them in the form of applesauce, pie filling, jelly, cider, and dried apple rings.

Crab apples are closely related to apples but have smaller fruit that is usually more tart. Grow them the same way, but prune and thin less.

Planning

Selecting plants. Choose a one- or two-year-old tree that's ½″–¾″ in diameter. There are hundreds of apple cultivars for you to choose from. To help you decide, consider how you want to eat your apples. Plant cultivars such as 'Rhode Island Greening' or 'Rome Beauty' if you mostly want to cook the fruit, or cultivars such as 'Jonagold' or 'Honeygold' if you want fresh eating apples. Consider disease-resistant cultivars such as 'Liberty' or 'Freedom'. Different apples ripen from midsummer to late fall, so you can choose several cultivars to lengthen your harvest. There are even cultivars such as 'Newtown Pippin' that not only keep well in storage but also improve in flavor.

Most cultivars of apples need cross-pollination: You need at least two different cultivars in order to get fruit. Certain cultivars, such as 'Mutsu' and 'Winesap', do not produce fertile pollen and can't pollinate other cultivars, so you will need three different cultivars in order to get fruit. These nonfertile, nonpollinating cultivars are called triploids.

Select your rootstock thoughtfully. If you have plenty of space and don't mind ladders, a seedling or other standard rootstock is fine.

Seedling rootstocks are also the best choice in very cold areas. Otherwise, choose a dwarfing rootstock. 'M.111' is a semidwarf (65–85 percent of full size) that tolerates heavy soils and drought and is reasonably hardy for a semidwarf. 'MM.106' is also a semidwarf (45–65 percent of full size) but is less tolerant of wet soil, drought, and cold. 'Interstem M.9/MM.111' (50 percent of full size) tolerates extremes in soil drainage but needs staking the first few years. 'Interstem M.9/MM.106' (50 percent of full size) makes a strong, well-anchored tree. 'MARK' (30–40 percent of full size) usually doesn't need staking and is very cold-hardy, but it may break in very windy sites. 'MM.26' (30–40 percent of full size) and 'M.27' (15 percent of full size) require good drainage and staking. 'M.9' (25–35 percent of full size) needs staking and grows well in moist soil or even clay but grows poorly in light, dry soil. Check with your nursery or local extension office to find a rootstock to match your site and needs.

Selecting a site. Choose a site with full sun and well-drained soil. If you can, avoid low spots where frost tends to settle. If you

---

∽ AT A GLANCE ∽

APPLE

Site: Full sun; avoid frost pockets; slopes are good.

Soil: Moderately fertile and well-drained.

Spacing: Dwarfs: 6'-8' apart. Semidwarfs: 12'-15' apart. Standard trees: 25'-30' apart.

Seasons to bearing: Dwarfs: one to three years. Semidwarfs: three to five years. Standard trees: five to seven years.

can't, plant a late-blooming cultivar such as 'Red Rome' or one such as 'Wagener', whose blossoms are somewhat frost-resistant. If you can help it, don't plant where an apple tree grew previously.

When to plant. Plant apple trees in either early spring or fall. Avoid fall planting in areas with very cold winters.

Spacing. Eventual size of an apple tree depends on the rootstock, the scion, and the soil fertility. A standard tree (one that is full-size, not a dwarf) needs 25'–30' of space. Semidwarf trees need 12'–15' of space. Dwarf trees can be 6'–8' apart.

For a greater harvest. If you want to cram more trees into a given space (for a greater selection and more fruit), plant dwarf trees.

Soil Preparation

Apple trees prefer moderately rich soil with good drainage and a pH between 6.5 and 6.8. Start preparing the soil a season before planting. Adjust pH and build up fertility by fertilizing and growing cover crops. For more details, see Chapter 2 and "Custom Care for Tree Fruits" on page 61.

Planting

For complete instructions on planting apple trees, see "Perennial Crops" on page 111. Be sure the graft union of a dwarf or semidwarf tree is higher than ground level so the scion won't root and negate the rootstock effect. Cut tall, unbranched trees back to 3'. See "Pruning at Planting Time" on page 145 for more details.

If your tree has a dwarf rootstock, it will need staking to compensate for the less vigorous roots. Drive a sturdy wooden or metal stake into the ground near the tree. Tie the tree loosely to the stake. Wrap the trunk to protect

it from sunscald, and install a hardware-cloth sleeve to protect it from rodents. Spread a layer of organic mulch over the area.

Growing Guidelines

Water and mulch. Apple trees need a regular supply of water throughout the growing season. They are especially thirsty from bloom through petal-fall, and the last two weeks prior to harvest. Dwarf trees are more drought-susceptible than standard trees. Maintain a thick organic mulch to help reduce water loss.

Feeding. Spread 5–10 pounds of compost out to the drip line in late winter each year. Shoots on a well-nourished, young apple tree should grow 1'–2' in a season; those on a mature, bearing tree should grow 6"–10". If growth is less than that, give them an inch or so of compost the following spring.

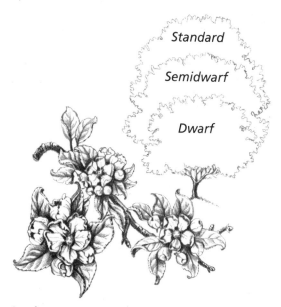

Apples are attractive trees. They range from 6- to 8-foot-tall dwarfs to giants 30 feet tall or taller.

Training. Train apple trees to central leader or modified central leader form. Standards can be trained to open center form. See "Pruning Trees" on page 142 for instructions.

Thinning. Thin young fruits to about 6" apart and no more than one fruit per spur. Remove damaged, misshapen, and puny fruits.

Problem Prevention

In late winter, spray dormant oil. If aphids, mites, or scale were a problem last year, spray oil just as buds are swelling.

In late winter, hang codling moth traps. About two weeks before bud break, hang one or two pheromone traps per tree to help control codling moths.

If you had a big problem with them the previous year, traps alone may not do the job. Hang one pheromone trap (for up to 5 acres). Check the trap weekly. When you catch the first codling moth, wait two weeks and then spray with a mix of ryania and *Bacillus thuringiensis* var. *kurstaki* (BTK), mixed according to label directions, plus soap (1 teaspoon per gallon) and molasses (1 tablespoon per gallon). See "Troubleshooting Fruit and Vegetable Pests" on page 182 for a description of codling moths and the damage they cause.

If you have quite a number of fruit trees, you may want to try mating disruption to control codling moths. See "Pheromones" on page 159 for suggestions.

When green shows, spray lime-sulfur. If apple scab has been a problem, spray once with lime-sulfur. Be sure to do it before bloom. See "Troubleshooting Vegetable and Fruit Pests" for a description of the symptoms of apple scab.

When green shows, spray kelp. Kelp sprays may increase fruit set and improve bud hardiness. Spray three times: when you first see green, when leaves are ½" long, and when the buds are fat and pink.

As buds swell, hang white sticky traps. White sticky traps hung in your trees will tell you when tarnished plant bugs appear, and the traps can help control them. Use one to four traps per tree (depending on tree size) for control or one trap for monitoring. If tarnished plant bugs were a problem last year, spray sabadilla as buds show pink (especially if your sticky traps have caught the pest).

When petals fall, spray calcium. Calcium sprays may reduce internal fruit breakdown (water core) and corky spots just under the skin. If either was a problem last year, spray three to five times at three- to five-week intervals.

When petals fall, hang plum curculio traps. East of the Rocky Mountains, plum curculio can be a major problem during the six weeks following apple bloom. Make green, sticky sphere traps by spray-painting red ones with 'Granny Smith' apple green paint before coating them with sticky coating. Spray a rotenone/pyrethrin mix as soon as any plum curculios are caught. Also, during their active period, you can jar plum curculios out of your trees twice daily, knocking them onto a sheet; then destroy them by dumping them into a bucket of soapy water. Spread beneficial nematodes under the trees to help reduce plum curculio larvae in soil. Allowing chickens to live beneath your trees also helps decrease curculio problems. There is no effective organic spray; rotenone and pyrethrins may be somewhat effective but must be repeated frequently, and most gardeners don't feel that's a good thing to do. See "Troubleshooting Fruit and Vegetable Pests" on page 182 for a description of plum curculios and the damage they cause.

When leaves expand, spray sulfur. If apple scab has been a problem, spray sulfur when weather is wet or humid and the temperature is above 59°F. Respray after each rain or once a week. Stop in midsummer if the weather stays warm and dry and there is little scab present.

After fruit set, thin. Well-spaced fruits are less likely to be attacked by insects or succumb to diseases. Thinning also results in bigger fruits.

Five weeks after bloom, hang apple maggot traps. Apple maggot is a pest in the eastern and central states. Trap the adults on sticky red spheres hung in your trees. Use one trap per dwarf tree, four to eight traps per standard tree. Hang the traps at eye level and 2'–3' within the tree. See "Troubleshooting Fruit and Vegetable Pests" on page 182 for a description of apple maggots and the damage they cause.

In early summer, replace codling moth lures. Six to eight weeks after you put out the traps, you'll need to put new lures in. If you catch any codling moths, spray immediately with a mix of ryania and *Bacillus thuringiensis* var. *kurstaki* (BTK), mixed according to label

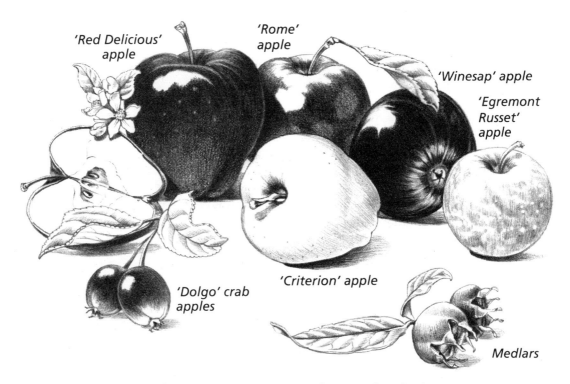

'Red Delicious' apple

'Rome' apple

'Winesap' apple

'Egremont Russet' apple

'Dolgo' crab apples

'Criterion' apple

Medlars

Apples boring? Hardly. When you grow your own, there are hundreds of cultivars to choose from. Apples are red, yellow, and green with white, pink, or yellow flesh. And the flavor! Sprightly, winy, citrusy— the variety is endless. Cut-open apples show a star of seeds. Here's a ripeness tip: Ripe apples have dark seeds; unripe apples have blond ones.

directions, plus soap (1 teaspoon per gallon) and molasses (1 tablespoon per gallon). Repeat every five to seven days as long as you catch new moths.

Throughout summer, watch for fire blight. Look for any shoot with blackened leaves and the curled stem tip typical of fire blight. Immediately cut 6″ below visible symptoms and destroy prunings. Sterilize clippers in alcohol between cuts. See "Troubleshooting Fruit and Vegetable Pests" on page 182 for a description of fire blight.

Summer through fall, pick up dropped fruit. Dropped fruit may harbor insect pests that will crawl out to pupate in the soil. Break the life cycle of the pests by frequently gathering and destroying dropped fruit.

In fall, deal with fallen leaves. Apple scab overwinters on dry infected leaves. Rake them up and compost them or simply bury them with mulch where they lay.

In fall, renew mulch. Rake loose mulch away from trees in early fall. In late fall, after the leaves have fallen and the rodents have found winter homes elsewhere, respread mulch and top it with new to make a 6″–12″ layer.

In winter, remove mummies and cankers. Diseases overwinter in mummified fruits; pick them off and destroy them. Cut diseased branches 6″ below any visible symptoms of disease and destroy prunings.

Gathering the Harvest

For best flavor and storage, pick fruits carefully and at the right moment. Pick summer apples fully ripe. Winter apples finish ripening in storage, so harvest them slightly underripe. You will know an apple is ripe when its underlying skin color changes from grass green to pale green or yellow, and if the fruit comes off when you give it a gentle lift and

---

🐝 FRIENDS & RELATIVES 🐝

APPLE

Medlar (*Mespilus germanica*) is a fruit that resembles an apple and is, in fact, closely related. A medlar fruit is small and brown and its calyx end (the end opposite the stem) is flared open. Pick the rock-hard fruits in the fall after leaves have dropped from the plant and let them soften indoors. When ready to eat, they are brown and mushy and taste like spicy applesauce.

Plant medlars in full sun in well-drained soil. The best-tasting cultivar is 'Nottingham', which, like other medlars, is self-fruitful. Medlars are rarely bothered by pests.

---

twist. For a sure test, take a sample bite every few days. Underripe apples taste green or starchy. Ripe apples taste sweet and juicy. Overripe apples get mealy.

Length of storage varies, ranging from only a few weeks for early cultivars to a half a year or more for late cultivars. Store apples at near-freezing temperatures and at high humidity. Only store undamaged apples with stems intact.

Fall and Winter Care

Protect trees from rodents by keeping mulches away from trunks and enclosing them with hardware-cloth sleeves. Make trees less appetizing to deer by hanging bars of deodorant soap or mesh bags of human hair in the branches. Paint lower trunks with diluted latex paint to ward off sunscald. See "Problem Prevention" on page 276 for other winter tasks that help control insects and diseases.

Late winter is the time to prune your young apple trees. See "Pruning Trees" on page 142 for details on when and how to prune and train your apple trees. Many apples bear their fruit on short growths called spurs. Thin out crowded and unproductive spurs.

Container Growing

Choose trees on very dwarfing rootstocks, such as 'M.9' or 'M.27'. Once your plant reaches full size, repot it every year when it is dormant, and prune back the roots and tops. In very cold areas, protect the roots in winter as shown in the illustration on page 240.

Propagation

Propagate new apple trees by grafting scions onto rootstocks. Apples are easy to graft by any of the common grafting methods described in Chapter 11. *

APRICOT

Prunus armeniaca. Rosaceae.
Deciduous tree. Zones 5–9.

Apricot, which originated in the mountains of Asia, is one of the most delectable of all fruits. The fully ripe fruits ship poorly, so just about the only way you can experience the lusciousness of a truly ripe apricot is to grow your own.

Unfortunately, apricots are not the easiest fruit to grow. They grow best where summers are hot and dry and winters are cold with little temperature fluctuation. Apricots bloom very early, so their blossoms are often wiped out by late frosts.

Nonetheless, if you have the space, consider planting apricots and resigning yourself to sporadic harvests. Breeders are constantly developing new cultivars with greater pest resistance and adaptability, making apricot growing more feasible all the time.

Selecting plants. Choose cultivars adapted to your particular climate and tolerant of pest problems in your region. Most cultivars of apricot are self-fruitful.

Site. Plant apricots in full sun. The trees bloom very early in the season, so choose a site not prone to late-spring frosts, such as on a north-facing slope or a few feet away from a north wall. Do not plant in low-lying areas.

Soil. Apricots require perfectly drained soils—ideally, a light-textured soil such as a sandy loam without any impervious layers deeper down. Apricots tolerate soil pH from 5.5 to 8.0. See "Custom Care for Tree Fruits" on page 61 for how to prepare and enrich the soil prior to planting.

Yield. A standard tree yields 3–4 bushels; a dwarf tree yields half as much.

Spacing. Space standard trees 25' apart each way. Plant dwarf trees 12'–15' apart.

Seasons to bearing. Expect your first crop two seasons after planting (barring late frost).

Planting and growing. Except in mild-winter areas, plant in spring. See "Perennial Crops" on page 111 for details.

If your tree is not branched, cut the trunk back so it is 3' tall at planting. Mulch the tree with 6"–12" of organic mulch.

Apricots can be trained to open center or central leader form. See "Pruning Trees" on page 142 for when and how to prune and train.

Thin apricots only if fruit set is very heavy.

Thin fruits to about 2″ apart.

For yearly feeding recommendation, see "Feeding" on page 438. Shoots on a well-nourished mature tree grow 1′–1½′ per year.

Apricots are subject to many of the same pest problems as peaches. See "Problem Prevention" on page 438 for ways to avoid them.

Harvesting. For best flavor, harvest apricots when they are slightly soft and readily part from the branch. The fruits will not ripen further after harvest. Store fresh fruits at high humidity and near-freezing temperatures for no longer than a week or two. Freeze or dry surplus fruit.

Fall and winter care. See "Fall and Winter Care" on page 440 for guidelines. Apricots bear fruit mostly on wood that is one to three years old.

Container growing. For container growing, plant dwarf apricots. Use a container at least 1½′ deep and wide. Once your plant reaches full size, repot it every year just before growth commences in spring, and prune back the roots and top. In very cold areas, protect the roots in winter as shown in the illustration on page 240.

Propagation. Propagate apricot trees by grafting. Because the trees bleed when cut, bud grafting, which causes only a small wound, is the method of grafting commonly used. Apricot seedlings are the preferred rootstock, but you can use peach or plum rootstocks.

Friends and relatives. Plumcots are hybrids between apricots and plums. Fruit characteristics of plumcots vary, depending on how much apricot or plum is in the parentage of a particular cultivar. Pollination needs also vary, with some cultivars being self-fertile and others requiring pollination by another plumcot, plum, or apricot. Plumcots are adapted from Zones 6 to 9. Check catalogs for pollination needs and hardiness of specific cultivars. ✳

ARTICHOKE

Cynara scolymus. Compositae. Perennial. Zones 8–10. Grown as an annual in cooler zones.

The big, bold plants of artichokes, sometimes called globe artichokes, have thistlelike silver foliage and handsome fleshy flower buds. Boil or steam the immature buds until they are tender enough for you to pull off individual scales (leafy bracts). Dip each scale in butter and scrape the flesh off its base with your teeth. Once you've removed all of the scales, scrape away the hairy "choke," cut off tough stem parts, and eat or pickle the tender heart.

Selecting plants. If you live in a mild coastal climate like northern California, where artichokes thrive, you can grow the standard 'Green Globe Improved' as a perennial. Where growing seasons are shorter, plant early cultivars, such as purple-budded 'Violetto', as annuals. For plants that produce buds sooner than artichokes started from seeds, start with root divisions, where available.

Site. In northern California, any sunny site with moist but well-drained soil will do. Gardeners elsewhere in the country need to create similar cool, moist conditions. Where summers get hotter than about 80°F, plant artichokes in light shade and mulch the roots with 3″ or more of compost to keep them cool. Since artichokes grow up to 5′ tall, choose a site where they will not shade smaller plants. If you grow them as perennials, put them where they won't interfere with annual vegetable crops.

Soil. Amend the planting site with 6″ of compost or aged manure. Consistently moist soils promote the best growth, but only where good drainage keeps the fleshy roots from rotting. In a well-prepared bed, perennial artichokes can grow and produce well for three or four years.

How much to plant. If your area lends itself to artichoke production, you might grow a dozen plants to have enough for eating fresh and pickling. Where the climate is less than ideal, experiment with a few plants before you commit a lot of garden space.

Spacing. Space young plants 2′–3′ apart in rows 3′–4′ apart, according to cultivar size.

Days to maturity. Artichokes take at least 110–150 days from seeds and 100 days from divisions to produce a bud after planting. Most do not flower until the second year of growth.

Planting and growing. Start artichoke seeds indoors a couple of months before the last expected spring frost; give them light and springlike (60°–70°F) temperatures. These plants may produce buds the first year, but more likely they will not. If you soak the seeds for two days and refrigerate them in moist sand for four weeks before sowing, your plants may flower earlier. When you plant a seedling or division, set the crown just above the surface of the soil to keep it dry. Water well anytime the soil begins to dry out, and mulch

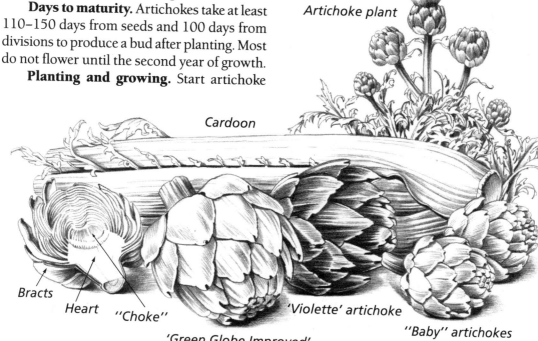

Artichoke plant

Cardoon

Bracts

Heart *"Choke"*

'Green Globe Improved' artichoke

'Violette' artichoke

"Baby" artichokes

Dramatic globe artichokes bear substantial flower buds that are considered a delicacy. Large buds yield leaflike bracts, each with a tasty bit of flesh at its base. Under the bracts lies the inedible "choke" and the succulent heart. Smaller buds are eaten whole. Cardoon is grown for its celery-shaped leaf stalks.

thickly. Apply fish emulsion fertilizer monthly in spring and early summer.

Near commercial artichoke fields, your crop may suffer from artichoke plume moths whose larvae tunnel into developing buds. Handpick the moths and eggs when you see them, and inject *Bacillus thuringiensis* (BT) into tunnels that appear in the buds. Clean up old artichoke leaves in the fall and burn them to eliminate overwintering places for pests. Aphids and red spider mites are quick to attack plants stressed by hot or dry conditions.

Gophers also love artichokes. Wendy Krupnick, trial garden manager for Shepherd's Garden Seeds in California, recommends surrounding the fleshy parts of the roots (extending about 6"–12" beneath the soil surface) in ½"-wire-mesh cages.

Harvesting. Harvest the flower buds once they are firm and meaty but before they start to open. The first and largest heads will grow from the tips of the main stem. If your growing season is long enough, sideshoots will produce smaller "baby" artichokes.

Fall and winter care. Where winter temperatures fall below 20°F, protect artichoke plants from freezing by covering them with 8" or more of loose mulch. You also can dig the plants carefully in fall—try not to break the delicate fleshy part of the roots—and put them in large nursery pots or tubs. Keep the potted plants indoors under fluorescent lights in a cool room, or store them—dormant—in a cellar or a garage that won't get colder than 20°F.

Container growing. Artichokes are hard to keep going in containers for longer than several months. Their long fleshy roots need room to expand and plenty of moisture and fertility. For best results, fill a half-barrel with a medium combining 3 parts growers mix to 1 part compost.

Propagation. To divide plants, dig them up when they are dormant in fall or spring. Cut off a portion of the root and crown that has at least two growth buds. Replant immediately. You also can save open-pollinated artichoke seeds (if you let any flowers mature), but expect variation in the quality of the resulting plants.

Friends and relatives. Cardoon (*Cynara cardunculus*) is a bold, bitter-flavored relative with similar growing requirements grown for its fleshy leaf stems. Like-named Jerusalem artichoke (*Helianthus tuberosus*) is a different vegetable; see the Jerusalem Artichoke entry for details. ✳

ASIAN SPECIALTIES

The food crops and cuisines of Asia reflect the rich diversity of its people, climate, and geography. A frequent highlight of Asian cooking is rapidly cooked fresh vegetables, so it's a perfect cooking style for home gardeners. Many gardeners now grow Asian produce to prepare ethnic dishes at home and experiment with new crops.

Traditional ethnic dishes are a must if you grow Asian specialty crops, but don't stop there. Many of them add interest and variety to green and pasta salads. Substitute them for more familiar vegetables in casseroles, steamed greens, soups, and pickles to provide a new dimension in flavor or form. You'll find their uses limited only by your imagination and flavor preferences.

Some Asian crop names can be confusing. Their names, in many languages and dialects, reflect their widespread popularity. Different systems for spelling these names create inconsistencies like bok choy and pak choi. Some descriptive names are misleading. One name can even describe different crops. The common names used in this entry are either the Chinese or Japanese common name.

Common Vegetables

Many crops from Asia are easy to grow because they are closely related to crops that are familiar to us. Unless otherwise noted, refer to the related entries (such as Cabbage and Beans, for example) for complete care information on these crops.

Cabbage-Family Crops

Cabbages. Chinese cabbage (*Brassica rapa*, Pekinensis group), a barrel-shaped or cylindrical heading cabbage with a delicate, sweet flavor, is often called Chinese celery cabbage in the United States. In China, some call it wong bok. It is hakusai in Japan. Napa-type cultivars produce thick, oval heads; michihli-type cultivars form tall, narrow heads.

Bok choy (*B. rapa*, Chinensis group), meaning "white vegetable" in Chinese, is a nonheading cabbage. Pak choi is a common alternate spelling, and it is sometimes known as Chinese mustard cabbage. Its white, celerylike stems and dark green leaves can vary in color and size depending on the cultivar.

Flat cabbage (*B. rapa* var. *rosularis*), often called tatsoi (its Japanese name), is another nonheading cabbage. It forms a rosette of dark green, spoon-shaped leaves and is noted for its cold-hardiness.

Cook the bok choys, flat cabbage, and Chinese cabbages like cabbage. Their tender, mild leaves and stems make excellent additions to salads. You can process the heading cabbages into tender sauerkraut. If they bolt, eat the tender stalks and flower buds like broccoli.

Mustards. Strong-tasting mustards are favorites, especially pickled or boiled quickly in soup. Dai gai choy (*Brassica juncea* var. *rugosa*), or "big mustard" in Chinese, is often sold in Asian groceries. Other mustards have smaller leaves (*B. juncea* var. *foliosa*) or curly leaves (*B. juncea* var. *crispifolia*).

Komatsuna (also called spinach mustard, *B. rapa*, Perviridis group) and mizuna (also called kyona, *B. juncea* var. *japonica*) are popular greens in Japan. The mild, young leaves are good to eat raw. Cook stronger-tasting leaves as you would cabbage.

Broccoli. The flowering bok choys are grown for their broccoli-like flower buds, stems, and leaves. Usually marketed as choy sum, meaning "vegetable heart" in Chinese, they include many *Brassica rapa* cultivars. Harvest stems at the base before the buds open. Cut again when the plants send up more shoots. Lightly stir-fry or steam the shoots.

Chinese broccoli (*B. oleracea*, Alboglabra group), or gai lohn in Chinese, is especially well-loved. Grow and harvest it like flowering bok choys. It is often steamed and served with oyster sauce but can be used as a substitute in any dish calling for broccoli.

Radishes. Daikon (*Raphanus sativus* var. *longipinnatus*) is one of the most common crops grown in Japanese home gardens. These white radishes can reach 2′ long. Plant and care for them like regular radishes. They can have green or pink shoulders and be tapered, cylindrical, or round. The flesh is usually white but can be green or pink. The mild or hot, crisp, juicy roots are good to eat fresh, cooked, or pickled. They are also loved in China, where they are called lobok.

Cucumbers, Squash, and Melons

Popular cucurbit-family members include Asian cucumbers (*Cucumis sativus*). They are long, slender, and usually burpless; they don't need peeling; and they grow like other cucumbers. For straighter fruit, just give them a trellis to climb.

American gardeners make sponges from mature luffa squash (*Luffa acutangula* or *L. aegyptiaca*); young luffas are an ingredient in oriental cooking. Kabocha squash (*Cucurbita maxima*), also called Japanese pumpkin, describes many Japanese winter squashes. They are orange-fleshed, dry, sweet, and grown like other winter squashes.

Bitter melon (*Momordica charantia*) is a warty green melon borne on a beautiful vine.

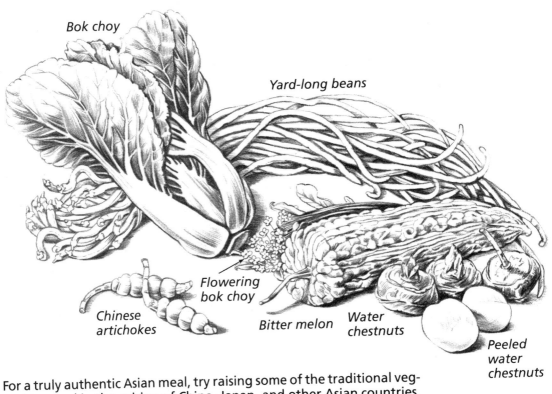

Bok choy

Yard-long beans

Flowering bok choy

Chinese artichokes

Bitter melon

Water chestnuts

Peeled water chestnuts

For a truly authentic Asian meal, try raising some of the traditional vegetables used in the cuisine of China, Japan, and other Asian countries. Crops like bitter melons and yard-long beans look and taste exotic but are grown just like familiar watermelons and pole beans.

It has a strong flavor that can be toned down by blanching. The winter melon (*Benincasa hispida*), or doan gwa in China and tohgan in Japan, is also called winter, wax, or white gourd. It looks like a watermelon covered with a white waxy layer. Peel it before cooking the white flesh. It keeps for up to six months in dry conditions at 55°–59°F. The vines of moh gwa (*B. hispida* var. *chieh-gua*), Chinese for "hairy melon" or "fuzzy melon," bear 4"–8" fuzzy fruits. Grow all of these melons as you would other heat-loving melons.

Beans and Peas

Soybeans (*Glycine max*) are usually processed into soy products like tofu, soy sauce, and miso, which are staples throughout Asia. Japanese people also munch them fresh as shelled beans. Called edamame, they are harvested when the beans just fill the pod, boiled for five minutes, then popped into the mouth. In China, they are also sprouted. The bean sprouts often used in Asian cuisine are sprouted mung beans (*Vigna radiata*). See the Sprouts entry for directions on how to start bean sprouts.

The yard-long bean (*Vigna unguiculata* subsp. *sesquipedalis*), a hot-climate cowpea relative, is also called dow gauk in China, sasage in Japan, Chinese long bean, and asparagus bean. Its tender beany flavor is best when picked young. Adzuki bean (*Vigna angularis*) also likes hot weather. Azukis, their Japanese name, also called Chinese red beans and hong dou or "red bean" in Chinese, are used in soup, cooked with rice, or made into a sweet paste for desserts.

Snow peas (*Pisum sativum* var. *macrocarpon*), the flat edible pods considered a trademark of Chinese stir-fries, actually originated in the Mediterranean. The tender leaf buds and shoots of any edible pea variety are a delicacy in China. Try them raw or very lightly cooked.

Onions and Garlic

In Asian cuisine, Japanese bunching onions (*Allium fistulosum*) serve the role of scallions. Bunching onions have long, thick, white stalks that divide without bulbing. Garlic chives (*A. tuberosum*), also called Chinese chives and gow choy in Chinese, are hardy perennials with flat, garlicky leaves. The flowering stems are prized when young and tender, but the yellow, blanched leaves, formed by covering the clumps with boxes or black plastic tunnels, are considered best.

Pepper and Eggplant

Asian cultivars of peppers and eggplants vary in color, shape, size, and flavor. Search catalogs of specialty seed companies, seed collector organizations, or seed swap columns in gardening magazines for sources. Most of these plants need hot summers for best results.

Other Crops

Chinese celery is a selection of common celery with narrow, stronger-flavored stalks. Cilantro, a name showing its fame in Mexico, is also called Chinese, Vietnamese, or any Asian country's parsley. All cultivars bolt quickly but are still edible—just stronger flavored. See the Herbs and Spices entry for more information on cilantro.

On about a half-acre, many Japanese gardeners grow their family's rice, which is a staple of many Asian diets. In cold regions, Asian people eat wheat in the form of noodles and breads, usually steamed but also baked, fried like tortillas, or deep-fried.

Spicy annuals such as Thai basil and other Asian basils (*Ocimum basilicum*) and perilla (*Perilla frutescens*) add zing to many dishes. With purple stems and an anisey aroma, Thai basil is delicious stir-fried with chicken and hot peppers. Perilla has red or green, frilly, cinnamony leaves. It is hardy, reseeding itself readily. Often served fresh with raw fish, it is said to neutralize the stomach parasites that may be in the fish.

Other Specialty Crops

Gardeners with a special bent for Asian cuisine will be happy to discover they can also grow many of the less familiar oriental crops. Some of these crops are related to common North American plants, although we wouldn't think of all of them as food plants.

There isn't room in this entry to give complete cultural information for all of the plants listed below. Some are covered in entries elsewhere in this book; look there for culture. If there is not a main entry for a plant that interests you, check the references on Asian crops listed in "Recommended Reading" on page 511 for additional information.

Greens

Vegetable amaranth (also called Chinese spinach, *Amaranthus tricolor*), is cousin to grain amaranth, pigweed, and the ornamantal lovelies-bleeding. It has many ethnic names, reflecting the wide popularity of its large, tender, colorful leaves in Asia, the Caribbean, and Africa. Unlike most greens, vegetable amaranth thrives in hot weather. Its culture is similar to grain amaranth. (See the Grains entry for details.) Cut the central stem at the plant's base when it has grown to 1'. You can cut it a second time when the leaves grow back. In Asia, the lime green or red leaves are stir-fried with garlic. They also lend a colorful flair and mildly wild flavor to salads.

Mild-flavored water spinach (*Ipomoea aquatica*) is related to sweet potatoes and morning glories. It has long, arrow-shaped leaves and hollow stems. It grows in water or moist soil. Seeds germinate readily indoors, but plants need warmth and moisture to thrive. You can root cuttings from bunches bought at a grocery store. Harvest new growth at the plant's base when it is 1'–2' long, and keep harvesting as growth continues. Cook it lightly, as you would regular spinach. See the Sweet Potato entry for culture.

Garland chrysanthemum, also known as edible chrysanthemum and shungiku, is grown for its young leaves and strong-tasting yellow flowers. See the Greens entry for culture.

Herbs and Flavorings

Daylily buds. These buds, called gum jum (Chinese for "golden needles"), provide a subtle muskiness to many dishes. Any daylily bud is edible cooked or fresh. Yellow and orange ones are considered best, with *Hemerocallis fulva* and *H. minor* used in China. Collect buds in the morning after the dew dries and just before they open. Dry them for future use.

Lemongrass. This perennial tropical grass, *Cymbopogon citratus,* has a sweet, lemony flavor. Grow it outdoors in frost-free areas. In cold climates, grow lemongrass in pots and move indoors to a sunny windowsill during the winter. Harvest it by dividing the clumps and removing the stalks needed. The white swollen base is chopped fine and used fresh for cooking. Dried lemongrass leaves are common in herb teas; see the Tea entry for suggestions.

Sesame. Sesame (*Sesamum indicum*) is a 1½'-tall annual that needs 90–120 warm days to produce a crop. Start plants indoors in northern areas. Seeds can be a creamy white, red, or black. (Black are deemed the most flavorful.) The seeds' toasted aromatic oil is cherished as a seasoning. Sesame seed paste, called tahini in the United States, is used in sauces.

Mushrooms. Many kinds of mushrooms are popular in seafood, vegetable, and meat dishes. The black mushroom—or shiitake, as it is called in Japan—is probably best known. Most Asian cooks buy mushrooms dried or canned.

Underground Crops

Bamboo. Shoots of bamboo rhizomes are good eaten sliced thin in salads or stir-fried. Bamboos in the *Phyllostachys* genus are best for eating; *P. dulcis, P. nuda,* and *P. aurea* are cold-hardy. Other bamboo genera are edible but bitter. To prepare bitter types, boil for ten minutes, drain, and repeat until the bitterness is gone.

Bamboo grows well in all but swampy sites. Be sure to learn about the growth habit of any bamboo before planting it. In warm climates and loose soil, many kinds of bamboo are highly invasive. An alternative is to plant bamboo in large tubs set above or buried in the ground. Surrounding the plant with an underground barrier, planting it by a sidewalk or regularly mown lawn, or committing to harvest *all* of the shoots are other ways to control its growth. Dig the shoots before they emerge above ground to prevent them from being bitter and tough.

Ginger. One Asian method for preparing the roots of ginger (*Zingiber officinale*) is pickling.

Do this by pouring vinegar over sliced or shredded raw ginger for a unique sweet-and-sour flavor.

Gobo. The long roots and distinctive taste of gobo (*Arctium lappa*) are prized in Japan. We know it better as the common weed called burdock. Young roots that snap when bent are best. Rub off just the skin to keep the flavorful flesh next to the skin intact, then cook or eat raw. If bitter, soak the roots in cold water for about an hour.

Gobo is a biennial that will form large roots when grown in well-drained, deeply worked soil. Sow seeds in early spring. To improve germination in cool areas, sow seeds indoors and plant them out when young, before the taproot develops. Space or thin to 4"–9" apart. The young leaves are good to eat when cooked quickly. Harvest the roots in summer and fall. You can also sow seeds in fall. Small plants will overwinter and are ready for harvest the following spring or early summer.

True yams. True yams (*Dioscorea* spp.) are lovely hardy perennial vines with edible tubers. One species, cinnamon vine (*D. batatas*), has insignificant flowers that release a cinnamony aroma. Plant bulblets produced on the stems, shoots from the tuber, whole young tubers, or the top of mature tubers in deep, light, well-drained, fertile soil. Train the vines up supports. Frost kills the vines to the ground. Harvest smallish tubers after the first season and larger ones, up to 2' long, after the second year. The tubers get woody with age. Store them like sweet potatoes. Cook the underground tubers like potatoes: baked in their skin or peeled and boiled for a starchy vegetable.

Kudzu. Kudzu (*Pueraria lobata*), a rampant weed in the southern United States, is an important starch source in Asia. Southern gardeners whose gardens have been invaded by kudzu may gain some satisfaction from eating its roots. The leguminous vine can grow 25′ and have roots weighing up to 80 pounds. Cook the roots as you would potatoes.

Chinese artichoke. The Chinese or Japanese artichoke (*Stachys affinis*) is a perennial mint grown for its small, pearly white, spiraled roots. They add a crisp, nutty crunch to salads when raw. Cooked lightly, they are like water chestnuts. Plant the tubers about 2″ deep, 6″–12″ apart. Give them a rich, light soil, full sun, and plenty of moisture. Like other mints, they quickly grow out-of-bounds. Control them by growing them in tubs or planters. Harvest the tubers in the fall. The ones you will inevitably miss at harvest time will form the following year's crop.

Water Lovers

Asian populations are focused near major rivers, and the people cultivate many edible plants growing along the river's edge, such as Old World arrowhead (*Sagittaria sagittifolia*), Chinese lotus (*Nelumbo nucifera*), water chestnut (*Eleocharis dulcis*), violet-stemmed taro (*Xanthosoma violaceum*), and wasabi (*Eutrema wasabi*). These plants bask in sunshine above the river while rooted in soil covered with flowing water.

No river in your backyard? You can grow these plants in a tub garden. All of these plants except for the lotus will also grow in garden soil. Plant them in a wet spot near a gutter downspout or where water from an air conditioning unit drips. If the soil dries out, the plants will go dormant, as they would in the wild, until moisture returns.

Where winters are cold, lift the roots or corms, bury them in damp sand, keep them cool without being frozen, and replant them outside when it becomes warm again. Leave them alone if your winters do not freeze. Except for wasabi, these plants grow easily when given the warm, wet conditions they crave. Quality wasabi roots are notoriously difficult to grow, although its leaves, also edible, grow vigorously.

Harvest the roots or corms at the end of the growing season. Wasabi is best harvested during its second year when the roots are stronger flavored. You can also harvest and eat lotus leaves, flowers, and seeds whenever they are available.

Peel the roots or corms and cook them like potatoes. Water chestnuts are good raw, but if you're cooking them, they should be cooked quickly to keep them crisp. Boil sliced lotus roots, with their round, concentrically arranged air holes, in soup. Grate raw wasabi root and eat it immediately, before it loses its horseradish-like pungency.

Fruits and Nuts

Fresh fruits, favored as snacks or desserts in Asia, include apples, oranges, plums, and pears. The kiwi is native to China and is popular. With much of Asia in the tropics, longan, lychee, mango, and other tropical fruits are cultivated and enjoyed. Jujube, sold as dried red dates in Asian groceries, is often stewed in chicken soup for a nourishing tonic broth. Chestnuts, ginkgo nuts, and nuts more familiar to many United States gardeners add a special touch to many dishes. See the Apple, Chestnut, Exotic Crops, Kiwi, Nuts, Orange, Pear, Plum, and Small Fruits entries for growing information on these plants. ✳

ASPARAGUS

Asparagus officinalis. Liliaceae. Perennial. Zones 2–9.

Tender green or purple-tinged young shoots of asparagus are early harbingers of spring. Typically steamed and served with butter or a sauce, asparagus spears are equally delicious steamed and served chilled. Asparagus is grown virtually everywhere in the United States except Florida and the Gulf Coast, where conditions are too wet or too mild to satisfy its dormancy requirement. The fernlike plants are attractive and long-lived; a well-tended planting may produce for 20 years or more.

Planning

Selecting plants. The list of asparagus cultivars is relatively short, making selection easy. Look for resistance to asparagus rust and Fusarium wilt. When possible, choose cultivars adapted to your region. For example, 'U.C. 157' is well-suited to West Coast weather; 'Jersey Giant' grows well in the East and Midwest. All-male cultivars offer higher yields.

Selecting a site. Plant asparagus as you would any long-lived perennial, keeping in mind that it may remain in place for 20 years or more. Choose a site in full sun with protection from strong winds, which can break the fernlike plants. Asparagus tolerates some shade, but full sun promotes vigor and helps minimize disease problems. Good drainage is also important; excess moisture encourages root rot. To avoid accidentally plowing up the plants in the spring, grow them away from annual vegetable plantings.

When to plant. Plant asparagus seedlings or crowns in early spring, as soon as you can work the soil and the soil temperature reaches 50°F. Beware of air temperatures below 40°F, however; frosts and freezes can kill the growing points on young plants.

How much to plant. Grow 20–40 plants for every person in your family. One seed packet produces about 60 plants.

Spacing. Allow 1½'–2' between plants in rows spaced 3'–4' apart.

For a greater harvest. Try planting asparagus after a cover crop that adds lots of organic matter to the soil. Fertilize and mulch each year to keep plants productive.

Soil Preparation

Asparagus thrives in light, sandy loam with a pH between 6.5 and 7.5. High levels of organic matter promote two other favorable conditions—quick warming and good drainage. Add 10–20 pounds of compost—1"–2" over the soil surface—to every 100 square feet of planting space. Work in the compost and cultivate the soil to at least 10" deep to accommodate this crop's extensive root system. Make raised beds if the site has poor drainage.

✿ AT A GLANCE ✿
ASPARAGUS

Site: At least one-half day of sun; protection from strong winds.

Soil: Evenly moist, well-drained, light, sandy loam that is rich in organic matter; pH of 6.5–7.5.

How much to plant: 20–40 plants per person.

Spacing: 1½'–2' between plants in rows 3'–4' apart.

Seasons to bearing: Begin harvesting after two to three seasons of growth.

Planting Indoors

Sowing seeds. Asparagus plants grown from seeds are less prone to transplant shock than those started from crowns, and the seedlings will eventually outproduce plants grown from crowns. Sow seeds indoors 8–10 weeks before planting time. To reduce disease problems, soak seeds in compost tea for five minutes before sowing. Plant single seeds 1½″ deep in peat pots and keep them in a sunny location. Seeds germinate best if the soil temperature is about 75°F. Germination takes 7–21 days.

Seedling care. After the seeds sprout, lower the temperature to 60°–70°F. Once the danger of frost is past, plant the seedlings (now about 1′ tall) 2″–3″ deep and 3″–5″ apart in a nursery bed. When tiny flowers appear, look at them with a magnifying glass. Female flowers have well-developed, three-lobed pistils; male blossoms are larger and longer. Weed out female plants—they produce fewer spears.

Planting Outdoors

Sowing seeds. In milder climates, plant seeds directly into a nursery bed as soon as you can work the soil. Sow two seeds per inch in rows 1½′ apart. They take about 30 days to germinate, so mark the rows with quick-growing radishes. When asparagus shoots are 3″ tall, thin them to 4″ apart. At the end of August, transplant the male plants to a permanent home. (See "Seedling Care" above for information on how to tell male asparagus plants from female ones.)

Buying crowns. Crowns are available from nurseries and mail-order seed companies. Buy one-year-old crowns; two-year-old crowns are more prone to transplant trauma. If possible, purchase male plants, which generally produce higher yields than female plants. Be sure the roots are fresh, firm, and healthy looking. Plant crowns immediately after you purchase them, or keep them in slightly moistened sphagnum moss.

Planting crowns. Before planting, soak crowns for 10–15 minutes in compost tea. Dig trenches 6″–10″ deep and 1′ wide. Leave 3′–4′ between rows. Build a 2″ mound of soil or compost down the center of each trench. Set the crowns 1½′–2′ apart with their roots draped over the mound. Cover with 2″ of soil. Every two weeks, add about 2″ of soil until the trench is filled and the soil is slightly mounded over the bed. Sprinkle alfalfa meal (1–2 pounds per 100 square feet) over the beds, then mulch with 6″–12″ of leaves or other organic mulch.

Setting out transplants. Transfer seedlings from the nursery bed to their permanent location the following spring, when they are about 1′ tall. Plant as you would crowns. (See "Planting Crowns" above for details.)

Growing Guidelines

Water and mulch. Keep soil evenly moist, but not wet—a handful of soil should form a loose ball without sticking to your fingers. After you harvest the spears each year, add 6″–12″ of leaf mulch. As asparagus crowns grow, they push up toward the soil surface and the resulting spears become smaller and less tender. Mound about 1″–2″ of soil over the beds every spring to keep the crowns well-covered and the shoots large and tender. To produce white asparagus, blanch the shoots by mounding soil up around them as they emerge.

Feeding. Every year, add 10–15 pounds

of compost per 100 square feet of growing space.

Problem Prevention

Select resistant cultivars. Choose cultivars that resist rust and Fusarium wilt.

Before planting, disinfect seeds. To prevent Fusarium wilt, soak seeds in a 10 percent bleach solution (1 part bleach to 9 parts water) for two minutes. Rinse in clear water for one minute before sowing.

At planting, plant in raised beds. Good drainage helps prevent crown rot and problems stemming from waterlogged soil, such as slow growth.

During the growing season, put up windbreaks. Blowing soil can damage the spears; strong winds may blow down foliage.

Before a freeze, cover spears. Unprotected spears may turn brown and soft or they may die.

At harvest time, don't overharvest. Build up the length of the cutting season gradually. Otherwise, production may be diminished in future years.

At harvest time, harvest daily if temperatures exceed 90°F. Heat can cause bracts to open prematurely.

Gathering the Harvest

Some gardeners harvest asparagus in its second season of growth, but waiting until the third season lets plants establish healthy root systems. Pick sparingly the first time—over about 2 weeks. Extend your harvest gradually in subsequent seasons, until you are harvesting for about 8 weeks (or up to 12 weeks in California).

Harvest spears in early spring when they are 6″–10″ high and the tips are still firm and closed. Use your fingers to snap the spears off at, or just below, ground level; don't cut them with a knife, or you may injure the crowns. Asparagus is best when fresh, but you can refrigerate it for up to one week. Set spears upright in 1″–2″ of water and refrigerate. Don't let the spear tips get wet, or they'll rot. Can or freeze surplus spears.

Extending the Season

Plant twice as much asparagus as you would ordinarily. Harvest spears in half of the bed until early summer. After the plants in the unharvested half of the bed leaf out into ferns (usually in late July), cut them down. Pick spears that emerge from these plants into October.

Fall and Winter Care

When the foliage becomes dry and brittle, mow it down and add a leaf mulch to protect the roots during the winter.

Propagation

You can collect your own asparagus seeds. Asparagus is dioecious; you need both male and female plants for seed production. Cross-pollination does occur but, since there are so few different asparagus cultivars, seeds usually produce plants similar to the parent plant. If you want to save seeds, gather red asparagus berries before the first expected fall frost. Crush the berries in a bag, then soak them in water to wash away the pulp. Collect seeds that sink to the bottom; air dry them for a week before storing. ✳

AVOCADO

Persea americana. Lauraceae.
Evergreen tree. Zones 9–10.

The nutlike flavor of avocado fruits, or alligator pears, adds a delicious twist to salads, dips, and sandwiches. In tropical areas, these native American trees can reach 30′–60′ and may live for 50 years. Avocados also make beautiful houseplants, but they will very rarely bear fruit indoors. Avocados are related to cinnamon and camphor, and crushed leaves of Mexican cultivars have a spicy aroma.

Selecting plants. There are three races of avocados: Guatemalan, Mexican, and West Indian. Florida gardeners can choose between Guatemalan avocados, with large, pale green to dark purple fruits that have hard, thick skin, and West Indian avocados, which have smooth, leathery skin. Thin-skinned Mexican avocados grow well in California, but not Florida. Plant at least two cultivars, and more than three if you want to harvest fruit over a longer period of time.

Florida gardeners can try cultivars such as 'Brogdon', 'Choquette', 'Hall', and 'Lula'. California gardeners can try 'Pinkerton', 'Anaheim', and 'Hass'. New avocado cultivars are constantly developed. Check with local nurseries for the best ones for your area.

Site. Avocados prefer full sun and are fairly salt-tolerant.

Soil. Avocados grow best in well-drained soil with a pH between 5.5 and 7.0.

When to plant. Plant in mid-March, when weather is cool and danger of frost is past. Avocado trees grown in pots can be planted any time of year, but it's best to avoid starting new trees during hot summer months.

How much to plant. Plant two trees for every person in your family.

Spacing. Plant trees 30′–40′ apart.

Seasons to bearing. Trees started from seeds bear in five to seven years. Budded trees usually bear within four years.

Planting and growing. Plant avocado trees as you would any tree. See "Perennial Crops" on page 111 for directions. Do not prune the tree at planting.

Check soil daily and add water only if needed during the first week. During the first year of growth, water every 7–10 days when the weather is dry. During the second year of growth, water every 10–14 days, and then as needed. Mulch with organic material around the trunk to conserve moisture and suppress weeds. Don't allow mulch to touch the trunk.

Avocados do not usually require much fertilizer. If your young trees are not growing vigorously, try an application of compost in early spring to midsummer. If new leaves are turning yellow, you may have a specific deficiency. Have the soil tested, and then add an amendment that supplies the needed nutrients.

Trees growing in sandy, limestone soils need foliar sprays of copper, zinc, and manganese for the first five years; after that, only zinc and manganese. Trees grown in alkaline soil need a yearly application of iron chelates. Test your soil for these nutrients, and follow recommendations for applying foliar sprays. Do not fertilize when trees are in bloom.

Home growers of a few avocado trees usually do not have many pest problems. To control scale, spray with horticultural oil. To reduce chances of fungal diseases, space trees widely and trim back surrounding trees to increase light and air circulation in humid climates.

Pruning. Avocado trees need little pruning. Remove dead wood as needed, shorten branches that droop to the ground, and pinch back upright shoots to maintain a height of 20′–30′.

Harvesting. Deciding when to harvest can

be tricky because most cultivars are green when mature. Inquire about expected harvest times when you buy your trees. Avocados do not ripen on the tree but usually are ready to eat three to eight days after harvesting. To check readiness, pick one fruit, leaving a short stem attached. Keep it on the kitchen counter for a few days. If the stem doesn't shrivel or turn dark, the fruit is mature; it's safe to pick others of the same size.

To harvest, clip fruit from branches. Use a long pole for top fruit. Wear gloves to avoid scratching fruit. Don't pick all of the fruit at once. Store it on the tree until it starts falling off, then pick all remaining fruit.

If you harvest more avocado fruit than you can use fresh, puree it, adding lemon or lime juice. Pack it into freezer containers, and freeze. You can use avocado puree to make tasty dips, or add it to fruit salad.

Propagation. Avocado cultivars do not come true from seed. You can start your own rootstocks from seeds. Use seeds from known trees of Mexican cultivars because they are the most cold-hardy. Cut a ⅛"-thick slice from the top and bottom of each seed to speed germination. Bury the seeds in moist sand, with the pointed end up. Germination takes 30 days in warm weather. When the seedling has six leaves, transplant it to a nursery bed. When the seedling rootstock trunk is about ½" in diameter, it is ready for budding. Graft buds onto the shaded side of the trunk to help prevent them from drying out. Cut back the rootstock once the bud begins to grow out. Grafting is most successful during cooler winter months. You can also cleft-graft additional cultivars onto an existing tree to make a multicultivar tree. ✳

BANANA
Musa spp. Musaceae. Tree-like perennial. Zones 9–10.

Originally native to Southeast Asia, bananas are now grown in humid tropical areas around the world. Banana plants will also grow and produce fruit indoors if given enough light and heat. Fruits eaten raw are called bananas; cultivars for cooking are called plantains.

Selecting plants. There are more than 40 cultivars available. 'Dwarf Cavendish' is recommended for Florida and other humid climates.

Site. Plant in full sun in a frost-free area that's protected from wind. Bananas are not salt-tolerant.

Soil. Grow bananas in rich soil with high humus content and good drainage.

How much to plant. Plant three to four plants of different cultivars per household.

Spacing. To allow room for the main stalk and three suckers, space plants 8' apart.

Seasons to bearing. The first fruiting will occur 12–15 months after planting, the second fruiting one year later. After that, expect at least one bunch each year.

Planting and growing. Bananas are grown from suckers, the new growth appearing at the base of the central stalk. To plant a sucker, dig a hole 3' in diameter and 2' deep. Add a mixture of equal parts of compost, sand, and potting soil to fill the hole three-quarters full. Position the plant in the center of the hole and finish filling it in with the soil mix. Water well to eliminate air pockets. Remove any damaged leaves. Mulch heavily to conserve moisture.

Water daily for three weeks. When new growth appears, water three times per week. Established plants usually don't need extra water.

Bananas are heavy feeders. Four weeks after planting, apply ½ pound of balanced blended organic fertilizer per plant. Continue monthly feedings, gradually increasing the amount to 2 pounds per plant at fruiting. Make a yearly foliar application of manganese, zinc, and copper. When suckers appear, remove all but three for best central plant growth and fruiting.

The flowers at the base of the flower cluster develop into fruits. Flowers at the tip have only stamens; they can be cut off to send more nourishment to the clusters of banana fingers.

Harvesting. Pick bananas when yellow. After fruiting, cut off the stalk and chop it into small pieces for mulch or compost.

Fall and winter care. Cover with blankets for protection against freezing weather.

Container growing. Banana plants in containers need a combination of warmth, bright light and high humidity year-round. Use supplemental light in winter to keep the plants alive. Daytime temperatures should be 75°F or higher and nighttime temperatures should be at least 67°F. Fertilize frequently.

Propagation. Start bearing clumps using healthy suckers or corms. ✳

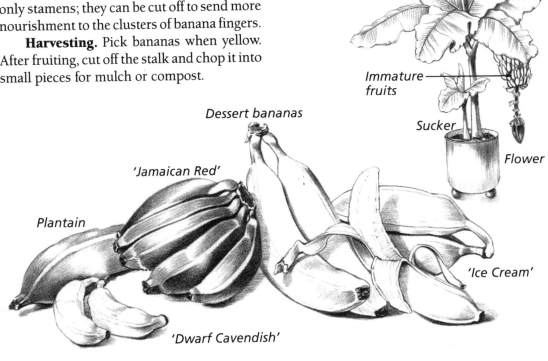

Immature fruits

Sucker

Flower

Dessert bananas

'Jamaican Red'

Plantain

'Ice Cream'

'Dwarf Cavendish'

Bananas include both the sweet, yellow-skinned treats we love for desserts and snacks and the stout plantains, which are cooked before serving.

BASIL

Ocimum basilicum. Labiatae. Annual.

Early Greek and Roman physicians advised that you shout and curse as you sow basil seeds, to ensure the best growth. Beginning herb growers will soon find that this is unnecessary. Given warm, sunny conditions, basil is easy to grow. Its warm aroma and vibrant green color are great additions to most vegetable, fish, and poultry dishes. Add a few chopped fresh leaves to summer salads and sauces, or use larger quantities to make pesto, a mixture of ground basil, garlic, Parmesan cheese, pine nuts, and olive oil.

Selecting plants. For a taste sensation, try lemon, licorice, or cinnamon basil. For a variety of leaf types, look for lettuce-leaf basil, with crinkled leaves; 'Piccolo Verde Fino', with tiny leaves; 'Purple Ruffles', with crinkled purple foliage; or 'Dark Opal', with shiny, deep purple leaves. Bush basil and 'Spicy Globe' form compact mounds.

Site. Basil grows best in a sunny spot.

Soil. Plants prefer a well-drained soil with lots of organic matter. Keep soil pH around 6.0.

How much to plant. For plenty of leaves for cooking, plant 6–12 plants. Small-leaved cultivars (like bush and lemon basil) will be less productive than large-leaved types (like sweet and lettuce-leaf basil).

Spacing. Plant small-leaved types 6″–8″ apart. Large-leaved cultivars need 1′–1½′ between plants.

Days to maturity. You can harvest basil as early as six weeks after transplanting outdoors.

Planting and growing. Sow seeds indoors six weeks before the last expected frost. Cover seeds lightly (about ⅛″ deep). Seeds of most cultivars germinate within five days at a soil temperature of 70°F; keep seedlings at 65°F. Seeds of purple-leaved cultivars germinate best in 82°F soil; keep seedlings at 75°F. Supply plenty of light. Keep the soil evenly moist.

Plant seeds and plants outdoors after danger of frost is past and when soil temperatures average 50°F or more. To have lots of fresh basil all season, make successive sowings at two- to three-week intervals until midsummer. To promote leaf growth, pinch off blossoms as they form.

Harvesting. Regular harvesting encourages bushy growth. Begin harvesting terminal leaves as soon as plants have several pairs. Harvest carefully to avoid bruising the foliage. If necessary, rinse the leaves gently, then dry them thoroughly in a lettuce spinner before using or storing.

Fresh basil stores best at about 40°F. At colder temperatures, foliage quickly turns black. To preserve basil for winter use, get the best flavor by freezing chopped or mashed leaves mixed with olive oil, in ice cube trays or sealed plastic bags. Use about 3 cups of packed leaves for each ¼–½ cup of olive oil. Add frozen cubes to winter soups. To make pesto, thaw the cubes and add the remaining ingredients. To preserve basil in vinegar, add 1 cup of packed fresh leaves to 1 quart of vinegar.

Extending the season. Basil is very cold-sensitive. If frost is expected, cover plants with clear plastic supported by hoops or stakes. Grow basil indoors in winter from summer cuttings (small-leaved cultivars work best) or from seeds.

Container growing. Low-growing types,

like bush basil, are the best choice for containers. Tall cultivars may need staking. Monitor the amount of moisture in the soil since basil won't tolerate drying out completely. Place pots in full sun away from strong winds.

Propagation. To save seeds, harvest seed-stalks when their color darkens. Basil may also be started from cuttings. ✳

BEAN

Phaseolus spp. Leguminosae. Annual.

When it comes to variety and versatility among vegetables, beans can't be beat. There are even several types of the common green bean (*Phaseolus vulgaris*), including snap or string beans, shell beans, and dry beans. Some beans can be considered snap, shell, and dry beans because they can be used in all three ways.

Beans are further divided into bush and pole types: Bush beans are erect and generally need no support. Pole beans produce long vines that require staking or trellising.

Lima beans (*P. limensis* or *P. lunatus*) are the best-known relatives of green beans. The butter bean (*P. lunatus*) is especially popular. The lima bean, whose name is derived from the capital city of Peru, is very cold-sensitive and should be planted at least two weeks after the last expected spring frost. The large, light green seeds are eaten fresh or dried.

In general, beans are a good source of iron and calcium, as well as many vitamins, including A, B_1, B_2, and C. Dry beans are an excellent source of protein and are a good nutritional complement to grains.

To learn more about the wide variety of beans you can grow, see "Friends and Relatives" on page 300.

Planning

Selecting plants. In general, bush beans mature faster and are less sensitive to drought and extreme temperatures than pole beans. However, pole beans usually produce a greater overall yield, and they take up less space in the garden. If you live in an area with hot, dry summers, try planting heat- and drought-resistant cultivars such as 'Tendercrop'. For cooler regions, early-maturing beans are best. If you plan to preserve beans, choose cultivars recommended for canning and freezing. For a bit of color, plant yellow wax beans, such as 'Sungold'. If you're thinking about growing

❧ AT A GLANCE ❧
BEAN

Site: Needs at least one-half day of sun.

Soil: Prefers a light, sandy soil with good drainage; pH of 5.5–6.8.

How much to plant: Bush beans: 10–15 plants per person. Pole beans: 3–5 hills per person.

Spacing: Bush beans: 4"–6" between plants in rows 1½'–3' apart. Pole beans: 6"–9" between plants in rows 3'–4' apart.

Days to maturity: Bush beans: 48–60 days. Pole beans: 62–68 days.

dry beans like pinto or kidney beans, keep in mind that they generally require a long growing season (at least 85 days).

Whenever possible, choose cultivars that resist or tolerate diseases such as bean mosaic, anthracnose, rust, and powdery mildew.

When to plant. Begin planting one to two weeks after the last expected frost, when the soil has warmed to at least 60°F; at lower soil temperatures, seeds may rot. Air temperatures at night should be at least 40°F and daytime temperatures at least 50°F. Lima bean seeds germinate best when the soil temperature is about 85°F. Frost can damage young plants. You can make repeated sowings throughout the season. In very hot weather (85°F or higher), flowers may drop, reducing harvest.

How much to plant. Plant 10–15 bush bean plants per successional planting or 3–5 hills of pole beans per person. Two ounces of seeds should cover 25' of row.

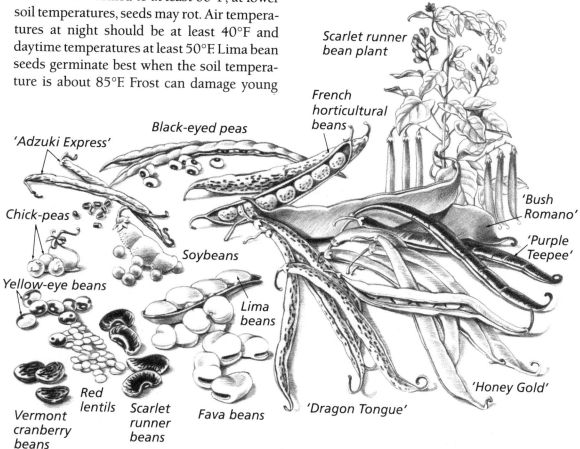

Scarlet runner bean plant

French horticultural beans

Black-eyed peas

'Adzuki Express'

'Bush Romano'

'Purple Teepee'

Chick-peas

Soybeans

Yellow-eye beans

Lima beans

Red lentils

Scarlet runner beans

Fava beans

'Dragon Tongue'

'Honey Gold'

Vermont cranberry beans

Be bold with beans! Plant a dramatic scarlet-runner-bean tepee. Try snap beans with yellow, purple, or striped pods, and some meaty shell beans as well. Make room for robust dry beans in a rainbow of colors and patterns.

Spacing. Plant bush beans 2″–4″ apart; allow 1½′–3′ between rows. Pole beans need more room: Plant seeds 4″–6″ apart in rows spaced 3′–4′ apart.

Plant bush limas 3″–6″ apart in rows 1½′–3′ apart. For pole types, allow 8″–12″ between plants and 3′–4′ between rows.

Rotation. Plant beans before or after heavy-feeding crops such as corn, celery, or tomatoes.

For a greater harvest. Interplanting beans with carrot-family plants may encourage predatory wasps. Interplanting with potatoes or other crops can help prevent Mexican bean beetles from finding your plants as easily. Or plant beans with celery and corn, which may enhance beans' growth. To get the most out of your garden, plant pole beans; they'll produce about three times as many beans as bush types in the same amount of space. Pick beans often to keep plants productive; when you harvest the immature pods, you encourage new blossoms to form. Plant early- and late-maturing cultivars to extend the season and increase the overall yield.

Soil Preparation

Beans will grow in almost any type of soil, rich or poor. For best results, soil should be light, sandy, and well-drained, with a pH of 5.5–6.8. Beans require phosphorus and potassium for healthy growth. (Dry beans need more phosphorus than snap beans.) If your soil tests low in either, check the "Fertilizer Options" table on page 50 and add an apropriate fast-acting source. Beans are legumes, and the bacteria that grow in nodules on their roots will supply some of the crop's nitrogen needs. Adding too much supplemental nitrogen can delay maturity and reduce the harvest.

Work in 5–10 pounds of compost per 100 square feet. Cultivate to at least 8″. Beans will grow well in traditional flat rows, except in heavy soils. They also thrive in raised beds. At planting, leave soil somewhat rough to provide air space, but be sure the surface is smooth enough for seeds to emerge.

Planting Outdoors

Sowing seeds. Before planting, soak seeds in compost extract for 20 minutes. To help beans fix nitrogen in the root nodules, treat seeds with an appropriate commercial inoculant. Plant one to two weeks after the last expected frost. Be sure the soil temperature is at least 60°F; seeds germinate best when the soil is 80°F. Sow seeds 1″–2″ deep. Space bush beans 2″–4″ apart; pole beans, 4″–6″ apart. For bush beans, allow 1½′–3′ between rows; for pole beans, space rows 3′–4′ apart. If you are planting pole beans in a circle of hills with tepee-style supports, sow six to eight seeds per hill; allow 3′–5′ between hills. Erect the tepee anytime from before planting until the young plants get their first two leaves. Insert a stake into each group of plants and tie the stakes together about 5′ above the ground. Germination normally takes 7–14 days.

Growing Guidelines

Thinning seedlings. Thin bush beans to 4″–6″ apart and pole beans to 6″–9″ apart. In hills, thin to three or four plants per hill.

BEAN SEEDLING

Seeds   Cotyledons   First true leaves

Water and mulch. Keep soil constantly moist but not soggy. Watering is especially important during the germination period and when pods are developing. Be careful not to overwater; too much moisture can cause stunted growth and pod drop. Don't spray water directly on flowers and leaves, or the blossoms may drop and diseases may spread. To keep soil moist and cool and to help control weeds, mulch with 3″–6″ of grass clippings after the seedlings emerge. Sowing a grass or legume living mulch may help reduce Mexican bean beetle problems; be sure it is kept 4″–5″ from the bean crop, and keep it mowed. Keep the area free of weeds; beans don't compete well with them. When cultivating, be careful not to disturb the bean plants' shallow roots.

Feeding. If your soil was well-prepared at planting, you won't need to add fertilizer during the season. For an extra boost, however, you can spray young plants with kelp extract.

Training. Provide your pole beans with support, such as a stake, a trellis, or a tepee made of four to eight poles tied together at the top. Put the support in place at planting time or when the seedlings have developed two leaves.

Problem Prevention

Select resistant cultivars. Plant cultivars that resist or tolerate bean mosaic, curly top virus, anthracnose, rust, powdery mildew, and other common bean diseases.

Before planting, apply parasitic nematodes to the soil. You will be less likely to have problems with pests, including seedcorn maggots, root knot nematodes, and wireworms.

At planting time, soak seeds in compost tea before sowing. Seedlings will be less likely to be affected by diseases such as root rot.

At planting time, avoid planting beans where you have grown them in the past three years. Otherwise, you may have recurring problems with pests and diseases.

After planting, cover the bed with clear plastic. This will help warm the soil and promote germination. It will also discourage root rot and other problems associated with cool, wet soil. Remove the plastic immediately after seeds germinate, or the seedlings may get too hot.

When seedlings emerge, cover plants with floating row cover. Row cover will prevent bean leaf beetles, potato leafhoppers, leafminers, flea beetles, and other pests from devouring your beans. You can also use a row cover to protect late crops from cold injury.

During the growing season, avoid overwatering. If the soil becomes waterlogged, you may have problems with root rot or with nitrogen deficiency, which can cause stunted growth and yellowing of leaves.

When plants have two true leaves, spray kelp extract. Foliar feeding will prevent nutrient deficiency symptoms. For example, a zinc deficiency will cause pods to drop.

During the growing season, don't touch wet plants. Avoid cultivating or harvesting when the plants are wet. Touching wet bean plants can cause disease spores to spread.

Immediately after harvest, compost the plants. This is a good idea if you've had problems with bean beetles in the past.

Gathering the Harvest

You can harvest beans up until frost. Pick snap beans when they are tender and about as thick as a pencil; they should snap when you break one in half (hence the name snap bean).

They're overmature if the seeds have begun to fill out the pods. Harvest shell beans when the pods are plump but still tender. Pick beans every couple of days to keep the plants productive. To harvest bush beans, carefully pinch off the pods with your fingers. Cut off pole beans with scissors. You can keep pods in plastic bags for one to two weeks in the refrigerator, or freeze or can the surplus.

Pick pods of dry beans when they have

❧ FRIENDS & RELATIVES ❧

BEAN

Don't limit your bean patch to green beans and limas. Try some of these unusual beans as well. Unless otherwise noted, plant and care for these beans as you would green beans.

Adzuki bean (*Vigna angularis*) is widely cultivated in Japan. The plant bears long, thin edible pods, and small nutty-flavored seeds.

Broad bean (*Vicia faba*) thrives in cool, moist conditions and withstands light frost. In the United States, broad beans, also called fava or horse beans, are grown primarily for livestock feed. Home garden cultivars are mild flavored and can be eaten like snap beans, shell beans, or dry beans. Some people have an allergic reaction to broad beans.

Chick-pea (*Cicer arietinum*), also known as garbanzo bean, tastes rather like a chestnut. Try chilled cooked chick-peas in salads.

Cowpea (*Vigna unguiculata*) thrives in areas with long, hot summers. Black-eyed peas (*V. unguiculata* subsp. *unguiculata*) are a type of cowpea that produces seeds with dark spots. Eat the pods cooked or harvest the dry seeds.

Hyacinth bean (*Dolichos lablab*), often called lablab bean, is a climber with lavender flowers. You can use hyacinth beans as snap beans, shell beans, and dry beans.

Lentil (*Lens culinaris*) is native to Asia. The small, flattened seeds are highly nutritious and used in soups, chili, and many other dishes.

Mung bean (*Vigna radiata*), popular in the Orient, has small yellow-green seeds, which can be used fresh or dried or eaten as bean sprouts. The pods are also edible.

Scarlet runner bean (*Phaseolus coccineus*) is a climbing perennial native to South America. It produces scarlet flowers and black-and-red–speckled seeds. You can eat young pods whole or eat just the beans, fresh or dried.

Soybean (*Glycine max*) is a highly nutritious bean that is an important protein source in many parts of the world.

Tepary bean (*Phaseolus acutifolius* var. *latifolius*) is a twining annual native to the Southwest and Mexico. The round edible seeds can be many different colors.

Winged bean (*Psophocarpus tetragonolobus*) is also called asparagus pea, princess pea, goa bean, and bin dow. This twiner from Asia bears edible fruit up to 9" long that appears to have wings.

Yard-long bean (*Vigna unguiculata* subsp. *sesquipedalis*), or asparagus bean, is a native of Asia and produces 1'–3'-long pods.

turned brown and the seeds have hardened. (You'll be able to hear the seeds rattling inside the pods.) If the weather is too damp for the beans to dry, harvest the plants and hang them upside down indoors. Shell the beans when they are completely dry and place them in an airtight jar, along with a packet of dried milk to absorb moisture. Store in a cool, dry spot for up to a year.

Extending the Season

Beans are generally difficult to transplant. However, you may want to start plants indoors if you live in an area with a short growing season. Sow seeds in peat pots about four weeks before the last expected frost date. Let them grow six weeks, then harden them off and transplant.

Whether you direct-seed or set out transplants, warm the soil by covering it with black plastic for several weeks before planting. To further extend the season, look for early cultivars that can be planted before the last expected frost. Plant both bush and pole types; the pole beans will be ready to harvest one to two weeks after the bush beans and will continue bearing fruit when the bush crop is no longer productive.

Plant successive crops of bush beans every two to three weeks up to seven to ten weeks before the first expected frost date in fall. You can plant two crops of pole beans if your growing season is long enough; to determine if there is enough time for a second harvest before the first expected frost, check the number of days to maturity for the cultivar you have selected. If you're planting lima beans, keep in mind that bush limas are ready to harvest 65–78 days after sowing seeds; pole lima beans take 88 days or more.

Protect your late plantings by covering them with a row cover. If temperatures drop to 45°F or below, the beans may become pitted and brown. Freezing temperatures will kill mature plants.

Fall and Winter Care

After the crop has winter-killed, mow the plant debris and mulch. Or you can turn the bean stalks under to improve the soil for next season's crop.

Container Growing

You can grow bush or pole beans in containers. For best use of vertical space, plant pole beans; place the container against a wall with a trellis attached, or put stakes right in the container. If you are growing bush beans, be sure the planters are large enough—for example, at least 6″ wide × 6″ deep for two plants.

Propagation

You might think that an easy way to save bean seeds is to gather pods that you missed harvesting earlier when it's garden cleanup time. Unfortunately, these seeds may be of an inferior quality and may tend to produce late-maturing plants.

Instead, decide right at planting which section of a bean row will be your plants for seeds. (Don't bother saving seeds from hybrid cultivars; they don't come true from seed.) Leave at least 150′ between your seed plants and other bean cultivars to prevent cross-pollination. Treat the plants well during the growing season; rogue undesirable plants. At the end of the season, let the pods dry on the plants and collect and store seeds as described in "Gathering the Harvest" on page 299. ✴

BEET

Beta vulgaris, Crassa group. Chenopodiaceae. Biennial grown as an annual.

Beets are best known for their firm, sweet-tasting roots, which are cooked or pickled and used in salads, soups, and other dishes. The tender, nutritious leaves are eaten as greens. Mangels and sugar beets are close relatives that are grown for livestock forage and sugar production.

Selecting plants. Beet cultivars offer roots of different colors and shapes: red, purple, gold, or white; round, oval, or cylindrical. If your weather is severe, look for cultivars that tolerate extreme temperatures. To stock your root cellar, look for beets with good keeping qualities. Select small-rooted cultivars for canning or pickling whole. Cylindrical cultivars such as 'Formanova' provide lots of uniform-size slices for cooking and processing with little waste. Where leaf spot has been a problem, grow disease-tolerant cultivars.

Site. Beets perform best in full sun but tolerate partial shade.

Soil. Light, sandy loam permits rapid, uninterrupted growth for tender roots. Moist, fertile, well-drained soil with a pH of 6.0–6.8 is ideal. Test the soil and amend as necessary. Work in 15–20 pounds of compost for every 100 square feet of soil.

Till the soil thoroughly to a depth of at least 1'. Prepare traditional flat rows or wide rows. In heavy or poorly drained soils, prepare 6"–8"-high raised beds instead. See "Custom Care for Root Crops" on page 56 for more information on soil preparation.

How much to plant. Grow 5'–10' of fresh beets per person. For canning, sow a 10'–20' row for each beet eater.

Spacing. Space plants 2"–4" apart; allow 12"–20" between rows. When plants are 2"–3" tall, thin them to 4"–6" apart.

Days to maturity. Harvest beet roots 56–70 days after sowing seeds. Baby beets are ready sooner. Beet greens are ready to harvest in just 30–45 days.

Planting and growing. Plant beets in early spring, as soon as you can work the soil. Optimum germination occurs when soil temperatures reach 80°F, but you can plant when the soil warms to above 45°F and the air temperature is 50°–65°F. Beets can withstand freezing temperatures, but plants exposed to two to three weeks of temperatures below 50°F after the first leaves have developed may go to seed prematurely.

To provide the nitrogen that beets need, try planting your beets where legumes, such as beans or peas, previously grew. Unless you amend the soil generously first, avoid planting beets after heavy feeders such as potatoes or melons.

Soak seeds in compost tea for 15–20 minutes before planting them. Direct-sow seeds ½" deep and 2"–4" apart in rows that are spaced 12"–30" apart. For an ongoing harvest of tender roots, plant every 20–30 days from early spring through midsummer. You can plant beets again about four to seven weeks before the first expected frost date in your area. Temperatures above 75°F may make roots light-

BEET SEEDLING

Seeds   Cotyledons   First true leaves

colored and internal rings more pronounced.

Most beet seeds produce a cluster of seedlings, so you'll need to thin these when they emerge. When plants are 2″–3″ tall, thin again to 4″–6″ apart.

Keep the soil evenly moist but not wet. Apply 4″–8″ of mulch when plants first emerge to help maintain soil moisture and limit weeds. Lack of moisture causes tough, stringy roots and may make plants go to seed. Hand-weed to avoid damaging beets' shallow roots.

When the first true leaves have fully expanded, drench beets with a solution of fish emulsion and kelp extract to encourage rapid growth. (Mix 1 tablespoon of fish emulsion and 2 tablespoons of kelp extract with 1 gallon of water.) Apply 1 cup of solution for every 2′ of row. Repeat weekly until the plants are 2″–3″ tall. Applying this solution also prevents the hard, black spots and stunted growth caused by boron deficiency. Use row cover when plants emerge to prevent problems with leafminers and flea beetles. Remove the cover when the weather gets hot.

Harvesting. Harvest roots when they are 1½″–3″ wide. Pull them out carefully to avoid bruising them. Remove any dirt, then cut the tops off; leave at least 1″ of the stem to prevent the roots from bleeding. Refrigerate for several weeks, or layer in a box filled with sand or peat and store in a cool spot for two to five months. Freeze, can, or pickle the surplus.

Extending the season. Sow seeds in the fall when air temperatures are 50°–65°F. Cover the row with 8″–12″ of straw for the winter. When daytime temperatures reach 50°–60°F in the spring, remove several inches of straw every few days until plants are exposed.

Container growing. Beets do well in containers at least 6″–12″ deep.

Propagation. Garden beets cross-pollinate with other beet cultivars and varieties, including sugar beets, and also with chard. Beet pollen is lightweight and readily windborne; avoid having more than one beet or chard cultivar in flower at a time. To produce seeds of these tender biennials, sow a few seeds late in the season, so the roots will be only 1″–2″ in diameter by fall. Harvest the roots before the first expected frost and select those with the best color, shape, and size for your seed crop. Trim the tops, leaving about a 1″ stub. Pack the roots in moist sand or sawdust and store over the winter in a cold (33°–45°F) place. Replant the roots in spring and allow them to flower and set seed. Where winters are mild, sow beets in the fall to overwinter in the garden; thin to 1½′ apart in the spring. Pull the plants when seeds at the base of the stalk ripen. ✷

BLACKBERRY

Rubus spp. Rosaceae. Perennial with biennial canes. Zones 5–9.

Blackberries bear rich-tasting purple to black berries with an edible central core. They are delicious fresh, baked, or preserved. For growing information, see the Brambles entry. ✷

BLUEBERRY

Vaccinium spp. Ericaceae. Deciduous shrub.
Zones 3–9.

Blueberries are only recently cultivated plants. As little as 100 years ago, our grandparents and great-grandparents had to hunt for wild bushes if they wanted a blueberry treat.

Nowadays, you can choose from three species of blueberry to grow: highbush, rabbiteye, and lowbush. The highbush blueberry (*Vaccinium corymbosum*), Zones 4–7, is most common. This shrub, growing about 6′ high, is native mostly to the eastern seaboard. Rabbiteye blueberry (*V. ashei*) is native to the Southeast and is grown there as far north as Zone 7. It is more heat- and drought-tolerant and can grow as tall as 15′. In the Northeast, the cold-hardy lowbush blueberry (*V. angustifolium*), Zones 3–7, is an important commercial berry. The best qualities of highbush and lowbush blueberries are combined in hybrids known as midhigh blueberries.

Selecting plants. Some cultivars and types require cross-pollination; others are partially self-fertile. Plant more than one cultivar to ensure good fruit set and to extend the harvest season. Berry size varies among cultivars. Large fruits are best for fresh eating; small fruits are better for pancakes and muffins.

Site. Although blueberries tolerate partial shade, they fruit best in full sun.

Soil. Blueberries require soil that is very acidic, high in organic matter, and very well drained. It's wisest to test the pH the season before planting. If needed, add sulfur to lower the pH to 4.0–5.0. To further acidify the soil, also mix a bucket of acid peat moss or composted sawdust into each planting hole.

If you live where soil is very alkaline, make a mix of equal parts sand and acidic peat moss. Use this mix to make a raised bed or to replace your native soil excavated from a hole 1½′ deep and at least 2′ in diameter.

For more detailed information on soil preparation and cover crops, see "Custom Care for Small Fruits" on page 62.

How much to plant. Each blueberry bush will yield between 5 and 20 pounds of fruit each year depending on the size of the bush.

Spacing. Plant highbush blueberries 6′ apart each way. Plant rabbiteye blueberries 8′ apart each way. Lowbush blueberries spread underground by rhizomes; set plants 2′ apart each way and the area will fill in within six years.

Seasons to bearing. Plants usually bear two to four years after planting.

Planting and growing. Plant blueberry bushes according to the general planting instructions in "How to Plant" on page 104. Put down 6″–12″ of organic mulch at planting. Keep soil constantly moist but not soggy. Remove the blossoms the first year so that plants can put their energy into shoot and root growth.

To prevent problems with blueberry maggot, hang red spheres coated with a sticky coating near your bushes before the first berries turn blue. Use one trap for each highbush plant or one trap for several lowbush plants. Leave the traps in place until you finish harvesting the fruits.

Cover bushes with netting to prevent birds from stripping fruits from the plants.

Harvesting. A blueberry that has just turned blue is not at its best for eating. Wait a few days for full sweetness and aroma. Tickle clusters of blue fruits, and the ripe ones will drop into your hand. Keep the berries refrigerated at near-freezing temperatures with high humidity for no longer than two weeks.

Fall and winter care. Remove loose, dry mulch each fall and clear away any fallen berries; they can harbor disease organisms. Then put down a fresh layer of mulch. Each spring, top mulch with 1 pound of blood meal per 10' of row.

Prune plants in winter, preferably late winter just before growth begins. On highbush cultivars, remove wood that is more than four years old, drooping to the ground, or crowding the center. Prune away spindly twigs. Prune rabbiteye cultivars similarly, but less severely.

Prune lowbush blueberries by cutting all stems to ground level. Pruned plants will not bear the season following pruning, so prune a different half of your planting in alternate years.

Keep an eye out for rabbits, which like to munch on blueberry stems in winter. Repel them by sprinkling bonemeal or blood meal on your plants. Reapply the repellent after rains.

Container growing. Choose midhigh blueberries for growing in containers. Use a potting mix composed of equal parts acid peat moss and either sand or perlite. Fertilize plants as needed with seed meals. If your tap water is alkaline, acidify it with ½ teaspoon of vinegar per quart of water before applying. Repot plants every few years during the dormant season,

Juneberry flowers

Lowbush blueberries

Blueberry flowers

'Darrow' blueberries

Bog cranberry flowers

Juneberries

'Elliott' blueberries

'Bluejay' blueberries

Bog cranberries

Plump blueberries are the critical ingredients in our favorite muffins. Juneberries also have sweet and juicy fruits, with a hint of almond flavor, and are less picky about soil conditions than blueberries. Cranberries are another American tradition, and, yes, they can be grown without a bog.

pruning back the roots and tops at that time. In very cold areas, protect the roots from cold during the winter as shown in the illustration on page 240. The plants do not need light in winter.

Propagation. Highbush and rabbiteye blueberries are difficult to propagate. Take softwood tip cuttings as soon as bushes complete their first flush of growth for the season. Set the cuttings in a mix of equal parts peat moss and sand in a sheltered, partly shaded location.

For lowbush blueberry, take softwood cuttings before shoot growth ceases. Lowbush blueberry can also be propagated by digging up rhizomes while the plants are dormant, then planting them in the rooting medium.

Friends and relatives. Bog cranberry (*V. macrocarpon*—the Thanksgiving cranberry) and lingonberry (*V. vitis-idaea* var. minus) are closely related to blueberry and require similar soil conditions. The bog cranberry requires a somewhat wetter soil. Both are creeping, evergreen plants that produce tart, red fruits. Neither plant needs annual pruning.

The word huckleberry is often used interchangeably with blueberry, but true huckleberries belong in a different genus (*Gaylussacia*). Huckleberries resemble blueberries, but huckleberry fruits contain bony seeds. Soil and growing requirements are the same.

Juneberry (*Amelanchier* spp.), sometimes called serviceberry or shadblow, has fruits that resemble blueberries in look and taste. These ornamental plants, adapted to Zones 3–8, are unrelated to blueberries botanically. They range from shrubs to medium-size trees. Juneberries are not finicky about soil pH and are rarely bothered by pests. ✳

BRAMBLES

Rubus spp. Rosaceae. Perennial with biennial canes. Zones 3–9.

Brambles include raspberries (Zones 3–8); blackberries (Zones 5–9); hybrids between the two species, such as tayberry, boysenberry, and loganberry (hardiness varies, but most are adapted only to Zones 8–9); and representatives of other species, such as wineberry, or *Rubus phoenicolasius* (Zones 5–8). There are red, gold, black, and purple types of raspberries.

Raspberries and blackberries are considered gourmet treats but not because they're hard to grow. They just don't ship well. Grow your own summertime treats. Once you've had your fill of fresh berries, just toss the surplus into a container and into your freezer, or make jam.

Planning

Selecting plants. Choose tissue-culture plants or one-year-old dormant plants with lots of roots. Brambles are self-fertile, so you can plant just one cultivar. In general, the hardiest are fall-cropped red and yellow raspberries, then summer red and yellow raspberries, followed by purple raspberries, black raspberries, blackberries, and then hybrid brambles.

Buy only virus-free plants because virus infection is the number one disease problem for brambles. Ask your local extension office or nursery what other diseases and pests cause serious problems in your region and which cultivars are resistant. Yellow raspberries may tempt birds less than other raspberries.

Selecting a site. Brambles do best in well-drained soil and full sun with plenty of air movement. In very windy locations, provide a windbreak to reduce cane breakage and thorn damage. To avoid soilborne diseases such as crown gall or Verticillium wilt, choose a site where brambles or other hosts to these diseases have not grown for a few years. (Tomatoes and peppers host Verticillium wilt; grapes and members of the Rosaceae family host crown gall.) Avoid diseases by choosing a site as far as possible from wild brambles. Keep black and red raspberries separated if you can. Most brambles will bear sparingly if you plant them in shade, but they will be more prone to disease problems than those planted in full sun. Wineberries are the exception and do well in shade.

When to plant. Plant brambles in spring or fall. Mulch is especially important following fall planting to prevent frost from heaving plants out of the soil. Green tissue-culture plants may be planted all summer.

Spacing. Space rows of raspberries at least 7'–8' apart to allow room to walk and work between them. Red and most gold raspberries spread underground, so plant them 2'–3' apart

in rows and allow them to fill in the row. Black raspberries don't spread underground and are planted in hills 2½'–4' apart. Purple raspberries are somewhere between reds and blacks in spreading ability and usually spread slowly. Plant them 1½' apart in a row or singly in hills as you would black raspberries.

Blackberries are larger plants than raspberries and need more room. Put rows 8'–10' apart, or more for thorny cultivars. Plant thorny cultivars 3'–4' apart in rows. Thornless cultivars need 4'–6' between plants.

For a greater harvest. Brambles do well in raised beds or individual raised hills.

Soil Preparation

Brambles thrive in well-drained, fertile soil that is rich in organic matter, with a pH of 5.5–6.5. Get perennial weeds under control before planting brambles. See "Custom Care for Small Fruits" on page 62 for details on preparing soil for planting.

Planting

See "How to Plant" on page 104 for planting guidelines. Soak bareroot plants in compost tea for 20 minutes before planting and dust roots with a mixture of 2 cups of kelp and 1 cup of bonemeal prior to planting. If you are planting canes, cut them back to the ground after planting to reduce caneborne diseases. If you are planting tissue-culture plants, spray them with an antitranspirant to reduce water loss from the leaves.

Growing Guidelines

Water and mulch. Brambles demand a steady supply of water throughout the growing season. Drip irrigation is ideal because it

Red raspberries

Black raspberries

Red raspberry flowers

Black and red raspberries have different plant habits. Red raspberries (and most yellows) bear fruit on the tip of the cane and spread by suckers. Black raspberries bear fruit on side branches and don't make suckers.

offers a steady supply of water without wetting the foliage. Brambles have shallow roots and thrive under a thick organic mulch.

Feeding. Add 10–15 pounds of compost per 10′ of row in late winter every year. Black raspberries are especially heavy feeders, so you may want to give them a little extra.

Training. Supporting your brambles makes it easier for you to harvest the fruit and exposes the canes to better air circulation and sunlight, decreasing diseases. Some brambles will grow fine without trellising, but berries are easier for gardeners to pick when brambles are trellised.

The most basic trellis for a row of brambles consists of one or more wires stretched between posts set firmly in the ground. Your trellis can be as simple as a single wire 4′–5′ off the ground to which you tie the canes after pruning. Or it can be as complex as three wires on each side of the row at 2′, 3′, and 4′ with the canes sandwiched between. Use 7′ posts set 2′ into the ground for raspberries and 8′ posts set 2½′ deep for blackberries.

A particularly effective bramble trellis is called a V-trellis. (See the illustration and explanation of this type of trellis on page 135.) Black or purple raspberry plants can also be tied to sturdy individual stakes.

Black and purple raspberries and erect blackberries require pruning during the growing season. See "Brambles" on page 135 for information on how to prune these plants.

Individual canes of all brambles begin to die when the summer harvest is complete. Prune off the spent canes at ground level after they finish fruiting to help reduce disease problems and to make room for the new canes to grow.

Thinning. Do not thin fruits, but do thin the *canes* during dormant pruning.

Problem Prevention

As buds show green, spray lime-sulfur. If powdery mildew (fruit or shoot tips covered with white powder) or cane diseases (canes discolor, wilt, and die in midsummer) were a problem last year, spray lime-sulfur in the spring just as the buds are first showing green.

When flower buds appear, spray rotenone. If raspberry fruitworm (tiny, yellow-white larvae feeding inside ripe berries) were a problem last year, spray rotenone and/or pyrethrins now. Repeat just before flowers open. Pick up and destroy dropped fruits. Spread beneficial nematodes to help control soil population.

As fruit first forms, spray compost tea. Compost tea sprays can help prevent gray mold. Spray in early morning on a clear day so foliage will dry fast.

As fruit begins to color, spray sulfur. If gray mold was a problem in previous years and it is humid or wet, spray sulfur. Respray after rains. Pick molded berries into a separate container and get them out of your patch. Next winter, leave fewer canes per plant or per foot of row.

In summer, watch for disease symptoms. Yellow patterns on leaves or small, crumbly berries could be symptoms of viral diseases.

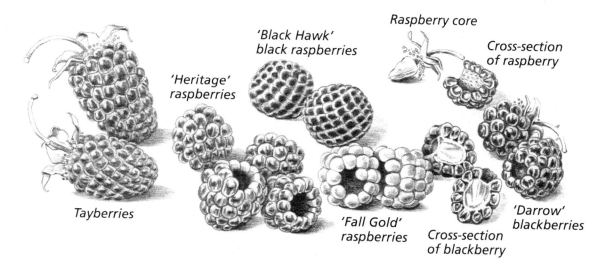

'Black Hawk' black raspberries

Raspberry core

Cross-section of raspberry

'Heritage' raspberries

Tayberries

'Fall Gold' raspberries

Cross-section of blackberry

'Darrow' blackberries

Raspberries and blackberries are great additions to your food garden. Raspberries come off their cores when ripe and are shaped like a thimble or hat. Blackberries stay attached to their cores; when they are ripe, the core separates easily from the stem. Tayberries are a cross between raspberries and blackberries.

Orange pustules on blackberries and black and purple raspberries indicate rust disease. Dig up and destroy all such plants immediately.

In summer, watch for wilted canes. Cane dieback is caused by borers or cane diseases. Look for a small entry hole near the base of the wilted area. Prune off and destroy infested canes or cane tips, borer and all. If canes are discolored and don't have an insect entry hole, a disease is at work. Cut the cane off at the base and destroy it.

When harvest is done, cut out spent canes. The canes will die anyway, so get them out of the patch now and reduce disease problems.

In fall, renew mulch. When leaves start to drop, rake back loose, dry mulch. After the weather gets cold and after mice have found winter nests elsewhere, rake mulch back into the row and add new mulch on top.

Gathering the Harvest

For best flavor, pick bramble fruits when they are thoroughly ripe. The ripe fruits are soft and come free from the plant with little force. Unripe fruits will not ripen after they are picked. Pick into shallow containers (three to four berries deep) to prevent crushing. The fruits are perishable, so store them no longer than two or three days at temperatures just above freezing and at high humidity.

Fall and Winter Care

Fall and winter is the time for pruning some of these brambles. See "Brambles" on page 135 for specific information on pruning brambles. Be sure to ruthlessly limit the width of your row to 1' or you and your crops will suffer.

Container Growing

With their thorny stems and spreading habit, brambles are not ideal container plants— and surely are not plants for terraces and other intimate settings where people will gather. Nonetheless, if you are willing to put up with their limitations as container plants, you can grow brambles in containers. Repot yearly when the plants are dormant. In very cold areas, protect the roots in winter as shown in the illustration on page 240.

Propagation

Bramble plants are easy to propagate— almost too easy, you may think as you fight back an expanding patch. Don't propagate virus-infected plants. If you know the plants personally and they bear good crops of well-formed fruits, you can probably take a chance and propagate them. Red, yellow, and suckering purple raspberries are propagating throughout the growing season. Just transplant some of the suckers that have ventured outside of the row. Black and nonsuckering purple raspberries and blackberries send up only occasional suckers and are usually propagated by tip layering. In late summer, bend branch tips to the ground, cover them with soil, and use a rock to hold down the soil and branch, if necessary. The following spring, cut off and transplant the rooted tip. ✳

BROCCOLI

Brassica oleracea, Botrytis group. Cruciferae. Annual.

Broccoli probably isn't the first thing that pops into your mind when someone mentions edible flowers. But what we call broccoli heads are really just clusters of tightly packed flower buds waiting to open. This common dinner side dish is rich in vitamins A, B, and C, as well as calcium, phosphorus, and iron. According to "The Broccoli Doctor," Paul Talalay, M.D., a specialist in molecular pharmacology on staff at Johns Hopkins Hospital in Baltimore, broccoli contains sulforaphane, an anticancer enzyme. Eat broccoli raw in salads or with dips. Or steam it or use it in stir-fries or soups.

Selecting plants. Choose from early, middle, and late cultivars. Hybrids tend to be more productive than open-pollinated cultivars. If you've had problems in the past, look for cultivars that are tolerant to problems like hollow stem, black rot, and downy mildew. 'De Cicco' is the standard open-pollinated cultivar. Slow-growing 'Romanesco' forms a pale green cauliflower-like head that spirals to a peak; it has a mild broccoli taste.

Site. Broccoli needs full sun; partial shade will reduce head size. To minimize disease problems, allow three years between plantings of broccoli and other cabbage-family plants. Since broccoli is a heavy feeder, it thrives after a legume, such as peas, or a clover cover crop.

Soil. Broccoli needs a fertile, humus-rich soil with a pH of 6.0–6.8. Lighter soils are best for spring planting, heavier soils for fall. Dig in a legume cover crop or 30 pounds of compost per 100 square feet. Work the soil to a depth of at least 8".

How much to plant. One gram of broccoli seeds averages 200 seeds and will sow about 20' of row or produce 150–180 seedlings. Plan on five to ten plants per person. Between the main head and sideshoots, one plant can give 2 pounds of broccoli.

Spacing. Allow 15"–18" between plants for spring plantings, 1½'–2' for fall plantings. Leave 2'–3' between rows.

Days to maturity. Broccoli will mature 55–78 days from transplanting.

Planting and growing. Get the best from your spring broccoli by setting out transplants. Direct sowing is a viable option only for later plantings, when the soil temperature is over 50°F but the air is cool (between 60° and 75°F). Broccoli seedlings are especially vulnerable to excess heat (over 80°F) and drying out. Though they may appear to recover, they probably won't produce much. If either extreme occurs, your best bet is to start over again with new seedlings. For more details on seedling care and transplanting, see the Cabbage entry.

Broccoli needs a regular supply of moisture to produce good heads. Excessive moisture will stunt or kill it. If your soil tends to get waterlogged, plant in raised beds. Mulching with legume hay, grass clippings, or straw will keep soil temperatures down and soil moisture even. Mulch will also reduce weed competition. Or use a living mulch for fall-planted crops; cultivate twice after planting and then underseed with clover, oats, or rye.

Rich, well-balanced soil will prevent many broccoli problems. Use tolerant or resistant cultivars, and space plants properly to allow good air circulation. Covering young plants or transplants with floating row cover will save them from cabbageworms, flea beetles, and root maggots. Broccoli is very sensitive to air pollution, so if ozone and sulfur dioxide are high, you may observe some leaf damage. The cold, rainy weather of fall can bring on diseases that cause heads to rot. Cultivars with dome-shaped heads tend to be less disease-prone since water drains off of them quickly.

For more complete information on general crop care and pest-prevention techniques, see the Cabbage entry.

Harvesting. Harvest while heads are still compact, before the buds start to open into flowers. Cut the stem at a slant, 4"–6" below the head. Heading broccoli will continue to produce sideshoots in the axils of the leaves; you can get four to six cuttings of shoots per plant over several weeks. The thick stems are edible, though you may want to peel them first. The leaves are tough but are usable in soups.

When you bring your broccoli inside, soak the heads in salt water (1–2 tablespoons of salt per gallon of water) for 30 minutes before cooking or storing. This will drive out any cabbageworms hiding in the heads. Broccoli will keep for little more than a week in the refrigerator if wrapped in plastic. The best way to store broccoli for longer periods is to blanch and freeze it.

Extending the season. For an early crop, start plants indoors ten weeks before the last expected frost. Set plants out after five to six weeks. Covering plants with floating row cover will extend the season in the fall. Cultivars such as 'Green Valiant' can withstand temperatures as low as 20°F, as long as the weather is evenly cool. If warm spells alternate with sudden frosts, 27°F can be cold enough to freeze plants. Where temperatures stay above 40°F, broccoli will grow all winter.

Fall and winter care. After harvest, pull up the plants, roots and all, and compost them.

Propagation. See the Cabbage entry for propagation information. Broccoli seeds last three years under good storage conditions.

Friends and relatives. For a tangier, more mustardy flavor, try sprouting broccoli (*Brassica oleracea*, Italica group). It produces longer stems and small clusters of buds, rather than large heads. Broccoli raab (*B. rapa*, Ruvo group) is actually a turnip raised for its leaves, young stems, and bud clusters. See the Turnip entry for details on growing broccoli raab. ✳

BRUSSELS SPROUTS

Brassica oleracea, Gemmifera group.
Cruciferae. Biennial grown as an annual.

Brussels sprouts are one of the most underrated vegetables around. Many people proclaim a lifelong aversion to this cabbage relative, having been subjected to soggy, overcooked, bitter sprouts. But once you've experienced the sweet, nutty taste of frost-touched, garden-fresh sprouts, you won't want to be without them.

Brussels sprouts are a good source of vitamins A, B, and C, as well as phosphorus, iron, and potassium. According to Paul Talalay, M.D., a specialist in molecular pharmacology on staff at Johns Hopkins Hospital in Baltimore, brussels sprouts contain sulforaphane, an anticancer enzyme. The sprouts are most delicious after a frost or two. For best flavor, steam them lightly and serve with butter or margarine.

Selecting plants. Open-pollinated and hybrid cultivars are available. Hybrids tend to have stronger root systems, making them less prone to leaning, and their sprouts mature more evenly. For an ornamental edible, try 'Rubine', which produces showy red sprouts.

Site. Brussels sprouts grow best in full sun. To avoid pest and disease problems, allow three years between plantings of cabbage-family plants. Brussels sprouts grow well after legumes like peas and beans. Do not plant after other heavy feeders, such as tomatoes and potatoes.

Soil. Brussels sprouts need a pH of 5.5–6.8. They grow well in either flat rows or raised beds. Well-prepared, rich soil is especially important because brussels sprouts have such a long growing season. Work the soil to a depth of at least 8″ and incorporate a legume cover crop or 30 pounds of compost per 100 square feet.

How much to plant. One gram of brussels sprouts seeds contains 100–200 seeds and will direct seed 25′ or start 80–150 plants. For an ample supply of sprouts, plant five to eight plants per person. Each plant should yield about 1 quart or 1½–2 pounds of sprouts.

Spacing. Allow 1½′–2′ between plants and 2′–3′ between rows. When mature, these plants can reach 2½′–3′ tall.

Days to maturity. Sprouts are ready in 90–110 days from transplanting.

Planting and growing. In most parts of the country, it's best to start this cool-loving crop indoors five-and-a-half months before the first expected fall frost. Set plants out after five to six weeks. Where growing seasons are long, you can direct-sow fall crops in July; in mild-winter areas, time your crop for winter-to-spring harvest. Soil temperatures must be over 50°F for good germination. See the Cabbage entry for more information on seed starting and seedling care.

Feed plants at transplanting and once a week for three weeks with a kelp-and-fish-emulsion drench (1 tablespoon of each in 1 gallon of water). Apply 1 cup per plant. If your soil is not very rich, side-dress with 1 shovelful of compost per plant or 1 cup of soy meal before cultivating. Work the side-dressing into the soil immediately. Be careful not to damage roots by hoeing too close to plants.

Brussels sprouts need steady moisture. This is especially important when air temperatures rise over 80°F; hot, dry spells will stunt sprout formation. Mulching with legume hay, grass cuttings, or straw will keep soil temperatures down and moisture levels steady while eliminating weed competition. Alternatively, underseed a clover cover crop when brussels sprout plants are well-established and you have cultivated twice for weeds.

As sprouts form in the leaf axils, snap off the leaves beneath them. Three to four weeks before harvesting, when sprouts reach ½″–¾″ in diameter, you have a choice: If you want sprouts to ripen all at once, pinch off the growing point (the cluster of leaves at the very top of the main stem). This gives the plant the signal to concentrate on sprout formation. If you let the plant develop naturally, your sprouts will mature over a longer period, extending the harvest.

Brussels sprouts suffer the same pests and diseases as cabbages, though they seem to be more tolerant. Gray aphids sometimes cluster on brussels sprouts in the fall. Remove pests with a blast of water or spray with insecticidal soap. For more complete growing guidelines and problem prevention tips, see the Cabbage entry.

Harvesting. Harvest the sprouts, starting from the bottom of the stem, when they reach 1"–2" in diameter. Brussels sprouts are best eaten fresh, although you can store them for up to three weeks in a plastic bag in the refrigerator. Or preserve them for up to one year by blanching and freezing.

Extending the season. To prolong the harvest in cold climates, dig up entire plants and replant them in a greenhouse or cold frame for picking through the winter. Or, where snow cover is reliable, bend the plants down to the ground and let them get covered with snow. Eat the sprouts when the snow recedes.

Fall and winter care. When the harvest is over, pull plants out with their roots and compost them. Chopping or shredding the tough, woody stems will help them break down faster.

Propagation. To produce seeds, brussels sprout plants must be exposed to temperatures under 45°F for one to two months. In their second season, they send up a seedstalk. Seeds last four years in storage. See the Cabbage entry for more complete propagation information. ✳

CABBAGE

Brassica oleracea, Capitata group. Cruciferae. Biennial grown as an annual.

Traditional heading cabbage may not be the trendiest vegetable in the garden, but it's one of the most dependable. This classic cole crop has been grown for centuries for its large heads of crunchy leaves. Chop up garden-fresh cabbage for a summer slaw, or store the heads for a winter batch of sauerkraut. If you feel adventurous, try growing some of the oriental cabbages, such as Chinese cabbage, napa, komatsuna, bok choy, tatsoi, and others. Cabbage and its relatives, including broccoli, kale, and kohlrabi, are collectively referred to as brassicas, crucifers, or cole crops.

Planning

Selecting plants. There are four basic types of heading cabbage: smooth-leaved green, smooth-leaved red, crinkled-leaved green and crinkle-leaved red types (also known as savoys). From among these, you can choose early cultivars for a late-spring crop, or mid-season and storage cultivars for late-summer to fall harvesting.

Selection and breeding have developed cabbages that are particularly well-suited for eating fresh, for storing, or for processing into sauerkraut. You can also find disease-resistant or disease-tolerant cultivars.

Selecting a site. Cabbage needs full sun. It will grow in any well-drained, moderately fertile soil, but for first-rate production, it needs soil that is rich in humus. If you have a choice of planting sites, choose a light, sandy soil for your spring plantings; plantings for fall harvest prefer heavier, moisture-retaining soil. Avoid sites where cabbage or other brassicas grew the previous three years.

CABBAGE

Site: Full sun.

Soil: Rich, sandy loam; pH of 6.0–6.8.

How much to plant: Five to ten plants per person.

Spacing: 15"–24" between plants in rows 2'–3' apart.

Days to maturity: 62–120 days from transplanting.

When to plant. Brassicas thrive in cool weather. Start early cultivars indoors and set them out before the last expected frost so they'll mature before hot weather arrives. Or direct-sow around the time of the last expected frost. For fall crops, start plants or direct-sow seed from mid-May (in cooler areas) to mid-June (in warmer areas). In the South, you can start cabbages in October and set them out six weeks later for a late-winter or early-spring crop.

How much to plant. Cabbage seeds are very small. One gram of seed contains from 100–200 seeds, enough for a 20' row. Seed packets usually contain enough seeds to produce 80–90 plants. Plant five to ten cabbages per person.

Spacing. Early cultivars need 15"–18" between plants. Later cultivars, and those developed for processing or storage, need 2' between plants. Allow 2'–3' between rows.

Rotation. To minimize disease problems, allow three years between plantings of all brassicas. As you plan your rotations, keep in mind that cabbages are heavy feeders. They do not thrive when planted after other heavy feeders, like potatoes. But they do grow well after a legume cover crop, like clover.

For a greater harvest. Cabbages and their kin produce better if conditions are right for steady growth. Set out vigorous, healthy plants, and make sure they have a regular supply of moisture from either rain or irrigation. Humus-rich soil is another key to high yields. Add ample amounts of organic matter to the soil to keep humus levels high.

Soil Preparation

Before planting, incorporate your cover crop, or work in well-matured compost at the rate of at least 30 pounds per 100 square feet. Dig or till the soil to a depth of 8". Brassicas grow well in either flat rows or low raised beds. Where water drainage is poor, raised beds are critical to keep roots out of water-logged soil. Beds that are raised more than 6", though, may dry out too quickly and get too warm for these crops.

Planting Indoors

Sowing seeds. For early cabbages, start plants indoors eight to ten weeks before the last expected frost. Plant two to three seeds per inch in flats or two seeds per cell in individual cells. Sow seeds ¼"–½" deep. For optimum germination, keep the soil at 75°–80°F.

CABBAGE SEEDLING

Seeds   *Cotyledons*

First true leaves

Cabbage seeds germinate within ten days.

Seedling care. Once the seedlings emerge, they need full light and good air circulation. Reduce the soil temperature to around 65°–75°F; keep the air temperature around 60°F during the day and 50°F at night.

If you start the plants in flats, prick them out when they develop their first set of true leaves. Transplant them into another flat, spacing the seedlings at least 1″ apart. In cells, thin them to one plant per cell.

Regular watering and fertilizing are critical. Once a week, feed the seedlings with compost tea. Or prepare a kelp-and-fish-emulsion mixture (1 tablespoon of kelp extract and 1 tablespoon of fish emulsion per gallon of water), and use this to water your seedlings.

Hardening off transplants. Four weeks after sowing, place the seedlings in a cold frame to harden off for a week or two before transplanting to the garden. If you do not have a cold frame, set plants outside during the day and move them back in at night for a week; then leave them out for a week before transplanting. Protect seedlings from wind, but allow them to experience the natural fluctuation of temperatures. Make sure you water your seedlings regularly; they'll dry out quickly outdoors.

Planting Outdoors

Sowing seeds. For mid-season and storage crops, you can sow seeds directly in the garden, from about two weeks before the last expected frost until two to three weeks after. If your soil is crusted, rake to break up the surface and form a fine seedbed. Sow seeds thinly, ½″ deep, in rows 2′–3′ apart. Keep the soil evenly moist for good germination.

Buying transplants. Most growers prefer to use transplants to get a jump on weeds and to avoid the extra soil preparation necessary for direct sowing. Look for sturdy, stocky plants free from flea beetles or cabbageworms. The leaves should not be yellowed or brown; stems should be firm and unscarred.

Setting out transplants. Set hardened transplants into the garden about four weeks before the last expected frost, when soil temperatures are 40°F or higher. Row cover can help shield plants from cold temperatures. For extra protection, set each transplant in a shallow dip, 2″–3″ below the soil line, or plant them in a shallow trench. This will protect the small plants from wind and hold moisture as well. Once the plants are established, fill the dip by pulling soil in around the stem with a hoe.

Water transplants well to settle the soil around the roots. To give them a boost, apply 1 cup of a kelp-and-fish-emulsion mixture (made by mixing 1 tablespoon of kelp extract and 1 tablespoon of fish emulsion per gallon of water) at the base of each plant.

Growing Guidelines

Thinning seedlings. Thin seedlings to 15″–18″ apart for early cultivars and every 2′ for late cultivars. Snip the extra plants off at ground level to avoid damaging the roots of the remaining plants. Use the thinnings in salads.

Water and mulch. Cabbages and other brassicas need a steady supply of moisture. To keep the soil evenly moist and cool, mulch with a 6″–8″ layer of hay, straw, or grass clippings. Cultivate thoroughly to destroy any weed seedlings before laying the mulch.

For fall crops, you may want to plant a

living mulch instead. That way, your cover crop will be in place for winter even before the harvest is over. Once the cabbages are established, cultivate thoroughly and broadcast low-growing clover, oats, or rye. By harvest, the cover crop will be well-established, and it will not mind you trampling it as you collect your cabbages.

Feeding. Water with 1 cup per plant of the kelp-and-fish-emulsion mixture (see "Setting Out Transplants" on the opposite page) for the first three weeks after transplanting. If your soil is not very rich, you may want to side-dress with compost or soy meal. Just before cultivating, sprinkle a shovelful of compost or a cup of soy meal around each plant, and incorporate the amendment as you hoe. This is especially beneficial for early crops.

For more tips on crop care for highest yields, see "Custom Care for Leafy Crops" on page 60.

Problem Prevention

Select resistant cultivars. If your cabbage crops have had problems in the past, look for disease-resistant cultivars. You can choose from cultivars that are resistant to Fusarium wilt, splitting, and tipburn. Some cultivars are tolerant of black rot, Alternaria blight, and downy mildew. In the future, you

'Jade Pagoda' michihli-type Chinese cabbage

'Primavoy' green savoy cabbage

'China Pride' napa-type Chinese cabbage

'Ruby Ball' red cabbage

'Polar Green' cabbage

Smooth or crinkly, crisp and colorful, cabbage is a reliable, easy-to-grow crop. Wide spacing produces the largest heads; closer spacing yields smaller heads—a plus for small families.

may be able to find cultivars that are resistant to cabbage loopers.

Grow buckwheat or dill nearby as a habitat for wasps. Beneficial wasps will lay eggs in cabbageworms and parasitize them, reducing crop damage.

Try companion planting to combat pests. Alternating rows of brassicas and garlic may help reduce flea beetles on the brassicas.

Before planting, balance soil fertility. Cabbage and other brassicas need a high rate of available nitrogen, potassium, phosphorus, and calcium. Adequate boron is also very important for cole crops. Nutrient imbalances can produce diseaselike symptoms and lower yields. Nitrogen deficiency causes leaves to turn yellow, beginning with the oldest ones. Excessive nitrogen can cause hollow stems. Potassium deficiency causes small, soft heads and poor coloring in red cabbages. Calcium deficiency can cause browning of both outer and inner leaf tips. Boron deficiency causes cracked, corky leaves, water-soaked stems, and hollow heads.

Maintaining even soil moisture and side-dressing with compost should prevent these problems. If symptoms do occur, spray plants with kelp extract and water with fish emulsion for short-term relief. Test your soil before the next growing season, and add necessary nutrients to balance soil fertility levels.

At planting, space plants correctly. Proper spacing will allow good air circulation around the plants. Crowded plantings produce small heads and are more prone to diseases.

At planting, protect transplants with cutworm collars and/or tar paper squares. Cutworms and root maggots are two major threats to your brassica seedlings. Protect young stems from cutworm damage by making cardboard collars. Cut toilet paper or paper towel tubes into 2″–3″ sections. Slide them over your transplanted seedlings, and push the collars about halfway into the soil. They'll last until your seedlings are past the susceptible stage.

Tar paper squares discourage root maggot flies from laying their eggs next to the seedlings. Cut 6″–8″ squares from tar paper, and make a cut from one edge to the center. Cut a small hole in the center of the square, so it will fit snugly around the stem but lie flat on the ground. Place one square around each seedling. Leave the squares in place until the end of the season.

Another approach is to mix a slurry of shredded newspapers and water and pour a collar around each plant. The slurry hardens and keeps off both cutworms and root maggots. Or purchase root-maggot-eating nematodes and water them into the soil around each plant.

At planting, cover plants with row cover. Row cover will protect new transplants from flea beetles and other flying pests, including root maggot flies. Be careful to cover plants thoroughly. Openings or holes will allow pests to enter and multiply undisturbed.

During the growing season, keep the soil evenly moist. Dry spells can cause bolting (flowering) or buttoning (the formation of tiny heads). A dry spell followed by heavy rain can cause heads to crack. If you plan to delay harvesting of mature heads, twist the entire cabbage plant a half-turn and pull up slightly; this breaks some of the roots and reduces excess water intake.

During the growing season, watch for cabbageworm butterflies. Those small white butterflies fluttering around your cole crops are the adult stage of imported cabbageworm. Their yellow egg masses hatch into velvety green caterpillars, which chew large, ragged holes in leaves. When you see the adults, start checking plants every day or two for signs of the larvae. Handpick light infestations, or spray with *Bacillus thuringiensis* var. *kurstaki* (BTK) at one- to two-week intervals.

Gathering the Harvest

A cabbage is ready to harvest when the head is full and firm. Cut the stalk at the base of the head with a sharp knife. It's best to harvest them in the morning, when the heads are cool. Early cabbages don't store well, so cut them as needed for fresh use. Storage-type cabbages will keep for two to three months in a cool, humid root cellar, with temperatures just above 32°F and 90 percent humidity. Cut off all rotted or damaged outer leaves. Space heads so their leaves do not touch.

Extending the Season

Begin the season with extra-early cultivars, such as 'Early Jersey Wakefield'. Extend the harvest in the fall with frost-hardy cultivars such as 'Custodian', which can withstand frosts down to 20°F.

Fall and Winter Care

After harvesting, pull out the remaining stems with roots attached and add them to your compost pile.

Propagation

Cabbages, like many other brassicas, are biennials, meaning that they don't flower and set seed until their second year. In most areas, you can leave a few plants in the garden to overwinter for seed production. For extra protection, mound soil around the stems, or cover with a layer of loose mulch. If winters are severe in your area, dig mature plants and set them in containers. Keep the dormant plants in a cool, humid place, such as a cold cellar. Replant them into the garden in early spring, where they should flower and set seed. Slashing an X into the top of cabbage heads will help the flowerstalk emerge. Collect seeds from the browning seed head. Properly stored seeds should last four years.

A word of warning: Cabbage and other cole crops will readily cross-pollinate. If you plan to save seeds, separate flowering cultivars and related crops by at least 300'; 1,000' or more is preferable. ✳

🐜 FRIENDS & RELATIVES 🐜

CABBAGE

Cabbage has many close relatives in the vegetable garden. For more information on these crops, check out the following entries: Broccoli, Brussels Sprouts, Cauliflower, Collard, Kale, Kohlrabi, Mustard, Rutabaga, and Turnip.

There are also many related Asian vegetables, which we tend to lump together as Asian cabbages. Napa and michihli are two common types of Chinese cabbage (*Brassica rapa,* Pekinensis group). Napa produces thick, oval heads; michihli forms tall, narrow heads. You'll find more information on Chinese cabbage and its relatives—including bok choy, tatsoi, Chinese broccoli, and komatsuna—in the Asian Specialties entry.

CAROB

Ceratonia siliqua. Leguminosae. Evergreen tree. Zones 9–10 and warmer parts of Zone 8.

Also known as Saint John's bread, carob was an important food in biblical times. This Mediterranean tree grows in Florida and flourishes in southern California, Arizona, parts of Nevada, Texas, and New Mexico. Ground pods make a chocolate-colored powder used in candy and desserts.

Selecting plants. Some types of carob bear male and female flowers on separate trees; others are self-pollinating. Be sure to ask your supplier which type you are getting and plant accordingly.

Site. Carob flourishes in a Mediterranean-type climate with cool winters and hot, dry summers.

Soil. This plant grows in well-drained soils ranging from heavy loam to sandy and rocky hillsides.

How much to plant. Two carob trees should yield enough for four people.

Spacing. Plant trees 30′ apart.

Seasons to bearing. Grafted trees bear in five to six years. Seedling trees bear in eight to ten years.

Planting and growing. To grow trees from seeds, scarify the seeds, and soak them in water until they swell. Plant seeds in flats indoors. When seedlings have two true leaves, transplant them to 1′-deep pots. When the trees reach 2′–3′, plant them outdoors. In most areas, fertilizer is not necessary. Carob is fairly trouble-free. In humid areas, it may suffer from fungal diseases that cause ripening pods to turn moldy.

Harvesting. Use a long pole to knock the pods onto a canvas tarp on the ground. Gather the ripe brown pods before winter rains begin to keep them from rotting.

Fall and winter care. Freezing temperatures can kill trees. Protect them by sprinkling them with water until the temperature rises above freezing. ✷

CARROT

Daucus carota var. *sativus.* Umbelliferae. Biennial grown as an annual.

Crunchy, sweet carrot roots add color and nutrition to a gardener's diet. This cool-season crop makes a tasty raw snack and is equally good cooked or added to soups or stir-fries.

Planning

Selecting plants. Most carrots are orange, but they come in red, yellow, white, and even purple. Some have distinct cores, others are coreless. Match cultivars to your garden's soil. Short-rooted and blocky carrots fare better in heavy or shallow soils than long-rooted ones. Long, tapered roots perform best in deep, loose soil. Use short-season cultivars for succession planting. Look for bolt resistance where drought is common.

Selecting a site. Carrots do best in full sun and deep, loose, moderately rich, evenly moist soil with a pH between 5.5 and 6.8.

When to plant. Plant carrots in early

CARROT

Site: Full sun to light shade.

Soil: Deep, loose, moist, and well-aerated; pH of 5.5–6.8.

How much to plant: 5'–10' of row, or 30 plants, per person.

Spacing: 3"–4" between plants in rows 16"–30" apart.

Days to maturity: 50–95 days from seed to harvest.

spring, when the soil temperature reaches 45°F and as soon as you are able to work the soil. Seeds germinate best when the soil is 80°F. Carrot seedlings tolerate air temperatures as low as 45°F but grow slowly under such conditions; optimum growth occurs at 60°–70°F. Temperatures above 80°F promote short, spindly roots with poor color and flavor.

How much to plant. Allow about 30 plants—roughly 5'–10' of row—for each person.

Spacing. Sow about six seeds per inch in rows separated by 16"–30". Or broadcast seeds in 1'–1½'-wide raised beds.

Rotation. This crop does well when planted after legumes: The extra nitrogen gives carrots an early boost. Amend the soil when following heavy feeders such as peppers. If you leave a few carrots in the ground over winter, the flowers they produce the following season will attract beneficial insects to your garden.

For a greater harvest. Make successive plantings two to three weeks apart until temperatures warm up. For a fall harvest, direct-seed 85–100 days before the first expected frost.

Soil Preparation

Give your carrots a deep, loose, well-aerated bed to grow in. Light, sandy, moderately rich soil with a pH in the range of 5.5–6.8 is ideal. Amend the soil with 10 pounds of compost per 100 square feet to provide a balance of nutrients. Apply nitrogen moderately—too much can cause hairy, misshapen roots. Thoroughly cultivate the soil to at least 1' deep, and prepare rows or raised beds. For details, see "Custom Care for Root Crops" on page 56.

Planting Outdoors

Sowing seeds. Sow seeds directly in the ground ¼"–½" deep. Plant about six seeds per inch in rows spaced 16"–30" apart. Carrots germinate slowly, taking from one to three weeks to sprout. Sow quick-germinating radish seeds with your carrots to mark the rows; the radishes help break the surface crust for the carrots, too.

Growing Guidelines

Thinning seedlings. When the tops are 2" tall, thin carrots to 1" apart; in two weeks, thin again to 3"–4" apart.

Water and mulch. Keep the soil constantly moist; uneven moisture can make roots

CARROT SEEDLING

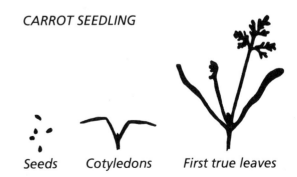

Seeds   *Cotyledons*   *First true leaves*

crack. After seedlings emerge, mulch with 5″–8″ of grass clippings or legume hay. Hand-pull weeds.

Feeding. Carrots benefit from applications of compost tea from emergence until the tops are 5″–8″ high. Apply 1 cup per foot of row every 10–14 days.

Problem Prevention

When preparing soil, apply parasitic nematodes to the soil. Used before planting, parasitic nematodes help to prevent and control problems with root knot nematodes, carrot weevils, carrot rust flies, wireworms, and other pests.

Delay planting until early summer. Carrot rust flies lay their eggs on carrots planted early in the season; their larvae tunnel into the roots. Plant after June 1 in most areas.

After planting, cover the seedbed with row cover. Protect early carrot plantings from carrot rust flies and carrot weevils by keeping adults from laying eggs atop your seedbed.

During the growing season, keep roots covered. Exposure to light makes carrots bitter and turns their shoulders green. Keep about 2″ of soil or mulch over the roots.

In fall, mulch before cold weather. Freezing soil can crack roots and leave them soft and water-soaked. Apply 8″–12″ of mulch in fall.

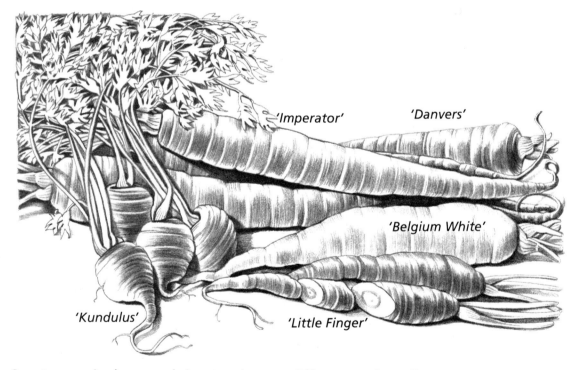

Carrots come in shapes and sizes to suit many different garden soils. Long, tapered roots need deep, loose soil to attain their classic carrot shape. Try short, ball-shaped or blocky cultivars in shallow, heavy, or rocky soil.

Gathering the Harvest

Harvest carrots when they are large enough to use. Pull a few to check their size. Loosen the soil with a fork, then gently pull them out of the ground. Watering before you harvest makes pulling easier. Brush off excess soil and twist off the tops. Refrigerate unbruised carrots, or layer them in moist sand or sawdust and store them in a root cellar for up to four months. You may also can, freeze, or dry carrots.

Extending the Season

Extend your harvest into the winter months by mulching the bed with 8″–12″ of grass clippings or legume hay before the ground freezes. Add a marker to help you find your crop under snow.

Container Growing

Carrots grow well in containers, where they can have optimum soil conditions. Short or ball-shaped cultivars need less rooting space.

Propagation

Carrots are insect-pollinated, and their cultivars cross-pollinate freely with each other and with Queen-Anne's-lace (*Daucus carota* var. *carota*). Separate blooming carrots and Queen-Anne's-lace by at least a mile, or cage plants to exclude insects. ✳

CAULIFLOWER

Brassica oleracea, Botrytis group. Cruciferae. Biennial grown as an annual.

The sweet, mild taste of garden-fresh cauliflower is more than worth the extra effort it takes to grow. With some special attention and good weather conditions, this cool-season crop will reward you with large, tightly packed flower heads (also known as curds). Cauliflower is a favorite for eating raw with dips. It's also great steamed, stir-fried, curried, or baked in a casserole.

Selecting plants. You can choose from white-, purple-, and even green-headed cauliflower. Purple cauliflower tastes more like broccoli and turns green when cooked. Most cultivars of white-headed cauliflower need to be protected from the sun to produce their snowy white curds; a few cultivars are self-blanching. If you've had bad luck with your cauliflower crop in the past, look for cultivars that are tolerant to problems such as high temperatures, hollow stem, and purple tinge.

Site. Cauliflower grows best in full sun; partial shade will reduce head size. Careful rotations are important to prevent pest and disease problems; avoid planting cauliflower and related cabbage-family crops where brassicas have grown in the last three years.

Soil. Cauliflower needs soil rich in organic matter and nutrients. The ideal pH range is 6.0–6.8, though it can tolerate a pH as high as 7.4. Before planting, turn under a legume cover crop or work in 30 pounds of compost per 100 square feet. Loosen the soil to a depth of at least 8″.

How much to plant. One gram of seed contains about 200 seeds; this is enough to direct-sow 25′ or start 150–180 plants. Figure on three to five plants per person. A single good-size head can weigh over 2 pounds.

Spacing. For spring plantings, allow 15″–18″ between plants; for fall plantings, 1½′–2′. Leave 2′–3′ between rows.

Days to maturity. Heads are ready 50–125 days from transplanting.

Planting and growing. For spring crops, start plants indoors ten weeks before the last expected frost. Set them out after four to five weeks, when the soil temperature is at least 50°F. For fall crops (or winter crops in the South), you can direct-sow seed, or start plants in flats or a seedbed and then transplant.

Cauliflower requires a steady supply of moisture. Mulching with legume hay, grass clippings, or straw helps preserve moisture and keeps soil cooler. Feed with a kelp-and-fish-emulsion mixture (1 tablespoon of kelp and 1 tablespoon of fish emulsion per gallon of water) at transplanting and once a week for three weeks. Apply 1 cup per plant. See the Cabbage entry for more details on seedling care, transplanting, and general plant care.

Unless you've chosen self-blanching cultivars, you'll need to blanch your cauliflowers to produce those pure white curds. Wait until the developing head reaches 2″ in diameter and starts pushing through the inward-curving leaves that cover it. Then use straw, raffia, or twine to tie the outer leaves loosely over the head. The head will reach harvestable size in 2–14 days, depending on the temperature. Purple and green cauliflower do not need blanching before harvest.

More than any other vegetable, cauliflower is sensitive to weather conditions. Heat can cause browning of curds or stem rot. Dry spells or extremes of cold or heat can cause bolting (premature flowering), buttoning (formation of tiny heads), or ricy curds (separation of heads into small ricelike sections). Drastic fluc-

tuations in temperature can cause leaves to grow among the curds. Some gardeners start a few cauliflower plants every week, hoping that at least some will get the right weather conditions.

Brown or discolored curds may be a sign of boron deficiency. Insufficient phosphorus can cause some white heads to become tinged with purple. For details on preventing these and other problems, see the Cabbage entry.

Harvesting. Pick cauliflower when the heads are full, but before the curds begin to separate. Cut through the stem under the head, leaving a few "wrapper" leaves for protection. Curds bruise easily, so handle with care.

Before preparing or storing cauliflower, soak it in salt water for 30 minutes to drive out any unnoticed cabbageworms that may be lurking in the heads. Cauliflower will keep for about a week in the refrigerator if wrapped in plastic. It does not store well in a root cellar. The best way to store cauliflower for longer periods is to blanch and freeze it.

Extending the season. For an early crop, you can start plants indoors. Covering plants with floating row cover may protect them from mild frosts in the fall. Self-blanching cultivars with good leaf coverage of the head will withstand moderate frosts. If heads freeze, they are still edible, as long as you harvest them before they thaw.

Fall and winter care. After harvest, pull out plants with their roots and compost them.

Propagation. To get your cauliflower to produce seeds, you must either have a very long growing season or expose the cauliflower to temperatures under 45°F for one to two months. Seeds last four years in storage. ✽

CELERY

Apium graveolens var. *dulce*. Umbelliferae.
Biennial grown as an annual.

Given plenty of moisture, nutrients, and time to grow, celery produces crisp, flavorful leafstalks for use in everything from salads to soups and casseroles. The leaves add zest to soups and are more nutritious than their stalks. And celery seeds produce delicious sprouts.

Selecting plants. Celery cultivars offer either traditional green stalks or so-called self-blanching golden stalks; both types have similar growing requirements. Avoid problems by choosing blight- and disease-resistant cultivars.

Site. Celery thrives in cool, moist locations. It tolerates light shade better than most crops but should receive at least one-half day of sun. Celery grown in the shade tends to be lanky and strong flavored. A heavy feeder, celery does well planted after legumes.

Soil. Moist, richly organic loam soil with a pH in the range of 6.0–6.8 is best for celery. Work in 10–20 pounds of compost per 100 square feet and cultivate to a depth of about 4″. Prepare traditional flat rows or raised beds no more than 6″ high for planting. Celery needs lots of moisture and withstands water-logged conditions better than most crops. Leave the soil surface rough and cover with a layer of grass clippings or legume hay. To give your celery an extra boost, apply blood meal (½ pound for every 10′ of row) before mulching. See "Custom Care for Leafy Crops" on page 60.

How much to plant. Plant approximately six plants for every person in your family. One seed packet generally produces more than any one family will need—400 plants or more.

Spacing. Space rows 18″–40″ apart and allow 6″–12″ between plants.

Days to maturity. Plants are ready to harvest 90–120 days after transplanting.

Planting and growing. Celery requires a long growing season and is normally grown from seedlings set out in the spring. Buy transplants from your local nursery, or start seeds 70–84 days before you intend to transplant. To speed germination and prevent problems with blight, presoak seeds in compost tea. Seeds may take two to three weeks to germinate. Give seedlings a bright location (out of direct sunlight) where nighttime temperatures are 60°–65°F and daytime temperatures are 65°–75°F. Don't let them dry out!

When plants are 5″–6″ tall, harden them off, then set them out. You can transplant one to two weeks before the last expected frost, as long as both the air and soil are at least 40°F. Air temperatures of 75°F or above can slow the growth rate of mature plants and cause leaf edges to turn brown. Celery needs plenty of water during the growing season to remain tender and flavorful. Mulch with 8″–10″ of legume hay or grass clippings to keep the soil cool and moist. Weed gently to avoid damaging celery's shallow roots.

Satisfy celery's need for nutrition with a solution of 1 tablespoon of fish emulsion and 2 tablespoons of kelp extract in 1 gallon of water. Drench each plant with ½ cup of the solution at transplanting time and every week thereafter until plants are 6″–8″ tall. Blanch celery plants to produce longer, pale, mild-flavored stalks. Golden cultivars are described

CELERY SEEDLING

Seeds   Cotyledons   First true leaves

as self-blanching, but they may also be blanched for improved flavor and tenderness. (See "Blanching Celery" on this page for details.)

Rotate celery plantings to avoid most disease problems. Handpick hungry caterpillars.

Harvesting. Begin harvesting celery when the stalks are large enough to use, up until the first frost. Cut individual stalks as needed, beginning with the outer ones, or cut the root of the plant just below the crown. Stalks keep for several weeks in plastic bags in the refrigerator. If they start to wilt, refrigerate them in a container of cold water. To store celery for a few months, put the plants in a box, mound moist sand or soil around the roots, and keep in a cool, humid, dark place.

Extending the season. Mulch plants thickly to continue your harvest into the winter. In the South, grow celery as a winter crop.

Propagation. Insects pollinate this carrot relative, which can cross with other celery cultivars and also with celeriac. But cross-pollination rarely poses a problem for home

> ## BLANCHING CELERY
>
> Although blanching destroys certain nutrients in celery, many people prefer the milder taste and increased tenderness that result from this procedure. To blanch, simply mound soil or mulch up around the stalks as they lengthen so that light can't reach them. (Keep the leaves exposed.) You can also keep a row of them out of the sun by placing boards vertically on either side of the plants and securing them with stakes.

gardeners, since it's unusual to have more than one cultivar flowering at a time.

Friends and relatives. For a taste treat, try celeriac (*Apium graveolens* var. *rapaceum*). Its large turniplike root is eaten raw or cooked. A relatively trouble-free crop, celeriac needs constant moisture for healthy growth. ✳

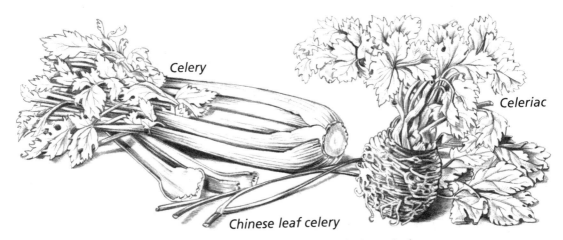

Celery

Celeriac

Chinese leaf celery

Celery is grown for its long, crunchy leafstalks. Its close relative celeriac produces a large, celery-flavored root. Chinese celery grows like common celery but has narrow, stronger-flavored stalks.

CHARD

Beta vulgaris, Cicla group. Chenopodiaceae.
Biennial grown as an annual.

This prolific relative of the beet is also known as Swiss chard, perpetual spinach, and leaf or spinach beet. Its succulent, mild-flavored leaves can either be eaten raw or cooked like spinach.

Selecting plants. Some chard cultivars have white stalks and veins; others feature bright red veins and stems or entirely red leaves.

Site. Chard grows best in full sun but tolerates partial shade.

Soil. Easy to grow in most soils, chard prefers rich, well-drained soil and a pH of 6.0–6.8.

How much to plant. Grow three to five plants for each chard consumer in your household.

Spacing. Leave 5″–8″ between plants in rows 1½′ apart.

Days to maturity. Chard matures in 50–65 days from seed.

Planting and growing. Make your first planting two to four weeks before the last expected frost; sow successive plantings until late summer. Direct-sow seeds ½″ deep and 1″–3″ apart. When plants are 6″–8″ tall, thin to 5″–8″ apart. Chard bears light frost and extreme temperatures better than most greens.

Harvesting. Pick outer leaves as soon as they are large enough; inner leaves will continue to grow. Refrigerate for up to two weeks.

Extending the season. After the first light frost, use row cover to extend the harvest into winter. Grow as a winter crop in mild areas.

Container growing. Compact, fast-growing chard makes a fine container crop.

Propagation. Chard cultivars cross-pollinate with one another and also with beets. Keep seed pure by having only one cultivar in flower at a time. ✳

CHERRY

Prunus spp. Rosaceae. Deciduous tree.
Zones 4–9.

Cherries have been cultivated since the dawn of civilization, but only in the past few hundred years have there been any deliberate efforts to improve them. Although there are many native species, cultivated cherries are Old World fruits that originated in western Asia. The familiar 'Bing' and 'Lambert' sweet cherries trace their lineage back to a load of seedling cherry trees brought from Iowa by ox cart to Milwaukie, Oregon, in the nineteenth century. Many of today's cultivars trace back to those two cultivars.

Tart cherries and sweet cherries differ not only in fruit flavor but also in tree habit. Sweet cherry (*Prunus avium*) is a naturally large tree, somewhat finicky about environmental conditions. It does not tolerate climates where winters are frigid (it is hardy to Zone 5), or where summers are hot or rainy. Tart cherries (*P. cerasus*) are small, spreading trees and much more tolerant of cold winters (it is hardy to Zone 4) and hot and wet summers. Duke cherry (*P. × effusus*) is more commonly cultivated in Europe and is probably a natural hybrid between sweet and tart cherry. In fruit flavor and tree shape, Duke cherries are intermediate to sweet and tart cherries, although they're generally less productive.

Thoroughly ripe cherries—even tart cher-

CHERRY

Site: Full sun with good air circulation and not prone to late-spring frosts.

Soil: Tart cherry tolerates many soil types; sweet cherry needs deep, well-drained soil. A pH of 6.0–6.8 is ideal.

Spacing: Standard sweet cherries: 20'–30' apart. Standard tart cherries: 15'–20' apart. Dwarf cherries: 8'–12' apart.

Seasons to bearing: Two to seven years.

ries, if you let them soften on the tree—are delicious fresh. The flavor of fresh cherry pie needs no further description. You may also dry, freeze, or can any cherries.

Planning

Selecting plants. Choose a one-year-old sweet cherry tree ½"–¾" in diameter and 4'–5' tall with one to three branches. Choose two-year-old tart cherry trees the same size.

Most cultivars of sweet cherry need cross-pollination. Not all cultivars are compatible, so check with your nursery for which ones you need. A few sweet cherries, such as 'Garden Bing' and 'Stella', are self-fruitful. Tart cherries are self-fruitful. Most Duke cherries need cross-pollination from a late-blooming sweet cherry such as 'Hudson'.

'Windsor' sweet cherry and 'North Star' tart cherry resist brown rot. Sweet cherries are prone to cracking, so if your springs are rainy or your summers are humid, choose a soft-flesh, noncracking cultivar. Bigarreau (firm-fleshed) types are more prone to cracking than guigne (soft-fleshed) types. Tart cherries of the amarelle or Kentish type, such as 'Meteor' and 'Montmorency', have light-colored flesh and colorless juice. Morello or griotte types, such as 'Northstar', have red juice and darker flesh. If birds are a problem, try a yellow-fruited sweet cherry cultivar or some of the new late-summer-bearing bush cherries such as 'Jan' and 'Joy', which bear tart-type fruit.

Sweet cherries are grafted onto seedling rootstocks. 'Mazzard' is a good rootstock for heavier, wetter soil. 'Mahaleb' is better for light soil and droughty conditions. If you do not have space for a full-size tree, consider planting a tart cherry or a dwarf sweet cherry. Dwarf trees may be either genetic dwarfs (cultivars that are naturally dwarf) or full-size cultivars grafted to a dwarfing rootstock such as 'Colt'.

Selecting a site. Cherries need full sunlight. Sweet cherry blossoms open early, so the ideal site is a north-facing slope. Avoid sites near wild chokecherries (*P. virginiana*), as those trees can harbor and spread viral diseases to cultivated cherries.

When to plant. Where winters are mild, plant in fall. Otherwise, plant in spring.

Spacing. Full-size sweet cherry trees need 20'–30' of space. Tart cherry trees need 15'–20' of space, and dwarf trees need 8'–12' of space.

For a greater harvest. Cherry trees do well in raised beds or individual hills. Birds love to eat cherries. The surest way to frustrate birds is to net or cage your entire tree.

Soil Preparation

Cherry trees prefer a moderately rich soil with a pH of 6.0–6.8. Good drainage is essential for sweet cherries. For information on soil preparation, see "Custom Care for Tree Fruits" on page 61.

Planting

Plant cherry trees as you would other fruit trees. See "Perennial Crops" on page 111.

Growing Guidelines

Water and mulch. Cherry trees grow best with an even supply of moisture through the growing season, especially up until harvest. Maintain a thick, organic mulch.

Feeding. Spread 5–10 pounds of compost out to the drip line in late winter every year. Shoots on a well-nourished, young cherry tree should grow about 1½′ in a season; those on a mature, bearing tree should grow about 8″. Do not expect this much growth from dwarf trees. If growth is less than this, increase the amount of fertilizer the following year. Don't fertilize after midsummer or the new growth may not harden before winter.

Training. Train sweet cherry trees to a modified central leader form. When the leader is 6′ high, cut it back to a weak side branch. Prune sweet cherry trees as little as possible. Mature sweet cherry trees and genetic dwarfs need little pruning. See "Pruning Trees" on page 142 for directions.

Tart cherries are naturally spreading. Train them to an open center form.

Thinning. Cherries do not need thinning.

Problem Prevention

Cherries share many of the same problems as peaches. See "Problem Prevention" on page 438 for general guidelines. (Ignore control for peach leaf curl.) Cherries are also bothered by a few problems that rarely affect peaches, including black knot, cherry leaf spot, cracking, black cherry aphids, and cherry fruit flies. If necessary, add the following steps to the routine described in the Peach entry.

In late winter, prune out diseased branches. Watch for black knot in addition to diseases described for peach trees. Affected branches have swollen, knobby black galls.

As buds swell in spring, spray lime-sulfur. In addition to the diseases listed for peach, if cherry leaf spot or black knot were a problem last year, spray now. If black knot was a problem last year, spray again after one week.

Cherry leaf spot causes small, circular purple spots on leaves. The centers of the spots eventually drop out, leaving a little hole. Leaves may yellow and drop early, and trees may eventually die. Spray sulfur every 10–21 days until leaf drop if weather is wet or humid and if the spots are spreading.

Don't spray lime-sulfur between petal-fall and harvest. Use only sulfur because lime-sulfur discolors cherry fruit. Once fruit is harvested, you can use lime-sulfur again.

After fruit set, spray calcium. If your sweet cherries tend to crack, spray chelated calcium three times, starting when the fruits are about ¼″ and repeating every 10–14 days.

In early summer, watch for aphids. Look for sticky honeydew or tiny, black insects and black, sooty mold on leaves. If there aren't many, ignore them. If infestation is severe, spray insecticidal soap. Encourage natural predators by growing nectar-producing flowers such as dill and buckwheat near your trees.

When nights are cool and days are warm, watch out for powdery mildew. This disease results in twisted leaves and a powdery coating on leaves and fruits. Control with sulfur sprays.

A few weeks after bloom, hang traps for cherry fruit fly maggots. Cherry fruit fly larvae burrow into cherry fruits and feed near the stone. Infested fruits are shrunken and drop early. Use the same traps you use for apple maggots; see "Five Weeks after Bloom, Hang Apple Maggot Traps" on page 277 for details. If they were a severe problem last year, spray rotenone when the first adults are trapped or as the fruit begins to color.

As fruit begins to color, net trees. Birds relish cherries and can clean off a tree in next to no time. Drape netting over the tree and fasten the edges so no birds can sneak in, or build a netting-covered cage with a door for you to go in and out of instead. Mylar bird tape or scare balloons may reduce damage. Move them around every few days so the birds won't get used to them.

Gathering the Harvest

Determine when to harvest your cherries by waiting until they are fully colored, then sampling a few. Fruits will not ripen after harvest. Tart cherries for cooking can be picked firm or ripe. For best storage, leave the stem attached. Pick carefully to avoid damaging the spur, which will bear the following year's fruit. Do not delay picking cherries. When the weather is hot and muggy, the fruits ripen, then rot, quickly. Pick ripe fruits quickly if rain falls on them because the fruits absorb water through their skin and may crack.

Store fresh cherries at high humidity and near-freezing temperatures. Firm-fleshed sweet cherries will keep for up to three weeks; tart cherries will keep for up to one week.

Fall and Winter Care

See "Fall and Winter Care" on page 440 for details.

Container Growing

Choose naturally dwarf trees (such as genetic dwarf sweet cherries or 'Northstar' tart cherry) or trees grafted on dwarfing rootstocks. Use a container at least 1½' deep and wide. Once your plant reaches full size, repot every year just before growth commences in spring, pruning back the roots and top at that time. In very cold areas, protect the roots in winter as shown in the illustration on page 240.

Propagation

Propagate cherries by bud grafting. See Chapter 11 for details. ✳

❧ FRIENDS & RELATIVES ❧

CHERRY

Because of their tolerance for both drought and cold, western sand cherry (*Prunus besseyi*) and Nanking cherry (*P. tomentosa*) are grown for their fruit in areas where sweet and tart cherries won't bear reliably. Sand cherries are used mostly for jellies and jams rather than for fresh eating. Nanking cherries are good for both. Sand cherry is used as a dwarfing rootstock for stone fruits and has been hybridized with plums to produce cold-resistant hybrid plums and so-called cherry-plums. For more information on cold-resistant plums, see the Plum entry.

CHESTNUT

Castanea spp. Fagaceae. Deciduous tree.
Zones 5–8.

Perhaps no other tree played as important a part in the history of the United States as the American chestnut (*Castanea dentata*). Its sweet, high-energy nuts fed wildlife, livestock, and people. Its timbers were raw materials for furniture, fences, barns, and houses. Tragically, by the 1940s, a fungal disease accidentally introduced from China had spread throughout the American chestnut's natural range, from Maine to Florida and westward to the Ohio River Valley, virtually eliminating the species.

The Chinese chestnut (*C. mollissima*) is resistant to the fungus, so most chestnut trees planted today are Chinese-American hybrids. Both the European chestnut (*C. sativa*) and American chestnut can survive only outside of the American chestnut's natural range in areas where the blight hasn't spread. The chinquapin (*C. pumila*), a small chestnut native to the eastern United States, is also susceptible to the blight, but its fast-growing bush habit lets it bear before its branches succumb to the disease.

Selecting plants. Unless you live in an isolated area where blight isn't a problem, choose blight-resistant cultivars.

Site. Choose an airy, open spot. Avoid frost pockets.

Soil. Chestnuts tolerate a wide range of soils, but it should be deep, fertile, and well-drained, with an acid pH (5.5–6.0).

How much to plant. Chestnut trees are not self-fruitful, so you'll need at least two trees of different cultivars for pollination to occur. Pollination occurs by wind, so plant

The multispined husks of Chinese chestnuts have an unmistakable look and feel. They burst open to reveal glossy, smooth nuts within. Chinese chestnut trees also double as ornamental landscape plants, with their dense, dark green foliage and graceful catkins (male flowers).

your trees no more than 200' apart. A ten-year-old tree can produce 60 pounds of nuts, and yields increase as the tree matures.

Spacing. Chestnuts do best with full sun, so plant them 20'–40' apart.

Seasons to bearing. Grafted chestnut trees will begin to bear in three to four years from transplanting.

Planting and growing. Plant chestnut trees as you would any tree. See "Perennial Crops" on page 111 for directions. Water well daily for the first few days after planting. Continue to water weekly during the growing season for the first several years whenever rain is scarce. Keep the area beneath the tree well-weeded, or mulch with wood chips or any mix of organic matter. To avoid excessive early growth that can be winter-killed, wait until the tree's second year to fertilize. Spread a thin layer of well-rotted manure or a blended organic fertilizer with a good nitrogen value beneath the tree once or twice a year in spring.

The chestnut gall wasp, a new threat accidentally imported from Asia, is spreading throughout the South. It lays its eggs inside chestnut buds, which then swell into galls. Prune and destroy these infested shoots as soon as galls begin to form.

Harvesting. Pick up fallen chestnuts daily to prevent the chestnut weevil from laying its eggs inside the smooth shell. Remove burrs, and spread the chestnuts in a dry place for five to ten days to cure. Discard any that have weevil grub exit holes. Store the nuts in containers in the freezer for up to one year.

Fall and winter care. Prune lightly in the first years, then prune annually in late winter to maintain an open, strong central leader shape with scaffold branches. Remove any dead wood. See "Pruning Trees" on page 142 for directions.

Propagation. You can create new trees by grafting cultivars onto seedling rootstocks grown from the same tree. ✷

CHICORY
Cichorium intybus. Compositae. Biennial grown as an annual.

Chicory is closely related to endive; see the Endive entry for culture. Loose-leaved chicories resemble dandelion leaves. Heading chicories are called radicchio. Roasted chicory roots make a coffee substitute. ✷

CHIVES
Allium schoenoprasum. Liliaceae. Perennial. Zones 3–10.

Most gardeners grow chives for the mild, onion-flavored leaves, although the plants also produce attractive and edible pink flowers in spring. Add the freshly snipped greens to any soup, salad, omelet, or vegetable dish. The flowers are wonderful in salads or vinegars. Chives lose their delicate flavor when cooked, so add them to recipes just before serving.

Selecting plants. 'Forescate' is a selection with ornamental rose pink flowers. For a change of pace, try garlic chives (*Allium tuberosum*), which have a hearty garlic zing.

Site. Chives require full sun. Shady, damp environments reduce plant vigor.

Soil. Plant chives in soil that drains well. Work a light application of aged compost into the soil before planting. Avoid heavy applications of nitrogen. Keep soil pH around 6.0.

How much to plant. Start with one to three clumps for two people. Chives will multiply quickly.

Spacing. Plant seedling clumps and divisions 5″–10″ apart.

Days to maturity. Begin snipping greens when they're about 6″ tall. Harvest lightly the first season.

Planting and growing. In late winter, broadcast seed in pots or trays indoors and cover with ¼″–½″ of growing medium. Seeds germinate within two to three weeks when kept at 60°–70°F. When seedlings are at least 2″ tall, use a knife to cut them into clumps 2″–4″ square. Transplant clumps outdoors in early spring as soon as the soil can be worked. In hot climates, plants benefit from an organic mulch in summer, but keep mulches away from the base of plants to avoid pest and disease problems. Divide every three years to keep clumps vigorous.

Harvesting. Throughout the growing season, use a sharp knife or scissors to cut foliage as needed, leaving at least 2″ of growth behind. Harvest blossoms at any stage.

To preserve chives for winter use, dry them in the microwave for best results. Place chopped greens on microwave-safe paper towels, then turn the oven on high for two minutes. Repeat until the greens are crisp and dry. Store in airtight containers. Chives freeze poorly.

Extending the season. In the fall, trick potted plants into dormancy by allowing them to freeze outdoors for three to four months, then bring them inside to begin new growth. Keep chives near a sunny window, or place the tops several inches below plant growth lights.

Fall and winter care. Stop harvesting at least three weeks before frosts begin, then prune away dead leaves and blossoms.

Container growing. In pots with drainage holes, plant clumps of chives in growing medium amended with compost. Keep the soil moist.

Propagation. Harvest seed heads as soon as they mature and remove the seeds or divide established clumps. *

COLLARD

Brassica oleracea, Acephala group. Cruciferae. Biennial grown as an annual.

Although commonly associated with southern gardens, collards thrive in cool weather, and their sweetness increases after a frost. This cabbage relative is great cooked for greens or in stir-fries.

Selecting plants. Open-pollinated and hybrid cultivars are available. Hybrids mature earlier and tend to be more productive.

Site. Collards prefer full sun.

Soil. Collards grow best in loose, rich soil with a pH of 5.5–6.8 and a steady supply of moisture. Before planting, incorporate a legume cover crop or 30 pounds of compost per 100 square feet.

How much to plant. One packet of seeds will sow approximately 100′ of row. Plan on five to ten plants or 4′–6′ of row per person.

Spacing. Allow 2′ between plants and 2′–3′ between rows.

Days to maturity. Collards are ready to harvest around 60 days from transplanting. Thinnings are ready earlier.

Planting and growing. Set out plants or direct-sow seeds when the soil temperature reaches 50°F. For complete growing guidelines and problem prevention, see the Cabbage entry.

Harvesting. Start picking when the lowest leaves are 8″–12″ long. Harvest individual leaves as needed from the bottom up throughout the season.

Extending the season. For an early crop, start indoors ten weeks before the last expected frost.

Fall and winter care. Collards withstand temperatures down to 20°F. In you live in a mild-winter climate, you can harvest collards all winter. When the harvest is over, pull out the plants and compost them.

Propagation. See the Cabbage entry for details on propagation and seed saving. ✻

CORN
Zea mays. Gramineae. Annual.

A native American crop, corn, or maize, was cultivated some 4,000 years before Europeans set foot in the New World. While livestock eat most of the corn produced in the United States, home gardeners know that sweet corn (*Zea mays* var. *rugosa*) is this crop's crowning glory. The flavor of a fresh-picked ear, delivered directly to a pot of boiling water, is deemed worthy of all of the space, water, fertilization, and care needed to produce it. And it's good for you, too. Corn is a source of vitamins A and B. The corn-and-beans combination known as succotash provides nearly complete protein.

Other varieties of this versatile crop are grown for their dry kernels. Learn more about popcorn (*Z. mays* var. *praecox*) in "Friends and Relatives" on page 339. Flour, cornmeal, and grits are made from dent corn (*Z. mays* var. *indentata*) and flint corn (*Z. mays* var. *indurata*). Dent and flint corns are grown the same way sweet corn is; see "Friends and Relatives" on page 339 for harvesting instructions.

Planning

Selecting plants. Most sweet corn is white, yellow, or bicolored (yellow and white) and is further divided into three major groups: standard, sugar-enhanced, and super-sweet. Standard cultivars do not contain any of the special genes that make modern corns taste so sweet. Standard hybrids such as 'Silver Queen' are still popular choices with home gardeners looking for traditional sweet corn flavor. Standard open-pollinated cultivars, including old familiar selections such as 'Golden Bantam', 'Country Gentleman', and 'Butter and Sugar', also offer traditional sweet corn flavor and the opportunity to save your own seed. Sugar-enhanced corn is sweeter and more tender than standard types, while super-sweet cultivars stay sugary for days after harvesting. When

---

❧ AT A GLANCE ❧
CORN

Site: Full sun; needs wind for pollination.

Soil: Rich, well-drained loam with a pH of 5.5–6.8; evenly moist but not wet.

How much to plant: 15–40 plants per person.

Spacing: 7″–15″ apart in rows 30″–42″ apart.

Days to maturity: 65–90 days from seed to harvest.

---

selecting corn cultivars for your garden, keep in mind that super-sweets can cross-pollinate with other non-super-sweet cultivars and types, resulting in starchy, tough kernels. Separate unlike types by time or space. To prevent disease problems, choose cultivars that tolerate or resist common corn diseases. Look for cultivars to suit the length of your growing season. For example, early-maturing cultivars are ideal for areas that have cold, damp springs. Dwarf cultivars produce 4"–5"-long ears and are ideal for small gardens.

When to plant. Plant early-season cultivars about two weeks after the last expected frost; mid-season corn goes in about seven to ten days later, as do late-season cultivars. Sow only if the soil temperature is at least 50°F and nighttime air temperatures are at least 40°F.

Corn germinates poorly in cool soil and does not tolerate frost. Many modern extra sweet hybrid types are especially sensitive to cool soil. Optimum growth occurs in 65°–75°F weather and increases up to 90°F but declines at temperatures of 100°F or above. In the fall, you can sow seeds nine to ten weeks before the first frost date, depending on the cultivar.

How much to plant. Each corn plant usually produces one or two ears. Since the germination rate for corn is only about 75 percent, sow three seeds for every plant you want to grow, then thin to the strongest seedling. For fresh use, grow at least 15 plants for each family member. Allow 30–40 plants per person for freezing or canning.

Spacing. Plant corn in rows spaced 2½'–3½' apart. Sow seeds every 7"–15" in the

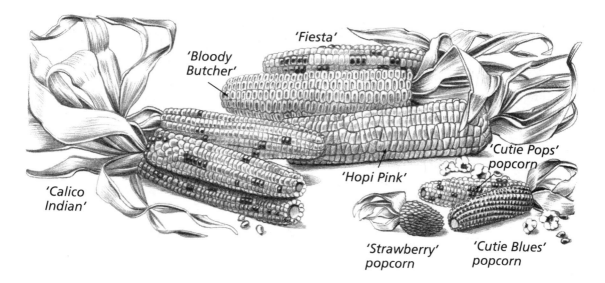

'Fiesta'
'Bloody Butcher'
'Cutie Pops' popcorn
'Hopi Pink'
'Calico Indian'
'Strawberry' popcorn
'Cutie Blues' popcorn

Dry corns offer kernel colors beyond the yellow and white of sweet corn. Grow red, blue, pink, and variegated ears of these dry corn crops for decorations, popcorn, or colorful cornmeal.

HAND-POLLINATING CORN

If you have only a small plot of corn, you may get ears with only a few kernels and a lot of gaps where a silk didn't get pollinated. To fill your corn's ears evenly and completely, try the following method: Choose a morning when the wind is calm. Look for several plants whose tassels are just beginning to shed pollen. Shake the tassels gently into a small paper bag to collect the pollen, then sprinkle the collected pollen onto the greenish silks of all of the developing ears of corn. Repeat this process once or twice over the next few days.

rows and thin plants to 15″ apart. (You can space rows of dwarf cultivars as close as 2′ apart.) Plant several short rows to form a block to ensure complete pollination. To avoid cross-pollination, separate super-sweet corn from other types of corn by staggering planting times or maturity dates so they will not be shedding pollen at the same time or by planting them 200–400 yards from one another.

Rotation. Rotate corn with other crops to prevent recurring pest or disease problems. Corn planted after alfalfa may suffer less wireworm damage, and the alfalfa improves the soil, as do beans and clover. Try growing pole beans with corn; the stalks provide support for the beans.

For a greater harvest. Plant early-, mid- and late-season cultivars to stretch your corn harvest over the longest possible time or make small plantings every three to four weeks. But don't try to squeeze in extra plants; corn that is planted too closely produces fewer ears. To ensure even pollination, hand-pollinate your crop. (See "Hand-Pollinating Corn" on this page for instructions.) Corn may benefit from an interplanting of soil-enriching legumes, such as peas or beans. And a corn–bean combination may also discourage fall armyworms on corn and leafhoppers on beans. Winter squash will grow amid cornstalks, too, and it helps to suppress weeds.

Soil Preparation

Corn grows best in rich, moist, but well-drained loam soil with a pH of 5.5–6.8. If your soil drains poorly, plant your crop in raised beds. To prepare the soil, work in compost at a rate of 20–30 pounds per 100 square feet. Corn is a heavy feeder and needs an ample supply of nutrients—especially nitrogen—for healthy growth. See "Custom Care for Fruit Crops" on page 58 for sources of readily available nutrients. Cultivate the soil to a depth of 4″ or so to accommodate corn's relatively shallow root system. Prepare your rows and cover the bed with clear plastic for two to four weeks before planting to help warm the soil for early crops. When you are ready to sow the seeds, remove the plastic.

Planting Outdoors

Sowing seeds. To aid germination and prevent disease, soak corn seeds for 15 minutes in compost tea. (Presoaking is especially important for super-sweet corn, which needs more moisture than the other types.) Direct-sow seeds 1″–2″ deep, placing three seeds every 7″–15″. Corn seeds normally germinate in seven to ten days.

Growing Guidelines

Thinning seedlings. Thin plants when they are 2"–4" tall. To avoid damaging surrounding plants, thin by cutting extra seedlings at ground level. Leave 15" between standard-size plants and 7" between dwarf cultivars.

Water and mulch. Keep the soil evenly moist but not wet. Never let young plants dry out, and supply plenty of water when tassels begin to appear. Water plants from below; water sprayed over plants can wash the pollen away. To control weeds and help conserve moisture, mulch with straw or legume hay. Or plant a cover crop of subterranean clover, white clover, or sweet clover between the rows and keep it mowed.

Feeding. Corn benefits from periodic fertilization. When leaves first emerge, drench the roots of each plant with ½ cup of compost tea; repeat weekly for three to four weeks. Just before the plants silk, spray with kelp extract (2 tablespoons per gallon of water).

Problem Prevention

Select resistant cultivars. Stop problems before they start by choosing cultivars that resist or tolerate diseases such as maize dwarf mosaic, bacterial wilt, northern or southern corn leaf blight, rust, and corn smut.

Avoid planting corn where grass has grown recently. Many corn pests dwell in sod and may feast on your corn seed and seedlings.

Before planting, apply parasitic nematodes to the soil. Keep wireworms, seedcorn beetles, and other soil-dwelling pests in check.

Plant early but only if the soil is warm. Problems with corn earworms tend to increase as the season progresses, so the earlier you plant, the better. However, corn seeds germinate poorly in cool soil and are more likely to suffer from rotting and insect damage, so wait to sow seeds until the soil temperature reaches at least 50°F.

At planting, plant corn in a block instead of a few long rows. Block planting promotes even pollination, necessary for well-filled ears of corn.

After planting, cover the area with a row cover. Discourage pests from feeding or laying eggs on young corn. Cover the area loosely with one large piece of row cover so that the corn has plenty of room to grow. Secure the extra row cover so that the wind doesn't blow it away. Loosen extra fabric as the corn gets taller. To allow pollination, remove the cover when tassels form.

When plants emerge, mulch to control weeds growing near the stalks. Johnsongrass and other weeds can be a breeding ground for maize dwarf mosaic. They also compete for water and nutrients that are essential to corn's growth.

When plants emerge, put cutworm collars around plants. If you have a small planting, this is the easiest way to deter cutworms.

CORN SEEDLING

Seeds   *Cotyledon*   *First true leaves*

When plants emerge, spray with an antitranspirant. If you've had problems with rust in the past, apply an antitranspirant every few weeks as a preventive measure. Stop when plants begin to show silk.

When plants are 1′ tall, hang phero-mone traps. (If your plants are covered with floating row cover, hang traps when you remove the cover.) Pheromone traps can help determine when adult moths of corn earworms,

European corn borers, or fall armyworms appear in your area. Check traps every few days. When any of these moths are caught, begin checking your corn every two to three days for signs of larvae feeding. If any of the upright, topmost leaves, or later the ears themselves, have feeding holes, spray plants (don't forget the undersides) with *Bacillus thuringiensis* var. *kurstaki* (BTK) to prevent further injury. Reapply weekly. If worms were a big problem last year, spray plants with ryania or a commercial rotenone/pyrethrin mix as soon as the first moth is caught.

When silks appear, apply BTK. Sprinkle granular *Bacillus thuringiensis* var. *kurstaki* (BTK) on the silks as soon as they emerge. To slow worm activity once they make it into the ears, apply a few drops of mineral oil to the drying silks or inject the tip of the ear with parasitic nematodes. If moths are active, spray plants in the evening to prevent the insects from laying eggs.

As ears ripen, discourage animal pests. Try using visual scare devices or scent repellents or surrounding your crop with a three-strand electric fence. A family dog is also handy for making hungry critters think twice before coming near your corn.

Gathering the Harvest

Sweet corn is ready to harvest 65–90 days after planting, depending on the cultivar. Normally, you can harvest corn in the same crop within a one- to three-week period. Look for brown, damp silks, and pick the ears when the kernels are plump and tender and when milky liquid spurts out when you poke them. (If the liquid is clear and watery, it's too soon; if there's no liquid, the kernels are too ripe.) Corn tastes

Tassel

Immature ear

Silk

Ripe ear

Harvest sweet corn when the silks are brown and damp to the touch. Press your thumbnail into a kernel; milky liquid is another sign of readiness.

best when it is picked in the late afternoon. Harvest by twisting the ear off of the plant in a downward direction. Because the sugar in corn quickly converts to starch, eat or preserve corn immediately after harvesting. The sugar-enhanced and super-sweets hold their sweetness and may be kept in the refrigerator a few days longer than standard cultivars. Freeze or can any surplus.

Extending the Season

If you live in an area with a short growing season, you can start seeds indoors about four weeks before planting time. Keep in mind, however, that transplanting corn is tricky. Grow your corn in peat pots to avoid damaging the roots, and check the soil temperature before you transplant the seedlings. To get a head start on sowing seeds outdoors, warm up the soil by covering it with clear plastic. To harvest up until the first expected frost, try planting early-, mid-, and late-season cultivars at the same time, or plant early types at two- or three-week intervals until early summer.

Propagation

All corn varieties and cultivars cross-pollinate, and corn pollen is windborne over distances of a quarter-mile or more. To maintain the purity of any seeds you save from your corn crop, your best bet is to isolate a few ears for seed production and to hand-pollinate them.

Common methods of isolation include separating corn crops by time—planting cultivars that tassel at different times—or by distance—leaving enough space between cultivars to limit crossing. However, only physical barriers can reliably keep your seed crop from crossing.

Choose about a dozen developing ears on which the silks have formed but not yet emerged. Pull down the leaf that partly surrounds the young ear, and cut off the leafy tip of the ear, leaving the cob intact. Cover the ear with a paper bag. The silks will grow out of the cut tip; pollinate them following the steps in "Hand-Pollinating Corn" on page 336. Keep the ears covered until the silks turn brown—you may have to replace the bags occasionally. When you remove the bags, mark your seed crop to prevent accidental harvesting. Let these ears dry on the stalks, then harvest and dry further indoors. ✻

❧ FRIENDS & RELATIVES ❧

CORN

Popcorn (*Zea mays* var. *praecox*) produces kernels that explode into a tasty, low-calorie snack when heated. Try growing your own popcorn from among the many available cultivars. Suit your tastes with white or yellow popcorn in standard (open-pollinated) or hybrid cultivars. Cultivars such as 'Japanese Hulless' feature hulls (the hard outer skins) that are more likely to shatter when the corn pops, leaving only tender kernels. Grow popcorn as you would sweet corn, but don't harvest the ears until after the first hard frost to allow the kernels to mature and harden. If the corn has not dried out completely by then, finish the drying process in a cool, dry spot inside. Store the kernels in tightly sealed jars.

CUCUMBER

Cucumis sativus. Cucurbitaceae. Annual.

Originally from India or southern Asia, cucumbers are among the most ancient of cultivated vegetable crops. Modern cultivars represent 3,000 years of breeding and combine characteristics of cucumber strains from China, Asia, and the Mediterranean. Cucumbers are most often used to add a cool crunch to salads, but they also may be pureed into cold soups or salad dressing, transformed into appetizers, pickled, or cooked briefly and served as a hot vegetable.

Planning

Selecting plants. There are many modern hybrids that produce bumper crops of cucumbers like those typically sold in stores. Long-fruited oriental cucumbers, slender Middle Eastern ones, ridged Armenians, or small-fruited pickling cultivars are also available.

Seed catalogs highlight three genetic traits to keep in mind: burpless, gynoecious, and nonbitter. Burpless cultivars do not form the chemical compounds that cause people to burp. Most burpless cultivars are long-fruited oriental types and produce impressive yields.

Gynoecious cucumbers produce all or mostly female flowers and tend to produce earlier than nongynoecious ones. To ensure fruit set, plant a few seeds of a normal cultivar usually included right in the seed packet to provide male flowers. Gynoecious cucumbers tend to set fruit all at once, so they're not the best choice for an extended harvest from a single planting.

Nonbitter cultivars don't form the bitter compounds that can develop in the fruits of drought-stressed plants. The absence of these chemicals in the leaves also deters cucumber beetles. See "Problem Prevention" on page 343 for more details about this pest.

Catalogs list slicing and pickling cucumbers separately, but young fruits of most slicing cucumbers may be pickled, and large fruits of picklers may be eaten fresh. If you plan to make a quantity of pickles, grow one cultivar for slicing and a small-fruited one for pickling.

When to plant. Cucumbers need warm soil and don't tolerate frost, so wait for warm spring days and soil temperatures above 60°F to plant. Schedule your last sowing of the season ten weeks before the first expected fall frost.

How much to plant. For fresh eating, three plants of a slicing cucumber will produce plenty for a family of four. Since cucumbers are perishable and produce heavily and all at once, plant two or three crops a year to spread out the harvest. Plant at least three plants for effective pollination. You'll want pick-

---

❧ AT A GLANCE ❧
CUCUMBERS

Site: Full sun, or full morning sun and less than three hours of afternoon shade.

Soil: Well-drained sand or clay loam with a pH of 6.0–6.8.

Spacing: Grow trellised plants, 6"–10" apart, or grow in 2'-wide hills spaced 4'–6' apart with three plants per hill.

Days to maturity: 55–70 days from seed, depending on the cultivar.

GROWING GREENHOUSE CUCUMBERS

In Europe, the most popular culinary cukes were developed for greenhouse culture and they bear mild, slender fruit. These don't require pollination to form fruit. When grown outdoors and pollinated by bees, they still taste good but often become curved and bumpy. They grow best outdoors if kept securely covered with floating row covers. Several seedless hybrids (called parthenocarpic) also don't need pollination. They'll produce well in a greenhouse, in walk-in plastic tunnels, or under row covers.

ling cucumbers to produce all at once: Grow 15–20 plants of picklers to make 24 pints of pickles.

Spacing. Grow long-fruited cucumbers on a trellis to help keep the fruits straight. Space trellised plants 6″–10″ apart. Short, blunt slicers and pickling cucumbers can be trellised or allowed to run on the ground. When planted in hills and allowed to run, grow three plants to a 2′ wide hill, with the hills spaced 6′

CUCUMBER SEEDLING

Seeds   *Cotyledons*   *First true leaves*

apart. Space hills planted with compact, bush-type cucumbers 4′ apart.

Rotation. Grow cucumbers after legumes or leafy greens but not after corn or other cucurbits. In many areas, cucumbers can be grown on a trellis that has been used earlier in the spring for peas.

For a greater harvest. Succession-plant so you always have young plants coming along; cucumber plants are highly productive but short-lived. Allow four weeks between your sowings.

Pick fruits as soon as they reach the size you want. Plants with overripe fruits on them may stop flowering prematurely. Short-vined cucumbers are ideal for intercropping with upright plants such as tomatoes and peppers.

Soil Preparation

Enrich the planting site with a 2″ layer of compost, rotted manure, or a blended organic fertilizer, working it in well. In soil that is low in organic matter, add leaf mold, rotted sawdust, or another humusy soil amendment to help the soil hold moisture. In acidic soil, choose a site that was recently limed, and sprinkle it with wood ashes.

Planting Indoors

Cucumbers may be direct-sown, or you can get an early start by planting some seeds indoors. In late summer, it may be easier to start seedlings indoors than outside in hot, dry soil.

Sowing seeds. Sow seeds indoors three weeks before you plan to set them out. Use 3″-wide peat pots or other individual containers. Fill containers to the top with any good potting soil. Plant seeds ½″ deep, using two to three seeds per container. Firm the soil gently with your fingers. Water well, then place in your sunniest windowsill or beneath a plant growth light in a warm, 75°F room.

Seedling care. Make sure seedlings receive very intense light, and keep them warm and constantly moist. A few days after germination, thin to one seedling per container. Water whenever the soil feels dry to the touch. Bottom watering is best. Begin adding a few drops of fish emulsion to the water after the first true leaf has unfurled.

Hardening off transplants. Begin hardening off seedlings soon after germination. Don't expose them to temperatures below 55°F. Drench the roots with weak compost tea the day before transplanting.

Setting out transplants. Set plants in prepared soil so that they are ½"–1" deeper than they grew in containers. Water well. If very hot

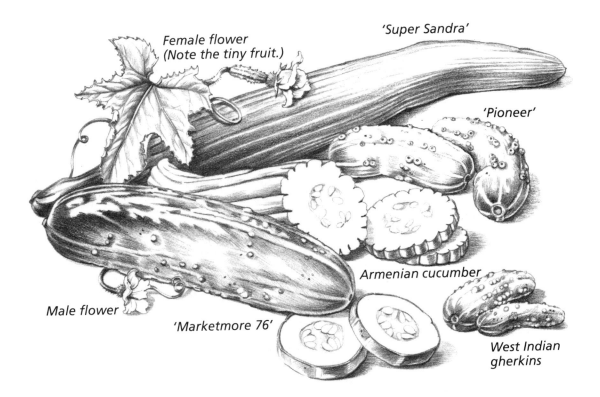

Female flower (Note the tiny fruit.)

'Super Sandra'

'Pioneer'

Male flower

'Marketmore 76'

Armenian cucumber

West Indian gherkins

Crisp, crunchy cucumbers grow on vines that trail across a garden bed or can be trained up stakes or a trellis. Whether you're growing short, fat pickling cukes or long, slender slicing types, remember that bees and other insects must carry pollen from male flowers to female flowers for fruit to be produced. European types are only seedless if not pollinated.

weather follows transplanting, cover the plants with floating row cover, boards held up with bricks, or some other shade cover for two days. You also can cover the plants with row covers immediately after transplanting.

Planting Outdoors

Sowing seeds. Sow seeds ½″ deep in prepared rows, hills, or beds. Sprinkle the seeded area lightly with compost, leaf mold, or other organic material to keep the soil from crusting. Water well, and keep the soil moist until the seeds germinate, usually within five to ten days. If soil temperatures are below 60°F, try covering the seeded soil with a sheet of clear plastic for three to five days, or until the first seedlings appear. When sowing a late crop in hot soil, soak the seeds in water for one day before planting. After sowing, cover the area with burlap, boards held up with bricks, or some other shade cover for two days. Shading keeps the soil cool and moist until germination and helps get your crop off to a fast start.

Growing Guidelines

Thinning seedlings. Thin seedlings to proper spacing when they have two or three true leaves.

Water and mulch. Cucumbers need plenty of water. For best quality, they should grow quickly and continuously. Drought stress can cause some cucumbers to taste bitter, especially at the stem end of the fruit. It's normal for leaves to wilt on hot days, but they should recover by nightfall. Prolonged wilting into the evening hours indicates water stress or disease problems.

Mulch trellised cucumbers with grass clippings or other organic material to suppress weeds and help hold soil moisture. Vines grown on the ground shade the soil, but mulch keeps fruits away from soilborne rots and insects. To mulch a large space quickly, cover the the soil with newspapers laid six sheets thick and held in place with straw or grass clippings.

Feeding. Cucumbers grown in improved soil don't need supplemental feeding. Spraying plants with a kelp-and-fish-emulsion product (1 tablespoon of kelp and 1 tablespoon of fish emulsion per gallon of water) while they are in full flower may improve fruit set and plant vigor. Yellowish green leaves or reddish leaf veins indicate a nutritional problem: Use a balanced organic fertilizer to correct it. See "Custom Care for Fruit Crops" on page 58 for more information.

Training. Be creative when trellising cucumbers. Use a fence, tomato cages, tripods made from three stakes or bamboo poles, or a trellis attached to sturdy posts. Tie vines to the trellis loosely with strips of soft cloth. You don't have to trellis every vine; some can scramble along the ground. Before new vines set fruit, gently move them to keep them in bounds.

Problem Prevention

Select resistant cultivars. Cultivars resistant to powdery mildew and numerous other diseases are available. No resistance is available for bacterial wilt, which causes plants to wilt and die suddenly. Cucumber beetles spread bacterial wilt and are less likely to feed on nonbitter cultivars, but spider mites *prefer* nonbitter cultivars.

At planting, scatter radish seed over the area. Where insect problems are severe, plant a few radish seeds in the area where cucumber vines will run. When allowed to flower, radishes seem to repel or confuse pests.

**After planting, cover the area with float-
ing row cover.** Cucumbers are much loved by
both cucumber beetles and squash bugs. Floating row covers can virtually eliminate problems with both pests; they are easiest to use
with compact, bush-type cultivars grown on
the ground. With some gynoecious cultivars,
the row covers may be left on until flowering is
well under way. When growing normal cultivars,
remove the covers when the first female blossoms appear.

Gathering the Harvest

Cucumbers mature very quickly. Pick them
often so the plants remain productive. Fruits
may become oversized if left on the vine even a
day too long. With slicing cucumbers, keep
fruits picked so that each plant has only two
or three growing fruits at a time.

To pick cucumbers, hold the stem with
one hand and pull the fruit with the other.
Harvest fruits when they are young and the
seeds inside haven't begun to harden. Gather
pickling cucumbers when they are very young
and the seeds are still quite soft. If possible,
harvest fruits in the morning, and refrigerate
immediately. Don't wash them until you're ready
to use them.

Extending the Season

In cool climates, prewarm prepared cucumber hills by covering them with black plastic
for two weeks before planting seeds or seedlings.
Use row covers or cloches at transplanting to
keep the plants warm during their first days in
the garden. Try growing your first sowing of
cucumbers under plastic tunnels. In fall, extend
the productive life of your plants by covering
them with a blanket during the first frost.

Fall and Winter Care

When early crops decline in midsummer,
compost the vines and plant a fall legume
such as bush beans. After your last crop in fall,

compost the vines, cultivate the soil, and sow a hardy cover crop or mulch the site.

Container Growing

Compact, bushy cultivars with small fruit are best for container culture. Water them frequently and feed every two weeks with manure tea or fish emulsion. In large containers, a tripod of small stakes helps increase yields and makes the crop look more attractive. You can underplant tomatoes or peppers with cucumbers.

Propagation

You can save seeds of nonhybrid cucumbers. Allow fruits from a disease-free plant to mature. Dark sores on stems and fruits indicate anthracnose; unusual angular crinkling of leaves indicates cucumber mosaic virus. Both diseases can be carried on seed. Ripe fruits are yellow and have hard rinds. Remove the hard-shelled seeds, wash in lukewarm water, and dry at room temperature on wax paper for a week. Store in airtight containers in a cool, dark place. ✳

CURRANT
Ribes spp. Saxifragaceae. Deciduous shrub. Zones 3–7.

Currants are small, often thorny shrubs that bear clusters of glistening, translucent fruit. See the Gooseberry entry for further description and culture. ✳

DILL
Anethum graveolens. Umbelliferae. Annual.

Dill is the herb to grow if you savor the taste of homemade pickles. Both the seeds and leaves are excellent flavoring ingredients for pickles, fish, cheese, potatoes, and salads. You can add the seeds at the beginning of cooking, but wait to add the fresh or dried foliage (often referred to as dill weed) until just before serving.

Selecting plants. Most dill produces many seeds and few leaves. Choose new cultivars like 'Dukat' or 'Fernleaf' for abundant foliage.

Site. Dill grows best in full sun.

Soil. Plants grow vigorously in almost any garden soil. Make sure the site has good drainage, and maintain soil pH around 6.0.

How much to plant. For two adults, start with a band of seeds 6″ wide and 3′–4′ long. Make successive sowings every two to three weeks until late summer. Frequent sowing ensures that you'll have plenty of foliage throughout the season, plus seeds at the right time for making pickles.

Spacing. If you're growing dill for seeds, thin seedlings to 6″–12″ apart in rows or beds. To encourage leafy, foliage-producing types, broadcast seeds lightly in bands or beds; thin seedlings to stand about 6″ apart.

Days to maturity. Begin harvesting leaves approximately eight to ten weeks after sowing.

Planting and growing. Sow the seeds outdoors in early spring or fall. Germination requires 21–25 days at 60°–70°F. Cover seeds lightly with soil, then keep the soil moist to encourage uniform germination.

Seed-producing types grow tall and may require staking. Caterpillars may be attracted to foliage; remove them by handpicking. Rabbits and woodchucks can destroy your dill patch overnight. Prevent their damage by covering small plants with floating row cover.

Harvesting. Harvest foliage throughout the season. Leave several inches of stem with at least one node for a second harvest. Harvest seeds when they are dry and light brown for best flavor. To collect the seeds, drop the seed heads into a paper bag as you harvest.

Avoid washing seeds or foliage. Wrap fresh foliage in paper or cloth toweling, then store in plastic bags in the refrigerator for up to one week. Air dry both seeds and foliage, or use a microwave to dry the leaves. Freeze leaves whole or chopped. A good way to preserve dill for use in pickle recipes is to add whole leaves to jars of vinegar; then use both the dill and the flavored vinegar to make the pickles.

Extending the season. Dill withstands light frosts. Plant it in cold frames, or cover garden plants with clear plastic row cover when heavy frosts arrive. Dill grows poorly indoors.

Container growing. Sow seeds directly into pots with a rich, well-draining medium. Place pots in full sun away from strong winds.

Propagation. Dill seeds are easy to save for next year's crop. ✳

Edible Flowers

Whether you sprinkle petals on top of a salad, make a flower-flavored sorbet, or garnish a plate with a single bloom, edible flowers add color and zest to any meal. Many common vegetables, fruits, and herbs bear edible flowers. Squash, pumpkins, dill, and chives are perhaps best known, but you also might want to try flowers of apples, elderberries, blackberries and other brambles, plus oranges and other citrus trees. Even the petals of sunflowers are edible. Edible herb blossoms include basil, fennel, garlic, marjoram, mint, mustard, oregano, rosemary, sage, and thyme.

Many ornamental plants also have edible flowers. Try using rose petals or tulip petals as a colorful addition to salads. Daylilies are a traditional part of Asian cooking. See the Asian Specialties entry for details. Bee balm (*Monarda didyma*) petals make a minty tea. Pinks (*Dianthus* spp.) have a mild, spicy taste. Violets (*Viola* spp.) are nice fresh or crystallized (coated with granulated sugar). The tiny red-purple flowers of the eastern redbud (*Cercis canadensis*) are edible, and so are the white, bell-shaped flowers of yuccas (*Yucca* spp.).

Many annual flowers are also edible. The starlike blue flowers of borage (*Borago officinalis*) have a mild cucumber flavor, as do the leaves. Try them floating in a cold soup. Cornflower (*Centaurea cyanus*) petals add blue, white, or pink color to salads. Johnny-jump-ups (*Viola tricolor*) and pansies (*V. × wittrockiana*) add a cheerful range of edible color all season long.

Sweet marigold (*Tagetes lucida*) flowers have a tarragon flavor, as one might expect from one of its other common names—Mexican tarragon. See the Mexican Specialties entry for other uses. Signet marigold (*T. tenuifolia*) flowers have a citrus flavor. The jewel-tone flowers of nasturtium (*Tropaeolum majus*) have a sweet, peppery flavor. Try them stuffed with a savory cheese spread. Nasturtium leaves are also very tasty. Try them in salad or float one in a chilled soup for a waterlily-leaf effect. Pot marigolds (*Calendula officinalis*) and safflowers (*Carthamus tinctorius*) are used as a substitute for saffron to color foods yellow. Snapdragon (*Antirrhinum majus*) flowers have a sweet flavor.

Harvest and Storage Tips

Harvest edible flowers just before you're ready to use them in a meal. The best blossoms are newly opened or have petals that are just beginning to unfold. Leave an inch or two of stem to make handling easy, and don't hold them by the petals.

Avoid washing the delicate petals. (A layer of mulch helps keep them clean in the garden.)

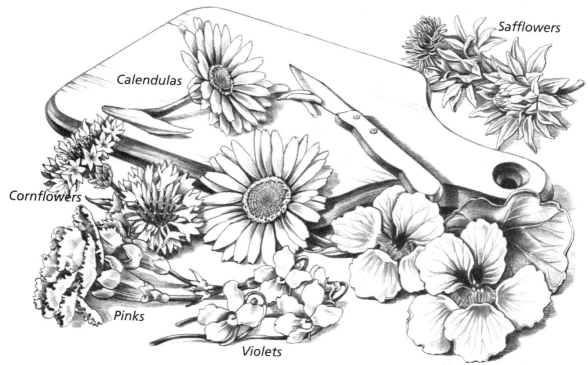

You can use edible flowers whole or remove the petals and sprinkle them atop a salad for added color. All edible flowers make attractive garnishes to decorate a serving tray or individual plate. Since edible flowers are delicate, add them to food just before serving.

If necessary, swish blossoms in cold water and allow them to air dry. Or use a towel to pat them gently.

You can store most edible flowers for several days if you pack them in layers between paper towels in containers in the refrigerator. Resealable plastic bags make great storage containers if you trap a bubble of air inside with the flowers to prevent the bag from collapsing. Or leave several inches of stem intact when you pick blossoms, then store them like cut flowers in a vase of water inside the refrigerator.

Use flowers whole, or pull the petals from their centers. Remove the stems before using, and add the petals or blossoms to foods just before serving. Since blossoms are tender and don't hold up to mixing, just toss them on top of foods. Large flowers, like squash or pumpkin blossoms, can be stuffed with dip, chicken salad, or pâté. Or shred them with your fingers before adding the bits of color to a salad.

Unsafe Blossoms

Don't try eating the flowers of just any plants: Many are poisonous. When you harvest blossoms, be absolutely sure you know what they are. Here's a list of some of the commonly grown plants with flowers that should *not* be consumed: cardinal flower (*Lobelia cardinalis*), crocus, daffodil, delphinium, foxglove (*Digitalis* spp.), iris, lily-of-the-valley, monkshood (*Aconitum* spp.), and nightshade-family members, including eggplant, Madagascar periwinkle (*Catharanthus roseus*), oleander (*Nerium oleander*), peppers, and tomatoes. If you buy flowers, make sure they have been grown for eating; florists' flowers are often heavily sprayed. ✳

EGGPLANT
Solanum melongena var. *esculentum.*
Solanaceae. Perennial grown as an annual.

A staple vegetable in Greek, Italian, and various Asian cuisines, eggplant deserves more respect from Americans as a delicious food crop. Homegrown eggplant, picked at its youthful perfection, is never bitter or tainted by gritty seeds. The plants are a bit less cold-tolerant than tomatoes, but otherwise are very easy to grow.

Selecting plants. Cultivars with light-colored skins often bear the sweetest fruits, but even dark-skinned eggplant is never bitter when properly grown. Fruit shape varies from round, bite-size baby types (which are ideal for grilling on skewers) to long, slender oriental types to the more familiar blocky fruits we think of as eggplants and large and small oblong fruits. Unusual striped cultivars are available. Explorers take note: Some heirlooms require short-day climates and do not grow well in the North.

Site. Eggplant prefers full sun.

Soil. Plant eggplant in moderately rich, well-drained loam. Eggplant is highly susceptible to Verticillium wilt, a soilborne disease. Where this disease is present, grow eggplant in sterilized potting soil in containers. (See "Container Growing" on the opposite page.)

How much to plant. Depending on the size of the fruits and your eggplant appetite, you will need two to three plants per person.

Spacing. Set plants 20″–24″ apart in raised beds or double rows 20″–24″ apart.

Days to maturity. Oriental and baby eggplants may bear fruit within 60 days after transplanting, but some cultivars need much longer—up to 100 days of warm weather.

Planting and growing. Start eggplant seeds indoors four to six weeks before the last spring frost is expected. Handle the plants like tomatoes. The only difference between the two crops is that eggplant likes slightly warmer conditions. When the plants are set out, cover them with floating row cover to keep them warm and protect them from flea beetles. Left unprotected, young plants often have their leaves ravaged by this pest and then outgrow the damage by midsummer.

Harvesting. The best eggplant fruits are so young that the seeds are barely visible when you cut them open. The skins should be glossy and tight. Cut fruits from the plants with an inch of stem attached, and store them in the refrigerator.

Extending the season. Use black plastic mulch, clear plastic tunnels, or cloches to cre-ate warm conditions for eggplants while cool spring weather prevails. In fall, cover plants with blankets or other frost covers to nurse them through the first cold nights. Some eggplant cultivars tolerate cold weather and light frosts surprisingly well.

Fall and winter care. When cold weather kills the plants, pull them up and compost them. Cultivate the soil, then cover with mulch or plant with clover or another legume.

Container growing. Many compact, small-fruited eggplants make ideal container vegetables. Besides being deliciously productive, the lavender to purple star-shaped flowers are quite attractive. In cool climates where eggplant does not grow well in an open garden, try growing plants in containers placed near a brick wall that heats up in the afternoon.

Propagation. Allow nonhybrid fruits to ripen until the skin loses its gloss and begins to shrivel. Cut fruits open, scoop out the seed cavity, and tear the pulp into small pieces to dry. Pick out seeds after a few days. Rinse clean, air dry, and store the seeds in a cool, dry place. To remain true to type, eggplant cultivars must be grown at least 150′ apart. ✻

ENDIVE

Cichorium endivia. Compositae.
Biennial grown as an annual.

Add a new dimension to your salads with tangy-flavored endive and escarole. Most American gardeners recognize frilly leaved endive as endive but call the broad, lettuce-leaved type escarole. Both types of endive produce a loose head with a creamy-colored, mild center and full-flavored outer leaves.

Grow a few different kinds of endive and its close relative chicory (see "Friends and Relatives" on page 351) to cut young for mixed green salads; allow part of your crop to mature into leafy rosettes or loose heads. You can add mature leaves to soups, stews, or casseroles or braise them for a side dish.

Selecting plants. Select extra-cold-tolerant types for late fall and winter harvests. Match cultivars to your intended uses. Endive loses quality quickly after reaching maturity. Self-blanching endive cultivars eliminate the need to tie up leaves or cover plants before harvesting.

Site. Select a garden site with full sun and shelter from strong winds. Endive tolerates partial shade and benefits from it in hot weather.

Soil. Endive thrives in fertile, well-drained soil. A raised bed amended with a 1″–2″ layer of compost is ideal.

How much to plant. A family of endive lovers may use a 3′ row per person each season. Since endive is best eaten the moment it matures, start a plant or two every couple of weeks to stagger your harvest over the growing season, suggests Robert Johnson, owner of Johnny's Selected Seeds in Maine.

Spacing. If you plant in single rows, leave at least 1′ between rows and 8″–10″ between plants, depending on the mature size of the cultivar. In a wide row, give each plant 8″–12″ on all sides. Crowded plants, says Johnson, have more trouble with bottom rot. If you keep young plants clipped small for mesclun (a mixture of different salad greens), you can space them as close as 3″ apart, says organic market gardener Molly Bartlett of Silver Creek Farm in Ohio. In cold weather, close planting lets endive's tough outer leaves protect the tender inner greens.

Days to maturity. You can harvest endive 40–50 days after sowing, depending on the cultivar and the weather.

Planting and growing. Endive needs much the same conditions as lettuce. Endive seldom bolts when the weather turns warm in summer—although it does pass its prime quickly. For best growth, plant when temperatures will remain between 60° and 70°F, in spring or late summer. Young endive plants that are exposed to temperatures below 50°F for ten days or more may bolt prematurely. Direct-sow seeds ¼″–½″ deep after frost, or start it indoors. If you start with seedlings, set the root balls slightly higher than their original depth to discourage bottom rot.

To keep endive mild and sweet flavored, encourage quick growth. Keep the soil moist, mulch with black plastic or straw, and fertilize every two weeks with a dilute solution of fish emulsion.

Pest problems are few. Control caterpillars with *Bacillus thuringiensis* (BT) and aphids with insecticidal soap. Like lettuce, endive can develop tipburn. Avoid plantings that will mature in hot, dry weather.

If you want a milder-flavored endive head,

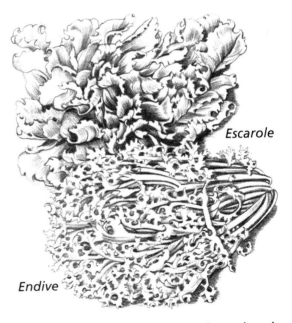

Escarole

Endive

Greens of broad-leaved escarole and curly leaved endive are tangy additions to salads. Blanching the heads makes the leaves more tender.

blanch the leafy heart. When a head nears maturity and is perfectly dry, tie the outer leaves securely over the head. Blanch for 5–21 days, depending on the cultivar and weather conditions. Or try Johnson's easy French blanching method: Cover the central head with an empty 4"–6"-wide margarine tub for three to four days before harvest. Slower-maturing cultivars benefit from longer blanching periods as long as temperatures remain cool. Blanching in hot, humid weather encourages rotting.

Harvesting. For mesclun, harvest 2"–3"-long unblanched leaves. Bartlett recommends cutting the plants back to ¾"–1" from the ground; they'll resprout for a second harvest. Or let plants mature into leafy heads.

Extending the season. For an early harvest, start endive and chicory seeds indoors under plant growth lights; plant seedlings out after three to four weeks. In mild climates, direct-sow seeds in August or September to harvest in winter or early spring.

If you have more endive than you can eat in the fall, dig up extra heads and plant them in buckets of moist sand. In cool root-cellar temperatures (just above freezing), endive plants may keep for two to three months, as long as the leaves and heart are free of excess moisture. Trapped water promotes rapid rotting in storage.

Container growing. You can grow full-size endive plants in 1- or 2-gallon nursery containers filled with 3 parts potting mix to 1 part compost. Keep the soil moist and the pot insulated from temperature fluctuations. Smaller pots, or even flats, are roomy enough to grow a crop of endive to harvest young for mesclun.

Propagation. Endive usually self-pollinates, so collected seeds normally produce plants that resemble the parent. Harvest seeds from the slowest-bolting plants for best results. Since endive is a biennial, you'll have to wait until the second season of growth to harvest seeds.

Friends and relatives. Chicory (*Cichorium intybus*) is closely related to endive and is grown in much the same way. Leaf chicories resemble light green, dark green, or red-tinged dandelion greens or leaf lettuce. Chicories that form heads are called heading chicory or radicchio. Water chicory regularly to prevent bolting and interior browning of heading types. Heading and leafy chicories reach harvest size in 50–70 days, depending on type, and will hold in the garden for several weeks. Some radicchio cultivars need to be cut back in late summer to stimulate a tight head to form in the fall. Newer cultivars are better suited to the United States and form heads without intervention.

Certain chicories known as witloofs are forced indoors to form tender, blanched heads called Belgian endive or chicons. The roots are grown outdoors, requiring 110 days to grow to harvestable size. To force witloof chicory, dig the roots in fall and cut off the tops 2" above the crown. Trim the roots to 8" and bury them upright in a container of moist sand or peat moss. Cover the container to maintain complete darkness and humid conditions; keep it moist and at 50°–60°F. Harvest the pale sprouts when they reach 4"–6" tall. Under good conditions, a second crop may sprout.

Chicory roots are also dried, roasted, ground, and brewed to make a coffeelike drink. ✳

EXOTIC CROPS

The tropical and subtropical areas of China, Southeast Asia, Africa, India, and the Americas are an exciting source of new tastes and textures for your eating enjoyment. These fruits and vegetables only grow well in climates where freezing temperatures are a rare occurrence, or in the greenhouse. A few can be grown in tubs and moved inside for the winter. Southern gardeners can try some of these crops outside; just look for the crops that will survive your winter low temperatures. Please note: The temperatures given below apply to plants that are at least a few years old. Young plants are less hardy and will need protection during cold spells.

You'll find separate entries for the following exotic crops: Avocado, Banana, Carob, Feijoa, Fig, Grapefruit, Guava, Kiwi, Lemon, Lime, Olive, Orange, Pineapple, and Pomegranate. You can also find information on some traditional Central and South American crops in the Mexican Specialties entry.

The tropics and subtropics are an incredible source of edible crops that you may never have seen or tasted. Here's a list of some tropical fruits and vegetables:

Acerola. Acerola (*Malpighia glabra*), also called Barbados cherry, is hardy to about 30°F. The shrub grows to 10' and is native to Texas, Central America, and the West Indies. Its fruit is lobed, thin-skinned, and bright red and has yellow-orange flesh with a high vitamin-C content. Acerolas will grow in poor soil, but adding water and fertilizer will increase fruit size. Propagate by cuttings; seeds are hard to sprout. Eat fruits fresh or make them into preserves.

Annonas. A number of trees in the annona family (*Annona* spp.) are cultivated for fruit. Cherimoya (*A. cherimola*) growing tips are hardy to 29°F; the trunk is hardy to 25°F. Custard apple (*A. reticulata*) is hardy to 28°F. Soursop (*A. muricata*) and sugar apple (*A. squamosa*) are slightly less hardy. Atemoyas are a cherimoya/custard-apple cross. They are all nearly evergreen trees that grow to 16'–25' in their native Peru. The fruits resemble large heart-shaped apples covered with thick, alligatorlike skin. The white flesh has a pleasing aroma and contains many hard, glossy, black seeds. Annonas do best in light, deep, fertile soil. Cherimoya flowers especially need daily hand-pollination for good fruit production. Graft cultivars to seedling rootstocks or raise seedling trees. Soak seeds for one or two days before planting. To enjoy the fruit, scrape the ripe flesh out of the skin, remove the seeds, and chill. Soursop flesh is best sweetened and used in juice or frozen desserts.

Artocarpuses. The best known of the fruits in the artocarpus family (*Artocarpus* spp.) is the breadfruit (*Artocarpus altilis*), which is not hardy below 35°–40°F. Jackfruit (*A. heterophyllus*) is hardy to 27°F, and kwai muk (*A. hypargyraeus*) is hardy to 20°F. They are all evergreen trees and are native to Malaysia. Breadfruit grows to 60', jackfruit to 50', and kwai muk to 20' in the tropics. The club-shaped fruits are yellow when ripe. Breadfruits are up to 1' long and jackfruits are up to 3' long, while kwai muk fruits are only about 1" long. Artocarpuses grow best in low, moist regions of the tropics. Breadfruit is propagated by transplanting suckers or root cuttings. Most breadfruits are seedless; those that do have seeds are called breadnuts and can be grown from seed. Jackfruit and kwai muks are also grown from seeds. Plant fresh seeds where they will remain. Unripe fruits are cooked and eaten as a starchy vegetable. Roasted fruit resembles bread. Breadnut seeds are cooked and eaten. The pulp surrounding the seeds of ripe jackfruit and kwai muk fruit is eaten raw.

Cacao. Cacao (*Theobroma cacao*) isn't hardy below 35°–40°F. The tree grows to 25′ in its native Central and South America. Seeds (cocoa beans) are borne in pods that form directly on trunks and large branches. Cocoa grows in wet, lowland tropical areas. To enjoy, open the pods and remove the seeds from the airy, delicious flesh. The seeds can be made into chocolate liquor, cocoa, and chocolate, but the process is somewhat involved.

Caper. Caper (*Capparis spinosa*) is not hardy below 35°–40°F. Capers are the pickled flower buds of a small prickly shrub that grows to 5′ and is native to Mediterranean regions. Some cultures eat the sprouts, which resemble asparagus. Pickled nasturtium flower buds are similar to capers and make a good substitute.

Capulin. Capulin (*Muntingia calabura*), also called strawberry tree, is hardy to about 28°F. It is a fast-growing but short-lived tree that grows to 20′ and is native to the West Indies. Capulin fruit looks like little red cherries and has sweet, strawberry-textured flesh. The trees like full sun and rich, moist soil. They will bear fruit in two years from seed or in one year from an air layer. Eat the fruits fresh or cooked.

Carambola. Carambola (*Averrhoa carambola*), also called star fruit, is hardy to 35°–40°F. The tree grows to 30′ in its native Southeast Asia. The small, green leaves are lacy; the blooms are tiny and purple. Healthy trees bear huge numbers of yellow, waxy, ridged fruit. Carambolas grow in sun or shade in rich soil and need high humidity. They are not salt-tolerant. Graft named cultivars onto seedling rootstocks to propagate. They grow quickly from seeds

but fruit quality will be variable. Ripe fruit is yellow with brown-tipped ridges. When cut crosswise, slices are star shaped. Eat out of hand or raw in salad. Fruits are best when fully ripe. The skin can be eaten, but remove the seeds. Lightly cooked fruit may be sweeter.

Cassava. Cassava (*Manihot esculenta*), also called tapioca, yuca, and manioc, isn't hardy below 35°–40°F. The shrubby perennial grows to 9′ and is native to the lowlands of Central America. The tall, cleft, palmlike foliage is quite attractive. It needs moderately fertile soil and 8–11 warm months to produce a crop. Plant 4″–6″ stem cuttings 4′ apart each way. The long tuberous roots must be cooked before eating to destroy the poisonous prussic acid they contain. Cassava is made into puddings, flour, and our familiar tapioca.

Ceriman. Ceriman (*Monstera deliciosa*), also called Swiss cheese plant and hurricane plant, isn't hardy below 35°–40°F. The fast-growing herbaceous vine grows to 30′ in its native tropical Mexico. The large, leathery leaves have slitlike holes, and the plant grows to form thick matlike clumps. The 10″ calla-lily-shaped flowers develop into green, pineapple-flavored fruits that look like large ears of corn. Ceriman grows in rich, moist, well-drained soil. Propagate by stem cuttings. It is widely used in landscaping for a tropical effect. Fruit ripens only a few inches at a time. Put it in a glass of water and pop off segments as they ripen. Fruit cannot be eaten green because of high oxalic-acid content. Ripe fruit is used in salads and for jelly.

Coconut. Coconut (*Cocos nucifera*) is hardy to 35°–40°F. Coconut palm trees grow to 100′ and are native to the moist tropics. Trees bear both male and female flowers, but two trees are required for good pollination. Trees need little care and can be grown from seeds. Space plants 25' apart. Large flower clusters form about the fourth year. Ripe nuts drop naturally. Drain milk by opening two "eyes" at the end of the nut with an icepick. Put the nut in the freezer for one hour for easier cracking. Crack the nut with a hammer and use a screwdriver to loosen and remove meat from the shell.

Coffee. Coffee (*Coffea arabica* and other spp.) isn't hardy below 35°–40°F. The shrubby tree grows to 15' and is native to tropical Africa. It can be grown as a houseplant. The leaves are glossy and dark green, and fragrant white flowers are followed by red ½"-long fruits. Each fruit contains two seeds or coffee beans. To grow a tree, separate the seeds from the pulp of a ripe berry and plant them in a sandy starter mix. Kept well-watered, they should sprout in five or six weeks. Trees may also be propagated by hardwood cuttings. To process your harvest, remove the beans and dry them in the sun. Then roast, grind, and brew them.

Date. Dates (*Phoenix dactylifera*) are hardy to 25°F. Date palm trees grow to 100' and are native to the Persian Gulf area. Leaves are grayish or bluish, with sharp tips. Fruits are cylindrical and yellow when ripe, with soft, buttery flesh. The grow best in hot, dry desert areas. Male and female flowers are borne on separate trees, so plant at least one male and one female tree. Propagate by transplanting suckers. Plant 30' apart. Eat dates fresh or dried. Dried fruits have dark skins. Clusters ripen more evenly if they are cut and hung in a warm, dry place to mature.

Downy myrtle. Downy myrtle (*Rhodomyrtus tomentosa*) is hardy to 27°F. It is a tropical Asian shrub and grows to 8'. Leaves have a downy gray underside. Bluish purple fruit is about ½" in diameter, with a fuzzy purple skin and many small seeds. Downy myrtle likes moist, acid soil with sun or light shade. It is

fairly salt-tolerant. Grow it from seeds or cuttings. Enjoy the fruit fresh or make it into pies and preserves.

Eugenias. Many of the eugenias (*Eugenia* spp.) are grown for their fruits. Cherry-of-the-Rio-Grande (*Eugenia aggregata*) is hardy to 20°F. Grumichama (*E. brasiliensis*), pitanga (*E. uniflora*), and pitomba (*E. luschnathiana*) are slightly less hardy. Eugenias are evergreen trees 15'–50' tall in their native Brazil. They have dark green, glossy leaves. The white blooms are followed by fruits that taste somewhat like sweet cherries. They grow well in rich, moist soil, they like full sun, and they are only fairly salt-tolerant. Propagate by seeds or cuttings. Eat the fruits fresh or in pie or preserved as jelly or jam.

Jaboticaba. Jaboticaba (*Myrciaria cauliflora*) is hardy to 27°F. The evergreen tree grows to 40' in its native Brazil. Grapelike fruits with tough purple or white skin are borne right on the trunk. The pulp is juicy, with a few small seeds. Trees grow slowly and prefer rich, moist soil. Seedlings may take 12 years to fruit. Grafted trees bear in 6 years. To enjoy, remove the skins and eat the grape-flavored fruit fresh or make preserves or wine.

Loquat. Loquat (*Eriobotrya japonica*), also called Japanese medlar and Japanese plum, is hardy to 12°F (Zone 8). The evergreen tree grows to 25' and is native to China. Leaves are long and stiff, dark green on top, and fuzzy light green underneath. The 3" yellow fruits are thin-skinned and juicy. The tree likes full sun and light, rich, moist soil. It is useful for beach plantings but is susceptible to fire blight. Graft cultivars onto seedling rootstocks to propagate. Fruit quality and hardiness of seedlings may be variable. Plant trees 20'–24' apart. Eat the fruit fresh, poached and chilled, or preserved. (Use not-quite-ripe fruit for preserving.) The skin may be removed or eaten; seeds must be removed. When cooking loquats, leave a few seeds in until just before serving to improve flavor and help thicken juice.

Lychee. Lychee (*Litchi chinensis*) is hardy to 26°F. Lychee trees grow to 40′ and are native to China. Leaves are shiny green and leathery; new growth is coppery red. The small, round or oval fruit is borne in clusters. Fruit has thin, leathery, red to purple skin; flesh is white and juicy. Trees like deep, loamy soil, full sun, and plenty of moisture. They are not salt-tolerant and need wind protection when young. Grow them from seeds and by air layering. Seedling trees may not bear fruit for many years. To enjoy the fruit, peel and eat the translucent flesh, discarding the seeds. Flesh may also be added to stir-fry dishes. The longan (*Euphoria longana*) is closely related to lychee and is grown and used the same way but is slightly more hardy.

Mamoncillo. Mamoncillo (*Melicoccus bijugatus*), also called genip and Spanish lime, is hardy to about 30°F. It is a slow-growing tree to 60′ and is native to the Caribbean and tropical America. Its leaves are shiny and green.

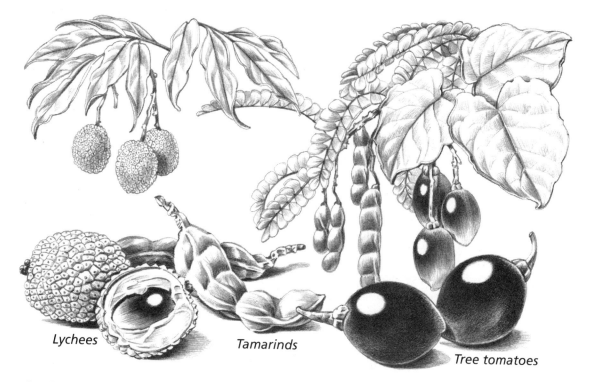

Lychees   *Tamarinds*   *Tree tomatoes*

The fruits of the lychee tree have a bright red, thin, leathery shell surrounding grapelike pulp and a single seed. Tamarind fruits resemble lima bean pods, with a brittle outer shell and shiny seeds embedded in tart flesh. The pulp is used in drinks, preserves, and chutneys. The fruits of tree tomatoes resemble garden tomatoes inside but have a lemony pineapple flavor.

The 1″ fruits have thick, green skin with juicy pulp and can be astringent when not fully ripe. Mamoncillo trees do well in dry areas. Grow them from seeds. To enjoy the fruit, peel it, remove the large seed, and eat it fresh.

Mango. Mango (*Mangifera indica*) is hardy to 30°F. The nearly evergreen, spreading trees grow to 100′ in their native India. Leaves are long, pointed, and deep green. The peachlike fruit varies in shape and size, and the skin can be green or colored like a beautiful sunset. Mangoes grow well in full sun and are fairly salt-tolerant. Graft cultivars onto a four- to six-week-old seedling rootstock to propagate. Seedling trees will vary in fruit quality. To enjoy fruits, cut out the large central seed, score the flesh into cubes, and invert the skin to pop the flesh out. Flesh can be frozen for later use. Mango is related to poison ivy and has caustic sap. Those sensitive to poison ivy may be irritated after touching the skin of this fruit. Wear gloves when picking.

Natal plum. Natal plum (*Carissa grandiflora*) is hardy to 25°F. The evergreen, spreading shrub grows to 18′ in its native South Africa. Leaves are glossy, thick, and green; branches have short, heavy thorns. Fruit is oval shaped and wine colored. Natal plums grow well in many soils and are salt-tolerant. They are easy to grow from seeds or cuttings. Eat the fruit fresh or cook it into sauces or jelly. Fruit exudes a white, milky sap, which disappears when sugar is added or when the fruit is cooked.

Papaya. Papaya (*Carica papaya*) is hardy to 31°F. The treelike herb grows to 25′ and is native to tropical America. The plant has a tuft of lobed green leaves at the top of the trunk. Most plants bear both male and female flowers; a few bear one or the other. Fruit is melonlike and weighs up to 20 pounds, with many shiny, black seeds in a central cavity. Plants like full sun and rich, well-drained soil and are not salt-tolerant. Seedling plants will flower in as little as five months. Papaya plants produce for only three or four years, so replant regularly. To enjoy ripe fruits, cut them in half lengthwise, scoop out the seeds, and eat the flesh with a spoon. Green fruits can be cooked and served as a vegetable. Papayas contain papain, a potent protein-digesting enzyme, and can be used as a natural meat tenderizer.

Passionfruit. Passionfruits (*Passiflora* spp.) are members of the passionflower family that are cultivated for their fruits. They include purple granadilla (*P. edulis*), yellow granadilla (*P. laurifolia*), sweet granadilla (*P. ligularis*), and others. Most are hardy only to 30°F. A hardy species (Zone 5), maypop, is described on page 471. Passionfruit vines bear striking flowers and a wide range of yellow, orange, or purple fruit. The egg- to apple-size fruits have a leathery skin and contain numerous crunchy black seeds in aromatic, juicy, tart, gelatinous flesh. Passionfruit vines aren't picky about soil but are highly susceptible to nematodes. They can be grown in pots. Grow plants from seeds or cuttings. To enjoy a passionfruit, scrape the pulp out of the skin and eat it as is, or blend it briefly and use it in beverages and desserts.

Pouterias. Pouterias (*Pouteria* spp.) are a group of trees native to Central America. Canistel (*P. campechiana*), also called egg-fruit, is hardy to about 28°F. Sapote (*P. sapota*) is less hardy. Canistel trees grow to 50′; sapote trees grow to 90′. Canistel fruit is round to top-shaped with thin yellow-orange skin and dry flesh resembling a hard-cooked egg yolk. Sapote fruit has thick, russet-brown skin and sweet, reddish flesh. Pouterias prefer sun and clay soil and are fairly salt-tolerant and wind-resistant. To propagate, graft superior selections onto a seedling rootstock or raise seedlings. Be patient: Seeds take three to six months to sprout. You can eat the fruit fresh or cooked. Sapote is often used to make a thick, marmalade-type preserve.

Ramontchi. Ramontchi (*Flacourtia indica*), also called Madagascar plum, is hardy to 26°F. The dense, rounded shrub or tree grows to 45' in its native South Asia. The glossy, deep green, leathery leaves are pale green underneath. Some plants have sharp spines. The ½" purple or deep red fruit has soft flesh with several small seeds. Ramontchis grow well in most soils and are fairly salt-tolerant. Propagate from seeds, suckers, or cuttings or by grafting. Growth can be rapid, so trees need frequent pruning. Eat the somewhat astringent fruits fresh or in preserves.

Sapodilla. Sapodilla (*Manilkara zapota*) is hardy to 27°F. In the wild, trees grow to 100', but cultivars are much shorter. The 4" round fruit has scruffy brown skin and yellow to brown flesh. Its flavor ranges from pearlike to brown-sugar-like. The milky sap is chicle—the original base for chewing gum. Trees thrive even in poor soil but require good drainage. To propagate, graft desirable types to a seedling rootstock. To enjoy the fruit, peel, remove seeds (if there are any), and eat it fresh.

Star apple. Star apple (*Chrysophyllum cainito*) is hardy to 29°F. The evergreen tree grows to 35' and is native to tropical America. Leaves are dark green above with silky golden brown undersides. The 4" round, purple or green fruit has sweet, white flesh. Star apples like full sun, tolerate poor soil, and are wind-resistant. They need warm temperatures year-round to produce fruit. Propagate from seeds or by air layering or grafting. Fruit is excellent fresh when fully ripe.

Tamarind. Tamarind (*Tamarindus indica*) is hardy to 28°F. The tree grows to 80' and is native to tropical Africa. The plump, brown pods are 3"–7" long. The pulp surrounding the flat, glossy seeds has a pleasing acid flavor. Trees grow well on limestone soils in semi-arid areas. Propagate from seeds (seeds remain viable for several years) or by grafting or budding. Seedling trees are slow to bear. Space trees 15'–20' apart. Use the tangy flesh as a flavoring and in beverages, preserves, and chutneys. Worcestershire sauce is flavored with tamarinds.

Tree tomato. Tree tomato (*Cyphomandra betacea*), also called tamarillo, is hardy to 35°F. The herbaceous shrub grows to 8' and is native to Peru. Its thick stems become somewhat woody with age. The yellow, red, purple, or

---

TO LEARN MORE

If you want to learn more about growing your own exotic crops, consider joining the California Rare Fruit Growers (CRFG). The members of CRFG share information through meetings and a quarterly magazine called *The Fruit Gardener* and a network of expert specialists. Despite the name, it is not limited to California. For information, write to: CRFG, c/o Fullerton Arboretum, California State University, Fullerton, CA 92634.

even striped fruit resembles a juicy tomato with a lemon-pineapple flavor. Fruits have many hard, flat seeds. Yellow-fruited types are the mildest, so start with those first. Tree tomatoes need rich, moist soil and good drainage. Grow them as you would a tomato or eggplant (see their individual plant entries for details). Tree tomato will bear in large tubs. It fruits in one-and-one-half to two years when grown from seeds or cuttings. Roots are easily disturbed. Pick fruits when they are just beginning to soften. Cut them in half and squeeze the juice as you would an orange, or remove the skin and eat the flesh raw, stewed, or made into jelly.

White sapote. White sapote (*Casimiroa edulis*) is hardy to 22°F. The evergreen tree grows to 50′. The 3″–4″ yellowish green to orange fruits have sweet, custardlike, cream-colored flesh. Trees grow in any soil as long it is well-drained, but they prefer sandy loam soil. To propagate, graft desirable types onto a seedling rootstock. Seedlings may take ten years to bear. Pick fruits carefully and allow them to soften at room temperature. Eat the custardy flesh as is. ✳

FEIJOA

Feijoa sellowiana. Myrtaceae. Evergreen shrub. Zone 9.

Native of South America, the feijoa, or pineapple guava, bears fleshy, edible petals followed by minty pineapple-flavored fruit that is excellent fresh or in jellies and conserves.

Selecting plants. Select a grafted tree of a known cultivar. 'Nazemetz' and 'Coolidge' are self-fertile and have excellent flavor. Some cultivars need cross-pollination.

Site. Feijoa needs full sun, but avoid south-facing walls because high summer temperatures prevent fruit set and cause sunscald.

Soil. Plant in well-drained soil with a pH of 5.5–7.0. Feijoa is somewhat salt-tolerant.

How much to plant. Each plant produces 50–100 pounds of fruit.

Spacing. Plant trees 15′ apart. Plant them closer in a hedge.

Seasons to bearing. Feijoa plants bear fruit in two to three years.

Planting and growing. Feijoa plants tolerate some drought, but benefit from regular watering. Cover the ground with an organic mulch to conserve water and cushion falling fruit.

Harvesting. Carefully pluck the sweet petals without destroying the developing fruit. Gently shake branches every few days to loosen ripe fruit. Fruits keep for a week in refrigeration.

Fall and winter care. Prune lightly to shape the plant and stimulate some new growth.

Container growing. Plants cannot tolerate temperatures below 15°F, yet they need a cool period before growth can begin in spring. Keep in a cool, bright room in winter.

Propagation. You can grow feijoa from seeds, but seedlings may not produce high-quality fruit nor bear for five years or more. Propagate cultivars by grafting or layering or by cuttings taken in autumn. ✳

FIG · 359

FENNEL

Foeniculum vulgare. Umbelliferae.
Perennial grown as an annual.

You'll find two kinds of fennel in seed catalogs and produce markets. Common fennel produces an abundance of seeds and feathery leaves. Florence fennel (*Foeniculum vulgare* var. *azoricum*) is grown primarily for its swollen leaf base. Both types are used in salads and soups or with fish. Since the heat of cooking destroys the delicate anise flavor, wait until just before serving to add fennel to your recipes.

Site. Plant in full sun for best growth.

Soil. Fennel grows well in most rich, well-drained soil. Keep the soil pH around 6.5.

Spacing. Thin plants to 6″–12″ apart.

Days to maturity. Begin snipping foliage eight to ten weeks after planting. Florence fennel needs 65–90 days for bulb formation.

Planting and growing. Sow seeds directly into the garden as soon as the ground can be worked. Cover the seeds lightly and keep them moist. Sow successive crops at two- to three-week intervals, if the climate permits, for tender foliage all season.

Harvesting. Pick leaves throughout the season, taking older leaves first. Pick seed heads at any stage, although seeds have the most flavor when mature and dry. Harvest Florence fennel when the leaf base begins to thicken; cut just below the swollen area.

Extending the season. Get an early start by sowing fennel indoors in deep pots filled with rich, well-drained medium. Move pots outdoors in spring; cover them if frost threatens.

Both types of fennel tolerate light frosts. In early fall, lengthen the growing season by covering garden plants with clear plastic if heavy frost is predicted.

Propagation. Allow plants to go to seed and collect for future crops. ✳

FIG

Ficus carica. Moraceae. Deciduous tree.
Zones 8–10 and Zones 6–7 with protection.

For a delicious, nearly trouble-free fruit crop, try growing figs. They're easy-to-grow even in the North, where they need winter protection. The yellow, green, or black fruits are pear-shaped, hollow, and fleshy. The flowers are borne inside the fruit, and the flower-filled centers are pink, red, or purple. The fruit is nutritious and is best eaten fresh even though it can also be dried, canned, pureed, or frozen.

Selecting plants. Cultivars are available in a range of fruit shapes and colors. Select self-pollinating ones adapted to your climate.

Site. Plant figs in full sun; they tolerate heat well. In the North, select a protected, south-facing site to provide added winter protection. Figs are moderatly salt-tolerant.

Soil. Plants require good drainage but will adapt to pH (anywhere from 5.5 to 8.0 is fine) and a wide range of soils (including sandy, clayey, and loamy).

How much to plant. Plant three or four fig trees per family. Plant several cultivars for variety and to spread out your harvest.

Spacing. Plant 5′–25′ apart, depending on the cultivar and the region of the country. In the North, where they need winter protection, plants will not grow as large as they will in the South.

Seasons to bearing. Plants should produce fruit the first year after planting.

Planting and growing. Plant as you would any young tree. Mulch well, feed with a balanced fertilizer twice a year, and spray monthly with kelp extract during the growing season. Figs don't require training or formal pruning; thin or head back branches to control size.

Generally, figs do not suffer from insect or disease problems in North America. Keep birds away with netting. Spread wood ashes around the base of trees to keep ants from climbing up to the fruits. If nematodes are a problem in your area, solarize the soil for 60 days the summer before you plant. Resistant cultivars are available.

Harvesting. In warm climates, harvest in June and again in late summer. In colder areas, expect one harvest in late summer to fall. Check trees daily in season, and pick fruit that's not quite ripe. Ripen at room temperature for a day or two. Ripe fruits are soft, and their skin may begin to split. Figs spoil easily but will keep for a week in the refrigerator. Store them in brown paper bags in covered containers. For drying, cut large figs in half; small figs can be dried whole. Prick fruits with a fork to speed drying.

Fall and winter care. In areas north of Zone 8, protect figs from freezing temperatures. In warmer parts of Zone 7, wrapping with burlap or old blankets is generally sufficient. North of that, bury figs to insulate them. In late fall, prune to about 6', remove spreading branches, and tie remaining branches together with rope. Dig a 2'-deep trench as long as the tree is tall, starting right next to the root ball. Line it with boards. Dig soil away from the roots opposite the trench. Wrap the tree in plastic, bend it into the trench, and fill in with straw or dried leaves. Cover with a board, and shovel soil over it. Resurrect trees in spring after danger of hard frost is past.

Container growing. Figs can be grown in large containers such as half-barrels.

Propagation. Use a shovel to cut suckers that sprout from the roots throughout the growing season; replant or share them with friends. Figs can also be air-layered or grown from cuttings. ✳

FILBERT

Corylus spp. Betulaceae. Deciduous tree or multi-stemmed shrub. Zones 3–8.

Filberts, also known as hazelnuts, are native to northern temperate regions. The European filbert (*Corylus avellana*) is widely grown in the Pacific Northwest, but is threatened by the eastern filbert blight. The native American filbert (*C. americana*) and beaked filbert (*C. cornuta*) have resistance to this blight, but unfortunately, their nuts are less desirable than those from European filbert trees. Researchers hope to develop resistant hybrids.

Selecting plants. 'Winkler' is a dependable American filbert with good nut quality. It's also the only filbert that's self-fertile; all others need pollinators to produce nuts. 'Winkler' is also smaller and bears earlier than many other cultivars. American and beaked filberts are hardy to Zone 3.

Some of the older European cultivars, such as 'Hall's Giant' and 'Barcelona', have a fair amount of resistance to blight. Turkish hazelnuts (*C. colurna*) can have some resistance to the blight once they reach maturity. European filberts are hardy to Zone 4; Turkish hazelnuts are hardy only to Zone 5.

Most filberts need to be planted near at least two other cultivars for best pollination.

Site. Filberts can tolerate partial shade but do best in full sun.

Soil. A well-drained, sandy loam is best, but filberts will survive shallow soils and tolerate a wide range of soil types.

How much to plant. A mature filbert bears 20–25 pounds of shelled nut meats each year. See page 416 for an illustration of filbert nuts.

Spacing. Most filberts, with the exception of the tree types, grow in a V-shape with multiple branching trunks. To create an attractive hedge, plant filberts in a row about 3½' apart. If you are short on space, plant several trees in a cluster, leaving 3'–5' between trees.

Seasons to bearing. Filberts will start bearing small crops in two to three years.

Planting and growing. Prepare the planting site and plant as you would any tree. See "Perennial Crops" on page 111 for directions.

Water well daily for the first few days. Continue to water weekly for the first several years during the growing season whenever rain is scarce. Keep the area beneath the tree well-weeded, or mulch with wood chips or any mix of organic matter. (Don't allow the mulch to touch the trunk of the tree.) To avoid excessive tender, early growth, wait until the tree's second year to fertilize. Then, spread a layer of well-rotted manure or a blended organic fertilizer with a good nitrogen value beneath the tree once or twice a year in spring.

If squirrels or birds are a problem and your filbert trees are small, consider covering your trees with netting. To control the filbertworm, harvest promptly and destroy infected nuts.

Harvesting. Nuts are ripe as soon as you can separate the nut from its husk—about one month before they would start to drop. Pick them off the tree or shake them onto a tarp spread beneath the tree. Spread them in shallow layers in a warm, airy place to dry until they are crunchy. They'll keep for up to one year in their shell in a cool place; if you crack them, store the nut meats in a refrigerator or freezer.

Fall and winter care. Remove dead wood regularly. Clean up old nuts and debris from around the tree.

Propagation. Filberts can be grown from seeds or propagated by grafting or layering. ✳

GARLIC

Allium spp. Liliaceae. Perennial grown as an annual.

European immigrants brought this pungent, easy-to-grow bulb with them when they came to America; since then, garlic has become a staple in many gardens.

Selecting plants. The two commonly grown types of garlic are soft-neck garlic (*Allium sativum* subsp. *sativum*) and hard-neck garlic (*A. sativum* subsp. *ophioscorodon*). Soft-neck garlic—also known as silverskin or artichoke garlic—is the type usually sold in grocery stores and tends to have the longest shelf life. Hard-neck garlic—also known as top-setting garlic, serpent garlic, or rocambole—produces mild bulbs and curiously twisted flowerstalks. It is important to note that a cultivar that is a hard-neck in one region of the country may be a soft-neck in another region, so don't be surprised if sets from far away turn out different than their description.

Site. Garlic grows best in full sun.

Soil. Plant in humus-rich, well-drained soil with a pH of 6.0–7.0.

How much to plant. Expect to harvest 5–10 pounds of garlic from 20′ of row. The average garlic bulb weighs 2–3 ounces and yields six to eight plantable cloves.

Spacing. Plant cloves 6″–8″ apart in rows or beds.

Days to maturity. Spring-planted garlic requires 120–150 days to reach maturity. However, the best quality and yields are from fall-planted garlic, which you harvest the following year in midsummer.

Planting and growing. Purchase garlic bulbs from seed catalogs or other garden suppliers—not the grocery store. Store-bought bulbs are usually adapted for commercial production and may not grow well in your area. Often, the best garlic you can get is from local growers. If they have success with a given cultivar in your area, chances are that you'll have good luck, too.

Select firm, healthy-looking bulbs that are free of insect and disease pests. Use your fingers to separate the individual cloves. Work carefully to avoid bruising the cloves, and try to keep their skins intact. Plant only the largest cloves, saving the small ones for cooking. Push individual cloves into prepared soil, 1″–2″ deep, root-end down. Cover them loosely with soil.

In most parts of the country, the best time to plant garlic is around mid-October. Plant a week or two earlier in very cold climates or later in the Deep South. Between the time of planting and winter freezing, the cloves will establish an extensive root system that helps to hold them in place during spring thaws. Shoots and roots will resume growth in early spring. Once the soil thaws, garlic needs consistently moist soil until the tops begin to die. Fertilize by spraying leaves every two weeks with fish emulsion or kelp extract, or side-dress with a light application of blood meal. Mulching with compost will control weeds and provide extra nutrients.

To plant garlic in the spring, prepare the soil the previous fall so you can plant as soon as the ground has thawed. Prepare and plant cloves as you would in fall, as described above.

If you're growing hard-neck, watch for the flowerstalks in early summer. Some growers cut the stalks back to the leaves so the plant can put all of its energy into bulb formation. Try adding the delicately flavored flowerstalk to stir-fried dishes.

In the home garden, garlic is rarely bothered by pests. To prevent disease problems, avoid planting garlic in low-lying areas where air circulation is poor. Destroy bulbs with any sign of disease, like molds, mildew, wilted foliage, or soft spots. To control diseases and insect pests, rotate garlic beds for two years with just about any crop other than onions. Or plant clumps of garlic scattered throughout the garden to foil insect pests. If your crops have had problems in the past with soil-dwelling pests like onion maggots or wireworms, apply parasitic nematodes to the soil at planting time. For more tips on controlling potential garlic pests, see the Onion entry.

Harvesting. Fall-planted garlic is commonly ready for harvest in late June or early

July. Spring-planted garlic usually isn't ready until the end of the season. When leaves begin to turn brown, pull several bulbs and break them apart. If it's too early, cloves will be unsegmented and difficult to separate. Leave the remaining bulbs for a week or two, and check again. If you leave bulbs in the soil too long, the outer skins begin to deteriorate, resulting in lower quality and poor keeping ability. A rule of thumb is to harvest when 75 percent of the foliage is brown. When in doubt, harvest early.

Use garlic fresh or cure it first for storage. Cure garlic in a hot, dry, dark, and airy place for a few weeks. Lay whole plants on the floor, or hang them in loose bunches from the ceiling. After several weeks, trim away the leaves and roots, then fill open-mesh bags with bulbs and hang them in a well-ventilated room at 60°–90°F. For long-term storage, keep the bulbs at 32°–35°F and 65 percent relative humidity.

Under these conditions, you can store garlic for five to eight months. To store garlic in the freezer, peel the cloves and place them in a container, then freeze.

Although most commonly grown for its bulbs, garlic also produces flavorful leaves. Snip a few leaves from each plant as needed. Use them like chives or for a tangy garlic pesto.

Container growing. For winter greens, plant several cloves in a small pot placed on a sunny windowsill; harvest the leaves as needed.

Propagation. Save your largest bulbs to replant for next season's crop.

Friends and relatives. Elephant garlic (*A. ampeloprasum*, Ampeloprasum group) forms large, garlic-shaped bulbs with a mild garlicky flavor. It is more closely related to leek than it is to garlic. Grow as you would garlic, spacing cloves 10″–12″ apart. Elephant garlic is partial to mulch. Elephant garlic doesn't store as long as true garlic does. *

GINGER

Zingiber officinale. Zingiberaceae. Perennial. Zones 9–10.

Most of the ginger you'll find at the market is grown commercially in the tropics, but it's not difficult to grow at home. Ginger's flavor is spicy, hot, and sweet at the same time. Fresh ginger is an excellent aid for digestion—make tea from the fresh root slices, then add a dab of honey. Add fresh or powdered ginger to beverages, cakes, and cookies. Toss chopped, fresh gingerroot with salads.

Selecting plants. Buy the aromatic rhizomes from herb and specialty plant dealers, or from your produce market. Pick rhizomes that are full—not dry and shriveled—with plenty of eyes (dormant buds).

Site. Ginger prefers a warm, humid environment and partial shade.

Soil. In the garden, ginger requires a well-drained, fertile soil.

Days to maturity. Sections of root can be harvested as soon as six months after planting.

Planting and growing. In Zone 7 and north, grow ginger indoors in pots, moving them outdoors to semishade in summer. Fill containers with any potting mix that includes sand and compost. Plant roots horizontally in beds or pots, loosely covered with soil. Keep the soil moist.

Harvesting. With potted ginger, slide both plant and soil from the pot. Use a sharp knife to trim away leaves and fibrous roots, cut as much rhizome as you need, and replant the rest. To harvest ginger in the garden, use your hands or a trowel to dig down into the soil next to the root. Use a knife to cut off small pieces, and then replace the soil. Rinse the root, then store it in the refrigerator by wrapping it in paper towels and placing it in a plastic bag.

Propagation. Replant sections of root. ✳

GOOSEBERRY

Ribes hirtellum and *R. uvacrispa.*
Saxifragaceae. Deciduous shrubs.
Zones 3–7.

Gooseberries thrive in cool summer weather and are especially enjoyed in northern Europe. The thorny bushes are somewhat notorious in North America as alternate hosts of white pine blister rust. This disease requires the presence of both a susceptible *Ribes* and pine trees. Although white pine blister rust rarely kills *Ribes,* it can be devastating to pines. Because of this, growing of *Ribes* was seriously restricted by federal law in the 1920s. Research subsequently proved that only blight-susceptible black currants pose a threat, and the federal ban was lifted in 1966. Since then, popularity of gooseberries has again been on the increase. Some states still have bans, so check before you plant.

Selecting plants. If you want gooseberries for fresh eating, choose a dessert cultivar, such as 'Achilles' or 'Hinnomaki Yellow'. If powdery mildew or leaf spot diseases are problems where you live, plant a disease-resistant cultivar, such as 'Poorman' or 'Leepared'. Gooseberries are self-pollinating.

Site. Plant gooseberries in either full sun or partial shade.

Soil. Gooseberries tolerate light or heavy soils that are slightly acidic. Mulch around plants to keep soil cool and moist.

How much to plant. The average yield is about 10 pounds of fruit per bush.

Spacing. Space bushes 6' apart.

Seasons to bearing. Expect your first crop the second season after planting.

Planting and growing. Gooseberries leaf out in early spring, so plant bareroot bushes in the fall. If you must plant in spring, do so as soon as the soil can be worked. See "How to Plant" on page 104 for instructions. Plant bushes slightly deeper than they stood in the nursery.

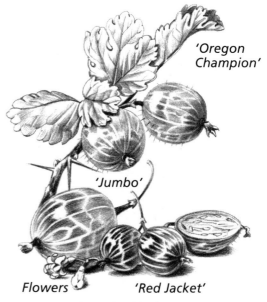

'Oregon Champion'

'Jumbo'

Flowers

'Red Jacket'

Thorny gooseberry bushes bear a sweet treat in a kaleidoscope of colors. They are wonderful for preserves and fresh eating.

After planting, cut away at ground level all but six shoots. Apply water and mulch.

Two diseases that may need control by spraying are powdery mildew and leaf spot. For mildew, spray with lime-sulfur, sulfur, or baking soda beginning at bud break and every couple of weeks thereafter, or following heavy rain. For leaf spot, apply bordeaux mixture just after leaves appear.

Potential insect pests include imported currantworm, gooseberry fruitworm, and currant borer. Control the first two pests with sprays of rotenone/pyrethrin mix as soon as you note damage. Control the borer by cutting off stems below where the borer entered.

Harvesting. For cooking, pick gooseberries slightly underripe. Allow dessert gooseberries to fully ripen on the bush for fresh eating. To negotiate the thorny branches at harvest, hold a branch up with one gloved hand while you strip the berries with your other, ungloved hand.

Keep harvested berries out of direct sunlight. Store fresh gooseberries at near-freezing temperatures and high humidity for no longer than two to four weeks.

Fall and winter care. Feed your plants between late fall and late winter, before you replenish mulch. Gooseberries need moderate amounts of nitrogen and relatively high amounts of potassium and magnesium. Spread 3 pounds of cottonseed or soybean meal plus ½ pound of wood ash, or a mulch of strawy manure, beneath each bush. To supply magnesium, use dolomitic limestone when you lime.

Prune gooseberries in winter by thinning out all but six new shoots and removing wood that's more than three years old. Except for lanky shoots, which need shortening, prune branches away at ground level. When thin-

'Red Lake'

'Ben Nevis'

'White Versailles'

Black currants have the most intense flavor, while pale whites have a delicate taste. You can eat ripe currants fresh from the bush, but they're most popular in preserves, jellies, and juices.

ning new shoots, selectively remove those drooping to the ground.

Container growing. Plant gooseberries in pots at least 1½' wide and deep in regular potting soil. Repot, cutting back some roots, every fall. In very cold areas, protect the roots in winter as shown in the illustration on page 240. The plants don't need light in winter.

Propagation. Propagate gooseberries by taking hardwood cuttings in fall. Plunge each cutting into well-drained soil up to its top bud. Mulch to prevent frost heaving during winter. Tip layering also works well.

Friends and relatives. Gooseberries are closely related to currants. Black currant (*R. nigrum*) and red and white currants (hybrids of *R. rubrum, R. sativum,* and *R. petraeum*) bear clusters of smaller fruit. Jostaberry (*R. nidi-*

grolaria) is a hybrid of black currant and goose-berry and has characteristics from each of the parents. Choose cultivars resistant to white pine blister rust (especially for black currants) and/or mildew.

Currants and jostaberries are grown just like gooseberries. Black currants are suitable for hedges, in which case set bushes only 3'

apart. Prune jostaberrries and red or white currants the same way as gooseberries. Black currants bear on one- and two-year-old wood, so when you prune, cut away wood that's more than two years old.

Currants don't store quite as long in the refrigerator as gooseberries do, so use them within a week or two. *

GRAINS

It's the unusual backyard gardener who has tried raising grains. Most gardeners assume that grains are difficult to grow on small plots, but those who experiment find that's not so. Even more valuable to many gardeners, most grains help build your soil, and many of them produce an excellent straw mulch. You can till the stalks that remain after harvest—especially those of buckwheat, flax, and rye—into your soil to add valuable organic matter. Except for barley and rye, the plants discussed in this section are not traditional cereal grains, but they can be ground into flour or eaten whole, like rice. You'll find more detailed information on four of the most common grains in the Corn, Oats, Rice, and Wheat entries.

Growing Grains

It's easy to seed small quantities of grain by hand, either by broadcasting the seeds or sowing them in rows. It can be difficult to find small quantities of grain seed for planting. Refer to "Sources" on page 507 for suggested sources, try striking a deal with a local farmer who grows them, or buy some at the health food store.

Most grains are fairly pest-free when planted in small patches in the appropriate site and soil conditions. Harvest grains by cutting them with a sickle or scythe. Separating the seeds from the seed head and removing the hulls from the seeds requires some special techniques; see "Processing Grains" on page 370 for directions.

Amaranth

Amaranth (*Amaranthus* spp.), a close relative of pigweed, is a highly nutritious, versatile food plant. You can eat the seeds whole like rice, pop them like popcorn, or grind them into flour. The greens of some species are also eaten; see the Greens entry and the Asian Specialties entry for information on the types of amaranth that are grown for greens. Many grain amaranth cultivars have bright red or purple seed heads. *A. cruentus* and *A. hypochondriacus* are the two main grain species. (*A. cruentus* is the type used for popping.) Choose white-seeded cultivars, which tend to have better flavor and texture than black-seeded ones. Amaranth is drought-tolerant and grows in even the worst soils in any bright, sunny spot.

Plant amaranth seeds in spring, after the soil warms to 65°F. Seedlings growing in cool, wet soil are prone to damping-off. Direct-seed ¼″ deep with about 4″ between seeds in rows 1½′ apart. If your season is short, start seeds indoors and transplant seedlings to the garden no more than three weeks later. You'll need only a few grams of seed to plant a 200-square-foot bed. Amaranth is slow to establish. Weed diligently early on. When seedlings are 3″ tall, thin them to 10″–12″ apart. Feeding by tarnished plant bug, the only widespread pest of grain amaranth, can cause seeds to taste bitter. Webworms and blister beetles sometimes feed on the leaves of young plants but rarely cause any real damage. Handpick them if infestations are heavy.

Though it will keep on flowering until the first fall frost, amaranth will ripen most of its grain about 90 days after sowing. Rub flower heads between your hands to test ripeness. When ripe, seeds will fall out readily. You can expect to harvest 25–30 pounds of seeds from a 200-square-foot plot.

Barley

Barley (*Hordeum vulgare*) is most familiar as little pearls found in soups or stews. It's also an essential ingredient in brewing beer. Look for hull-less barley cultivars to eliminate tedious hulling and beardless cultivars, which won't stick you when you're harvesting. Barley performs best in full sun but will endure some shade during the day. It does not require highly fertile soil but does best with a balanced pH and good drainage.

Plant barley in spring as soon as you can work the soil. In Zone 7 and south, you can also plant barley about three or four weeks before the first expected fall frost. You'll need ¾–1¼ pounds of seeds for a 200-square-foot bed. For best results, sow in rows 14″ apart. Cover barley seeds with about an inch or so of

soil. Water during germination if weather is dry. Barley has few pest problems.

Spring-planted barley will ripen in 60–70 days; winter-planted barley will ripen about 60 days after the ground thaws in spring. The seed head is ripe and ready to harvest when it darkens from light tan to golden brown. You can reasonably expect to reap about 25 pounds of barley from a 200-square-foot bed.

Buckwheat

Besides making great flour for pancakes and a high-carbohydrate Japanese pasta called soba, buckwheat (*Fagopyrum esculentum*) sports beautiful white flowers that attract many beneficial insects to your garden. Choose a large-seeded type for the best texture and flavor. Buckwheat prefers a sunny, well-drained site, but it will grow just about anywhere.

Plant buckwheat anytime after your last frost through late summer—whenever you have a two-month window in your rotation. If you live in a hot climate, plant buckwheat in the fall; it doesn't flower well in hot weather. You'll need 6–10 ounces of seeds to produce a dense stand in a 200-square-foot bed. Broadcast the seeds over a tilled bed and rake the soil lightly over it. Water during the first three weeks of growth if weather is dry. Then, leave it be—it's highly drought-tolerant. To ensure that you have a full crop, pull as many weeds as you can until the crop is well-established.

Buckwheat will continue to flower until a hard frost. But after 60–65 days, most of the seedpods will be heavy and turning golden brown. Stalks will be yellowing. When you see these signs, your buckwheat is ripe and ready to harvest. You can expect to reap about 10–15 pounds of buckwheat from a 200-square-foot patch.

Flax

Flax (*Linum usitatissimum*) is commonly grown for its fiber, which is spun into linen or made into paper. It is also grown for its protein-rich seeds, which are used whole or ground in baking or as hot cereal and are pressed to make linseed oil. Select cultivars that are resistant to wilt and rust if you have a choice, or buy whole seeds at a health food store and plant that. Flax grows best in cool, dry conditions, so plant it in an area that gets some shade and drains very well. A well-cultivated bed with a moderate amount of humus will do just fine.

Plant flax as soon as you can work the soil in early spring. You'll need 3–5 ounces of seeds to plant a 200-square-foot plot. Broadcast seeds to make a dense stand so that the plants will grow tall rather than branched. Tall plants produce heavier seed heads. Cover the seeds with an inch or so of soil. Flax doesn't compete well with weeds, so pull weeds conscientiously. Keep soil evenly moist for the first month, then hold off on the water, because flax is prone to wilt and rust—two diseases that are often caused by excess moisture.

Your flax seeds will be ready to harvest in about 70 days. Wait until the seed heads turn from their characteristic blue to a paler gray and are dry to the touch. You can reasonably expect to reap 8–10 pounds of flax seeds from a densely planted 200-square-foot bed.

Millet

Millet is the staple grain in some parts of China. Birds like it, too, and related types are included in almost any birdseed mixture. Pearl millet (*Pennisetum americanum*) is the best for eating as a whole grain, while the proso type (*Panicum miliaceum*) is more commonly ground

into flour. *Don't* buy wild millet, which is a highly invasive weed. Millet likes sunny, dry conditions. It yields well in a moderately fertile soil and can grow in somewhat poor soil.

Plant millet almost anytime from the last expected spring frost to about six weeks before the first expected fall frost. You'll need about ½ ounce of seeds to plant a dense 200-square-foot patch. Broadcast seeds thickly and rake to cover them with 2″–3″ of soil (to protect the seeds from birds). Millet is relatively drought-tolerant and pest- and disease-free, and it will outcompete most weeds.

You can begin harvesting 40–50 days after seeding. Don't wait too long, or birds will eat it first. Harvest heads that are heavy and densely covered with plump seeds. A 200-square-foot plot of millet will reliably yield 25–30 pounds of seeds.

Quinoa

Quinoa (*Chenopodium quinoa*), a close relative of amaranth, is an ancient grain that has been rediscovered. Its leaves make tasty greens for salads; the seeds are eaten whole like millet or ground into flour. Quinoa produces seed heads in a variety of colors, including yellow, green, and pink. A native of the mountains of South America, it will not produce much grain at low elevations, especially when days are extremely hot and nights are warm. Chilean strains of quinoa grow well at moderate elevations (2,000′–4,000′); choose Bolivian strains if you garden at a higher elevation (above 4,000′). Plant in a low-lying spot where cool air collects at night. It does best in a sunny, dry, moderately fertile spot, but it will grow in damp conditions.

Plant quinoa after the soil warms to 60°–65°F. Sow seeds 1″ deep in rows 4″ apart. A few ounces of seeds will plant a 200-square-foot plot. If the weather is dry, water during the germination period, then slowly cut back on watering. When seedlings are 2″–3″ tall, thin them to 8″ apart. Quinoa has few pest problems. It can suffer from fungal diseases when the conditions are wet late in the season.

Quinoa ripens in 70–80 days, depending on the cultivar. When the stalk's head is plump with small, yellow seeds, the grain is ready for harvest. Under favorable conditions, you can expect to reap about 15–20 pounds of quinoa from a 200-square-foot plot. Quinoa seeds are naturally covered with a bitter-tasting compound called saponin, which can be removed with thorough washing. Place the grain in a porous cloth bag and soak it in several changes of water to rinse the saponin away. Wash only the grain you intend to use right away, or be sure that the washed grain is fully dry before you store it.

Rye

Rye (*Secale cereale*) is a hardy grain that makes a somewhat coarse flour. It is often mixed with wheat flour to make bread. When you buy seeds, be sure not to pick up rye*grass* seed; ryegrass is a fine cover crop, but it doesn't produce grain. Tetraploid ryes grow faster and

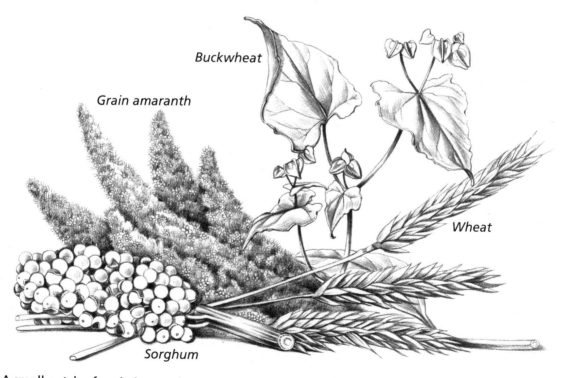

A small patch of grain in your backyard won't supply all of the flour for your baking, but it's an exciting treat to have bread made from grain you've raised yourself. Wheat, sorghum, grain amaranth, and buckwheat are just four of the many common and uncommon grains that will grow well in backyard plots.

produce more grain than standard rye. Rye needs full sun but will grow in damp or dry soil with absolutely minimal fertility.

Plant rye in mid- to late fall or early spring. It will germinate at air temperatures as low as 33°F, but it won't really grow much unless the temperature is 40°F or higher. Rye will not germinate in soil that is warmer than 85°F. Broadcast rye seeds thickly, then rake soil lightly over them. You'll need ¾–1¼ pounds of seeds for a 200-square-foot plot.

Rye demands little care. There is one disease you need to be on the lookout for, which is called ergot. Ergot produces an ugly black fungus that grows in the seed head of rye plants; it is poisonous to humans and animals. Plant certified disease-free seeds, or store seeds for one year before planting. (The disease organism doesn't live that long.) If you see black growths instead of plump grains in any of your seed heads, do *not* eat the grain.

Rye planted in fall will ripen 40–50 days after the soil reaches 40°F in spring. Rye sown in early spring will ripen in 65–70 days. Harvest when seed heads are full and the stalks and heads turn golden brown. You can expect to reap 15–20 pounds of rye from a 200-square-foot plot.

Sorghum

Commonly thought of as feed for livestock or as a source of syrup, grain sorghum (*Sorghum* sp.) seeds can be ground into a flour that makes a heavy, doughy bread when mixed with wheat flour. Use it alone to make tasty, unique cookies. Select grain-type sorghum cultivars for eating. Light-seeded or yellow endosperm types make the best flour. Choose a sunny, well-drained site for your patch. Grain sorghum suffers from many diseases, so plant resistant cultivars. If you live in a cool, damp climate favorable to disease problems, consider planting a less susceptible grain.

The rule of thumb for planting grain sorghum is to wait until ten days after the date recommended for sowing corn in your area; like corn, sorghum does not do well in cool, wet soils. You'll need about 1 ounce of seeds to plant a 200-square-foot plot. Plant seeds 1″–2″ deep and about 4″ apart in rows 18″–20″ apart. Thin seedlings to 8″ apart when they are 3″–4″ tall.

Grain sorghum is ready for harvest about 70 days from seeding. Gardeners with short growing seasons will need to harvest sorghum before it is completely ripe and hang it to dry in a sheltered area because it will mold outdoors in wet fall conditions. In regions with longer seasons, bring your sorghum in when the seed head is dry to the touch and is turning brown. Sorghum will produce 15–20 pounds of grain in a 200-square-foot plot.

Processing Grains

There are some important intermediate steps between harvesting grain and eating it. These include threshing (beating the seed heads to separate the grain from the husks) and winnowing (separating the grain from the chaff and little bits of straw). Some types of grain also need to have the tough hull, or seed coat, removed.

Consult descriptions of individual crops to decide when the crop is ripe. In general, if you have a grain crop with stalks that are turning yellow and a period of wet weather is forecast, harvest before the rain and bring the grain inside to finish drying in a shed, garage, or barn.

Large-scale grain growers use combines to harvest their crops, but you can cut your grains by hand with a sickle, a scythe, or a traditional Japanese harvesting tool called a kama, which has a honed steel blade at a right angle to its handle. (Whichever you use, be sure the blade is sharp.) To use a sickle or kama, firmly grasp a handful of stalks and cut them about 1' below the seed head. A scythe works best when you rotate your whole body from the hips up in a rhythmic swinging motion. Once the grain is cut, bind the stalks with straw or twine and hang them to dry.

After the seed heads are thoroughly dry, thresh them by whacking the seed heads against the inside wall of a barrel until the seeds are jarred loose and fall to the bottom. Or scatter the stalks on a sheet spread on a hard surface and beat the seed heads with a flail (a broomstick or a toy baseball bat works well) until the seeds are separated from the straw. The drier the seed head, the more readily the seeds will fall out.

To winnow the threshed grain, pour your threshed seeds from one container to another in a stiff breeze or in front of the airstream from a fan until the chaff and straw have blown away. Be sure the wind isn't so stiff that your seeds blow away!

You can eat any of the grains mentioned previously (except quinoa and standard barley) without any further preparation before cooking. Standard barley will need to be hulled; see the Rice entry for details. You can crack grain or make flour with a hand or electric-powered mill. Many high-powered blenders or juicers will grind grain into flour, but check the owner's manual before you try it with yours.

Propagation

Saving seeds from grain plants is easy because the grain is the seed. Be sure to save some from the heaviest, plumpest seed heads (before threshing) and store them in airtight containers in a cool, dark place. ✳

GRAPE

Vitis spp. Vitaceae. Deciduous vine.
Zones 4–10.

Grapes were one of the first cultivated fruits, with written descriptions of grape growing and wine making dating back thousands of years. Cultivars such as 'Muscat' and 'Petite Sirah' were known to the ancient Romans and are still available today.

You can carry on this grape-growing tradition—viticulture—in your own backyard. If you live where summers are sunny and dry and winters are mild (Zones 10 through 6 or 7, depending on the cultivar), you can grow the grape of antiquity, commonly called vinifera, or European wine grape (*Vitis vinifera*). These grapes are generally sweet, with mild flavor, and suited to fresh eating, drying, or wine making.

American, or fox, grape (*V. labrusca*), is native to the Northeast. Adapted from Zones 4 to 7, Americal grapes tolerate more cold, humidity, and pests than vinifera grapes. If you have tasted 'Concord', with its strong "foxy" flavor, you know what a typical American grape is like. These grapes are best for fresh eating, jelly, and juice. Breeders have crossed vinifera and American grapes to produce what are called French or French–American hybrids, combining qualities of both parents.

A third type of grape commonly grown is another native American, the muscadine grape

GRAPE

Site: Warm and sunny.

Soil: Deep, moderately fertile, well-drained.

Spacing: Muscadines: 15'–20' between plants in rows 10' apart. Other grapes: 8' between plants in rows 8' apart.

Seasons to bearing: Two to four years.

(*V. rotundifolia*). Muscadines are hardy to Zone 7. They grow wild and are adapted to the warm, humid climate of the Southeast. Muscadine vines are robust plants producing small clusters of large berries, which are usually eaten fresh or made into jelly or wine.

Planning

Selecting plants. Choose one-year-old dormant plants. American, hybrid, and muscadine grapes can be on their own roots or grafted. Vinifera grapes must be grafted on a phylloxera-resistant rootstock.

Grapes are self-fertile, with the exception of muscadines. If you are planting muscadines, check with your supplier to see if you need a pollinator.

Select cultivars adapted to your region in terms of season length, winter cold, summer humidity, and pests. Dry, hot areas of the West provide the best conditions for vinifera grapes. In cooler regions of the West, and north of the Carolinas in the East, plant American grapes. In the Southeast, plant muscadine grapes. French hybrids can be grown over many regions, depending on the hardiness, days needed for ripening, and pest resistance of specific cultivars. Consult descriptions in nursery catalogs so that you can choose cultivars best adapted to your region and use for the fruit.

It is very important to choose disease-resistant cultivars, especially in areas with humid summers. More resistant cultivars are released every year, so check with your supplier about new ones that may be available. Here are a few to choose from now:

'Beta', 'Campbell's Early', 'Cascade', 'Chancellor', 'De Chaunac', 'Delaware', 'Elvira', 'Fredonia', 'Hunt', 'Ives', 'Scuppernong', 'Sheridan', and 'Worden' are somewhat resistant to black rot.

'Baco Noir', 'Cascade', 'Catawba', 'Concord', 'De Chaunac', 'Delaware', 'Fredonia', 'Ives', and 'Niagara' resist Botrytis.

'Canadice', 'Cayuga White', 'Ives', and 'Steuben' resist powdery mildew.

'Aurora', 'Baco Noir', 'Canadice', 'Cascade', 'Concord', 'Foch', 'Himrod', and 'Steuben' resist downy mildew.

'Concord', 'Delaware', and 'Niagara' are resistant to anthracnose, one of the diseases that cause cane dieback.

Selecting a site. Grapes thrive in heat and full sun. The ideal site is a south-facing slope with sandy or loamy soil and a pH of 5.0–6.0. Avoid poorly drained sites. To further lessen the chance for disease, make sure drying breezes are unobstructed by fences, shrubs, or buildings. Stay away from wild grapes, as they may increase your disease and insect problems.

When to plant. Plant grapes in either early spring or fall.

Spacing. Plant vigor and the training system you intend to use both determine how far apart you should plant your grapes. Generally, space vinifera, American, and hybrid grapes with 8' between plants in rows at least 8' apart.

Muscadines are strong growing vines, so they need 15′–20′ between plants in rows at least 10′ apart.

For a greater harvest. Plant grapes in raised beds or individual raised hills.

Soil Preparation

Grapes—especially vinifera grapes—grow well in many different types of soils. The most important requirement is depth and good drainage. See "Custom Care for Small Fruits" on page 62 for how to prepare your site for planting.

Planting

Prepare your vine for planting by shortening lanky roots back to 1½′ and trimming dead or injured roots back to healthy tissue. Soak the roots in a bucket of compost tea for 20 minutes before planting. Just prior to planting, dust roots with a mixture of 2 cups of kelp and 1 cup of bonemeal. If crown gall is a problem in your area, dip roots in an anti-crown-gall inoculant before dusting with kelp and bonemeal.

Dig planting holes deep and wide enough to accommodate the roots. See "Perennial Crops"

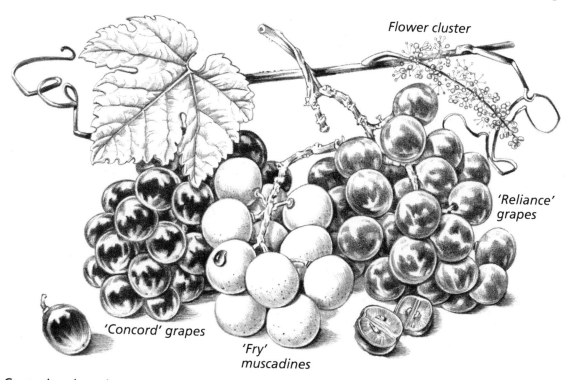

Flower cluster

'Reliance' grapes

'Concord' grapes

'Fry' muscadines

Grapevines have been cultivated from time immemorial. In temperate regions, European (vinifera) grapes, American (lambrusca or 'Concord' type), and their hybrids bear a wide range of fruit for fresh eating, drying, and beverages. In warmer regions, muscadine grapes are a better choice.

on page 111 for more details on how to plant. Make sure the graft on grafted vines is at least 2″ above ground level. To keep the graft from drying out on grafted vines, pile a mound of loose soil up over the graft and leave the soil in place for two months. Cut back the newly planted cane to two to four buds. Pound a sturdy wooden or metal post into the ground next to your plant. Finally, spread an organic mulch around the plant.

Growing Guidelines

Water and mulch. Grape roots spread deep and wide. Except in dry regions, supplemental watering often is unnecessary once plants are established. In dry regions, let the soil dry as grapes finish ripening and thereafter to help vines harden up for the winter. Maintain 6″–12″ of organic mulch under the vines.

Feeding. Add 10–15 pounds compost per 10′ of row each year in late winter.

Training. Grapes need a trellis or other support and lots of pruning every winter. The grape trellis illustration on page 136 shows one trellis option. "Pruning Perennial Vines" on page 140 discusses and illustrates how to prune grapes.

Thinning. When your vine sets an especially heavy crop, thinning is necessary. Do this while the fruits are still small and hard. Cut off some fruit clusters completely. On the clusters that remain, especially on cultivars with very tight or large clusters, cut off some of the little branchlets to open up the clusters.

Problem Prevention

When buds swell in spring, spray lime-sulfur. If diseases were a problem last year, spray now. Black rot shows up as light orange-brown spots on leaves and green fruit. Ripening fruits turn brown, then black, and shrivel into raisinlike mummies. Powder and downy mildew shows up as a white coating on shoot tips and leaves. Fruits ripen unevenly.

When buds show green, spray kelp. In early spring when leaf buds start to open, spray plants to increase bud hardiness and fruit set. Repeat every two to four weeks until fruits are set.

When buds show green, spray fungicides. If diseases were a problem last year, spray now. Use copper for black rot and downy mildew; use sulfur for powdery mildew. Do not spray copper while flowers are open; spray sulfur or lime-sulfur instead. Spray when weather is wet or humid and the temperature is above 59°F. Respray after each rain or once a week. Stop in midsummer if the weather stays warm and dry and there is little disease present.

When fruit buds appear, hang grape berry moth traps. Grape berry moths are a pest east of the Rockies. Early-season larvae feed on leaves and roll leaf edges over. Summer larvae attack fruits. Infested fruit is webbed together and often colors prematurely. If they were a pest last year, hang one trap to monitor arrival. Spray *Bacillus thuringiensis* var. *kurstaki* (BTK) one week after you catch your first moth. Repeat every few days until no new moths are caught. Raking and destroying fallen leaves in fall will help control them. If you have quite a few vines, you may want to try mating disruption to control grape berry moth. See "Pheromones" on page 159 for suggestions.

When fruits set, bag clusters. Small paper bags protect fruit from insects, diseases, and birds. Cut a small hole in the bottom corner of a paper bag to allow water to escape. Slip the bag over the cluster and fold the top so it fits tightly around the stem, then staple the bag closed. Leave enough space in the bag for the fruit to grow.

In summer, watch cane dieback. Various diseases cause stunting or death of entire branches. Prune off affected canes 6″ below elongated, sunken spots and destroy.

In late summer, remove leaves around fruit. Removing some leaves allows air to circulate around developing fruits, minimizing diseases such as botrytis bunch rot. Botrytis-infected clusters turn brown, soggy, and moldy.

In late summer, protect ripening fruits from birds. Birds peck holes in fruits, which not only ruins them but also attracts bees and wasps. Bag individual bunches or drape netting over the whole plant.

In fall, renew mulch. Rake loose, dry mulch away from vines in early fall. In late fall, after all of the leaves have fallen and the rodents have found winter homes elsewhere, respread the old mulch and top it with new to make a 6″–12″ layer.

In fall, deal with fallen leaves. If grape berry moth or black rot was a problem, rake up and destroy leaves, or bury them under mulch.

In winter, remove mummies. Diseases such as black rot and botrytis overwinter in mummified fruits. Pick them off and destroy them.

Gathering the Harvest

Do not pick grapes underripe because they will not ripen further after harvest. With American, vinifera, and French hybrid grapes, pick whole bunches when all of the berries in the cluster are fully colored and full-flavored. Spot-pick muscadine berries because they do not ripen evenly on the bunch. Pick frequently because ripe berries on some muscadine cultivars tend to drop.

You can store some cultivars of vinifera grape—'Emperor' and 'Ribier', for example—for

as long as six months at temperatures near freezing and high humidity. American grapes are more perishable, keeping, at most, for two months. Muscadine grapes are the most perishable. Even a cultivar that stores well, such as 'Carlos', will keep no more than two weeks at an optimum storage temperature of 35°–40°F.

Fall and Winter Care

In the fall, soon after the leaves drop, clean up diseased fruits and leaves. Prune your grapevine each winter when the plant is dormant. If your winters are very cold, wait to prune until after the coldest weather has passed. Pruning close to budbreak results in sap bleeding from wounds, but this does not harm the plant. How to prune grapes is explained and illustrated in "Pruning Perennial Vines" on page 140.

No matter what system of training you use, balance your pruning to the growth and productivity of your plant. You want canes that are 5′–6′ long and about as thick around as a pencil. If your vine didn't grow long enough or fat enough canes or if it set a poor crop the previous season, prune more severely than you did last year (leave fewer total buds). If your vine grew excessively long canes or lots of thick "bull" canes, prune less severely than you did last year (leave more buds).

Container Growing

If you want to grow grapes in containers, choose a nonvigorous cultivar, such as 'Delaware'. Provide some sort of supports for the vine, such as three or four stakes set around the edge of the pot, and coil the growing shoots around the supports. Once your plant reaches full size, repot it every year when it is dormant. Prune the tops more severely than you would a vine planted in the ground. In very cold areas, protect the roots in winter as shown in the illustration on page 240.

Propagation

The easiest way to propagate American and hybrid grapes in quantity is taking hard-wood cuttings. When the vine is dormant in the fall, cut canes into pieces with three nodes, with the upper cut on each piece just above the top node and the lower cut just below the bottom node. Keep cuttings cool and moist through the winter, then plunge them up to

their top buds and 6″ apart in spring in well-drained soil. Transplant the rooted cuttings in autumn or the following spring.

Muscadines are more difficult to root by cuttings, but layering is usually successful. When the plant is dormant, bend a growing cane to bare soil, then weight it down with a stone, leaving the tip exposed. By the end of the growing season, roots will have grown where the stem touches the soil. Cut off the rooted stem and transplant it.

Graft vinifera grapes to rooted American or hybrid cuttings or to special rootstocks. Any type of graft is suitable. ✳

GRAPEFRUIT

Citrus × paradisi. Rutaceae. Evergreen tree. Zones 9–10.

Grapefruits on the "half-shell" are well-known to breakfast fans. Grapefruits are also delicious peeled and eaten in sections like an orange. See the Orange entry for further description and culture. ✳

GREENS

Nothing beats garden-fresh greens for soups, salads, and savory side dishes. Plant a patch of greens in sun and fertile, humus-rich soil, and you'll have nutritious, flavorful foliage throughout the season. Many greens adapt well to growing in containers—a plus for small-space gardeners.

Greens are great as cooked vegetables. Try them lightly steamed, or mix them into stir-fries or soups. Enjoy the garden-fresh good-ness of fresh greens by adding them to salads. Try one kind at a time, or combine a variety of greens for a real taste sensation.

More and more seed companies are offer-ing mesclun—a mixture of different salad greens. The specific ingredients of mesclun can vary widely, depending on your tastes. Buy a pre-pared mesclun or make your own, following the recipes in "Super Salad Mixes" on the oppo-site page. Or combine a variety of your favor-ite greens for your own personalized blend. Mix the seeds together at planting time, or sow them separately and combine the greens as you harvest.

Among the greens, standard favorites include beet greens, chard, chicory, collards, endive, kale, lettuce, mustard greens, spinach, and turnip greens. For specific information on growing these popular crops, see their indi-

vidual entries. More uncommon greens include vegetable amaranth, beetberry, dandelion, Good King Henry, orach, sea kale, sorrel, and many others. For tips on raising vegetable amaranth and other Asian greens, see the Asian Specialties entry. Growing details for many other greens are given below.

Arugula

Arugula (*Eruca vesicaria* subsp. *sativa*) produces rosettes of slightly hairy leaves with a tangy, distinctive taste. It is also known as rocket, roquette, and rugula. This fast-growing annual salad green is very easy to cultivate; in fact, it grows wild in some areas. Arugula also grows well in window boxes and containers.

Plant in full sun, but provide afternoon shade during hot spells. Prepare a site with humus-rich soil by digging or tilling the top 4"–5"; rake to create a fine seedbed. Sow tiny seeds ¼" deep in early spring. Make successive sowings every two weeks until early summer; sow again in late summer for a fall crop. Plant 1'–2' of row per person at each sowing. Thin to 6"–10" between plants, with 16" between rows. Keep plants evenly moist and protect them from pests with floating row cover.

Start harvesting six weeks from sowing. Pick as needed when leaves are 4"–6" long. This cool-season plant tends to bolt in heat. Harvest the edible stems and flowers, or let a few plants set seed; collect the seeds or let them self-sow.

Malabar Spinach

Malabar spinach (*Basella alba*) is also called vine or summer spinach. The thick, succulent leaves of this vine have a delicate flavor and a high nutritional value. A native of India, Malabar spinach thrives in warm, humid weather and is a perennial in mild climates. Start plants indoors eight weeks before the last expected frost, and set them out after all danger of frost is past. Space plants 3' apart near a fence or trellis that you can train them up. Cut the young, tender leaves as needed; steam or add to salads.

Beetberry

Beetberry (*Chenopodium capitatum*) has triangular leaves that are tasty raw in salads or cooked like spinach. The other name for this annual plant, strawberry blite, comes from the pulpy orange fruit that dots the flower stems. The raw fruit is mild-flavored and adds a splash of color to a salad.

Seeds may be difficult to find—check specialty seed companies or seed exchanges—but it's worth the search. Plant in full sun in humus-rich soil. Sow seeds ¼" deep in spring. Leave 8"–10" between plants if you're growing them for leaves, 12"–16" for fruit. Allow 1½'–2' between rows. Keep soil evenly moist for best growth.

Plants are ready to pick 90 days from seed. Harvest leaves when they are 8"–10" long. Later in the season, harvest fruit from the stems. Beetberry is very hardy and can overwinter under snow cover or straw mulch.

Salad Burnet

Salad burnet (*Poterium sangisorba*) is a hardy perennial plant with leaves that have a mild, cucumberlike taste. Enjoy the young leaves raw in salad, or use them to flavor vinegars. Burnet grows in any soil with full sun. Direct-sow ½" deep outdoors in early spring; germination takes eight to ten days. Thin to 8"–10" between plants. Burnet reseeds profusely. It will keep growing even during winter if mulched.

Corn Salad

The iron-rich, spoon-shaped leaves of corn salad (*Valerianella locusta*) make a mild addition to early-spring or late-fall salads. Corn salad is also known as lamb's lettuce and mâche. This easy-to-grow crop likes full sun and reseeds easily. Leave 4" between plants. When leaves are 3"–4" tall, cut the entire rosette at ground level. See "Arugula" on page 377 for more complete growing information.

Cress

The plants we commonly call cresses are grown for their peppery, vitamin-rich leaves. Garden cress or peppergrass (*Lepidium sativum*) and curly cress (a curly selection of *L. sativum*) are annuals; upland or winter cress (*Barbarea verna*) is a biennial. Grow these easy crops as you would arugula. See "Arugula" on page 377 for details. The similarly flavored watercress (*Nasturtium officinale*) is a perennial. Watercress thrives in a few inches of cool, running water. You can also grow it in any good garden soil if you keep it quite moist. Or plant it in a large pot and keep the pot sitting in a deep saucer filled with a few inches of water.

Dandelion

In your lawn, dandelion (*Taraxacum officinale*) can be a weed; in your garden, it's a great source of early-spring greens. Plant seeds ½" deep in spring to midsummer. Thin to 10" between plants, 1½'–2' between rows. Harvest lightly about six weeks after planting, or wait until the following spring. Pick the young leaves of established plants as needed until warm weather makes them turn bitter. Try dandelion greens raw in salads or steamed like spinach. Remove spent blooms to avoid self-sowing, or use the flower heads for making wine.

Garland Chrysanthemum

Garland chrysanthemum (*Chrysanthemum coronarium*) is an annual grown for its young leaves and strong-tasting yellow flowers. Also known as edible chrysanthemum and shungiku, it grows best in cool temperatures. For growing guidelines, see "Arugula" on page 377.

Good King Henry

Good King Henry (*Chenopodium bonus-henricus*) goes by many names, including fat-hen, mercury, and all-good. This hardy perennial grows best in sun and rich soil but can survive in infertile soil and partial shade. Sow seeds ⅛" deep in rows 1'–2' apart. Keep the seedbed moist for four to six weeks for good germination. Thin to 1′ between plants. In fall, cut plants down and protect crowns with a layer of mulch. In early spring, harvest the 10″–12″ arrow-shaped young leaves and use them like spinach. Later on, cut the flowering shoots and prepare them like asparagus.

Lamb's Quarters

A familiar garden weed, lamb's quarters (*Chenopodium album*) thrives in humus-rich soil. It grows very much like its relative, beetberry. See "Beetberry" on page 377 for growing information. Unlike beetberry, lamb's quarters is not frost-hardy. The plants can grow 8′–10′ tall, especially in fertile soil, but the leaves are good to eat only when young and tender.

Orach

As one of the oldest cultivated plants, orach (*Atriplex hortensis*) has many names, among them mountain spinach. The plant looks like a big lamb's quarters with broad, arrow-shaped, pale green or reddish leaves. The mild young leaves are good raw in salads or steamed like spinach.

To grow this annual, follow the guidelines given in "Arugula" on page 377, but leave 15″–18″ between plants and 2′ between rows. Orach grows well in alkaline soil and tolerates drought. Pinch back the flowers to encourage branching and fresh new leaves. If you let a few plants flower, orach reseeds easily.

Purslane

Many gardeners think of purslane (*Portulaca oleracea*) only as a common weed, but experienced greens-growers cultivate it for its foliage. Mildly acerbic in flavor and succulent in texture, the leaves and thin stems are useful raw in salads or in a stir-fry. The thicker, bottom portions of stems add body to soups and make good pickles.

Arugula

Garden sorrel

Purslane

Don't waste those weeds! Many common plants that we think of as weeds are great sources of greens. Pick plants like arugula, purslane, and garden sorrel for super salads and savory side dishes.

This heat-loving, drought-tolerant crop is very easy to grow. It prefers full sun and loose, sandy soil. In spring after danger of frost is past, just press the seeds into the soil and water them. Make small successive sowings every two to four weeks until late summer. Thin to stand 4"–6" apart. Harvest as needed, but leave at least 1" of stem to regrow. Purslane is not frost-hardy but reseeds easily.

Sea Kale

Sea kale (*Crambe maritima*) is a perennial with bluish green leaves and white flowers. Like asparagus, sea kale is valued for its early shoots. Direct-sow seeds in early spring, 2'–3' apart. Mulch over winter in cold areas; topdress with compost in spring. You can begin harvesting the third spring after planting. In late winter, as shoots begin to appear, cover them with an inverted basket. When shoots are 6"–8" long, cut them like asparagus. Harvest young plants for one to two weeks and older plants for three to four weeks. After harvesting, remove the basket and let the plant regrow.

Sorrel

For zesty perennial greens, try garden sorrel (*Rumex acetosa*) or French sorrel (*R. scutatus*). The common garden weed is smaller and tastier than the cultivated French type. Both plants lend a lemony flavor to sorrel soup or a sharp tang to a salad. Sorrel has no pests and few growing problems. It prefers acid soil and tolerates partial shade. Direct-sow early in spring, 1/2" deep. Thin to 1½' between plants, with 1½'–2' between rows. Cut large leaves as needed for a continuous supply.

Tyfon

Tyfon (*Brassica rapa* ✕) is a mild-flavored cross between turnip and Chinese cabbage. Direct-sow this fast-growing, cold-tolerant crop 1/2" deep in early spring or midsummer; in mild areas, try it as a winter crop. Thin to 6" apart. In about 90 days, harvest leaves as needed, or cut the whole head about 1" above the crown. (It will resprout.) Use the leaves fresh in salad or as cooked greens. ✳

GUAVA

Psidium guajava. Myrtaceae. Evergreen shrub or small tree. Zone 10 and warmer parts of Zone 9.

These small evergreen trees originated in the American tropics. The white or red flowers later turn to round to oval fruits with pink, red, or white centers with many small seeds. Guava juice is a delicious treat, or make guava shortcake, jams, jellies, and guava paste, which adds spice to apple pie. Strawberry guava (*Psidium littorale* var. *longipes*) is a more cold-tolerant species.

Site. Plant in a sunny, sheltered spot.

Soil. Grows well in many types of soil.

How much to plant. Start with one or two trees. Plant more, if needed.

Spacing. Space trees 25'–30' apart.

Seasons to bearing. Guavas often bear fruit the first year after planting.

Planting and growing. Plant in early summer at the beginning of the rainy season. Plant as you would any tree; see "Perennial Crops" on page 111 for directions. Feed three times a year with alfalfa meal, blood meal, or fish meal. Foliar-feed with kelp or fish emulsion.

Prune lower branches if tree form is desired. Don't overprune; fruit is borne on one- to three-year-old wood. Whiteflies can be a problem. Releasing predatory wasps is effective on a neighborhood-wide basis.

Temperatures below 29°F can kill trees to the ground, but the roots will resprout.

Harvesting. Pick fruit daily as soon as it begins to ripen and fall.

Propagation. Guava grows from seeds. It can also be air-layered or grafted.

Friends and relatives. Pineapple guava, which is commonly known as feijoa, is different from guava. See the Feijoa entry for details. ✳

HERBS AND SPICES

Herbs and spices are natural additions to your garden-fresh fruits and vegetables. There's simply nothing like fresh tomatoes sprinkled with basil, or a fresh bay leaf added to spaghetti sauce. And when it comes to spices, there's nothing quite like cinnamon in cider or apple pie, or vanilla beans in ice cream. While you can grow most herbs in your garden, most spices are native to tropical climates. Although tropical spices can't be grown outdoors in most parts of North America, to get the best flavor—both from your homegrown fruits and vegetables and from the spices—it's a good idea to know what spices you are buying and how to use them.

In this encyclopedia, you'll find individual entries on many herbs. See the individual entries for Basil, Chives, Dill, Fennel, Garlic, Ginger, Horseradish, Marjoram, Mint, Mustard, Oregano, Parsley, Rosemary, Sage, and Thyme. You'll also find information on using herbs in the Asian Specialties, Italian Specialties, Mexican Specialties, and Tea entries. You'll find information on even more herbs in the table "Growing and Using Herbs" on page 382.

Exotic Spices

Although you'll probably buy your spices, not grow them, you can take steps to make sure you use ones that are as flavorful as possible. The shelf life of spices is short, so buy them in small amounts. You can store whole and ground spices in sealed containers in the freezer for up to one year. When appropriate, buy your spices whole, then grind them at home right before using. To grind or powder your own spices by hand, use a mortar and pestle. Other tools to use are pepper mills, coffee mills, miniature food processors, and spice grinders. Use the guidelines below for buying and using the most popular spices.

Allspice (*Pimenta dioica*). Aromatic allspice is the dried berry of a 30' evergreen tree grown in the tropics. The berries are picked green, then dried. Buy whole allspice and add it to slow-cooked soups, stews, pickles, and mulled cider. Grind the dried berries and add them to baked goods, including pumpkin pie.

Cardamom (*Elettaria cardamomum*). A perennial herb grown in India, cardamom is collected as small, unripe seedpods, then dried. Buy the seeds whole, then crush or grind them

(continued on page 386)

Growing and Using Herbs

In the garden or in the kitchen, herbs are easy to grow and delightful to use. The blossoms and foliage add texture and fragrance to arrangements and ornamental garden beds. Herbs attract honeybees and other beneficial insects. Some help to repel garden pests. In the kitchen, herbs are common ingredients in all kinds of dishes, from soups and stews to beverages and desserts. Sprigs of fresh herb leaves or blossoms also are an attractive garnish. Use this table to help you select herbs that will grow well in your conditions.

NAME AND FAMILY	CULTURE	HARVESTING AND DRYING	USE(S)
Angelica (*Angelica archangelica*) Umbelliferae	Biennial or perennial. Grow from seeds. Likes part shade and cool, damp, slightly acid soil. Grows 5′–8′ tall. Space 3′ apart. Deadhead to prolong life of plant, or allow to self-sow. Zones 4–9.	Harvest stems, roots, and leaves. Harvest sparingly the first year.	Candy the stems. Eat roots and stems fresh. Add leaves to vegetables while cooking. Seeds make a sweet tea.
Anise (*Pimpinella anisum*) Umbelliferae	Annual. Grow from seeds. Likes full sun and light, poor, slightly acid, well-drained soil. Dislikes heat and high humidity. May need staking.	Snip the licorice-flavored leaves with scissors as needed. Collect seeds when they fall easily from the head. To preserve, dry the stems, leaves, and seeds.	Add leaves to salads. Use seeds to flavor baked goods or tea.

Fenugreek

Bay

Hops

NAME AND FAMILY	CULTURE	HARVESTING AND DRYING	USE(S)
Bay (*Laurus nobilis*) Lauraceae	Tender shrub. Buy nursery plants. Grow in containers in the North and bring indoors in winter. Likes full sun to part shade and fairly rich, slightly acid, well-drained soil. Zones 8–10.	Harvest leaves with scissors as needed.	Add whole fresh or dry leaves to soups, stews, sauces, and meats at the beginning of cooking time; remove before serving. Add dry leaves to potpourris or wreaths.
Caraway (*Carum carvi*) Umbelliferae	Biennial. Grow from seeds or cuttings. Likes full sun to part shade and light, fertile, slightly acid soil. Mulch to keep soil cool and moist. Zones 3–7.	Cut plants when seeds become brown and almost loose. Hang in paper bags; collect when thoroughly dry.	Use in rye bread or tea; add to soups and stews during the last 15 minutes of cooking.
Chervil (*Anthriscus cerefolium*) Umbelliferae	Annual. Grow from seeds. Likes part shade and moist, humus-rich, slightly acid soil. Dislikes heat. Will self-sow.	Harvest the licorice-flavored leaves with scissors as needed. Leaves dry poorly.	Add fresh leaves to dishes just before serving, since heat destroys the flavor.
Cilantro (*Coriandrum sativum*) Umbelliferae	Annual. Grow from seeds. Likes full sun to part shade and moderately rich, slightly acid, well-drained soil. Seed every 2–4 weeks for continuous harvest. Will self-sow.	Pinch fresh leaves as needed when plants are growing vigorously. Seeds of this plant are known as coriander. Harvest and dry seeds when they are brown, before they shatter.	Use leaves in Mexican cuisine.

Caraway Chervil Anise Hyssop

(continued)

Growing and Using Herbs—Continued

NAME AND FAMILY	CULTURE	HARVESTING AND DRYING	USE(S)
Cumin (*Cuminum cyminum*) Umbelliferae	Annual. Grow from seeds. Likes full sun and average, well-drained soil.	Cut plants when seeds become brown and almost loose. Hang in paper bags; collect when thoroughly dry. Yield tends to be small.	Grind the dry seeds and use them to flavor Mexican cuisine.
Fenugreek (*Trigonella foenum-graecum*) Leguminosae	Annual. Grow from seeds. Likes full sun and rich, warm, well-drained soil.	Harvest pods as they start to open. Shell the seeds; dry in the sun.	Use seeds in baked goods for maplelike flavor. Add ground seeds to curries. Leaves are used as a vegetable in Indian cuisine.
Hops (*Humulus lupulus*) Cannabaceae	Perennial. Buy nursery plants or grow from cuttings. Likes full sun and deep, fertile, slightly acid soil. Plants need a fence or trellis to climb on. Zones 3–7.	Collect catkins when they are brown to amber colored. Dry them in an oven (125°–150°F) or food dehydrater. Use promptly.	Conelike catkins are the hops used in making beer.
Hyssop (*Hyssopus officinalis*) Labiatae	Perennial. Grow from seeds. Likes full sun to part shade and light, well-drained soil. Zones 3–9.	Pick the leaves and blossoms as needed. Flowers are attractive to bees and butterflies.	Use leaves and blossoms in salads.
Saffron (*Crocus sativus*) Iridaceae	Perennial. Plant the corms in spring or fall. Likes full sun to part shade and light, well-drained soil. Zones 6–9.	In the fall, collect and dry individual dark yellow stigmata from inside flowers.	Use in rice dishes for flavor and color.

NAME AND FAMILY	CULTURE	HARVESTING AND DRYING	USE(S)
Savory, summer (*Satureja hortensis*) Labiatae	Annual. Grow from seeds. Likes full sun and average, well-drained soil.	Harvest leaves continuously once plants are growing vigorously. For best foliage flavor, cut just before flowering. Dries well.	Use leaves fresh and dried in bean, egg, and fish recipes.
Savory, winter (*Satureja montana*) Labiatae	Perennial. Grow from seeds, cuttings, or divisions. Likes full sun and poor to average, well-drained soil. Zones 6–9.	Harvest leaves continuously once plants are growing vigorously. For best foliage flavor, cut just before flowering. Dries well.	Use leaves fresh and dried in poultry and bean recipes. Blossoms are attractive to bees.
Sesame (*Sesamum orientale*) Pedaliaceae	Annual. Grow from seeds. Likes full sun and average, well-drained soil. Prefers warm, southern climates.	Cut the stalks as soon as the uppermost pods are green. Hang in bunches to dry in a paper bag. Seeds fall easily when dry. Yields are usually low.	Use seeds in baked goods and candies.
Tarragon, French (*Artemisia dracunculus*) Compositae	Perennial. Buy nursery plants; seed-grown plants do not have true tarragon flavor. Likes full sun to part shade and light, slightly acid, well-drained soil. Dislikes hot, dry climates. Zones 4–8.	Snip foliage with scissors as needed all summer, as long as plants are growing vigorously. Preserve by drying.	Add to salad vinegars.

just before adding to curries, coffee, or baked goods. Store them in the dark.

Cinnamon (*Cinnamomum zeylanicum*). Cinnamon is the bark of a small tree grown in Ceylon and India. The sweet, spicy bark is harvested as curled quills or sticks, then dried. Buy cinnamon in small quantities, since flavor deteriorates quickly. Add the sticks to hot beverages and potpourri. Use ground cinnamon in baked goods, sprinkle it on fresh summer fruits, and add it to tomato sauces paired with ricotta cheese.

Clove (*Syzygium aromaticum*). Cloves are the flower buds of a tropical evergreen tree that resembles bay. Even the leaves have a clove scent. Flower buds are harvested before they bloom, then dried. Buy whole or ground cloves. Whole cloves are difficult to grind by hand. Stick whole cloves into roasting meats, or add them to hot beverages. Add ground cloves to fruit dishes and baked goods.

Nutmeg and mace (*Myristica fragrans*). Nutmeg is a nutlike seed enclosed within a fruit that is harvested from a tall evergreen tree grown in tropical countries. Mace is the fleshy skin lying over the seed. After harvesting, nutmeg and mace are dried separately. Nut-

meg has a sweeter flavor; mace is robust. Buy whole nutmeg and grate it as needed for baked goods, pies, and sauces. Buy powdered mace and use it in vegetable dishes, especially with spinach.

Pepper (*Piper nigrum*). Black pepper, harvested from a tropical vine, is made from dried, unripe fruits. Buy pepper whole, then grind just before using; flavor deteriorates quickly when ground. Add whole peppercorns to slow-cooking dishes, since ground pepper becomes bitter with long cooking.

Turmeric (*Curcuma domestica*). A perennial herb from tropical Asia, turmeric yields an underground rhizome similar to ginger. Mature rhizomes are boiled, peeled, dried, then powdered. Add turmeric to curry recipes or to color foods a warm yellow.

Vanilla (*Vanilla planifolia*). Vanilla is an orchid that is a perennial vine. It is trained to grow on posts or trees in the tropics. Its white flowers yield long pods called vanilla beans. The pods are harvested unripe, then cured and made into an extract that is used to flavor baked goods and hot beverages. You can buy the beans as well, and add the flavorful seeds to ice cream or baked goods. ✳

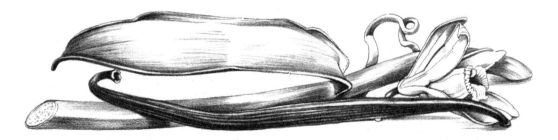

Vanilla is a climbing orchid with thick, fleshy leaves and white flowers, which are followed by flavorful pods.

HORSERADISH

Armoracia rusticana. Cruciferae. Perennial. Zones 5–9.

Horseradish is known for its hot, mustard-flavored roots. Add it grated to mayonnaise for sandwiches, or use it as a condiment with beef. Toss the tender leaves into salads.

Selecting plants. Buy dormant horseradish root cuttings in early spring or fall. Look for root cuttings that are straight, with a crown of buds at the top.

Site. Grow horseradish in full sun.

Soil. Horseradish prefers a site with abundant moisture. Humus-rich, heavy soil, free of stones or other obstructions and with a neutral pH, is best. Prepare beds in late fall or late winter. Loosen the soil to a depth of 1'–2' for the best root growth.

How much to plant. For most families, one plant will provide plenty of root to harvest.

Spacing. Space new roots 1'–2' apart.

Days to maturity. Harvest horseradish in early to late fall of the first year, or in early spring the following year.

Planting and growing. In spring or fall, plant root pieces 1'–1½' deep. If the soil is dry, water thoroughly after planting. Horseradish spreads quickly and can escape the borders of your garden. To prevent its spread, plant the roots in the ground in bottomless containers 20"–24" deep. Small plastic trash containers with their bottoms cut out work well.

Harvesting. Dig roots in spring or fall. Break or cut off what you need and replant the rest. Brush off the soil, and store roots in the refrigerator, in dry sand in a cool cellar, or buried shallowly in garden soil covered with straw bales to prevent freezing. Store fresh roots for up to three months. For longer storage, grate and store in vinegar.

Propagation. Take root cuttings in spring or fall. ✳

ITALIAN SPECIALTIES

Growing "Italian-style" can be as simple as planting some new cultivars of your standard garden crops. That's because Italian cuisine today makes extensive use of tomatoes, peppers, and eggplant. These crops, all native to the Americas, were unknown in Italy until Columbus and other explorers brought them back to Europe. Other common vegetables, including beans, squash, and a variety of greens, also figure prominently in Italian cooking. Of course, you'll also want to grow some of the herbs that frequently flavor Italian dishes. Grow basil, parsley, marjoram, mint, oregano, rosemary, sage, and thyme to season your Italian specialty crops.

Common Vegetables

Traditional Italian cultivars may look different or have a different texture than the plants you usually grow, but they have the same growing requirements. See the individual plant entries for cultural information on these crops.

Tomatoes. No Italian garden is complete without some paste tomatoes such as 'San Marzano'. The meatier types such as 'Principe Borghese' are used in fresh sauces, dried, or preserved in olive oil. For salad tomatoes with an Italian bent, grow 'Costoluto Genovese'.

Peppers. Italian-style sweet peppers include bell-shaped cultivars and elongated types sometimes called frying peppers. Thick-walled bell peppers are most often roasted. The thinner-walled frying peppers are sautéed or eaten raw. Grow 'Corno di Toro' and 'Marconi' peppers for frying. You can even grow your own 'Pepperoncini' for pickling.

Eggplant. If you like eggplant, try growing 'Violette di Firenze', which bears large, lavender fruit with exquisitely creamy flesh, or 'Listada di Gandia'.

Squash. Summer squash also features prominently in Italian cuisine. 'Tromboncino' bears elongated, pale green fruits with crisp flesh on long vines that need trellising. Zucchini and 'Cocozelle' squash are also traditional. Italians eat squash blossoms, too. Try them in frittatas (baked omelets) and risottos (rice cooked in meat stock and seasoned with Parmesan cheese or saffron). Or stuff them with cooked mixed vegetables and Romano cheese seasoned with garlic and parsley. Dip in egg, then flour, sauté in olive oil, and top with Romano cheese.

Beans. Snap beans, shelling beans, chick-peas, and fava beans are all popular vegetables. 'Green Anellino' is an Italian-style pole snap bean. Shelling beans are used green or dried. The most common are 'Borlotto', 'Cannellini', and 'Spagna Bianchetti'. If you can't find these, 'Vermont Cranberry' beans are similar to 'Borlotto' and you can use butter beans for 'Spagna Bianchetti'.

Greens. Bitter or spicy greens are an important part of any Italian garden. Domesticated dandelion, arugula, mustard, garden cress, watercress, and endive stand out in salads and add spark to vegetable and pasta dishes. Radic-chio and other chicories are also important. 'Red Treviso' and 'Verona Red' are traditional radicchio or heading chicories, but 'Adria', 'Giulio', and 'Alto' may perform better in this country. For leaf chicory, try 'Biondissima Trieste' and 'Catalogna'.

Spinach, chard, and leaf lettuce are favored milder greens. Italian cultivars of chard such as 'Argentata' and 'Monstruoso' have wider midribs than American ones, and the broad stems are used as a vegetable in their own right.

Other common vegetables. Where the climate permits, you may want to grow globe artichoke. Italian markets offer small purple artichokes as well as the larger green type. The purple ones are said to be more tolerant of cold temperatures. Try 'Violetto' or 'Purple Sicilian'.

Italians also serve beets sautéed or in a sweet-and-sour sauce; 'Chioggia' is one beet to try. Finally, onions add flavor to many Italian dishes; try 'Rossa di Milano' and 'Red Florence'.

Vegetable Specialties

For truly traditional Italian cuisine, try growing the following less well known crops.

Black salsify. Also known as scorzonera, black salsify is a different plant than salsify. It has a long, thin root that is creamy inside its black skin. Both scorzonera and salsify have a sweet, faintly oyster flavor. See the Salsify entry for culture.

Broccoli raab. Also called rapini, broccoli raab forms a small broccoli-like head, which is harvested and eaten with about 6″ of stem and leaves. It is typically prepared by blanching in boiling water for a few minutes to reduce bitterness. Then, it's chopped coarsely and sautéed in olive oil with garlic and onions. Try tossing it with hot pasta. It is sometimes sold as 'Di Rapa' broccoli or sprouting broccoli. See the Broccoli entry for culture.

Cardoon. Cardoon, or *cardoni,* a close relative of globe artichoke, is grown for its celery-shaped leafstalks. Blanch the thick, fleshy leafstalks before harvesting by wrapping them in burlap or paper. Eat the tender inner stalks raw or braise them. Or dip sections in egg batter, sauté until lightly browned, sprinkle with grated cheese, and serve. See the Artichoke entry for culture.

Fennel. Bulb fennel, also called Florence fennel or *finocchio,* is eaten raw and thinly sliced in salads or cooked in a variety of ways. Its licorice flavor is more pronounced when it is eaten raw, more subtle when cooked. Try it sautéed in olive oil. See the Fennel entry for culture. ✳

JERUSALEM ARTICHOKE

Helianthus tuberosus. Compositae. Perennial. Zones 2–9.

Jerusalem artichokes, sometimes called sunroot, reliably produce a harvest of mild-flavored tubers, year after year. A species of sunflower, Jerusalem artichokes are native to North America, not the Middle East. They probably got their misleading name from the Italian word *girasole,* which means "turning toward the sun," as sunflowers seem to do. You are unlikely to confuse them with artichokes, although these potatolike tubers were once described as artichoke flavored.

Jerusalem artichoke plants, which may reach 12′ tall, spread by rhizomes. Each rhizome is tipped with a fleshy tuber that has flavor and texture similar to a water chestnut. Peel off the skin and slice the tender root into salads, sauté it lightly in a stir-fry, or boil half a dozen for a mashed-potato-like dish. David Cavagnaro, a garden manager at Heritage Farm for Seed Savers Exchange in Iowa, shreds the tubers into slaw.

Selecting plants. You can grow the brown-skinned, white-fleshed Jerusalem artichokes sold in grocery stores. Or seek out cultivars with tubers of different sizes and skin colors—such as red, violet, or golden. They all taste and store similarly, says Cavagnaro, so choose the cultivar you find prettiest. To save cleaning time and trouble, look for tubers with smooth, round surfaces, instead of dirt-trapping knobs. If you want the crop to be ornamental, too, find cultivars that produce small, golden, sunflower-like heads—some don't.

If space is limited, grow a cultivar with shorter rhizomes. This makes it easier for you to dig up all of the tubers in fall, leaving less chance for the plants to escape and spread. Cultivars such as 'French Mammoth White' produce tubers in an easy-to-find clump beneath the plant. 'Golden Nugget', which has an elongated yellow tuber, has semi-invasive 1′–2′-long rhizomes, and 'Fuseau', which has slender, yam-shaped tubers, has quite invasive 3′-long runners that are easy to miss. Cavagnaro's favorite is 'Smooth Garnet', a ruby-skinned type with rhizomes of moderate length.

Site. Select any sunny garden site, preferably on the northern side of the garden where the tall plants will not shade other crops. Use the sturdy, fibrous stalks as a windbreak or to support climbing beans.

Soil. You'll have good luck growing Jerusalem artichokes in well-drained soil of average fertility, but they will produce tubers even in poor sites. Tubers grown in clay soil are harder to clean, however. For a large, exceptional harvest, give the plant rich, deep soil. In a garden of fertile Iowa loam, Cavagnaro once harvested two heaping wheelbarrow loads of sizable tubers from a 15' row of Jerusalem artichokes.

How much to plant. One Jerusalem artichoke plant can yield 2–10 pounds of tubers, depending on the cultivar and the growing conditions.

Spacing. Set whole or cut tubers about 4" deep, 1'–2' apart in rows 2'–3' apart.

Days to maturity. You can dig tubers of some cultivars as early as 90 days after spring planting. Or plant in fall and harvest the following fall.

Seasons to bearing. Jerusalem artichokes will produce tubers the first season whether you plant in spring or the previous fall.

Planting and growing. Plant new tubers in spring after the last expected frost. Broken Jerusalem artichokes don't store well, but you can replant them after your fall harvest to produce the following year's crop. Make sure each cut or broken piece you plant has several eyes on it. If your Jerusalem artichokes spread too quickly, surround the bed with an underground "fence" of 1'-wide boards inserted into the top 1' of soil to limit the rhizomes. This plant does not need high fertility to produce well, but a little compost or fertilizer won't hurt. Whenever you have extra compost, work it into the bed before planting or use it as a mulch after planting. If the plants tend to stay small, add some extra nitrogen and potassium in the form of fish emulsion and wood ash. Mice and voles enjoy dining on Jerusalem artichoke tubers during winter. Eliminate these losses by digging the tubers in fall and storing them in damp sand in a cool root cellar.

Tubers

Jerusalem artichokes are a perennial sunflower that produces nutty-flavored edible tubers.

Harvesting. Although tuber formation begins in mid-season, the tubers don't reach their full size until fall. Harvest after frost turns the upper portions of the plant brown; cool weather sweetens the tubers. When you harvest, comb the entire bed to find all of the tubers you can; any you leave will sprout into new plants in spring.

Extending the season. If you mulch the bed deeply—with 1' of leaves—to keep the soil from freezing, you can continue digging up the tubers all winter long.

Propagation. Cultivated forms of Jerusalem artichokes seldom produce seeds. Propagate them easily by dividing the tubers into small pieces with one or two growth buds each.

Friends and relatives. Maximilian sunflower (*Helianthus maximilian*), also called pencil-thin sunroot, is another perennial sunflower with thin, edible roots. Its culture is the same as Jerusalem artichoke. ✳

KALE
Brassica oleracea, Acephala group.
Cruciferae. Biennial grown as an annual.

Kale is a reliable, fast-growing, cool-season crop. This leafy cabbage relative is a superior source of vitamins A, B, and C, as well as calcium, iron, and potassium. Enjoy kale raw in a salad, or steam it, stir-fry it, or add it to soups.

Selecting plants. Open-pollinated and hybrid cultivars of kale are available. Hybrids tend to mature earlier and produce more heavily.

Site. Kale grows best in full sun, but it does appreciate some shade in hot climates.

Soil. Kale thrives in a light, humus-rich soil with a pH of 5.5–6.8. Incorporate a legume cover crop, or work in 30 pounds of compost per 100 square feet before planting.

How much to plant. One gram of seeds sows 20' of row. Plant 5'–10' of row per person.

Spacing. Allow 1' between plants and 2' between rows.

Days to maturity. Kale matures 50–65 days from direct-sowing or 30–40 days after transplanting.

Planting and growing. Set plants out or direct-sow in early spring or midsummer. Kale is prone to the same pests and diseases as cabbages, though not as badly. See the Cabbage entry for complete growing guidelines.

Harvesting. Begin picking kale leaves when they reach 8"–12" long, starting at the bottom of the plant. Or make several successive sowings and harvest entire plants when they are 1' tall. Flavor improves after frost. Kale keeps for up to two weeks in the refrigerator in vented plastic bags; freeze for longer storage.

Extending the season. For an early crop, start seeds indoors ten weeks before the last expected frost.

Fall and winter care. After harvest, tear out plants and compost them.

Propagation. See the Cabbage entry for details on propagating kale. ✳

KIWI

Actinidia spp. Actinidiaceae.
Deciduous vine. Zones 3–9.

People in eastern Asia have been enjoying the fruits of native kiwi vines for centuries. Late in the nineteenth century, western explorers introduced kiwi vines to other parts of the world, mostly as ornamentals. In New Zealand, however, the fruit's value was recognized, and commercial plantings were established. The fuzzy kiwi owes its popularity to its delicious, sparkling green flesh and a name change, years ago, from "Chinese gooseberry" to "kiwifruit."

The fuzzy kiwi (*Actinidia deliciosa*) is hardy in Zones 7–9. *A. arguta* and *A. kolomikta*, both commonly dubbed hardy kiwi, stand more cold than fuzzy kiwi, tolerating winter lows in Zones 4 and 3, respectively. Hardy kiwis bear grape-size fruits with smooth, green, edible skins and slightly sweeter flavor than the larger fruits of fuzzy kiwi.

Kiwis are good eaten fresh as well as canned, dried, or made into wine. Avoid overcooking the fruits or else you will drive away the flavor and cause the fruit to become muddy green in color and more tart.

Selecting plants. Except for a few cultivars, such as 'Issai' (*A. arguta*) and 'Blake' (*A. deliciosa*), most kiwis need pollination from a separate male plant. Even self-fruitful cultivars may yield larger and more fruit when a male pollinator is present. Plant one male vine to pollinate up to eight females. You can tell a male vine from a female vine by its flowers; male flowers have a large tuft of stamens, while female flowers have a small green kiwifruit in the center of a ring of stamens.

Site. Kiwi bark is susceptible to winter injury, and leaves emerging in early spring are susceptible to frost injury. To avoid these hazards—and they are hazards even to hardy kiwis—choose a site located on a north-facing slope or shielded from low winter and early spring sun by a building or trees. Shade tolerance in kiwis corresponds with cold-hardiness, with the hardiest kiwis being fond of some shade.

Soil. Kiwis demand well-drained soil with a pH of 5.0–6.5. If your soil does not drain sufficiently well, set plants atop a raised mound of earth. Kiwis are not drought-tolerant, however; water during dry spells.

How much to plant. A mature, bearing fuzzy kiwi vine yields about 200 pounds of fruit. Expect about 100 pounds from a hardy kiwi vine.

Spacing. Space vines 15' apart.

Seasons to bearing. Depending on the cultivar, your first harvest will be from two to six years after you plant.

Planting and growing. You can let kiwi plants clamber over decorative pergolas and arbors, but for best fruit production, train the vines on a trellis.

Build a sturdy trellis with T-posts every 15'. Make the T-posts by bolting a 6'-long 2 × 4 crossarm to one end of an 8'–9'-long 4 × 4 or 6 × 6 post. Set the post into the ground so that the crossarm is 6' above the ground (or slightly less if you're short) and at right angles to the row of posts. Stretch five strands of 12-gauge wire from crossarm to crossarm along the length of the trellis: one in the center right above the posts, one at each end of the crossarms, and the remaining two halfway between the others.

Plant vines equidistant between the T-posts. Tie a string from the center wire to the base of the vine so that the new growth can grow up the string. When the shoot, which will be a plant's permanent trunk, reaches the center wire, pinch out the tip and train shoots that grow from the topmost two buds along the wire in opposite directions. These two shoots—called cordons—will be permanent arms from which fruiting shoots will grow.

Prune vines occasionally during the growing season. Cut back shoots growing off the trunk between ground level and the cordons, as well as any rampant or tangled shoots. As soon as blossoming ends, prune male plants back sharply, removing much of the previous year's growth.

Pest problems are few on kiwi, but the plant is among the many enjoyed by Japanese beetles. Handpick these pesky pests into soapy water; use milky disease (*Bacillus popilliae* and *B. lentimorbus*) to control the grubs.

Kiwi does suffer from one unique pest problem: cats. The vines' effect on cats is similar to catnip's. Mature plants can withstand the chewing and clawing that sometimes results, but protect the bases of young plants with a cylinder of chicken wire.

Harvesting. For long-term storage, harvest kiwis while they are still firm. First, cut open a few fruits. Black seeds indicate that the fruits are mature enough to harvest. At high humidity and near-freezing temperatures, you can store firm fruits for many months. Before eating kiwis, let them soften, either on the vine or out of cold storage. To speed ripening, put firm fruits in a paper bag with an apple.

Fall and winter care. The bark on young kiwi vines—even the cold-hardy species—is susceptible to winter injury, especially in direct sunlight or when winter temperatures fluctuate. After the ground freezes in winter, protect young trunks by wrapping them with cornstalks, burlap, or similar materials.

Prune your kiwi vines during winter dormancy. On young plants that you are still training to fill the trellis, shorten each developing cordon, leaving about 2′ of growth from the previous season. This heading forces fruiting arms to grow out from the cordons. Thin these fruiting arms to 1′ apart, then drape or tie them across the outside wires.

Cut cordons on mature plants back to 7′. Each winter, cut back the fruiting arms, or the laterals growing off these fruiting arms, to a length of 1½′. Occasionally rejuvenate old fruiting arms by cutting them back to within a few inches of the cordon.

Container growing. Kiwis can be grown in containers, but you need to provide a trellis or some other support for the rampant growth. For ease of management, grow weaker sorts such as *A. kolomikta* cultivars or 'Issai'.

Propagation. Kiwi seeds germinate readily after stratification, but the resulting plants will, of course, be either male or female. The females will produce fruit of variable quality. The seedlings are very susceptible to damping-off in their initial slow development.

The easiest way to propagate a cultivar is by softwood cuttings, which often root in two to four weeks. Use ripened wood near the bases of new shoots for cuttings.

If you want more rapid initial growth and you have a rootstock, propagate by grafting. Use a dormant scion, and join it to the rootstock in midwinter or after shoots begin to grow in spring, using a whip-and-tongue or cleft graft. *

KOHLRABI

Brassica oleracea, Gongylodes group.
Cruciferae. Biennial grown as an annual.

Curious-looking kohlrabi tastes like a cross between turnip and cabbage but has a milder, sweeter flavor than either of those crops. Enjoy the crunchy "bulbs" (really swollen stems) raw, or steam them and serve with butter.

Selecting plants. Green and purple cultivars are available; they generally taste the same.

Site. Plant in full sun.

Soil. Kohlrabi grows well in light, humus-rich soil with a pH of 5.5–6.8. Incorporate a legume cover crop, or work in 30 pounds of compost per 100 square feet before planting.

How much to plant. One seed packet will sow 30' of row. Sow 3'–5' of row a person.

Spacing. Allow 3"–6" between plants and 1'–3' between rows.

Days to maturity. Kohlrabi matures 40–75 days from seed.

Planting and growing. Set out plants or direct-sow in early spring or late summer. Compared to the other members of the cabbage family, kohlrabi is relatively problem-free. See the Cabbage entry for complete growing information.

Harvesting. Pick kohlrabi when the bulb is 2"–3" in diameter. Cut the stem just below the bulb. You can also eat the leaves as greens. Kohlrabi will keep for one to two weeks wrapped in plastic in a refrigerator. Or store it in a cool, moist cellar for up to three months.

Extending the season. Start plants indoors ten weeks before the last expected frost and set out after six weeks. In the South, kohlrabi will grow throughout the winter when temperatures are 40°F or higher.

Fall and winter care. After you've cut the bulb, pull the roots and compost them.

Propagation. See the Cabbage entry for details on propagation and seed saving. ✳

LEEK

Allium ampeloprasum, Porrum group.
Liliaceae. Biennial grown as an annual.

This close relative of the onion has been a favorite of European gardeners for centuries. The long, thick, white stalks of this hardy plant have a wonderfully sweet, subtle flavor that enhances salads, soups, stews, or any dish to which you would normally add onion. Along with potatoes, it is a key ingredient in vichyssoise. The leaves of leeks can be chopped up and used as a garnish.

Selecting plants. Since leeks require a fairly long growing season, look for cultivars that mature quickly or are extremely hardy. The faster-growing leeks are generally smaller and less hardy than other cultivars.

Site. Give leeks a sunny site, if possible. They will tolerate partial shade.

Soil. Leeks will grow in most types of soil, but thrive in well-drained loam with a high organic matter content and a pH of 6.0–7.0.

How much to plant. Grow about eight to ten plants for every person in your family.

Spacing. Allow 4"–6" between plants in rows 12"–16" apart. You can also grow leeks in intensive beds, spacing plants 2"–6" apart.

Days to maturity. Leeks are long-season vegetables that take 70–150 days or longer to reach maturity from seed. Plants often will grow larger if left in the ground after they mature.

Planting and growing. If you live in an area with a long growing season, direct-sow leek seeds ½" deep in early spring. Otherwise, start plants indoors up to 12 weeks before the last expected spring frost. Seeds germinate in 10–14 days. Seedlings grow best in temperatures of 55°–60°F at night and 65°–70°F during the day. After the last expected frost, set out transplants when they are about 8" tall. Plant them 6" apart in individual holes or a trench 6" deep, covering all but 1" or so of the leaves. As the leeks grow, blanch the stalks by filling in the trench gradually and/or mounding soil or mulch around them to exclude light. This will make the stalks longer and more tender.

Keep the bed well-weeded and evenly moist but not soggy. Fertilize plants with compost tea every four weeks or so during the growing season. Mulch the crop to control weeds. Leeks share pest and disease problems with onions; avoid planting leeks where onions grew the previous year.

Harvesting. Begin harvesting leeks when the stalks are large enough to use; their flavor improves after a light frost. Pull or dig them carefully. You can refrigerate leeks for a few weeks, or store them in moist sand or soil in a cool place for six to eight weeks.

Extending the season. Try sowing seeds of fast-growing cultivars in the winter in a cold frame to get a jump on the season. Where temperatures stay above 10°F, harvest leeks throughout the winter. For an early-spring harvest in colder areas, plant seeds in summer. Lift plants before the first expected hard frost and store them in the cellar; replant in spring. Or mulch thickly and overwinter leeks in the garden.

Fall and winter care. When the first hard frost is predicted, cover your plants with a 1' layer of straw or other mulch. Harvest plants as needed throughout the winter.

Propagation. To save seeds, simply allow a few plants—preferably the best ones—to flower in their second year of growth. Pick the umbels in the fall and let them dry. Beat or rub the dry heads vigorously to release the seeds. ✳

LEMON

Citrus limon. Rutaceae. Evergreen tree. Zones 9–10.

Acid-tart lemons are essential for lemonade, lemon meringue pie, and many other piquant treats. See the Orange entry for further description and culture. ✳

LETTUCE

Lactuca sativa. Compositae. Annual.

If you choose the right cultivars and stagger planting dates, you can easily grow all of the lettuce you can eat, and some to share with the neighbors, too! Lettuce is at least 90 percent water but offers plenty of vitamins A and B. Use lettuce as a main ingredient in salads, or cook it as a novelty in soups or as a side dish.

Planning

Selecting plants. Leaf lettuce is quick and easy to grow. It's ideal for early and late plantings. Romaine, or cos, lettuce has long,

---

❧ AT A GLANCE ❧
LETTUCE

Site: Tolerates partial shade; thrives in light shade in summer; does well in humid spots.

Soil: Loam soil that is well-drained and moderately rich; needs constant moisture; pH of 6.0–6.8.

How much to plant: Plant 15–20 leaf lettuce plants or 7 head lettuce plants per person.

Spacing: Leaf lettuce: 6–12" between plants in traditional rows 1'–3' apart, or in intensive beds with 6"–9" between plants. Head lettuce: 8"–14" between plants in traditional rows 1'–3' apart.

Days to maturity. Leaf lettuce: 40 days from seed to harvest. Head lettuce: 70 days from seed to harvest, or 20–35 days from transplanting to harvest.

---

crunchy leaves. Head lettuce forms a dense clump or rosette of leaves. Head or semihead types include iceberg lettuce and butterhead, or Boston, lettuce. Look for heat- and bolt-resistant cultivars for summer crops. Also look for disease-resistant cultivars.

When to plant. Lettuce does best in temperatures of 60°–65°F. The soil temperature should be at least 35°F. If the weather gets hot (80°F or higher), lettuce will bolt and turn bitter. For planting times, see "Planting Indoors" and "Planting Outdoors" following.

How much to plant. A ¼-ounce packet of seeds covers a 100' row and produces about 50 pounds of leaf lettuce or 80 heads. Plant 15–20 leaf lettuce plants or 7 head lettuce plants per person.

Spacing. For traditional rows, space leaf lettuce 6"–12" apart and heading plants 8"–14" apart. Allow 1'–3' between rows. In intensive beds, space leaf lettuce 6"–9" apart.

Rotation. Good preceding crops for lettuce are legumes and root crops. Avoid planting lettuce directly after broccoli; lettuce is sensitive to the chemical compounds released from broccoli crop residues as they break down.

For a greater harvest. For best results, grow lettuce in areas shaded lightly by overhanging trees or by tall crops such as corn. Interplanting lettuce with other crops, such as cabbage, creates humid microsites for the lettuce.

Soil Preparation

Lettuce will grow in most soils but prefers a moderately rich, well-drained loam with a pH of 6.0–6.8. Lettuce is a heavy feeder. See "Custom Care for Leafy Crops" on page 60 for details on enriching the soil before planting.

Cultivate the soil shallowly but finely before planting lettuce. If planting seeds, rake the surface smooth. Transplants can tolerate a rougher planting bed.

Planting Indoors

Sowing seeds. Start head lettuce indoors 35–49 days before you plan to set it out. Don't bury seeds in flats; they need light to germinate. Seeds germinate in seven to ten days.

Seedling care. Keep plants moist. The

LETTUCE SEEDLING

Seeds   *Cotyledons*   *First true leaves*

optimal growing temperature for transplants is 55°–65°F during the day and 50°–55°F at night.

Hardening off transplants. Begin this process at least one week before setting out.

Planting Outdoors

Sowing seeds. Leaf lettuce is best sown directly in the garden. Sow seeds directly in the ground two to four weeks before the last expected frost date. Try broadcasting seeds lightly over a wide row, and gently rake them in. Don't bury seeds—they require light for germination. For rows, sow seeds thinly ¼" deep in rows 1½' apart. Heading types do better when started as transplants.

Lettuce seeds germinate best at soil temperatures of 40°–80°F. Seeds will not germinate if the soil is over 85°F; germination is slowed if the soil temperature drops to 35°F.

For a steady supply of leaf lettuce, plant every 15–20 days in the spring and every 10–15 days in the summer. Plant heading types at shorter intervals. Shade plants in the summer.

Buying transplants. Choose plants that are compact and dark green.

Setting out transplants. Immediately water transplants well and mulch thickly.

'Black-Seeded Simpson'

'Gemini'

'Paris Island'

'Sitonia'

'Royal Oak Leaf'

With lettuce, iceberg is just the tip of the iceberg. Leaf lettuce has smooth or frilly leaves that range in color from green to red. Romaine, or cos, lettuce produces long, crunchy leaves. Butterhead lettuce has loosely folded, tender outer leaves and a yellow heart.

Growing Guidelines

Thinning seedlings. When they are 3″–4″ tall, thin plants to 6″–12″ apart in traditional rows or 6″–9″ apart in intensive beds. Use thinnings in salad. In intensive beds, rake lightly to weed and thin at the same time.

Water and mulch. Lettuce needs constant moisture for rapid growth. After thinning seedlings or at transplanting, put down a 6″–8″ layer of straw, legume hay, or grass clippings. To avoid disturbing the shallow roots, hand-weed as needed.

Feeding. For plants growing in poor soil, feed weekly with fish emulsion (1 tablespoon per gallon of water) or compost tea from transplanting until the plants are 3″–4″ tall. Plants growing in well-prepared soil don't need fertilizing.

Problem Prevention

Select resistant cultivars. Choose cultivars that resist bolting or tipburn or diseases such as mosaic virus, downy mildew, and bottom rot.

After planting, cover plants or seedbed with floating row cover. Covering plants will prevent feeding by aphids, leafhoppers, flea beetles, and other pests.

After planting, erect a chicken-wire fence or use repellents. Otherwise, your lettuce may be eaten by four-legged creatures.

During the growing season, keep soil evenly moist but don't overwater. Too much water will cause the plants to rot. Too little water will cause slow growth and lead to a poor harvest. Water in the morning. That way, the leaves will have a chance to dry by evening and are less likely to become diseased.

Gathering the Harvest

Leaf lettuce matures about 40 days from seeding. Start harvesting outer leaves when they are still small to encourage the inner leaves to grow. If your crop begins to bolt or is threatened by a hard frost, harvest the entire plant. Head and romaine lettuce mature about 70 days from seeds and 20–35 days from transplants. When the heads are firm, harvest by cutting the plant at ground level. For crisp lettuce, harvest in the morning and eat that day. You can store most lettuce in the refrigerator for one to two weeks; iceberg lettuce keeps for up to three weeks.

Extending the Season

You can sow lettuce seeds outdoors six weeks before the last expected frost under floating row cover or clear plastic tunnels. (Keep the plastic at least 3′ from the leaves.)

🐜 FRIENDS & RELATIVES 🐜

LETTUCE

Celtuce (*Lactuca sativa* var. *angustana*) is grown primarily for its edible central seedstalk. It's both heat- and frost-tolerant. You can harvest it two ways: First, pick the outer leaves when they're less than four weeks old. After that, cut off the central seedstalk when it is about 1″ in diameter.

You can use both the leaves and the stalks in salads or in steamed or stir-fried dishes. Be sure to peel the bitter outer skin off of the stalk before you eat it.

For a fall harvest, plant leaf lettuce seeds at least seven weeks before the first expected frost; plant heading types about ten weeks before frost, depending on the cultivar. If you protect heading types under clear plastic tunnels, you can continue planting up until five weeks before first fall frost. You can also try overwintering young lettuce plants under a heavy layer of mulch.

Container Growing

Lettuce grows beautifully in containers. Tuck it in at the edges of large containers where you're growing other vegetables or herbs, or even flowers.

Propagation

Lettuce is self-pollinating but may occasionally cross with nearby cultivars. Plant in very early spring, or plant in fall and overwinter plants under heavy mulch. Spring-planted lettuce will bolt during the summer; fall-planted lettuce will bolt in the following spring. Since bolting is not a desired characteristic for lettuce, collect seeds from the last plants that bolt. You can keep unused seeds for up to five years. *

LIME
Citrus aurantiifolia. Rutaceae.
Evergreen tree. Zone 10.

Limes are the least cold-hardy of the citruses, but the tangy fruits are a gourmet treat. See the Orange entry for further description and culture. *

MARJORAM
Origanum spp. Labiatae.
Perennial grown as an annual.

The aroma and flavor of sweet marjoram (*Origanum majorana*) are something similar to mild oregano. Use the leaves fresh or dried in salads or egg dishes, stirred into soups, or rubbed on roasts. The dried leaves are aromatic additions to potpourri, wreaths, and arrangements.

Site. Grow marjoram in full sun.

Soil. Marjoram grows in most well-drained soils with a neutral pH.

How much to plant. Two to three plants will supply enough marjoram for two people.

Spacing. Space plants 8″ apart in all directions.

Days to maturity. Begin harvesting five to six weeks after transplanting outdoors, or when plants are growing vigorously.

Planting and growing. Sow seeds indoors in a well-drained medium six to eight weeks before the last expected frost. Cover seeds shallowly and keep the soil moist. Move plants outdoors after the danger of frost is past.

Harvesting. Harvest leaves during the growing season. Hang bunches to dry in a cool, airy place away from sunlight. Rub the dry bunches in your hands to remove the leaves; discard stems, or crumble and add to potpourri.

Fall and winter care. In cool climates, lift the whole plant from the soil in early fall. Break the root system into several parts, then plant the pieces in pots to bring indoors. Left on a sunny windowsill, potted marjoram plants will provide light harvests for winter meals. In spring, move plants back to the garden.

Propagation. Sow seeds indoors in early spring. Divide plants in fall or take cuttings anytime.

Friends and relatives. Pot marjoram (*O. onites*) has a peppery flavor and grows well in hanging baskets. Oregano (*O. vulgare*) is sometimes refered to as wild marjoram. ✳

MELON

Cucumis melo and *Citrullus lanatus*.
Cucurbitaceae. Annual.

Sweet, succulent melons are one of the special pleasures of summer breakfasts and cold lunches. Their flavor, aroma, and high amounts of vitamins A and C make melons a healthy delicacy. Most of the melons we grow, including muskmelons, honeydews, casabas, and crenshaws, are variations of the same species (*Cucumis melo*). Watermelons are less closely related but are grown the same way. Small watermelons (*Citrullus lanatus*) and orange-fleshed muskmelons, often called cantaloupes, are easy crops for beginning gardeners. Some melons require more gardening skill or a perfect climate, but all are grown in much the same way.

Planning

Selecting plants. The most popular melons are green-fleshed honeydews, watermelons, and orange-fleshed muskmelons. For gardeners seeking something different, there are many other choices—green-fleshed muskmelons, orange-fleshed honeydews, and seedless or yellow-fleshed watermelons.

Muskmelons are the easiest to grow. Place high priority on resistance to powdery mildew in areas where this disease is common.

Powdery mildew typically develops while the melons are ripening and robs them of flavor.

Unless you are really cramped for space, try long-vined cultivars, not short-vined or bush-type ones. Long vines usually are associated with superior flavor and texture because they have more leaves and can put more energy into fruit production. If you do grow short-vined cultivars, thin fruits to two per plant to keep the leaf-to-fruit ratio high.

Most muskmelons have soft-textured flesh; cultivars described as very firm-fleshed, or crisp, will have flesh that crunches like a cucumber. Slow-growing, crisp-fleshed casaba and crenshaw melons need substantial heat. They are best grown where summers are long and warm.

❧ AT A GLANCE ❧
MELON

Site: Full sun.
Soil: Moderately rich, well-drained soil with a pH of 6.0–6.8.
Spacing: 8"–12" apart in rows 6'–10' apart or two plants per hill, with the hills spaced 2'–3' apart.
Days to maturity: 75–90 days from seed, depending on cultivar.

Very large-fruited watermelons need a long warm season, too, but small icebox types will grow in all but the coolest climates. Seedless watermelons are grown just like seeded ones, but seeds have to be started indoors and pampered through the germination process.

When to plant. Melons need very warm soil and won't grow well in soil cooler than 60°F. They don't tolerate frost. Sow seeds outdoors two weeks after the last expected spring frost; for indoor sowing, start seeds one week before the last expected spring frost. For fall planting, add three weeks to the days-to-maturity rating of the melon you are growing and plant that long before the first expected frost.

How much to plant. Bushy, short-vined muskmelons and watermelons will produce two or three good fruits per plant; long-vined types will produce five. Ripening tends to be uniform, meaning that all of the fruits usually mature in a three-week period.

Spacing. Space plants 8″–12″ apart in rows 6′–10′ apart. Or plant melons in hills, two plants per hill, with the hills spaced 2′–3′ apart.

Rotation. Plant melons after legumes, tomatoes, peppers, or leafy greens but not after other cucurbits or corn.

For a greater harvest. Plant melons once in late spring and again three to five weeks later. If space is tight, let them to run between upright crops like tomatoes, peppers, okra, or sunflowers, or along a block of widely spaced corn.

Soil Preparation

Melons resent extremely acidic soil, so choose a spot that has recently been limed or is naturally alkaline. Dig two shovelfuls of compost or rotted manure into each hill or planting hole within a row. If you are using a purchased organic fertilizer, choose one that is rich in nitrogen. Shape the cultivated soil into raised hills or a raised row, raked flat on top. In cool climates, cover the prepared soil with black plastic for two weeks to warm the soil before planting. See "Custom Care for Fruit Crops" on page 58 for a more detailed discussion.

Planting Indoors

Melons often are started indoors in cool climates because they need every day of warm summer weather they can get. For best results, melons sown indoors need strong light, constantly warm conditions, and large transplantable containers such as 3″ peat pots. Handle the seedlings just like cucumbers. (See "Planting Indoors" on page 341 for details.)

Seedless watermelons need to be started indoors. They have thick, sticky seed coats that sometimes clamp down over the emerging sprout. To help them along, mist the sprouts with water to keep the seed coat soft. If it still refuses to let go, gently open it out, using two hands, and free the seedling leaves. Once the seedlings emerge, grow seedless watermelons just like regular ones. Seeds of a pollinator are included in packets of seedless watermelon seeds because they do not produce sufficient pollen by themselves.

Planting Outdoors

Sowing seeds. Soak seeds in compost tea for 15 minutes before planting them. Plant seeds ½ inch deep, with four or five per hill or spaced along the row. If you have clay soil that tends to develop a crust on its surface, scatter grass clippings, sawdust, or straw thinly over the planting before watering well.

Setting out transplants. Harden off seedlings for a week before setting them out. If you have used black plastic to prewarm the bed, cut holes in the plastic and set the plants in shallow holes. With or without black plastic mulch, set the plants ½″–1″ deeper than they were growing in their containers. Water each plant thoroughly after transplanting.

Growing Guidelines

Thinning seedlings. When direct-sown seeds are showing at least one true leaf, thin them to two plants per hill. In rows, thin to 2′–4′ intervals, depending on the vigor of the cultivar.

Water and mulch. Melons need 1″ of water a week while they're young, but flavor often improves if the plants become gradually drier as the fruit ripens. At the same time, big plants need more water than small ones. Watch mature plants closely and water if they appear stressed by heat and drought. Never allow melons to dry out completely since a heavy rain after a long dry spell can cause ripening melons to split.

Because melons sprawl, keeping weeds under control is a challenge. Disturbing the vines when weeding interrupts the flow of nutrients to ripening fruits, which increases the risk that they may be ripe on one side but green on the other. To prevent this problem, weed thoroughly just as the vines begin to run, then mulch with an 8″ layer of straw or hay. The mulch will control weeds and also provide a clean resting place for ripening melons.

If your melon patch is so large that deep mulching is impractical, sow a low-growing cover-crop such as clover between rows or hills. Melons don't do well with plants growing close to their crowns, but you can cover the soil between the melons with plants that lure bees and other beneficials, such as alyssum, marigolds, radishes, and basil.

Training. The fruits of most melons are so large that they cannot be grown on trellises. Small-fruited melons can be trellised, but support individual fruits with nets or slings.

Problem Prevention

Select resistant cultivars. In addition to resistance to powdery mildew, look for tolerance or resistance to Fusarium wilt.

Control pests. The insects that sabotage other cucurbits—cucumber beetles, squash bugs, and squash vine borers—can wreak havoc in the melon patch. These pests usually shun watermelons, and squash bugs and borers prefer squash, but cucumber beetles often devastate muskmelons and honeydews by infecting them with bacterial wilt, which causes plants to wilt and die suddenly. Row cover offers the best protection against this pest.

At planting time, use row cover. Besides creating a warm, moist atmosphere for seedlings, row cover applied at planting time protect plants from birds and insects. Remove it a week after the first flowers appear or sooner, if plants are cramped.

MELON SEEDLING

Seeds   Cotyledons   *First true leaves*

Fertilize. From the time they begin growing vigorously until the first blossoms appear, melons need a steady supply of nitrogen. If growth is less than robust, drench plants weekly with a solution of 1 tablespoon of fish emulsion per gallon of water. Later, when the plants are in full flower, spray them with a kelp-based foliar spray on a mild, cloudy afternoon.

Gathering the Harvest

One of the trickiest aspects of growing melons is knowing when they're ripe. Many muskmelons develop a thick netting over the rind, and the rind beneath becomes a lighter shade of green, or even yellow, as they reach full maturity. Other melons "slip" from the vine when ripe. With "full slip" types, harvest after the melon forms its own scar where the stem attaches to the fruit; you should be able to pull the melon free with a gentle tug.

Watermelons are tricky, too. When ripe, the curled tendril at the stem end dries to brown, the underside of the melon turns yellow or cream-colored, and the melon will yield a deep, resonant sound when thumped. Or you can be scientific and count off 35 days from the time the fruit sets and begins to grow.

Most melons will ripen a little bit more for two or three days after they're picked. Store melons at room temperature until they are totally ripe, then refrigerate for several weeks. Melons can be pureed or cut into balls and frozen.

Extending the Season

Prewarming the soil with black plastic helps melons grow better in cool climates.

🐦 FRIENDS & RELATIVES 🐦

MELON

The balsam pear, or bitter melon (*Momordica charantia*), is edible only when soaked and blanched to decrease its bitterness. It makes a nice ornamental vine. Various Asian melons produce small, slightly sweet melons with thin rinds. Their texture is similar to a potato. All are grown like conventional melons. See the Asian Specialties entry for more on Asian melons.

Fall and Winter Care

When the last melon is harvested, turn under the vines and plant a cover crop. Or gather the vines and compost them, cultivate the soil, and plant turnips, lettuce, or another leafy green suitable for growing in fall.

Container Growing

Melons are difficult to grow in containers since the fruits develop several feet away from the main crown of the plant.

Propagation

To save seeds from nonhybrid cultivars, allow a melon from a disease-free plant to ripen until the vine dies back or the melon begins to soften. Scoop out the seeds, wash them in warm water, and allow them to dry on a sheet of wax paper for several days. Store in an airtight container in a cool, dark place. ✳

MEXICAN SPECIALTIES

Anyone who loves the traditional foods of Mexico and the American Southwest can easily fill their gardens with plants used in this pungent, diverse cuisine. In fact, you're probably already growing many of the vegetables and herbs used in traditional Mexican cuisine. Beans, peppers, and tomatoes are perhaps most closely associated with Mexican cooking, but garlic, onions (both green and yellow), spinach, green beans, potatoes, squash, and turnip greens also play important roles in traditional Mexican recipes. Corn, which is ground into flour and cornmeal, and rice, which is used mainly as a side dish with beans, are the principal grains. You'll find growing information on these crops in their individual plant entries.

Most basic Mexican vegetables and herbs—or at least fair substitutes for them—will grow anywhere in the continental United States without much problem in containers, in the ground, or indoors. In the North, it's harder to coax some crops into peak flavor and performance than it is in the South or Southwest. Look for cultivars recommended for your region and, in short-season areas, get a jump on the growing season by starting plants indoors in flats, and use row cover after transplanting outdoors to keep the plants warm.

Common Vegetables

For truly authentic Mexican food, try growing some of the traditional cultivars of beans, peppers, tomatoes, and corn.

Beans

Pinto beans, black beans, and chick-peas (also called garbanzo beans) are the staples of Mexican dry bean cuisine. They're used in burritos, soups, stews, pastes, and casseroles.

Pinto beans are drought-tolerant and not picky about soil but they need a long season to mature; they're not tough enough to withstand freezing temperatures just when they're maturing. While there's no substitute for the native flavor of pinto beans, reasonable short-season substitutes include kidney beans, white pea beans, navy beans, and marrow beans, which are similar to white navy beans, only larger.

Virtually all of the black beans do well in the North. 'Black Turtle' and 'Black Mexican' are popular cultivars. Use them in soups and casseroles, and boil and mash them for burritos.

Dried chick-peas are used whole in many recipes; they're also ground to a powder or cooked and mashed for fritters and fried cakes. It's easy to cook dry chick-peas. They freeze well, and their nutty taste is delicious for snacking and in salads. Try them in place of noodles in your favorite pasta salad.

Peppers

According to an old Texas folk saying, the trick to raising really hot hot peppers is simple: Plant peppers when you're angry, and don't talk to anyone while you're doing it. Whether this is true or not is anyone's guess; what does seem to hold true is that peppers grown in cooler climates are more likely to have a milder flavor than those grown further south.

When it comes to selecting peppers to grow, you'll find a variety of types listed, most with several different cultivars. Often both hot and mild forms are available. Ancho, jalapeño, cayenne, and chili peppers are traditional Mexican types. For best results with peppers, look for cultivars adapted for your region, especially in northern, short-season climates.

Stuffing peppers. Mexican cooks stuff fresh peppers with rice, meat, or cheese. You can also cook and marinate dried 'Ancho' peppers or large dried red California chili peppers and then stuff them. Northern gardeners can try 'Crimson Hot', a large red pepper that's about the size of a Hungarian wax pepper but has a hotter flavor. Jalapeños, probably the most popular of the hot peppers, are good stuffed with cream cheese and served as appetizers or snacks.

Sweet or bell peppers. Sweet bells aren't used as frequently as hot peppers in Mexican cuisine, but there's a place for them in the garden and on the table—especially if someone in your family doesn't like hot peppers. Use sweet peppers raw, stuff them, or fry them with onions as a colorful side dish. (Cultivars in shades of red, green, orange, yellow, purple, lavender, white, and chocolate brown are available.) Or add them to sauces or soups. Good choices are 'Big Bertha', 'Golden Summer', and 'Sweet Chocolate', which turns a deep chocolate color before ripening to red.

Mild to medium-hot peppers. 'Relleno' peppers, from which *chiles rellenos* are made, mature in about 75 days and are fine for northern gardens. The mildly hot 'Manzano' is used in salsas and soups. It requires a long season to mature—grow it in containers in the North.

Two good Mexican chili peppers for short-season climates include those packaged under the 'New Mexico' or 'Colorado' series. Both are good for *chiles rellenos;* 'Colorado' is also good roasted and peeled or dried.

Although 'Serrano' peppers are not recommended for the Midwest, they're sold for gardens west of the Cascades in the Pacific Northwest. Mexican cooks use them fresh or cooked in sauces, or as a piquant garnish. 'San Felipe', a cayenne, is very productive, is fine for northern gardens, and bears early. Fresh cayenne peppers can be used as a substitutes for jalapeños. 'Mexi Bell' is a hot bell pepper.

Very hot peppers. Jalapeños, perhaps the best known of the hot peppers, turn red when ripe but are picked and used at all stages of their development for salsas, guacamole, nachos, and more. They also can be pickled, either alone or with onions and carrots. Or stuff them as described in "Stuffing Peppers" on this page if you like very hot foods.

'Anaheim' chili peppers are definitely on the list of very hot peppers, as are green chilies and 'Red Cherry' peppers. 'Chimayo' chilis are used green for *chiles rellenos* or dried in the red stage for chili powder. They're strung and hung to dry as *ristras,* the strings of peppers that have become a symbol of the Southwest. 'De Arbol', a small-fruited chili pepper, is a good choice for southern states and produces with some success in the North. 'Ring of Fire', a cayenne, produces in 60 days from transplant to harvest. 'Habañero' peppers ripen to orange and are used to add fire to chili and salsa.

Chiltepin (*Capsicum annuum* var. *aviculare*) is an interesting, very hot pepper from Mexico and southern Arizona. It bears pea-size fruit and is a perennial in frost-free areas of the Southwest. In the North, it makes a good container plant. Start chiltepins early indoors; they take up to 200 days to produce ripe fruit from seeds. When ripe, use them in salsa if you dare, and set aside some to dry for your pepper shaker.

Tomatoes and Tomatillos

Tomatoes in all forms are an essential ingredient in Mexican cooking. You can use hybrid tomatoes or try some unusual cultivars. Probably the most uniquely Mexican contribution to the tomato world is a group of old

Native American cultivars that are hollow, like bell peppers, and used for stuffing. 'Large Ribbed Zapotec' is fluted—some say ruffled—with many hollow cavities. Other commercially available cultivars are ribbed 'Mexicali' and 'Yellow Ruffled', which do well in most of the country.

Tomatillo (*Physalis ixocarpa*) is a traditional vegetable that's a relative newcomer to many seed catalogs. It produces prolifically with little pampering in most parts of the United States. Sometimes referred to as a husk tomato, the tomatillo is actually a large version of the ground cherry. It looks like a small green tomato with a husk. See the opposite page for an illustration of a husked and unhusked tomatillo. Its hard, green, tart fruit makes a delicious, mild green sauce called *salsa verde* that goes well with tacos and *chiles rellenos*. Tomatillos are also good cooked with meats, added to casseroles, and used in place of tomatoes for salads. Their firm texture, not as juicy as a green tomato, gives depth to a sauce.

Tomatillos are easy to grow and they thrive almost anywhere. If you harvest a bumper crop, pull back the husks and braid them as you would garlic. To freeze them, remove the husks, wash the fruit, and store them whole in freezer bags.

Corn

The types of corn used in traditional Mexican cooking are flour, flint, and dent corn. Flour corn is ground into flour. Flint and dent corn are hard corn used for making cornmeal. Cornhusks are used to wrap tamales. In the North, it's difficult to grow traditional cultivars that thrive in Mexico and the Southwest. However, there are several suitable substitutes. 'Mandan Bride' is a good substitute for traditional flour corn. 'Nothstine Dent', 'Hickory

---

PREPARING TOMATILLOS

When cooking tomatillos, follow these directions from Sue Dremann, co-owner of Redwood City Seed Company in California. Remove the husks from the tomatillos, put them in water, and bring to a boil. Boil for a couple of minutes, then drain and rinse several times. Return the tomatillos to the pot, add water, and boil a second time. Then drain again and rinse several times. This process eliminates the sticky slime on the fruit and should also improve the taste. When the fruits are cool, slip off the skins. Cooked tomatillos can be mashed, blended, or roasted. See "Tomatoes and Tomatillos" on page 405 for ideas for how to use cooked tomatillos.

King', and 'Bloody Butcher', a red corn, are reliable cornmeal corns.

Herbs

Traditional Mexican herbs are strongly flavored, aromatic, and vigorous. Most can be grown outdoors in most parts of the country. (See the Herbs entry for growing information.) Two well-known herbs used in Mexican cooking are anise (*Pimpinella anisum*) and cilantro (*Coriandrum sativum*). Anise leaves and seeds, which have a sweet licorice flavor, are used in soups, stews, breads, and desserts. The leaves also are good in salads. Chopped cilantro leaves add zest to chicken, chili, stews, and fresh vegetables. Cilantro has a completely different flavor than its seed, coriander, which is used as a condiment. Following are some less-well-known Mexican herbs.

Epazote. Also called wormseed, goosefoot, Mexican tea, and Jerusalem oak, epazote (*Chenopodium ambrosioides*) is a tough annual herb. Its leaves make an attractive garnish and give a peppy flavor to Mexican food. Plants reseed prolifically in the fall and epazote flourishes in most regions if given moist soil, partial shade, and plenty of room. (It is considered a weed in many places.) One or two plants are enough for most gardens. Add a couple of fresh sprigs or 2 teaspoons of dried epazote to a pot of beans during the last 15 minutes of cooking as an aid to prevent flatulence.

Yerba buena. The English meaning of yerba (or hierba) buena is "good herb." A tender perennial related to summer savory, yerba buena (*Satureja douglasii*) is often added to a pot of soup at the end of cooking. It gives a refreshing flavor to meatballs in savory tomato broth. Yerba buena enjoys loose, well-drained, evenly moist soil and full sun.

Mexican tarragon. Although it is com-

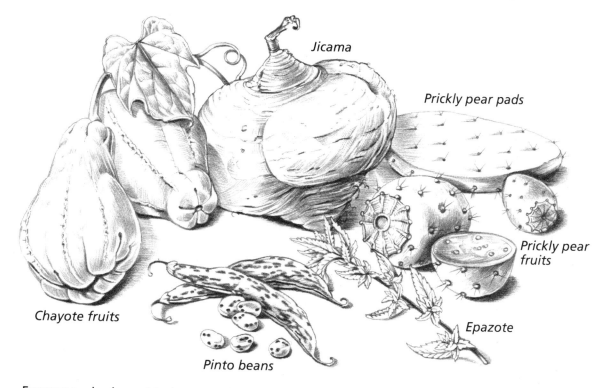

Jicama

Prickly pear pads

Prickly pear fruits

Epazote

Chayote fruits

Pinto beans

Everyone who loves Mexican cuisine recognizes beans, tomatoes, and peppers, but not many gardeners are familiar with the less-well-known Mexican specialty crops. Chayote is a melon relative that can be used like summer squash. Jicama, a tuberous root that tastes like a water chestnut, is a tropical relative of pinto beans. Both are in the pea family. The fruits and pads of prickly pear cactus and epazote, a pungent herb, are two other traditional Mexican crops.

monly called *yerbanis,* winter tarragon, Texas tarragon, and Mexican mint marigold, Mexican tarragon (*Tagetes lucida*) is actually related to ornamental marigolds. Hardier and easier to grow in the Southwest than French tarragon, Mexican tarragon is used in cooking green corn and chayote squash and in seasoning salads, fish, and fowl. Its anise-scented leaves are also used to make tea and vinaigrettes. It reseeds readily and prefers full sun and loose, well-drained soil. North of Zone 8, grow it from seeds as an annual.

Mexican oregano. Similar in flavor to true oregano but more pungent, Mexican oregano (*Lippia graveolens*) is used in chilies, chicken marinades, bean dishes, and red wine vinegar. It is a woody shrub that isn't hardy north of Zone 10; grow it in containers in the North.

Other Specialty Crops

Other Mexican specialties require longer growing seasons and are best grown in the Southwest and South or in tropical climates. These include cumin (*Cuminum cyminum,* which is also known as *comino*), prickly pear cacti (*Opuntia* spp.), and mesquite beans. Peanuts and pine nuts (also called piñon) are traditional Mexican foods, too. For growing information on peanuts, see the Peanut entry; for information on pine nut culture, see the Nut entry. Banana leaves, called *hoja de platano,* are used for wrapping tamales and grilled fish. They're also chopped and used in various dishes because they have a flavor similar to licorice. See the Banana entry for information on growing this tropical favorite. Try growing these crops in containers so that you can bring them

indoors to provide a long growing season.

Avocado leaves. The chopped leaves of Mexican cultivars of avocado are used in tamales and sprinkled over refried beans. When dried and ground, they have a somewhat nutty, anise taste. For more information, see the Avocado entry.

Chayote. Also known as mirliton, chayote (*Sechium edule*) has a crisp texture like a cucumber and tastes like summer squash. It is a perennial that overwinters in frost-free areas. Harvest young fruit at 4″–6″ and use them like summer squash. Mature fruit are cooked in stews and chowders and made into fritters. The large roots are much like potatoes. To try growing a store-bought chayote: Put it in a warm place (such as on the top of the refrigerator) until it sprouts, then plant it the garden.

Hoja santa. This semi-woody perennial bears large, heart-shaped leaves (8″ × 10″ or more) that have a scent similar to sassafras or licorice. Hoja santa (*Piper auritum,* sometimes listed as *Piper sanctum*) is as ornamental as it is useful. The leaves are used for wrapping fish, chicken, or tamales, and they are used as a seasoning.

Jicama. Also known as yam bean and Mexican potato, jicama (*Pachyrhizus tuberosus*) produces a long, white, tuberous root that tastes like a water chestnut or mild radish. It needs rich soil, lots of sun and water, and a warm, five- to nine-month growing season. Grow it from seeds sown indoors or directly into the ground in moderate climates. It is delicious in salads and soups and marinated in lime juice. Beware of the seeds and pods of this tropical plant—they are poisonous. ✳

MINT
Mentha spp. Labiatae. Perennial.
Zones 5–9.

Mint is one of the most popular and most familiar herbs. Its sweet flavor has been added to just about everything, from the candy jar to the medicine cabinet. Grow mint to scent the garden air, then add it to both sweet and savory recipes. Pennsylvania Dutch farmers recommend that you plant mint where water drips—near water pumps and outdoor spigots—because mint thrives in very moist conditions.

Selecting plants. Peppermint (*Mentha × piperita*) and spearmint (*M. spicata*) are probably the best known species. A few others to try include apple mint (*M. suaveolens*), with fuzzy, gray-green leaves; orange mint (*M. × piperita* var. *citrata*), with smooth, dark green leaves that have a citrus scent and taste; and Corsican mint (*M. requienii*), a creeper with tiny but powerfully fragrant leaves.

Site. Most mint species grow well in full sun, although they usually prefer partial shade.

Soil. Mint grows best in a rich, moist, well-drained soil with neutral to slightly acid pH. Use a garden fork to work compost into garden soil before planting. Avoid using compost with weed seeds or planting in weedy sites since weeds are difficult to remove once they become established in a patch of mint.

How much to plant. Since mint spreads quickly, one or two plants of each type will usually produce all the mint you need for fresh use and drying.

Spacing. Space plants 1′–1½′ apart in all directions.

Days to maturity. When grown from cuttings or divisions, growth is vigorous enough to withstand light harvesting the first year.

Planting and growing. Plant cuttings or divisions in spring. Seeds or purchased seedlings are a less reliable way of getting a specific mint. Mints cross-pollinate easily, so mint seeds don't always produce the exact plant promised. Peppermint, for example, is a sterile hybrid that doesn't produce seeds and must be grown from cuttings or divisions.

To keep mint from spreading uncontrollably underground, plant it in open-ended cylinders—like clay drainage tiles or bottomless pots—that are at least 1′ deep. If you use clay containers, be sure to sink the rims below the soil surface, otherwise they'll wick water out of the soil. You'll need to install a barrier above ground, too. Position metal or plastic lawn edging 2″–4″ high around the border of the planting.

An established patch of mint needs heavy pruning to encourage the growth of tender shoots. To keep plants vigorous, divide them in the fall every one to two years and replant into soil enriched with compost. Each spring, mulch with compost to fertilize and help retain soil moisture.

Harvesting. Harvest foliage regularly until two to four weeks before fall frosts are expected. To dry mint, harvest it just before bloom for maximum flavor.

Extending the season. For winter harvests in cool climates, start seedlings in pots outdoors in midsummer, then move them indoors. Or pot up clumps of mint from your garden in late summer or early fall, then leave them outdoors to freeze for at least four weeks before moving them inside. You can simulate this process by placing pots in the refrigerator for one week in early fall, then in the freezer for three to four weeks. Let pots thaw out in a cool place for a few days, and then move them to a sunny windowsill or place them under plant growth lights.

Container growing. Mint grows well in containers. Provide water regularly and feed with liquid kelp or fish emulsion every two weeks.

Propagation. To propagate mints, divide plants in fall or take cuttings from upright stems or runners in early spring or fall. ✳

MUSHROOM

If you love growing something that's a bit unusual, mushrooms are a crop for you. You can grow them indoors in a basement or under the kitchen sink, or you can grow them outdoors in a shady part of your yard. All you need to grow a wide variety of mushrooms are some basic supplies, which are readily available from mail-order specialists, and a sense of adventure.

The unique flavors of the different species make for tasty soups, sauces, main dishes, and breads. A good way to taste-test fresh mushrooms is to slice a few and sauté them in butter. This brings out the flavor of the mushroom and is a good way to compare species. Mushrooms can be preserved by drying, pickling, canning, or freezing.

Getting Started with Mushrooms

Understanding a bit about mushroom life cycles will help get you started with your first crop. Mushrooms don't have roots, leaves, stems, flowers, or seeds. Instead, their life cycle begins with spores, which germinate and form a thick network of slender filaments called a mycelium. When conditions are right (or during the appropriate season, depending on the species), the mycelium produces fruiting bodies, or the part we know as mushrooms. The cycle begins again when the mushrooms mature and produce spores.

Since they don't have chlorophyll, mushrooms can't produce food the way green plants do. Instead, they absorb nutrients directly from the medium in which they're growing. That's why a rich substrate is important to growing mushrooms. Button mushrooms, for example, like a substrate of compost and/or strawy manure; other species, such as shiitakes, grow on wood.

To grow your own mushrooms, you'll order a ready-to-grow kit or spawn, which is mycelia of the species you want. If you buy spawn, you'll use it to inoculate a substrate, which varies depending on the species you're growing, and then you'll wait for the mycelia to spread. Once conditions are right, fruiting bodies, or mushrooms, will form. Spawn you buy will be growing on a carrier material such as grain or straw; mushrooms that grow on wood like shiitakes will be inoculated on pieces of wood. See "Sources" on page 507 for a list of companies that sell mushroom-growing supplies.

Indoor Cultivation

Probably the best way to grow your first crop of mushrooms is with a kit. A variety of kits are available, including inoculated boxes of compost for growing button mushrooms

(*Agaricus bisporus*), as well as kits for growing shiitake mushrooms (*Lentinus edodes*) and oyster mushrooms (*Pleurotus* spp.) All will produce mushrooms over several weeks or months if cared for according to the directions.

You'll need more equipment if you want to start your own small-scale indoor mushroom-growing operation. In addition to spawn and substrate, you will also need boxes to grow the mushrooms in. It's also possible for you to prepare your own substrate. Button mushrooms can be grown on composted straw and manure. See "Recommended Reading" on page 511 for books on growing mushrooms.

Mushrooms don't need total darkness to grow well, but they will flourish in cool (55°–60°F), dimly lit areas where other plants refuse to grow. Consider growing them in a cool basement, under the kitchen sink, or in a garage. Throughout the process, it's important to keep the growing area clean, provide ventilation without drafts, and keep the area humid and the substrate slightly moist. (Too much water kills spawn.) The main enemies of homegrown mushrooms are bacterial diseases, invasive airborne spores of other fungi, and insects.

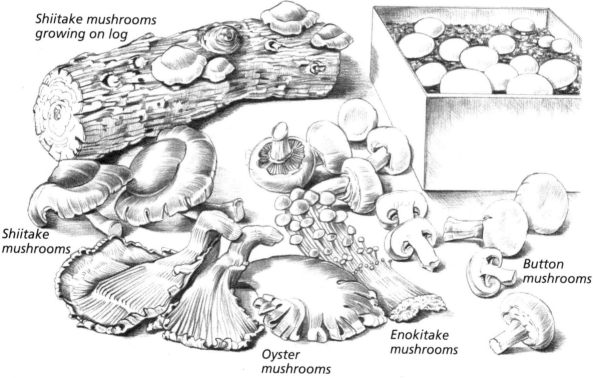

Button mushroom kit

Shiitake mushrooms growing on log

Shiitake mushrooms

Oyster mushrooms

Enokitake mushrooms

Button mushrooms

It may seem strange at first to grow mushrooms, but they're generally easy to grow, both indoors and out. Button mushrooms, an indoor crop, are probably the best known. Enokitake mushrooms can also be grown indoors. Kits for growing shiitake and oyster mushrooms either indoors or out are also readily available.

Outdoor Cultivation

If you like surprises, you'll love growing mushrooms in your own backyard. For wood-inhabiting mushrooms, like shiitakes, you can order either order inoculated logs or sterilized plugs or patches that contain mycelium, which you use to inoculate logs. Other mushroom species come as spawn, which must be inoculated into the proper substrate (generally specially prepared compost, which is also available commercially). Once you get mushrooms established, they'll generally bear one or more crops a year for several years. Shiitakes, oysters, and morels (*Morchella* spp.) are three types you can buy for growing outdoors.

For the most part, mushrooms prefer moist, shady areas that are rich in decaying organic material. Usually, spawn is either laid out in spring for a fall harvest or in fall for a spring harvest. This gives the mycelia time to spread throughout the growing medium. Fruiting depends on the temperature sensitivity of the species.

If you are growing mushrooms, especially outdoors, it's important to harvest with care. A good field guide is an important harvest tool. Closely examine the mushrooms you're harvesting in case the planting has become infested with nonedible or even poisonous species. When in doubt, don't eat. ✳

MUSTARD

Brassica spp. Cruciferae. Annual or biennial.

Mustard is the name given to a few species of peppery-flavored greens in the cabbage family, including *Brassica juncea*, and *B. rapa*. A host of adjectives—red, brown, Chinese, Indian, Japanese—identify various leafy species. Many also have alternate names, such as mizuna and komatsuna, that reflect their Asian origins. Young mustard leaves are delicious mixed with other greens in salad. Pick larger leaves to steam, stir-fry, or use in soup.

The mustard that you spread on your hot dog is made from the seeds of white mustard (*Brassica hirta*) or black mustard (*B. nigra*); these two species also produce tasty young greens. If your mustard bolts, blend the seeds with vinegar for a mustard spread, or add them whole to spicy dishes.

Selecting plants. Choose cultivars that are slow to bolt for spring sowing and cold-tolerant cultivars for fall and winter crops.

Site. Plant mustards in full sun. Use handsome red or frilly leaved mustards as ornamentals as well as food plants.

Soil. Like most greens, mustard grows best in a rich, moist soil that is high in nitrogen. Work 1"–2" of rotted manure shallowly into the soil before planting.

How much to plant. Plant a 3' row of mustard greens per person. Make a single 15' row for seed production.

Spacing. To snip young leaves for salads or for a harvest of seeds, space your mustard plants 3"–6" apart in rows 2' apart or in a 2'–3'-wide bed. If you intend to let the leafy rosettes swell to their full size, give each plant 10"–30" on all sides, depending on the mature spread of the cultivar. Look on the seed packet for this information.

Days to maturity. Harvest mustard greens 25–50 days after sowing, depending on the weather and the cultivar. Seeds mature in about ten weeks.

Planting and growing. Like their cabbage cousins, mustards prosper in cool weather. In spring, direct-sow mustard seeds ¼″ deep about four weeks before the last expected frost. Sow seeds in late summer for a fall harvest. Where mild winter temperatures or available cold-frame space permit it, sow cold-tolerant mustards in fall for winter harvest. Cool weather reduces bolting and mellows the flavor of the greens.

Encourage quick growth by providing about 1″ of moisture a week; fertilize every two weeks with a dilute solution of fish emulsion (1 tablespoon of fish emulsion per gallon of water). Although mustards go to seed more slowly than most lettuces, once they send up a flowerstalk, the foliage becomes bitter and the plant deteriorates. Protect young plants with a floating row cover to prevent flea beetle damage.

Harvesting. Gather small, tender mustard leaves beginning when they are about 3″ long or, for more flavor, pick larger leaves or the entire head. In cool weather, you can harvest greens over several weeks. To harvest seeds, cut off the pods once they turn brown but before they are dry enough to shatter. Hang the pods to finish drying over paper or in a paper bag, for easy seed collection. Crush the pods gently with a mortar and pestle to remove the seeds.

Container growing. Try growing mizuna in an 8″–10″-diameter pot indoors under plant growth lights, where it makes a handsome-looking—and tasty—houseplant.

Propagation. Different cultivars within the same species may cross-pollinate unless they flower at different times or are separated by at least 100 yards. ✳

NATIVE AMERICAN CROPS

Whether you realize it or not, you are probably growing a garden full of crops that are native to North, South, and Central America. The list of important crops originally developed by Native Americans includes some of our best-known vegetables, fruits, and grains. These include amaranth, beans, corn, squash, tomatoes, and sunflowers—plus root crops such as potatoes and peanuts.

Many of our best-loved fruit and nut crops are also native to the Americas and were gathered and used by native peoples. These include many bramble fruits such as raspberries and blackberries but also cloudberry (*Rubus chamaemorus*), American dewberry (*R. flagellaris*), and black raspberry (*R. occidentalis*). Grapes, including American grape (*Vitis labrusca*) and muscadines (*V. rotundifolia*), are also native fruit crops, as are blueberries, cranberries, and elderberries. Native nut crops include hickory, pecan, and black walnut. Greens such as fiddleheads, lamb's quarters, chicory, dill, sassafras, and sumac and root crops such as groundnuts (*Apios americana*) also were important to Native Americans.

Beyond their basic food value, many plants have long played a central role in native religions. Corn, beans, and squash are called the "Three Sisters of Life."

If you want to learn more about native American crops, try growing some of the ancestors of our modern hybrids. See "Sources" on page 507 for sources of native and heritage cultivars. Also see the Mexican Specialties entry for information on traditional crops of Mexico and the Southwest. ✳

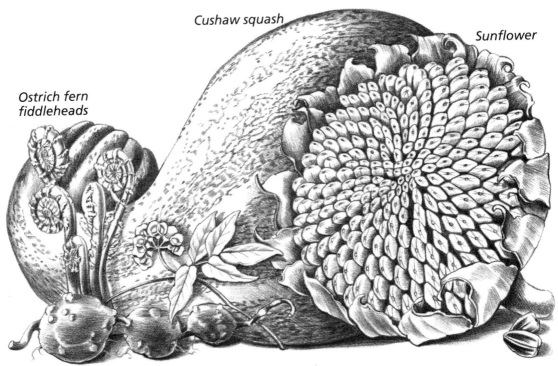

Cushaw squash

Sunflower

Ostrich fern fiddleheads

Groundnut tubers and flower cluster

Native Americans developed many of our most important crops, such as corn, beans and squash, including cushaw squash, which is used for baking and grows well in the long, hot summers in the South and Southwest. Other native foods include sunflowers; groundnuts, a twining herb that produces tubers that were ground to make cakes; and the fiddleheads of ferns, which are among the first edible greens in spring.

NUTS

No matter where you live, there's probably a native species of nut tree already thriving near you. If you're interested in planting your own trees to raise nut crops, you'll need to be a patient gardener. Most nut trees need at least three years of growth before they begin to bear, but the rewards are worthwhile. Nuts are some of the most vitamin-packed, health-giving foods you can grow.

While nuts can be high in fat, most of it is in beneficial forms—monounsaturated and polyunsaturated—which can help control serum cholesterol. Nuts are high in fiber and have immunity-strengthening nutrients, including zinc, folate, and iron. Nut meats store well for many months. And as an added benefit, nut trees beautify your landscape and provide shade. Most nut trees, especially pecan (*Carya illinoinensis*), beeches (*Fagus* spp.), and hickories (*Carya* spp.), are graceful and beautiful shade trees.

Most nut trees can adapt to a range of sites. They generally need little special care once established. Most nut trees are not self-fertile. You'll need to plant two different cultivars of each species in order for pollination to occur. Either a local nursery that sells nut trees or your local extension office should be able to recommend the right combination of cultivars for your area.

Propagation of named nut tree cultivars is best done by grafting. Trees that sprout from the nuts of an improved cultivar have a very slim chance of being as good as the parent tree. Grafted trees also bear crops sooner than seedling trees.

Nuts for Cold Climates

Gardeners in the North are most likely to succeed with black walnuts, English or Persian walnuts, butternuts, hickories (*Carya* spp.), filberts, and chestnuts. These trees can also withstand the rigors of northern winters and still produce good crops of nuts. Pecans are less hardy, but a few cultivars will bear nuts as far north as Pennsylvania. Most pecans are more suited to the southern states.

You'll find information on black walnuts, English or Persian walnuts, and butternuts in the Walnut entry. Filberts, chestnuts, and pecans have individual entries under their own names. Hickories are described below.

Hickories. Hickories are in the same genus (*Carya*) as pecans. They are mostly uncultivated, though a few cultivars of some species have been selected for superior nut quality. 'Yoder No. 1' and 'Grainger' are shagbark hickories (*Carya ovata*). 'Keystone' is a shellbark hickory (*C. laciniosa*). Mockernut (*C. tomentosa*) and sweet pignut (*C. glabra*) are tasty but not cultivated. A hican is a cross between hickory and pecan. Several hican cultivars are available. See the Pecan entry for culture of hickories and hicans.

Nuts for Warm Climates

Some less hardy nuts need mild winters and long, dry summers. These tender trees include the almond and the pistachio (*Pistachia vera*). Both do well on the West Coast, particularly in California. While the southern United States may be warm enough for these nuts, the region is too humid. Pecans, however, do quite well in the southern United States.

You'll find information on growing almonds in the Almond entry and information on growing pecans in the Pecan entry. Information on growing pistachios is below.

Pistachios. Pistachios are small, deciduous trees and are hardy through Zone 9. They bloom late and thus escape early-spring frosts. Male and female flowers are borne on separate trees, so you'll need at least one of each to harvest nuts. Harvest pistachios by knocking them from the tree to a tarp on the ground when most of the outer hulls pop off and the inner shell splits when gently squeezed. Put the nuts in a bag and hit it with a board to shell them, then float them in a bucket of water. The

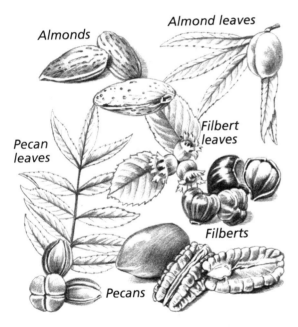

Almonds, pecans, and filberts are three popular nuts for backyard nut growers. Almonds grow best in dry, hot climates, while pecans and filberts grow well in many areas of the United States. For information on growing these nuts, see the Almond, Filbert, and Pecan entries.

good nuts will sink. Let dry, then freeze them for storage.

Nuts for Hot Climates

There are also many well-known nuts that grow well only in the heat of the tropics. Here are descriptions of a few of them.

Brazil nuts. Brazil nut (*Bertholletia excelsa*) is native to the Amazon basin. The nuts have chocolate-brown shells and are borne in clusters of a dozen or more enclosed in a woody globe.

Cashews. Cashew (*Anacardium occidentale*) is native to tropical America but can be grown in sandy soil in southern Florida. The cashew plant is a member of the poison ivy family. The nuts must be roasted before shelling to eliminate their poisonous oil.

Macadamia nuts. Macadamia nuts (*Macadamia integrifolia* and *M. tetraphylla*) are native to subtropical Australia. They grow best in rain forest areas such as Hawaii, where they are a major crop.

Unusual Nuts

Among the dozens of tasty nuts collected for food are some that have fallen out of popularity and many that simply have never become well-known. Below you'll find descriptions of some easy-to-grow nuts that are often overlooked.

Pine nuts. Also called pignolias or piñons, pine nuts are large, edible seeds borne on slow-growing, long-lived, small trees that may take decades to bear regularly. In North America, these include several species of piñon pines (*Pinus edulis, P. monophylla,* and *P. quadrifolia*), which tolerate hot, arid conditions, steep slopes, and poor soil but must have good drainage.

Piñon pines are hardy through Zone 7. Southern gardeners can also try Italian stone pine (*P. pinea*), which is the pine nut of southern Europe. It is hardy through Zone 8. More northern gardeners can plant Swiss stone pine (*P. cembra*), which produces edible nuts and is hardy through Zone 3.

Ginkgo. Ginkgo (*Ginkgo biloba*) nuts, a popular food in China and Japan, are produced only on female trees. The small nuts are encased in a fleshy fruit that smells foul when it rots. For this reason, most ginkgo trees sold are male, but female trees are available from a few nurseries. Plant one of each for nut production. Seedlings are very slow to bear. Enjoy the green, almond-size nuts roasted, boiled, or steamed. Trees tolerate a wide range of soils and poor drainage.

Monkey puzzle tree. The monkey puzzle tree (*Araucaria araucana*) is named for the difficulty a monkey might have climbing it. It has sharp spikes for leaves and an almost geometric growth pattern. Native to South America and hardy to about −10°F, it will start to bear football-size nut clusters in about 10–15 years. Each cone contains up to 300 nuts that taste like chestnuts and fall from the cluster gradually. There are male and female trees. Plant one of each for nut production.

Beechnuts. Both American and European beech trees (*Fagus* spp.) produce small edible nuts. If you've never seen one, it's because the nuts are very popular with wildlife. Nuts are small and sweet and can be shelled by hand. This deciduous tree needs a moist but well-drained location. Plant at least two for nut production.

MORE NUTTY INFORMATION

Growing backyard nuts can be a satisfying, active hobby, complete with special equipment (nutcrackers and squirrel barriers), expert skills (grafting), and, best of all, a chance to swap nut stories with other nut fanciers. Nut-grower groups can be invaluable sources of information. Their members include people who are eager beginners, farmers, commercial growers, and hobbyists as well as professional horticulturists.

There may be a nut-growers' association in your state. Northern nut growers can write to: The Northern Nut Growers Association, c/o Ken Bauman, Treasurer, 9870 South Palmer Road, New Carlisle, OH 45344. Southern nut growers can contact: The Southern Nut Growers Association, c/o Eve Elliot, 1729 Unice Ave. N., Lehigh Acres, FL 33971.

Acorns. Several species of oaks (*Quercus* spp.) were an important food source for North American natives, who removed bitter tannins by soaking or boiling the acorn meats in water. Oaks vary greatly in the amount of tannins their acorns contain. Acorns from most red oaks are too bitter to eat, but a sweet, low-tannin cultivar, 'Ooti', has been developed by acorn-eating enthusiasts. 'Ashworth' is a sweet bur oak selection. Use caution when sampling acorns; they are classified as poisonous by the Food and Drug Administration. ∗

OATS
Avena spp. Gramineae. Annual.

Highest in protein of the cereal grains, versatile oats are tasty rolled as a hot breakfast or ground into flour for bread or cookies.

Selecting plants. Choose white oats (*Avena sativa*) for early-spring plantings that ripen in early summer. If your winters are mild (Zone 7 and south), sow red oats (*A. byzantina*) in the fall for a spring harvest. Ask a local farmer or extension agent to recommend cultivars. Hull-less cultivars eliminate dehulling but have not yet been tested in all climates. Try a small planting to see how they thrive in your area.

Site. Sow oats in a partially sunny spot that is as weed-free as possible. Oats like damp conditions. Seed heads will not fill well in dry conditions, so if you're growing oats in full sun or well-drained soil, take extra care to keep your soil moist.

Soil. Oats will grow well even in poor soils. Too much fertilizer, particularly nitrogen-rich types, will cause the stalk to grow tall but weak, and then it will fall over. Cultivate before planting to eliminate weeds.

How much to plant. A densely sown 200-square-foot patch will yield 15–20 pounds of dehulled oats.

Days to maturity. White oats mature 60–70 days after sowing. Red oats mature 30–40 days after spring soil temperatures reach 40°F.

Planting and growing. You can seed 200 square feet with about ½ pound of oats. Plant white oats as early in spring as you can work the soil; you can even clear snow off of a prepared seed plot for early sowing. Sow an equal amount of red oats in mid- to late fall, three to four weeks before the first frost is expected. Broadcast the seeds by hand. After sowing, cover the seeds with 1″ of soil for best results; uncovered seeds may still germinate. To minimize competition for moisture and soil nutrients, pull or hoe any weed seedlings that emerge when the oat seedlings do.

Providing moisture shouldn't be too difficult because oats are generally planted during the wettest times of the year. If it's a dry season, apply supplemental water.

Oats (especially small patches) don't have any significant insect pests but occasionally suffer from crown rust and Septoria leaf blight. Many cultivars are resistant to both. Help prevent crown rust in northern regions by removing buckthorn (*Rhamnus* spp.) plants from the area—the shrubs are hosts to the disease. Crop rotation helps minimize both diseases.

Harvesting. Cut your stand when the seed heads have just begun to harden and the stalks are turning yellow and brown. Use a sharp sickle or scythe to cut at least 7″–8″ of stalk with the seed head. Bundle the stalks and hang them to finish drying in a well-ventilated spot.

The bundles are dry when the seed heads are crumbly and the stalks no longer have any green on them. Thresh and winnow them after they dry. See "Processing Grains" on page 370 for instructions.

After threshing and winnowing, you must remove the hull. To do this, first roast the oats at 180°F in the oven for about one hour to dry out the hulls. Then run the oats through a grain grinder or high-powered blender or juicer to remove the hulls and winnow them from the groats (cracked grains). You can eat the groats as is or grind them further into flour.

Propagation. The oat grain is the seed, so save some (before dehulling) from your stoutest plants with full seed heads. Store the seeds in an airtight container in a cool, dark place. ✳

OKRA

Abelmoschus esculentus. Malvaceae. Annual.

Okra's affinity for warm weather can be traced to its African origin. Actually an edible relative of hibiscus and cotton, young, tender okra pods are an essential ingredient in Creole gumbo. Pods also may be pickled, cooked alone or with tomatoes, or sliced and breaded with seasoned cornmeal and fried until crispy and brown.

Selecting plants. Cultivars vary in size and length of time to flowering. Where summers are cool, plant dwarf, quick-maturing cultivars.

Site. Okra requires full sun.

Soil. Okra will grow in almost any soil that is not infested with root knot nematodes.

How much to plant. For fresh use, eight to ten plants produce enough pods for two people. Grow 30 or more plants for pickling or freezing.

Spacing. In a 3'-wide bed, sow seeds in two rows that are 1½' apart, spacing seeds 4" apart. When seedlings are 8" high, thin plants to 2' apart. Bushy cultivars may need wider spacing.

Days to maturity. Okra matures 50–65 days from seeds sown in warm soil.

Planting and growing. Heat- and drought-tolerant, okra needs warm soil to germinate and grow well. Pests seldom bother it, but root knot nematodes cause stunting.

Harvesting. Using a sharp knife or pruning shears, cut 3"–4"-long pods with their stems attached. Pods longer than 5" will be tough.

Extending the season. In late summer, cut off the top 2' of each plant to encourage development of bearing sideshoots.

Fall and winter care. After frost, turn plants under or pull them up and compost them.

Container growing. Don't try to grow okra in containers because the yield is low for the amount of space occupied.

Propagation. In midsummer, let pods from one plant mature. After frost, crush the dry pods and gather the seeds. ✳

OLIVE

Olea europaea. Oleaceae. Evergreen tree. Zones 9–10.

Olives are long-lived, ornamental, evergreen trees with silvery gray leaves. In Mediterranean climates, where they flourish, there are specimens known to be 1,500 years old, although plants bear their best crops before they are 50 years old. In North America, olives fruit best in the hot central valleys of California, in southern Arizona, and in Florida during drier-than-normal seasons. The oily fruit is the source of an important cooking and salad oil, the unripe fruit is processed into green olives, and the ripe fruit is processed into black olives. Olives cannot be eaten right off the tree because they contain a bitter compound that must be neutralized by processing before use.

Selecting plants. A number of cultivars are available; some are best for oil; others, for fruit. Cultivars are often grafted onto seedling rootstocks, which help trees withstand wind.

Site. Grow in full sun with some wind protection. Olives thrive in long, hot summers and grow best in areas where January temperatures are between 40° and 50°F. Olives need some winter chilling to produce flowers but are killed if temperatures drop below 12°F.

Soil. Olives require well-drained soil but will adapt to many soil types, including poor soil. Sandy or clay loam is best. Olives will tolerate a pH of 5.5–8.5.

How much to plant. Plant two or three trees for home use.

Spacing. Space trees 35′–40′ apart.

Seasons to bearing. Plants bear four to five years after planting.

Planting and growing. Plant olive trees as you would any tree. See "Perennial Crops" on page 111 for complete instructions. Train plants to an open center form during the first three years. (See "Pruning Trees" on page 142 for more information about this technique.) Fruit is borne on one-year-old wood. Annually prune away spindly branches. Fertilize annually with a few cups of a good source of nitrogen such as blood meal or cottonseed meal. Avoid overfertilizing trees or you will encourage too many fruits to set. Plants are not receiving enough fertilizer if they are growing less than 4″ per year.

Olives generally have few major diseases in dry climates. Rake up and destroy any leaves or fruits that show spots or other signs of disease. Cut out swellings on the trunk and limbs, caused by olive knot, as well as cankers that appear. If trees set an extra-heavy crop, thin fruit to no more than three to five olives per 1′ of branch. Ripening a very heavy crop can cause trees to begin bearing in alternate years.

Harvesting. For pickling, harvest olives green or when fully colored (black). For oil pressing, harvest them black. Commercially pickled olives are treated with lye to remove the bitter taste, but they can also be prepared either by salting or by a lactic acid fermentation process similar to that used for making dill pickles. Check with your local extension agent for complete instructions.

Fall and winter care. In case of a severe freeze, spray plants with water, use grove heaters like those used in citrus groves, or wrap trees in blankets.

Container growing. Olives will grow in containers and make attractive houseplants when light is adequate.

Propagation. Grow olives from softwood cuttings taken in fall. Cultivars are often grafted onto seedling rootstocks. ✴

ONION

Allium cepa, Cepa group. Liliaceae.
Biennial grown as an annual.

Cooks around the world revere the common garden onion for its versatility in the kitchen. The sweet-to-pungent taste of this hardy plant adds zing to salads, soups, stews, and side dishes, and you can store the bulbs for several months. Onion cultivars are often divided into two groups: bulbing and bunching. Bulbing onion cultivars produce bulbs of various shapes and sizes. Bunching onion cultivars are grown for their delicate-tasting stems and generally are harvested before they form bulbs.

ONION

Site: At least one-half day of sun.

Soil: Richly organic, well-drained loam with a pH of 6.0–6.5; constantly moist, but not wet.

How much to plant: About 40 plants per person.

Spacing: 1"-4" between plants in rows 1'–2' apart.

Days to maturity: Varies with cultivar and method. 100–160 days from seed to harvest. Green onions: Harvest in 45 days from transplants or sets. Bulb onions: Harvest in 90 days from transplants or sets.

Bunching onions are commonly called green onions, scallions, and spring onions.

Planning

Selecting plants. Garden onions vary in shape, size, color, and flavor. Some produce small bulbs that are well-suited for pickling. Others, such as the Spanish or Bermuda types, are large with a sweet, mild flavor. Still others are used as green onions. Colors range from white or yellow to red or purple. White onions generally are more susceptible to problems than red, purple, or yellow ones. Start onions from seeds to have your choice of the largest selection of cultivars.

Bulb onion cultivars differ according to the amount of daylight needed for bulb formation. Some require as few as 12 hours, others as many as 16. If you live in the North, select a long-day cultivar; southern gardeners should look for short-day types. If you plan to store onions, choose cultivars that are good keepers. You can avoid many problems by planting onion cultivars that resist or tolerate diseases and pests.

When to plant. You can grow onions from seeds, seedlings, or sets (small bulbs grown the previous year). Sets mature quickly and are easy to grow, but they offer the most limited cultivar selection. A long growing season is necessary to produce bulbing onions from seeds. Plant in early spring, as soon as you can work the ground and as soon as the soil temperature is at least 40°F—about four to six weeks before the last expected frost. Where late summer temperatures don't go above 75°F, you can also plant green onions four to six weeks before the first expected fall frost. In mild climates, plant in fall for a winter or spring harvest. Onions grow best in air temperatures of 55°–75°F. Although this crop can tolerate temperatures as low as 30°F, freezing soil can make the bulbs soft and waterlogged. When temperatures reach 85°F or higher, soft, gray, watery bulbs may result. Onions generally need cool temperatures in the early stages for top growth and warm temperatures later for bulb formation.

How much to plant. One pound of sets covers about a 50-foot row. An ounce of seeds is enough to plant a 100-foot row.

Spacing. Allow 1"–4" between plants in traditional rows spaced 1'–2' apart. Use 1"–2" spacing if you have loose, fertile soil and intend to thin out some plants for use as green onions.

Rotation. Don't plant onions after alfalfa, oats, or wheat, all of which can encourage onion thrips. Wireworms infest both onions and sweet potatoes, so don't rotate these crops with each other. To limit recurring wireworm problems, avoid growing onions in the same place within three years.

For a greater harvest. To get the most out of bulbing onions, plant them close together and thin them before the bulbs mature; use the thinnings as you would green onions. Some gardeners claim that onions do well planted with lettuce, though there is no proof.

Soil Preparation

Onions thrive in fertile loam soil that doesn't dry out quickly. Because they are shallow-rooted, onions are sensitive to both drought and soggy conditions. The pH should be between 6.0 and 6.5. Cultivate the soil to a depth of at least 8″. Work in 20 pounds of compost per 100 square feet. If your soil drains poorly, plant in raised beds. See "Custom Care for Root Crops" on page 56.

Planting Indoors

Sowing seeds. To start onions from transplants, sow seeds indoors 10–12 weeks before you intend to plant outdoors. Presoak seeds in compost tea, then plant 10–12 seeds per inch, ½″–1″ deep. Allow 4″ between rows. Seeds germinate in soil temperatures as low as 45°F; optimum germination occurs at about 75°F. Germination usually takes 10–14 days.

Seedling care. Grow seedlings in temperatures ranging from 55° to 65°F. Thin plants,

---

ONION-PLANTING TIP

If you're starting onions from seeds, try mixing in a few radish seeds as you sow. When the radishes emerge, you'll know just where the slower-growing onions are. The radishes will also attract any root maggots that would ordinarily head straight for your onion crop. Be sure to pull and destroy maggot-infested radishes.

---

leaving the strongest to grow to nearly pencil thickness.

Planting Outdoors

Sowing seeds. Direct-seed onions in early spring as soon as you can work the soil. Sow one to five seeds per inch at a depth of ½″–1″. Allow 2′ between rows.

Buying sets and transplants. You can purchase onion sets from garden stores in the spring. Transplants are available through catalogs. Choose firm, small sets—about ½″ in diameter. The larger the set, the more likely it is to bolt.

Planting sets and transplants. Before planting, soak sets or transplants for 15–20 minutes in compost tea to prevent disease, then dust bonemeal powder on the roots. Plant as soon as the soil temperature reaches at least 40°F and you can work the soil. Plant sets pointed-side-up, 1″ deep and 2″ apart in rows 14″ apart. Set transplants stem-end-up, 1″–1½″ deep and 4″ apart. Keep rows 16″–24″ apart.

Growing Guidelines

Thinning seedlings. For large, full-term bulbs, thin plants to 3″–4″ apart when they are large enough to use as green onions and

ONION SEEDLING

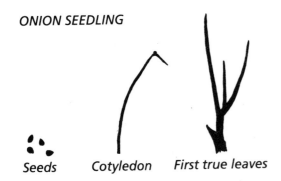

Seeds　　*Cotyledon*　　*First true leaves*

then eat the thinnings.

Water and mulch. Keep the soil evenly moist but not wet. (Transplants need more water than sets.) Dry conditions slow growth, making onions more prone to pest problems and splitting. Excess moisture promotes rot. To keep weeds down and conserve moisture, put down 8″–10″ of mulch when the soil warms up, or plant a legume cover crop at least 4″ from your onions, and keep it mowed.

Feeding. Before you mulch, apply ¼–½ pound of alfalfa meal for every 10′ of row.

Problem Prevention

Select resistant or suitable cultivars. Cultivars are available that resist or tolerate problems such as pink root, Fusarium bulb rot, onion maggots, onion leaf blight, smut, and onion smudge. Select cultivars that are suited to the daylength in your area. Otherwise, the plants may bolt before forming bulbs.

For a few weeks before planting, warm the soil with clear plastic. Plants will be less susceptible to purple blotch, smut, and other diseases that attack crops in cool soil.

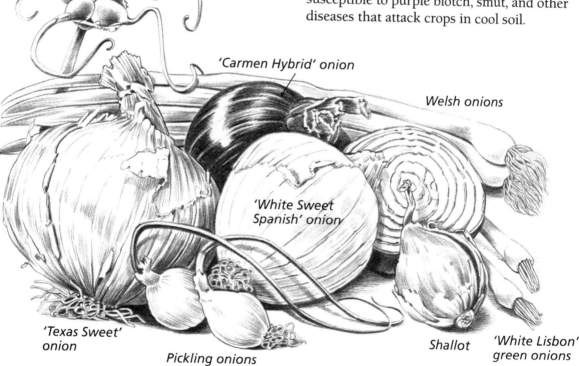

Top-setting onion head

'Carmen Hybrid' onion

Welsh onions

'White Sweet Spanish' onion

'Texas Sweet' onion

Pickling onions

Shallot

'White Lisbon' green onions

Most bulb-forming onions (or their sets) are grown from seeds. Perennial Welsh onions divide over time for an endless supply of green onions. Top-setting onions form tiny bulbs atop their stalks; these bulbs root when they touch the ground. Shallots produce clusters of underground bulbs. Any type of onion can be harvested at the "green onion" stage.

CURING ONIONS

To cure onions after harvesting, leave them outdoors for a few days to dry. Spread them on wire mesh held up off the ground, or keep them in a sheltered location such as a shed. If the bulbs are exposed to the sun, cover them to prevent sunscald. Lay them out so the tops of some onions cover the bulbs of others.

When the papery outer skins are completely dry and brittle and the tops are withered looking, prepare the onions for storage by cutting the tops off about 1" above the bulb and placing them in mesh bags. Or braid the tops together for a decorative effect. Hang braids or mesh bags of onions in a cool, dry spot to store them.

Before planting, apply parasitic nematodes to the soil. If added at least a week before planting time, these parasites can help control such pests as cutworms and onion maggots.

Before planting, presoak seeds, sets, or roots in compost tea. This will help prevent diseases such as damping-off from affecting your crop.

Avoid planting onions near asparagus. Both crops are prone to the same kind of rust.

After planting, cover plants or planted area with floating row cover. Protect your crop from onion maggots by keeping the adult flies from laying eggs on young plants.

During the season, keep soil moist and cover it with mulch. When temperatures rise to 85°F or above, onion bulbs may become gray and water-soaked.

When bulbs begin to mature, reduce moisture levels. Cut back on watering, especially near harvest time, to keep the necks from rotting.

Harvest onions carefully. Bruised bulbs are more likely to rot in storage. Avoid damaging the bulbs with your digging tool, and lay them gently in the sun to cure.

Gathering the Harvest

You can begin harvesting onions as soon as they are big enough to use as green onions. Bulbing onions are fully mature when the tops turn yellow and start to fall over. To speed the maturation process, knock the tops over with the back of your rake. Wait a few days until the tops turn brown, then carefully lift the bulbs out of the ground with a spading fork. To reduce the risk of rotting in storage, cure the bulbs to make sure their necks are completely dry. See "Curing Onions" on this page for instructions.

After curing, store the bulbs in a cool, dry place such as the cellar. Warm, humid conditions cause onions to sprout and rot. Onions will keep for several months if they are completely dry and stored in a cool, well-ventilated spot. For best results, choose cultivars that store well.

Extending the Season

Lay one or two layers of clear plastic over the bed to warm the soil two to four weeks before spring planting. Plant successive crops beginning four to six weeks before the last expected frost and ending two weeks afterward. Plant several cultivars—some that are good as green onions, some that produce bulbs for fresh eating, and some that store well. Overwinter your bulbs by covering them with a thick layer of mulch.

🐛 FRIENDS & RELATIVES 🐛

ONION

Top-setting onions (*Allium × proliferum*) produce clusters of small bulbs on the tops of the stalks, as well as an underground bulb. Commonly called Egyptian or tree onions, they are planted in the fall and harvested in two stages: first in the spring as green onions, and again in summer or fall for the little bulbs at the end of the stems. Propagate by planting the small bulbs.

Multiplier onions (*A. cepa*, Aggregatum group), often called potato onions, divide underground to form a cluster of bulbs. They are propagated by underground bulbs. Shallots are probably the best-known members of this group. Easy to grow, they produce a white, brown, red, or gray bulb with a mild, garlicky flavor. Multiplier onions are also grown as green onions.

Welsh onions (*A. fistulosum*), also called Japanese bunching onions, are popular in China and Japan. These relatively trouble-free perennials produce very slender, elongated bulbs and are used primarily as green onions.

To learn about other onion relatives, see the Chives, Garlic, and Leek entries.

Propagation

Onions are biennial and flower their second year. Store sound, fall-harvested bulbs over winter in a cold, dry place. Replant in spring, 3″–4″ apart in rows 3′ apart. Overwinter bulbs in the ground in mild climates. Insects carry pollen from one onion umbel to the next, and cultivars cross-pollinate freely. Separate flowering cultivars by at least 100′ if you're saving seeds. Harvest flower heads as soon as black seeds appear. Air dry the seed heads for several weeks, then gently rub off the seeds. ✳

ORANGE

Citrus sinensis. Rutaceae. Evergreen tree. Zones 9–10.

Oranges are a favorite tree in many Florida and California home gardens. They are native to Southeast Asia.

Selecting plants. Choose several orange cultivars to lengthen your harvest. There are three types of sweet oranges: Oranges such as 'Valencia' have a long ripening season (including summer); navel oranges, such as 'Washington Navel', ripen in winter, are seedless, and have excellent flavor; blood oranges, such as 'Ruby', have deep red juice and flesh and ripen in spring.

Choose a tree with a straight trunk, sturdy graft, and unblemished, healthy green leaves. Select a young tree without fruit because it will have a stronger root system and establish faster. Oranges are self-pollinating, so one tree of each cultivar is sufficient.

Site. Choose a site with sun or partial

shade, protected from strong winds.

Soil. Oranges thrive in well-drained, deep, fertile soil with a pH of 6.0–6.5. Avoid soils where salt accumulation is a problem. If your native soil is not suitable, try planting citrus in a raised bed with purchased topsoil mixed with compost. Avoid planting citrus in turf—keep the soil beneath oranges mulched.

Spacing. Oranges are naturally dwarf. Plant trees 15′ apart.

Seasons to bearing. Oranges bear four years after planting.

Planting and growing. Plant bareroot trees when danger of frost is past but when weather is still cool. This is also the best time for planting container plants, but you can plant them throughout the year. Shade new trees if you plant in the heat of summer.

Plant trees in holes about 1′ in diameter and 1½′ deep. See "Perennial Crops" on page 111 for more details. Be sure to keep the graft union 6″ above soil level.

If lawn planting is your only option, clear sod from an area at least 3′ in diameter for each tree. After planting, you can mulch the cleared area with gravel. Outline with bricks or edging to prevent grass from reinvading the area.

Orange trees need consistently moist soil. Young trees are easily lost to moisture stress. Water trees once a week for the first year of growth. Drip irrigation helps conserve water and keeps trees from drying out. Oranges are quite sensitive to salt buildup. Have your water checked for salt content, and avoid watering trees with salty water.

Spread a thin layer of compost or well-rotted manure, or a few handfuls of cottonseed or blood meal out to the drip line of each tree several times a year. In Florida, feed young trees in February, May, and October. In California, feed in January or February and continue every six weeks until early September. Feeding produces tender new growth. Later feeding may cause leaf and branch loss in cold winters.

Orange trees are self-shaping. You only need prune out crossing branches and head back upright growth to limit tree size.

Avoid viral diseases by planting only virus-free stock. Encourage beneficial insects by creating sheltered areas with small-flowered plants. Beneficials will help keep down populations of scale, mites, and whiteflies—three of the major pests of citrus. If snails are a problem, install copper trunk barriers. If scale and mealybugs have been a problem in your area, you may want to plan for regular sprays of horticultural oil to prevent further outbreaks.

Harvesting. Record the harvesting time of each tree you plant. Watch trees for fruit that shows mature color, but keep in mind that color is not a reliable indicator of ripeness. When you think the fruit is ready to harvest, pick a sample fruit for tasting. Fruit should taste sweet, not acid.

You don't have to pick the fruit all at once; ripe oranges can remain on the tree for up to three months. Some gardeners never bother to pick; they just wait until the perfectly ripe fruit falls to the ground. However, if you notice birds pecking the fruit, pick all of the fruit immediately. Some can be juiced and frozen or canned. You can store oranges in an extra refrigerator for several months. For best flavor, be sure to let them warm to room temperature before eating.

Extending the season. If a freeze is predicted when you have several trees full of ripe oranges, try in-ground storage. First dig a large hole. Then put fruit in plastic bags and place them in the hole. Cover the hole with a board, and shovel the dirt on top. Open the hole when you're ready to use the fruit.

Fall and winter care. When cold weather hits, you must act fast to protect trees. One measure is to leave sprinklers aimed at your fruit trees running through the night.

You can also try wrapping trees in old blankets and quilts. Don't use plastic; contact with cold plastic can damage trees. You can build special shelters for the trees and cover the shelters with plastic. Add heat in the shelter with an electric light bulb or kerosene lantern. You can also try making tree shelters out of palm fronds or large cardboard boxes, such as refrigerator boxes.

After the weather warms up again, usually by noon the following day, unwrap the trees or they may wilt from overheating.

Container growing. Some orange cultivars are naturally dwarf and adapt well to container culture; a 5-gallon pot is sufficient for some trees. During the summer, put them outdoors in a sheltered, partially shaded spot. Keep trees thoroughly watered. In the winter, move them indoors to a place where they will get at least half a day of sun. Mist leaves frequently to keep the humidity high, and main-

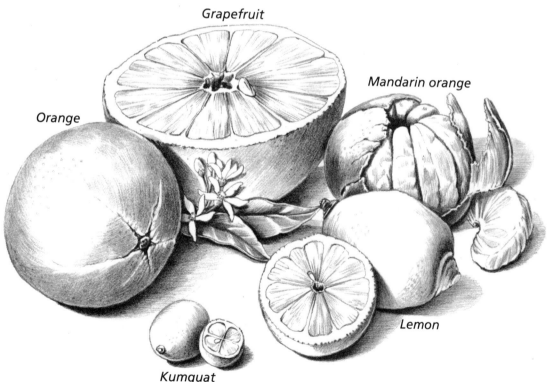

For fresh eating or juicing, it's hard to beat the citrus family. The fragrant flowers and shiny evergreen foliage also make these trees an attractive ornamental for any yard.

tain warm days (70°–75°F) and cool nights (45°–55°F). Apply liquid fertilizer such as kelp extract at least once a month. Hand-pollinate with an artist's brush.

Friends and relatives. There is a wide range of citrus types you can choose from to vary your eating pleasure. They are all grown and harvested like oranges. Some are a bit hardier than orange, some a bit less. Here are the common eating types:

Calamondin (× *Citrofortunella mitis*) is a cross between mandarin orange and kumquat and hardy to 20°F. The small tree thrives in containers and the 1½″ round, orange fruits taste like tart mandarin oranges.

Grapefruit (*Citrus × paradisi*) is as hardy as orange. Trees grow 30′–50′ tall. Select cultivars with pink flesh, such as 'Star Ruby', or white flesh, such as 'Marsh'. Many gardeners harvest grapefruits by waiting for the perfectly ripe fruits to fall to the ground.

Kumquat (*Fortunella* spp.) is hardy to 18°F. They grow to 12′ and are often pruned as bushes. The small oval fruits are usually cooked and sweetened for desserts and relishes. 'Meiwa' is a sweet cultivar you can pick and eat right off the tree.

Lemon (*Citrus limon*) grows best in California. Most cultivars are less hardy than oranges but hardier than limes. Lemon trees grow to 20′. Other gardeners can try 'Meyer', which is hardy to 17°F and grows well in containers. 'Ponderosa' is a dwarf cultivar suited to containers that bears almost basketball-size fruit.

Lime (*Citrus aurantiifolia*) is generally less hardy than orange and only grows in warm, protected, areas. Limes are large shrubs or small trees. 'Bearss' is the hardiest (to 28°F). 'Persian' is a natural dwarf only 2′ tall and well-suited to container growing.

Mandarin orange (*Citrus reticulata*), or tangerine, is slightly hardier than orange, surviving 20°F. Trees grow to 8′. Cultivars to try include 'Satsuma', 'King', 'Clementine', 'Dancy', and 'Ponkan'.

Rangpur lime (*Citrus × limonia*) is not a true lime but is probably a cross between lemon and mandarin orange. It is hardy to 20°F and produces lime-flavored fruit. ✳

OREGANO

Origanum spp. Labiatae. Perennial. Zones 5–10.

Oregano is reputed to banish sadness—no wonder it's such a popular herb. Many species and cultivars are available, and each offers a different version of the oregano flavor and aroma—you'll have to sniff around to determine which you like the best.

In the kitchen, use fresh or dried oregano in tomato recipes, or add fresh leaves to pots of bean or lentil soup. Tie several branches into a bundle and use it as a brush to baste grilled meats with oil. Planting oregano among your beans may increase your bean harvest. In the home, sprinkle dried oregano leaves around pet beds to help repel fleas.

Selecting plants. If you want the strong-flavored oregano commonly used in tomato sauces, try Greek oregano (*Origanum heracleoticum*, also called *O. hirtum* or *O. vulgare* subsp. *hirtum*), which produces white flowers.

Be aware that many seeds and plants labeled "true oregano" are actually wild marjoram (*Origanum vulgare*). Wild marjoram produces attractive clusters of purple flowers, but its leaves have very little flavor. Golden oregano (*O. vulgare* 'Aureum') is an attractive golden-leaved cultivar with a mild oregano flavor.

Site. Grow oregano in full sun. Leaves are said to have less flavor when grown in shade.

Soil. Plant in well-drained soil that has a neutral to slightly acid pH. Oregano thrives in dry, rocky gardens.

How much to plant. For two people, one or two plants should provide plenty of fresh foliage all season. If you plan to preserve the leaves for winter use, you may want to start with three or four plants.

Spacing. Space plants 1'–1½' apart in beds or rows.

Days to maturity. You can begin snipping oregano when plants are at least 6" tall.

Planting and growing. Since oregano cross-pollinates freely, its seedlings tend to be variable in flavor and aroma. For specific cultivars, buy plants from a nursery, or trade cuttings or roots with a friend.

If you choose to grow oregano from seeds, sow indoors eight to ten weeks before the last expected frost; leave the seeds uncovered. Set seedlings out into the garden after all danger of frost is past. A light organic mulch will keep the soil evenly moist and add some nutrients. Apply the mulch well away from stems and leaves to allow air circulation and prevent disease problems. Watch for spider mites and aphids, especially on plants growing in containers. If pests appear, use a strong spray of water to wash them off.

Harvesting. Harvest as needed throughout the summer. To promote bushy growth, you can prune plants severely right before flowering, cutting just above the lowest leaves; plants soon leaf out again. Oregano dries well. Spread the leaves on a screen, or hang bunches up to dry and strip the leaves from the stems before storing.

Fall and winter care. To help Greek oregano overwinter in cold climates, cover it with a loose mulch or bring it indoors.

Container growing. Most oregano species and cultivars grow well in containers. Place pots in sun to partial shade. Use a potting mix that contains sand to promote good drainage.

Propagation. Take stem cuttings in spring or fall. Divide plants in spring.

Friends and relatives. Mexican oregano (*Lippia graveolens*) is not a true oregano, but it has a very similar flavor. It is very cold-sensitive and must be grown in a greenhouse or on a sunny windowsill in cool climates. ✳

PARSLEY

Petroselinum crispum. Umbelliferae.
Biennial grown as an annual.

The next time you dine out, don't throw away the parsley on your plate—nibble on it instead. Parsley's high chlorophyll content makes it a natural breath freshener. Besides its common use as a garnish, this vitamin-rich herb blends well into a wide variety of recipes. Add dried or fresh parsley to rolls, breads, biscuits, sauces, and soups.

Selecting plants. Curly parsley (*Petroselinum crispum* var. *crispum*) is good for garnishes or as a seasoning. Or try flat-leaved, or Italian, parsley (*P. crispum* var. *neapolitanum*), which gourmets say has better flavor.

Site. Grow parsley in full sun to partial shade.

Soil. Parsley likes a humus-rich, moist, well-drained soil with a pH around 6.0. Prepare beds or rows with plenty of compost or aged manure, worked in to a depth of 6″.

How much to plant. Start with 6–12 plants for two people.

Spacing. Set plants 8″–10″ apart in all directions.

Days to maturity. Begin harvesting leaves from seedlings as soon as plants are growing vigorously, eight to ten weeks after planting.

Planting and growing. Sow seeds indoors six to eight weeks before the last expected frost or outdoors when the soil temperature averages 50°F. Southern gardeners can sow seeds outdoors in fall for spring harvest. Plant the seeds ¼″ deep; they need darkness to germinate. Parsley transplants poorly, so sow the seeds in peat pots if you're starting them indoors. Set plants out into the garden after all danger of frost is past, and make sure to keep the soil evenly moist.

Parsley is rarely bothered by pests, but you may have to handpick an occasional caterpillar—usually the larvae of the black swallowtail butterfly, which are green caterpillars with white-spotted black stripes. When weeding or picking, avoid disturbing the plant's sensitive crown and root. Keep organic mulches pulled away from the crown to promote air circulation and prevent diseases.

Start parsley from seeds sown indoors or outdoors. Germination may take as long as six weeks, so be patient. To speed sprouting, soak the seeds in warm water overnight before planting. Or freeze the seeds in ice cubes, two to three seeds per cube, then plant the cubes.

Harvesting. Use scissors to harvest outer stems first, leaving the tiny center leaves to grow for the next picking. Harvest regularly throughout the season. A mulch will help to prevent soil splashing up on the leaves and keep them from getting gritty. If the foliage does get dirty, swish it around in a basin of water, then rinse it thoroughly and pat dry before using. Salad spinners, those handy kitchen tools made for drying lettuce, also work well to dry parsley.

Not only is parsley wonderful when used fresh but it also dries and freezes well. Chop the foliage when it's plentiful in summer, then freeze it in resealable plastic bags or dry it for winter use.

Extending the season. In fall, cover plants with clear plastic to encourage growth until the soil freezes and plants become dormant. Northern gardeners may be able to coax a spring harvest from overwintered parsley. Side-dress the plants with compost or alfalfa meal just as the new growth starts. Cut off the flowerstalks as they emerge from the center of the plant. (If allowed to flower and set seed, parsley will die, although it may self-sow.) For winter use, start new seedlings in pots in mid-summer and bring them indoors in fall, or sow seeds in summer in an open cold frame and close the top of the frame when winter temperatures arrive.

Container growing. Plant parsley in pots filled with any mix that includes compost and sand. Bring indoors in fall for winter use.

Propagation. Parsley plants will flower and set seed their second season. Collect seeds or let them self-sow for next season's crop. ✳

PARSNIP

Pastinaca sativa. Umbelliferae.
Biennial grown as an annual.

The hardy, white roots of parsnips store well in the ground all winter long. Prepare parsnips like carrots; their sweet, nutty taste enhances soups and stews, and they're tasty when steamed and served with butter.

Selecting plants. Parsnip cultivars differ mainly in the length of their roots. Try short-rooted plants in heavy soils; those with long roots do better in deep, loose soils. Cultivars resistant to canker are available.

Site. Choose a site that receives full sun.

Soil. Like carrots, parsnips need soil that is deep, loose, fertile, and well-drained; sandy loam with a pH of 6.0–6.8 is best. To prepare for planting, remove rocks and break the soil down into fine particles. Cultivate to a depth of 1'–1½', working in 3–5 pounds of compost per 100 square feet. Don't use fresh manure; excess nitrogen causes parsnips to produce forked roots.

How much to plant. Grow about 25 plants for each person in your family.

Spacing. Allow 4"–6" between plants in rows spaced 20"–24" apart.

Days to maturity. Parsnips are ready to harvest 80–120 days from sowing.

Planting and growing. Since parsnip seeds quickly lose their viability, use fresh ones each year. To speed germination, soak seeds overnight before planting. Direct-seed in early spring as soon as you can work the soil. If you live in an area with mild winters, plant in late fall for a spring harvest. This cool-season crop can withstand temperatures as low as 40°F. For best results, grow parsnips when air tempera-tures are 60°–65°F. Roots that mature in temperatures above 75°F are generally of poor quality. Sow seeds thickly at ½" deep; leave 20"–24" between rows. Keep the soil evenly moist but not wet. Seeds germinate in 2–3 weeks. When the seedlings are 1" tall, thin to 4"–6" apart. Mulch to conserve moisture, and pull weeds to keep them from competing with the young plants.

Harvesting. Leave parsnips in the ground until after the first frost; freezing tempera-tures make the roots taste sweeter. Dig the roots and store them like carrots (see "Gathering the Harvest" on page 323), or mulch the row and leave the roots in the ground over winter. Add a marker for finding midwinter harvests in snow.

Extending the season. Even if your climate is cold, you can overwinter parsnips by covering them with a thick layer of hay; dig the roots as you need them. Parsnips lose quality when new growth begins; harvest them before spring.

Container growing. Short-rooted parsnip cultivars grow well in containers.

Propagation. Saving this hardy biennial's seeds takes two seasons. Select the largest and longest-storing roots from your harvest for seed production and replant them in the spring. Plants will flower and set seeds. Parsnips are insect pollinated and do cross with one another, but other cultivars rarely are present to contribute to a cross. As the seed heads turn brown in late summer, shake them into bags to catch the seeds.

Friends and relatives. A similar crop, skirret (*Sium sisarum*), is grown and used like parsnips. *

PAWPAW

Asimina triloba. Annonaceae.
Deciduous tree. Zones 5–8.

Pawpaw is a native cold-hardy fruit with a banana-pineapple-mango flavor—hence, its common names Michigan banana, Hoosier banana, and poor man's banana. Pawpaw is the northernmost member of the custard apple family. The tree's long, drooping leaves lend an exotic air to the landscape. Enjoy pawpaw fruits fresh or cook them, being careful not to use too much heat, which drives away the flavor. Traditional favorites include pawpaw pudding and marmalade.

Selecting plants. Choose pot-grown plants of named cultivars such as 'Overleese' or 'Sunflower'. Most pawpaws need cross-pollination, so plant at least two seedlings or two different cultivars. Pawpaws transplant poorly and seedlings produce variable fruits.

Site. Pawpaw can tolerate some shade but will fruit best in full sunlight.

Soil. Plant pawpaws in well-drained soil having a pH of 5.0–7.0. Mulch thickly with leaves or straw to keep the roots cool and moist and to cushion falling fruit.

How much to plant. An average yield is 1 bushel per tree.

Spacing. Space pawpaw trees 15' apart.

Seasons to bearing. Seedlings bear in about six years. Grafted plants bear in two to three years.

Planting and growing. You can set potted trees in the ground at any time. Bareroot trees should be dug and planted in spring, just before bud break. Take care when planting to preserve as much of the taproot as possible. Shade seedlings for their first two years.

If your trees bloom but set little fruit, try hand-pollination. When pollen is dusting off flowers' anthers, pick off a flower, remove its petals, and rub the anthers against the central stigmas of flowers on another plant.

Harvesting. Pick pawpaws dead-ripe, or just as they begin to soften to finish ripening indoors. Either way, the fruit is ready to eat when the greenish yellow skin turns brown or black. Tree-ripened fruits have a stronger flavor.

Fall and winter care. Prune lightly to remove wayward branches. Shorten shoots to stimulate fruitful new growth on an old tree.

Container growing. Because of its taproot, pawpaw doesn't do well in containers.

Propagation. Sowing seeds is an easy way to propagate a pawpaw, but you have to wait six or more years until you taste your first fruit. Sow seeds in the fall where you want trees, or stratify seeds by keeping them cool and moist for two months (refrigerated in a bag of moist peat moss) before planting.

Fruit quality on the resulting seedlings is not predictable, but they make good rootstocks on which to graft high-quality cultivars. Whip-and-tongue and most other types of grafting work well. Graft just as the buds on the rootstocks are beginning to expand.

You can also propagate pawpaws by transplanting suckers or taking root cuttings, but this requires more care. To transplant a sucker, push a shovel into the ground around the sucker to sever its roots from the mother plant. Leave the sucker in place for one year before digging it up for transplanting. Be sure to dig deeply and carefully to get the entire taproot.

Take root cuttings, pencil-thick pieces of root, from around the dormant mother plant. Cut the pieces into 4″ lengths.

Friends and relatives. To find out more about pawpaw's tropical cousins, see "Annonas" on page 352. ✳

PEA

Pisum spp. Leguminosae. Annual.

The garden pea (*Pisum sativum*) has been a favorite for centuries. This cool-season vegetable is rich in vitamins A and C, as well as protein. To enjoy peas at their best, pick the pods when they are plump, then shell and eat the sweet, juicy seeds immediately. For information on edible-podded peas and dry peas, see "Friends and Relatives" on page 300.

Planning

Selecting plants. Wrinkled-seeded cultivars are generally sweeter than smooth-seeded types and are more commonly grown by home gardeners. You can choose from among bush cultivars (also called dwarf) or climbing cultivars. Climbers require support but make better use of space and produce a larger overall yield than bush types. Grow both early-maturing cultivars and late-maturing cultivars to spread out the harvest. Disease-resistant and heat-resistant cultivars are available. If you plan to freeze some of your harvest, select one cultivar recommended for freezing.

When to plant. Plant peas as soon as the ground can be worked and the soil has reached 40°F. Peas can withstand cold, but freezing temperatures may damage plants. Peas grow best at temperatures between 60° and 65°F. Pods may become tough and woody or may not develop at all in temperatures above 75°F, so don't plant too late in spring. For fall harvest, don't plant until daytime temperatures are consistently below 80°F—in cold-winter areas, about six to eight weeks before the first expected frost date. In mild-winter areas, sow seeds in fall for an early-spring crop.

How much to plant. Allow 40 pea plants per person. One pound of pea seeds will cover a 100' row.

Spacing. Allow 2″–3″ between plants. For bush peas, space rows 2' apart; plant climbing types in rows 3' apart or in double rows 6″–8″ apart with a trellis between the rows. Allow 3' between each double row.

Rotation. Like other legumes, peas are a good crop to plant before heavy feeders such as corn that need lots of nitrogen.

For a greater harvest. Inoculate pea seeds to promote nitrogen fixation and increase yields. For bush types, try broadcasting the seeds in 1½'-wide rows. Plant early-, mid-, and late-maturing cultivars at the same time, then plant them again two weeks later. Grow fall crops in the shade of corn or pole beans.

Soil Preparation

Peas will grow in almost any well-drained soil, but the pH should be between 5.5 and 6.8. Test the soil and amend it as necessary. Before planting, spread 5–10 pounds of compost per 100 square feet. Cultivate the soil to a depth of at least 8″. Plant peas in flat rows or make raised beds if the soil is heavy or drains poorly.

ᴄ◦ AT A GLANCE ᴄ◦

PEA

Site: Full sun; will grow in partial shade.

Soil: Well-drained soil with high organic matter is best; pH of 5.5–6.8.

How much to plant: 40 plants per person.

Spacing: Bush types: 2' between rows. Climbing types: 3' between rows. Both types: 2″–3″ between plants.

Days to maturity: 56–75 days from seed to harvest.

🐝 FRIENDS & RELATIVES 🐝

PEA

Below you will find descriptions of some popular peas. For information on black-eyed peas, chick-peas, cowpeas, and princess peas, see "Friends and Relatives" on page 300.

Snow peas (*Pisum sativum* var. *macrocarpon*), or edible-podded peas, produce tender, succulent pods that are eaten raw or added to stir-fried dishes. Harvest when the pods are young and flat and the seeds are small and immature.

Snap peas (*P. sativum* var. *macrocarpon*) bear tender pods with juicy seeds, both of which are edible. Pick when the pods are plump and bulging with mature seeds. Snap peas are deli-

cious raw or cooked like snap beans.

Dry peas (*P. sativum* var. *sativum* and *P. sativum* var. *arvense*), or field peas, are grown for their seeds. Harvest them when the pods have turned brown. Shell the peas, then spread them out to dry for three weeks, or place them in a pan in the oven for three to four hours at 120°F. Cool the peas, then store them in airtight containers. Add them to soups or use them like dried beans. Prepare split peas by gently crushing dry peas with a mortar and pestle to break the seed coat and separate the two halves. Winnow to remove the seed coats; see "Processing Grains" on page 370 for instructions.

Planting Outdoors

Sowing seeds. Before planting, soak seeds in compost tea for 20 minutes. Sow seeds directly in the ground four to six weeks before the last expected frost. Plant 1″–2″ deep and 1″ apart. Seeds germinate in one to two weeks.

Growing Guidelines

Thinning seedlings. Thin plants to 2″–3″ apart when they are 2″–3″ tall.

Water and mulch. Keep soil moist, but don't overwater. Peas like cool, humid soil; however, soggy conditions can cause plants to rot or reduce yields. When plants are 3″–5″ tall, mulch with 4″–8″ of grass clippings. Pull

weeds gently by hand to avoid injuring pea plant roots.

Training. Climbing peas require support. Provide a 5′–8′-tall trellis at planting time or when seedlings are about 3″ tall.

Problem Prevention

Select resistant or tolerant cultivars. Cultivars are available that resist or tolerate

PEA SEEDLING

Seeds   Cotyledons   First true leaves

Fusarium wilt, downy mildew, pea root rot, and mosaic viruses.

Before planting, apply parasitic nematodes to the soil. This will help control cutworms and other pests.

When seedlings appear, cover plants with row cover. Row cover prevents leafhoppers, leafminers, cucumber beetles, caterpillars, pea weevils, and other pests from feeding on your crop.

Every two weeks, spray young plants with kelp extract. This will help prevent micronutrient deficiencies.

Gathering the Harvest

Peas are ready to pick about three weeks after flowers appear. Harvest plump pods that are just beginning to look bumpy; if the pods are discolored or shriveled, the peas are past their prime. Use scissors to cut the pods from

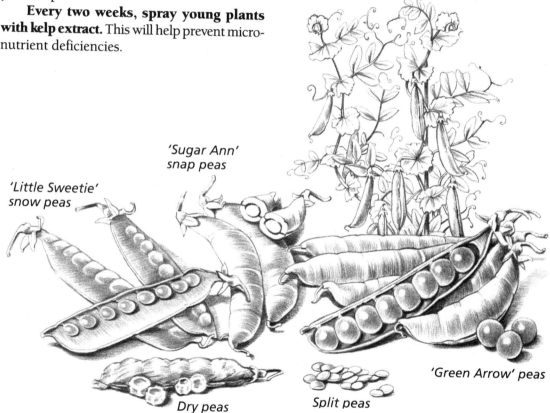

'Little Sweetie' snow peas

'Sugar Ann' snap peas

Dry peas

Split peas

'Green Arrow' peas

Eating fresh peas is one of the pleasures of having a garden. Growing snap peas and snow peas saves you the trouble of shelling. But watch out—some edible-podded cultivars have strings running down each pod that you must remove before eating. Opt for "stringless" cultivars for the easiest picking and fastest eating.

the plant, or pull them off very carefully; otherwise, you may uproot the plant. Harvest daily to keep the plants productive. Because the sugar quickly turns to starch, it's best to eat fresh peas immediately. Refrigerate the surplus for up to one week. You can also freeze or can peas.

Extending the Season

To get a head start on spring planting, cover the bed with clear or black plastic to warm the soil. When planting a fall crop, mulch and provide partial shade to keep the soil cool and moist.

Propagation

Plan to grow plants especially for seed saving—don't just save seeds of the pods you missed at harvest time. Follow the same procedure you would for saving seeds from bean plants. Refer to "Propagation" on page 301 for directions. ✳

PEACH

Prunus persica. Rosaceae. Deciduous tree. Zones 5–9.

Few fruits are more luscious than a thoroughly ripe peach. Once you've had your fill of fresh ones, dry, can, or freeze the rest.

Nectarines are just fuzzless peaches. They have smooth skin and are somewhat more prone to brown rot. They are grown and used just like peaches.

Planning

Selecting plants. Choose one-year-old trees that are ½" in diameter with one to three branches. Most peaches are self-fertile, so you need only one to get a crop. Cultivars that are not self-fertile such as 'J. H. Hale' and 'Chinese Cling' need a second cultivar to produce a crop.

Choose your cultivars with care. Peach trees, like other temperate-zone trees, require a period of cold weather before they will resume growth in spring. But peaches will burst into flower the first warm spell after their chilling requirement is met, making them more susceptible to frost-nipped flowers than some other fruit trees. If your winters are very mild, grow a "low-chill" cultivar such as 'Desert Gold' that needs only a short period of cold weather. If you get cold winters, you need a "high-chill" cultivar. If you plant a low-chill cultivar in the North, you will get frosted flowers in that January warm spell. If you plant a high-chill cultivar in Georgia, your tree will bloom erratically, if at all.

Peaches aren't known for their problem resistance, but there are some cultivars out there if you look. 'Elberta' and 'Red Bird' have some resistance to brown rot. 'Frost', 'Red Haven', and 'Stark EarliGlo' resist peach leaf curl.

⮿ AT A GLANCE ⮿
PEACH

Site: A warm site in full sun, not prone to late-spring frosts.
Soil: Well-drained and fertile.
Spacing: Full-size trees: 15'–20' apart. Grafted dwarf trees: 8'–12' apart. Genetic dwarfs: as close as 3' apart.
Seasons to bearing: Two years.

'Earlired', 'Harbrite', and 'Loring' resist bacterial leaf spot. 'Elberta', 'Harbrite', and 'Reliance' resist canker disease. Peachtree borers aren't as fond of 'Dixie Red', 'Elberta', or 'Jubilee'. Ask your local extension office what the serious problems are where you live, what cultivars resist them, and which cultivars are suited to your climate. Narrow the list according to color, season, and what you want to use them for.

Most peaches are grafted on seedling rootstock. 'Nemaguard' and 'Okinawa' are resistant to nematodes. 'Siberian C' increases hardiness if your winters stay cold but not if winter temperatures fluctuate.

Full-size peach trees don't grow very large, but if space is very limited, plant dwarf peaches. Some are natural (genetic) dwarfs; others are grafted onto dwarfing rootstocks.

Selecting a site. Peaches need full sun. In short-summer areas, select a south-facing site out of the wind. Excellent drainage is a must. The blossoms open early, so avoid frost pockets. North-facing slopes are ideal where late-spring frosts are common. Avoid sites where peaches grew previously. Avoid sites near wild chokecherries—they can harbor viral diseases.

When to plant. In mild-winter areas, plant in spring or fall. Elsewhere, plant in early spring.

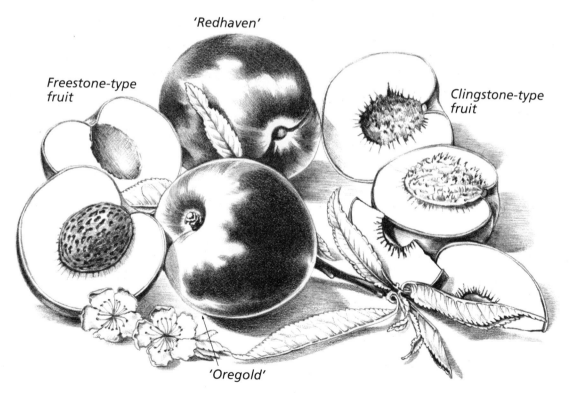

'Redhaven'

Freestone-type fruit

Clingstone-type fruit

'Oregold'

Soft, melting peaches are the taste of summer. Cultivars range from white to deep yellow-orange. Clingstones stay firmer when cooked; freestones are favorites for fresh eating and drying.

Spacing. Plant full-size peach trees 15′–20′ apart. Space grafted dwarf trees 8′–12′ apart and genetic dwarfs as close as 3′.

For a greater harvest. Peach trees live 10–15 years. Set out new trees in a new site every 4–5 years. The new trees will be in full production just as the old ones are declining.

Soil Preparation

Peach trees prefer a fertile soil with a pH between 6.0 and 7.0. Start preparing your soil a season before planting. Adjust the pH and build up fertility with fertilizer and cover crops. See "Custom Care for Fruit Crops" on page 58. If you have any doubts about your drainage, make raised beds.

Planting

See "Planting Trees" on page 145 for complete instructions on planting peach trees. Be sure the graft union of a grafted dwarf tree is higher than ground level so the scion's trunk won't root and negate the rootstock's dwarfing effect. Cut tall, unbranched trees back to 3′. See "Pruning at Planting Time" on page 145 for more details.

Growing Guidelines

Water and mulch. Peach trees need a regular supply of water throughout the growing season. Maintain an organic mulch under the trees.

Feeding. Spread 5–10 pounds of compost out as far as the tree's dripline in late winter. After petal-fall, spread 2 cups of bonemeal and 1 cup of alfalfa meal. (If flower buds are killed by frost, skip this second feeding.) Shoots on a well-nourished, young peach tree should grow about 3′ in a season; those on a mature, bearing tree should grow about 1½′. Expect about half as much growth from dwarf

trees. If growth is less than this, increase the amount of fertilizer the following year. Don't fertilize after midsummer, or the new growth may not harden before winter.

Training. Train peaches to an open center form. See "Pruning Trees" on page 142 for how and when to prune and train your peach tree.

Thinning. Thin fruit after June drop (the natural drop of some fruits in early summer) to 6″–8″ apart, removing damaged fruit first.

Problem Prevention

In late winter, prune out diseased branches. Cut off branches with bacterial canker lesions—sunken, elliptical patches or cracks that may ooze a reddish gum—a few inches below cankers. Paint cuts with a slurry of lime-sulfur. Cut off any other odd-looking twigs and remove any mummified fruits. Destroy prunings. Delay other pruning until bloom.

In late winter, spray dormant oil. If scale insects or aphids were a problem last year, spray trees with dormant oil. If you plan to spray lime-sulfur or sulfur, spray dormant oil at least three weeks before you'll be spraying any sulfur compound.

As buds swell in spring, spray lime-sulfur. Lime-sulfur helps control overwintering bacterial leaf spot, brown rot, and peach scab spores. Bacterial leaf spot causes dark, sunken spots on fruit that turn into cracks. Peach scab shows up as olive green spots on fruit. Brown rot is described on page 178. If you saw any symptoms last season, spray now.

Don't spray peaches with copper. Copper and copper-containing compounds can defoliate peaches. Use lime-sulfur or sulfur instead.

As buds swell, hang pest traps. If peach tree or twig borer damage was a problem last year, hang one or two pheromone-baited traps per tree to help control them.

If oriental fruit moth damage was a problem last year, hang one or two pheromone-baited traps per tree to help control them this year. Or use one (for up to 5 acres) to see when the pest appears. Check the trap every few days. Wait 10–14 days after first oriental fruit moth is caught, and spray trees with *Bacillus thuringiensis* var. *kurstaki* (BTK) plus molasses or pyrethrins plus rotenone. See "Troubleshooting Vegetable and Fruit Pests" on page 182 for a description of this pest and the damage it causes. If you have quite a few fruit trees in your landscape, you may want to try mating disruption to control these moths. See "Pheromones" on page 159 for suggestions.

If tarnished plant bugs were a problem last year, hang one to four white sticky traps per tree (depending on tree size) to help control them. Or use one trap to tell you when the bugs appear. Spray trees with sabadilla when you catch your first tarnished plant bug. Attacked fruits have sunken, corky pockets. See "Troubleshooting Vegetable and Fruit Pests" on page 182 for a description of this pest.

When green shows, spray kelp. Kelp increases fruit set and bud hardiness. Spray three to six times: when you first see green, when leaves are ½" long, when the buds are fat and pink, and then every three to four weeks all summer to help reduce disease, including peach leaf curl.

At bloom, prune. Delayed-dormant pruning just before to just after bloom helps decrease the chance of pruning-induced cold injury and helps prevent canker disease development.

At bloom, spray sulfur. If it is wet or humid and 70°F or more when your peaches have open flowers, spray sulfur to help control brown rot.

When petals fall, hang plum curculio traps. Plum curculio can be a major problem east of the Rocky Mountains. See "When Petals Fall, Hang Plum Curculio Traps" on page 276 for details.

As new leaves appear, remove distorted ones. Peach leaf curl is a fungal disease that causes crinkled, curly leaves. Remove and destroy them.

After fruit set, thin. Well-spaced fruits are less likely to be attacked by insects or succumb to diseases, and you'll get bigger fruits. Thin fruits to 6"–8" apart, beginning with damaged fruits.

If shoot tips wilt, remove them. Oriental fruit moth larvae and peach twig borers attack new growth. Snip off the twig a few inches below the damage and destroy.

Summer through fall, pick up dropped fruit. Dropped fruit may harbor insect pests, which will crawl out of the fruit to pupate in the soil.

If dark spots appear on fruit, spray sulfur. Peach scab and bacterial leaf spot can cause dark spots and cracks on fruit. Spray sulfur or lime-sulfur every 10–21 days until harvest if weather is wet or humid and spots are spreading.

Six weeks after bloom, replace pheromone lures in traps. Freshly baited traps will control pests for the rest of the season.

As fruits begin to color, spray sulfur. Fruits become susceptible to brown rot infection again now. If the weather is wet or humid and below 85°F, infection can occur in a few hours. In order for sulfur to protect the fruit, it needs to be there before these conditions occur. Remove and destroy rotting fruits the second you see them.

In early fall, check and winterize trunks. Peach tree borer larvae bore into the bark near the soil line and up about 1'. Remove any wire or plastic guard and pull the soil away from the trunk an inch or so down. Examine the trunk. If you find borer holes or gummy ooze, dig the borers out with a sharp flexible wire, or squirt beneficial nematodes into the holes. To reduce sunscald injury and protect wounds from canker disease, paint the trunk from the soil to the first branch with a mixture of white latex paint and lime-sulfur, diluted according to label instructions. Return soil and guards to their original position.

In fall, renew mulch. Rake old mulch away from trees in early fall. In late fall, after all of the leaves have fallen and the rodents have found winter homes elsewhere, respread mulch and top it with new mulch to make a 6"–12" layer.

Gathering the Harvest

On the average, expect 2–3 bushels of fruit from a full-size tree. Pick fully ripe fruits carefully. Ripening doesn't continue after harvest. Ripe fruit shows no green, is slightly soft, parts easily from the stem when you lift with a slight twisting motion, and tastes delectable. A ripe peach is highly perishable. You can store slightly underripe fruits for two to four weeks at high humidity and near-freezing temperatures.

Fall and Winter Care

In the fall, clean up leaves and mummified fruits and winterize your trunks. (See "In Early Fall, Check and Winterize Trunks" on page 439 for instructions.) Wait until bloom time to prune. See "Problem Prevention" on page 439 for instructions on how to prune.

Container Growing

Choose genetic dwarfs or trees on dwarfing rootstocks for container growing. Use a container at least 1½' deep and wide. Once your plant reaches full size, repot it every year just before growth commences in spring, and prune back the roots and top. In very cold areas, protect the roots in winter as shown in the illustration on page 240.

Propagation

Peaches are usually propagated by budding. Grow your own rootstock from peach pits. You also can propagate peaches on their own roots by either hardwood or softwood cuttings. *

PEANUT

Arachis hypogaea. Leguminosae. Annual.

Whether they're fresh-roasted, chopped, or ground into that American staple, peanut butter, there's a place for peanuts in almost any meal. They can be eaten as a snack, used in baking, sprinkled over desserts, or added as a garnish to stir-fried dishes and salads. They are also a fascinating crop to grow. Peanut plants produce small yellow flowers at the tip of special branches near the base of the plant. If a flower is pollinated, the petals drop off and the branch, or "peg," grows downward and buries its tip in the soil where the nut then develops.

Selecting plants. Nut size varies with cultivar. Short-season cultivars such as 'Early

Spanish' are more likely to succeed in northern gardens.

Site. Peanuts need full sun and very warm conditions.

Soil. Peanuts prefer light sandy loam. Except for Spanish-type cultivars, peanuts can adjust to well-drained clay.

How much to plant. Under ideal conditions, a peanut plant produces a few pounds of unshelled nuts.

Spacing. Plant seeds 6″ apart and thin to 1′ apart after a month. Space rows at least 2′ apart.

Days to maturity. Peanuts mature in 100–150 days, depending on the cultivar.

Planting and growing. Remove the shells but leave the skins on the seeds. Plant in deeply worked soil at least two weeks after the last expected frost, when the soil is warm. Keep plants well-weeded and the soil crust-free. Hill up soil around the plants when they're about 1′ tall so the pegs can easily work their way underground.

Harvesting. In the South, harvest peanuts when the tops start to yellow and the nuts are mature. In the North, the tops may not yellow before frost, so dig a sample peanut in mid-fall to test maturity. Immature nuts have soft shells and pale skins; mature nuts have hard shells and pink or red skins. Dig whole plants with nuts and roots intact, shake off the soil, and dry them in the sun for several days. Then hang them in an airy place for several weeks to dry further. Remove the nuts and store in paper, cloth, or burlap bags. Roast unshelled peanuts before eating, if desired. Boil uncured immature nuts in plain or lightly salted water, shells and all, and eat them as snacks.

Extending the season. In cool climates, use black plastic mulch to prewarm the soil for two weeks before planting.

Fall and winter care. Compost plants after removing the nuts.

Container growing. Choose a container that is at least 1½′ across so there is plenty of room for the pegs to work their way into the soil.

Propagation. Collect mature, unshelled nuts from disease-free plants and store them in a cool, dry place. ✳

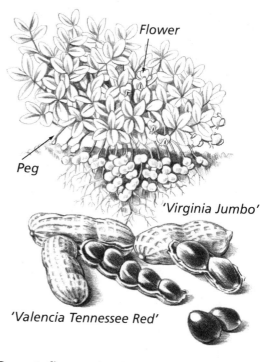

Flower

Peg

'Virginia Jumbo'

'Valencia Tennessee Red'

Peanuts flower above ground. After pollination the flower stems, or pegs, burrow into the ground and form the familiar nuts. They thrive in warm weather and need a minimum of 100–110 frost-free days to bear a crop.

PEAR

Pyrus communis and hybrids. Rosaceae.
Deciduous tree. Zones 4–9.

Pears are versatile fruits that keep for a long time in storage and dry, freeze, and can well. In Europe, "hard" pear juice, known as perry, is made from snow pear (*Pyrus nivalis*) cultivars, some with such colorful names as 'Merrylegs' and 'Devildrink'.

Planning

Selecting plants. Choose a one-year-old tree, ⅝"–⅞" in diameter and 4'–5' tall with one to three branches. Pears generally need cross-pollination, so you must plant at least two cultivars to get fruit. A few cultivars can't pollinate specific cultivars or any cultivars at all. Check with your nursery when you order.

Fire blight is a problem mostly where summers are hot and humid. You can still grow pears in such regions if you plant resistant cultivars such as 'Kieffer', 'Magness', and 'Moonglow'.

Pear rootstocks come in a range of sizes. 'Bartlett' seedlings make full-size trees. Dwarfing rootstocks offer the full range in tree size, from 30' down to 8' high. The rootstock series 'OH × F' ('Old Home' × 'Farmingdale') offers fire blight resistance and results in trees with a range of sizes, from very dwarf ('OH × F 51') to full size ('OH × F 97'). Quince rootstock is quite dwarfing.

Selecting a site. Plant pears at a sunny site with plenty of air movement.

When to plant. Plant pear trees in either early spring or fall.

Spacing. Eventual size of a pear tree depends on the rootstock and the soil fertility. Spacing ranges from 15'–20' apart for a full-size tree to 8'–12' for a dwarf tree.

For a greater harvest. Pears tend to be upright growing, and upright branches are not very fruitful. Encourage early and abundant fruiting by using lots of weights and spreaders. See "Spreading Fruit Tree Branches" on page 136 for how and when to do this.

Soil Preparation

Pear trees prefer a moderately fertile soil with a pH between 6.0 and 6.5. Good drainage is nice but not essential. For information on soil preparation, see "Custom Care for Tree Fruits" on page 61.

Planting

Plant pear trees like other fruit trees. See "Perennial Crops" on page 111.

Growing Guidelines

Water and mulch. The water and mulch requirements for pears are the same as for apples. See "Water and Mulch" on page 275.

Feeding. Pears need the same feeding as apples. See "Feeding" on page 275 for details.

❧ AT A GLANCE ❧

PEAR

Site: Full sun.

Soil: Tolerates many soils but prefers well-drained, moist soil with a pH of 6.0–6.5.

Spacing: Full-size trees: 15'–20' apart. Dwarf trees: 8'–12' apart.

Seasons to bearing: Three to six years.

If you have a mature pear tree that consistently puts out too much new growth, replace the mulch with turf grass to help reduce the moisture and nutrients available to the tree.

Training. Train pear trees to a central leader or modified central leader form. Spread branches whenever possible. Prune as little as possible. See "Pruning Trees" on page 142 for how-to instructions.

Thinning. A month or two after bloom, thin fruits to leave one or two per cluster. Spot-pick mature fruits during harvest to allow the fruits that remain to mature and grow larger.

Problem Prevention

Pears are closely related to apples and are prone to many of the same problems. Follow the steps in "Problem Prevention" on page 276. Pears have one additional common problem: pear psyllas. Pears in general are also more susceptible to fire blight than apples are. Both problems are encouraged by soft, succulent growth, so limit fertilizer applications. Prune with thinning cuts to avoid stimulating suckering.

In late winter, spray dormant oil. If psyllas were a problem last year, spray oil just as buds are swelling. Psyllas are $\frac{1}{10}$"-long red or

'Bosc' pear

'Bartlett' pears

'Hosui' Asian pear

'Red Bartlett' pears

Melting and buttery or crisp and flavorful, a ripe pear is a special treat. When the seeds darken to brown or black, the fruit is ready to pick. Pears are attractive trees with clouds of white flowers, shiny dark leaves, and vivid fall color. They bloom late and usually escape frost damage. Why not make a few fruiting pears part of your landscape?

green insects that suck plant juices. As they feed, they release a sticky honeydew, which supports the growth of black sooty mold. Sooty mold black washes off; fire blight black doesn't.

When the flower buds swell, spray strep-tomycin or copper. If fire blight was a problem last year, spray trees just before flowers open. Repeat every four days during bloom and every five to seven days until fruit appears. As soon as you see any fire blight, prune it out.

During fruiting, eliminate pear psyllas. If you find any of this pest affecting your trees when they are fruiting, spray them with insecticidal soap or superior oil.

Gathering the Harvest

Except for 'Seckel', which should be picked ripe, pick pears before they are ripe. A pear is ready for harvest when the green color lightens and the stem of the fruit parts readily from the spur when you lift up on the fruit with a slight twist. Allow pears to soften and ripen indoors at a temperature of 65°–70°F.

For storage, keep fruit at high humidity and temperatures near freezing. The length of storage varies with the cultivar. Remove the fruit from storage to soften and ripen before you eat it.

Yield varies greatly with tree size, averaging 1 bushel for a dwarf tree to 3–5 bushels for a standard tree.

Fall and Winter Care

See "Fall and Winter Care" on page 278 for details.

🐝 FRIENDS & RELATIVES 🐝

PEAR

Asian pears (hybrids of *Pyrus pyrifolia*, *P. ussuriensis*, and *P. bretschneideris*) have been enjoyed for thousands of years in Asia. The fruits are crisp, very juicy and sweet, and often round. Grow Asian pears the same way you grow European pears. If their bloom times overlap, they can cross-pollinate each other. There are two differences: Train Asian pears to open center or modified central leader form, and allow Asian pears to ripen on the tree before harvesting them.

Container Growing

Choose pears grafted on dwarf rootstocks. Once your plant reaches full size, repot it every year when it is dormant, pruning back the roots and tops at that time. In very cold areas, protect the roots in winter as shown in the illustration on page 240.

Propagation

Propagate pears by grafting them onto pear or quince rootstocks. Quince rootstocks result in dwarf trees that fruit at an early age. Some pear cultivars, such as 'Bartlett', are incompatible with quince rootstocks. In such cases, select a compatible rootstock. Check with your nursery for more details. ✳

PECAN

Carya illinoinensis. Juglandaceae. Deciduous tree. Zones 6–9.

These long-lived, spreading trees are native to the wide floodplains of the Mississippi, Missouri, and Ohio rivers. In the South, pecan trees can grow up to 150'. For a good crop of nuts farther north, select cultivars that will mature in a shorter growing season. Late-spring or early-fall frosts can destroy a crop. Pecans also like steady summer heat, with little difference between day and night temperatures. In the Deep South, too much humidity can hamper pollination and promote disease.

Pecan nuts are wonderful when shelled and eaten. For a sweet, sinful dessert, try pecan pie, or add chopped pecans to breads and cookies. They are also a nice topping for yogurt or ice cream.

Selecting plants. Buy from a nursery as close to your location as possible. Make sure the rootstock of your tree can handle the winter temperatures in your area if you are buying from a nursery farther south. For an illustration of pecan nuts and leaves, see page 416.

Site. Plant pecan trees on a flat area, if possible. Pecans are very susceptible to winter-kill and spring frost damage. Avoid little valleys or depressions where cold air settles.

Soil. Pecans do best in deep, fertile, well-drained soil.

How much to plant. Pecans are not self-fruitful. They need another pecan tree planted nearby that will have male flowers in bloom when the female flowers of the other are open. Check with your local extension office for a list of pecan cultivars and recommended pollinators for your state.

Spacing. Plant trees at least 35' apart—50' is preferable. Maximum spacing for adequate pollination is about 100'.

Seasons to bearing. Budded or grafted trees will yield small crops in four to seven years.

Planting and growing. Prepare the planting site and plant as you would any tree. See "Perennial Crops" on page 111 for directions.

Water well daily for the first few days. Continue to water weekly during the growing season for the first several years if rain is scarce. Keep the area beneath the tree well-weeded, or mulch with wood chips or any mix of organic matter. To avoid excessive, tender early growth, wait until the second year to fertilize. Then spread a thin layer of well-rotted manure or a blended organic fertilizer with a good nitrogen value beneath the tree once or twice a year in spring.

To help control pecan aphids, grow a cover crop of crimson clover, hairy vetch, red clover, or white clover around the trees to attract their natural predators.

Pecan weevils can be a major pest. They tend to appear in larger numbers every two years. They look quite similar to plum cucurlios, which are illustrated on page 187. Since pecan weevils tend to stay under the tree or trees where they hatch, they are possible to control. In late July, mow any vegetation below the tree as short as possible. Get a piece of floating row cover large enough to cover the ground under the tree at least out to the drip line or a little farther. Cut a slit into the center and fit the cover snuggly around the trunk and spread it over the ground. Roll the edges of the slit together and use a stapler or clothespins to seal it. Seal the outside edges with soil, or tack it down every few feet. Now any hatching weevils will not be able to get to your pecans. Leave the cover in place through harvest. A few weevils may fly in, so collect and destroy any nuts that drop prematurely.

Harvesting. Harvest promptly. Pecans are ripe when they fall or they can be knocked from the tree. Remove the husks and cure nuts on wire mesh screens or hang them in mesh bags. After about two weeks, freeze in or out of the shell for long-term storage.

Fall and winter care. Prune in late winter to a central leader shape; remove branches with narrow crotch angles. See "Pruning Trees" on page 142 for directions.

Propagation. Propagate pecans by budding or grafting. Be sure to use a rootstock chosen for hardiness or insect and disease resistance. ✱

PEPPER

Capsicum annuum var. *annuum*. Solanaceae. Perennial grown as an annual.

One of the greatest culinary treasures discovered in the New World five centuries ago is the pepper. Native to tropical areas of North and South America, various peppers are now culinary mainstays from Hungary to California. Sweet peppers can be stuffed, pickled, added to sauces, or eaten fresh in salads. Spicier peppers are a mainstay of many cuisines, including Mexican, and can be used to spice up anything from dips and sauces to main dishes. There are even peppers grown primarily as ornamental plants in front yard flower beds.

Planning

Selecting plants. Finding the right peppers to suit your palate is an adventure, for there are dozens of variations in flavor, color, size, and shape from which to choose. Small-fruited cultivars usually produce many more peppers than large-fruited ones. They'll also set fruit better under very hot or cold conditions. On the other hand, large, thick-walled peppers tend to be sweetest, especially when allowed to ripen completely. Sweet peppers come in green, yellow, red, orange, or purple, and even blue, white, and chocolate brown.

Sweet peppers come in a variety of shapes. Bell peppers can be blocky and lobed or elongated. Pimentos and paprikas are heart-shaped, and bananas are long and narrow. The easiest sweet peppers to grow are probably medium- to small-size bell peppers (either square or elongated) and mild banana types. Pimentos, paprikas, and very large bells grow best where summers are long and warm because the fruits take a long time to mature. Little cherry peppers and small pepperoncini, on the other hand, tend to be fast and prolific.

Caribbean-type peppers, such as 'Cubanelle', popular for grilling and frying, are a category all their own. Fruits tend to be long and narrow and have a mild but not really

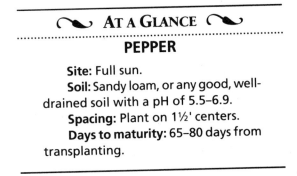

❧ AT A GLANCE ❧
PEPPER

Site: Full sun.
Soil: Sandy loam, or any good, well-drained soil with a pH of 5.5–6.9.
Spacing: Plant on 1½' centers.
Days to maturity: 65–80 days from transplanting.

sweet flavor that's packed with pepper taste. They're grown just like sweet peppers and often produce continually from midsummer to frost.

Hot peppers are quite variable as well, and some are much, much hotter than others. Several modern hot peppers have been developed specifically for people who want piquant flavor but not so much heat that the pepper taste is hidden. Depending on the cultivar, jalapeño peppers may be very hot or only slightly hot, but there is no such thing as a mild cayenne.

See the Mexican Specialties entry for more information on hot pepper types and cultivars.

Selecting a site. Peppers need warm soil that's well-drained, and they do best in full sun. They'll tolerate a site that gets strong morning sun and isn't shaded until late afternoon. In windy areas, shelter from cold winds is helpful.

When to plant. Peppers are a warm-weather crop and grow best when the soil is at least 65°F and night temperatures stay above 50°F. Wait until at least a week after the last expected spring frost to plant them. Depending on the cultivar, plants may be set out until 12 weeks before the first expected fall frost. See "Extending the Season" on page 450 if you live where summers are cool.

How much to plant. For mild peppers, plant at least three plants per person—more if you plan to freeze or pickle them. With hot peppers, one or two plants per person should be sufficient.

Spacing. In traditional rows, space peppers 1½' apart. Or grow them in double rows or wide raised beds, with 1½' between plants in all directions. A 4' × 6' raised bed will support eight plants. If you are growing only one or two hot pepper plants, let them serve as accents in various corners of the garden.

PLAY IT SAFE WITH HOT PEPPERS

The chemical compound that makes peppers hot, called capsaicin, does not readily wash off human skin. If you get capsaicin on your hands and then touch your eyes, it can be a very painful experience. Capsaicin is most concentrated inside hot peppers around the seeds. Wear rubber gloves when cutting up hot peppers. Surgical gloves (sold at medical supply stores) give good protection. Locate hot pepper plants where young children will not be tempted to pick them.

Rotation. Plant peppers after legumes but not after potatoes, eggplants, or tomatoes.

For a greater harvest. Plant large- and small-fruited cultivars, including some that mature early. In hot-summer areas, large-fruited peppers may not bear until early fall since they don't set fruit well when temperatures are above 90°F. A few small-fruited plants will supply some peppers in the heat of summer. Also, small-fruited peppers tend to set fruit in cold weather better than large-fruited ones, so they are a good choice in cool climates.

Soil Preparation

Peppers like warm, well-aerated soil. Loosen soil to a depth of 1' or more, and add 1 large shovelful of compost per plant to raised beds, or add 20–30 pounds of compost per 100' row.

Planting Indoors

Sowing seeds. Pepper seeds are grown much like tomato seeds, except they don't need to be planted in the larger 3″ pots or cells. Use 1½″ cells or 2″ peat pots. Peppers germinate best when the planting medium is kept somewhat dry. They also prefer somewhat warmer temperatures than tomatoes; temperatures between 70° and 80°F are ideal. See "Sowing Seeds" on page 494 for more information. Plant seeds seven or eight weeks before you want to plant your seedlings out.

Seedling care. Pepper seedlings need good light and warmth. The best temperatures for strong growth range between 65° and 75°F in the daytime and 60°–65°F at night. Feed seedlings weekly with a weak liquid fertilizer, such as fish emulsion (1 tablespoon per gallon of water).

Hardening off transplants. Harden off peppers much as you would tomatoes. See "Hardening Off Transplants" on page 496.

Planting Outdoors

Buying transplants. Look for plants with thick stems and dark green leaves. If they already show flower buds but you are not yet ready to set them out, transplant them to larger pots and feed weekly with fish emulsion (1 tablespoon per gallon of water) or compost tea.

Setting out transplants. Move plants to the garden two to three weeks after the last expected frost, when soil temperatures reach 60°–65°F. Don't expose plants to temperatures below 40°F. Protect them with plastic tunnels or cloches until mild weather returns.

PEPPER SEEDLING

Seeds   Cotyledons   First true leaves

In cool climates, warm the soil with black plastic for a week before planting, and use cloches to keep the plants warm for three weeks after transplanting.

In hot climates, set out peppers in the late afternoon or evening. If their first few days in the garden will be sunny ones, cover each plant with an upside-down cardboard box that's propped up on one side, or shade them with burlap for two to three days. Water often for the first two weeks after setting plants out. Heat and moisture stress can seriously delay new growth.

Growing Guidelines

Water and mulch. Peppers appreciate moderate, even moisture around their roots but tolerate drought better than tomatoes or eggplants.

Mulch reduces weed problems and helps retain soil moisture. Black plastic mulch also helps keep the soil warm. When mulching peppers with straw, grass clippings, or legume hay, keep the mulch pulled back 2″ from the plants.

Living mulches such as clovers also can be a boon in the pepper patch, but keep them mowed. For best results, grow nitrogen-fixing cover crops between rows, and use mulch around the plants themselves.

Feeding. If you enrich each planting hole with a shovelful of compost, your peppers may not need supplemental fertilizer. But if you want to make sure, drench plants with fish emulsion or kelp-and-fish-emulsion mixture weekly from transplant to first bloom. Side-dressings of kelp can help offset potassium deficiency, and bonemeal can provide needed phosphorus. Avoid excessive nitrogen, which can cause rampant growth of leaves but not many fruits. See "Custom Care for Fruit

Crops" on page 58 for more information. Spray plants with Epsom salts (1 teaspoon per gallon of water) when first blossoms appear.

If your peppers are growing well but not setting fruit, the problem may not be nutritional; it could be the weather. Peppers flower and set fruit in temperatures between 65° and 85°F. Purplish or yellow leaves may indicate nutritional deficiency, but low productivity during very hot or very cold weather does not.

Training. When they load up with ripening fruits, peppers tend to fall over. The plants will continue producing in a prone position, provided a thick mulch keeps ripening fruits from touching the ground. A single 3'–4'-tall stake, pushed 10″ into the soil, gives the plants ample support. Stake peppers when they are 1' tall or taller by tying the plants to stakes with two or three strips of soft cloth.

In windy areas, a sturdy string trellis is ideal. Place 3'–4'-tall stakes between plants, and weave plastic twine around plants, crossing the twine at each stake to create a figure-eight weave.

Some gardeners prefer to grow peppers unstaked. The advantage of this practice comes in late summer, when early frosts may be followed by several weeks of mild weather. Prostrate plants are easy to cover with blankets to get them through early frosts. They also may stay a little warmer when they hug mulched ground.

Peppers come in a delicious array of shapes, sizes, colors, and flavors. Bell peppers are mild and can be eaten green or ripe. 'Corno di Toro', 'Cubanelle', and 'Sweet Banana' have thinner flesh and are often used for frying but are also quite mild. 'Anaheim' peppers can be medium to quite hot, and most jalapeño cultivars are very hot.

Problem Prevention

Select resistant cultivars. Peppers that are resistant to tobacco mosaic virus may also show resistance to less common viruses. Small-fruited hot peppers often have high levels of natural resistance to these diseases.

At planting, place paper collars around seedlings. Take this precaution at transplant time to prevent cutworms from cutting down seedlings.

Plant in raised beds. Imperfect drainage can aggravate problems with Verticillium and Fusarium wilts, which sometimes affect peppers. Raised beds give pepper roots a healthy edge against these and other diseases.

Before planting, solarize soil. Where nematode infestations are severe, solarize soil prior to planting peppers and add chitin to the soil. In addition, give peppers extra water to make up for the root loss caused by this pest.

Gathering the Harvest

Most peppers can be eaten when they are green and underripe, although the flavor improves as they ripen. Most peppers change color when ripe. Small, thin-walled peppers like cayennes tend to color up rapidly. Heirloom cheese peppers, on the other hand, ripen very slowly. Sweet bell peppers that show stripes of yellow, red, or orange will continue to ripen when harvested and stored at room temperature. Ripening stops when peppers are refrigerated.

Cut bell peppers from the plants with a sharp knife or pruning shears, leaving at least 1/2″ of stem attached. Cayennes and some other peppers usually pop off with ample stem attached when pulled from the plants. Always use a cutting tool if you find yourself having to twist and tug to get peppers picked.

Juicy, thick-walled peppers can be stored in plastic bags in the refrigerator for up to two weeks. Or wash your peppers, cut them into strips, blanch them for 30 seconds in boiling water, and freeze them. Peppers also may be pickled.

Small, thin-walled peppers start drying the moment you pick them. To dry hot peppers like cayennes, lay them in a single layer in a very warm place (like an attic) until they are beyond leathery but not quite crisp. Then store them in airtight jars. Hot peppers with thick walls, like jalapeños, are harder to dry. Freeze or pickle them instead.

Extending the Season

To get an early start in spring, prewarm the soil with black plastic, and use cloches or plastic tunnels after the plants are set out. In fall, covering the plants with blankets during the first freeze or two may keep them producing for several more weeks.

Some small-fruited peppers can be dug in late summer, potted, and grown indoors throughout the winter. For best results, prune the plants back by one-third just after potting.

❧ FRIENDS & RELATIVES ❧

PEPPER

Tabasco peppers (*Capsicum frutescens*) are grown much like other peppers, although they grow best in warm, humid climates. The peppercorns from which black pepper is made are the seeds of an unrelated plant, *Piper nigrum*. See "Pepper" on page 386 for more information about this plant.

Grow them in your warmest, sunniest windowsill. Set them back in the garden in late spring.

Fall and Winter Care

When a hard freeze blackens your peppers, pull up the plants and compost them.

Container Growing

Peppers will grow well in containers, provided they have good drainage.

Propagation

Pepper seeds are easy to save. Let a pepper ripen completely, pick it, cut it open, and tap out the seeds with a knife. Allow the seeds to air dry on a paper towel. If you save seeds, plant mild and hot peppers at opposite ends of the garden to keep them from cross-pollinating.

If bacterial spot has been present, soak the seeds in a solution of ¼ cup of bleach and 1 cup of water for ten minutes. Pour them out into a strainer, and dry the seeds again before storing them in a cool, dry place. ✳

PERSIMMON

Diospyros spp. Ebenaceae. Deciduous tree. Zones 5–10.

Ripe Asian persimmons (*Diospyros kaki*), or kakis, are honey-sweet and have a smooth, soft texture; so-called non-astringent cultivars can be eaten crisp. Asians are adapted from Zones 7 to 10.

Fruits of the American persimmon (*D. virginiana*), a native of the eastern United States, are smaller, drier, and richer-tasting than Asian persimmons. Americans persimmons are adapted from Zones 5 to 10.

Selecting plants. Gardeners in warm regions can plant non-astringent Asians. Where winters and summers are cooler, plant astringent Asians. These cultivars are puckery and unfit to eat until they soften. In still colder climates, plant American persimmons, most of which are inedible until they are soft. In northern areas, make sure you choose a cultivar capable of ripening within your growing season.

Persimmon trees usually are either male or female, but most female cultivars of Asians and a few female cultivars of American persimmons bear fruit without pollination. Some cultivars are edible while they are crisp only if they have been pollinated; without pollination, wait to eat the fruit until it has softened. Descriptions in nursery catalogs will tell you whether or not cultivars offered require pollination.

Site. Persimmon trees fruit best in full sunlight. Plan before you plant because the trees become large with age.

Soil. Persimmons tolerate almost any soils except those that are waterlogged.

How much to plant. Yields vary with cultivar and climate, but expect 200 pounds or more per tree.

Spacing. Space trees 15′ apart.

Seasons to bearing. Grafted trees often bear some fruit the year after planting. Transplanted suckers and trees grown from root cuttings will take a few more years. Seedlings are slow to bear.

Planting and growing. Persimmon trees

have a long taproot, so they need special care in planting. Set potted trees in the ground at any time, but plant bareroot trees in spring, just before bud break. Take care when planting to preserve as much of the taproot as possible. Roots regenerate slowly, so water the tree weekly during the first season.

Harvesting. Harvest ripe Asian persimmons by clipping the fruits from the tree. Many cultivars of American persimmon drop their fruits when they are ripe, so mulch under trees to cushion their fall.

Do not pick fruits of astringent cultivars until they are very soft and their skins are almost translucent. Pick fruits of non-astringent cultivars while they are fully colored yet firm. Pick American persimmons when the fruits are very soft or fall to the ground. Slightly underripe persimmons will ripen off the tree. Speed ripening by placing fruits in a bag with an apple.

Store persimmons for up to two months at temperatures just above freezing.

Fall and winter care. Prune persimmons in winter. Train young trees to an open center or modified central leader form. See "Pruning Trees" on page 142 for instructions. Shorten long branches or support them with stakes. Wrap the trunks of young trees with burlap or tree tape to prevent sunscald.

As your tree comes into bearing, prune to stimulate some new growth, which will bear fruit the following season. Also shorten some one-year-old branches to thin the fruits. American persimmon often drops branches that have fruited, so little further pruning is needed.

Propagation. Grafting is the most common way to propagate cultivars. Asian, date plum (*D. lotus*), and American persimmon can all serve as rootstocks. Asian persimmon is the least cold-hardy of the three. Date plum is adaptable to many soils but is incompatible with some Asian cultivars and subject to disease problems. American persimmon is the

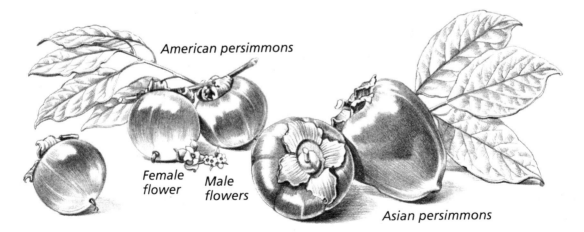

American persimmons

Female flower

Male flowers

Asian persimmons

Asian persimmon was once the most popular fruit in Asia. American Indians dried loaves made from pulped American persimmons. Persimmons cook into mouthwatering pies, cakes, cookies, and puddings.

most cold-hardy and tolerates the widest range of soil conditions. However, it is difficult to transplant.

Join persimmon stock and scion by whip grafting, bark grafting, or cleft grafting just as buds on the rootstock are pushing out.

Propagate ungrafted trees by transplant-ing suckers or by taking root cuttings.

Plant persimmon seeds to grow rootstocks for grafting or if you want to develop new cultivars. Stratify seeds for two to three months immediately after extracting them from the fruit. Seedlings first begin to bear fruit when they are about six years old. ✳

PINEAPPLE

Ananas comosus. Bromeliaceae. Perennial. Zone 10.

Fresh, homegrown pineapples picked at the peak of ripeness are among the most delicious fruits in the world. They're made into juice, eaten fresh as dessert, and used in salads, and they can be cooked or canned.

Selecting plants. 'Honey Gold' bears fruits up to 15 pounds. 'Smooth Cayenne' foliage is nearly free of spines. 'Variegated' is an attractive ornamental and bears white, honey-sweet fruits.

Site. Pineapples grow well in sun or partial shade.

Soil. Plant pineapples in well-drained soil enriched with organic matter. They tolerate a pH of 5.5–6.0.

How much to plant. Grow five or six pineapple plants per family.

Spacing. Plant a bed with rows 2'–3' apart with plants 1½' apart.

Seasons to bearing. Pineapples bear in one-and-a-half to two-and-a-half years. Plants grown from suckers bear faster than those grown from crowns.

Planting and growing. Buy plants. Or cut the crown of leaves from the top of a fruit. Remove leaves from the bottom 1" of stalk; dry the stalk for a few days to prevent rotting. Plant the stalk in well-drained soil in a pot or in the ground, just deep enough to keep it from tipping over. Water frequently; mulch between plants. Feed plants four times a year with compost or another balanced fertilizer. Keep soil out of the crown. Plants survive temperatures to 28°F but do not grow below 55°F. Remove plants that have fruited; the bed will produce crops from suckers for several years. Thin suckers to ensure adequate spacing.

Harvesting. Fruits are ready to harvest when they begin to soften and are very fragrant.

Fall and winter care. Protect plants if temperatures dip near freezing by covering them with a blanket.

Container growing. Grow in large containers. If temperatures dip near freezing, protect the plant by moving the plant into a sunroom or other sunny area where temperatures never drop below 40°F.

Propagation. Plant crowns or suckers that arise from the base of the plant or the base of the fruit as described in "Planting and Growing" above. ✳

PLUM

Prunus spp. Rosaceae. Deciduous trees and shrubs. Zones 4–10.

Unless you live in a truly frigid climate or in the tropics, you can find a plum suited to your garden. Although there are many species of plum, the most important, from the standpoint of the gardener, are the European plum (*Prunus domestica*), the damson plum (*P. insititia*), the Japanese plum (*P. salicina*), and various species of wild American plums (*Prunus* spp.). Plant breeders also have created hybrids between American and Japanese plums, combining the cold hardiness of the former with the fruit quality of the latter. With such a broad genetic base, cultivated plums offer a wide diversity in fruit and plant characteristics: sweet, melting dessert fruits or tangy, firm cooking fruits, in shades from yellow to blue to almost black, and ranging in size from as big as a cherry to as big as an apple. Of the species, American plums are the most cold-hardy, followed by European and damson, then Japanese plums.

When is a plum a prune? A prune plum is a type of European plum—'Italian Prune' and 'Stanley' are examples—that has a firm flesh with enough sugar in it to dry naturally. Even if you are not interested in drying them, prune plums are delicious for fresh eating.

Planning

Selecting plants. For Japanese plums, choose a one-year-old tree ½″ in diameter. For European plums, choose two-year-old trees.

Plums vary in the degree of winter cold they can tolerate, so choose cultivars suited to your winter temperatures. European and dam-

son plums are hardy in Zones 4–9. Japanese plums are less hardy—Zones 6–10. Some of the native American plums are extremely hardy and drought-tolerant.

When choosing a cultivar, be sure to look for those that have resistance to diseases that are common in your region. 'AU-Rosa', 'Crimson', and 'Ozark Premier' resist brown rot, canker, black knot, and leaf spot. 'Redheart' resists brown rot, canker, and leaf spot. 'AU-Producer', 'AU-Roadside', and 'Homeside' resist canker, black knot, and leaf spot. 'AU-Amber' resists canker and leaf spot. 'President' resists canker and black knot. 'Bradshaw', 'Formosa', 'Milton', 'Santa Rosa', and 'Shiro' resist black knot. 'Crimson', 'Damson', 'Green Gage', 'Simon', and native American plums resist leaf spot.

Pollination needs vary with the types of plums you choose. Most European plums, including damson plums, do not need cross-pollination, so one tree will set fruit. Most Japanese plums do need cross-pollination from either another Japanese type or an American type. American plums also need cross-pollina-

---

❧ AT A GLANCE ❧

PLUM

Site: Full sun, not prone to late-spring frosts.

Soil: Well-drained, moderately fertile with a pH of 6.0–6.8.

Spacing: Full-size trees: 15'–20' apart. Dwarf trees and bushes: 8'–12' apart.

Seasons to bearing: Two to five years.

tion from either an American type or a Japanese type. The hybrids are the most complicated of the lot as far as pollination needs. They need cross-pollination, usually from an American type, sometimes from a specific American type. Look for this information in nursery catalogs.

Rootstock choice can influence your tree's success. Apricot and certain peach rootstocks (such as 'Nemaguard') are resistant to destructive nematodes. Choose 'Damas', 'Myrobalan', or 'Mariana' rootstocks for heavy or poorly drained soils. 'Mariana' is the hardiest standard-size rootstock. Plums are not large trees to start with, but if you want a dwarf tree, get one on 'Pixie' rootstock. *P. besseyi* is a hardy dwarfing rootstock, but it suckers profusely. Avoid *P. besseyi* rootstock on windy sites, or stake trees on this rootstock.

Selecting a site. Plums need full sunlight to remain healthy and produce top-quality fruit. The blossoms open early, especially on Japanese types, so slopes are ideal sites. North-facing slopes are best because they warm up later in spring and delay flowering for a few days. Avoid sites where frosty air collects. Soil needs to be fairly well drained, but plums will tolerate less perfect drainage than peaches or sweet cherries will. Japanese and American cultivars prefer sandy or loamy soil, while European cultivars can do well in clayey soil.

When to plant. Except where winters are mild, plant plum trees in spring, as soon as the soil is dry enough to be worked. In mild-winter areas, plant in late fall.

Spacing. Full-size trees of vigorous cultivars need 15'–20' of space. Plant less vigorous cultivars, such as some of the bushy American hybrids, as well as trees on dwarfing rootstocks, 8'–12' apart.

For a greater harvest. Plums do well in raised beds or individual hills.

Soil Preparation

Plum trees prefer a moderately rich soil with a pH between 6.0 and 6.8. Correct poor drainage and adjust pH. For information on soil preparation, see "Custom Care for Tree Fruits" on page 61. Of the plum species, Japanese plums require the most fertile soils, so give them a little extra food.

Planting

See "Perennial Crops" on page 111 for complete instructions on planting plums. Be sure the graft union of a grafted dwarf or standard tree is higher than ground level so the scion won't root and negate the rootstock effect. Cut tall, unbranched trees back to 3'. See "Pruning at Planting Time" on page 145 for more details.

Growing Guidelines

Water and mulch. Plum trees need a regular supply of water, either from irrigation or natural rainfall, throughout the growing season. Maintain a thick, organic mulch beneath your trees.

Feeding. Feed plums as you would feed peaches. See "Feeding" on page 438 for recommendations.

Training. Plum cultivars vary in their growth habits. Train spreading cultivars, such as many of the Japanese types, to open center form. Use a modified central leader form for cultivars that are more upright growing. See "Pruning Trees" on page 142 for details.

Thinning. When plums are about ½" long, thin small-fruited cultivars to 1"–3" apart and large-fruited cultivars to 4"–5" apart.

Problem Prevention

Plums are closely related to peaches and are prone to many of the same problems. Plums have an additional common problem that it shares with cherries: black knot. Plums are also prone to bacterial leaf spot. Follow the steps in "Problem Prevention" on page 438, but ignore the reference to peach leaf curl. Plums benefit from kelp sprays right through leaf drop in fall. Add the following steps as needed to the routine described in the Peach entry.

In late winter, prune out diseased branches. Watch for black knot. Affected branches have swollen, knobby, black galls.

As buds swell in spring, spray lime-sulfur. If black knot was a problem last year, spray now. Repeat after one week.

Bacterial leaf spot causes small, angular black spots on plum leaves. Leaves may turn yellow and drop prematurely. Spray lime-sulfur every 10–21 days until leaf drop if weather is wet or humid and if the spots are spreading.

Gathering the Harvest

For fresh eating or drying, pick plums when they are thoroughly ripe. A ripe plum is fully colored and slightly soft. Store the fruits for to two to four weeks by keeping them at high humidity and near-freezing temperatures. Prune plums, with their firm flesh and high sugar content, keep better than other types. Yields vary with climate and cultivar, but expect to harvest 1–3 bushels from a plum tree.

Fall and Winter Care

Plums need the same fall and winter care as peaches. See "Fall and Winter Care" on page 440 for details. Japanese plums need the heaviest pruning because they bear much of the crop on young wood and because their otherwise-heavy crop loads would break limbs. The other types of plums need only moderate thinning and shaping each year.

Container Growing

For container growing, plant plums that are naturally dwarf (such as the American types) or trees grafted on dwarfing rootstocks (such as *P. tomentosa* or 'St. Julien A'). Use a container at least 1½' deep and wide. Once your plant reaches full size, repot it every year just before growth commences in spring, and prune back the roots and tops at the same time. In very cold areas, protect the roots in winter as shown in the illustration on page 240.

Propagation

Propagate plum trees by budding. Where the growing season is long, graft in June and the bud will push out growth the same season you graft. Where seasons are short, bud later in the summer for growth the following growing season. Suitable rootstocks include plum, as well as Myrobalan (*P. cerasifera*), peach, and apricot. ✳

🐝 FRIENDS & RELATIVES 🐝

PLUM

Plumcots are hybrids of apricots and plums. See "Friends and Relatives" on page 280 for details.

POMEGRANATE

Punica granatum. Punicaceae. Deciduous or semi-deciduous shrub or tree. Zone 8.

Pomegranate is an ancient fruit that originated in the Middle East. Pomegranate plants are highly ornamental, especially in summer with their orange-red flowers. The shiny leaves turn clear yellow in autumn, and the decorative fruits carry on the show even after the leaves drop.

Selecting plants. Pomegranates are self-fruitful. 'Wonderful' bears full-size fruit. 'Nana' is a shrub and bears small fruit.

Site. Pomegranate thrives best in hot, dry climates. If extra warmth is needed in summer and winter, plant near a south wall.

Soil. Pomegranate tolerates a wide range of soil, but prefers a well-drained soil with a pH of 6.5–7.0.

How much to plant. The average yield for a productive, full-size plant is 100 pounds of fruit.

Spacing. Space plants 15' apart or, for a hedge, 6' apart. Set dwarf cultivars as little as 3' apart.

Seasons to bearing. Pomegranates bear in three to four years.

Planting and growing. Water plants in arid climates or sandy soils. Pomegranates generally are pest-free.

Harvesting. Cut fruits off as soon as they turn fully red. Slightly underripe fruits will store for many months if kept cool and dry.

Fall and winter care. Prune lightly to shape the plant and remove dead wood and suckers.

Container growing. 'Nana' is well-suited to growing in containers as small as 1 gallon.

Propagation. Propagate with hardwood cuttings. After leaves drop, cut 6" sections of pencil-thick wood that grew that season. Stick cuttings in a growing medium with only their tips showing. Transplant rooted cuttings in one year. ✳

POTATO

Solanum tuberosum. Solanaceae. Annual.

Potatoes offer everything a gardener could want—ease of culture, long storage potential, and endless versatility in the kitchen. The varied forms and colors of potatoes make them a fun crop to grow. Originally from South America, potatoes are the world's favorite root crop.

Planning

Selecting plants. Potato cultivars vary greatly in size, flavor, texture, interior and exterior color, and the amount of time it takes them to mature. All grow best in cool or mild weather and resent extreme heat and dry soil. To grow a successful crop, look for cultivars that will do well in the growing conditions in your garden. In northern areas where the weather stays mild all summer, consider large, slow-maturing baking potatoes. In warm climates with short cool seasons, it's best to choose smaller, fast-maturing cultivars.

You'll also want to think about your family's food preferences when choosing potatoes for your garden. There are multipurpose types that hold their quality when served many different ways—baked, mashed, fried, or boiled, but many potatoes are best suited to a particular mode of preparation. In general, the finest

---

Site: Full or nearly full sun, with good air circulation.

Soil: Any good garden soil that drains well; pH of 5.0–6.8.

Spacing: Leave 1' between plants in rows 3' apart or plant in raised beds on 1½' centers.

Days to maturity: 90–120 days, depending on cultivar and climate.

---

spuds for boiling and roasting are small red-skinned potatoes. Waxy, elongated fingerling types make superior potato salad. Potatoes with a high starch content are the best bakers.

Several serious potato diseases are easily spread from infected tubers. Always buy seed potatoes that are certified to be disease-free.

Selecting a site. Potatoes need plenty of sun and good drainage. Reject sites where rainwater quickly accumulates and areas where the soil becomes hard and compacted less than 15″ below the surface. Coarse, sandy loam is ideal, but potatoes will grow in clay soil, provided it does not stay extremely wet.

When to plant. As long as the soil is dry enough to work, you can plant potatoes four weeks before the last expected spring frost. The soil should be at least 40°F. Potatoes grow best when daytime temperatures are 60°–69°F yet are usually hardy when exposed to light freezes. Temperatures below 25°F may kill young leaves, but new sprouts should appear within two weeks.

Except in areas where springs are short and summers are hot, you can continue planting until 12 weeks before the first expected fall frost. In warm climates, plant potatoes twice a year: in late winter and again in late summer for a fall crop. Avoid growing potatoes when temperatures are above 90°F. High temperatures may cause mature potatoes to discolor inside.

How much to plant. Each potato plant will produce 3–4 pounds of potatoes, sometimes more. Medium-size, all-purpose potatoes usually yield more than fingerlings or other smallish cultivars. To grow 50 pounds of potatoes, you will need a 15' row or a raised bed 4' wide and 6'–8' long.

Spacing. In single rows, space plants 1' apart with 3' between rows. Or grow them in intensive raised beds or double rows with 1½' of space on all sides.

Rotation. Grow potatoes after corn or beans but not after tomatoes or peas.

For a greater harvest. In cool climates, plant early, mid-season, and late-maturing cultivars for an extended harvest season. Mulching with straw reduces pest problems and improves yields.

Soil Preparation

Potatoes prefer well-aerated soil that is loosened to a depth of more than 1'. If your soil is heavy and compacted, grow potatoes in raised beds or rows to give them plenty of loose root space. Take care not to compact the soil around potatoes. Use boards or stepping stones between rows or beds to avoid walking on the soil.

Potatoes love moderately rich soil, well-endowed with potassium, phosphorus, calcium, and magnesium and with a pH between 5.0 and 6.8. To assure strong growth, work 20–30 pounds of compost into 100' of row. Don't worry about breaking up every clod; if kept well-mulched, potatoes grow quite well in chunky soil.

Planting

Two to three weeks before planting day, set seed potatoes in a bright, 65°–70°F place to encourage them to sprout. Up to two days before planting, cut seed potatoes into pieces with a sharp knife, making sure each piece has at least two eyes—the puckered places where sprouts develop. If the potatoes already have sprouted, handle them gently to keep the sprouts from breaking off.

Plant the cut pieces in prepared soil, 2″–4″ deep, with the cut side down. Cover lightly with straw, leaves, or hay to prevent crusting. A few weeks later, after the plants have emerged, mulch again until the mulch is 6″–8″ deep. Clean straw or legume hay are best.

Growing Guidelines

Water and mulch. Potatoes like constantly moist soil and may need supplemental water in dry weather. Extreme fluctuations in soil moisture can lead to cracked, knobby tubers. Thick mulch helps retain soil moisture, reduces pest problems, and protects the tubers from sun.

Feeding. When grown in good soil and hospitable weather, potatoes need no supplemental fertilizer. To alleviate possible nutritional stress in poor soil, drench each plant with 1 cup of compost tea a month after

Potato plant

'Norkotah Russet'

'Yukon Gold'

'Blossom'

'Purple Peruvian'

Well-worked, constantly moist soil, a thick layer of mulch, and a cultivar suited to your region are the ingredients for great potatoes. There are lots of different types to choose from, including mealy-fleshed baking potatoes, fingerlings for salads, red-skinned ones for boiling with parsley—even heirloom cultivars that have blue or yellow flesh.

planting, and again ten days later. As the plants become larger, mix 2 tablespoons of powdered or liquid kelp into 1 gallon of compost tea, and spray plants with this solution until they're dripping wet. Repeat every two weeks. If the soil is low in phosphorus, add 2 teaspoons of rock phosphate to the spray solution. Always spray on a cloudy day or early in the morning to avoid injuring potato leaves.

Problem Prevention

Select resistant cultivars. Especially in areas where potatoes are grown commercially, grow disease-resistant cultivars.

After plants sprout, spray compost tea. Blights that cause dark blotches on leaves may be slowed by spraying or drenching plants every two weeks with compost tea.

During the season, handpick Colorado potato beetles. Gather both adults and larvae of this leading potato pest whenever you see them. Use *Bacillus thuringiensis* var. *san diego* (BTSD) to control large larval outbreaks.

During the season, protect tubers with soil or mulch. Sunlight will turn tubers green and make them inedible. Protect tubers from sunlight by hilling up soil over plants or applying additional mulch when the tubers swell and the plants begin to die back.

Gathering the Harvest

Potato stems and leaves turn brown as tubers become fully mature, but you don't have to wait for the plants to die back to start eating your homegrown potatoes. Harvest when the tubers reach the size you want for new potatoes. If you plan to store your harvest, make sure the skins don't peel off easily when you gently rub them with a finger.

Gather potatoes on a cloudy day or late in the afternoon. Protect them from sunshine at all times. Potatoes exposed to light develop a green color as well as bitter chemical compounds that are poisonous.

If the soil is loose, you may be able to harvest your potatoes by simply pulling up the browning foliage of the plants. Then use your fingers to explore the hole left behind. If you find more potatoes in the soil, use a turning fork to gently loosen the soil on the outside of the row. Lift the tubers by hand. Gently wash harvested potatoes with cool water and your fingers—not a brush. Don't attempt to remove every speck of soil or you may damage the skins. Dry the tubers in a single layer on newspapers or an old towel. Scratches and other places where the skins were damaged in harvesting usually heal when the tubers are cured. To cure, spread potatoes in a single layer in a dark, 50°–60°F place for two weeks. Then pack loosely in boxes or bags and store at about 40°F.

In cool climates, potatoes are fine candidates for long-term storage in a cool basement or root cellar. In warm climates, keep harvested potatoes in the coolest part of your house throughout the summer, and move them to an unheated place during the winter months.

Extending the Season

You can leave potatoes in the ground until frost and harvest then, but they're most nutritious when gathered and cured as soon as they mature. If you live in a warm climate, take potatoes that have begun to sprout and plant them in late summer for a fall crop.

Fall and Winter Care

Potato foliage often harbors fungal diseases, so gather up the plants and compost them instead of turning them under. After the space is cleaned, cultivate it and sow a soil-building cover crop such as clover, or plant an edible legume.

Container Growing

Potatoes are easy to grow in large containers if they get sufficient sunshine. Shallow wooden boxes, wooden packing crates with the bottoms removed, or half-barrels make good potato containers. To get maximum yields, let plants grow out the top and sides of containers.

Propagation

If you see no evidence of disease on your potatoes, set aside some of the best tubers for use as seed potatoes the following year. Don't plant the ones that sprout prematurely in storage. Buy certified disease-free seed potatoes if yours may harbor diseases. Spots that are soft, sunken, or discolored are obvious clues that problems exist, but some potato diseases, especially viruses, may be passed on from potatoes that appear to be sound. ✳

PUMPKIN
Cucurbita spp. Cucurbitaceae. Annual.

Orange orbs of pie and jack-o'-lantern fame, pumpkins are just winter squashes. Giant pumpkins can weigh 700–800 pounds. See the Squash entry for culture. ✳

QUINCE
Cydonia oblonga. Rosaceae.
Deciduous tree. Zones 5–9.

Quinces have been enjoyed for thousands of years. The fruit is shaped like a cross between an apple and a pear and has a yellow, fuzzy skin. When ripe, most quinces are hard and astringent and are inedible raw but delicious cooked into jelly or added to applesauce or apple pie. "Flowering" quinces, such as *Chaenomeles* spp., bear showy flowers. The fruits are edible but not very tasty.

Selecting plants. Quince trees are self-fertile, so you only need to plant one tree to get fruit.

Site. Quinces need full sun. The flowers open late, so spring frosts are not a hazard.

Soil. Quinces prefer well-drained, moderately rich soils.

How much to plant. The average yield for a tree is 1 bushel of fruit.

Spacing. Plant quince trees 15' apart.

Seasons to bearing. Quinces bear fruit in three to four years.

Planting and growing. Train quinces either as an open center tree or as a multi-stemmed shrub. See "Pruning Trees" on page 142 for instructions.

Quinces are susceptible to many of the same diseases as apples and pears, although less so.

Harvesting. Pick late in the season when they're fully colored and fragrant. Frost does no harm. Handle carefully—they bruise easily. Refrigerate for up to two months.

Fall and winter care. Prune to remove dead, diseased wood, and thin the center of the plant if crowded.

Container growing. Quince can be grown in a container 1½′ deep and wide, or larger. Prune the top and roots each winter.

Propagation. Propagate by hardwood cuttings or by grafting onto seed-grown rootstocks. ✳

RADISH

Raphanus sativus. Cruciferae. Annual.

Few crops are as easy to grow as radishes. This mild- to peppery-flavored root crop pops up readily under conditions that hinder less-hardy crops. And you can harvest radishes in as few as three weeks after sowing seeds. Spring radishes are typically eaten raw. White, carrot-shaped daikon (Japanese) radishes (*R. sativus* var. *longipinnatus*) are also steamed, stir-fried, or grated into a condiment. Radish sprouts and green seedpods are edible and taste much like the roots.

Selecting plants. Try a few different colors and shapes. Look for heat tolerance and resistance to soilborne diseases. Grow winter radishes to use in Asian cooking or to store.

Site. Grow radishes in full sun to partial shade, alone or interplanted with other crops.

Soil. Radishes grow in any type of soil, but they prefer light, sandy loam with a pH between 5.5 and 6.8. Loosen soil to a depth of 8″ and work in 10 pounds of compost per 100 square feet.

How much to plant. Radishes grow and pass their prime quickly; sow successive plantings every ten days of a few feet of row per person.

'Summer Cross Hybrid'   'April Cross'

'Snow Belle'   'French Breakfast'   'Plum Purple'

Quick-growing, crisp, and colorful, spring radishes, such as 'French Breakfast', 'Snow Belle', and 'Plum Purple', can satisfy even the most impatient gardener. Also called winter radishes, slower-growing, longer-keeping daikon types like 'April Cross' and 'Summer Cross Hybrid' flavor many Asian dishes.

RADISH SEEDLING

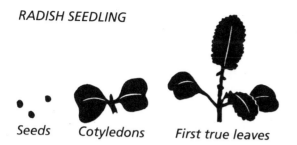

Seeds   Cotyledons   First true leaves

Spacing. Space rows 8″–18″ apart, planting eight to ten seeds per foot. Thin to one plant every 2″.

Days to maturity. Spring radishes mature in three to five weeks. Winter types mature in 55–60 days.

Planting and growing. Sow seeds in the garden, ½″ deep, as soon as you can work the soil. Plant every ten days until daytime temperatures are consistently above 75°F; resume planting when temperatures begin to cool in the fall. High temperatures and drought make radishes tough, strong-tasting, and prone to pest problems. Mulch to conserve moisture.

Harvesting. Pull spring radishes when they reach up to 1″ in diameter, cut off tops, and refrigerate. Pull winter types soon after the first frost and store in a cool, moist area.

Extending the season. Radishes tolerate cool soil. Grow early or late crops under row cover.

Container growing. Radishes grow well in any container with sufficient root space. Select one deep enough to accommodate the roots of your chosen cultivar.

Propagation. Bees carry pollen from radish to radish, and cultivars cross freely with one another over distances of up to ¼ mile. Allow only one cultivar to flower at a time when saving seeds, or cage a few plants and hand-pollinate them. Spring radishes produce green seedpods by midsummer; pull plants and hang them to dry when the pods turn yellow. Crush the pods and remove the seeds. Save seeds of biennial daikon as you would those of beets. ✳

R ASPBERRY

Rubus spp. Rosaceae. Perennial with biennial canes. Zones 3–8.

Raspberries are easy to grow yet costly to buy. Make yourself feel rich by planting some this year. Choose from red, purple, black, or yellow. See the Brambles entry for culture. ✳

R HUBARB

Rheum rhabarbarum. Polygonaceae. Perennial. Zones 2–8.

Known in pioneer times as the pie plant, rhubarb is a long-lived perennial with delicious tart leaf petioles (stems)—but poisonous leaves. Use the petioles in pies, crisps, and jams. Or stew them with sugar, then add them to oatmeal or puree them into a sauce for broiled fish.

Selecting plants. If you are buying from a nursery, look beyond the old-fashioned standby, 'Victoria', which has tart green flesh that cooks to a brown color. Newer cultivars like 'Chipman's Canada Red', 'MacDonald', and 'Valentine' have sweet, succulent red stalks that look as good as they taste. 'Giant Cherry' grows well where winters are short or mild.

A rhubarb division offered by a neighboring gardener is likely well-suited to your climate, but ask about the plant's tendency to bolt. Rhubarb cultivars, including 'Victoria', that bolt regularly, produce fewer large-size stalks; their energy goes into flower and seed production, says David Cavagnaro, a garden manager at Heritage Farm for Seed Savers Exchange in Iowa.

Site. Rhubarb thrives in cool locations and full sun. In warmer climates, plants benefit from light shade but form longer, thinner stems.

Soil. Rhubarb needs deep, moist but well-drained soil. Before planting, prepare a hole at least 1½' deep and 3' wide. Loosen the soil and enrich it with a 6″ layer of compost. Add a handful of bonemeal if your soil is low on phosphorus.

How much to plant. You can harvest 2–6 pounds of rhubarb each season from a full-size plant. Cool, moist weather tends to increase productivity, while warm, dry conditions may reduce your harvest.

Spacing. Space plants 3'–4' apart in rows 6' apart.

Seasons to bearing. You may lightly harvest rhubarb one year after planting small divisions or nursery plants. Gradually increase the number of stalks and the length of time you pick in the second and third years of growth. Expect healthy plants to produce fully in the fourth year.

Organic market gardener Molly Bartlett of Silver Creek Farm in Ohio transplants good-size rhubarb divisions in early spring. They produce large, tempting stalks in May, which she harvests lightly without damaging the plants.

Planting and growing. Set the crowns of rhubarb divisions 1″–2″ below the soil surface. Set container-grown plants level with the soil surface or slightly lower if the surrounding soil is likely to settle. Keep the plants moist, and mulch in spring and fall with several inches of straw or grass clippings. Keep mulch away from the crown to avoid rot problems. Remove any seedstalks that form—they sap the plants' energy. Fertilize every year in early spring by spreading a few inches of compost over the area.

Rhubarb is generally trouble-free. Slow growth of older plants is a signal that they need dividing. Rhubarb curculio, a ½″-long, yellow-gray beetle, damages stalks and crowns by boring holes in which to lay its eggs. Hand-pick adult curculios and destroy nearby curly dock (*Rumex crispus*), which is an alternate host. Control severe infestations with rotenone.

Harvesting. Harvest lightly one year after planting. Pick only stems that are at least 1″ thick the second year; then harvest for one to two months in the third year. Snap off rhubarb stalks by twisting them sharply at the base. Or cut them off with a sharp knife, using care to avoid injuring underground buds. Cut off and compost the leaves as you harvest. Starting when the leaves are expanding in the spring, you may pick one-third to one-half of the new shoots from a full-size plant. Cool, moist weather encourages plants to produce fat new stalks; keep picking until thin stalks begin to emerge.

Longtime rhubarb grower Judith Dilkie of Ontario, Canada, harvests a second time in fall when she cleans up the bed for the season. To harvest longer stalks, try putting a bottom-less bushel basket over the plant until the stems reach the desired length; the stems stretch up longer—and stay paler—in the limited light.

Extending the season. If you have extra rhubarb plants, try forcing one in the winter. In fall, transplant it into a tub of moist planting mix or sand. Leave the tub outdoors in 28°–50°F temperatures for seven to nine weeks, then move it into cool (55°–60°F), bright indoor conditions. Keep the soil moist; stalks will appear in about a month. Harvest when they reach 1'–1½' long.

Fall and winter care. Compost old rhubarb leaves after they die back in fall or winter.

Propagation. Propagate rhubarb by dividing large root clumps. Slice them into pieces with a spade, or work the twisted roots apart with your hands. Seeds from most rhubarb, except 'Victoria', produce poor-quality plants. Seedlings take four to five years to reach harvesting size. ✳

RICE
Oryza sativa. Gramineae. Annual.

You don't need to turn your backyard into a paddy or swamp to grow a family-size quantity of rice. While rice is a semitropical plant often grown in flooded paddies, it will grow in wet soil in temperate conditions.

Selecting plants. Choose an "upland" cultivar of rice because it will produce grain in cooler conditions and require less water than traditional rice. One upland cultivar to try is 'M-101'. To produce grain, rice needs 40 consecutive warm days (above 70°F) and nights (above 60°F) falling within a 120-day frost-free period. If your season is too short, compensate by starting rice seeds indoors in cell packs.

Site. Select a partially shaded, damp site. A low-lying area or any plot where water doesn't drain away immediately will produce the best yields. You can help retain moisture by digging a trench 1½' wide and 6" deep around the plot. Use the soil you dig out to build a berm (or levee). Line the trench and the berm with plastic. This will keep soaking rains or water you supply from running out of your plot.

Soil. Rich loam full of organic matter is best. Don't add high-nitrogen fertilizer—that leads to too much stalk and less flower and seed head. Enrich soil before planting by tilling in a 1" layer of finished compost or well-rotted manure in early spring.

How much to plant. A 200-square-foot patch should yield 20 pounds of rice.

Spacing. Set transplants 3"–4" apart in rows 9" apart. Once they are established, thin plants to about 6".

Days to maturity. Rice matures in 120–200 days, depending on the cultivar and climate.

Planting and growing. About 2 ounces of rice will seed a 200-square-foot patch. Before planting, immerse the seeds in 5 gallons of lukewarm water with a few tablespoons of salt added. Swirl the water. Remove the seeds that float; they are not viable. Let the viable ones soak overnight to speed germination. Weed thoroughly before you plant; rice doesn't compete well with weeds. Water thoroughly before you plant; rice will even root through standing water.

Check frequently to be sure your rice patch never dries out, and water as needed. Mulch around your thinned seedlings with wheat straw to retain moisture and suppress weeds.

Rice does not have any major insect pests,

but it is prone to fungal diseases. Remove patches of broadleaf signalgrass and barnyard grass near your rice patch since they can host fungal diseases that also attack rice.

Harvesting. When the seed heads become heavy and start to turn brown (about 30–40 days after the rice stalks flower), allow the soil to dry out a bit. When about 85 percent of the seed heads are golden brown, cut the stalks and bundle them. Hang the bundles to dry in a well-ventilated spot for two weeks to two months. Once the bundles are dry, they're ready for threshing and winnowing. See "Processing Grains" on page 370 for instructions.

Removing rice hulls from the winnowed grain by hand with a mortar and pestle is labor-intensive. You can adapt the Corona grain mill into a rice dehuller with a public-domain invention. (To get the plans to adapt the grinder, send along a SASE to: I-Tech, 22974 W. Sheffler Road, Elmira, OR 97437.) Add the potassium-rich rice hulls to your compost pile.

Propagation. Unthreshed rice grains are rice seeds. Save some from the stoutest stalks with the plumpest seed heads to plant next year. *

ROSEMARY

Rosmarinus officinalis. Labiatae. Perennial. Zones 8–10.

Rosemary's rich, pungent aroma makes it one of the most well-loved plants in the herb garden. Use the fresh or dried foliage to scent homemade bread and rolls or to flavor roasted meat and potatoes.

Selecting plants. Many cultivars are available, varying in habit, hardiness, and color. For hanging baskets, try 'Prostratus', also known as trailing or creeping rosemary. Northern growers should try the cultivar 'Arp', which is reportedly hardy to at least 18°F and perhaps lower.

Site. Plant in full sun to light shade.

Soil. Rosemary needs excellent drainage. Plant in light soil with a near-neutral pH.

Planting and growing. Set plants outdoors after all danger of frost is past. Let the soil surface dry out between waterings. Light pruning for the first two years encourages bushy growth.

Harvesting. Harvest throughout the season. Preserve rosemary by drying or by adding the fresh leaves to oil, vinegar, honey, or jellies.

Fall and winter care. In cold climates, experiment with overwintering techniques. Heavy mulches and wind barriers (like an overturned bushel basket stuffed with straw) may help. Or grow your rosemary in a pot and set it—pot and all—in the garden in spring. Bring it indoors in fall.

Container growing. Rosemary makes an excellent potted plant. Use any potting mix that includes compost and sand. Sunny, enclosed but unheated porches are good locations for potted plants during cold winters.

Propagation. Sow seeds indoors several months before setting plants in the garden; seedlings grow very slowly. Propagate established plants in spring or fall by taking cuttings of semi-woody growth or by layering. *

RUTABAGA

Brassica napus, Napobrassica group.
Cruciferae. Biennial grown as an annual.

Rutabagas, also known as swedes or swede turnips, are a dependable cool-season root crop. A good source of vitamins A and C, rutabagas are also very high in potassium. Use them in soups and stews or steam them and mash them with butter.

Selecting plants. Few cultivars are offered for commercial sale in this country. Look to seed exchanges or specialty seed companies for cultivars that differ in flesh color, storage quality, or disease resistance.

Site. Rutabagas prefer full sun.

Soil. Rutabagas grow well in light soil with a pH of 5.5–6.8. Avoid planting where cabbage-family crops grew in the past three years.

How much to plant. One gram of rutabaga seeds contains an average of 300 seeds and sows 50' of row. Sow 5'–10' of row (10–20 plants) per person. Plants should produce 1 pound of rutabagas per 1' of row.

Spacing. When the plants are 6 inches high, thin them to 4"–6" between plants and 1½'–2' between rows.

Days to maturity. Rutabagas take 95–100 days from seed to harvest.

Planting and growing. Direct-sow ¼"–½" deep. Most growers plant one crop in mid-June to mid-July for a fall harvest. The Cabbage entry offers more information; see "Growing Guidelines" on page 316 and "Problem Prevention" on page 317.

Harvesting. Mature roots are 4"–8" in diameter. Harvest after a few good frosts for best flavor. Cut off tops ½" above the root. Rutabagas will keep for three to five weeks in a cool, dry place. Or store for up to six months in a root cellar at 32°F and 90 percent humidity.

Fall and winter care. Clear any remnants of plants out of the garden and compost them.

Propagation. Save seeds and propagate as you would for cabbages; see "Propagation" on page 319 for details. ✳

SAGE

Salvia officinalis. Labiatae. Perennial.
Zones 4–9.

Common sage, with its pebbly, grayish leaves and purple-blue flowers, is equally at home in herb gardens and in ornamental gardens. The fresh or dried leaves of this flavorful herb blend well with a variety of meats and vegetables, including tomatoes, beans, and potatoes. Add the colorful, edible flowers to salads.

Selecting plants. Common green-leaved sage is the plant most often grown for culinary use. Cultivars include 'Purpurea', with reddish purple leaves, and 'Aurea', with green leaves edged in golden yellow. These colorful cultivars are more ornamental than common sage but tend to be less cold-tolerant.

Site. Sage needs full sun to partial shade.

Soil. Plant in a humus-rich, well-drained soil and a neutral to slightly acid pH (6.0–7.0).

How much to plant. For two people, one or two plants should provide plenty of foliage after the first year.

Spacing. Allow 1½'–2' between plants.

Days to maturity. Snip leaves sparingly during the first year of growth; harvest as needed in following years.

Planting and growing. Although sage is most often sold as a potted plant, it is easy to start from seeds. Sow seeds indoors six to eight weeks before the last expected frost. Seeds germinate within three weeks at 60°–70°F. Move the seedlings to the garden after the danger of frost is past. Divide plants every three to five years in spring or fall to keep them vigorous.

Harvesting. Pick leaves throughout the season to use fresh or to dry. Store dry leaves in the refrigerator or freezer to preserve their flavor.

Propagation. Sow seeds indoors in early spring. Take stem cuttings in summer or fall. Divide in spring. Layer in spring or fall.

Friends and relatives. Pineapple sage (*S. elegans*) is a tender perennial with brilliant red flowers and pineapple-scented foliage. Use it for tea and for flavoring jelly. ✳

SALSIFY

Tragopogon porrifolius and *Scorzonera hispanica*. Compositae. Biennials grown as annuals.

These two deep-rooted crops, white-skinned salsify (*Tragopogon porrifolius*), or oyster plant, and black-skinned black salsify (*Scorzonera hispanica*), or scorzonera, resemble slender parsnips, but they are not sweet. They have smooth flesh. Harvest them fresh in midwinter. Peel salsify's roots and boil them with a little lemon juice to keep them from browning. Leave black salsify's flavorful black skin intact when boiling it. You also can sauté, french fry, or bake both kinds of roots.

Site. Give both plants a sunny spot where the 2'–3'-tall plants can grow undisturbed. Excess fertility can make the roots hairy or forked.

Soil. Both types of salsify grow roots at least 8" long and need a light soil, about 1½' deep. In shallow or heavy soils, plant in raised beds.

How much to plant. Grow a 5'-long row to harvest about 5 pounds of roots.

Spacing. Grow plants 2"–4" apart in wide beds or in rows 1'–2' apart. Thin if the young plants become overcrowded.

Days to maturity. Roots mature in 120–150 days.

Planting and growing. Sow seeds directly into your garden, ½" deep, four to six weeks before the last expected spring frost. When large seedlings are exposed to extended cold, the plants tend to bolt in midsummer. In zones with mild winters, plant in fall for a spring harvest.

Harvesting. Dig the mature roots in fall after a couple of frosts; store them in moist sand in a cold root cellar. Eat the young shoots from overwintered plants as you would asparagus.

Extending the season. In late fall, cover the bed with a bale of hay so the soil won't freeze. You can dig the roots all winter long.

Propagation. Both species come true from seed, which is produced in the second year of growth. ✳

SMALL FRUITS

From buffalo berry to salal, little-known small fruits are an exciting new field for home gardeners to dabble in. Why grow them? Some, such as cornelian cherry and highbush cranberry, not only provide fruit but are beautiful ornamentals as well. Others provide good food and cover for wildlife yet yield abundantly enough for you to share the harvest. These plants are generally tough, requiring little more from you than planting and harvesting. For information on common small fruits, see the Blueberry, Brambles, Gooseberry, Grape, and Strawberry entries.

Buffalo Berry

Buffalo berry (*Shepherdia argentea*) is also called Nebraska currant because it looks and tastes rather like red currant. The fruits grow on an erect, thorny shrub 6'–20' tall. It has silvery leaves and grows in Zones 2–6. Plants are either male or female. Harvest the fruits after frost, then eat them fresh, dried, or cooked into conserves or jelly.

Buffalo berry is free from pest problems and tolerates dry soils. Plant bushes—at least one male for every few females—in full sun. The bushes need little pruning. Propagate new plants by seeds or hardwood cuttings. Do not allow seeds to dry out, and stratify them before sowing.

Cornelian Cherry

Cornelian cherry (*Cornus mas*) makes a wonderful ornamental small tree (to about 25') and is adapted from Zones 4 to 8. The trees begin blooming in early spring and stay awash with small yellow blossoms for weeks. The cherries, which look like sweet cherries, hang on the tree from late summer into autumn. The leaves turn mahogany red in autumn.

Some cultivars, such as 'Alba', produce yellow fruits. The cherries are tart but become less so if you let ripe fruits hang on the plant or ripen in a bowl indoors. Use the fruits for conserves and to flavor drinks. Another dogwood species, *C. kousa*, also has edible, though insipid, fruits.

For best fruiting, plant in full sun. Plants are only partially self-fertile, so plant two seedlings or two different cultivars for maximum yields. This tree is not choosy about soil and requires minimal pruning. Prune off suckers and low branches to form a small tree, or allow it to grow into a multi-stemmed clump. Cornelian cherry has no serious pest problems. You can start trees from seeds, but seeds often require two or three years to germinate. Cuttings root with difficulty.

Elderberry

This fruit is well-known as an ingredient of jellies, pies, and wines. Elderberry (*Sambucus canadensis*) is a deciduous shrub growing 6'–10' tall and adapted from Zones 2 to 9. The plant has large compound leaves and tends to produce suckers. Fruits are purplish black and hang in large clusters from the branches. The flavor is mild, and the clusters of drooping white flowers are also edible. For best fruiting, plant a cultivar such as 'Adams', 'Kent', or 'York'. Other edible species include European elder (*S. nigra*) and blue elderberry (*S. glauca*), a native of western North America.

Elderberry tolerates a wide range of soils

in full sun or part shade. Plants are partially self-fruitful but yield better crops if another elderberry (a seedling or a different cultivar) is growing nearby. Once a plant reaches bearing age, prune it each winter to thin out excess suckers and remove all wood older than three years. Propagate new plants by sowing seeds (following warm then cool stratification), taking cuttings, or transplanting suckers.

Highbush Cranberry

Highbush cranberry (*Viburnum trilobum*) isn't related to the the bog cranberry of Thanks-giving fame, but its fruit is tart and red. The fruits are borne on an attractive 6'–10' shrub with clusters of white flowers in spring and reddish orange leaves in autumn. If left un-harvested, the fruits will hang decoratively from late summer almost through the winter.

Each highbush cranberry fruit has a single seed that must be strained out when the fruit is cooked into jam or jelly. 'Phillips' and 'Went-worth' are among the best-tasting cultivars. Don't confuse highbush cranberry fruits with the look-alike but less palatable fruits of European cranberry bush (*V. opulus*). Many other viburnums, such as nannyberry (*V. lentago*), and black haw (*V. prunifolium*), bear tasty fruits.

Plant highbush cranberries in well-drained

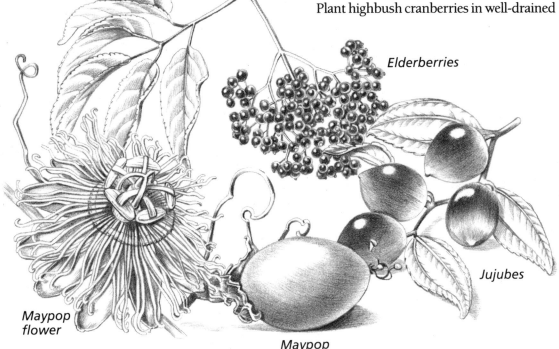

Elderberries

Jujubes

Maypop flower

Maypop fruit

Discover the tastes and beauty of uncommon small fruits. Mild-flavored elderberries make wonderful jam, pie, or homemade wine. The intricate, pale lavender maypop flower stays open for only one day. Jujube fruits left hanging on the tree darken and shrivel, and the sugars concentrate, leading to another common name for the fruit: Chinese date.

soil. Plants tolerate partial shade but fruit better in full sun. The only pruning required is to periodically remove old, unproductive wood. Do so during the dormant season. Propagate new plants by softwood or hardwood cuttings.

Jujube

Ripe jujube (*Ziziphus jujuba*) fruits have a shiny, mahogany skin, and crisp white flesh similar to that of apples. They can be as small as cherries or as large as plums. The plant is a small tree (up to 30' tall) that is native to the Orient and will grow in Zones 5–10. The leaves are shiny and the branches droop downwards, especially when the tree is laden with fruit. Some plants are armed with large spines. The trees flower over a long period. The Indian jujube (*Z. mauritiana*) is a cold-tender tree that also produces edible fruits.

Jujube tolerates almost any soil but needs full sun and hot weather. Plants tolerate drought well. Avoid tilling the soil around the tree because any root damage induces suckering. Some cultivars need cross-pollination and others don't, but these needs may depend on climate. Cross-pollination increases fruit set and size even with self-fertile cultivars. The trees drop some small branches at the end of the season and require little pruning. Propagate jujube cultivars by grafting or, if the cultivar is growing on its own roots, by taking root cuttings or transplanting suckers.

Maypop

Maypop (*Passiflora incarnata*) is a cold-hardy species of passionfruit. Maypop fruit is similar to passionfruit. The plant is a perennial vine whose roots are hardy from Zones 5 to 10 but whose stems die back to the ground each winter. New shoots poke through the ground relatively late in spring but then grow rapidly to 20' or more, climbing by tendrils. Suckers may appear a few feet from the mother plant. The plant is very vigorous and can become a weed at the southern end of its range. Blossoms first appear when shoots are about 4' long and continue to appear until frost.

The inside of the egg-size fruit is filled with air and seeds, each of which is surrounded by a tasty gelatinous pulp. The pulp tastes rather like canned fruit punch. Maypop can be crossed with the less hardy passionfruits to combine their fruit quality with its hardiness.

Maypop plants need cross-pollination, so plant at least two plants. 'Incense', a cultivar selected for ornamental flowers, is pollen-sterile so it cannot be used for pollination. Plants do best in full sun. Provide support—a fence or even a shrub—on which vines can climb. Hand-pollinate in late morning for best quality and maximum yield of fruit. Harvest fruits as they drop to the ground. Maypop is easy to propagate by seeds, shoot cuttings, and root cuttings.

Mulberry

The fruits of mulberries (*Morus alba, M. rubra, M. nigra,* and hybrids between *M. alba* and *M. rubra*) are shaped like blackberries but can be black, red, lavender, or white in color. The berries can be intensely sweet, but in the better cultivars, such as 'Illinois Everbearing', the sweetness is balanced by just the right degree of tartness.

Mulberry is a medium to large tree whose deciduous leaves vary in shape even on the same plant. The tree is long-lived, but cold-hardiness varies with species and cultivar. Generally, white mulberry is the most cold-hardy, to Zone 5. Black mulberry is the least cold-hardy, to Zone 7, and grows well only on the West Coast.

Black mulberry cultivars, such as 'Black

Persian', produce the best-quality fruits. Some hybrids of red and white mulberry, such as 'Illinois Everbearing', are also good. Ripening continues over the course of several weeks. The fruits are very soft. Harvest the fruits in quantity by shaking them off of the branches onto a clean cloth spread on the ground. Harvest fully ripe fruits for fresh eating or drying, but for jams and pies, harvest fruits when they're slightly underripe.

Plant mulberries in full sun. Choose a location where the falling fruit will not stain walkways or vehicles. Although some female trees may need a male pollinator, many cultivars set fruit without pollination. Once trees are trained to a sturdy framework, little or no further pruning is necessary. Birds are fond of mulberries, but mature trees usually bear enough fruit for birds and humans. Propagate mulberries by sowing fresh seeds, taking hardwood or softwood cuttings, or by grafting.

Rose Hips

Rose hips are the fruit of the rose (*Rosa* spp.). They are bright red or orange, up to 1″ in diameter, and sometimes covered with soft bristles. All rose hips are edible. Hips from *R. rugosa*, *R. villosa*, and *R. moyesii* are the ones most commonly eaten.

R. rugosa is a suckering bush growing 2′–8′ tall, with crinkled (rugose) leaves. It grows from Zones 2 to 9; *R. villosa* and *R. moyesii* are cold-hardy only to Zone 6. The carmine red, or sometimes pink or white, flowers appear throughout the season. The flowers are large and intensely fragrant.

The fruits are extremely rich in vitamin C. The flavor is mild, somewhat tart. Because the fruits are very seedy, cook and strain them before using them in jam or fruit soup. Dried,

the fruits make a healthful and tasty tea. Among the best cultivars for fruit production are 'Alba', 'Frau Dagmar Hartopp', and 'Scabrosa'. Pick the fruits as soon as they have fully colored.

R. rugosa requires full sun. The bushes tolerate any soils except those that are waterlogged. The bush even does well growing in sands along ocean beaches. Unlike many other roses, pests are not a problem. In winter, look for branches that have become old and unproductive and prune them to ground level or to a vigorous sideshoot. Propagate new plants by taking cuttings or transplanting suckers.

Salal

Salal (*Gaultheria shallon*), sometimes called shallon, is related to blueberry, with small, dark purple, blueberry-like fruits. The flavor is aromatic and tart—excellent for jelly.

The fruits are borne on an evergreen shrub with attractive reddish stems. White or pink blossoms dangle from the stems in spring. Salal grows 2′–6′ high and is adapted from Zones 6 to 9. Plant salal in full sun or part shade in very acidic soil (with a pH of 4.0–5.0). Prune only enough to shape the plant. ✳

TO LEARN MORE

If you're interested in finding out more about the less common fruits, a great way to do it is to join the North American Fruit Explorers (NAFEX). This organization publishes a quarterly magazine called *Pomona* and a handbook. Members also meet and swap plants and information. For more information, write to: NAFEX, Route 1, Box 84, Chapin, IL 62628.

SPINACH

Spinacia oleracea. Chenopodiaceae. Annual.

Cultivated in temperate regions around the world, spinach is compact and relatively easy to grow. Its tender, dark green leaves contain more of vitamin A and B$_2$ than any other commonly grown vegetable, and they are a good source of iron.

Planning

Selecting plants. Spinach cultivars produce either smooth or savoy (crinkled) leaves. Look for cultivars that are heat-tolerant, very hardy, or disease-resistant to match the growing conditions in your region.

When to plant. Sow seeds directly in the ground as soon as soil temperatures reach 35°F and you can work the soil. Plant every 14–21 days until daytime temperatures are consistently above 75°F. You can also plant spinach in the fall as soon as temperatures fall below 75°F, up to one or two weeks before the first expected frost date. Long days and temperatures above 75°F encourage mature spinach to bolt. Young plants may bolt if exposed to temperatures below 40°F for one to two weeks after they come up. Spinach grows best in cool (60°–65°F) weather, but temperatures of 20°F or below can freeze leaves and kill plants.

How much to plant. Grow approximately 30 plants for every person in your family. One seed packet should sow about 30' of row.

Spacing. Traditional flat rows help retain moisture, especially areas that are dry. Space spinach plants 2"–6" apart in rows that are 1'–3' apart.

Rotation. Since spinach can withstand light to moderate frost, it is a good crop to grow after warm-weather vegetables.

For a greater harvest. This cool-season crop thrives when interplanted with tall crops that provide both light shade and a humid microsite in the summer. Celery prefers similar growing conditions and is a good companion to spinach. Spinach yields are greatest in heavy loam soils.

Soil Preparation

This leafy vegetable grows in any moist, well-drained, moderately rich soil. Spinach usually reaches harvest size earlier in sandy soil; crops in clay soil tend to produce later harvests. A soil pH in the range of 6.0–7.0 is optimal; spinach grows poorly in very acidic soils. Before planting, work in 10–15 pounds of compost per 100 square feet. Add a source of available nitrogen, such as blood meal, to promote rapid growth. Dig the soil to a depth of at least 4", rake the surface smooth, and mulch with grass clippings, legume hay, or decomposed leaves to keep the soil cool and moist. See "Custom Care for Leafy Crops" on page 60 for more information.

❧ AT A GLANCE ❧
SPINACH

Site: Sun to partial shade; needs a cool, moist site.

Soil: Heavy, fertile loam that is moist, but not soggy; pH of 6.0–7.0 (won't tolerate pH below 5.0).

How much to plant: About 30 plants per person.

Spacing: 1'-3' between rows, 2"-6" between plants.

Days to maturity: 37–45 days from seed.

Planting Outdoors

Sowing seeds. To speed germination, soak seeds for 15–20 minutes in compost tea, then direct-sow ½" deep. Optimum soil temperature for germination is 70°F, although spinach seeds will germinate (slowly) at temperatures as low as 35°F. Germination rates decline significantly when the soil warms to 85°F and above.

Growing Guidelines

Thinning seedlings. Thin seedlings to 6" apart when they are 4"–5" tall. Enjoy the thinnings in early-season salads.

Water and mulch. Constant moisture promotes rapid growth and prevents bolting. Keep the soil evenly moist but not wet. Water heavy soil one or two times a week; spinach growing in light, coarse soil may need watering every other day. When seedlings emerge, mulch with 3"–6" of straw, legume hay, or grass clippings to conserve moisture and limit weeds.

Feeding. Spinach is a heavy feeder. When the first true leaves are fully expanded, drench plants with a solution of fish emulsion and kelp extract. Mix 1 tablespoon of fish emulsion and 2 tablespoons of kelp extract per gallon water; apply 1 cup of the solution for every 1' of row. Fertilize weekly until the plants are 2"–3" tall.

SPINACH SEEDLING

Seeds   Cotyledons   *First true leaves*

🐞 FRIENDS & RELATIVES 🐞

SPINACH

Spinach suffers when the heat is on, but a few other crops stand ready to take its place in your garden and on your table. Try these unrelated spinach stand-ins, all of which thrive under hot conditions: vegetable amaranth, Malabar spinach, New Zealand spinach (*Tetragonia tetragonioides*), or orach.

Of these heat-tolerant substitutes, New Zealand spinach is perhaps the most spinachlike in terms of flavor and use. A hot-weather crop that is rarely troubled by pests, New Zealand spinach endures drought and saline soils, too. Direct-sow seeds one to two weeks before the last expected frost; harvest in 55–70 days. Pick about 4"–6" of branch tips together with the leaves, or cut whole plants above the ground when they are small; the stem will resprout.

Information on vegetable amaranth appears in the Asian Specialties entry; read the Greens entry to learn more about Malabar spinach and orach.

Problem Prevention

Select resistant cultivars. 'Melody', 'Indian Summer', and other cultivars resist mosaic virus and downy mildew, two common foliar diseases of spinach. Prevent white rust problems by growing 'Fall Green' and other rust-tolerant cultivars.

Before planting, balance soil fertility. Add compost, plus an additional nitrogen source, to the soil before planting to ensure an adequate supply of all of the nutrients spinach needs. If you suspect a nutrient deficiency, have your soil tested and amend it accordingly.

Grow spinach only in cool weather. Hot temperatures encourage Fusarium wilt and other fungal diseases, as well as promote bolting.

When plants are 4″ tall, thin to improve air circulation. Good air movement discourages fungal diseases such as downy mildew, white rust, and anthracnose.

After planting, cover the area with floating row cover. Use row cover over young plants to thwart attacks by flea beetles and caterpillars. As long as temperatures remain moderate, you can leave the row cover on until you are ready to harvest.

During the season, destroy leaves with light-colored tunnels or blotches. Leafminers can spread quickly unless controlled. Till the soil at the end of the growing season to prevent leafminer problems.

Gathering the Harvest

Spinach is ready to pick 37–45 days after seeds are sown. Harvesting usually extends over two to six weeks, but hot weather may shorten the harvest by causing plants to bolt. Harvest spinach when the leaves are large enough to use. Pick the leaves gradually, beginning with the outer ones; inner leaves will continue to grow. If the crop begins to bolt, harvest entire plants by cutting at ground level. Refrigerate fresh spinach for up to a week. Blanch and freeze extra leaves for cooked use.

Extending the Season

Sow spinach in February in a cold frame; your crop will be ready to harvest in March. Choose heat- and bolt-resistant cultivars, and give them light shade to extend the growing season into the warmer months. For fall crops, plant hardy cultivars. You can overwinter spinach plants by covering them with 8″–12″ of straw. When daytime temperatures reach 50°–60°F in the spring, gradually remove a few inches of straw each week. In the South, plant spinach in late fall as a winter crop.

Propagation

The wind carries dustlike spinach pollen over distances as great as 1 mile. Since spinach cross-pollinates readily, maintaining seed purity is difficult for the home gardener. If you're willing to chance it, eliminate small, early-seeding plants, and let a few of your best plants go to seed. Pick seeds in summer after they've ripened on the plant; store in a cool, dry place. ✳

SPROUTS

Sprouts are a great indoor crop you can grow any time of year, no matter what the weather. And they're not only easy to grow, they'll add new flavors and greater nutrition to your family's meals. The best way to decide what you want to sprout is to do some experimenting. Each kind of seed has its own timetable, but all require the basics crucial to germination: air, water, and temperatures between 50° and 70°F.

Sprouting Methods

Sprouting is done by soaking seeds in water overnight, then draining and sprouting them at room temperature. While they're sprouting, the seeds need to be rinsed frequently with water. And, although darkness is not necessary for germination, some sprouts, such as mung beans, develop a better flavor when grown in darkness or very dim light.

You don't need much equipment to get started in sprouting, but if you want to grow a lot of sprouts, there are automatic sprouters, special sprouting jars, and compact layered setups that accommodate several types of sprouts at once.

Sprouting Step-by-Step

Before investing in the latest equipment, see how well you like the routine and results of sprouting by growing a few batches the old-fashioned way, using a wide-mouthed jar covered with muslin or a nylon stocking.

Be sure to select untreated seeds for sprouting; seeds sold specifically for sprouting are a safe bet. For best results, start by sprouting small batches of seeds. That way you can experiment with what size batch is best, and you won't end up wasting any. Start with 1–2 tablespoons of small-seeded sprouts like alfalfa or about ¼–½ cup of larger ones, such as mung beans. For soaking and rinsing, consider using distilled water if chlorination or other variables make your tap water less than tasty.

Here's a new twist on the old-fashioned jar-and-stocking method that uses a plastic jug for rinsing and draining the seeds:

1. Immerse the seeds in cool water overnight in a clean glass quart jar. Cover the top with a piece of muslin or a nylon stocking secured by a rubber band.

2. The next morning, remove any floating seeds and drain excess water from the jar.

3. Cut the top off of a clean plastic 2-quart jug, and poke some small holes (no larger than

---

SPROUT SENSE

Here are some ways to use sprouts besides eating them raw as snacks or in salads and sandwiches:

• Steam bean sprouts with cooked rice. When sautéed with onions and mushrooms, bean sprouts add more taste and nutrients to main dishes.
• Stir wheat sprouts into oatmeal a minute before it's done.
• Try peanut-butter-and-alfalfa-sprout sandwiches.
• Replace lettuce with alfalfa sprouts in tacos and other Mexican dishes.
• Whip alfalfa sprouts with lightly seasoned tomato juice in the blender for a nourishing beverage.
• Add sprouts to pancakes, breads, casseroles, and cookies.

---

the seeds you're sprouting) in the bottom. Then transfer the seeds to the plastic jug. Cover the jug with a stocking secured by a rubber band.

4. For the next two to three days, rinse the seeds twice daily with a gentle stream of cool water. Use plenty of water each time, swishing it around in the jug as it drains out the bottom. Drain immediately each time, and keep the jug in indirect light. (You can set the jug in a saucer so it doesn't drip.) In hot weather, rinse three times daily. If your house isn't air-conditioned, rinse more often, and keep your jug in the coolest part of the house to avoid molds and fungi.

5. Seeds should be sprouting by the third day. Continue daily rinsing as in Step 4 until the sprouts have greened up and/or are of desired length and flavor. Daily rinsing helps keep sprouts from souring. You can start a

new batch of seeds as soon as the first one has started germinating to ensure a continuous supply of sprouts.

6. Refrigerate sprouts in sealed glass or plastic containers. Use a salad spinner to reduce excess water.

Seeds for Sprouting

One easy way to decide how to use your sprouts is to think of them as either light or heavy. So-called light sprouts are grown from small seeds. They're fairly delicate, wilt easily when cooked, and are often eaten raw. They're at their best in salads and sandwiches and can also be used as toppings for baked potatoes. They're also good as last-minute additions to scrambled eggs, omelets, quesadillas, and grilled cheese sandwiches. Light sprouts include adzuki, alfalfa, cabbage, clover, fenugreek, mustard, onion, and radish.

Heavy sprouts, grown from larger seeds, are harder to keep fresh because they turn sour more easily. (Frequent rinsing usually takes care of this.) Heavy seeds include most beans and peas—chick-peas (also called garbanzo beans), cowpeas, green peas, lentils, lima and kidney beans, mung beans, soybeans, and other legumes, plus wheat. Add them during

Alfalfa sprouts

Mung bean sprouts

Unsprouted mung beans

Sprouts are easy to grow either the old-fashioned way, in a jar covered with muslin or a nylon stocking, or in a specially designed sprouter. Fenugreek, mung beans, and alfalfa are just three of the many types of seeds that are delicious when sprouted and added to salads and other dishes.

the last few minutes of cooking a stir-fry dish or soup.

Other sprouting seeds to try include corn, millet, oats (the whole sprouting type only), rye, sesame, sunflower, triticale, and watercress. Almonds and pumpkin seeds are ready to use after less than a day of soaking, without sprouting. Soak almonds for 12 hours and use them in breads, desserts, and dressings. Pumpkin seeds soaked for 8 hours are good in breads, cereals, desserts, dressings, snacks, and yogurts. If you want to sprout seeds other than those listed, be sure to do some research. Sprouted tomato and potato seeds, for example, are poisonous.

Troubleshooting

Sprouting is easy but not without its problems. Seeds that are infested with insects or that aren't viable won't germinate. They will usually float to the surface during soaking (Step 1 on page 476) and can be discarded. If insects float to the top, discard the entire batch of seeds and the batch it came from. Moldy sprouts are caused by unsanitary containers. Some sprouts will sour if you don't rinse them often enough. Contaminated water, too much heat or cold, or inadequate ventilation can also spoil your crops. And forgotten sprouts germinating in your pantry will remind you with a sour odor. ✽

SQUASH
Cucurbita spp. Cucurbitaceae. Annual.

Squash are among the easiest food crops to grow. Fast-growing summer squash (*Cucurbita pepo*) include crooknecks, zucchinis, and scallops or pattypans. These can be steamed, stuffed, roasted, and even grated into quick breads and muffins. Winter squash, including pumpkins (*C. pepo, C. maxima, C. mixta,* and *C. moschata*), are rich sources of beta carotene and other important nutrients. When properly cured and stored, they retain their flavor and texture for several months.

Planning

Selecting plants. The main question to keep in mind when planning your squash crop is what types of squash your family likes to eat. All are notoriously productive, and planting too much of a type that's not to your liking can be a weighty mistake. Gardeners tend to separate squashes into three categories—summer squash, winter squash, and pumpkins—based on how they use them. Summer squashes are harvested when tender and immature, while winter squashes are harvested when hard and ripe. Pumpkins are just winter squashes that look "pumpkiny." All three need the same growing conditions and care.

Say summer squash, and many people think of long, dark green zucchini cut raw into

---

∾ AT A GLANCE ∾
SQUASH

Site: Full or almost full sun.

Soil: Any good garden soil that drains well; pH of 5.5–6.8.

Spacing: Bushy cultivars: in hills 2'–4' apart. Vining types: in hills 3'–8' apart.

Days to maturity: Summer squash: 45–50 days. Winter squash and pumpkins: 85–110 days.

---

salads or sautéed with butter. But that's just the beginning. There are yellow zucchini and pale green, round zucchini. Yellow crooknecks and straightnecks will add variety in your summer casseroles. And be sure to plant some scalloped or pattypan squash for stuffing. A few cultivars are even selected to produce lots of flowers for stuffing. Most summer squash cultivars are bushy plants, though some may flop over and sprawl a few feet as the season progresses.

Don't plant entire seed packets of all of these kinds of summer squash, or you'll have squash to feed your family, friends, acquaintances, and everyone else within a few square miles of your garden. Instead, try planting one or two plants of a few different summer squashes instead of all one cultivar. They are all as easy to grow as the familiar zucchini.

Winter squashes tend to be vining plants, though some bush cultivars are available. They are usually served as a starchy vegetable or sweetened and used to make "pumpkin" pie. The seeds are usually removed either before cooking or before serving. The seeds can be roasted and eaten. Winter squashes can be white, yellow, tan, orange, dark green, or bluegray, and some are spotted or striped. They range from single-serving size to hulking monsters that take many meals to eat.

Three of the most familiar types of winter squash are the dark green, ribbed acorn; the golden-tan, club-shaped butternut; and the

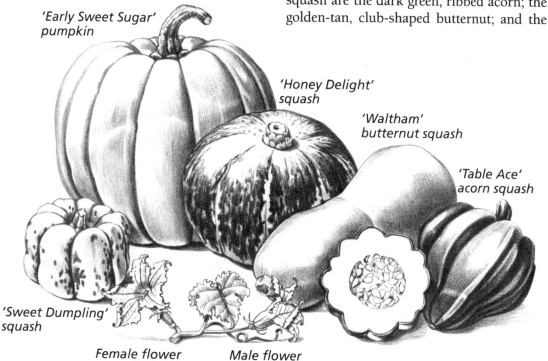

'Early Sweet Sugar' pumpkin

'Honey Delight' squash

'Waltham' butternut squash

'Table Ace' acorn squash

'Sweet Dumpling' squash

Female flower   Male flower

Winter squash are ideal for storing the garden's bounty through the winter. All squashes bear male and female flowers that are edible. Female flowers have a tiny fuzzy, green fruit just below the blossom.

squat, dark green buttercup with its gray button.

The Japanese have developed a number of fine kabocha-type cultivars with dry, flaky, sweet flesh such as 'Honey Delight'. Also try 'Chestnut', which is reputed to taste like its namesake.

Delicata types are very sweet, excellent for stuffing, and need no curing. They are sometimes called sweet potato squash. Try 'Sweet Dumpling' for single-serving stuffers.

Hubbards are the traditional New England squash. Try a cultivar such as 'Blue Ballet' for hubbard flavor in a manageable size.

Many other heirloom types and cultivars are also available. Calabaza or Cuban types have sweet, moist flesh. Cushaw types are often used for pies and baking. 'Tahitian', or melon squash, is an old culivar with rich, sweet flesh that can even be eaten raw.

One unique type of winter squash is the spaghetti squash. The pale yellow, oblong fruits have mild-flavored, yellow, spaghetti-like flesh.

If pumpkin pie is your goal, don't limit yourself to orange jack-o'-lantern-shaped fruits. Try making pie with any yellow- or orange-fleshed squash. If seeds to snack on appeal to you, consider planting a naked seed cultivar such as 'Lady Godiva' or 'Eat-All'.

When to plant. Squash grows best in warm soil. Sow seeds 2 weeks after the last expected spring frost, or when soil temperature reaches 60°F. Summer squash can be planted until 8 weeks before the first expected fall frost. Sow winter squash up to 15 weeks before the first expected fall frost.

How much to plant. Limit summer squash to three to four plants per person and two to three per person with winter squash. Grow more than one type to keep the harvest interesting.

Spacing. With bushy, upright cultivars,

grow two plants per hill, with hills spaced 2'–4' apart. Long-vined winter squash and pumpkins need 3'–8' between hills. Or grow them along the garden's edge and let them ramble. Cultivars with long vines need plenty of space to run but may be trained up a trellis if the fruits are not too heavy.

Rotation. Plant after a legume or leafy greens and not after corn if cucumber beetles are a recurring problem.

For a greater harvest. Succession-plant summer squash two or three times during the summer. Harvest at least twice a week to keep the plants productive. Plant both early-maturing winter squash, such as acorns or butternuts, and some late maturers, like buttercups.

Soil Preparation

Squash grows best in moderately rich soil. For best results, plant them in hills enriched with compost or rotted manure. You can plant pumpkins and winter squash in old compost

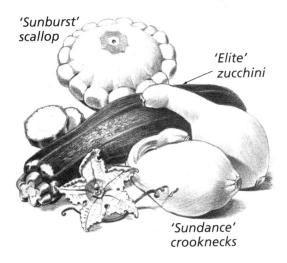

'Sunburst' scallop

'Elite' zucchini

'Sundance' crooknecks

Summer squash come in a variety of shapes and sizes. For best flavor and texture, harvest them when they're young and tender.

heaps at the garden's edge. Loosen the site with a spade or digging fork before planting.

Planting Indoors

Sowing seeds. Squash may be direct-sown, or you can get an early start by planting some seeds indoors.

Seedling care. Seedlings become large very quickly: Sow seeds in 3″ containers three weeks before you plan to set them out. Handle the seedlings just like cucumber seedlings; see "Planting Indoors" on page 341. If transplanting is delayed for more than a few days after the first true leaf appears, move seedlings to larger containers.

Planting Outdoors

Sowing seeds. Just before planting, soak seeds in compost tea for 15 minutes to improve germination. Plant seeds 1″–2″ deep, depending on their size, in predampened hills, with three to four plants per hill. To prevent soil crusting, scatter a thin layer of sawdust, grass clippings, or rotted leaves over seeded beds.

Seedling care. Cover seedlings with row cover to protect them from squash bugs and cucumber beetles. Hill soil up around the stem if it is more than 1″ from the soil line to the first set of leaves.

Growing Guidelines

Thinning seedlings. When direct-sown seeds have at least one true leaf, thin them to two plants per hill.

Water and mulch. Squash need average watering, between ½″ and 1″ per week. Organic mulches such as straw or grass clippings help keep soil moist and cool but make pest control more difficult. Squash can be grown without mulch except in very dry areas, since the leaves are large and will shade the surrounding soil.

SQUASH SEEDLING

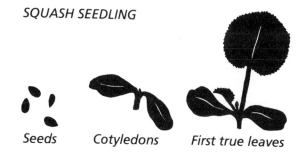

Seeds   Cotyledons   First true leaves

Feeding. If plants lack vigor, drench them every two weeks with a kelp/compost-tea mixture. Avoid strong nitrogen fertilizers, which encourage excessive leafy growth. See "Custom Care for Fruit Crops" on page 58 for more information.

Problem Prevention

At planting, sprinkle radish seeds over hills. Many gardeners report that radishes repel squash pests. Let the radishes remain as bedfellows all season.

After planting, cover the area with floating row cover. Cucumber beetles, squash bugs, and squash vine borers are the most common pests of squash. Cucumber beetles and squash bugs suck plant juices, but, most important, spread bacterial wilt, a common disease that causes plants to wilt and die suddenly. Row cover keeps both pests at bay. Remove it when female blossoms appear to allow pollination.

After removing floating row cover, control borers. Squash vine borers feed inside squash stems, especially plants of *C. pepo*, which includes summer squash, most pumpkins, and a few winter squash. Borers generally attack within 6″ of where the plants emerge from the soil. Wrapping this section of stem with cloth can deter them, as can heaping soil over it. Cultivars that develop supplemental roots as they run may continue to grow despite borer damage to the main crown.

If few or no fruits form, hand pollinate flowers. Most squash produce only male flowers at first, followed by a mixture of male and female flowers a week or so later. (See the illustration on page 479 to identify male and female flowers.) If female flowers are opening and withering without setting fruit, they may not be receiving enough pollen. Bees and other insects normally pollinate squash, but you can help. Use a small paintbrush to collect pollen from male blossoms and transfer it to the female flowers. Or pick a male blossom, place it over a female one, and tap it to release the pollen. Poor pollination also can cause the blossom ends of squash fruits to shrivel. This is seldom a problem if four or more plants are flowering at the same time.

Gathering the Harvest

Harvest all squash by cutting fruits with 1″ of stem attached. Pick summer squash when they are small, harvesting every day or so, because fruit quality deteriorates with age. Store it in the refrigerator. Gather winter squash and pumpkins when the rind is hard enough to resist puncturing with a fingernail. Or wait until the plants begin to die to gather winter squash and pumpkins. Clean harvested squash with a damp cloth. Disinfect fruits destined for long-term storage by dipping them in a solution of 1 part bleach and 6 parts water. Be sure to dip the stem end, where rotting usually begins. After cleaning, cure winter squash in a well-ventilated place at room temperature for ten days. Then move to cooler storage where temperatures range between 50° and 55°F.

Extending the Season

In cool climates, prewarm hills by covering them with black plastic, and start seedlings indoors. If the soil temperature remains below 70°F, cover the hills with clear plastic for two days after sowing outdoors, or use row cover.

Fall and Winter Care

Compost summer squash when plants begin to fail, and cultivate the soil to expose any hidden insects. Compost winter squash plants after harvest. Plant a fall cover crop such as annual rye or clover if time allows.

Container Growing

For container culture, use compact, bushy cultivars that bear small fruits. Feed the cultivars every three weeks with compost tea or another liquid organic fertilizer. Hand-pollinate to ensure fruit set.

🐝 FRIENDS & RELATIVES 🐝

SQUASH

Gourds are related to squash and are grown just like them. A few types of gourds are harvested and eaten like summer squash when they are immature. Luffas (*Luffa acutangula* and *L. aegyptiaca*), also known as sponge gourds, are edible when young and are likened to green beans and okra. They're best eaten when 6″–8″ long. Luffas need very warm conditions and a trellis for best performance. Bottle gourds (*Lagenaria siceraria*) are edible and tasty when young. Cucuzzi bottle gourd fruits are thin and edible up to 2′, and they taste much like green beans. Another bottle gourd is the source of the dried gourd shavings that are an essential ingredient in sushi.

Propagation

Squash seeds are easy to save. If you grow only one cultivar, allow only fruits from a disease-free plant to mature. (Mature summer squash have hard rinds and brown stems.) Look for mottled foliage that indicates viral diseases and circular sores on leaves and fruits that indicate anthracnose. Do not save seeds from squash that show any of these signs. If you grow more than one cultivar, you will need to sequester your mother flower and hand-pollinate it. See "Cross-Pollinated Crops" on page 262 for details. Cure the fruits at room temperature for two weeks, remove the seeds, and wash in several changes of water. Dry seeds in a single layer for a week, and store in a cool, dark place. *

STRAWBERRY

Fragaria × ananassa. Rosaceae. Perennial. Zones 3–10.

Wild strawberries have been eaten since antiquity, but the garden strawberry as we now know it is a relative newcomer to gardens, the result of crossing two native American wild strawberries. After two centuries of breeding, strawberries are now available with resistance to pests and the ability to ripen at various times during the growing season.

Planning

Selecting plants. Although strawberries are self-fruitful, consider planting two or more cultivars to spread out the harvest season. Nursery catalogs list cultivars as early-, mid-, or late-season ripening. June-bearing strawberries ripen a single crop in spring or early summer. Everbearing strawberries bear two crops each season, one in spring and the second in fall. Day-neutral types fruit throughout the growing season.

The amount of runners, or horizontal stems, that strawberries produce varies with type and cultivar. Runnering generally increases from day-neutral to everbearing to June-bearing types. Cultivars resistant to diseases such as Verticillium wilt, red stele, and leaf spot are available. Strawberries also are subject to viral diseases, so purchasing disease-free plants is important.

Also consider the fruit characteristics of different cultivars. The flavor intensity, size, and firmness varies with cultivar. Firmer cultivars are better for freezing and preserving.

Selecting a site. Full sun is best. Avoid low-lying areas where spring frosts are apt to injure the early blossoms. If possible, also avoid ground in which grass, tomatoes, potatoes, peppers, or eggplants were recently growing because these plants harbor pests common to strawberries.

When to plant. Where winters are cold,

❧ AT A GLANCE ❧
STRAWBERRY

Site: Full sun. Avoid low-lying areas prone to spring frosts.

Soil: Rich, well-drained soil that is high in organic matter.

Spacing: 1 square foot per plant.

Seasons to bearing: 4–12 months from planting.

plant strawberries in early spring, as soon as you can work the soil. Where winters are mild, plant strawberries either in late winter or in fall.

Spacing. Each plant needs about a square foot of space for sufficient air circulation and light. There are two basic ways to manage strawberries: removing all of the runners or just letting them do their own thing.

If you remove all of the runners, you will be following the hill system. Stagger plants 1′ apart in double rows with 1′ between the rows. (Space the less vigorous day-neutral cultivars just 7″ apart in double rows 7″ apart.) Leave 4′ walkways between the double rows. Pinch out all runners as they form. Unless you have lots of time on your hands, select cultivars that don't make very many runners if you choose this method.

If you let the runners root wherever they touch down, you will be following the matted row system. Space plants 2′ apart in single rows with 4′ walkways between the rows. Let the runners root where they may; just mow or cultivate the walkways to keep the strawberry bed only 1½′ wide. This method suits busy gardeners.

Strawberry plant

Alpine strawberry plant

'Earliglow'

'Vesper'

'Guardian'

'Tristar'

There are strawberry cultivars suitable to nearly any climate, from Florida heat to Canadian cold. Alpine strawberry fruits are small but have an intense, wild flavor. Alpine strawberries are too small to harvest in quantity, so for filling your freezer or making jam, rely on the larger fruits of garden strawberries.

Soil Preparation

Strawberries thrive in a fertile soil that is rich in organic matter and has a pH of 5.5–6.5. To prepare the soil, it's best to plant a cover crop in your strawberry patch the season before you intend to plant strawberries. See "Custom Care for Small Fruits" on page 62 for details. Consider soil solarization as a means to deal with potential weed and disease problems.

If the soil drains poorly, rake it into raised beds 6″ high and 2′ wide. In general, growing strawberries in raised beds seems to increase early rooting and results in better first-season growth.

Planting

Plants usually are sold bundled together and bareroot. If you cannot plant immediately, moisten the roots, put the plants in a plastic bag, and refrigerate them. When you are ready to plant, cut all the roots back to 4″ with a pair of scissors. Soak the roots in compost tea for 15–20 minutes just prior to planting, then dust roots with 1 cup of kelp plus 1 cup of bonemeal. Plant strawberries as you would any herbaceous perennial. See "Bareroot Plants" on page 112 for directions.

Tuck a mulch of straw or pine needles 2″ deep around each plant. Then give each plant a pint of water to settle the soil and get growth off to a good start. Pinch off all flower buds for three months after planting so that your plants channel their energy into growing strong roots.

Growing Guidelines

Water and mulch. Strawberries need constantly moist soil, especially at planting and from flowering until fruits just start to color. When fruits begin to mature, let the soil dry out between waterings. Maintain a straw mulch around plants.

Feeding. Kelp sprays improve fruit set and enhance bud hardiness. Apply two or three sprays of kelp/compost-tea (2 tablespoons of kelp per gallon of tea) from when blossoms form in the spring until just prior to full bloom.

Fertilize strawberries in early summer, after the spring or early-summer harvest. Make a mixture of 1 tablespoon of fish emulsion in 1 gallon of compost tea. Pour on 2 cups of the mixture per 1′ of row.

Training. Renovate your bed after harvest by removing old plants and excess young plants. The vigorous young plants that you leave should each have about 1 square foot of space.

Problem Prevention

Start with good planting stock. Purchase certified disease-free plants from a nursery rather than planting plants you get from friends. Also, choose cultivars that are resistant to pest problems in your area.

In spring, protect blossoms from frost. If frost threatens, throw a blanket or some other covering over the plants.

When fruits begin to color, spray sulfur. If you've had problems with gray mold in the past and if humidity is high or weather is wet, a preventive spray of sulfur is advisable. Reapply after rains.

When fruits begin to color, spray compost tea. If weather is dry or if your plants haven't suffered previous problems with gray mold, a compost tea spray should be sufficient to prevent gray mold infection.

As fruits begin ripening, cover with

netting. Birds like to peck at strawberries. The only sure protection is netting.

As fruits begin ripening, go on slug patrol. Control slugs by handpicking them at night and trapping them in shallow saucers of beer. Exclude them by installing copper flashing around your strawberry bed. Or sprinkle the ground with wood ashes or diatomaceous earth; renew these materials following rains.

At harvest, pick off all berries. Don't leave rotting berries in the field; put them into a separate container for disposal. Removing these rotting fruits prevents them from spreading disease to sound fruits.

Right after harvest, renovate your bed. Renovation thins the planting and helps slow the buildup of disease organisms. Cut off all leaves with a mower set on high or with hand shears. Gather leaves and compost, or, if they are diseased, dispose of them in a sealed container with household trash. Thin out plants, leaving those that are youngest and most vigorous. Remove every single weed. Spread a 1″ layer of compost over the beds, remulch, and water thoroughly.

Replant a new bed every two or three years. Pests build up in a strawberry bed after about four years, decreasing productivity. By planting a new bed at a new location every two or three years, you have a new bed coming into full production just as you take out an old bed.

Gathering the Harvest

Junebearers yield their first crop during the growing season after planting. Other types yield a late-summer harvest. Expect about a quart of berries per plant.

Pick strawberries when the fruits are red and separate readily from the stem. The fruits are highly perishable, so store them fresh no longer than about a week, at temperatures just above freezing and high humidity.

Fall and Winter Care

In late fall when the plants are dormant, cover your beds with mulch to protect the crowns from cold and prevent plants from heaving. Spread enough of a fluffy, weed-free, organic material, such as straw, pine needles, cornstalks, or mulch hay, so that it is 2″–3″ deep after settling.

Alternatively, drape floating row cover over the plants. Weight down the edges with stones or boards to prevent it from blowing away.

In late winter (or early spring in northern areas), watch for new growth beneath the mulch.

🐛 FRIENDS & RELATIVES 🐛

STRAWBERRY

Not all wild strawberry species have been forgotten. Among the most popular is the Alpine strawberry, a runnerless type of the wood strawberry (*Fragaria vesca*). Alpine strawberries bear small but highly flavored berries from late spring through fall. They don't make runners, so they are ideal for busy gardeners. They also make a good edible edging for flowerbeds. New Alpine strawberry plants can be propagated by crown division but are usually propagated by seeds. Sow the seeds in early spring, barely covering them with soil, then transplant the seedlings when they begin to crowd. The seeds germinate erratically and grow very slowly at first, so be patient.

When pale new leaves begin to grow beneath the mulch, pull the mulch back off of the crowns to give them light. Tuck the mulch around the plants as a summer mulch to keep the soil cool and moist and to keep the berries clean.

Container Growing

For container plantings, grow strawberries that throw out few or no runners, such as the day-neutral or Alpine strawberries. For a novelty, plant day-neutrals in hanging baskets—runners will fruit in midair.

Use any potting mix suitable for houseplants. Discard old plants when their crowns turn woody, and replace them with young plants. When winter comes, bring plants indoors if you want the harvest to continue. Give the plants abundant light and cool temperatures. Otherwise, leave the containers outside, but protect them from cold as shown in the illustration on page 240.

Propagation

Propagate garden strawberries by transplanting rooted runners. To propagate cultivars that make few runners, divide the crowns with a sharp knife, and plant the crown pieces separately. *

SUNFLOWER
Helianthus annuus. Compositae. Annual.

Sunflowers grow with ease as long as they are in full sun. For snacking, roast the seeds at 275°F for about 45 minutes. Crack and remove the shells, or eat the seeds shells and all.

Selecting plants. Dwarf cultivars make the most of small gardens. For a harvest of seeds for snacking, choose single-stalked cultivars with big gray-and-white-striped seeds. 'Sundak' is a dwarf plant with a full-size seed head and seeds. Many sunflowers produce small, black, oil-type seeds, which are fine for birds but not for eating out of hand.

Site. Plant tall sunflowers where they won't shade low-growing crops.

Soil. Grow in average, well-drained soil.

How much to plant. Each large seed head head yields 3–6 ounces of seeds.

Spacing. Give large sunflowers 1'–3' of open space on all sides; set smaller ones as close as 8" apart.

Planting and growing. Sunflowers take from 60 to 110 days to produce seeds, depending on the cultivar. Keep fertilizing and watering to a minimum. Once the seeds are set, cover the ripening heads to protect the seeds from hungry wildlife.

Harvesting. Let the mature seeds dry to a hard coat outdoors or cut the head with several inches of stem and hang it indoors to dry in a warm, airy spot. To remove the seeds, rub the head on wire mesh set over a bucket.

Propagation. Sunflowers can cross-pollinate. If you save seeds, grow cultivars that flower at different times.

Friends and relatives. Jerusalem artichoke is a perennial member of the sunflower clan that makes edible tubers. See the entry of the same name for more information. *

SWEET POTATO

Ipomoea batatas. Convolvulaceae. Annual.

The caramel flavor and aroma of sweet potatoes often are associated with holiday meals, but these nutritious tubers are delicious year-round. Even after being stored for six months or more, sweet potatoes are packed with vitamins A and C. Beyond baked sweet potatoes, casseroles, and pies, sweet potatoes can be paired with citrus fruits in salads or matched with carrots and chopped ginger in spicy side dishes. Cooked mashed sweet potatoes also work well as a fat-free butter substitute in quick breads and muffins.

Selecting plants. Cultivars vary in interior and exterior color, starch and moisture content, and long-term storage potential, as well as how fast they form tubers. Visit a farmers' market in early fall, purchase samples of different cultivars, and evaluate their flavor. If you find a favorite, use small to medium-size tubers as mother plants, and grow your own slips. (For directions, see "Planting and Growing" on this page.) Many seed companies sell either slips or parent potatoes of several common cultivars.

Site. Full sun is required, although sweet potatoes can tolerate some afternoon shade in warm climates.

Soil. Rich soil is not required, and a slightly acidic pH of 5.5 is ideal. In either sand or clay soil, adding organic matter will help keep the soil friable and promote good tuber development. Sweet potatoes are not heavy feeders, but they do require a good balance of soil nitrogen, potassium, and phosphorus.

How much to plant. A single, well-grown sweet potato plant produces four or more edible tubers. In terms of square-foot yield, a 5′ × 8′ raised bed containing 15 plants will pro-duce 30 to 40 pounds of tubers.

Spacing. Set root-bearing stems, called slips, 1′ apart in rows spaced 3′ apart. In raised beds, space plants 1½′ apart.

Days to maturity. Sweet potatoes mature in 70–100 days, depending on the cultivar.

Planting and growing. To grow your own slips, lay small tubers in a warm cold frame, covered with 2″–3″ of straw or compost, around the time of the last expected spring frost. Or to grow them indoors, stick toothpicks around the center of sprouting tubers and suspend them in jars of water, with the sprouting ends up. Grow them in a sunny window.

At least three weeks after the last expected spring frost, when the sprouts are 4″–6″ long and show tiny roots, break them off and plant them. Lay slips in damp soil and cover the stems so that only three leaves show above the surface. Keep moist for a week after planting.

Sweet potatoes form vines that run along the ground. The vine tips are edible when cooked as summer greens. Mulch the plants or let the vines form their own living mulch. Where space is tight, train the vines to run up a trellis.

Harvesting. After 70 days, check tubers of all cultivars and dig them when they reach the size you want. Sweet potatoes cannot be pulled up; they must be dug. Start digging at the outer edge of the planting, for some tubers will lie at least several inches from the plants' main crowns. After digging, wash the sweet potatoes with water and cure them in a warm (80°F) place for two weeks. Then store at cool room temperature, or about 60°F. Some fast-maturing cultivars with a high moisture content may be eaten without curing, but curing improves the flavor and nutrition of most sweet potatoes. The long-term storage potential of sweet potatoes varies with the cultivar. Sweet potatoes that mature slowly and have a high starch content store the longest.

Extending the season. In cool climates, cover the bed with black plastic two weeks prior to planting. Cut slits in the plastic for planting slips. Leave the black plastic in place all season to keep the soil temperature as high as possible. In warm climates, grow a fast-maturing cultivar along with one that takes longer to mature. Try intercropping sweet potatoes with okra, widely spaced corn, or other upright plants such as sunflowers.

Fall and winter care. After the tubers are dug, gather the vines and compost them. Cultivate the soil, and plant it with a legume or hardy cover crop. In warm climates, early crops may be followed by fall leafy greens.

Container growing. Sweet potatoes may be grown in half-barrels. Let the vines cascade or train them up a trellis to save space.

Propagation. Sweet potatoes are usually propagated from slips. (They flower and set seed only in warm, short-day climates.) Set aside small to medium-size, disease-free tubers to act as parents for next year's crop. Or purchase certified disease-free slips each spring.

Friends and relatives. Small sweet potatoes are often called yams, especially when they are accompanied by a caramel sauce. Yet sweet potatoes are quite different from true yams, which include over 500 species of the genus *Dioscorea*. True yams are starchier than sweet potatoes, and their culture is limited to tropical and semitropical areas. Most edible yams are large perennial vines. See the Asian Specialties entry for more information. ✳

Heat-loving sweet potatoes are grown for their delicious tubers, which are rich in vitamins A and C. The shoot tips can also be cooked as a flavorful green vegetable. The plants can be allowed to sprawl or trained up a trellis.

TEA

After a long day, there's nothing like the luxury of curling up with a steaming cup of tea. And when you've grown the ingredients yourself, the experience is all the more satisfying. No matter where you live, you can enjoy the pleasure of growing and mixing your own special herb blends.

The "Real" Tea

The standard cup of teabag tea comes from the leaves of *Camellia sinensis*. Tea leaves are picked year-round where this shrub thrives: in India, China, Thailand, and other tropical regions. In the United States, it's possible to grow your own tea if you live in the Southeast or Pacific Coast regions (Zones 7–9). The tea plant makes an attractive hedge with shiny, evergreen leaves and fragrant white blossoms. Plant in sun and average soil; mulch annually with compost. Save the prunings for your own homemade tea.

Herbal Teas

Even if you can't grow the "true" tea plant, you can still create many wonderful teas from the garden. The flavor of herbal teas will vary, depending on what plant part you use and whether the materials are fresh or dried. Following you'll find some suggestions of herbs that provide great-tasting teas, along with the parts you can use, the life cycle of the plant, and suggested growing conditions. Create a special tea garden, or mix these beautiful and versatile plants into your flower and vegetable gardens. Of course, always make sure you have correctly identified any plant before adding it to your teapot!

Minty Herbs

Mint is a popular flavor in all kinds of products, but it's especially nice in tea. Enjoy the following minty herbs.

MAKING HERBAL TEA

Herbal teas are great hot or cold. Try these recipes with your favorite herb combinations.

Hot Herbal Tea

For each cup of tea, measure 2 tablespoons of fresh herbs or 1 tablespoon of dry herbs into a nonmetallic tea pot or mug. Bring freshly drawn, cool water to a rolling boil in a separate container, then pour the water over the herbs. Allow to steep for five minutes. Strain before serving. Sweeten to taste.

Herbal Iced Sun Tea

Fill a gallon-size glass jar with freshly drawn cool water. Add 1–2 cups of fresh herb leaves and flowers—rinse them first if they're gritty—then place the jar in a sunny spot for four to eight hours. Strain before serving. Pour into glasses over ice. Sweeten to taste.

Anise hyssop (*Agastache foeniculum*) has sweet and minty fresh leaves and flowers. This perennial likes humus-rich soil in full sun or light shade.

Catnip (*Nepeta cataria*) has leaves with a mild mint flavor; use them fresh or dried. This perennial likes average soil in full sun or partial shade.

Mints (*Mentha* spp.) are perennials that produce leaves that can be used fresh or dried. See the Mint entry for complete growing guidelines.

Fruit-Flavored Herbs

Fruity herbs add a nice flavor and aroma to herbal teas. They also blend well with minty flavors. Experiment with these flavors.

Bee balm (*Monarda didyma*) leaves and flowers have a citrus flavor; use them fresh or dried. This perennial likes moist, humus-rich soil in full sun or light shade.

Chamomile includes German chamomile (*Matricaria recutita*) and Roman chamomile (*Chamaemelum nobile*). Their flowers have an apple flavor; use them fresh or dried. They like evenly moist soil in full sun to light shade.

Lemon balm (*Melissa officinalis*) leaves have a minty lemon flavor when fresh. This perennial likes average soil in full sun to light shade.

Licorice-Flavored Herbs

If you enjoy the flavor of licorice, try these herbs.

Angelica (*Angelica archangelica*) has licorice-flavored roots, leaves, and seeds; use them fresh or dried. This biennial or short-lived perennial likes moist soil and partial shade.

Anise (*Pimpinella anisum*) has licorice-flavored seeds and leaves; use them fresh or dried. This annual likes light soil and full sun.

Fennel (*Foeniculum vulgare*) has licorice-flavored seeds; use them fresh or dried. Fennel is grown as an annual. See the Fennel entry for complete growing information.

Savory Herbs

Many culinary herbs are as good in the teapot as in the soup pot. Try these for zesty tea.

Marjoram (*Origanum majorana*) leaves taste like sweet oregano; use them fresh or dried. This is a tender perennial. See the Marjoram entry for complete cultural details.

Rosemary (*Rosmarinus officinalis*) leaves and flowers have a pinelike minty taste; use them fresh or dried. This is a tender perennial. See the Rosemary entry for growing tips.

Sage (*Salvia officinalis*) leaves have a savory lemon flavor; use them fresh or dried. Sage is an attractive perennial with silver-gray leaves and blue flowers. See the Sage entry for growing information.

Harvesting and Storing

Use scissors and a basket to collect leaves and blossoms in the morning just after the dew has dried. Dry your tea ingredients hanging in bunches or spread them loosely on screens in a warm, dark, dry place with good air circulation. Or dry them on a cookie sheet in a warm oven (about 90°F) for three to six hours. The herbs are dry when they're brittle and crisp. After cooling, store them in tightly closed, labeled jars away from heat and light, for up to one year. ✳

THYME

Thymus spp. Labiatae. Perennial. Zones 5–9.

Thyme has so many culinary uses, but you might be surprised to learn it was once used in cough syrups, moth repellents, and embalming fluids. In the kitchen, add thyme to rice and bean dishes, vegetable soups, roasted meats, and chowder. Its flavor blends well with most vegetables, casseroles, and salads.

Selecting plants. Thyme plants grow in two forms: as upright plants up to 1½' tall (choose these for frequent picking) or as ground-covers that grow 1"–6" tall. Common thyme (*Thymus vulgaris*) is a shrubby type used for cooking. You'll find many other species and cultivars in a variety of colors and flavors, including silver, golden, lemon, and caraway thymes.

Site. Provide full sun to partial shade.

Soil. Thyme thrives in a well-drained, sandy soil with a neutral to slightly acid pH (6.0–7.0).

Spacing. Allow 1' between clumps.

Days to maturity. Begin harvesting sprigs during the first year from cuttings; snip seedlings sparingly until the second year.

Planting and growing. Thyme seeds germinate in three to four weeks at 55°F. Sow in flats, then use a knife to slice the tray of seedlings into clumps. Set plants out after danger of frost is past. Divide clumps every three or four years.

Harvesting. For the best flavor, harvest just before bloom. Strip leaves from the stems; use them fresh or dry them as described in "Harvesting and Storing" on page 491.

Fall and winter care. Mulch plants in winter to protect them from cold damage.

Container growing. Low-growing thymes are attractive in hanging baskets. Use any well-drained potting medium that includes compost.

Propagation. Layer or divide in spring. Take cuttings in summer. Sow seeds outdoors in fall or spring or indoors in early spring. ✳

TOMATO

Lycopersicon esculentum. Solanaceae. Annual.

There's no doubt about it, vine-ripened tomatoes are one of the best reasons to garden. Whether added to a salad or garnished with basil, nothing beats the taste of a succulent tomato ripened to perfection in a home garden. Another advantage of homegrown tomatoes is the unusual cultivars that gardeners can choose from. Plus, you only need a little space to grow an assortment of different tomatoes for special uses—cherry tomatoes for salads, big slicers for sandwiches, and firm-fleshed paste tomatoes for sauces, freezing, and canning.

Planning

Selecting plants. When you start considering which tomatoes to grow, you'll find two different types of growth habits—determinate and indeterminate—and three different major fruit types—slicing tomatoes, cherry tomatoes, and paste tomatoes. Disease resistance is another consideration. To choose the best tomatoes for your garden, grow and taste a variety of cultivars. Even if your garden is small, try growing at least three different cultivars each year, and make one of them a cultivar you've never grown before.

TOMATO

Site: Full sun or full morning sun and less than three hours of afternoon shade.

Soil: Moderately fertile clay or sandy loam with good drainage and a pH between 5.5 and 6.8.

Spacing: Staked tomatoes: 1½'–2' apart. Unstaked, uncaged tomatoes: 3'–4' apart. Caged tomatoes: Center 2'-diameter cages 4' apart.

Days to maturity: 90–140 days from seed; 60–90 days from transplanting, depending on the cultivar.

Determinate tomatoes tend to flower and set fruit all at once and then decline. Many modern cultivars listed as determinate blur the distinction between the types, though, because they produce all season. Cultivars described as strongly determinate usually are compact plants that require no pruning and minimal staking. So-called vigorous determinates need substantial staking or trellising to hold up the heavy crops they produce. If you prune them back after the first heavy crop of fruit ripens, they'll frequently bear a nice fall crop.

Indeterminate tomatoes produce over an extended period of time instead of setting one major crop. Most have long, sprawling vines rather than stocky limbs. You can let indeterminates sprawl or you can prune them by pinching out all or most of the suckers (the shoots that emerge between large leaves and main stems). Either way, you'll have to trellis, stake, or cage indeterminates to keep the fruit off of the ground.

Cherry tomatoes are popular for salads, snacking, and appetizers. They tend to be sweet, prolific, and easy to grow. Vigorous indeterminate cherry tomatoes do a very good job of setting fruit in hot weather, and they tend to be quite disease-resistant.

There are hundreds of juicy slicing tomatoes to choose from. As a general rule, large-fruited plants like beefsteaks don't produce as many fruits as cultivars that bear small or medium-size fruits. If you are a new gardener, start with a local favorite and then branch out into more unusual selections. Deep red tomatoes often deliver the most intense flavor. Yellow tomatoes often taste milder, and pink-fleshed ones tend to be firm, mild, and sweet.

Paste or processing tomatoes have small seed cavities, extra-thick walls, and fleshy inner membranes. They hold together well when cooked and yield thick sauce when processed. Most processing tomatoes are determinate, so they conveniently bear their main crop all at once.

In addition to these three major types, you'll also find special-use tomatoes, including stuffers, which are almost hollow inside; small pears, which are similar to cherry tomatoes; and various Italian heirloom cultivars, which have convoluted or elongated shapes.

Finally, look for disease resistance. In catalogs, you'll find that many cultivars have capital letters after the name. These indicate genetic resistance to several common diseases, including Verticillium wilt (V), Fusarium wilt (F), root knot nematodes (N), and tobacco mosaic virus (T). Your local extension agent can tell you if these diseases are common in your area. Disease resistance has nothing to do with tomato flavor, other than the fact that resistant tomatoes often continue to thrive long after nonresistant ones are dead. Most tomato diseases strike just as plants begin to set fruit.

When to plant. Tomatoes like warm soil and don't tolerate frost, so wait until warm spring days and soil temperatures above 60°F to plant. Begin setting out seedlings two weeks after the last expected spring frost, earlier under well-insulated cloches. See "Extending the Season" on page 497 for more information on getting an early start in the garden. You can set additional plants out until 12–14 weeks before the first fall frost is expected.

How much to plant. Where summers are long and warm, two plants per person of any type tomato usually yield enough for fresh eating. In cooler climates, where tomatoes do not produce as heavily, grow four plants per person. If you can or freeze tomatoes, grow six or more plants of a processing or paste tomato, plus plants for tomatoes that you intend to eat fresh.

Spacing. Spacing depends on whether you plan to stake or cage plants or allow them to sprawl, as well as on the vigor of the cultivar. Space staked plants 1½'–2' apart, 3'–4' if plants are allowed to sprawl. Most gardeners grow big, indeterminate tomatoes in 2'-diameter cages, with one plant per cage. For easy harvesting, space cages 4' apart. Allow enough space between plants to permit good sun penetration and air circulation.

Rotation. Plant tomatoes after beans, peas, or another legume. Never plant tomatoes after or next to potatoes; early blight, a common leaf spot disease, can quickly spread from one crop to another. Also avoid planting after eggplants and peppers, which are in the same family.

For a greater harvest. Stagger planting dates to extend the harvest season and reduce problems with pests and diseases. Unless you live where summers are very short, plant just a plant or two of an early cultivar for a quick first crop and plant a mixture of mid-season and late tomatoes for the bulk of your harvest. Include one cherry tomato because they resist diseases and nutritional disorders and set fruit under extreme temperatures. After tomatoes bear heavily in midsummer, try cutting some plants back to encourage healthy new growth and a fall crop of fruits.

Soil Preparation

Tomatoes respond best to moderately rich, deeply worked soil that is well-drained and rich in both major and minor nutrients. Potassium is more important than nitrogen. Tomatoes are sensitive to shortages of calcium and magnesium.

To make sure your tomatoes find the nutrients they need as they stretch their roots through the soil, dig two shovelfuls of good compost or rotted manure into each planting hole. Homemade compost made with manure, leaves, and grass clippings is usually sufficiently rich, but you may boost its nutrient content by mixing 1 cup each of bonemeal and greensand into 10-gallon wheelbarrow loads of compost. See "Custom Care for Fruit Crops" on page 58 for more information.

Planting Indoors

For many gardeners, learning the art of sowing seeds indoors begins with tomatoes. Fortunately, they're easy to grow from seeds. If you plan on experimenting with the wide variety of cultivars that are available, you'll have to grow them from seeds.

Sowing seeds. Sow seeds indoors six to eight weeks before you set them out. Use plastic cell packs or 2"–3"-wide peat pots, or sow seeds in rows in well-drained flats. (If you start early, 3″ containers are best.) Fill containers to the top with any good potting soil. For better germination and to control damping-off, soak seeds in compost tea for 10–15 minutes before sowing. Sow two or three seeds in individual containers, or space seeds 1″ apart in flats. Cover the seeds with ¼″ of soil. Firm the soil gently with your fingers. Water well. Seedlings will germinate in about one week. Once they germinate, move the pots to your sunniest windowsill or beneath a plant growth light in a warm (60°–85°F) room.

Seedling care. Make sure seedlings receive very intense light, and keep them warm and constantly moist. Daytime temperatures be-

'Beefmaster'

'Homestead'

'Snowball'

'Roma'

'Yellow Pear'

'Sweet 100'

You'll find a wealth of tomato cultivars to choose from. Fruit colors include red, orange, yellow, and even green.

tween 65° and 85°F and nighttime temperatures between 60° and 65°F are best for growing sturdy transplants. A few days after germination, thin to one seedling per container or transplant to individual containers. Water whenever the soil feels dry to the touch. Bottom watering is best. Begin adding a few drops of fish emulsion or compost tea to the water after the first true leaf has unfurled. If you must hold back seedlings that are large enough to plant, move them to roomier containers (4″) so root growth is not restricted.

Hardening off transplants. Begin hardening off tomato seedlings grown indoors (or purchased plants that were greenhouse grown) two weeks before transplanting. Set them outdoors on mild, warm days in a site protected from strong winds. Keep them outdoors continuously for three days prior to transplanting.

Planting Outdoors

Buying transplants. Look for young, vigorous plants with stocky, stiff stems. Bypass tall, spindly specimens and plants with dark spots on their leaves or leaves that are purplish or yellowish. Look closely for insects such as aphids and whiteflies on stem tips and both above and below leaves. Unless your transplants are going directly into the garden, move them to slightly larger containers and drench with a weak fish emulsion mixture.

Setting out transplants. Drench plants with weak compost tea before transplanting.

TOMATO SEEDLING

Seeds   Cotyledons   First true leaves

Put 1 cup of kelp meal and 1 cup of bonemeal into each planting hole. Set transplants so the lowest set of leaves is at soil level or remove all but the top few leaves and bury the plant horizontally. At least two sets of leaves should show above the soil line. Press the soil down gently and water well. Protect plants with cloches or row cover if nights remain cold or days are very windy. Remove cloches when plants show strong new growth.

Growing Guidelines

Water and mulch. Tomatoes need warm, constantly moist soil while they are young. In cool climates, use black plastic mulch to warm the soil. Where warm weather prevails, mulch tomatoes with 8″ of straw or another organic mulch after the soil is thoroughly warm. Install stakes or cages before you mulch.

Feeding. Seedlings planted in well-prepared soil need no supplemental fertilizer, but if soil is poor, feed plants with 1 cup of fish emulsion mixture weekly until the first blossoms appear. In long-summer areas, top-dress plants that are pruned back in midsummer with 2″ of compost. Or drench with fish emulsion or compost tea in late summer when vigorous new growth begins. See "Custom Care for Fruit Crops" on page 58 for more information. If lower leaves are blotchy and yellow, spray plants with a mixture of 1 teaspoon of Epsom salts per gallon of water.

Training. Some stocky, compact cultivars can be grown unstaked, but they take up more room than staked plants. Unstaked plants should be heavily mulched. Most tomatoes should be tied to sturdy stakes, restrained inside cages, or trained to grow on a trellis. Begin training plants when they are 1′ tall and growing vigorously. Tie compact determinate plants to sturdy 5′ or 6′ stakes, or place stakes between plants and weave taut twine in a figure-eight pattern between plants and stakes. Support sprawling indeterminate plants with cages or multiple stakes or tie them to a trellis.

Problem Prevention

At planting, place paper collars around seedlings. Take this precaution at transplant time to prevent cutworms from cutting down seedlings.

After the soil is warm, mulch heavily with straw. Fluctuations in soil moisture can lead to fruit cracking and blossom end rot. In northern areas, apply black plastic two weeks before planting instead.

During hot weather, apply kelp sprays to foliage on mild, cloudy days. This prevents calcium and magnesium deficiencies, which cause black spots on the blossom ends of fruit. The disorder is aggravated by hot weather.

During the growing season, pinch off speckled leaves. To reduce leaf loss from early blight, late blight, and other leaf spot diseases, remove infected leaves as soon as you see them, and spray affected plants with compost tea.

During the growing season, handpick tomato hornworms. If these colorful caterpillars are numerous, use *Bacillus thuringiensis* to bring them under control.

Gathering the Harvest

Tomatoes are ripe when they change color. For best flavor, leave the fruits on the plants for as long as possible. Some cultivars drop their fruits when they are ripe. Pick these up, wash them, and use them. You can also pick tomatoes when they just begin to show stripes of mature color and then ripen them at room temperature. Never store tomatoes in the refrig-

---

TOMATOES AND TEMPERATURE

Many tomatoes fail to produce fruits when temperatures are below 50°F or above 90°F. Try special cold- or heat-tolerant cultivars if you live where summer temperatures are either too warm or too cold. Small-fruited, indeterminate cultivars, such as cherry tomatoes, often flower continuously, and therefore give you more chances of seeing successful fruit set. In cool climates, choose early cultivars, such as 'Oregon Spring', which mature quickly and tend to tolerate cool conditions.

---

erator because cool temperatures cause them to lose flavor and texture.

Extending the Season

In cool-summer areas, use insulated cloches such as Wallo'Waters, plastic tunnels, or slitted row cover to create warm conditions for young tomato plants. In all areas, pick ripe fruits promptly to encourage extended production. When the first fall frost is expected, cover plants with old blankets or other covers to keep them growing for a few more weeks. Toward the end of the season, prune away leaves to help warm sunshine reach ripening fruit. When fall temperatures are consistently below 60°F, pick all mature green fruits and allow them to ripen indoors. Tomatoes picked when the outer color changes to a lighter shade of green will ripen off of the plants.

Fall and Winter Care

In late fall, pull up dead plants and compost them. After plants are pulled up, spread

---

🐝 FRIENDS & RELATIVES 🐝

TOMATO

Tomatoes have several relatives with similar cultural requirements. Tomatillo (*Physalis ixocarpa*) is one of its most common cousins. Also known as husk tomato, this annual bears tart green fruits that slowly ripen to yellow-green. See "Tomatoes and Tomatillos" on page 405 for more information on this plant.

Physalis peruviana, P. pruinosa, and *P. pubescens* are tomato relatives that have a variety of common names, including cape gooseberries, ground cherries, and strawberry tomatoes. They bear small, seedy, yellow fruits with papery husks. The fruits are husked and eaten fresh or they can be used to make preserves.

Pepino, or melon shrub (*Solanum muricatum*), is a tropical evergreen perennial also grown like tomatoes. Pepinos need a warm climate and bear oblong fruits that taste like melony cucumbers.

Garden huckleberry (*Solanum melanocerasum*) bears small blue-black berries that are used in muffins, pies, cakes, and preserves.

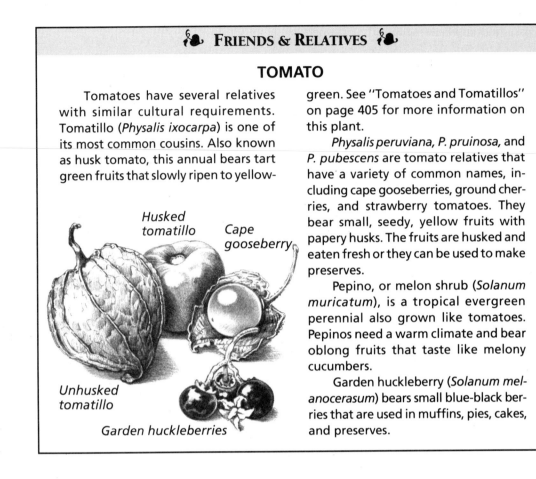

Husked tomatillo

Cape gooseberry

Unhusked tomatillo

Garden huckleberries

---

compost over the bed and cultivate the soil. If possible, sow a cover crop such as clover, wheat, or rye.

Container Growing

Tomatoes are easy to grow in large containers kept in a warm, sunny spot. Use a sandy potting soil enriched with compost or rotted manure. Feed and water weekly until blossoming begins, and then reduce fertilizer use to once every three weeks. Stake or trellis container-grown tomatoes to keep them upright, or grow sprawling cherry types in large hanging baskets.

Propagation

If you are growing more than one cultivar, plant those you wish to save seed from at the other end of the garden to reduce chance cross-pollinations. To save seeds, choose fruits from nonhybrid plants that show no evidence of disease. See "Harvesting Seeds" on page 263 for instructions on cleaning and storing tomato seeds. ✳

TURNIP

Brassica rapa, Rapifera group. Cruciferae.
Biennial grown as an annual.

Turnips are a versatile, easy-to-grow cabbage-family crop that thrives in cool weather. Try turnip's mild-flavored roots steamed and mashed with butter or margarine; cook the tops as greens. Overwintered turnips send up shoots, which are eaten like broccoli raab.

Selecting plants. Some cultivars, such as 'De Nancy', are mainly grown for roots; others, such as 'Seven Top', produce mostly greens.

Site. Turnips need full sun for best growth.

Soil. Plant in light, loose soil with steady moisture and a pH of 5.5–6.8. Before planting, incorporate a legume cover crop or 30 pounds of compost per 100 square feet.

How much to plant. One gram of seeds will plant 20′ of row. Figure on 8′–10′ of row per person.

Spacing. For roots, thin to 4″ between plants; for greens, allow 2″ between plants.

Leave 1′–1½′ between rows.

Days to maturity. Turnips mature 35–60 days from seed.

Planting and growing. Direct-sow turnips in early spring, as soon as the soil temperature reaches 50°F. Plant seeds ¼″–½″ deep in a fine seedbed. For more complete growing information on these cabbage-family crops, see "Growing Guidelines" on page 316.

Harvesting. Gather roots when they are 2″–3″ in diameter. Harvest leaves as needed at 8″–12″ tall, cutting at ground level. Roots keep in the refrigerator for two to three weeks in plastic bags. Or store them for up to five months in a root cellar at 32°F and 90 percent humidity.

Fall and winter care. In the South, turnips can grow all winter. Left in the ground, they will send up early shoots that you can harvest and cook as greens or use raw in salad. Pull out and compost any remains after harvest.

Propagation. For details, see "Propagation" on page 319. ✳

WALNUT

Juglans spp. Juglandaceae. Deciduous tree. Hardiness varies with species.

A string of delicious walnut species circles the world. Black walnuts (*Juglans nigra*) and butternuts (*J. cinerea*) are native to North America. English walnuts (*J. regia*), also called Persian or Carpathian walnuts, grow throughout Europe and Central Asia. The heartnut (*J. ailantifolia* var. *cordiformis*) is a fast-growing, wide-spreading walnut native to Japan. Walnuts are large trees, from 40′ to 100′ tall.

The English walnut, which is hardy in Zones 5–9, is the most widely cultivated. California and Oregon produce about 100,000 tons of English walnuts annually. Named for their European background, the Carpathian cultivars are hardiest and will produce crops in areas where winter temperatures reach −30°F.

Black walnuts, which are hardy in Zones 4–8, grow wild throughout most of eastern North America and are a favorite of backyard nut growers. There are many improved cultivars selected for nut kernel size and the ease of removing it from the very hard shell. Three of the best are 'Clermont', 'Rowher', and 'Thomas'.

Butternuts are hardy in Zones 3–7 and are sometimes called white walnuts. A few cultivars have been selected for their "crack-

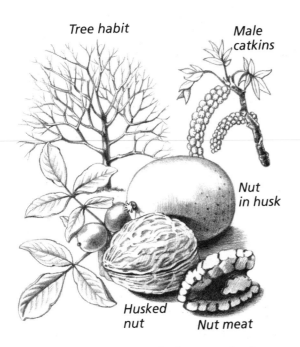

Tree habit

Male catkins

Nut in husk

Husked nut

Nut meat

English walnuts are stately, fast-growing trees. The male flowers are brownish green catkins; female flowers are inconspicuous.

ability" and sweet, mild flavor; try 'Craxezy'. Unfortunately, many wild trees now suffer symptoms of a new, accidentally introduced fungal disease. Butternuts may go the way of the American chestnut until resistant cultivars can be selected.

Heartnuts are hardy in Zones 5–8. The nut meats are heart shaped, mild flavored, and easy to extract from the shell.

Vigorous hybrid buartnuts (J. × bixbyi) are a cross between butternut and heartnut. Buartnuts are hardy in Zones 4–8 and combine the easy cracking and yields of the heartnut with the flavor and cold-hardiness of the butternut.

For information on juglone, a growth-inhibiting compound that is found in walnut trees and can affect nearby plants, see "The Black Side of Walnuts" below.

Site. Choose a site in full sun with deep, fertile, well-drained soil. Walnuts also tolerate slopes and slightly acid soils (6.0–7.0).

How much to plant. Plant at least two trees of each species you choose to ensure good pollination.

Spacing. Plant at least 25'–30' apart to allow good air circulation and light penetration.

Seasons to bearing. A grafted tree will bear in three to five years. Seedlings take longer to bear.

Planting and growing. Prepare the plant-

THE BLACK SIDE OF WALNUTS

Walnut trees aren't always good neighbors for other plants. Black walnut trees contain a growth-inhibiting substance called juglone. English walnut, pecan, hickory, and butternut trees also contain juglone but to a lesser extent.

Root contact can adversely affect juglone-sensitive plants. Juglone also leaches from leaves and nuts into the soil. It breaks down rapidly, especially in rich soil.

Tomatoes, potatoes, alfalfa, apples, blackberries, rhododendrons, azaleas, mountain laurels, and pines are very sensitive to juglone. The following plants also are somewhat sensitive: sweet peppers, lilacs, viburnums, autumn crocuses, peonies, magnolias, and crab apples.

Oddly enough, some plants grow normally, or even better than normal, near a black walnut tree. Edibles in this category include beets, snap beans, lima beans, onions, parsnips, sweet corn, dandelions, black raspberries, grapes, and mints.

ing site and plant as you would any tree. See "Perennial Crops" on page 111 for directions.

Water well daily for the first few days. Continue to water weekly during the growing season for the first several years whenever rain is scarce. Keep the area beneath the tree well-weeded, or mulch with wood chips or any mix of organic matter. To avoid excessive, tender early growth, wait until the second year to fertilize. Then spread a thin layer of compost or a blended organic fertilizer with a good nitrogen value beneath the tree once in spring.

To help control pests and disease, rake up dead twigs, fallen immature nuts, and leaves. Walnuts are susceptible to anthracnose, a fungal disease that causes leaves to blacken. Clean up dead, infected leaves and burn them or discard with household trash.

Harvesting. Harvest ripe nuts promptly. To interrupt pest cycles, destroy infected nuts.

English walnuts fall out of their husks to the ground when ripe. Black walnuts and butternuts fall still encased in spongy outer husks. Remove husks as soon as possible to allow the nut meats to cure. Place them on a hard surface and stomp on them, or hit them with a mallet and finish removing the husks by hand. Wear waterproof gloves—their juices can leave permanent stains. Then wash the nuts by stirring them in a bucket of water (empty nuts will float) or hosing them off in a basket.

Fall and winter care. Prune annually in early spring or late winter to open up the center of the tree and create a strong central leader with scaffold branches. See "Pruning Trees" on page 142 for directions. Remove dead branches regularly.

Propagation. Create new trees by grafting a piece of scion onto a rootstock chosen for hardiness or insect and disease resistance. ✳

WATERMELON

Citrullus lanatus. Cucurbitaceae. Annual.

What would a summer picnic be without a crisp, cool watermelon? See the Melon entry for culture. Don't miss trying a yellow-fleshed type. ✳

WHEAT

Triticum spp. Gramineae. Annual.

The staple grain in most North Americans' diets, wheat is easy to grow and looks striking in any garden.

Selecting plants. Wheat (*Triticum* × *aestivum*) comes in soft and hard types. Soft wheats produce a lighter flour used for making cookies, cakes, or pasta; the hard types are best for bread making because they have more

gluten, the protein that makes bread doughy. There are winter and spring cultivars of both hard and soft wheat. Spring wheat is of poorer quality and generally grown only in areas with extremely cold winters where winter wheat will not survive.

Durham wheat (*T. durum*) is also called semolina. It is the grain of choice for making pasta. Club wheat (*T. compactum*) is a soft wheat.

A few ancient types of wheat are enjoying

a revival. Emmer (*T. dicoccoides*) is also called German wheat. It is cultivated in mountainous areas of Europe. Kamut (*T. polonicum*), or Polish wheat, produces very large grains. It is reputed to be less allergenic than wheat, but can be used interchangeably. Spelt (*T. spelta*) is also reputed to be less allergenic and has a slightly nutty flavor.

Site. Wheat grows best in a bright, sunny spot that is well-drained.

Soil. If your soil is rich in humus, simply till before planting. If you want to boost organic matter content, spread a thin layer of well-rotted manure or compost before tilling. Wheat does not do well in acidic soils (7.0–8.5).

How much to plant. A 200-square-foot bed broadcast-planted or drill-seeded in rows will yield at least 20 pounds of grain, a good start for gardeners new to grain growing.

Spacing. Broadcast thickly over the bed or plant in furrows 6″ apart with about 1″ between seeds.

Days to maturity. Winter wheat is planted in mid- to late fall and ripens the following mid-spring; spring wheat is planted as early in the season as the soil can be worked and is harvested in early summer.

Planting and growing. You'll need ¾–1¼ pounds of seeds to plant a 200-square-foot bed. Weed the area when the wheat is still in the seedling stage. Supply water during a dry season, but don't overwater.

If your winter wheat comes up too fast due to warm fall and early-winter weather, clip shoots that grow taller than 4″–6″ before the hard frost. This will prevent lodging—toppling of tall plants whose roots aren't strong enough to support the plant in winter winds.

Hessian fly is the only significant pest of wheat. Resistant cultivars are available. Or time planting to avoid the pest. By sowing after its egg-laying period, usually in late summer or early fall, you can avoid the fly altogether. (Ask your local extension agent for your area's "fly-free" date.)

Lodging can also occur if soil is too wet or if plants get too much nitrogen. Wheat stalks that fall over will not form full seed heads. To minimize lodging, plant in a well-drained site and don't use high-nitrogen fertilizers.

Harvesting. Harvest wheat when the stalks turn yellow with just a few streaks of green and the heads begin to bow over.

You can use a scythe, sickle, or a Japanese *kama* to harvest your wheat. Leave enough stalk attached to build stooks, which are free-standing bundles of wheat. Try not to get weeds in your bundles because they can carry fungi that will damage the rest of the stook. You can also bundle it and take it inside to dry in a well-ventilated spot.

Allow bundled wheat to dry until the seed heads are hard and no hint of green remains on the stalk. Now your wheat is ready to be threshed and winnowed and turned into flour. See "Processing Grains" on page 370 for instructions.

Propagation. The grain is the seed. Save the grain from some of your healthiest plants by storing it in an airtight container in a cool, dark place.

Friends and relatives. Triticale (× *Triticosecale* sp.) is a cross between rye and wheat. It is the first modern man-made grain. The flour is low in gluten and is usually mixed with wheat for bread. ✳

Easy Crops by Region and Season

For your first garden, easy crops are your best bet. We asked expert gardeners from 11 regions for their thoughts on the easiest vegetable and herb crops for beginning gardeners. You'll find their recommendations listed below by region.

You'll notice that we mostly haven't given exact planting dates for these crops. Instead, we've used such terms as "early spring" or "as soon as ground can be worked in spring." That's because exact planting dates will vary depending on the local climate. Consult your local extension office to get an idea of when these dates might be for your garden.

Mid-Atlantic

Plant these cool-season crops in early spring.

Vegetables: Seeds or transplants of chard, kale, leaf lettuce, and spinach; seeds of radishes and turnips; broccoli transplants.

Herbs: Transplants of chives and thyme.

Plant these warm-season and cool-season crops in mid-spring to early summer.

Vegetables: Seeds or transplants of chard, kale, and leaf lettuce; seeds of summer squash and turnips; sweet potato slips.

Herbs: Seeds or transplants of basil and parsley; seeds of anise, borage, cilantro, dill, and summer savory; transplants of marjoram, mint, oregano, and sage.

Plant these cool-season crops in late summer.

Vegetables: Seeds or transplants of chard, kale, leaf lettuce, and spinach; turnip seeds; broccoli transplants.

Herbs: Transplants of mint, oregano, sage, and thyme; horseradish roots; garlic sets.

Midwest

Plant these cool-season crops as soon as ground can be worked in spring.

Vegetables: Seeds or transplants of leaf lettuce; sets of onions and potatoes; seeds of beets, carrots, and sugar snap peas.

Herbs: Chive transplants.

Plant these warm-season crops when danger of frost is past.

Vegetables: Tomato transplants; seeds of beans and New Zealand spinach.

Herbs: Transplants of lemon balm, sage, and thyme.

Plant these cool-season crops in mid-summer.

Vegetables: Leaf lettuce transplants; onion sets; seeds of beets and carrots.

Northeast

Plant these cool-season crops as soon as ground can be worked in spring.

Vegetables: Seeds or transplants of chard, leaf lettuce, and spinach; seeds of beets, carrots, parsnips, peas, radishes, and turnips; transplants of cabbage and cauliflower.

Herbs: Parsley transplants; dill seeds.

Plant these cool-season crops and fast-maturing cultivars of warm-season crops when danger of frost is past.

Vegetables: Seeds or transplants of chard, leaf lettuce, and spinach; seeds of beets, bush snap beans, carrots, corn, parsnips, radishes, and turnips; transplants of cabbage, cauliflower, and tomatoes.

Herbs: Transplants of basil, mint, and sage; lovage seeds.

Plant these fast-maturing, short-season crops one to two months before the first expected fall frost.

Vegetables: Leaf lettuce transplants; seeds or transplants of spinach; radish seeds.

Rocky Mountains: North and High Altitudes

Plant these cool-season crops as soon as ground can be worked in spring.

Vegetables: Seeds or transplants of chard, leaf lettuce, and spinach; seeds of beets, bush beans, carrots, kohlrabi, peas, radishes, and summer squash; sets, seeds, or transplants of onions; transplants of broccoli and cabbage; potato sets. (Note: At altitudes above 7,500 feet, omit the beans and summer squash.)

Herbs: Transplants of mint, oregano, sage, and thyme.

Plant these warm-season and cool-season crops when danger of frost is past.

Vegetables: Seeds or transplants of chard, leaf lettuce, and spinach; seeds of beets, bush beans, carrots, kohlrabi, peas, radishes, and summer squash; sets, seeds, or transplants of onions; transplants of broccoli and cabbage; potato sets.

Herbs: Transplants of basil, chives, mint, oregano, parsley, sage, and thyme; dill seeds.

Plant these fast-maturing, short-season crops one to two months before the first expected fall frost.

Vegetables: Seeds or transplants of leaf lettuce and spinach; radish seeds.

Rocky Mountains: Lower Altitudes

Plant these cool-season crops as soon as ground can be worked in spring.

Vegetables: Seeds or transplants of chard, leaf lettuce, and spinach; seeds of beets, carrots, kohlrabi, peas, and radishes; sets, seeds, or transplants of onions; transplants of broccoli and cabbage; potato sets.

Herbs: Seeds of caraway and dill; parsley transplants.

Plant these warm-season crops when danger of frost is past.

Vegetables: Seeds of bush beans, pole beans, summer squash, and sweet corn; transplants of eggplant, green peppers, and tomatoes.

Herbs: Transplants of basil, chives, mint, and sage.

Plant these cool-season crops in mid-summer.

Vegetables: Seeds or transplants of leaf lettuce and spinach; seeds of beets, radishes, and turnips; broccoli transplants.

South

Plant these cool-season crops in late winter.

Vegetables: Seeds or transplants of leaf lettuce and onions; seeds of bush sugar snap peas and radishes.

Plant these warm-season crops in early spring.

Vegetables: Seeds of bush beans, okra, and summer squash; transplants of peppers and tomatoes.

Herbs: Seeds of basil and dill; transplants of chives, oregano, parsley, rosemary, and thyme.

Plant these cool-season crops in late summer.

Vegetables: Seeds or transplants of collards and leaf lettuce; radish seeds; broccoli transplants.

Florida

Plant these cool-season crops from late summer to early fall.

Vegetables: Seeds or transplants of cabbage and leaf lettuce; seeds of carrots, collards, green onions, mustard, radishes, and turnips; potato sets.

Herbs: Transplants of mint and parsley.

Plant these warm-season crops in late winter.

Vegetables: Transplants of eggplant, peppers, and tomatoes; seeds of beans, cucumbers, okra, southern peas, summer squash, and sweet corn.

Herbs: Seeds or transplants of basil.

Gulf Coast

Plant these cool-weather crops in late winter (February or March).

Vegetables: Seeds or transplants of leaf lettuce and spinach; pea seeds.

Plant these warm-weather crops in early spring (late March or early April).

Vegetables: Seeds of bush beans, cucumbers, and summer squash; tomato transplants.

Herbs: Seeds of dill and fennel; transplants of mint and oregano.

Plant these heat-tolerant, warm-weather crops in late April.

Vegetables: Seeds of okra and southern peas; sweet potato slips; pepper transplants.

Herbs: Basil seeds; mint transplants.

Plant these cool-season crops in late September.

Vegetables: Seeds or transplants of broccoli raab, collards, kale, lettuce, mustard, and spinach; shallot sets.

Herbs: Parsley seeds; mint transplants.

Southwest

Plant these cool-season crops and fast-maturing or heat-tolerant, warm-season crops in early spring.

Vegetables: Seeds or transplants of bok choy, chard, lettuce, and spinach; seeds of beets, bush beans, carrots, early corn, radishes, snow peas, summer squash, and turnips; transplants of broccoli, cabbage, cauliflower, early tomatoes, and peppers.

Herbs: Transplants of basil, mint, oregano, parsley, rosemary, tarragon, and thyme.

Plant these cool-season and early warm-season crops in late summer to early fall.

Vegetables: Seeds or transplants of bok choy, chard, lettuce, and spinach; seeds of beets, bush beans, carrots, early corn, radishes, snow peas, summer squash, and turnips; transplants of broccoli, cabbage, cauliflower, and early tomatoes.

Herbs: Seeds of cilantro and parsley; transplants of chives, mint, oregano, sage, and thyme.

Coastal Northwest

Plant these cool-season crops in late winter.

Vegetables: Seeds or transplants of chard, kale, leaf lettuce, mustard, and spinach; seeds of beets and turnips; green onion sets.

Herbs: Cilantro seeds; transplants of chives, parsley, and thyme.

Plant these warm-season and cool-season crops in mid- to late spring.

Vegetables: Seeds of beets, bush beans, chard, kale, leaf lettuce, mustard, spinach, summer squash, and turnips; green onion sets.

Herbs: Seeds of cilantro and dill; transplants of basil, French tarragon, garlic chives, parsley, rosemary, and thyme.

Plant these cool-season crops in late summer.

Vegetables: Seeds of beets, chard, kale, leaf lettuce, mustard, spinach, and turnips; green onion sets.

Herbs: Cilantro seeds; transplants of oregano, parsley, rosemary, and thyme.

Southern California

Plant these warm-season crops and fast-maturing, cool-season crops from April to June.

Vegetables: Seeds of beans, radishes, summer squash, and sweet corn; transplants of peppers and tomatoes; seeds or transplants of endive and leaf lettuce.

Herbs: Transplants of basil, mint, oregano, parsley, rosemary, tarragon, and thyme.

Plant these cool-season crops from October to February.

Vegetables: Seeds or transplants of chard, endive, leaf lettuce, and spinach; seeds of beets, carrots, onions, radishes, and turnips; transplants of broccoli, cabbage, and cauliflower.

Herbs: Seeds of chervil, cilantro, and dill; transplants of chives and parsley.

USDA PLANT HARDINESS ZONE MAP

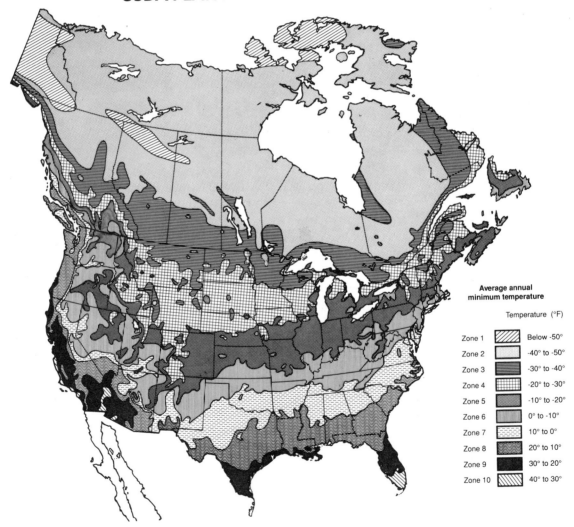

Average annual
minimum temperature

Temperature (°F)

Zone 1		Below -50°
Zone 2		-40° to -50°
Zone 3		-30° to -40°
Zone 4		-20° to -30°
Zone 5		-10° to -20°
Zone 6		0° to -10°
Zone 7		10° to 0°
Zone 8		20° to 10°
Zone 9		30° to 20°
Zone 10		40° to 30°

SOURCES

Seeds and Plants

The following companies offer fruit trees and bushes, vegetable seeds and sets, and herbs. Some are large companies that offer a wide range of crops and cultivars, and others are smaller businesses that specialize in a particular type of plant.

Adams County Nursery, Inc.
P.O. Box 108
Aspers, PA 17304
Fruit trees

Ahrens Nursery & Plant Labs
P.O. Box 145
Huntingburg, IN 47542
Berry plants from tissue culture

Bear Creek Nursery
P.O. Box 411
Northport, WA 99157
Fruit trees: scionwood, bud wood, budded trees, and rootstocks

Champlain Isle Agro Associates
Isle LaMotte, VT 05463
Tissue-culture bramble plants

The Cook's Garden
P.O. Box 535
Londonderry, VT 05148

Ed Hume Seeds, Inc.
P.O. Box 1450
Kent, WA 98035
Specializes in untreated vegetable seeds

Edible Landscaping
P.O. Box 77
Afton, VA 22920
Specializes in fruits

Harris Seeds
P.O. Box 22960
Rochester, NY 14692

Hastings
P.O. Box 115535
Atlanta, GA 30302
Specializes in plants for southern climates

Henry Leuthardt Nurseries, Inc.
P.O. Box 666
East Moriches, NY 11940
Specializes in small fruits and espalier fruit trees

Johnny's Selected Seeds
2580 Foss Hill Rd.
Albion, ME 04910
Vegetable and herb seeds

J. W. Jung Seed Co.
335 S. High St.
Randolph, WI 53957

Le Jardin du Gourmet
P.O. Box 75
St. Johnsbury Center, VT 05863
Vegetable seeds in small and inexpensive packets

Lilypons Water Gardens
6800 Lilypons Rd.
P.O. Box 10
Buckeystown, MD 21717-0010

Logee's Greenhouses
141 North St.
Danielson, CT 06239
Herbs

Meadowbrook Herb Garden Catalog
P.O. Box 578
Fairfield, CT 06430

Native Seeds/SEARCH
2509 N. Campbell Ave. #325
Tucson, AZ 85719
Southwestern native and heirloom vegetable and herb seeds

New York State Fruit Testing Cooperative Assoc., Inc.
P.O. Box 462
Geneva, NY 14456-0462
Annual membership fee; new and time-tested fruit cultivars

Nichols Garden Nursery
1190 N. Pacific Hwy.
Albany, OR 97321
Herbs and vegetables

North Star Gardens
19060 Manning Trail N
Marine on St. Croix, MN 55047
Specializes in berries

Owens Nursery
P.O. Box 193
Gay, GA 30218
Specializes in muscadines

Park Seed Co.
P.O. Box 31
Greenwood, SC 29647

Pinetree Garden Seeds
Route 100
New Gloucester, ME 04260
Inexpensive, small seed packets

Raintree Nursery
391 Butts Rd.
Morton, WA 98356
Specializes in fruits, nuts, and edible plants

Redwood City Seed Co.
P.O. Box 361
Redwood City, CA 94064

Ronniger's Seed Potatoes
Star Route
Moyie Springs, ID 83845

St. Lawrence Nurseries
R.R. 5, Box 324
Potsdam, NY 13676
Specializes in northern hardy fruits and nuts

Sandy Mush Herb Nursery
Route 2, Surrett Cove Rd.
Leicester, NC 28748
Specializes in rare and unusual plants

Seed Savers Exchange
3076 North Winn Rd.
Decorah, IA 52101
Annual membership fee; heirloom fruits and vegetables

Seeds Blüm
Idaho City Stage
Boise, ID 83706
Heirloom vegetable and herb seeds

Seeds Trust High Altitude Gardens
P.O. Box 4619
Ketchum, ID 83340
Specializes in seeds for high altitudes and cold climates

Shepherd's Garden Seeds
6116 Hwy. 9
Felton, CA 95018

Southmeadow Fruit Gardens
Box SM
Lakeside, MI 49116
Unusual fruit cultivars

Stark Bro's Nurseries & Orchards Company
Hwy. 54
Louisiana, MO 63353

Stokes Seeds, Inc.
Box 548
Buffalo, NY 14240

Territorial Seed Co.
P.O. Box 157
Cottage Grove, OR 97424
Vegetable seeds for the Pacific Northwest maritimes

W. Atlee Burpee & Co.
300 Park Ave.
Warminster, PA 18974

Well-Sweep Herb Farm
317 Mt. Bethel Rd.
Port Murray, NJ 07865

Whitman Farms
3995 Gibson Rd. NW
Salem, OR 97304
Currants and gooseberries

Specialty Crops

The following companies specialize in the crops of a particular ethnic background, in exotic crops, or in unusual crops. You'll find sources for mushroom growing kits and supplies, tropical and subtropical fruit trees, and rare seeds and plants from all over the world.

Brokaw Nursery
P.O. Box 4818
Saticoy, CA 93004
Avocado trees

Exotica Rare Fruit Co.
P.O. Box 160
Vista, CA 92085

Fungi Perfecti
P.O. Box 7634
Olympia, WA 98507
Mushroom-growing supplies

Hopkins Citrus and Rare Fruit
Nursery
5200 SW 160th Ave.
Fort Lauderdale, FL 33331

J. L. Hudson, Seedsman
P.O. Box 1058
Redwood City, CA 94064
*Rare seeds from around the
world*

Mushroompeople
P.O. Box 159
Inverness, CA 94937

Southern Exposure Seed
Exchange
P.O. Box 158
North Garden, VA 22959
Source of rice seeds

Sunrise Enterprises
P.O. Box 330058
West Hartford, CT
06133-0058
Asian vegetable seeds

Cultivar and Sources Reference Books

Refer to the books below when you want to find a source for a particular cultivar of a plant, especially if it's an unusual or heirloom cultivar. These books can also give you more comprehensive information on sources of plants and supplies. If your local library doesn't have these books, ask if they can acquire them for you through interlibrary loan.

Barton, Barbara J. *Gardening by Mail: A Source Book.* 3rd, updated and enl. ed. Boston: Houghton Mifflin Co., 1990.

Facciola, Stephen. *Cornucopia: A Source Book of Edible Plants.* Vista, CA: Kampong Publications, 1990. (Available from Kampong Publications, 1870 Sunrise Dr., Vista, CA 92084.)

Whealy, Kent, ed. *Fruit, Berry, and Nut Inventory.* 2nd ed. Decorah, Iowa: Seed Saver Publications, 1993. (Available from Seed Savers Exchange, Route 3, Box 239, Decorah, IA 52101.)

———. *Garden Seed Inventory.* 2nd ed. Decorah, Iowa: Seed Saver Publications, 1988. (Available from Seed Savers Exchange, Route 3, Box 239, Decorah, IA 52101.)

Gardening Equipment and Supplies

The following companies offer merchandise such as organic fertilizers, composting equipment, animal repellents and traps, beneficial insects and microbes, shredders, sprayers, tillers, row covers and shading materials, irrigation equipment, hand tools, and carts.

A. M. Leonard, Inc.
P.O. Box 816
Piqua, OH 45356

Bountiful Gardens
19550 Walker Rd.
Willits, CA 95490
*Also offers organically grown
herb and vegetable seeds*

DripWorks
380 Maple St.
Willits, CA 95490
Drip irrigation and pond liners

Gardener's Supply Co.
128 Intervale Rd.
Burlington, VT 05401

Gardens Alive!
5100 Schenley Place
Lawrenceburg, IN 47025

Harmony Farm Supply
P.O. Box 460
Graton, CA 95444

Johnny's Selected Seeds
2580 Foss Hill Rd.
Albion, ME 04910
Automatic venting arm for cold frames

Necessary Trading Co.
P.O. Box 305
422 Salem Ave.
New Castle, VA 24127
Soil amendments and organic pest controls; large quantities only

Peaceful Valley Farm Supply Co.
P.O. Box 2209
Grass Valley, CA 95945

Pest Management Supply
311 River Dr.
Hadley, MA 01035
Traps and pheromone lures

Raindrip, Inc.
21305 Itasca St.
Chatsworth, CA 91311

Smith & Hawken
25 Corte Madera
Mill Valley, CA 94941

The Urban Farmer Store
2833 Vicente St.
San Francisco, CA 94116
Water-conserving irrigation systems and other supplies

Soil-Testing Laboratories

The following companies will test soil samples from home gardens. Some companies also make recommendations for adding soil amendments based on test results. Be sure to mention that you need an organic recommendation—or you may get one that includes synthetic fertilizers.

A & L Agricultural Labs
7621 White Pine Rd.
Richmond, VA 23237

Biosystem Consultants
P.O. Box 43
Lorane, OR 97451

Cook's Consulting
R.D. 2, Box 13
Lowville, NY 13367

Timberleaf
5569 State St.
Albany, OH 45710

Wallace Labs
365 Coral Circle
El Segundo, CA 90245

RECOMMENDED READING

The following books provide a wealth of additional information on growing food crops. Your local Cooperative Extension Service office also has many helpful gardening publications, especially for pruning and trellising information, and problem-identification guides.

Adams, William D., and Thomas R. Leroy. *Growing Fruits and Nuts in the South*. Dallas, Tex.: Taylor Publishing Company, 1992.

Ashworth, Suzanne. *Seed to Seed*. Decorah, Iowa: Seed Savers Exchange, 1991.

Bartholomew, Mel. *Square Foot Gardening*. Emmaus, Pa.: Rodale Press, 1981.

Bradley, Fern Marshall, and Barbara W. Ellis, eds. *Rodale's All-New Encyclopedia of Organic Gardening*. Emmaus, Pa.: Rodale Press, 1992.

Brickell, Christopher. *Pruning*. New York: Simon and Schuster, 1988.

Bubel, Mike and Nancy. *Root Cellaring*. 2nd ed. Pownal, Vt.: Storey Communications, Garden Way Publishing, 1991.

Carr, Anna. *Good Neighbors: Companion Planting for Gardeners*. Emmaus, Pa.: Rodale Press, 1985.

Coleman, Eliot. *Four-Season Harvest: How to Harvest Fresh, Organic Vegetables from Your Home Garden All Year Long*. Post Mills, Vt.: Chelsea Green Publishing Co., 1992.

———. *The New Organic Grower: A Master's Manual of Tools and Techniques for the Home and Market Gardener*. Post Mills, Vt.: Chelsea Green Publishing Co., 1989.

Creasy, Rosalind. *The Complete Book of Edible Landscaping*. San Francisco: Sierra Club Books, 1982.

Ellis, Barbara W., ed. *Rodale's Illustrated Encyclopedia of Gardening and Landscaping Techniques*. Emmaus, Pa.: Rodale Press, 1990.

Ellis, Barbara W., and Fern Marshall Bradley, eds. *The Organic Gardener's Handbook of Natural Insect and Disease Control*. Emmaus, Pa.: Rodale Press, 1992.

Engeland, Ron L. *Growing Great Garlic*. Okanogan, Wash.: Filaree Productions, 1991.

Fischer, Bill. *Growers Weed Identification Handbook*. Oakland, Calif.: ANR Publications, 1985.

Galletta, Gene J., and David Himelrick. *Small Fruit Crop Management*. Englewood Cliffs, N.J.: Prentice Hall, 1990.

Genders, Roy. *Mushroom Growing for Everyone*. Winchester, Mass.: Faber and Faber, 1982.

Gershuny, Grace. *Start with the Soil*. Emmaus, Pa.: Rodale Press, 1993.

Gershuny, Grace, and Deborah L. Martin, eds. *The Rodale Book of Composting*. Emmaus, Pa.: Rodale Press, 1992.

Greene, Janet, et al. *Putting Food By*. 4th ed. New York: Viking Penguin, 1988.

Halpin, Anne Moyer, and the Editors of Rodale Press. *Foolproof Planting: How to Successfully Start and Propagate More Than 250 Vegetables, Flowers, Trees, and Shrubs*. Emmaus, Pa.: Rodale Press, 1990.

Harrington, Geri. *Grow Your Own Chinese Vegetables*. Pownal, Vt.: Storey Communications, Garden Way Publishing, 1984.

Hartmann, Hudson T., et al. *Plant Propagation: Principles and Practices*. 5th ed. Englewood Cliffs, N.J.: Prentice Hall, 1990.

Hill, Lewis. *Secrets of Plant Propagation*. Pownal, Vt.: Storey Communications, 1985.

Horst, R. Kenneth. *Westcott's Plant Disease Handbook*. 5th ed. New York: Van Nostrand Reinhold Co., 1990.

Hupping, Carol, et al. *Stocking Up III*. Emmaus, Pa.: Rodale Press, 1986.

Hylton, William H., and Claire Kowalchik, eds. *Rodale's Illustrated Encyclopedia of Herbs*. Emmaus, Pa.: Rodale Press, 1987.

Jeavons, John. *How to Grow More Vegetables Than You Ever Thought Possible on Less Land Than You Can Imagine*. Rev. ed. Berkeley, Calif.: Ten Speed Press, 1991.

Kourik, Robert. *Designing and Maintaining Your Edible Landscape Naturally*. Santa Rosa, Calif.: Metamorphic Press, 1986.

———. *Drip Irrigation for Every Landscape and All Climates*. Santa Rosa, Calif.: Metamorphic Press, 1992.

Larkcom, Joy. *Oriental Vegetables*. New York: Kodansha America, 1991.

Lovejoy, Sharon. *Sunflower Houses: Garden Discoveries for Children of All Ages*. Loveland, Colo.: Interweave Press, 1991.

Michalak, Pat. *Rodale's Successful Organic Gardening: Herbs*. Emmaus, Pa.: Rodale Press, 1993.

Michalak, Pat, and Cass Peterson. *Rodale's Successful Organic Gardening: Vegetables*. Emmaus, Pa.: Rodale Press, 1993.

Ogawa, Joseph M. and Harley English. *Diseases of Temperate Zone Tree Fruit and Nut Crops*. Oakland, Calif.: ANR Publications, 1991.

Ogden, Shepherd. *Step by Step Organic Vegetable Gardening: The Gardening Classic*. Rev. and updated. New York: HarperCollins Publishers, 1992.

Peirce, Pam. *Golden Gate Gardening: The Complete Guide to Year-Round Food Gardening in the San Francisco Bay Area and Coastal California*. Davis, Calif.: agAccess, 1993.

Pleasant, Barbara. *Warm-Climate Gardening: Tips—Techniques—Plans—Projects for Humid or Dry Conditions*. Pownal, Vt.: Storey Communications, 1993.

Reich, Lee. *Uncommon Fruits Worthy of Attention*. Reading, Mass.: Addison-Wesley Publishing Co., 1991.

Sherf, Arden F. and Alan A. MacNab. *Vegetable Diseases and Their Control*. 2nd ed. New York: Wiley, John, and Sons, 1986.

Van Atta, Marian. *Growing and Using Exotic Foods*. Sarasota, Fla.: Pineapple Press, 1991.

Wilson, Jim. *Landscaping with Container Plants*. Boston: Houghton Mifflin Co., 1990.

INDEX

Note: Page numbers in *italic* indicate illustrations and captions.
Boldface references indicate main encyclopedic entries in Part 2.